The Bloomsbury Companion to Jewish Studies

Other volumes in the series of Bloomsbury Companions:

Hindu Studies, edited by Jessica Frazier, foreword by Gavin Flood

Islamic Studies, edited by Clinton Bennett

Religion and Film, edited by William L. Blizek

New Religious Movements, edited by George D. Chryssides and
Benjamin E. Zeller

The Bloomsbury Companion to Jewish Studies

Edited by

Dean Phillip Bell

Bloomsbury Companions

B L O O M S B U R Y
LONDON · NEW DELHI · NEW YORK · SYDNEY

Bloomsbury Academic
An imprint of Bloomsbury Publishing Plc

50 Bedford Square 1385 Broadway
London New York
WC1B 3DP NY 10018
UK USA

www.bloomsbury.com

BLOOMSBURY and the Diana logo are trademarks of
Bloomsbury Publishing Plc

Hardback edition published 2013
This paperback edition published 2015

British Library Cataloguing-in-Publication Data
A catalogue record for this book is available from the British Library.

ISBN: HB: 978-1-4411-5857-4
     PB: 978-1-4725-8713-8
   ePDF: 978-1-4725-1326-7
   ePub: 978-1-4725-0540-8

Library of Congress Cataloging-in-Publication Data
A catalog record for this book is available from the Library of Congress.

Series: Bloomsbury Companions

Typeset by Newgen Knowledge Works (P) Ltd., Chennai, India
Printed and bound in Great Britain

Contents

Detailed Contents

List of Contributors

Judith R. Baskin, who received her PhD in Medieval Studies from Yale University, is the Philip H. Knight Professor of Humanities and Associate Dean for Humanities, College of Arts and Sciences, at the University of Oregon. She served as President of the Association for Jewish Studies from 2004 to 2006. Professor Baskin has written numerous scholarly articles. Her books include *Pharaoh's Counsellors: Job, Jethro, and Balaam in Rabbinic and Patristic Tradition* (1983), *Midrashic Women: Formations of the Feminine in Rabbinic Literature* (2002), the edited collections *Jewish Women in Historical Perspective* (2nd edn, 1998), *Women of the Word: Jewish Women and Jewish Writing* (1994), and *The Cambridge Guide to Jewish History, Religion, and Culture* (2010), coedited with Kenneth Seeskin, which won the 2011 National Jewish Book Award for Anthologies and Collections. Professor Baskin also edited *The Cambridge Dictionary of Judaism and Jewish Culture* (2011) and served as Post-Biblical Consulting Editor for *The Torah: A Women's Commentary* (2008), which was named the National Jewish Book Council Book of the Year in 2008. In her role as Associate Editor, she oversaw the addition of over two hundred new and revised entries on topics concerned with women and gender to the 2006 second edition of the *Encyclopedia Judaica*.

Elisheva Baumgarten earned a PhD in medieval history at the Hebrew University of Jerusalem. She is currently Senior Lecturer in the Department of Jewish Studies and the Gender Studies Program at Bar-Ilan University. Her academic interests include medieval history; social history and anthropology; and applications of gender methodology to medieval studies focusing primarily on Germany and Northern France in the High Middle Ages. She is the author of *Mothers and Children: Jewish Family Life in Medieval Europe* (2004) and *Practicing Piety: Religious Observance and Daily Life in the Medieval Jewish Communities of Northern Europe* (forthcoming). Baumgarten is the recipient of numerous academic awards and fellowships, including most recently a fellowship at the Herbert D. Katz Center for Advanced Judaic Studies at the University of Pennsylvania.

Dean Phillip Bell is Dean and Chief Academic Officer at Spertus Institute for Jewish Learning and Leadership in Chicago. He earned his BA at the University of Chicago and his MA and PhD at the University of California, Berkeley, and he has taught at the University of California, Berkeley, DePaul University, University of Illinois, Urbana-Champaign, Northwestern University, and the Hebrew Theological College. Bell has served as a member of the Board of Directors of the Association for Jewish Studies and President of the Midwest Jewish Studies Association. He previously served as Associate Editor and member of the Editorial Board of *Shofar: An Interdisciplinary Journal of Jewish Studies*, member of the Editorial Board of *Mo'ed-Researches in Jewish Studies*, and Associate Editor for the *Encyclopedia of Antisemitism, Anti-Jewish Prejudice and Persecution* (2003). He is author of *Sacred Communities: Jewish and Christian Identities in Fifteenth-Century Germany* (2001); *Jewish Identity in Early Modern Germany: Memory, Power and Community* (2007); *Jews in the Early Modern World* (2008); and, with Stephen G. Burnett, editor of *Jews, Judaism and the Reformation in Sixteenth-Century Germany* (2006).

Judah M. Cohen is the Lou and Sybil Mervis Professor of Jewish Culture and associate professor of folklore and ethnomusicology at Indiana University. He has authored *Through the Sands of Time: A History of the Jewish Community of St. Thomas, US Virgin Islands* (2004); *The Making of a Reform Jewish Cantor: Musical Authority, Cultural Investment* (2009); and *Sounding Jewish Culture: The Music of Central Synagogue* (2011). He has also coedited, with Gregory Barz, *The Culture of AIDS in Africa: Hope and Healing Through Music and the Arts* (2011). Cohen's recent essays and book chapters address subjects such as Jewish hip-hop, music in Jewish summer camps, and musical works associated with Anne Frank's diary and *The Merchant of Venice*. Cohen is currently at work on two projects: one exploring the ways that World War II–based narratives circulated among musical theatre creators, and a second exploring the musical world of nineteenth-century American Judaism.

Sergio DellaPergola, born in Italy, has lived in Israel since 1966. He holds a PhD from The Hebrew University of Jerusalem, is the Shlomo Argov Professor Emeritus of Israel-Diaspora Relations at the Hebrew University's Avraham Harman Institute of Contemporary Jewry, and the Institute's former chairman. He has published numerous books, including *Israele e Palestina: La forza dei numeri: Il conflitto mediorientale fra demografia e politica* (2007); *Jewish Intermarriage around the World* (coauthored with S. Reinharz, 2009); *Pertenencia y Alteridad— Judios en/de America Latina: cuarenta años de cambios* (coauthored with H. Avni, J. Bokser-Liwerant, M. Bejarano, and L. Senkman, 2011); and *Jewish Demographic Policies: Population Trends and Options in Israel and the Diaspora* (2011); as well as over two hundred papers on historical demography, the family, international migration, Jewish identification, and population projections in the Diaspora and in Israel. He has lectured at over 60 universities and research centers worldwide and served as senior policy consultant to the President of Israel, the Israeli Government, the Jerusalem Municipality, and many major national and international organizations. In 1999, he won the Marshall Sklare Award for distinguished achievement from the Association for the Social Scientific Study of Jewry.

Gil Graff is the author of two books and numerous articles in the field of modern Jewish history. His book *Separation of Church and State: Dina de-Malkhuta Dina in Jewish Law, 1750–1848* (1985) explores the Jewish encounter with modernity in western and central Europe. In *"And You Shall Teach Them Diligently:" A Concise History of Jewish Education in the United States, 1776–2000* (2008), he examines the personalities, events, and larger social forces that shaped various conceptions and structures of Jewish education in America. Graff earned a PhD at UCLA and holds a JD from UCLA School of Law. He has been a Lady Davis Fellow, Charlotte Newcombe Fellow, and Jerusalem Fellow, and a Visiting Scholar at the Oxford Centre for Hebrew and Jewish Studies. Graff has taught under-graduate and graduate students as an adjunct faculty member at American Jewish University, Hebrew Union College-Jewish Institute of Religion, Spertus Institute for Jewish Learning and Leadership, Touro College, and the Academy for Jewish Religion, California. Since 1993, Dr. Graff has served as Executive Director of BJE: Builders of Jewish Education, Los Angeles.

Leonard J. Greenspoon, a native of Richmond, Virginia, holds the Klutznick Chair in Jewish Civilization at Creighton University in Omaha, Nebraska. On the Creighton faculty since 1995, Greenspoon is also Professor of Classical & Near Eastern Studies and of Theology. In addition, he is a visiting professor at the Spertus Institute for Jewish Learning and Leadership in Chicago. From his days as a graduate student at Harvard University (from which he received his PhD in Near Eastern Languages and Civilizations), Greenspoon has been interested in translations of the Bible. He has written on topics ranging from the earliest translation of the Bible, the Septuagint, to versions of the Bible com-posed as recently as last year, and he has been involved in two Bible transla-tion projects as editor or consultant. He is author of *Textual Studies in the Book of Joshua* (1983) and *Max Leopold Margolis: A Scholar's Scholar* (1987), as well as editor or coeditor of an additional eight books. Greenspoon has also published in several areas of popular culture, including Jews (and, more generally, reli-gion) in comic strips and the use (or misuse) of the Bible in the daily press. He writes a column ("The Bible in the News") on the latter for *Biblical Archaeology Review* and incorporated all of these interests during his tenure as editor of *The FORUM*, published by the Society of Biblical Literature.

Michael Kotzin received a PhD in English Literature from the University of Minnesota and then joined the English Department faculty at Tel Aviv University, where he served for a dozen years. He then began a career in Jewish communal service, spending the past 25 years on the staff of the Jewish Federation of Metropolitan Chicago, including as Executive Vice President from 1999 until 2011. He currently holds the title of Senior Counselor to the President of the Chicago Federation. In 2004, Kotzin published an opinion column in *The Forward* calling for communal support to advance the growth of Israel Studies in American universities, and he was instrumental in establishing an Israel Studies Project at the Chicago Federation that currently supports programs at four major universities in Illinois. While continuing to direct that project, in the spring of 2013 he additionally returned to the classroom to teach a course at the University of Illinois at Urbana-Champaign on "Reflections on Zion: American Jewish Writers and Israel." Kotzin's publications on literary subjects include a book on *Dickens and the Fairytale* and essays on Dickens and other writers ranging from Thackeray, Wilde, and Conrad to C. S. Lewis and I. B. Singer. His publications on Jewish communal affairs include essays in works published by the Susan and David Wilston Institute of Jewish Policy Studies, the Divinity School of the University of Chicago, the Vidal Sasoon International Center for the Study of Anti-Semitism at the Hebrew University of Jerusalem, and the Archdiocese of Chicago.

Yehuda Kurtzer is President of the Shalom Hartman Institute of North America, overseeing the Institute's many educational initiatives for the leadership of the North American Jewish community. He previously served as the inaugural Chair of Jewish Communal Innovation at Brandeis University, where he taught courses in Jewish Studies and in the Hornstein Jewish Professional Leadership Program. He has also taught at the Hebrew College Rabbinical School and in adult and academic settings across the country. Kurtzer's new book, *Shuva: The Future of the Jewish Past*, deals with many of the central challenges facing contemporary Jewry, and offers new thinking on how contemporary Jews can and should relate to our past. He received his doctorate in Jewish Studies from Harvard University, with a focus on the Jews of the ancient Mediterranean Diaspora and their relationship to the rise of rabbinic piety. He is an alumnus of both the Wexner Graduate and Bronfman Youth Fellowships. Kurtzer also helped cofound Brookline's Washington Square Minyan, and coorganized the first two Independent Minyan Conferences. He lives in New York with his wife, Stephanie Ives, and their two sons.

Gary G. Porton received his BA in History from UCLA, his MA in Judaic Studies from the Hebrew Union College-Jewish Institute of Religion, Los Angeles, and his PhD in the History of Religions: Judaism from Brown University. He taught in the Department for the Study of Religion at the University of Illinois,

Urbana-Champaign, between 1973 and 2008, retiring as the Sarah and Charles Drobny Professor of Talmudic Studies and Judaism. Porton was cofounder of the Program in Jewish Culture and Society at the University of Illinois. He has published 7 books and 28 journal articles and chapters in books, along with numerous dictionary and encyclopedia entries. Most of his publications focus on Jews and Judaism in late antiquity as well as the rabbinic collections form that period.

Elie Rekhess is Visiting Crown Chair in Middle East Studies and Professor of History at Northwestern University. Rekhess earned his PhD at Tel Aviv University, and he has held numerous central advisory posts in Israel. Until his retirement in 2011, he served as a Senior Research Fellow in the Moshe Dayan Center for Middle Eastern and African Studies, Tel Aviv University, and headed the Program on Jewish-Arab Cooperation in Israel sponsored by the Konrad-Adenauer-Stiftung (1995–2010). He recently authored, edited, and coedited *Muslim Minorities in non-Muslim Majority Countries: The Islamic Movement in Israel as a Test Case* (2011); *The Arab Society in Israel: A Compendium* (2009); *Arab Youth in Israel: Caught between Prospects and Risk* (2008); *The Arab Minority in Israel: An Analysis of the "Future Vision" Documents* (2008); *The Arab Minority in Israel and the 17th Knesset Elections* (2007); *Together but Apart: Mixed Cities in Israel* (2007); *The Evolvement of an Arab-Palestinian National Minority in Israel* (2007); *The Municipal Elections in the Arab and Druze Sector: Clans, Sectarianism and Political Parties* (2005); and *The Arabs in Israel: A National Minority in a Jewish Nation State* (2005). He is currently completing two manuscripts, one on Islamic Fundamentalism in Israel and another on Communism and Arab Nationalism.

Marina Rustow is Charlotte Bloomberg Associate Professor in the Humanities in the Department of History at The Johns Hopkins University. With an undergraduate degree from Yale University and an MA and PhD from Columbia University, she previously taught at Emory University. Rustow's research focuses on the Jewish communities of the medieval Mediterranean and, more broadly, medieval Middle Eastern history. She is the author of *Heresy and the Politics of Community: The Jews of the Fatimid Caliphate* (2008). The recipient of numerous fellowships and awards, her current research focuses on documents from the Cairo Geniza and what they can tell us about the Jewish community that preserved them and the governments that produced them.

Acknowledgments

This book could never have come to be without the assistance and hard work of many people. Pride of place goes to the marvelous contributors to the volume, whose important scholarship and educational sensitivities inform all the content to follow. Valiantly combating the myriad projects already on their desks and risking time away from other professional and personal tasks, I thank them for all their energy, support, and efforts. The commissioning editors at Continuum and Bloomsbury—first Kirsty Schaper and then Lalle Pursglove—have been remarkable partners in the process of conceptualizing and completing this volume, with their keen eyes on the market and their dedication to growing an excellent and meaningful list.

The overarching concept for this book emerged over many years and in numerous conversations with colleagues, particularly at my home institution, Spertus Institute for Jewish Learning and Leadership, in Chicago. Spertus is a remarkable institution, which has its own rightful place in the history and development of the field of Jewish Studies. Founded in 1924 as the College of Jewish Studies in Chicago, Spertus provides a remarkable range of impressive educational offerings for graduate students as well as adult learners. Many of the themes and issues discussed in this book are taught regularly at Spertus, and in my two decades at Spertus I have benefited tremendously from conversations with the faculty and my many students. Particular thanks must be reserved for Barry Chazan, Director of the Master of Arts in Jewish Professional Studies program and Professor of Jewish Education at Spertus, and Yohanan Petrovsky-Shtern, Crown Family Professor of Jewish History at Northwestern University—good friends and valued colleagues, with whom I have bounced around many of the ideas pursued in this book. Without the nurturing environment created by Hal M. Lewis, the President and CEO, as well as Professor of Contemporary Jewish Studies and Jewish Leadership at Spertus, it is hard to imagine that this volume would ever have seen the light of day. Hal provides remarkable leadership, which he models on a daily basis, and he offers genuine, reflective, and stimulating conversation in a fabulous range of topics related to

Jewish Studies and the Jewish community. He is a close friend, colleague, and mentor, whose vision of and passion for Jewish Studies is played out throughout this volume and all of my scholarly endeavors.

In the end this work, like everything that I am blessed to produce, can never really be possible without the love and support of my family. My children—Malkaya, Chanan, Ronia, and Yair—each in their own very different ways, have always allowed me time away from them to pursue my scholarly interests. For that willingness and for the enthusiasm they offer me for even the remotest scholarship I practice, I am truly grateful. But the bulk of the thanks for this and for everything else I do goes to my wife Juli, who stands with me always, providing constant support and encouragement and giving of herself completely so that I can continue to engage in the work that is so meaningful to me. There is no better example of a selfless individual, who toils for others before herself. Her intelligence, wisdom, and wit inform and enrich every wonderful moment we are fortunate to have together. Having her as my best friend and soul mate is more than I could ever have asked or hoped for. As always, this work is dedicated to her.

1 Introduction

Dean Phillip Bell

Chapter Outline

The Development of Jewish Studies

How to define Jewish Studies is not a question with a simple answer. There has, in fact, been a great deal of discussion about the very definition of "Jewish Studies." Taking a broad approach, some have asserted that Jewish Studies is as old as Judaism itself. Internal scholarly production is evident in the biblical corpus, which has increasingly been seen as in conversation with itself (through inner biblical writing and exegesis) as well as with the broader Ancient Near East (especially through the engagement with and appropriation, or recasting, of surrounding culture, religion, and social values).[1] Similar observations could be made throughout the balance of Jewish history—with internal developments as well as external interests (not always positively motivated), in such areas as Christian Hebraism and ethnographical writing already in the Middle Ages and early modern period.[2] In fact, the study of various aspects of Jewish life and Judaism has been utilized for many different purposes, from self-identification to scholarly inquiry and attempts to missionize or demonize the Jews.

What we can say is that Judaism and Jewish history were objects of academic interest long before they were classified as a formal (or even informal) academic field or subdiscipline. Frequently—as is the case with many modern academic disciplines—the development of Jewish Studies has often been placed in the context of the intellectual and cultural revolutions of the nineteenth century that led to new philosophies and worldviews. It has been generally accepted that Jewish history, for example, took on radically new tones and functions in the aftermath of Enlightenment and Emancipation. According to the historian Yosef Haim Yerushalmi, in the nineteenth century, "For the first time it is not history that must prove its utility to Judaism, but Judaism that must prove its validity to history, by revealing and justifying itself historically."[3] In response to modern secularization, assimilation, and nationalism, Jews reconsidered their identity and how they and their religion fit into broader society. "The Jews in the early nineteenth century who first felt an imperative to examine Judaism historically did so," Yerushalmi argues, "because they were no longer sure of what Judaism was, or whether, whatever it was it could be viable for them."[4] In this model, Jewish history became the "faith of fallen Jews,"[5] reflecting a break with the past and a separation from Jewish collective memory. Judaism, in this sense was no longer an absolute and self-contained essence, but rather it evolved through time and needed to be understood in its various contexts.[6] No longer interested in memory (the alleged nourishing milk of premodern society), the modern Jewish historian, like other modern Jewish Studies scholars, was not content with the narrow focus of more traditional Judaism, but rather sought to recover a complete past, one that utilized a wide range of sources and explored a plethora of topics.[7]

Of course, the Jewish intellectual developments of the nineteenth century drew from and cultivated the broader philosophical orientations of the age. The early nineteenth-century Jewish writer Immanuel Wolf, for example, asserted that "the content of this special science [the study of Judaism] is the systematic unfolding and representation of its object in its whole sweep, for its own sake, and not for any ulterior purposes."[8] Jewish Study, in this scheme, was not to serve religious identity or polemics. "Scientific" approaches to knowledge revealed both continuities and innovations, however, and Wolf himself recognized a special, ongoing essence or spirit of Judaism. Therefore, *Wissenschaft des Judentums* (the scientific study of Judaism, which developed in the early part of the nineteenth century) itself, he asserted, "unfolds Judaism in accordance with its essence and describes it systematically, always relating individual features back to the fundamental principle of the whole."[9] This study of Judaism, for Wolf, proceeded on three levels—textual, historical, and philosophical.[10] Similarly, for the German Jewish scholar Isaac Marcus Jost, the Jewish historian had to grapple with the collective spirit of his people, at the same time that he was required to employ critical methods and approaches to historical data and sources in order to light his path and dispel dangerous errors.[11] The entire literary corpus of the Jewish people became, for Jost and others, fair game for evaluation:

> We consider the entire collection of Hebrew sacred literature a source of history although it was not all intended to be historical and even the actual historical books do not proceed from an historical point of view. . . . In this sense, the Holy Scriptures of the Hebrews become wholly excellent sources of history. They constitute a collection of popular accounts, thoughts, laws, speeches, poems, seldom separated into genres but rather meshed and interwoven, nearly always producing a clear portrait of the totality.[12]

Of course the scholars of the nineteenth century were not the first to ask difficult questions of sacred texts or explore the context of Jewish writings and historical experiences. The Bible itself provides evidence of internal debate, with ancient stories being erased, submerged, or re-crafted for a range of purposes—including the clarification of theological positions and the navigation of political disputes (internal and external). The rabbis were aware of the many tensions and gaps in the biblical texts and filled these gaps through Midrash, in ways that allowed oral traditions and religious law to be established. Even medieval chroniclers and exegetes were aware of apparent tensions in the biblical and rabbinic texts, and they were capable of approaching such challenges with creativity and finesse. Certainly in the seventeenth century, Baruch (or Benedict) Spinoza offered a severe challenge to the sacrality of the Bible. Spinoza has been equally hailed as the last medieval and the first modern Jew. While Spinoza contextualized the Bible (Hebrew Bible and New Testament), he continued to maintain that the Bible had important historical and ethical value, even if the context in which it was crafted was no longer completely relevant. As such, some have seen Spinoza as a secularist, but one in close negotiation with religious tradition and texts. Perhaps that makes Spinoza a Jewish Studies scholar in the modern sense, though one suspects that Spinoza himself would have rebuffed such anachronism.[13]

In any event, by the end of the nineteenth century, important aspects of Jewish Studies, particularly Bible and Semitics (an academic discipline including the study of the history, language, and culture of Semitic peoples) were receiving important and significant attention, though, as with the study of Jewish history, often by non-Jewish scholars. The results could vary, but at times such scholarship was used for polemically anti-Jewish purposes.

Jews, Jewish Studies, and Higher Education in America

Early Jewish Studies in America imbibed the nineteenth-century cultural and scientific approaches to Jewish Studies that could be found in Germany.[14] As in

Europe, Jewish Studies in America was not a particularly Jewish endeavor and Jews were typically and effectively excluded from the study of the Bible and religion in academic circles.[15] In these early years the number of Jewish scholars who were accepted or who reached the highest echelon of universities was quite small—Harry Wolfson at Harvard University and Salo Baron of Columbia University were not only the most renowned, but also among the few professors of Judaica.[16] The small number of Jewish students at institutions of higher education in America in the early part of the twentieth century likewise limited the focus of Jewish Studies and its connection with Jewish communities. That is not to say that Jews did not engage such issues—in Hebrew colleges (starting already in the late nineteenth century) as well as in developing seminaries and in the expanding work of innovative boards of Jewish education.[17]

In the late nineteenth and early twentieth centuries, a number of significant changes would lay the foundation for the expansion of Jewish Studies as a formal academic endeavor. Between 1881 and 1924, the Jewish population in America grew from 250,000 (less than 1% of the total population) to almost 4 million (more than 3%). This growth combined with the significant development of colleges and the dramatic increase of students enrolling in institutions of higher education. From the start of the third decade of the twentieth century into the mid-1960s, the number of institutions granting a bachelor's degree doubled and the number of bachelor's degrees conferred increased 11-fold; similarly the number of master's degrees conferred increased 35-fold and doctoral degrees 30-fold.[18] This general academic boom resulted in a remarkable surge in Jewish attendance at colleges as well[19]—growth that mirrored increasing Jewish college attendance in the USSR and key cities in central Europe, where Jews could comprise a third of college students in some locations.[20] The number of Jewish Studies courses in the United States expanded 90-fold (generally increasing 70% every three years) in the middle decades of the twentieth century.[21] Facilitating this increase were the many Jewish academics who migrated from Europe, especially Germany, in the 1930s and who taught in the middle of the twentieth century at various Jewish seminaries and Hebrew colleges.[22]

The easing of restrictions on the number of Jewish students and the integration of Judaica themes and courses into the broader university curriculum impacted student and faculty experiences beyond the classroom. They led to the development of robust Jewish student organizations, such as the Menorah Association at Harvard University, representing diverse Jewish interests of both an academic and personal nature. The activities of such associations did not, however, always meet with the approval of university officials, Jewish communal leaders, or Jewish students and faculty.[23]

Semitics and Hebrew were central Judaica fields in the early part of the twentieth century in American Higher Education, with increased enrollments in the late nineteenth century.[24] Over time, however, emphasis slowly shifted in other directions; particularly by the last third of the twentieth century, the focus of Jewish Studies began to wander to modern Hebrew, history, literature, and culture. According to a prevalent understanding of the situation:

> The pessimism of the 1920s, bracketed by academic anti-Semitism and the emergence of a "mass" urban constituency, slowly eroded as Jewish learning expanded into new subject areas under the aegis of parent disciplines that had fewer restrictions than Semitics and into new types of colleges. "Pluralist" justifications for university inclusion that gave roughly equal billing to "Jewish contributions" and to internal integrity replaced the unqualified universalism of the preceding generation.[25]

Still, statistics about general course offerings reveal little interest in new themes or methodologies before the 1960s,[26] and Jewish learning continued to lack independent status at the program or departmental level.[27]

What was originally a field (or fields) housed at a small number of prominent research universities gradually spread to many other institutions.[28] In addition, and following broader trends in the academy and American society, in the 1930s and the 1940s, Judaica scholars became increasingly concerned with pluralistic and universalistic issues,[29] helping to prepare the fuller integration of Judaica themes into the university curriculum by the 1960s. Even so, in this period Jewish learning was often still primarily related to Jewish communal work, where many of the great Jewish historian Salo Baron's students, for example, toiled in the middle decades of the century. This was a period of significant transformation of formal Jewish community organizations. For the first time, some individuals with scholarly inclinations, who would previously have only entered the rabbinate as a vehicle for study and professional opportunities, chose to enroll in the university for advanced Judaica training and to seek careers in Jewish communal service. This was also a period in which a substantial number of Israeli academics moved to locations outside Israel to find academic work. The conditions were ripe for enhanced needs and perceived attractiveness of university-based Jewish Studies, outside the traditional religious and educational institutions and parameters.

By the 1960s, new approaches to history and Hebrew language instruction emerged, resulting in proliferating enrollments and pedagogical advances.[30] Similarly, academic interest in Yiddish expanded and the theme of religion was more broadly absorbed into the humanities, after several decades of relative decline.[31] In the same vein, growing interest in the social sciences in the late 1940s and into the 1960s would add to the increasing diversity of academic methodologies and concerns, especially in Judaica study.[32]

It is customary to associate Jewish Studies as an academic area of interest with the revolutionary changes of the 1960s: the social and cultural movements that inspired civil rights movements and the emergence of ethnic and gender studies programs in America and elsewhere; the dramatic military victories of the State of Israel, particularly the Six-Day War, which strengthened Jewish sensibilities and identity; and the growth of interfaith dialogue, especially in the wake of the Second Vatican Council. Regarding the position of religion in the academy, a Supreme Court decision in 1963 further opened the way for teaching about religion in public institutions, even as it prohibited devotional exercises. While higher biblical criticism was being debated and, in some circles, Christian triumphalism and orientation was being challenged, religion itself was more broadly integrated into the university curriculum. Within the Jewish community, as Robert Alter noted already in the early 1970s, the changing nature of Jewish identity at the time and, in particular, the less self-conscious mind-set and willingness to be seen on campus of a new generation of Jews sparked interest in Jewish pasts (perhaps the result of what Alter labeled an incomplete process of assimilation) and Judaica programming.[33]

In addition to the factors noted above, the development of Israel and the scholarly advances in a number of academic fields have made Jewish Studies simultaneously a battle ground and an attractive and productive laboratory. Consider, for example, the increased attentiveness to minority groups as reflected in colonial and subaltern studies. On the one hand, Jewish history has been presented as a paradigm of minority success in the wake of persecution; on the other hand, Jews themselves have been the targets of demagogues airing political views, frequently about the Middle East, and cast as oppressors (particularly in anti-Zionist voices).

But there have been other, no less important or dramatic changes, as well. The long-awaited and much-needed infusion of women into the higher ranks of the academy has brought new emphases and sensitivities in different fields and an openness to explore issues of gender and other sociological concerns. As with many other fields, especially in the social sciences, Jewish Studies has been largely an interdisciplinary endeavor that has benefited from this broader connectivity and recalibration.

Some scholars have criticized more recent developments in Jewish Studies. According to one argument, the expansion of Jewish Studies to new fields and its preoccupation with new questions has watered down its focus and quality and dampened the attention and scope of treatment given to classical sources — especially rabbinic (as well as biblical). This is evident, some assert, in the narrowing specialization within Jewish Studies. Of course, many scholars would counter that that is the natural progression and development of an academic field. As specific themes and methodologies emerge they are by nature more specialized; as the field matures, scholars begin to forward broader syntheses and reevaluations of themes and methodologies.

One additional observation that has been hinted at, but not yet fully stated, should be offered here as well—namely, that Jewish Studies like other fields, and perhaps quite a bit more, can be highly localized. While there has been a good deal of interdisciplinary work and fecund cross-fertilization across fields, the focus of and approach to Jewish Studies has varied in specific regions. Jewish Studies is not the same in every country and may even differ by institution or institution type. Take the example of Germany. There, two quite divergent schools of Jewish Studies have developed over the past several decades. Proponents and practitioners of Judaistik, who traditionally have tended to teach and research in West Germany, have generally focused on Hebrew sources and on more traditional approaches to rabbinic and biblical topics. Jüdische Studien, on the other hand, which has been practiced more in East German circles, has tended to be concerned with social history and often makes primary use of archival materials in German. Over the years, polemical battles pitting individual personalities and quests for funding have led to some vociferous diatribes between some proponents of these schools. Even in this area, however, one senses that—ongoing differences notwithstanding—a blurring of the lines is occurring in Germany, as scholars cross schools, utilize a diversity of sources and methodologies, and explore an expanded palette of themes.[34] Similar observations could be made about Jewish Studies and its primary foci and agenda in other places across Europe, in South America, as well as in Israel and the Far East.

Jewish Studies, Judaism, and the Jewish Community

The role of the Jewish community and individual donors in the growth and focus of Jewish Studies should not be overlooked. The creation and composition of Jewish Studies departments and offerings (within or beyond any formal centers or programs) has frequently been determined by donor wishes and sensibilities or by university administrations who believe that significant philanthropy can be harvested by providing such academic focus. At the same time, and perhaps even more frequently, the form that Jewish Studies takes on campus is determined in part by the (often chance) makeup of the broader faculty at a given institution, with individual faculty members possessing some specialization or simply personal or professional interest in some aspect of Jewish Studies or a personal commitment within the local Jewish community. As a result, many programs present Jewish Studies as essentially a program or course in Holocaust or, increasingly, modern Jewish history or literature, frequently with an emphasis on Israel, or a series of courses that address the personal or research interest of individual faculty members.

As Jewish Studies have moved from rabbinical seminaries and Hebrew teachers colleges more firmly into secular university settings there have been both benefits and challenges. For some, the marketplace of ideas at the university allows for a thoughtful and objective examination of Judaica themes and Jewish history, nurturing fresh approaches and comparative perspectives that take into account diverse contexts beyond the Jewish community. The academy affords the opportunity to cultivate and practice critical thinking skills. Not surprisingly, for many Jewish Studies scholars, the university cannot and should not be considered a resource for Jewish religious education or continuity—something that many donors to such programs have clearly hoped they might become, especially given their frustration at the Jewish community's oft-limited success in engaging precollegiate youth.[35] As Arthur Green noted years ago,

> Jewish scholarship can no longer serve as the handmaiden of Jewish apologetics. The university scholar, unlike his seminary colleague, cannot teach that Judaism is the unique repository of truth, that it is "better," either morally or theologically, than other faiths, or even comfortably preach the values of its continued existence . . . the content of the professors' message can hardly dare to allow itself to be the same as that of the rabbis. Here the content of objective research has caught up with itself, and its implications can no longer be ignored.[36]

Of course, depending on one's position, such an observation—if we indeed accept the idealized notion of objectivity, and in particular academic objectivity—does not have to be a bad thing. As Green continues, "This is not to say that the effect of scholarship on the faith of Judaism is entirely corrosive—not at all. I believe it provides for a clearing of the air and helps to set Jewish theology on a creative and modern—or post-modern—course."[37] Such scholarship allows people to see the variation within Judaism and to focus upon contextualization and interpretation. And for some in the field of Jewish communal work, the broad knowledge of Judaica enriches the work of Jewish professionals, even as it makes them aware of the diversity of perspectives and practices in contemporary Jewish communities and throughout Jewish history.[38]

Differences in focus are of course also quite marked in different countries. Jewish Studies in Germany, for example, serves a primarily non-Jewish audience and it is heavily focused on modern themes that help to explicate modern German history and the horrific annihilation of Jews in the twentieth century. In Israel, on the other hand, Jewish Studies has become a field that is symbolized both by tradition and grappling with classical texts in Hebrew as well as iconoclastic scholarship. In many ways, particularly in the early years of the state, the role of Jewish Studies was related to national agendas and identities as a way to validate Jewish culture and political orientations—even as the same serves today as a means to criticize and challenge current political realities and trajectories.[39]

Cocurricular Jewish activities and the academic sought learning goals of Jewish Studies courses have been effectively separated by many faculty, who find it too dangerous to steer the line between the two. Still, by the very courses that they teach and the way that they approach them, faculty members do insert their own ideas about Judaism and Jewish society into the curriculum. Alter notes that

> any instruction in the humanities, though ideally critical and disinterested, is never value-free. Certain fundamental intellectual allegiances, aesthetic and perhaps moral preferences, surely come into play when a teacher decides on a curriculum, when he chooses emphases and approaches in the presentation of his materials, simply when he devotes himself to a particular field of study.[40]

For some in the academy, Jewish Studies should in fact not be targeted at Jewish students at all. According to this line of thought, the sign of its maturation as an academic field is that many non-Jewish students enroll in Jewish Studies courses. What is more, the enrollment of non-Jewish students in Jewish Studies courses adds to the vitality of programs and allows courses that would otherwise be saddled with low enrollments to continue.

The result is that the audience for Jewish Studies is even more diverse than its scholars. Jewish Studies courses attract a wide range of students with many different areas of interest, especially when such courses are constructed in comparative frameworks or address contemporary issues. Many students enroll in Jewish Studies courses because they are interested in themes related to religion, and Jewish Studies courses appear in Christian as well as Jewish seminaries. Many other students are interested in more general aspects of history, literature, art, language, and culture. Jewish students themselves are hardly an easily identifiable group, and they come from different denominational backgrounds; many do not affiliate with Jewish religious life on campus or at home. How a particular Jewish Studies course fits into their academic plans, fulfills a distribution requirement, or otherwise stirs their curiosity is often difficult to plan for or understand. At the graduate level, Jewish Studies offerings likewise draw an eclectic range of students, particularly as many graduate students have first or second fields outside of Jewish Studies. And although most adult learners do not take Jewish Studies courses for credit, the extent of Judaica offerings that are designed and delivered within the university (through continuing education and special courses, such as travel courses) and in other Jewish communal settings should not be overlooked. These courses are often taught by local university faculty, frequently at a sophisticated level, and they encourage the dissemination of current research and topics that allow for a vibrant connection between town and gown.

Jewish Studies Today

Over the past 40 years, Jewish Studies has blossomed into a vibrant and sophisticated academic field. Combining a variety of methodologies and addressing myriad issues associated with the history of Jews and the development of Judaism, both internally and in relation to other societies and cultures, Jewish Studies today is rich and interdisciplinary. It has evolved within the context of unique Jewish and communal orientations and concerns and as part of broader shifts in the academy.

According to the Association for Jewish Studies (AJS), one of the largest associations of Jewish Studies academics, there are more than 250 endowed professorships in Jewish Studies at 85 colleges and universities in North America. Many of these institutions offer minors or majors in Jewish Studies; many more offer individual courses in a range of Jewish Studies themes. The AJS itself has grown from a small circle of scholars focused on biblical and rabbinic topics to a professional association comprised of more than 1,500 members. It holds annual conferences in different locations across North America, which regularly attract a thousand participants and feature 700–800 academic presentations. The AJS also publishes a scholarly journal and offers travel and research grants, as well as online resources for its members.

Similarly, the European Association for Jewish Studies (EAJS) holds an annual conference and publishes a journal. According to its website,

> The main aims of the European Association for Jewish Studies (the sole umbrella organization representing this field of university studies in the continent) are the encouragement and support of the teaching of Jewish studies at [the] university level in Europe, and to further an understanding of the importance of Jewish culture and civilization and of the impact it has had on European cultures over many centuries. The EAJS was founded as a voluntary academic association in 1981, and the Association has since organized a number of international conferences in Jewish studies.[41]

More than 450 institutions of higher education that offer Jewish Studies courses in 28 European countries are listed by the EAJS. National associations can be found in nine countries: France, Germany, Italy, Netherlands, Poland, Russia, Spain, Switzerland, and the United Kingdom. The countries with the largest number of institutions related to Jewish Studies are in western Europe: Germany (110), the United Kingdom (87), Italy (50), France (32), and the Netherlands (29), though the number and scope of institutions offering Jewish Studies in some form in eastern Europe has increased, especially in Poland (27). These institutions and their programs are supported by 29 Judaica libraries. In terms of individual scholars, the nearly 1,200 EAJS members hail from 26 different countries, with the largest numbers from Germany (344), the United Kingdom (226), Italy (97), France (70), and Poland (60). Especially in Germany and eastern Europe, many Jewish Studies scholars are not themselves Jewish.

The World Union of Jewish Studies (WUJS) is likewise an umbrella association that provides important Jewish Studies resources. Established in 1947, WUJS is a parent body for Jewish Studies research for scholars, students, and intellectuals around the globe.[42] It is supported by the Israeli government and various Israeli institutions and foundations, with goals to unite scholars and institutions and provide a framework for regional research organizations; organize and sponsor international conferences; promote and disseminate Jewish Studies research; and establish foundations and award grants and prizes. These goals are met, in part, through the World Congress of Jewish Studies that meets in Jerusalem every four years. The 2009 Congress assembled 3,000 participants from 40 countries and featured 1,400 academic presentations.

Other, smaller and regional, Jewish Studies associations have also developed over the past several decades, including the Midwest Jewish Studies Association (MJSA) and the Western Jewish Studies Association (WJSA) in the United States, which along with the Jewish Studies program at Purdue University publish the academic journal *Shofar: An Interdisciplinary Journal of Jewish Studies* and which hold independent and joint academic conferences. The Association for Canadian Jewish Studies / l'Association d'études juives canadiennes, similarly was founded in 1976 (originally as the Canadian Jewish Historical Society / Société d'histoire juive canadienne). The association published the *Canadian Jewish Historical Society Journal* in the late 1970s and the 1980s and more recently the journal *Canadian Jewish Studies*. The multidisciplinary association is headquartered in Montreal, and it is focused on the promotion and dissemination of "historical research concerning the engagement of Jews to Canadian society."[43]

Jewish Studies is not limited to North America, Europe, and Israel, however. Other associations have been formed to advance Jewish Studies in diverse locations and in related fields. There are, for example, regional and national associations with smaller, but growing footprints. Consider the Australian Association of Jewish Studies and the Jewish Studies work being done in China through the initiatives of several individual faculty members and universities. There are likewise some theme-specific associations, such as the Latin American Jewish Studies Association, which hold a special caucus at the AJS's annual meeting.[44]

Jewish Studies as an academic field also reaches far beyond the confines of specifically Jewish Studies settings. Almost every major academic discipline in the humanities and social sciences engages Jewish Studies themes and includes scholars who spend at least some time researching and teaching issues that could be classified as Jewish Studies. According to a 2008 AJS membership survey, for example, a large percentage of AJS members also participate in the American Academy of Religion (22.3%), American Historical Association (19.6%), Society of Biblical Literature (19.3%), and Modern Language Association (14.5%), to cite just the largest. There are many scholarly associations that hold regular meetings and include numerous papers on Jewish Studies themes, such as the German Studies Association and the Sixteenth-Century Studies Conference, to give just two examples. Jewish Studies related papers are also presented in many different contexts at local, national, and international conferences that focus on specific topics.

While the nature and focus of Jewish Studies scholars obviously varies by discipline, age, personal interests, and geography (among other factors), a review of the membership data available for the AJS reveals some important information and useful, if tentative, conclusions. The AJS membership comprises a large and vibrant community of scholars. According to the respondents of the membership survey in 2008,[45] the gender balance is 53 percent male and 47 percent female and the median age is 50 (with 70% of members between the ages of 35 and 64). Nearly 79 percent of respondents categorized themselves as Democrats and 65 percent as politically liberal, much higher than typical American percentages. Ninety-two percent of the membership survey respondents were Jewish, most with clear religious affiliation: 21.3 percent Orthodox, 32.5 percent Conservative, 13.5 percent Reform, 3.9 percent Reconstructionist, and 0.9 percent Renewal. More than 18 percent identified themselves as Jewish, but nondenominational. More than 51 percent of AJS members work in public university settings; nearly 31 percent in private educational settings. More than 17 percent work in sectarian institutions of higher education—14.6 percent in Jewish and 2.8 percent in Christian ones. Sixty-three percent work in institutions that offer graduate degrees and just over 20 percent work at four-year colleges. Far fewer AJS members work in research institutes (3.8%) or two-year junior colleges (0.8%).

Departmental affiliations reveal clusters of foci among Jewish Studies academics: nearly 24 percent in history, over 16 percent in religion, and just above 11 percent in Near Eastern/Judaic studies. Other areas of focus include: English literature (5.7%), Rabbinics/Talmud (5.2%), sociology (4.2%), Bible (3.1%), Hebrew language and literature (2.9%), education (2.6%), comparative literature (2.3%), Romance languages (1.8%), and philosophy (1.3%). Underscoring the interdisciplinary orientation of Jewish Studies in North America today, approximately 25 percent of faculty members in Jewish Studies hold an exclusive appointment, while the rest hold joint appointments in Jewish Studies and another department or program (32.7%) or an appointment outside of Jewish Studies altogether (42.5%).

The wide range of Jewish Studies associations and activities and the profile of Jewish Studies academics reveal a diverse and engaged cadre of scholars who are comfortable within and beyond the Jewish community and Jewish topics. Indeed, Jewish Studies has grown dramatically over the past several decades and its growth has been encouraged by and helped to fuel developments in a variety of academic disciplines.

Future Orientations

Disparate and diverse topics and global concerns have affected Jewish Studies. In recent scholarship, Jews throughout history have been seen as both engaged with surrounding non-Jewish culture and often simultaneously inward looking, segregated, and distinctive.[46] Such tension has allowed scholars to explore with new inflections questions of Jewish identity and agency, with Jewish power in relation to non-Jews emerging forcefully in ways that parallel discussions of colonized and marginalized people in a variety of studies over the past three decades. Recent interest in acculturation (as opposed to assimilation), however, also raises the fresh question of how Jews took surrounding ideas and practices and crafted them within Jewish tradition to create new culture and praxis. More than the famous Jewish contributions to civilization—which had as one central goal to reinscribe Jews in society and history—this approach now recognizes that Jews and Judaism were also transformed in their exchange with the broader world. Of course, one can recognize vast continuity in Jewish history, religion, and thought. As David Biale notes, "And yet, such a definition [of culture that is focused on context and change] would be missing a crucial aspect of Jewish culture: the continuity of both textual and folk traditions throughout Jewish history and throughout the many lands inhabited by the Jews."[47]

Not surprisingly, then, Jewish Studies can mean a great many things to different people and Jewish Studies takes place in many fora, utilizing a range of scholarly tools, and assuming a variety of shapes. Jewish Studies are pursued at universities and seminaries of all stripes. They are also cultivated at Hebrew colleges and a plethora of research centers—some with a special focus on Jews and Jewish Studies[48] and some of a broader nature that touch upon themes related to Judaism and Jewish history or thought.[49] We have already had occasion to discuss the range of Jewish Studies associations. But these and other organizations and presses publish an impressive range of journals that address the full scope of Judaica.[50] Similarly, scholarly journals not focused on Jews or Judaism also provide regular and important articles on Jewish Studies topics.[51]

As can be seen from the essays in this volume alone, the diversity of sources and the span of languages that are addressed and utilized by Jewish Studies are vast. Particularly important scholarship in Jewish Studies appears regularly in English, Hebrew, German, French, and Italian. But both local/regional studies and broader syntheses appear in many other languages, notably Russian, Spanish, and increasingly Chinese, to name only a few.

As it stands now and as it will continue to develop, there are many ways to understand Jewish Studies. There are particular choice points to be made in determining approaches to and even divisions within the field. There are also certain topics that have emerged or appear to be emerging that will affect the trajectory of the field and help establish new narratives in many disciplines.

As in other maturing disciplines, the master narratives that have been regnant in Jewish Studies over the past century have slowly been revised through specialized study of particular themes, sources, and contexts. While some scholars observe in this sea-change reflections of broader academic agendas or, perhaps more critically, symptoms of the decreasing breadth of knowledge of contemporary colleagues, in many ways, these and other changes reflect the ripening and advancement of the entire field of Jewish Studies. The reassessment of traditional—and, in some cases, tired—narratives is a sign that Jewish Studies is vital and self-reflective. This is not to suggest that older or more traditional narratives are not, by necessity or lapse of time, valuable or even correct in details or broad outlines. Still, the opportunity to ask new questions or to consider issues of relevance today within the context of Jewish history and thought is not only useful, but necessary as well. Synthesis of more specific studies allows engagement with previous scholarship and the reconsideration of assumptions, while simultaneously staking out the ground for new research and laying the foundation for revised conclusions.[52]

As indicated above and throughout this volume, the turn to cultural studies has had an enormous impact on many aspects of Jewish Studies. Long-needed attention to diversity within Judaism and Jewish society has arrived—with important foci of research on gender, social stratification, and variation in local conditions, as well as the reconceptualization of how to define "traditional" and "normative" Judaism. The result has been treatment of themes that have not traditionally generated sustained attention—consider, for example, a renewed emphasis on Sephardic Jewry, innovative studies of Jewish women, and new discussions on Jewish power and polemic. The work on culture has also opened up fruitful discussions of arts and material culture,[53] refinements in how we view and understand assimilation and acculturation, and focus on little-studied issues such as daily life. This concern with internal diversity has developed in concert with new emphases on Jewish interactions with the outside world.

Of course, the outlines of Jewish Studies that have emerged in recent decades are indebted to earlier work and modern and contemporary developments. In addition to the many issues raised throughout this introduction, the Holocaust and the State of Israel have arguably contributed the most to the current state of Jewish Studies—both directly and indirectly. The Holocaust has, until recently, been the most discussed topic in Jewish history and theology over the past several decades. For a time, the Holocaust-dominated academic conferences, course offerings, and even the language of the discipline, with issues such as trauma, power and powerlessness, victimization, memory, ethics and religion, modernity, continuity, and identity informed by the Holocaust and infusing much of the discussion across the full range of subfields of Jewish Studies. Many historians have discussed the nature and implications of these developments.[54] The field of Holocaust Studies itself has become quite broad[55] and has been highlighted by intensive research that has both academic and practical implications. The fact that the Holocaust does not receive its own chapter in this volume testifies to how thoroughly the subject has informed Jewish Studies writ large and how impossible it is to do justice to the theme in a single volume. As the attentive reader will notice, the themes of the Holocaust filter into many chapters and they help inform the contours of modern Judaism and continue to impact the orientation and concerns of contemporary Jewish society. At the same time, it is fair to say that the themes in Holocaust Studies have themselves been impacted by some of the prevailing concerns of Jewish Studies more generally—consider the localization of studies, the emphases on diversity of experiences, and the questions of politics and power, for example.

In a similar way, the State of Israel has served as a flashpoint for much of the development in Jewish Studies. For some, the State of Israel has been placed within the context of responses to the Holocaust. Broader perspectives on the Jews in Palestine and the development of nationalism and Jewish relations with non-Jews, however, have raised many other questions. Longer-term discussions of homeland and exile have informed Jewish Studies for more than a century (even longer in some ways). The collection of materials and an academic environment and culture that possess internal concerns as well as international aspirations and foci have helped to raise some previously little-studied themes to greater prominence. As reflected in the rapid growth of Israel Studies, the scholarship being produced in Israel as well as the various religious, social, cultural, and political issues being addressed in Israel and in responses to Israel need to be considered in a review of Jewish Studies as an academic discipline— one that has a great deal of resonance beyond the walls of the academy.

There is one final and more general theme that should be singled out in the development of Jewish Studies today—"postmodernism."[56] While the term is often overplayed and insufficiently defined, the postmodern turn has been especially salient for Jewish Studies. This has been true for the implications of postmodernism for Jewish life today as well as the postmodern accents of contemporary scholarship in areas such as literature, anthropology, politics, and identity. Postmodernism has often been focused on rupture and discontinuity[57]—in some ways itself indebted to the discussions of the Holocaust. Much of the earliest work of a postmodern hue developed in the context of literary studies. A good deal of the deconstruction and post-structuralism of the past several decades has presented history as a literary genre and so in a sense fiction. After all, history—like everything—is a subjective representation based on the selective survival, use, and interpretation of sources by individuals asking particular questions and bearing unique personal and intellectual baggage and lenses. Indeed, interpretation must be seen in any body of writing—it forms part and parcel of all literatures and histories and cannot easily be isolated from the very narratives it explicates or produces. As a result, many conclude that there is no objectivity and indeed no essentialism; rather, everything needs to be contextualized and is the product of local conditions.[58] Of course, this raises tremendous questions about and challenges for understanding broad religious movements and historical development in Judaism and other subjects. Ironically, the resultant debates and recalibrations of traditional narratives have simultaneously been fecund and productive and, in some ways, restored some aspects of the traditional master narratives. Even recent discussions of secularization, for example, have returned to ground discussion in the context of more "traditional" religious orientations.[59]

The study of literature in postmodern contexts elevated the role of language in producing narrative and rhetoric. As Moshe Rosman has noted, according to this approach, "Language is a cultural code . . . it encrypts meaning [and] . . . encodes the values, ideologies, and power relations inherent in the culture it serves";[60] the deconstruction of such language has been seen as essential by many scholars for uncovering subjectivities, contingent meanings, and power interests. The literary focus of such postmodern trends extended beyond literature and has impacted the study of art and material culture as well.[61] In fact, in almost every social science and humanities discipline, this approach has fostered methodological innovation and directed attention to new themes and to the experiences of victims and minorities (religious, social, gendered)—that is those who have been discriminated against in the power narratives of the majority or victors, but who have, at the same time, been able to contest power relations and structures through the very same discourse (though inversions and subtle uses of the same languages and concepts). On the one hand, new interest in minorities has centered and even "legitimized" the study of Jews; on the other hand, it has at times placed Jews in the role of the majority and oppressors and presented rather negative interpretations of Jewish history and activity (as in critiques of Zionism and the State of Israel).

Postmodernity has had important sociological implications as well that have impacted Jewish society and so Jewish Studies. Among the issues that have had implications in both areas, consider: demographical shifts (including the growth of Israel and shrinkage of world Jewish communities, complicated by a large, but proportionately decreasing concentration in the United States); political, legal, and economic integration generating questions about assimilation and acculturation as well as Jewish and non-Jewish relations more broadly; multiplicity of identities (including syncretistic, pluralist, hybrid) that have resulted, in part, in growing questions of how to define Jews and Jewishness; social concerns that have prompted new attention on women and issues of sexuality; and the velocity and acceleration of change, prompted in part by expanding technology.[62]

The impact of any of these specific categories of themes has varied by field, scholarly school, and individual scholarly orientations and concerns. Details about specific developments in various fields emerge in the essays to follow. In some ways, then, Jewish Studies is no different from any other academic field. It has been impacted by the larger social and academic changes around it. And yet, by the very nature of many of its central sources and concerns, Jewish Studies is simultaneously traditional and innovative. There is a fine balance between these two realms, but in many ways the very tension is and has always been central to Jewish Studies as a field of academic endeavor. That may be part of its richness and complexity and may explain why it is often difficult to clearly define Jewish Studies.[63] At the same time, such tensions have helped to make Jewish Studies one of the most vibrant, engaging, and important fields in the academy—one that draws from and advances scholarship and teaching more generally.

A Note on This Volume

The dramatic growth and important academic contributions of Jewish Studies make a volume devoted to the state and future directions of Jewish Studies not only desirable, but necessary. While several encyclopedias, dictionaries, and edited volumes of essays have addressed the theme of Jewish Studies over the past several years, they have each done so from a very specific perspective— they have focused on particular issues and themes—or they have attempted to be comprehensive, all the while losing cohesion and consistency across the individual essays.[64]

In this volume, we offer an overview of Jewish Studies, in which individual chapters survey the key themes as well as the development and current trends of research in each subject area. This volume is designed for students and advanced scholars alike. It contains an alphabetical glossary of terms; select bibliography of key works in English; maps; and timelines. It can be used as the primary text for a range of thematic, survey, and comparative courses in Judaism, religion, and history. It is also a central resource for individuals steeping themselves, for personal or professional reasons, in to a specific Jewish Studies theme for the first time or seeking to garner a broad overview of the field (or better, fields) of Jewish Studies. Contributors to the volume are both accomplished researchers and seasoned educators. Each essay, therefore, engages broad disciplinary issues and topics that draw from current research.

The 12 essays of this volume have been divided into two parts. In Part I, we have focused on somewhat traditional chronological divisions of Jewish Studies—biblical and rabbinic (representing the formation of Judaism and Jewish society); medieval (the extended period from the close of the Talmud until the expulsion from Spain) as reflected in the rich and diverse experiences of Jews living under Islam and Christianity; early modern and modern (with the acceleration of life more generally and complex political and demographic developments). There has been significant growth in all these fields. As each of the essays reveals in its own way, the interdisciplinary nature of Jewish Studies and the use of diverse and exciting methodological innovations characterize the field as a whole. To this we have added, in Part II, five essays that focus on the contemporary period and several essential themes that have impacted the full scope of Jewish Studies, but which grow out of contemporary concerns and perspectives—namely, gender, arts and material culture, demography, and Israel Studies.

Notes

1. See the essay by Leonard J. Greenspoon in this volume; consider, as well, the important and still-engaging work of Nahum Sarna, such as (1966), *Understanding Genesis* (New York: Jewish Theological Seminary of America) or the recent efforts of Avigdor Shinan and Yair Zakovitch (2012), *From Gods to God: How the Bible Debunked, Suppressed, or Changed Ancient Myths and Legends,* Valerie Zakovitch (trans.). Lincoln: University of Nebraska Press.
2. See, for example, the recent work of Yaakov Deutsch (2012), *Judaism in Christian Eyes: Ethnographic Descriptions of Jews and Judaism in Early Modern Europe,* Avi Aronsky (trans.). Oxford: Oxford University Press, in which the author claims that European Christian ethnographers of the Jews and Christian Hebraists in the early modern period may rightfully stake claim to being the precursors of academic modern Jewish Studies professors.
3. Yosef Haim Yerushalmi (1982), *Zakhor: Jewish History and Jewish Memory.* Seattle: University of Washington Press, p. 84.
4. Ibid., p. 86.
5. Ibid.
6. Ibid., pp. 91–2.
7. Ibid., p. 94.
8. Michael A. Meyer (1974), *Ideas of Jewish History.* New York: Berman House, p. 152.
9. Ibid., p. 152.
10. Ibid., p. 153.
11. Ibid., p. 186.
12. Ibid., p. 184.
13. See the work of Steven Nadler, for example, including most recently (2011), *A Book Forged in Hell: Spinoza's Scandalous Treatise and the Birth of the Secular Age.* Princeton: Princeton University Press.

14. Daniel Greene (2011), *The Jewish Origins of Cultural Pluralism: The Menorah Association and American Diversity*. Bloomington: Indiana University Press, pp. 94 ff.
15. Alan Cooper (2002), "Biblical Studies and Jewish Studies," in Martin Goodman (ed.), *The Oxford Handbook of Jewish Studies*. New York: Oxford University Press, pp. 14–35.
16. See Greene, *The Jewish Origins of Cultural Pluralism*, pp. 109 f., for example, and Paul Ritterband and Harold S. Wechsler (1994), *Jewish Learning in American Universities: The First Century*. Bloomington: Indiana University Press.
17. Greene, *The Jewish Origins of Cultural Pluralism*, 98 ff.; and see Jonathan B. Krasner (2011), *The Benderly Boys and American Jewish Education*. Lebanon, NH: Brandeis University Press.
18. Ritterband and Wechsler, *Jewish Learning in American Universities*, p. 218.
19. Greene, *The Jewish Origins of Cultural Pluralism*, pp. 16–17.
20. Ibid., p. 17.
21. Ritterband and Wechsler, *Jewish Learning in American Universities*, p. 218.
22. For example, Norman F. Cantor (1991), *Inventing the Middle Ages: The Lives, Works, and Ideas of the Great Medievalists of the Twentieth Century*. New York: W. Morrow.
23. Greene, *The Jewish Origins of Cultural Pluralism*.
24. Ritterband and Wechsler, *Jewish Learning in American Universities*, p. 216.
25. Ibid., p. 217.
26. Ibid., p. 174.
27. Ibid., p. 173.
28. Ibid., pp. 220 ff.
29. Ibid., p. 174.
30. Ibid., p. 186.
31. Ibid., pp. 189, 192, 195 f.
32. Ibid., pp. 201 ff.
33. Robert Alter (1974), "What Jewish Studies Can Do?" *Commentary* 58:4 (October): 71–6, p. 73.
34. See the special issue of Dean Phillip Bell (ed.) (1997), "Historical Memory and the State of Jewish Studies in Germany," *Shofar: An Interdisciplinary Journal of Jewish Studies* (Summer).
35. See Alter, "What Jewish Studies Can Do?" who criticizes the unreasonable and unrealizable expectations of counterbalancing the poor Jewish education children received before college that reside behind such philanthropic acts (pp. 73–4). See the recent issue of *AJS Perspectives* (Fall 2012, "The Apocalypse Issue") for various contemporary responses to the question of how, if at all, Jewish Studies scholars see the connection of their academic work with the Jewish community.
36. Arthur Green (1986), "Jewish Studies and Jewish Faith," *Tikkun* 1:1: 84–90, p. 85. Or, as Bernard Dov Cooperman has written more recently, "But by competing in universal academe, we also inevitably redefine our goals and change our criteria for excellence. Instead of reinforcing identity and encouraging endogamy, our goal in Jewish academe has become to promote sophistication of thought, flexibility of mind, (self) critical analysis, and expansive creativity. These qualities will not always be seen as desirable to a community that encourages group cohesion in the face of perceived external and internal threats." See Bernard Dov Cooperman (2006), "Jewish Studies Professors and the Community: A Response," in *Shofar: An Interdisciplinary Journal of Jewish Studies* 24:3: 136–40, p. 138.
37. Green, "Jewish Studies and Jewish Faith," p. 87.
38. See Hal M. Lewis (2006), "The Jewish Studies Professor as Communal Leader," *Shofar: An Interdisciplinary Journal of Jewish Studies* 24:3: 127–35, in which the author

embraces the idea that the very critical training of the academy can be brought into fruitful exchange with communal needs and governance.

39. Martin Goodman (2002), "The Nature of Jewish Studies," in Goodman (ed.), *The Oxford Handbook of Jewish Studies*, pp. 1–13, p. 9.

40. Alter, "What Jewish Studies Can Do?" p. 75; of course, the limits of "objectivity" were no different in the many centuries when Jewish Studies was largely a non-Jewish activity—see also Goodman, "The Nature of Jewish Studies," p. 3.

41. http://eurojewishstudies.org/about-us/history-and-aims/ (last accessed November 25, 2012).

42. www.jewish-studies.org/?cmd=about (last accessed November 25, 2012).

43. http://acjs-aejc.ca/ (last accessed November 25, 2012).

44. For the developments in Israel Studies, see the essay on "The State of Israel Studies" in this volume.

45. The 2008 Association for Jewish Studies Membership Survey, sponsored by the Jewish Policy Archive, with the support of the Charles H. Revson Foundation and the Mandell L. and Madeleine H. Berman Foundation, and conducted by Steven M. Cohen and Judith Veinstein. Available on the AJS website: www.ajsnet.org/survey.pdf (last accessed November 25, 2012).

46. David Biale (2002), "Preface: Toward a Cultural History of the Jews," in David Biale (ed.), *The Cultures of the Jews: A New History*. New York: Schocken, pp. xvii–xxxiii, p. xxi.

47. Ibid., p. xxiv.

48. Consider, for example, prominent centers at the University of Pennsylvania, University of Michigan, The Hebrew University of Jerusalem, YIVO, the Center for Jewish History, as well as important centers in Oxford and Berlin.

49. Such as the institutes for advanced study, notably at Princeton.

50. For example, *Jewish Quarterly Review, Revue des Études Juives, Hebrew Union College Annual, AJS Review, Tarbiz, European Journal of Jewish Studies, Jewish History, Jewish Social Studies, Proceedings: American Academy for Jewish Research, Zion*; theme or period specific journals; older journals (German and Hebrew, e.g., *Monatsschrift für Geschichte und Wissenschaft des Judentums, Koroth*).

51. For example, the *American Historical Review, Sixteenth Century Studies, Past and Present*. For a very useful discussion of these themes, see Goodman, "The Nature of Jewish Studies," pp. 5–7, who also sketches in broad strokes the development of Jewish Studies as an academic field.

52. See Moshe Rosman (2007), *How Jewish Is Jewish History?* Portland: Littman Library of Jewish Civilization, p. 58, in which he attributes this change in part to postmodern sensibilities.

53. Now realizing that Jews, despite guild exclusions and Jewish restrictions, were producers and consumers of material culture and that such material culture provides invaluable sources—different from but no less important from the texts that have been mined and that have more typically defined the nature and scope of Jewish experience and Jewish scholarship.

54. See Peter Novick (1999), *The Holocaust in American Life*. Boston: Houghton Mifflin; see also the work of Dominick LaCapra, for example: (1994), *Representing the Holocaust: History, Theory, Trauma*. Ithaca: Cornell University Press; (1998), *History and Memory after Auschwitz*. Ithaca: Cornell University Press.

55. See, for example, Saul Friedlander (2002), "The Holocaust," in Goodman (ed.), *The Oxford Handbook of Jewish Studies*, pp. 412–44.

56. There are, of course, a range of other themes that could be discussed and that appear throughout the pages of this volume—but in most cases they have not had the same kind of impact on the field of Jewish Studies as a whole.

57. See Michel Foucault (1982; orig. 1972), *The Archaeology of Knowledge and the Discourse on Language*, A. M. Sheridan Smith (trans.). New York: Pantheon, p. 8.

58. See Rosman, *How Jewish Is Jewish History?* p. 4.

59. See, recently, David Biale (2011), *Not in the Heavens: The Tradition of Jewish Secular Thought*. Princeton: Princeton University Press.

60. Rosman, *How Jewish Is Jewish History?* pp. 2–3.

61. As Michel Foucault famously noted, the "document" is no longer a simple and inert item but a rich and multivalent monument that requires archaeological treatment. See Foucault, *The Archaeology of Knowledge and the Discourse on Language*, pp. 6–7.

62. For a discussion of the implication of these kinds of changes on Jewish education more generally, see Jonathan Woocher (2012), "Reinventing Jewish Education in the 21st Century," *Journal of Jewish Education* 78:3: 182–226.

63. And why we have generally refrained from labeling Jewish Studies as a "discipline."

64. See, for example, some of the general volumes listed in the Select Bibliography.

Part I

Judaism and Jewish Society from the Bible to Modernity

The Formation of Judaism and Jewish Society

The areas of biblical and rabbinic studies have remained the backbone of investigations into Jewish life and the development of Judaism. Both fields have witnessed remarkable expansion over the past several generations, with the adoption of new scholarly methods (including various literary study theories), increased use of comparative study, and the discovery and analysis of new documents and source bases. Introducing readers to these significant developments, the following two chapters also provide important orientation to the key texts and the outlines of historical and intellectual development of these formative epochs.

In "The Hebrew Bible," Leonard Greenspoon provides a detailed overview of the Hebrew Bible, focused on its central themes and books. In this way, Greenspoon is able to offer contents of the Bible that will be valuable to readers, but also important contextualization, comparing as he does developments in the Ancient Near East as well as internal biblical writing and exegesis. Reflecting current scholarly agendas, Greenspoon discusses the practices and processes of transmission and translation of the Bible, pointing to the role that varying manuscripts and traditions of biblical interpretation have played in understanding the Bible, at the time of canonization and today—here he discusses, for example, the Dead Sea Scrolls as well as the Masoretes. Along the way, Greenspoon assesses some of the central issues raised by archaeology, literature, and biblical criticism in approaching Judaism and Jewish society in contemporary scholarship. Advancing this discussion, Greenspoon reflects on the nature of Jewish scholarship on the Bible in the academy today, noting the central divergent approaches (such as synchronic and diachronic exegesis and gender considerations).

In "The World of the Rabbis," Gary G. Porton delivers a historical and theological overview of Palestinian and Babylonian Jewry in the first six centuries
of the Common Era. Presenting relations with Roman authorities—including
cultural engagement, political rebellion, and the destruction of the Temple—
Porton also assesses internal Jewish developments, with careful attention to
the diversity of Jewish movements and texts produced at the time in Palestine.
He proffers a similarly intricate review of the Jews and Judaism in Babylonia,
comparing Jewish communities and contextualizing Jewish political, religious,
and intellectual developments. Turning to central scholarly concerns, Porton
lavishes attention on the literary-critical methods that have been applied to
the rabbinic collections. He also considers the myriad ways in which Jewish
communal developments in late antiquity have been presented, with particular
attention to questions of rabbinic leadership and debates over the nature and
extent of Judaism's engagement with Hellenism. The relationship between rabbinic Judaism and early Christianity, which has been a much-debated theme in
recent scholarship, is also reviewed at length by Porton.

2 The Hebrew Bible

Leonard J. Greenspoon

Introduction: Where to Start

When we think about reading the Hebrew Bible from its start, most of us would turn to the first page—in a Hebrew text or a translation—and, without much further thought, commence reading at Genesis 1.1; that is, the first verse of the first chapter of the first book. This coincides with what we have done many times before—that is, begin at the beginning—and seems confirmed by the initial expression we meet in the text, which in the traditional English rendering goes like this, "In the beginning, God created the heavens and the earth."

Nonetheless, upon further reflection, there are many other options for where to start reading. For example, since the Hebrew Bible is largely the story of the people of Israel, we might start in the book of Exodus, which describes the liberation from Egypt. Or, since the Ten Commandments are typically seen to encapsulate the "heart" of biblical teaching, we might start with them. Or, since the ancient Hebrews were closely identified with the land of Israel (hence the term, Israelites), perhaps it makes better sense to start with the account of the conquest in the book of Joshua.

Moreover, the Hebrew expression traditionally translated as "In the beginning, God created . . ." might more aptly be rendered "When God began to create . . ."[1] This translation alerts careful readers to the fact that Genesis 1.1 is not really the beginning of history, but rather a moment in the account of

God's interactions with his creation. When we as readers encounter a story or an account in the middle of things, we sometimes speak of it as *in medias res* (which is simply Latin for "in the middle of things"). This format requires readers to have some prior knowledge of the topics they meet in their reading.

This is exactly what happens in Genesis 1.1. The phenomenon is most pronounced when the text says simply ". . . God created . . ." We are not given any introductory information about this character, "God," other than that he creates. Who is God? Where did he come from? What was he doing prior to the creation of our universe? And many other questions—most of these the writers of the Hebrew Bible don't deal with explicitly. It is assumed, as it were, that readers already know something about this "God," whose story is central to every verse, every chapter, every book of the Bible, even when he is not explicitly mentioned by name or implicitly by a defining characteristic.

The reader of the Hebrew Bible, in antiquity and in the modern world, is plunged into an account of God in action. Even if we decided to begin our reading of the Bible elsewhere in its text, we would not be far from this basic concept: we can know about God from what he does. And even when we accept the inadequacy of the human word to fully explore all aspects of the divine presence, we can acknowledge the value of this written word as carrying authority and distinctive meaning. This, at least, is a central teaching and affirmation of Judaism.[2]

Major Books and Themes

Creation, the Flood, and the Rest of Genesis

While it is true, ideally at least, that ancient and modern readers can share some of the same experiences when encountering the text of the Bible, it is also true that this is not always the case. This can be powerfully demonstrated in the two narratives that make up most of the first ten chapters of Genesis: Creation and the Flood. For today's readers, even those with little prior direct connection with the Bible itself, these stories, at least in their broad contours, are well known. Whether accepted in a literal fashion or interpreted as metaphorical or exemplary, these accounts are part of the literary and/or religious tradition broadly shared by residents of the Western world. They may elicit assent, criticism, or even indifference.

However, contemporary readers of the biblical stories of Creation and the Flood rarely exhibit surprise. And yet, that was exactly the desired response in antiquity. Similar stories circulated throughout the Ancient Near East. Creation by divine word, as in Genesis 1, can, for example, be paralleled by Egyptian accounts of the god Ptah. The general ordering of creation, including the fashioning of humans from the ground, is found in the Mesopotamian myth, the *Enuma Elish*. A universal flood, ordered by divine forces and culminating in the near destruction of all life, was a theme common to the Mesopotamian stories of Atrahasis, Gilgamesh, and others. There should be no doubt that the authors and the earliest readers (or hearers) of the accounts now enshrined in the book of Genesis were thoroughly familiar with the similar stories that had been told far and wide.[3]

Therefore, when the earliest readers of Genesis came to their initial encounter with these narratives, they would have felt as if they were entering familiar territory, since many of the details were already familiar to them. But they would also, as it were, feel as though the terrain of this territory was shifting before their eyes: It was not the gods, multiple deities, who brought about all of this, but the one God who created all. Humans were not bystanders or afterthoughts in the ages-old combat among warring gods. No, we are uniquely fashioned by God, in his image and with the capacity, and the responsibility, to know the difference between good and evil—and we must face the consequences for our choices. The oneness of God, then, is not a mere shift in characters in a familiar story. Rather, it is a fundamental reorientation of universal consequence—and also of individual significance. Everything is familiar; all is changed. That is another way of expressing the biblical message, from the first of its verses to the last.

Within the book of Genesis, to say nothing of the entire Hebrew Bible, acquaintance with extra-biblical material (i.e. ancient stories and laws found outside of the Bible) is not limited to its earliest parts. For example, in Abraham's search for an heir, he first adopts a household slave and then provides himself with a surrogate wife, before fathering a son with his wife Sarai (Sarah). Both adoption and surrogacy are among provisions found in Mesopotamian law. What makes them unique in the biblical setting is their incorporation into the narrative whereby Abraham seeks a means to carry out God's covenant promise that Abraham's progeny will be as numerous as the stars of the sky or the sands of the shore. Such a promise could not be fulfilled without Abraham's procuring at least one heir.

The last portion of the book of Genesis is comprised of a novella about Joseph, from his youth as a spoiled child to his rise to a position of unparalleled power in Egypt, through which he was able to preserve his family, including the very brothers who had plotted his death. As part of this extended narrative, the wife of one of Joseph's employers seeks to seduce him. Outraged by his refusal to acquiesce, she publicly accuses him of trying to seduce her. Through his actions, Joseph is portrayed as steadfast and incorruptible. A similar story, about Anubis and Bata, is found *In Egypt*. Again, the parallels serve not to dilute the power of the biblical story, but rather to highlight the strengths of Joseph and, through him, to serve as an example to his extended progeny about the need to remain true to God, no matter how appealing the alternatives may seem.

The Structure of the Hebrew Bible or Tanak

As we noted, the Hebrew Bible begins with the book of Genesis. This is the first of five books—the others are, in order, Exodus, Leviticus, Numbers, and Deuteronomy—that make up the Torah or the Five Books of Moses. The latter designation is based on the tradition that Moses was the author of all, or at least almost all, of this material. These five books comprise the Torah, which may be translated as "law" or, more broadly, as "instruction."[4] This is an apt designation, since it is in these books that God is portrayed as revealing the laws, statutes, and commandments that the people of Israel should follow. In the Jewish tradition, handwritten copies of the Torah are found in scrolls that are kept in an ark located in the front of the sanctuary in all synagogues. Each year, the Torah is read from beginning to end, on a weekly basis, announcing thereby the preeminent importance of this material for Jews and Judaism.

The second portion of the Hebrew Bible is called the Prophets or, in Hebrew, Nevi'im. The second section of this portion contains the Latter Prophets: the longer books of Isaiah, Jeremiah, and Ezekiel; and the briefer collections of the 12 Minor Prophets. The Former Prophets, the first section of this portion, is made up of the books of Joshua, Judges, 1 and 2 Samuel, and 1 and 2 Kings. At first thought, these books, which recount the history from the Israelite conquest of Canaan to the Babylonian destruction of Jerusalem, may seem an odd fit for a biblical portion called the Prophets. In this context, it is worth noting that the perspective or viewpoint of this history is a decidedly theological one, thoroughly consistent with the approach taken by the prophets. In short, what matters most in this world is not military or political might, but rather whether or not humans act in accordance with God. In general, those who do will succeed, even if (or, especially when) they are the underdogs in military prowess or political power. Selected portions from the Prophets, Former or Latter, are chanted weekly in the synagogue after the reading of the Torah portion. These are the Haftorot.

The third section of the Hebrew is a rather miscellaneous collection of works that are collectively known as the Writings (Ketuvim, in Hebrew). These include Psalms, Proverbs, Job, Ecclesiastes, Ruth, Daniel, Esther, and 1 and 2 Chronicles, among other compositions. The principle by which books were placed in Ketuvim is not entirely clear, nor was the ordering of these books secure until a fairly late period. Some of these books, for example Ruth and Esther, are annually read on Jewish holidays; others, especially Psalms, form part of traditional Jewish liturgy.

Although the terms "Hebrew Bible" and "Old Testament" are often used inter-changeably, they should not be. The Old Testament refers to one or another of the forms of the first part of the Christian Bible; as such, it is always followed by the New Testament. The Hebrew Bible is the Bible for Jews, in accordance with the contents and ordering described in the previous paragraphs. It may also be called Tanak (or Tanach or Tanakh), which is a term formed by joining the first letter of each of the three sections mentioned above: T(orah)-N(evi'im)-K(etuvim).

The Exodus from Egypt

In the Jewish traditions, the books of the Torah, and the weekly portions into which they are divided, are known by the first word (or significant word) they contain. Thus, the second book of the Torah is, in Hebrew, called "Shemot." Shemot means "names," and it is with names—specifically, the descendants of Jacob who go down into Egypt—that this book begins. Nonetheless, it is doubt-less true that the more common name for this book, Exodus, is more descriptive of its contents.

The first half of Exodus is given over to the details that lead up to the libera-tion of the enslaved Hebrews from Egypt. In all of this, attention is given to two figures: one human, Moses, and the other divine, the Lord God. It is Moses who is saved at birth, ironically by a daughter of the same Pharaoh whom Moses will confront later. Moses' encounter with the burning bush—or more precisely, with God as experienced in the burning bush—is decisive for Moses' sense of mission.

As a fallible human being, Moses at first tries to escape from his responsibili-ties. This is a theme played out frequently when God calls upon an individual, for example a prophet, to carry out a weighty task. Eventually, Moses acquiesces and, along with his brother Aaron, demands of Pharaoh that the Hebrew slaves be freed. Pharaoh's unwillingness to commit himself to this action, first agree-ing then reneging on his word, is attributed both to divine action (God hardens Pharaoh's heart) and to Pharaoh himself (who is said to harden his own heart). These alternating explanations appear to affirm, at one and the same time, that God has ultimate control and that humans are free to exercise their own will.

Eventually, after ten punishing plagues strike the Egyptians, Pharaoh gives his assent and then immediately chases after the fleeing Hebrews. The events of this dramatic scene are encapsulated to this day by Jews who annually cele-brate the Passover. At the Sea of Reeds (traditionally, the Red Sea), the Hebrews are able to pass over on dry land, while the Egyptian forces drown. Once again, God's power is demonstrated.

The Ten Plagues are among the prime examples of what some people refer to as miracles. But the Hebrew Bible itself has no word that can be thus translated.

Rather, the text refers to "signs and wonders," through which the Lord exhibits his supreme strength. For some people, it is important to devise a series of "scientific" explanations for the plagues, as well as for other "miraculous" events within the Bible. The text itself does not dwell on such explanations nor in fact does it support them. Rather, this narrative, along with many others, points to the tentative and tenuous nature of human existence. The Egyptians, vaunted as among the most powerful nation in the world, are brought low by the action of God. Through this same action, the Lord raises up the Hebrews or Israelites, freeing them to fulfill what might be termed their destiny as God's covenantly chosen people.

Alas, Moses is by no means the only human among the people of Israel. No sooner did the Israelites cross the Sea than they began to complain. Here they were in the wilderness with no certainty as to their future. Life in Egypt had been horrible, but it was known. Now, nothing was known, nothing sure. Why were the people of Israel unwilling to rely on God, given the fact that he had just shown his power and strength? Perhaps, it must be chalked up to human nature. In any case, it was the people's lack of faith in him (as exemplified in the Golden Calf and the fear-inducing report of scouts Moses sent into Canaan) that led God to allot 40 years (almost two generations) to wandering through the wilderness when the direct route to the Promised Land was a far briefer journey.

Biblical Law and Laws

The Israelites had many experiences during these years, including on occasion warfare and physical deprivation. But this was also the time during which the disparate people that made up the Israelites began to coalesce into the nation of Israel. Of preeminent importance in this regard was the giving of the Law or rather the giving of many laws. The most famous of the laws are the Ten Commandments, whose contents appear, with some differences in wording, at Exodus 20 and again at Deuteronomy 5. But the biblical text does not use the term "Ten Commandments," nor does it support the view that these ten expressions of God's will are inherently or intrinsically more important than any other laws of the Torah.

Nonetheless, the form of the Ten Commandments, which is not unique to them, but nonetheless unusual in the Bible, does add force to their statement. Each of the commandments is in the form of a direct imperative addressed to each individual. These commandments are not formulated, as are most biblical laws, in terms of "if . . . then." Rather, the Ten Commandments envision no exceptions, no extenuating circumstances, and no (what we might call) wiggle room. To be in a covenant relationship with God, the people of Israel, individually and corporately, take these commandments upon themselves as the means of regulating the entirety of their lives.

A portion of the remainder of the book of Exodus and almost the entirety of the following three books of the Torah are comprised of laws. While there is a rabbinic tradition that the number of laws is 613, it is also possible to arrive at different numerations. Far more important than the number of the laws is their nature. There are a few factors regarding biblical law that cannot be overestimated in importance.

First, according to the witness of the biblical text itself, all law was fashioned and promulgated by God, generally through the agency of Moses. Therefore, all biblical law is of divine origin. To disobey or to attempt to counteract one of these laws is not then (simply) a matter of breaking a law passed by a (human) congress or parliament. Rather, disobedience of the law is what we would term a "sin," a form of rebellion against God. Israel might be governed by judges, native kings, or foreign powers. None of those would change the sovereignty of God.

Along these lines, it should be noted, second, that biblical law covers all aspects of human life: public interactions with others, private moments with one's family, even time spent with oneself. Criminal law, civil law, family law, capital crimes, major crimes against persons or property, petty crimes, failure to observe one's obligations to religious establishments—all of these and more are within the scope of biblical law. What concerns God is everything and everyone within his covenant community, the people of Israel. Thus, it is not surprising that his pronouncements provide such overarching guidance.

Third, the collections of laws contained in the Torah are sometimes spoken of as codes. This, however, is inexact. Rather than containing a comprehensive section on family relations, for example, followed by a section on property rights and then one on crimes against fellow humans, etc., the laws of the Torah don't seem to follow any particular pattern, with dissimilar laws often juxtaposed for chapter after chapter. Moreover, the laws, while covering all aspects of life, are nonetheless not comprehensive; that is, we can quickly discern many situations that don't seem to be even mentioned. Thus it is that the biblical laws, as we have them, were probably more for the use of judges rather than for circulation among the general public. In this sense, they served as models, exemplifying principles that a judge could apply in modified form to actual circumstances.

Fourth, as it turns out, many of the biblical laws are similar to those found elsewhere in the Ancient Near East, for example in the well-known Code of Hammurabi from Mesopotamia. This should not be surprising, since in many ways all of the ancient peoples of this area governed themselves in a similar fashion. Within these patterns of similarity, the distinctive features of biblical law stand out even more starkly. Only in Israel were all people, from the poorest to the most powerful, subject to the same punishments. And only in Israel was the law elevated to the unique status of divine revelation.

Finally, however, it must be noted that there are sometimes disagreements between biblical laws seemingly dealing with the same topic; at other points, the laws are in tension with each other. This is most often the case where a law in Deuteronomy returns to the same subject mentioned earlier. Recognition of this phenomenon is at least as ancient as the naming of the fifth book as Deuteronomy, which means "a second law." No matter how such incongruities are explained, it seems most likely that we are witnessing the development of legal traditions within Israel as the result of the application of principles to actual circumstances. This last point was mentioned above, but deserves reiteration here.

By the end of the Torah, the Israelites had received their freedom and their law. They stand poised to begin the struggle for the last of the three necessary components to become the people of Israel: the acquisition of the Land. Alas, Moses, who had led them through the wilderness, was not allowed by God to be their leader in the conquest. That role was to be played by Joshua.

The Transmission and Translation of the Hebrew Bible

Most people today read or hear the Hebrew Bible in translation rather than in its original languages (Hebrew and Aramaic). Even though something is always lost when rendering a text from one language into another, there is nothing inherently wrong with reliance on a translation for appreciation and study of the Bible. Nonetheless, for Jews, it should always be kept in mind that the translation is not the original and that, where possible, the original Hebrew and Aramaic should be consulted.

There are many debates concerning the origins of the biblical text. For some, it was divinely dictated to humans, starting with Moses. For others, the text reflects the results of human interaction with God, a divine-human enterprise, so to speak. Still others understand the Hebrew Bible as a wholly human composition, as an ancient people sought to make some sense of the world as they experienced it.

Beyond these issues of theology are matters relating to probably more mundane questions, such as: Do we possess the original copy, or autograph, or any book of the Bible? The simple, straightforward answer is no. What are the oldest texts of the Bible that we have? The oldest copies of the Bible we have are from the Dead Sea Scrolls and date from as early as the mid-second century BCE. Is the wording of the Dead Sea Scrolls the same as in our Bibles today? The answer to this question is a bit more complex. In many cases, the wording is similar to or even exactly the same as in our Bibles today. In other instances, however, it is longer, shorter, or differently expressed. This diversity results from the apparent fact that prior to the end of the first century CE (i.e. after the destruction by the Romans of the second Jerusalem Temple in 70 CE) the text of the Hebrew Bible was "fluid"; in other words, it had not yet been fixed. Beginning from the second century until today, a version of the Hebrew Bible has been copied or reproduced with remarkable fidelity. It is not, however, possible to assert that this is "the" original.

A further "complicating" factor is the observation that biblical manuscripts prior to the tenth century CE (thus, including the Dead Sea Scrolls) did not explicitly indicate or mark vowels; in other words, the text was (almost) entirely made up of consonants. It is certain that in antiquity people who could read (a small minority overall) knew the vowels and would (automatically) put them in as they read out loud or to themselves. In the late tenth century CE, manuscripts that included the explicit marking of vowels in texts of the Hebrew Bibles began to appear. The group of scholars who produced this vocalized texts are known as Masoretes (or preservers), and the Bibles they produced are said to preserve the Masoretic Text (or MT). This text is standard within the contexts of Jewish worship and Jewish study of the Bible. It cannot, however, be stated with certainty that the vowels the Masoretes introduced were precisely the same as ancient readers utilized.

Thus, it becomes clear that reading the Bible in its original languages or translating the Bible into a modern language such as English is a formidable undertaking, requiring substantial preparation and care.[5] The task is made somewhat easier by recognizing that many people, as individuals or in groups, have in the past worked assiduously to understand the text of the Bible. There nonetheless remain a number of passages that are interpreted in decidedly different ways by different exegetes (i.e. interpreters). In such instances, the careful reader of the text, whether in Hebrew or in translation, would do well to consult commentaries and other aids in the process of arriving at one or more satisfactory explanations.

The Books of Joshua and Judges

As we observed in an earlier section, the Hebrew Bible or Tanak is divided into three portions, the second of which is designated as Nevi'im or Prophets. This section can itself be subdivided into the Former Prophets and the Latter Prophets. It is to the Former Prophets that we turn first. In the Hebrew Bible, the Former Prophets comprise the books of Joshua, Judges, 1 and 2 Samuel, and 1 and 2 Kings. We have already had occasion to note that this account of historical events and characters, like all such accounts, has a distinctive perspective: for the biblical writers of the Former Prophets, as for all writers of the Bible,

God and his interaction with humans is the starting point, and in fact the finishing line, for understanding everything that happens. While other observers might point to battlefield strategies or diplomatic posturing as the leading factors in success or failure, those who authored the books contained in the Former Prophets characteristically searched out human acceptance or rejection of God as the ultimate cause of victory or defeat.

Briefly outlined, the book of Joshua describes the conquest of Canaan, and the Canaanites, under the human general Joshua and God as commander in chief. As described in the battle accounts that take up the first half of this book, all (or almost all) Canaanites whom the Israelites encountered and defeated were put to death. With rare exceptions, no efforts were made to bring Canaanites into the fold. Their way of life, marked (according to the biblical writers) by idolatry and immorality, was completely incompatible with the values God proposed for his people. So "toxic," we might say, were the Canaanites and their way of life that only annihilation could be accepted, with very rare exceptions.

The conquest of much of the Land of Israel was followed by its allocation to the 12 tribes. This allocation included some of the land east of the Jordan River, as well as considerable properties in Israel itself. The great detail in which tribal borders are described bespeaks the seriousness with which the biblical writers understood the people's stewardship of the land. Land allotted to a particular tribe, or to a particular family in a tribe, was not to be permanently sold to outsiders. At the same time, there was the stark recognition that it was God himself, and not humans (individually or collectively), who actually laid claim to ownership of the land. As such, there was always the possibility—which alas became a reality—that the God who allowed Israel to possess the land could on some occasion dispossess them if circumstances demanded it.

Overall, the book of Joshua gives the impression that the Israelites conquered all of the land, even while allowing that certain areas and cities, Jerusalem included, were not in fact captured all at the same time. The incompleteness of conquest is one of the unifying themes of the book of Judges, which narrates a series of events in which the Israelites turn away from God by worshipping idols and thus failing to acknowledge the oneness of his divinity. After a period of time, on each occasion the Israelites repented of their evil ways, and God raised a deliverer to free the people from the hands of their enemies. These deliverers, who included a woman (Deborah) and a common-street thug (Samson) among others, are collectively known as the judges.

As described in the biblical text, these judges came from all segments of society and did not inherit their position because of family or other connections. Rather, the "spirit of God" fell upon them; in this sense, the judges were charismatic leaders. Although the chronology is not absolutely secure, it appears that Israel, or at least parts of Israel, was governed by judges for a period of nearly two hundred years.

As described in the final portions of the book of Judges and the early chapters of the book of 1 Samuel, the people of Israel themselves demanded a king as leader, so that they would be like all of the other nations that they knew. In fact, some form of monarchy, generally absolute monarchy, was the rule throughout the Ancient Near East.

1 Samuel–2 Kings

The biblical text itself is ambivalent about the establishment of a monarchy in Israel. On the one hand, no judge was sufficiently powerful to unite all of the people or to provide for the safety and sustenance of everyone. On the other hand, it was difficult anywhere in antiquity to envision a monarch who would not hold himself above the law and, possibly, above God. Whatever the theological or ideological considerations were, it is a fact that kingship was established in Israel, existed as a reality for many centuries, and remained in some respects an ideal long after the end of the biblical period.

The figure of Samuel, who was something of a judge and also a prophet, looms large in the transition from judges to kings. It was he who, at God's command, anointed Saul as the first king of Israel. It was also Samuel, again at God's command, who expressed divine displeasure with the halfhearted devotion of Saul. And finally it was Saul who anointed David, a shepherd from the tribe of Judah, as Saul's successor, thereby denying to Saul the opportunity to set up a dynasty. David's dynasty, on the other hand, was guaranteed by God so long as the ruling monarch remained faithful to God and his command.

David was first crowned king of Judah in the town of Hebron. After a relatively short period of time, he led his army in the conquest of Jerusalem, which became the political and subsequently religious capital of Israel. In retrospect, David's reign, as described in the books of 1 and 2 Samuel, was looked upon as a veritable Golden Age. Indeed, it was a period of considerable military success and political consolidation that paved the way for the even grander empire of David's son and successor, Solomon. At the same time, the writers or compilers of this section of the Bible do not overlook David's flaws and foibles, most notably his adulterous relationship with Bathsheba and his deliberate murder of Bathsheba's husband.

Solomon's succession, as described in the early chapters of the book of 1 Kings, was not without its own drama. But Solomon was successful in gaining power and enlarging Israel's borders and wealth to an almost unimaginable extent. He is also responsible for the construction of the Temple in Jerusalem, where the priests oversaw the offering of sacrifices on a regular basis.

However, Solomon was not steadfast in his relationship with God, allowing many of his myriad wives to bring the worship of idolatry into the center of Jerusalem itself. It is as if Solomon, consciously or not, altered his priorities from a primary commitment to wisdom to a primary desire for wealth. As a result, we are told, the Kingdom of Israel, which was (more or less) united under Saul, David, and Solomon, was divided at Solomon's death, the southern portion, Judah, remaining under Davidic kingship in Jerusalem, while the northern kingdom of Israel managed under an ever-changing series of dynasties, some lasting only a matter of months.

Looked at in terms of political or military might, the northern kingdom of Israel was almost always more powerful and wealthy than Judah. Its kings regularly allied themselves with powerful nations or joined with other smaller lands to rebel against the major powers that always sought to subjugate them. But, as we have observed more than once, the writers of the Hebrew Bible, in keeping with their understanding of God's perspective, were not impressed with the trappings of earthly power, which were typically accumulated at the expense of the poorer members of society and against the express commands of God.

Thus, the rebellion against the House of David that established the northern kingdom was also viewed as a rebellion against God. Although it took many centuries to happen, the fall of the northern kingdom, as described in the book of 2 Kings, was essentially a foregone conclusion from the biblical perspective. Their leaders had continued to deny the warnings and teachings of God as transmitted by a number of prophets, most notably (in the Former Prophets) Elijah and Elisha, whose activities are generously and memorably recounted at the end of the book of 1 Kings and the beginning of 2 Kings.

For the southern kingdom of Judah, however, greater hope seems to have been held out. After all, the covenant God made with David might be seen as protecting each of his descendants who ascended to the throne in Jerusalem. However, God's protection of David's progeny was dependent on devotion to God alone. While some of the Davidic kings, most notably Hezekiah and Josiah, filled their reigns with actions that benefited the populace and were judged pleasing to God, this was not indeed the case with all of the monarchs who ruled over Judah.

One king in particular, Manasseh, who was Josiah's grandfather and ruled for over half a century, was singled out for the particularly heinous nature of his kingship. Even if we accept that he, along with other rulers in the North and South, was constrained to act in accordance with the will of powerful overlords, there was no way—from the biblical perspective—to excuse Manasseh from personal responsibility for his activities. In fact, the biblical writers point to Manasseh's period of rule as the beginning of the end—thereafter, it was only a matter of time, as it were, before Jerusalem and the rest of Judah were captured and its leaders taken away into exile. This in fact happened under the Babylonian king Nebuchadnezzar.

The southern kingdom lasted considerably longer (from ca. 922 BCE–ca. 587 BCE) than did the northern kingdom (from ca. 922 BCE to ca. 722 BCE). This greater longevity might be said to result from the relatively better monarchs in Jerusalem in comparison with those who governed Israel. Be that as it may, nothing in Israel's previous history could compare to the abject circumstances that faced those taken into the Babylonian exile. Separated from their Temple and seemingly abandoned by their God, it is not difficult to identify the reasons why the people felt helpless and without hope. It was the difficult, but (as we will see) not insurmountable task of several prophets to provide this group of people with a thorough understanding of how they (and not God) had gone wrong and how things could be restored or even made better in the future.

Archaeology and the Bible

Before turning to the prophets, we should consider one further matter of particular, although not unique, relevance to the Former Prophets; namely, the connection (or lack of connection) between the biblical text and the discoveries of archaeologists in Israel and elsewhere in the Ancient Near East. Put most directly, the question is: Does archaeology support the Bible?

This is not, however, the most appropriate form for a query in this area. First of all, it supposes that all archaeological data are essentially of the same kind: in support of or raising serious doubts about the Bible. This is not in fact the case. Archaeologists can show, for example, that most of the Canaanite sites described as captured by the Israelites (in the latter part of the thirteenth century BCE, most likely) were not in fact destroyed or even inhabited at that time. On the other hand, archaeological finds do support, for example, exactly the wealth of the northern kingdom that the prophet Amos described and decried. The Jerusalem city wall at the time of Nehemiah appears to have been discovered; there is extra-biblical textual evidence that the Babylonians did in fact capture Jerusalem in the first part of the sixth century BCE and that the Assyrians threatened the capital city near the end of the eighth century. And yet there are (still) no remains that can be securely tied to the exodus from Egypt or to the centuries of servitude the Hebrews are said to have endured in Egypt.[6]

We can reconstruct in some detail daily life in Israel for certain periods, down to details of diet, clothing, and housing. And yet there is only one inscription that mentions, almost in passing, King David and his dynasty. Thus it is that archaeologists can illuminate some aspects of the biblical account and challenge other details. None of this should be particularly surprising, given the fact that the biblical writers were not attempting to reproduce and replicate with precision the past they were narrating. Rather, as has been true for all "historians," they selected what they wished to emphasize, perhaps embellishing as they went along, and downgraded or omitted other material, which another chronicler might have chosen to highlight.

Beyond these observations, it is also worth asking what it actually means to prove or disprove the Bible. Or, to put it another way, wherein does the "truth" of the Bible lie? Certainly, it would be disquieting for many readers if it turns out that the biblical narratives rest entirely on fiction and not at all on what did indeed happen. But, for believers, the truth of the Bible does not reside in "what" happened but rather in "why."

To demonstrate conclusively that the Babylonians captured Jerusalem is not the same as proving that this action occurred because of God's intense displeasure with the actions of the people of Judah. To find "hard" evidence that the Hebrews, once enslaved in Egypt, marched out through the Reed Sea does not prove that this occurred through the signs and wonders of God. In essence, the "why"—namely, the constant interaction of God with his creation—is not susceptible to proof or disproof by archaeologists. This is not to diminish or in any way demean the work of archaeologists. Rather, it is to acknowledge the value and validity of archaeology within those areas that are appropriate to it.

Biblical Prophecy: An Overview

Foretelling the future has, we can imagine, never been an easy task. Whether supported by tea leaves, the flight patterns of birds, or bumps on the human cranium, the future is, by its nature, uncertain. On the other hand, if the prediction is set in the distant future, the predictor can enjoy at least some period during which he/she might be correct. Or, if the prognostication is sufficiently vague, it may never be conclusively dismissed.

In the Ancient Near East, as in many other societies, foreknowledge was associated with the gods, who could, if they chose, reveal the future to select individuals, who might use a variety of methods to induce the deities to be forthcoming in their revelations. Such figures served prominently in royal courts and were undoubtedly regular figures on the streets and roads of every city and village. There is something comforting, for most humans, in knowing beforehand how things will turn out. And those who made a convincing show of these abilities were often well paid financially and in their access to political power.

Thus it is that the prophets of ancient Israel had their parallels in almost all neighboring societies. Almost everywhere revelations were associated with the gods, and the language used to convey these revelations were very similar from one society to another. Therefore, it cannot be said in general that prophets and prophecy were a uniquely Israelite phenomenon. This fact is acknowledged in the Torah in several passages that warn the people of Israel not to be led astray by "false" prophets, who invoked multiple deities or offered pronouncements that ran counter to Israel's monotheistic lifestyle. It is not likely that the biblical text would have referred to such non-Israelite figures if they did not actually exist and were not perceived as a real threat.

Nonetheless, there are many features of biblical prophecy that are indeed unique. For example, there is the observation that Israel was the home of a prophetic tradition that spanned many centuries. Whether we term Moses a prophet, as the biblical text does on occasion, or posit a later time for prophecy's origins in Israel, that is, near or at the beginning of the monarchy, the people of Israel were never without at least one prophet in their midst. As with the office of judge, the position of prophet does not appear to have been hereditary. Also in common with the judges, the prophets came from all strata of society and from diverse locales in the North and in the South, in the cities and throughout the countryside.

By and large, the message of the biblical prophets, unlike their cohorts elsewhere, was a negative judgment on society, especially in respect to how the wealthy and powerful dealt with the poor and powerless. A "true" prophet, as we see, was rarely, if ever, a cheerleader for the status quo. The prophet Jeremiah, as true a prophet as ever existed (from the biblical perspective), went so far as to declare that people should be suspicious of any (overly?) optimistic prophecies on the part of those who claimed to be speaking on behalf of/in the name of God.

And there should be no mistake about this: Israel's prophets, although they were not God's tape recorders, were God's spokesmen (and occasionally spokeswomen). The power of the prophet's words, their distinctive feature, was that they bore the majesty and the urgency of God himself. Thus, prophets often began their pronouncements with a phrase like "Thus says the Lord" or "This is the word of God." Moreover, in the prophecies themselves, the prophets often identified so closely with their message that they spoke in the first person (as if they were God) instead of the third person (i.e. describing what God said).

It is not possible for us to ascertain the truthfulness of prophetic narratives related to encounters with God. Or, to put it another way, it is (almost) impossible for us to judge whether or not prophets actually encountered God, who in some way instructed the prophets in what to say or do. However, a dispassionate reading of the words of the prophets as contained within the Latter Prophets of the Tanak leaves little doubt about the sincerity of the prophets: they truly believed that God had communicated with them and that they were given the task (which they might well have initially resisted) to communicate the divine word to its intended audience.

As observed earlier, the intended audience for the divine word, which was most often a word (or, more accurately, an extended series of words) of severe criticism, was frequently the ruling elite, consisting of the royal family and its retainers, military leaders, and others at the top of the social and economic ladder. These people, as individuals and as groups, were accused of oppressing the general public economically and, in this and myriad other ways, failing to adhere to the standards demanded by God of his people. Even those without great power were subject to the judgment of God, for they too went astray—and typically made few efforts on their own to mend their ways and repent.

On occasion, however, the intended audience of a prophecy was to be located outside of Israel. Nations great and small were also accountable to God for their actions; although such peoples were not in a covenant relationship with God, they were nonetheless responsible for the iniquities they committed, most often against Israel, but sometimes among themselves. Even when a nation like Assyria or Babylonia was used by God as a "rod of his anger" against his own people, that nation was not considered blameless for excesses in its conquests or for failing to realize what was the true cause of their successes.

It is generally maintained that the ultimate goal of a prophet's encounter with God was to learn what God wanted his people to know. While this is certainly one of the goals, it may well be that the prophets did not so much enter into the "mind" of God (if we may use this term), but rather into God's emotional life. For many people, the very idea that God had an emotional life will sound very strange; however, there are numerous biblical passages to support the contention that God could get angry, change his mind, or exhibit compassion.[7]

This insight encourages us to consider that God's judgments against his people were most often of a corrective nature, in that he hoped his people would turn back to him, or return to him, so that the promises of peace and prosperity could be, once and for all, fulfilled. In some instances, God, as portrayed by Israel's prophets, appears to be pleading with his people to repent. The prophets' exposure of sin was, then, not an end in itself, but a necessary step on the way to Israel's redemption.

In this light, passages in the second part of the book of Isaiah (generally known as Second Isaiah and dated to the last half of the sixth century BCE) are especially surprising and encouraging. Israel, then in the depth of the Babylonian exile, was soon to experience the unparalleled joy of returning to its land, the unqualified sense of acceptance by God, the unassailable sense that their period of abandonment and captivity was drawing to a close. This was, in effect, a culmination of all of the words of prior prophets. Alas, Israel's return to God, although undoubtedly sincere and promoted by many prophets in addition to Second Isaiah, was not long lived, and words of judgment came to predominate once again. According to Jewish tradition, Malachi was the last of the prophets. Whether it was he or someone else, the position of prophet did not continue in the postbiblical era.

Major and Minor Prophets

Because, as we maintained above, individual prophets retained their own personalities, peculiarities included, when they spoke or acted on behalf of God, we find that each prophet, although agreeing on general principles with all others, nonetheless exhibited his/her own distinctive features. All of this is on display in the 15 books that make up the Latter Prophets, as well as in some narratives, especially those that recount the activities of Elijah and Elisha, contained in the Former Prophets. It is conventional to subdivide the Latter Prophets into the Major Prophets—Jeremiah, Isaiah, and Ezekiel—and the 12 Minor Prophets. The words "major" and "minor" in this context are not judgments about the respective value or validity of the prophets involved, but simply a recognition of the fact that the books of the Major Prophets are far longer than the books of the Minor Prophets. One of the books of the Minor Prophets, Obadiah, is the shortest book in the Hebrew Bible, comprising only one chapter.

Although it is not possible here to discuss each prophet, we can note a few of the distinguishing characteristics of some of the prophets. For example, Isaiah, who lived at the end of the eighth and the beginning of the seventh centuries, was well connected and had ready access to the halls of power in Jerusalem. He also had priestly connections, as was also true of Ezekiel. Several chapters of the book of Isaiah describe the prophet's dealings with Judah's kings, whom he tried to influence in the direction that (he felt) God wanted. Isaiah was successful in some instances, less so in others.

Jeremiah, who began prophesying during the last years of Judah's monarchy, had a much stormier relationship with the monarchy. Efforts, ultimately unsuccessful, were made to silence him, and he endured harsh conditions for extended periods of time. Moreover, Jeremiah revealed, more than any other biblical prophet, the anguish he felt at having to deliver such harsh criticisms to his own people. Jeremiah also expressed the revulsion of a true prophet at the excesses and false promises offered by those whose claim to prophecy he rejected.

Ezekiel is probably the most peculiar person we meet in the Hebrew Bible. He has a mysterious, perhaps mystical vision of God and his throne chariot. He eats a scroll containing God's word to show his assent to the divine message. He acts out the travails of those who are to be exiled, and, although he describes himself as already in Babylonia, he has vivid, terrifyingly immediate visions of the degradation and ultimate destruction of those who were still resident in Jerusalem. On the other hand, the book of Ezekiel has the most easily discernible system of organization of any of the Latter Prophets: its prophecies are arranged in chronological order from the earliest to the latest.

Among the Minor Prophets, Amos is well known for having been plucked out of his pastoral life in the South to deliver scathing attacks against those who ruled in the North. Hosea, as he himself relates, was ordered by God to marry a woman of compromised virtue. Only in this way, God felt, could the prophet truly feel the sense of disappointment and abandonment that God felt when his people went "whoring" after other gods. And Jonah, most reluctant of biblical prophets, tried mightily, but of course unsuccessfully, to evade his divine commission, to speak to the people of the foreign capital, Nineveh, so as to lead them toward repentance and away from destruction.

Just above we mentioned the way in which one book of biblical prophecy, Ezekiel, was organized or arranged. In the case of the other books of the Latter Prophets, thematic, rather than chronological, considerations seem to have predominated. It is unlikely that any of the prophets are themselves responsible for the selection and organization of material in "their" book. Doubtless some prophets had disciples or other followers who gathered together, probably from memory at first, words they had heard or actions they had witnessed.

With the exception of the book of Isaiah, referred to earlier, there is no compelling reason to judge that any book of the Latter Prophets contains substantial additions of material later than the particular prophet himself. Thus, although it would be an error to equate the words attributed to the prophets with the precise expressions they uttered during their lifetimes, it will be equally erroneous, if not more so, to dismiss these collections as lacking in historical or theological bases. They remain invaluable witnesses to a unique heritage that believers understand to be rooted in God's revelation and relevant beyond the circumstances of time and space in which they developed.

The Book of Psalms

As we have had several occasions to note, the third section of the tripartite structure of the Tanak is Ketuvim or Writings (in some older sources, this section is sometimes referred to as Hagiographa or Sacred Writings). Manuscript evidence is clear that the ordering of books in this section was set later than for the Torah or Prophets. Although five of the books in Ketuvim now appear in the order in which they are read during the annual cycle of Jewish holidays, it is unlikely that this reflects the original ordering of these books, if indeed there was an earlier authoritative decision on this matter. Moreover, it is probable that at least some of the books in Ketuvim were among the last books of the Tanak to be written or at least to be recognized as canonical.

The first book of Ketuvim, in the present ordering, is also the longest book of the Tanak, Psalms. The book of Psalms, also known as the Psalter, contains 150 individual compositions, which have been organized in five parts, reminiscent as it were of the five books of the Torah. Traditionally, authorship of most, if not all of the Psalms was attributed to King David, whose name does indeed appear in the superscriptions (introductory verses) to many of the Psalms. However, there is widespread acceptance of the view that the Psalms reflect spiritual and social conditions over a vastly longer period of time than (simply) the reign of David. For example, a composition like Psalm 137 surely seems most relevant for the period of the Babylonian exile. Some interpreters, in fact, date certain Psalms as late as the second century BCE.

There are many different ways to divide up the Psalms. We can, for example, describe some of them as laments, others as pleas for divine assistance, and a third group as comprising prayers of thanksgiving. Or we can look at the poetic structure of the Psalms, some of which are quite short and straightforward, others of which (see especially Psalm 119) are elaborately fashioned constructions following seemingly complex patterns of thought and diction.

We could also look at the Psalms in terms of their possible or probable use. Most, if not all, of them would have played some role in Israel's structured practice of worship. Some of them may have been recited on a daily or other regular basis by the priests who officiated at the Jerusalem Temple. Others, designated Psalms of Ascent, were probably spoken or chanted by pilgrims as they climbed toward the heights, spiritual and spatial, of Jerusalem. Still others may have served individuals as they sought the appropriate words to address God in petition or thanks.

All of these uses are important when we consider that worship in ancient Israel, while it did include sacrificial offerings at the Jerusalem Temple, was also made up of prayers to accompany the offerings or to be recited apart from the Temple and its ritual. Thus, it is important to keep in mind that prayers were not an innovation that arose exclusively after the destruction of the Temple. Rather, as we can vividly experience through the lengthy prayer attributed to Solomon at the Temple's dedication (in 1 Kgs), prayer was central to the relationship between God and his people during the time the Temple stood, as well as before and after that period. The book of Psalms, then, or rather its contents allow us remarkably keen access to the religious life of ancient Israel. Just as Jews today characteristically worship through words and expressions taken from the biblical Psalms, so the Psalms functioned as an integral part of what we may call the prayer book of antiquity.

Wisdom Literature

Many of the books in Ketuvim exemplify the characteristics of what we speak of as "wisdom literature." This is especially true for the books of Proverbs, Ecclesiastes (Qohelet), and Job. Wisdom literature was a form of expression that the ancient Israelites held in common with other Ancient Near Eastern societies from Egypt through Mesopotamia. In fact, some of the sayings in, for example, Proverbs run parallel to similar literature in Egypt.

This is not at all surprising when we recognize that wisdom literature is rooted in humanity's experience with the world around us, an experience that in many crucial respects is almost, if not entirely universal, subject to many of the same constraints, as well as open to many of the same possibilities, regardless of where and when they are encountered. A lot of proverbial literature starts with observations of nature and continues with apt applications of the lessons thus gleaned to human life. Other sayings are anchored in common sense or reflect the realities of a society that, in spite of all efforts, does not necessarily reward the good and punish the evil. We are then urged on many occasions to be circumspect, just as curiosity and creativity can be commended in other circumstances.

Even though wisdom literature, as we can see, is not explicitly grounded in divine revelation or historical experience, it would nonetheless be a major mischaracterization to speak of wisdom literature as "secular." The author of the book of Proverbs, traditionally King Solomon, several times reminds us that "fear" (better, "awe" or "respect") of the Lord is the beginning of Wisdom. In order to fear, respect, or have awe for God, we must, from the perspective of the entire Hebrew Bible, know of Israel's past and ongoing relationship with God. This, as we might express it, forms the necessary and only substantial foundation for our further inquiries.

Here it is important to notice that the text of Proverbs does not equate "fear" of the Lord with the entirety of Wisdom; rather, a proper relationship with God is the starting point for the search to understand the universe, how it works, and our place in it. In this respect, wisdom literature counters any complacency that we already know all that we need to. Indeed, wisdom literature teaches us, we are put on earth in part to acquire knowledge, impart knowledge, and receive knowledge from others.

In and of itself, this quest for Wisdom may be thought of as leading to positive results or, on the other hand, as leaving us as humans very disappointed and frustrated. The first way of evaluating the quest for Wisdom may also be thought of as optimistic; that is, enabling humans to live the fullest possible life on earth, exhibiting concerns for others and reaping appropriate results for our charitable activities. This is, on the whole, the viewpoint espoused in the book of Proverbs: wisdom is rewarded; its opposite (more often described as foolishness than as evil) invariably leads to destruction.

We do not, however, have to be that astute as observers to recognize that life, as actually lived, does not always, or even most of the time, conform to this pattern. More than once, all of us have viewed, at near or far range, the downfall of the wise and good and the rise to power of those who exemplify none of the positive characteristics associated with Wisdom. What causes this? It is to the task of answering this sort of question that the authors of the books of Ecclesiastes and Job set themselves.

Traditionally, Solomon, seen as old and rather worn out by life, has been designated as the world-weary author of Ecclesiastes. Although this designation seems unlikely when we consider the language and style of this book, it is nonetheless the case that its author, whoever it was, cautions us against being overly committed to any idea or ideal. We will, he sagely observes, all die, king and commoner alike. Life is a struggle, and we might as well reconcile ourselves to this. While it is better to have someone with whom we can share our lives, piteous as they are, marriage is not a cause for great exaltation. Rather, it becomes marginally less burdensome for two rather than one to make their way through life, such as it is. The inclusion of the book of Ecclesiastes in the Tanak is cautionary for those who would give absolute value to the trappings of wealth and power. Yes, indeed, the wealthy and powerful are no better (or, in fact, worse) than all of the rest of us. If the book of Ecclesiastes were the only book of the Hebrew Bible, it would be almost unbearable to read it. But it is part of a larger collection and only in that context can it be fully understood and appreciated.

Much the same can be said for the book of Job, which is on the whole the most difficult book of the Hebrew Bible. Set adrift in a world without specification of time and probably of place and ethnicity, the book of Job, despite (or perhaps because of) its problematic nature, has an immediate appeal that transcends cultures and chronological periods. Job is a blameless man, whose seemingly senseless persecution is allowed and even abetted by God. Only in this way, it was determined, could God find out if Job's devotion to God was guided by faith or self-interest.

Most of the book is taken up by appeals from his so-called friends for Job to repent. He must be guilty, so they argue, of heinous sins in order to be punished so severely. But Job knows, as we the readers do, that he is innocent of any serious criminal activity. All he wants, really wants, is to have his chance to confront God face-to-face. And finally, near the book's end, he is given that chance. It is not, to say the least, a discussion among equals. In essence, God challenges Job's right to question him; after all, did Job create the world or was it God? In a difficult-to-understand response, Job does express repentance—but it is far from clear exactly for what or why he is repenting. In this way, the book of Job forces its readers to acknowledge the breadth and depth of the chasm that separates humans from God. Even under the best of circumstances, we can never fully know God or adequately account for his actions.

The Book of Esther, Daniel, 1 and 2 Chronicles

To complete this analysis of Ketuvim, and of the Tanak, we will look at several other books in this section. First is the book of Esther. This book, and the intriguing narrative it contains, is very well known to almost all Jews. It is read in full as part of the celebration of the holiday of Purim, which takes place annually in March or April. This holiday and its accompanying rituals and practices are based on this biblical book.

When the book begins, the reigning Persian monarch is holding a multiday (and night) celebration, complete with vast amounts of food and drink. His current wife Vashti refuses the royal command to appear before the drunken hordes (in the Jewish tradition, this command is for her to appear nude, except for her crown). Quickly dispatching this recalcitrant mate, the king embarks on an empire-wide search to find a more suitable queen. His choice is Esther, a woman whose Judaism is hidden from the king and his court. Esther and her cousin Mordecai are the heroes of the story. The villain is the courtier Haman, who broadens his hatred for Mordecai personally to a vendetta against all of Mordecai's people, the Jews. Esther, at first reluctantly, reveals her religion and her people's plight to the king, who duly executes Haman and his sons and allows the Jews to defend themselves against an onslaught he apparently could not countermand.

All ends well, at least for the "good guys." Esther and the king remain happily married, with Mordecai given powers of the highest order to govern on the king's behalf. There are a number of reasons to think that the author of the book of Esther had familiarity with many of the details of Persian court life. However, it is difficult to fit the leading characters of this narrative into any known historical sequence of the Persian Empire. Thus, it seems prudent to characterize the book of Esther as a whole as an exemplary tale that does not aim at describing an historical event so much as devising and depicting a way of life for Jews in the Diaspora (i.e. those living outside of the Land of Israel). They could indeed expect to face difficulties, some of them life-threatening. Remaining steadfast to God would ultimately prove the way out of such difficulties.

The book of Daniel is also set in the Diaspora, in this case the Babylonian court; at least this is true for the first half (i.e. the first six chapters) of the book. Here, the hero Daniel, alone or with his three compatriots, must overcome a series of challenges to their belief in God and the way of life he has ordained. Individually or collectively, they must choose whether or not to eat food prepared by others rather than in accordance with their traditions, to bow down to foreign deities rather than face the probably severe consequences of remaining true to their monotheistic faith, and to provide authentic interpretations of dreams or inscriptions that bear very negative messages for their Babylonian captors. Not only do Daniel and his friends pass all of these tests; they do so with flying colors.

The second part of the book of Daniel consists of a series of visions, some interpreted, others left open-ended, which Daniel receives from God. Perhaps, the connection between the narratives of Daniel's first part and the visions of its second is that, through the trials Daniel faced, he proved himself a worthy recipient of these visions. In any case, these visions are largely given over to a description of the end of time, when God and his human allies will engage the forces of evil in a series of cataclysmic battles of universal significance. The world as we know it will come to an end, replaced by a kingdom ruled by God and his human supporters. Although the time frame for these decisive activities remains shrouded in mystery, it is to be expected very soon rather than pushed off into the far distant future. All of these features of the visions are characteristic of apocalyptic thought, of which the second half of the book of Daniel is the primary exemplar in the Tanak.

Traditionally, the book of Daniel is dated to the Babylonian period, and all of its visions are viewed as, originally at least, predictions of future events. It seems more likely, however, that the book of Daniel, at least in its final form, is a product of a later time, during the mid-second century BCE, when the Jews, led by Judah Maccabee, sought to free themselves from their Seleucid overlords, who seemed determined to wipe out every vestige of Judaism and Jewish practice, including worship at the Jerusalem Temple. Because the Seleucids were so fully focused of these policies and were in fact aided and abetted by many Jews themselves, the threat thus posed was more serious and more central than any experienced by previous generations of Jews. It was in those dire moments that the visions of Daniel were composed, to offer hope to persecuted Jews that God would indeed decisively intervene—and in the near future. This same book of Daniel continues to offer hope to Jews and others who perceive that they are in a similar plight.

While going through the historical accounts of the Former Prophets, we had occasion to note that there is another "history" of Israel, especially during the time of the monarchies, elsewhere in the Tanak. This other "history" is contained in the books of Chronicles, whose author or editor was apparently also responsible for two biblical books that recount the experiences of Jews in the early postexilic period; namely, the books of Ezra and Nehemiah.

In many ways, the books of Chronicles follow the narrative, including the theological insights, of the books of Samuel and Kings. However, on occasion they notably depart from the earlier narrative. Thus, for example, there is no account of the David and Bathsheba incident in Chronicles. Moreover, it is in Chronicles, but not in Samuel-Kings, where we learn that God forbade David to construct the Jerusalem Temple because of the blood on his hands (even though this was the blood of conquered peoples). It is also in Chronicles alone that we find the story of King Manasseh's repentance. This monarch, the arch-villain of Judah in the account of Kings, fully repents from his evil ways in Chronicles.

It is inviting, but not necessarily productive, to attempt to determine, in these and other instances, which account is the most factual; that is, which account accords most closely with what actually happened. It is more productive, however, to seek out the theological or ideological motivations that led the different authors/editors to shape their narratives in the way they did. In order to do this, it is necessary to consider that the authors/editors of Chronicles were active at a much later date than those responsible for Samuel-Kings. During this later, postexilic period, it was apparently more useful to emphasize the positive features of David's personality and reign and the possibility, if not certainty, that even so egregious a sinner as Manasseh could be led to repent. History, in this sense, was shaped more by the perceived need to inculcate morals and provide positive exemplars than to (simply) convey details and facts.

After the Hebrew Bible: Interpretation and Scholarship

Inter-Biblical Exegesis

Interpretation of the biblical text is found within the Bible itself; thus, it is earlier than its transmission or translation. In the first part above, we had occasion to observe that a number of the laws of Deuteronomy serve to reconcile apparent contradictions in the legal pronouncements of Exodus-Numbers or to update such statements in the light of later conditions. In addition, as we noted, the authors/editors of the accounts contained in 1 and 2 Chronicles apparently had access to the material found in 1 Samuel–2 Kings, which they modified (through additions, omissions, and changes of nuance) to accord with their understanding of the needs of the audience whom they were addressing. There are many other cases of similar activity, which can be termed inter-biblical exegesis. This exegesis was already recognized in antiquity and continues to be the subject of fruitful study.

Biblical Interpretation in the Dead Sea Scrolls

Recognition that the legal traditions of the Bible were not static, but rather represented different stages of development, may well have influenced Jews to continue that development in the postexilic period. One of the most interesting places to examine this phenomenon is at Qumran, where the Dead Sea Scrolls were written, edited, and annotated by a group with close connections to the Essenes. These individuals, whose leaders claimed priestly descent and prerogatives, understood biblical texts, prophetic, legal, and narrative, as applying directly to their own circumstances from the mid-second century BCE until the mid-first century CE. Led, at least initially, by the Teacher of Righteousness, this group developed an exegetic form called the *pesher*; in general, a verse or two from biblical books considered prophetic (which included the book of Psalms) was followed by an extended interpretation, which sought to understand this community's past, present, and future through the application of sacred text to their own experienced or predicted circumstances. It is worth acknowledging, if not analyzing further, the parallel practice among those Jews who identified Jesus as the Messiah; they also fervently believed that Scripture provided a flawless blueprint for the travails, as well as the joy, they were destined to face.

A number of Dead Sea Scrolls also reflect the specific belief that biblical laws, given by God to Israel, were nonetheless susceptible to modification based on the changed circumstances of the Qumran community. It is possible, and not unhelpful, to state this with greater force: members of the Dead Sea Scrolls community saw it as their responsibility to modify biblical law on those occasions where such changes allowed legal principles to remain relevant for them and their contemporaries. The study of the relationship between biblical texts and their interpreters at Qumran remains an area in which substantive progress continues to be made.[8]

It has become increasingly clear that many phenomena at Qumran, which at first were judged unique to this community, are in fact applicable to other groups of Jews in the Second Temple/Hellenistic period.[9] There was, in fact, no single approach to the interpretation or application of Tanak that was imposed on all Jews.[10] This becomes apparent when, for example, we look at many of the renderings in the Greek translation of the Hebrew Bible that we call the Septuagint (produced from ca. 275 BCE to ca. 100 BCE). In every book of the Bible, to a greater or lesser degree, there are differences between the Hebrew that underlies the Septuagint and the Hebrew preserved in the traditional or Masoretic Text. Without trying to determine, where it is even possible, which text is original or earlier, it should readily be admitted that as a whole the Septuagint is a reliable witness to the Hebrew text its translators were rendering or to traditions they consciously chose to introduce into their "biblical" version. The study of the Septuagint as an invaluable repository for Hellenistic Jewish thought and practice is an increasingly attractive and productive topic for analysis and research.[11]

Biblical Interpretation among the Rabbis

The primary methods identified with Jewish exegesis of the Tanak come from the somewhat later period when the rabbis were centrally involved in discussions and disputations that led to the classical expression of Judaism in the Talmud and related texts.[12] In the context of this chapter, it is possible to touch upon only a few of the highlights of rabbinic exegesis, its principles, and results. Perhaps, the most important aspect to note is that the rabbis, individually and collectively, were not literalists. They did not believe that there was only one way to read a biblical text nor were they averse to metaphorical or open-ended readings that allowed later interpreters to build exegetical constructs of their own. *Peshat* is the plain reading of the text, which frequently differs from its literal reading.

In this regard, the rabbis did lay out more than one series of "rules" by which the text could be most profitably interpreted and applied. But these were not hard-and-fast regulations intended for mechanic application; rather, they were guidelines, allowing for freedom—albeit freedom within set boundaries. It is also characteristic of rabbinic exegesis, as for rabbinic activity in general, that one or more minority views were transmitted alongside the interpretation that received greatest support. Again, the goal was to nourish the interpretation tradition, not to starve it or beat it into submission to a unitary approach.

Among the most significant insights espoused by the rabbis was the contention that there is no extraneous or repetitious wording in the biblical text. Thus, the meanings of even near synonyms were probed to discern the nuances that less careful readers would simply gloss over. Recognizing the linear quality of Scripture, the rabbis acknowledged that on more than one occasion actions were not narrated in strictly chronological order. Because Hebrew does not have past perfect, the rabbis' judgments in this regard, as in so many others, are certainly subject to criticism. Nonetheless, the fecundity and dynamic nature of rabbinic exegesis should not be overlooked, nor should their openness to multiple interpretations be underestimated. In spite of centuries of study, this rabbinic material still offers many surprises for those who approach it in a non-dogmatic, unbiased manner.

Jews and/in the Higher Criticism of the Bible

Thus it was that some individuals expressed doubt with the traditional view that Moses was the author of all of the Torah. Nor did rabbinic interpreters ignore inconsistencies in the legal or narrative sections of the Tanak. But they did not mount anything close to an extended challenge to the authoritative status of the text or the inspired nature of its composition. Such challenges were raised, loudly and frequently, in predominantly Protestant circles of the late eighteenth century and throughout the nineteenth century, beginning in central Europe and rapidly spreading westward (but only hesitatingly, at first, eastward). In such circles, what was termed Higher Criticism became increasingly popular, challenging almost every traditional notion of what the Bible was and how it came into being. In particular, source criticism waged a frontal attack on the Torah as a unified composition, produced by a single individual (i.e. Moses) at a single time (i.e. during Moses' lifetime).

Familiarity with these new critical approaches to the Bible was a central feature among Enlightenment Jews, whether or not they accepted (wholly or even partially) the methods and results promoted by Protestant scholars. As Jews gained full (or at least fuller) access to the larger cultures and societies in which they lived, they would of necessity learn about these criticisms. For liberal, or more liberal Jews, critical scholarship liberated them from what they saw as the shackles and blinders imposed by traditional, parochial forms of education. They adopted, often enthusiastically, the methods of progressive Protestant scholarship. However, these Jewish scholars tended to be far more tentative in their embrace of the results of critical scholars, many of whom were not favorably disposed to Judaism or were out-and-out anti-Semites.[13]

More traditional Jews, large numbers of whom united under the banner of neo-Orthodoxy, rejected both the methods and results of critical scholarship. Some of them wrote, and apparently lived, as if critical scholars did not exist; others engaged and sought to combat what they understood as dangerous tendencies in the misunderstanding and misinterpretation of Sacred Writings.

Jews and/in the Academy

By the end of the nineteenth century, Jewish scholars were on the whole well established within the various academic fields associated with the study of the Bible. However, they still had to withstand several obstacles placed in their way. Rather complete dedication to analysis of the Old Testament did not always, or even regularly, translate into positive attitudes toward Jews and Judaism on the part of many Christian, especially Protestant, specialists. As racial, as well as religious hatred of Jews continued to grow unabated, all too many scholars read the prejudices of their day into their analysis of the Old Testament. Rarely if ever were the words of the Hebrew Bible interpreted in their own right; rather, they were seen, and judged, as if they were strewn, ever so haltingly, along a path that was moving forward and upward from the fallacies of the Hebrews to the truths of Jesus and his followers.

Much of the work of these specialists, produced at the leading universities especially of central Europe, was widely accepted. At the time, the anti-Jewish prejudices and biases that lay just below the surface typically went unnoticed or little noted. As a result, this scholarship entered into the realm of accepted and authoritative. Only in recent decades have scholars, Jewish and non-Jewish, taken the opportunity to peel away the layers of anti-Judaism that had inflected so much work for so many years. This does not invalidate a half century or more of research, since not all of it was, we might say, rotten to the core. But it does call attention to the fact that scholars do not work in a political or social vacuum and that, in order to evaluate their work, we must understand the context in which they produced it. This insight, which continues to demonstrate its validity, can also be applied far more widely.

Jewish scholars of religion in general, and the Bible in particular, were often not offered posts at major universities. This, coupled with blatant caps on the number of Jewish students admitted to such institutions, resulted in the establishment of a number of Jewish colleges of higher learning. These remained popular throughout the first half of the twentieth century in the United States and in some European countries. Fortunately, departments of Jewish Studies are now a mainstay in higher education throughout most of the world. This has allowed Jewish scholars to move to the forefront of research and to partake in almost all of the major academic projects being undertaken in the field of biblical studies. Thus, for example, Jewish specialists were among the earliest to be asked to author commentaries in the Anchor Bible Series. And Jews are editing volumes in the *Biblia Hebraica Quinta* edition of the Hebrew Bible, all of whose editors in previous editions were Protestants. Although leading Jewish scholars were occasionally found among the early presidents of the Society of Biblical Literature, their presence has been far more frequent, we might even say commonplace, in more recent years.

At the same time, Jews have established and maintained their own organs for study of the Hebrew Bible. Thus, there are sections devoted to biblical studies at the annual meetings of the Association for Jewish Studies, and Jewish presses, most notably the Jewish Publication Society of America (JPS), have made editions of the Bible and commentaries on the Bible one of their major emphases. However, as the recent demise of the JPS as an independent publisher demonstrates, Jewish study of the Hebrew Bible is so much a part of the mainstream today that it is not always possible, or perhaps even desirable, to maintain specifically Jewish contexts or auspices for its sponsorship or dissemination.

Does Distinctively "Jewish" Scholarship on the Bible Exist?

In this regard, it is worth contemplating whether indeed there exists an identifiably Jewish way of studying the Hebrew Bible. As it is, Jewish scholars, individually or collectively, are fully immersed in the major movements or methods that broadly define contemporary study of the Bible. For example, several Israeli archaeologists are among those forcefully espousing a minimalist view of the Bible; namely, that the Hebrew Bible contains only a very small amount of historically valid data, each piece of which needs to be verified through extra-biblical sources before it can be, even tentatively, understood as recording and conveying what "actually" happened.[14] At the same time, Jews, from archaeologists to textual critics, also number among the leading proponents of the maximalist view of the Bible, whereby readers are predisposed to accept as historical biblical accounts purporting to be so—not uncritically, of course.[15] This would, of course, accord with traditional Jewish methods of reading the biblical text. However, it would be a serious mistake to assume that only traditional Jewish exegetic approaches should, in today's academic world, be termed authentically Jewish.

We see a similar dichotomy when looking at other areas of contemporary biblical studies. For some Jewish scholars, the historico-critical approach, which emphasizes the varying disparate sources that went into the composition of the text as we now know it, is a necessity for anyone trying to arrive at a complete understanding of the Bible.[16] This approach gives exegetical preference to what are purported to be the diachronic elements of the text; that is, those that are said to support the view that the text as we have it is a composite of sources from different sources geographically, ideologically, and chronologically.

Synchronic study of the Hebrew Bible, also championed by Jewish scholars, emphasizes the form of the text as it now stands—and has indeed stood for many centuries. The vowels and cantillation marks that were added approximately a millennium after the consonants are generally given serious consideration in this approach as well. Contemporary synchronic approaches are more sensitive to literary techniques than were parallel studies in traditional Jewish sources.[17] Nor do most synchronic studies ignore the results of diachronic analysis. Nonetheless, a synchronic approach to the Hebrew Bible is, on the whole, more consistent with traditional Jewish exegesis than are diachronic approaches. As noted above, this is intended to be (simply) a statement of fact and not a value judgment.

Feminist and gay/lesbian studies have found a home in academia over the past few decades. And studies employing the insights derived from these fields are increasingly widespread in biblical studies. Not surprisingly, Jewish researchers have been leaders and creative followers in this phenomenon. Thus, there are women's commentaries and "queer" commentaries of the Hebrew Bible as a whole and of specific biblical books and sections in particular.[18] It is also not surprising that these collections have met with warm approval by some Jews and rather heated dismissal by others. A sympathetic reading of the Bible from the perspective of women or gays and lesbians is not something that we would immediately or easily identify with traditional Jewish sources. However, the authenticity, not to say the necessity, of such readings is fervently supported by many in today's society. Can it be said, using any sort of objective standards, that such interpretations are non-Jewish or, less provocatively, less Jewish than others?

These are among the questions raised by those trying to define a distinctly and distinctively Jewish approach to the Bible—and by those who resist any attempt to articulate such definitions.[19] Perhaps, a way out of such dilemmas is achieved by remembering, as we noted above, that the Hebrew Bible is not the same as the Old Testament. Even when the same methods, or variety of methods, are applied, at least some of the results will be different when the material is considered as either the entire Bible or the first part of the Bible. Since almost all serious scholars of the Bible are members of one or another faith community, it is not possible, and probably not desirable, for any of them to stand wholly outside of that community when they turn to scholarship. What we can ask for and expect is that all scholars define their commitments and the degree to which these commitments affect their research. It is reasonable to suggest that Jewish scholars share some distinctive commitments with other Jews and also have commitments in common with scholars who are not Jewish. Thus it is that although there is no single approach that unites all Jewish scholars of the Bible, there are characteristics that define them as part of a continuing tradition that values creativity over uniformity, careful contextual analysis over proof-texting, and reasoned discourse and analysis over vituperation and vitriol.

Notes

1. For an illuminating analysis of these different renderings, see the discussion of these verses in Harry M. Orlinsky (1969), *Notes on the New Translation of the Torah*. Philadelphia: Jewish Publication Society.
2. For introductions to the Hebrew Bible, the following are recommended. It is worth noting that all of these books are written by Jewish scholars. This listing is in chronological order, from earliest to the most recent: Samuel Sandmel (1978), *The Hebrew Scriptures: An Introduction to Their Literature and Religious Ideas*. New York: Oxford University Press; Adele Berlin and Marc Zvi Brettler (eds) (2004), *The Jewish Study Bible: Featuring the Jewish Publication Society TANAKH Translation*. New York: Oxford University Press; Marc Zvi Brettler (2005), *How to Read the Bible*. Philadelphia: Jewish Publication Society; and Marvin A. Sweeney (2012), *TANAK: A Theological and Critical Introduction to the Jewish Bible*. Minneapolis: Fortress Press.
3. These and other parallels adduced in this chapter can be read, in an accessible translation, in Victor H. Matthews and Don C. Benjamin (2006), *Old Testament Parallels: Laws and Stories from the Ancient Near East* (revised and expanded 3rd edn). New York: Paulist Press.
4. In addition to the source listed in the first note, extended treatments of the Torah can be found in the following: J. H. Hertz (ed.) (1961), *The Pentateuch and Haftorah*. London: Soncino Press; *The JPS Torah Commentary*. Philadelphia: Jewish Publication Society: *Genesis,* commentary by Nahum M. Sarna (1989); *Exodus,* commentary by Nahum M. Sarna (1991); *Leviticus,* commentary by Baruch A. Levine (1989); *Numbers,* commentary by Jacob Milgrom (1990); *Deuteronomy,* commentary by Jeffrey H. Tigay (1996); W. Gunther Plaut and David E. S. Stein (1995), *The Torah: A Modern Commentary* (revised edn). New York: Union for Reform Judaism; David L. Lieber and Jules Harlow (2001), *Etz Hayim: Torah and Commentary*. Philadelphia: Jewish Publication Society; and (2008), *The Jewish Bible: A JPS Guide*. Philadelphia: Jewish Publication Society.
5. On Jewish translations of the Bible, see (listed in chronological order): Max L. Margolis (1917), *The Story of Bible Translation*. Philadelphia: Jewish Publication Society; Harry M. Orlinsky (1974), *Essays in Biblical Culture and Bible Translation*. New York: Ktav;

Edward L. Greenstein (1989), *Essays on Biblical Method and Translation*. Atlanta: Scholars Press; Harry M. Orlinsky and Robert G. Bratcher (1991), *A History of Bible Translation and the North American Contribution*. Atlanta: Scholars Press; Frederick W. Knobloch (ed.) (2002), *Biblical Translation in Context*. Bethesda: University of Maryland Press; Leonard J. Greenspoon (2003), "Jewish Translations of the Bible," in Adele Berlin and Marc Zvi Brettler (eds), *The Jewish Study Bible*. New York: Oxford University Press, pp. 2005–20; Leonard J. Greenspoon (2009), "The King James Bible and Jewish Bible Translations," in David G. Burke (ed.), *The Translation That Openeth the Window: Reflections on the History and Legacy of the King James Version*. New York: American Bible Society, pp. 123–38; and Leonard J. Greenspoon (2009), "Versions, Jewish," in *New Interpreter's Dictionary of the Bible*. Nashville: Abingdon, Vol. 5, pp. 760–5. Among the most popular English-language versions in use today are the following. They typically include some commentary (often more extensive in some editions; abbreviated in others): Aryeh Kaplan (1981), *The Living Torah: The Five Books of Moses* (2nd edn). New York: Maznaim Publishing (subsequent volumes, incorporating Kaplan's insights and principles, have continued to appear); (1985) *TANAKH. A New Translation of THE HOLY SCRIPTURES According to the Traditional Hebrew Text*. Philadelphia: Jewish Publication Society of America (this is the first edition of the entire text, containing revisions from earlier publications of the Torah, the Prophets, and the Writings; in 1999 there appeared the first edition with Hebrew and English on facing pages, with some further revisions in the English translation); Everett Fox (1995), *The Schocken Bible: Volume 1. The Five Books of Moses. A New Translation with Introductions, Commentary, and Notes*. New York: Schocken (earlier versions of Genesis and Exodus also appeared); and (1996) *The Tanach: The ArtScroll Series/Stone Edition*. Brooklyn: Mesorah Publications (this text incorporates in revised form earlier editions as well as new material). Mesorah has also published a number of commentaries in different formats, some using the Stone Edition and others using different English-language versions.

6. For a lively discussion of these and related issues, see the works of William G. Dever. Especially relevant and accessible is his 2006 book *Who Were the Early Israelites and Where Did They Come From?* Grand Rapids: Eerdmans.

7. On this understanding of prophecy, see especially this classic work, Abraham J. Heschel (2001; 1st edn, 1962), *The Prophets*. New York: Harper Perennial Modern Classics.

8. On the Dead Sea Scrolls, probably the most accessible discussions are found in James C. VanderKam (2010), *The Dead Sea Scrolls Today* (revised edn). Grand Rapids: Eerdmans; from a distinctively Jewish perspective, this work by Lawrence H. Schiffman is recommended: (1994) *Reclaiming the Dead Sea Scrolls: The History of Judaism, the Background of Christianity, and the Lost Library of Qumran*. Philadelphia: Jewish Publication Society.

9. On this, see most recently Lawrence H. Schiffman (2010), *Qumran and Jerusalem: Studies in the Dead Sea Scrolls and the History of Judaism*. Grand Rapids: Eerdmans.

10. See, for example, the wide-ranging selections fruitfully gathered together in James L. Kugel (1999), *The Bible As It Was*. Cambridge: Harvard University Press.

11. On the Jewish context and character of the Septuagint, see these works by Leonard J. Greenspoon (2006), "The Septuagint," in *Encyclopaedia Judaica* (new edn). Jerusalem: Jerusalem Publishing House, Vol. 3, pp. 595–8; and (2010) "At the Beginning: The Septuagint as a Jewish Bible Translation," in Robert J. V. Hiebert (ed.), *"Translation Is Required": The Septuagint in Retrospect and Prospect*. Atlanta: Society of Biblical Literature, pp. 159–69.

12. For an accessible account that begins with this material, see Shai Cherry (2007), *Torah through Time: Understanding Bible Commentary from the Rabbinic Period to Modern Times*. Philadelphia: Jewish Publication Society.

13. On these and related developments, see most recently Alan Levenson (2011), *The Making of the Modern Jewish Bible: How Scholars in Germany, Israel, and America Transformed An Ancient Text*. New York: Rowman and Littlefield.
14. See especially the publications of Israel Finkelstein; for example, Israel Finkelstein and Neil Asher Silberman (2007), *David and Solomon: In Search of the Bible's Sacred Kings and the Roots of the Western Tradition*. New York: Free Press.
15. The works of William Dever, referred to above, fit comfortably into this perspective.
16. This case is made most forcefully and effectively by Marc Brettler—see his (2005), *How to Read the Bible*. Philadelphia: Jewish Publication Society.
17. See especially Robert Alter (1981), *The Art of Biblical Narrative*. New York: Basic Books; idem (2011), *The Art of Biblical Poetry* (2nd edn). New York: Basic Books; Adele Berlin (2007), *The Dynamics of Biblical Parallelism* (revised and expanded edn). Grand Rapids: Eerdmans; eadem (1994), *Poetics and Interpretation of Biblical Narrative*. Grand Rapids: Eisenbraun; James L. Kugel (1998), *The Idea of Biblical Poetry: Parallelism and Its History*. Baltimore: The Johns Hopkins University Press; and Meir Sternberg (1987), *The Poetics of Biblical Narrative: Ideological Literature and the Drama of Reading*. Bloomington: Indiana University Press.
18. For the former, see, among others, Tamara Cohn Eskenazi and Andrea L. Weiss (eds) (2007), *The Torah: A Women's Commentary*. Cincinnati: URJ Press; and Ellen Frankel (1997), *Five Books of Miriam: A Woman's Commentary on the Torah*. San Francisco: HarperOne; for the latter, Gregg Drinkwater, Joshua Lesser, David Shneer, and Judith Plaskow (2009), *Torah Queeries: Weekly Commentaries on the Hebrew*. New York: New York University Press.
19. See also efforts to rescue "Biblical Theology" from its seemingly secure status as a Christian discipline in works such as Jon D. Levenson (1987), *Sinai and Zion: An Entry into the Jewish Bible*. San Francisco: HarperOne; and, also mentioned above, Sweeney, *TANAK: A Theological and Critical Introduction to the Jewish Bible*.

3 The World of the Rabbis

Gary G. Porton

Introduction: Overview of the Rabbinic Period

This essay[1] focuses on Jews from the first through the sixth centuries CE. Alexander's arrival in Asia Minor initiated the Hellenistic world in which rabbinic Judaism would develop. At the beginning of the period, Jews resided mainly in Palestine, Egypt, and Mesopotamia. By the end of the period, Jews lived throughout the world: in Iraq, from Basra near the Persian Gulf to Sarari, Argiza, and as far as Kurdistan in the north; in North Africa Jews were spread from Sale, Tingus, and Abyla in the west, to Daphane and Pelusium in the east; Jews were in Spain, France, Italy, Greece, and Germany. However, it was in Syria-Palestine and in Babylonia that rabbinic Judaism developed and flourished.

Palestinian Jewry

Reconstructing the history of Palestinian Jews from Alexander's arrival in 333 BCE until the fall of Masada in 73/74 CE relies heavily on Josephus; information about the period after Masada comes mainly from the rabbinic collections.[2] The only major historical event in the earlier period for which we have extensive evidence outside of Josephus is the Maccabean Revolt.[3] For the later period, we have information from Roman sources, the Church Fathers, and the

Roman-Byzantine law codes. We now also possess some limited information from archaeological sites.[4]

Alexander arrived in Asia Minor in 333 BCE; Josephus recounts that he traveled to Jerusalem and was impressed by the High Priest and the Temple. Upon Alexander's death in 301, Palestine became the contested prize of the Seleucids in Syria and the Ptolemies in Egypt. Egyptian and Syrian forces constantly invaded Jewish territory, each challenging the other's authority over the Jews, and each seeking to provide a buffer for its own state. The Jews rose up against Syria in 167/166 and retook the Temple and rededicated it in 164, but the struggle with Syria continued. In 141, Simon Maccabee, the last surviving brother of Judah Maccabee who had led the revolt and retaken Jerusalem, captured the citadel, the last stronghold of Syrian forces in Jerusalem, but it was not until the death of Antiochus VII, in 129/128?, that John Hyrcanus, Simon's son, established an independent Jewish state. That nation remained free of foreign domination until Pompey entered Jerusalem in 63 BCE. From that point on, Rome controlled the Jewish community in Palestine, and all Jewish rulers governed at the pleasure of Rome.

The Herodeans

The Maccabean dynasty (the Babylonian Talmud calls the Maccabees Hasmoneans) begun by Simon ended when Herod the Great came to power in 37 BCE. Herod's parents were Idumaean and Nabatean, populations that Hyrcanus had forcibly converted to Judaism, so that Herod was a practicing Jew, but his "Jewish ancestry" could be challenged. Rome placed Herod in power, and he remained Rome's client throughout his rule, which was marked by his ruthless destruction of his enemies, many within his own family, and his numerous construction projects within and outside Palestine, including a complete redesign and expansion of the Temple in Jerusalem. Upon Herod's death, 4 BCE, his kingdom was divided among his three sons—Antipas, Archelaus, and Philip—but the unity and stability of Palestine was ended. The economy was in shambles with the end of Herod's massive construction projects, and Rome placed Palestine under the rule of a number of greedy, insensitive, and incompetent prefects.[5] The situation continued to deteriorate until 66/67 CE when the province rose in revolt against Rome. In 70 CE, the Temple was destroyed as a starving and contentious Jewish population in the city was withstanding the Roman onslaught. The war ended in 73/74 CE with the fall of Masada, a mountaintop fortress built by Herod in the southern part of the country.

Internal Jewish Developments

Along with his political history, at times Josephus turns his attention to the inner life of the Jewish community. Within this period, more precisely from the time of Alexandra Salome, ruler of the Palestinian Jewish community 76/75–67 BCE, Josephus introduces the Pharisees, Sadducees, and Essenes, which he styles as philosophies. The Pharisees and Sadducees also appear in the New Testament and in the rabbinic collections, implying that they were the major groups within the Palestinian Jewish community until the rise of the rabbinic movement. Previous generations of scholars accepted Josephus' claim that the Pharisees controlled the Jewish community, especially after the destruction of the Temple. However, modern scholarship has not only rejected Josephus' picture of the scope of the Pharisees' influence, but also much of the descriptions of the Pharisees and Sadducees in the New Testament and the rabbinic documents.[6] Many scholars identify Josephus' Essenes with the community at Qumran and the Dead Sea Scrolls.[7] While we may accept the broad outline of Josephus' history, the details with which he fills in his account are less certain.[8]

From the last quarter of the first century, the rabbinic collections—Talmud and Midrash—become our most informative sources about the Palestinian Jewish community and the inner development of Judaism. The rabbinic texts tell us that Yohanan b. Zakkai, whose disciples, according to tradition, carried him out of Jerusalem in a coffin before the city fell to the Roman troops, inherited the scholarly mantel of his teacher Hillel, the greatest Pharisees of the first century. The rabbinic movement essentially began when Yohanan established "an academy" at Yavneh after he fled Jerusalem. There, he began creating the outlines of a Judaism that could survive without the Temple.[9] Yavneh was the center of Pharisaic Judaism as it developed into rabbinic Judaism. Rabban Gamaliel II, who came to power upon Yohanan's death, traced his ancestry back to Hillel and reestablished the dynasty of Hillel around 80. Rabbinic tradition holds that under Gamaliel the Hebrew Bible was canonized and the basic outline of the Amidah, the prayer that replaced the sacrificial offering, was set. Following Gamaliel, Aqiba was the most important rabbi. Although, according to later tradition, he did not engage in his rabbinic studies until late in life, he continued the tradition of Hillel and set the parameters for the subsequent developments of Palestinian Judaism.

Despite the loss of the Temple and the destruction of Jerusalem in the failed revolt of 70, in 132, the Jews launched another revolt, which was even more challenging to the Roman forces. Sixty years after the destruction of Jerusalem and the Temple, Bar Koziba, the name by which Bar Kokhba of the rabbinic collections is known in the documents from the revolt, was able to mount a revolt against Rome that necessitated the intervention of the 10th legion. When Bar Koziba led his revolt, Aqiba seems to have proclaimed him the Messiah, a claim not widely accepted by Aqiba's colleagues. Aqiba, along with nine other leading sages, was martyred by the Romans. Bar Koziba was the last independent Jewish ruler of the Jews in Palestine in late antiquity.

Transitions

The destruction of the Temple and Yohanan's move to Yavneh mark one major transition point in the history of Palestinian Jews and Judaism. Similarly the defeat of Bar Koziba and Hadrian's response to the second revolt mark another crucial transition. Hadrian ploughed under the Temple Mount, erected a Temple to Jupiter in its place, and renamed the city Aelia Capitolina. At some point, either before or after the revolt, he also outlawed circumcision. He forcibly moved the Jews from Judea to the Galilee, divided a good deal of conquered land among his army officers, and forbade the Jews from entering Jerusalem except on the ninth of Av to mourn over the Temple's destruction. With the move to the Galilee, the center of rabbinic Judaism moved from Yavneh to Usha, and the second major phase of rabbinic Judaism began. At Usha, Aqiba's student Meir transmitted Aqiba's teachings and continued the line of Jewish thought that would culminate in the Mishnah during the rule of Judah ha-Nasi (Judah the Patriarch/Prince, d. 218 CE?), whom Rome recognized as the leader of the Jewish community and the rabbinic tradition as a great scholar. Although the Mishnah, our earliest rabbinic document and edited while Judah was in power, focuses its attention on the village and countryside, there were significant Jewish populations in regional centers, such as Sepphoris and Tiberias.

Under Judah (170–218?), the Patriarchate, the office of the political ruler of the Jews, reached its pinnacle. Judah had the blessing of the Roman authorities, even though they placed a Roman legion at his court to aid him if he encountered opposition to his authority. The legion would also ensure the Patriarch's loyalty to Rome. The failing Roman economy coupled with the devastation wreaked by the Roman legions during the Bar Kokhba revolt presented Judah and the Palestinian population with severe economic conditions, forcing Judah to open his storehouses to feed the population. Judah's good relationship with the Roman rulers became legendary.

The deteriorating economy of the Roman Empire naturally affected Palestine. Palestine was primarily an agricultural economy, with its olive oil prized throughout the empire. Jewish farms were at the subsistence level, although Palestine's geographical location made it an important location on several trade routes. Olives, grapes, and wheat were the main crops. Jews also engaged in a number of house-centered crafts, such as working with cloth, leather, flax, and the like.[10]

The instability of the Roman political system and the challenges to the empire from internal and external forces also affected Palestine. Some scholars have argued for uprisings in Palestine in the mid-fourth century amid this instability. On the other hand, the evidence of Jewish collaboration with the non-Jewish government is sound and widespread. Some Roman legal texts imply that the Patriarch held imperial honors as late as the early fifth century, shortly before many scholars speculate the Patriarchate ended. The Patriarch's demise did not mark the end of Palestinian Judaism, nor did it mark the end of rabbinic culture, according to many contemporary scholars.[11] But it did mark the end of Jewish political power within Palestine. Some have linked the final edition of the Palestinian Talmud to the waning of Jewish political power in the Land of Israel.

Babylonian Jewry

The other geographical center of Judaism in late antiquity was Babylonia, modern-day Iraq. Generations of scholars have relied primarily on the Babylonian Talmud, along with the rest of the rabbinic corpus and Geonic[12] chronicles[13] to reconstruct the history of Jews in Babylonia. Unlike the situation in Palestine, virtually the only information we have about the Jewish community, its leadership, and its relationship to the non-Jewish world comes from the rabbinic collections. While we can glean limited information about the Jews from Persian documents, they do not discuss the Jews in a way comparable to our information about Palestine from the Roman, Byzantine, and Christian writers.[14] In addition, we have virtually no archaeological information. While many scholars of Palestinian Judaism have placed the Jews within the context of Roman culture, only a few scholars, most notably Yaakov Elman,[15] have attempted to place Babylonian Jewish law and culture in the context of Sasanian law and culture.[16]

There was a Jewish community in Babylonia/Persia from at least the sixth century BCE after Nebuchadnezzar conquered Jerusalem. Although several groups of Jews returned to Palestine by the end of that century, many remained. The fact that Jews resided in the domains of both the Roman and Parthian Empires affected how both powers dealt with the Jews, with some suspicion. In addition, the growth and development of Christianity in the West affected Palestinian Judaism, but Christianity did not play the same role in the East, so that Babylonian Judaism was able to develop without the same challenge of Christianity's appropriation and reinterpretation of the Hebrew Bible and its claim to be the True Israel.[17] The Jews began their sojourn in Babylonia in northern Mesopotamia and the areas east of the Tigris: Assyria, Adiabene, Media, and Elam. Nisibis was the most important city of the Parthian period; Jewish sources mention a rabbinic academy in the city. During the Sasanian period, we find the Jewish centers in southern Mesopotamia near where the Tigris and Euphrates meet. Pumbedita, Nehardea, Sura, Mahoza, Seleucia, and Ctesiphon appear as important Jewish communities and rabbinic activity. Still, modern scholarship rejects the traditional picture that these were the sites of rabbinic academies throughout the period. At best, rabbis studied with individual sages in informal settings, finding another teacher upon the death of their master. Formal rabbinic academies are later creations.[18]

Parthian Rule

Probably around 120 BCE, the Parthians, a military aristocracy, took control from the Seleucids, who had ruled Babylonia from shortly after the death of Alexander. The former remained in power almost continually until 220 CE. The Parthians impinged as little as possible on the various ethnic groups within their empire, requiring only that they remain loyal and fight against any foreign invaders. They saw their Jewish subjects as important allies against the Seleucids and then the Romans once they gained control in Palestine. The Jews of both Babylonia and Palestine joined with the Parthians when Rome moved eastward and served as the formers' allies when they moved into Jerusalem, consistently favoring "any power but Rome." Within Parthia itself, the Jews were able to gain some political authority. Josephus relates the story of Anileus and Asineus who were able to establish an independent Jewish enclave in the Parthian Empire probably 20–35 CE. Josephus also recounts the story, elements of which also appear in rabbinic literature, of the conversion of the rulers of Adiabene, Helen and Izates, to Judaism, perhaps in the mid-thirties CE. The Babylonian Jews did not support the Palestinian revolts of 67–73/74 CE or 132–5 CE against Rome.

The two Jewish communities were not completely independent of each other. The rabbinic sources describe consistent and active contact between the Palestinian and Babylonian communities, but we don't know much about the inner life of the Jewish community or the rabbis during the Parthian period. The first-century leader of Pharisaic Judaism, Hillel, was a Babylonian Jew, implying that there was a religiously active segment of the community. Only two Tannaim[19] are mentioned in Babylonia, Hananiah and Judah ben Bathyra. At some point, the Babylonian Jewish community created an institution parallel to the Palestinian Patriarch, called the Exilarchate, but its origins are uncertain.

Sasanian Rule

Sasanian rule in Babylonian is coextensive with the rabbinic period. It began at round that date that Rav migrated from Palestine[20] to Babylonia and initiated the Amoraic[21] period, and it ended with the rise of Islam, 220s–620s. The Talmud records mostly cordial relations between the Jews and the Sasanian Emperors from Shapur I (239–70) until Yazdagird I (399–420), almost 200 years. The Sasanians engaged in military actions against Rome well into the fourth century, affecting the Jews in Asia Minor, Syria, and the Babylonian heartland, who were caught up in the ravages of the battles. Despite this fact, Samuel, the then leader of the Babylonian Jewish community, and Shapur I worked out an agreement whereby the Sasanian authorities allowed their Jewish population to oversee their community affairs as long as they did not interfere with the larger matters facing the national government. *Dina de Malkuta Dina*, that is, "the law of the land of the law," was Samuel's formulation, and it meant that the Jews would support Shapur in his struggles with Rome and any other foreign invaders, such as the Palmyrenes.[22] In return, Shapur would allow the Jews to manage their own communal affairs. In truth, within the wider empire, the Jews' affairs were minor and almost trivial. A close reading of the court cases in the Talmud suggests that the Jewish courts handled what we today would classify as civil cases, especially those that would be settled in small claims court, and family law, especially as it applied to the concerns of those of lower middle- to lower-class status. The rabbis' control of the community's religious calendar, ritual, and eating habits fits into this pattern. The Sasanian government would have cared little, if at all, about these matters. In addition, the rabbis had limited control of the village marketplaces and regulated intra-communal trade.

By enhancing the power of the Zoroastrian clergy, the Magi, the Sasanians virtually created a state-church. However, this situation is not comparable to the superficially parallel "marriage" between the Byzantine Empire and the Catholic Church, in the fourth century CE, because the Zoroastrian clergy exercised authority sporadically and in limited ways. While Zoroastrianism was the official religion of the Sasanian Empire, Kirdir (272–90) was the first priest to have achieved any real power; there are records of his attempts to persecute Jews, Buddhists, Brahmins, Nasoreans, Christians, Maktaks, and Zandiks, but the scope of these activities is unclear, and the Talmud mentions only occasional interference by the Magi, most likely in opposition to the Jews' use of fire, or of water for immersion, for both were holy to the Zoroastrians. Furthermore, the Magi may have objected to the Jewish practice of burying their dead instead of leaving them exposed above ground. But the Talmud does not mention any major persecution by the Magi.

The Sasanian monarchy began to weaken under Yazdagird II (438–57) and his son Peroz (459–84). Later Jewish sources[23] point to Zoroastrian persecutions of Jews during this time, which may be the result of their becoming stronger and the Sasanian rulers becoming weaker. While the Talmud does not mention any problems at this time, Geonic chronicles described prohibitions of Sabbath worship, closure of synagogues and schools, and the forced conversions of Jewish children. The reason for disagreement between the Talmud and Geonic sources is unclear, so that determining exactly what happened is virtually impossible.

Exilarchate

At the end of the fifth century, Mazdak, a Persian priest who had been influenced by Manichaeism, rose to prominence with the support of the king, Kavad (488–531). Apparently Mazdak deposed Kavad for a short time, 496–8, and Geonic sources state that Mar Zutra, the Exilarch, attempted to establish an independent Jewish state at that time. If the Amoraic rabbinic movement began at the same time as the ascension of the Sasanians to power, tradition states that the final editorial process of the Babylonian Talmud coincided with the waning of their power in the fifth century.

The Talmud suggests that the Exilarch was the political authority of the Jews and their representative to the Sasanian government. Although the Geonic sources list the Exilarchs, the Talmud is more ambiguous about the office. There is no reliable evidence of the existence of the Exilarch during the Parthian period, but the significance of that fact is unclear. Does it mean that there was no Exilarch or that we simply don't have enough information about the Parthian period? The Babylonian Talmud's descriptions of the Exilarch closely parallels its descriptions of the Palestinian Patriarch, which suggests that the Talmud may not be depicting him as he really existed: Davidic ancestry is attributed to both, both appear as representatives of the Jewish community before the non-Jewish political establishment, both had at their disposal an armed force supplied by the non-Jewish government, both appointed judges over Jewish courts, and both were wealthy. Be this as it may, if the figure actually existed at all, it bears noting that both Talmuds agree that the Exilarch appointed the supervisor of the Jewish markets, the *agoranomos*, although his exact duties in Babylonia are unclear. The Talmuds record a rocky relationship between the Patriarch and the rabbis in Palestine, and an even more competitive situation between the Exilarch and the rabbis in Babylonia. Our sources suggest that the Exilarch was much more independent of the rabbinic class than was the Patriarch.[24]

The Jewish population probably engaged in subsistence agriculture just as the non-Jews. The Babylonian Talmud promotes business, not agriculture, as the path to wealth. The Talmud names rabbis who became wealthy by trading in beer, flax, silk, linen, dates, and wine. As in Palestine, the Jewish farmers, traders, and businessmen interacted with their non-Jewish counterparts.

Interpretation and Scholarship

While the historians of Babylonian and Palestinian Judaism can agree on the broad outlines above, there is a good deal of debate concerning specific issues — the history of the Patriarch and the Exilarch, the scope of rabbinic authority, the nature of Jews' responses to Roman/Byzantine and Parthian/Sasanian rulers at any specific time, the nature of the economic life of Jews in both Palestine and Babylonia, the influence of the non-Jewish culture and environment on Jews/Judaism — to name only a few topics debated among scholars. However, contemporary scholars are posing much more fundamental questions to the rabbinic collections: Can they be used as sources of historical information at all, and if so, of what periods do they speak? Do the sources describe a Jewish community at odds with the cultures surrounding it, or do the collections describe a Jewish community interacting with the non-Jews and their government? Is it legitimate to gather the information on a topic from the full range of rab-binic documents or should we limit ourselves to studying each document on its own? These questions have important implications for constructing a picture of Judaism in late antiquity. The historical reconstructions above are based on the best nineteenth- and twentieth-century scholarship using those collections[25] as sources of reliable historical information. However, contemporary scholarship has raised serious questions on about this assumption as they have rethought the nature of the rabbinic collections and the information they contain.

Reading the Sources

Although the rabbinic documents are vastly different, they do share some essential traits. They are edited collections, not single-authored works. None of them reflects the thought or mind-set of one person, much less a person well known to us, such as Josephus, Philo, Livy, or Tacitus. We do not actually know who edited the various collections, even though later authorities, often Geonic, have assigned names of supposed authors or editors. Also, we have no reliable information concerning the processes of their creation, the forms individual passages had before their incorporation into later documents, from where edi-tors got what they included, what they chose to exclude, or their editorial prin-ciples in general. For example, the relationship between Tosefta and Mishnah remains a topic of extensive scholarly debate,[26] even though understanding the relationship between these two Tannaitic[27] collections is fundamental to evaluating the editing of the Mishnah,[28] what its editor(s) knew, what he/they rejected, and what he/they collected for the Mishnah.[29] We do not even know why these collections arose or what purpose(s) they were meant to serve. The original function of the Midrashim is also unclear. Most scholars argue the col-lections of Midrashim derive from the popular sermons the rabbis delivered in late antiquity. Others maintain the Midrashim are internal rabbinic creations meant to demonstrate the rabbis' expertise in manipulating Torah.[30]

A major innovation in current study is the application of a variety of liter-ary-critical methods to the study of the rabbinic collections.[31] Jacob Neusner was one of the first scholars consistently to apply literary-critical methods. He showed that the *sugyot*, the small units upon which all of the collections are based, were compiled in a limited number of literary forms. While not the first scholar to identify such literary forms, Neusner's *Development of a Legend*[32] and *The Rabbinic Traditions about the Pharisees before 70*[33] brought the work of the rabbinic texts' editors/collectors to the fore. An essential consequence of his work is the recognition that given the formulaic nature of the rabbinic collec-tions, we cannot *assume* that they contain the actual words of the ancient sages. Indeed, Neusner's work demonstrated that the different collections painted vastly different pictures of individual rabbis and of individual Pharisees, with later documents embellishing stories found in earlier collections. The divergent pictures of the sages found in different documents raised fundamental questions in Neusner's mind: Could we uncover "historical" information about the early sages? Could we actually discover what any sage said or thought? Why were the sages described so differently in the various documents? What were the sources from which the later collections drew their information? Did the later documents merely create information *de novo* to serve the editors' larger agenda? Exactly how did the various rabbinic collections relate to one another? Was it possible to construct an accurate historical reconstruction of the Jews from 1–600 CE from these texts?

Neusner concluded that we cannot discover reliable historical information about the early sages. Even if some of the information is accurate, obviously much is not, and none of it contains the actual words of the sage himself; in Neusner's mind, there thus was no way to distinguish the accurate and inaccurate materials. Perhaps Neusner's most controversial conclusion was that each rabbinic collection needed to be studied and evaluated independently of the other rabbinic documents. Each collection reflected the mind-set and world-view of its own particular editors, who pursued their own distinctive literary and theological agenda, appropriate to their own historical setting and location. Before we could even propose any synthetic studies that examined rabbinic Judaism overall, we needed to know what each collection told us about the thoughts of those who collated them.[34]

While Neusner's approach largely revolutionized how rabbinic documents would be studied, many scholars continue to propose a quite different assessment. Alexander Samely argues that one must read the array of rabbinic texts as an interrelated collection.[35] He writes, "[I]n reading them [rabbinic documents] in each other's light, one seems to be able to obtain enough additional information to determine the meaning of a given statement."[36] Even though the rabbinic collections come from different times and from different locations, in Samely's view the totality of rabbinic literature "constitutes a unified historical phenomenon."[37] Samely notes that all the rabbinic texts share a common language, the same few literary forms, express the same ideas, frequently in the same idiom, cite by name the same sages, refer to the same "historical" people and events, and all quote from the Hebrew Bible in the same fashion.[38] Furthermore the rabbinic collections do not contain the literary genre popular in the worlds in which the texts arose; they are distinctively rabbinic. They are not historical writings, "lives" of famous people, epics, extended fiction, tragedies, comedies, long speeches, or "systematic tracts on explicit philosophy, theology, grammar, mathematics, and all other theoretical or empirical sciences." Nevertheless, the array of rabbinic documents form "a unified historical phenomenon"; however, "the task of unifying themes and positions is entirely left to the reader."[39] For Samely, one cannot understand any single collection unless one refers to the other rabbinic texts. A reader finds unity and coherence only when he/she brings the various rabbinic collections into an interpretative relationship. Interpretation of a passage in one text, this is to say, depends on reference to many other texts, which likely provide the information and context for ideas expressed laconically elsewhere.[40]

The disagreement between Samely and Neusner is fundamental to the study of the rabbinic documents. Is each document a unique creation that stands on its own, or are they all interconnected, so that each document assumes the information in every other document? We know that later collections quote earlier documents and that one text may alter material found in another collection. Do the "authors" of each document follow an overall plan or not in amassing the materials for their document? Did the authors of each document know the totality of the materials in the other collections and *assumed* that their readers would know information that they did not bring to their new creation? While it is unlikely that we will ever conclusively answer these questions, it is important to recognize that Neusner's emphasis on the integrity and uniqueness of each text has opened up new and fruitful ways of understanding each document.

Scholarship on the Talmud

While the issues raised here extend to the study of all the rabbinic collections, much of what is new in the study of rabbinic texts can be illustrated by examining the work done on the Babylonian Talmud. Noting that the Babylonian Talmud is "entirely uniform, and the stylistic preferences exhibited on any given page characterize every other page of the document,"[41] Neusner focuses on the similarities that one finds among the various pages of the Talmud. He writes, "[P]eople everywhere [in the Talmud and in every location to which it refers], whatever the subject or problem turn out to speak in the same way, and . . . even to say the same thing about many things."[42] Neusner concludes that a "textual community" — his term for the group of men who finally edited the Talmud — imposed this unity on the diverse materials compiled into the Babylonian Talmud as they set out to define an elaborate plan for the social and political order of an entire people. Neusner argues that when the Talmud quotes other sources it reformulates those sources in such a way that they conform to final plan of the Talmud's editors. Everything looks and sounds the same because the final editors created a text in which everything was blended together to conform to their final plan.[43]

While recognizing the important work of the Talmud's editors, Richard Kalmin, among others, challenges Neusner's claim that they reworked the materials they incorporated into their text so much as to obliterate their distinctive traits. Kalmin argues that the editors/compilers of the Babylonian Talmud maintained the distinctive ideas of earlier as well as of later generations of sages:

one can see different opinions about dreams and dream-interpretations; the fixed opinions of Rav and Samuel; and the different technical terms employed to introduce early and later Amoraic opinions.[44] Kalmin thus argues that earlier Talmudic generations appear differently from later ones. This proves not only that the Talmud is composed of sources that were transmitted from earlier generations to the later Talmudic editors but also that its final editors did not change at least discernible amounts of what they received.

Christine Hayes, while accepting some of Neusner's ideas, poses important challenges to his work. Building on the work of Kalmin and Shamma Friedman,[45] Hayes rejects the claim that the final editors of the Talmud homogenized all of the material, so that one cannot set the smaller units into a diachronic relationship. She writes that "applying the term 'authorship' to the final redactors of the Talmud . . . obscures the degree to which the redactors were . . . constrained by the raw material they received, by the agenda set in earlier combinations and contextualizations of traditions, by the community in which they worked, and even by the genre of the work being produced."[46] Hayes argues that "with proper attention to the distinctive features of these [rabbinic] texts . . . some *relatively reliable* diachronic and cultural-historical analyses of rabbinic texts *beyond the level of redaction* become possible."[47] Hayes compares passages in the Palestinian and Babylonian Talmuds in order to ascertain how they differ in their treatment of specific legal issues. From there she argues about the differences between the Babylonian and Palestinian rabbinic communities. Hayes maintains that the Talmud's editors left us many indications of the "layers" of sources they combined, and these markers allow us to speak about specific generations of Babylonian sages.[48]

David Weiss Halivni has argued that the rabbis who produced the anonymous layer of the Talmud—known as the *Stammaim*—are the editors of the document as a whole.[49] Halivni's work, largely in Hebrew,[50] stands together with Shamma Friedman's work[51] in creating what many see as an accurate picture, as far as it is possible to draw such a picture, of the methods the final editors of the Babylonian Talmud employed in creating the document.

In Halivni's view, the final editors were crucial for the production of the Babylonian Talmud, reworking and creating a literary context for every tradition they received; still, Halivni holds that one can disentangle the Talmudic text in order to separate the layer of the final editors from the sources they brought together. For Halivni in contrast to Neusner, the Talmud can be used as a source for the history and ideologies of the rabbis of the generations prior to that of the Talmud's editors themselves.

Halivni specifically argues that all of the anonymous material in the Babylonian Talmud postdates the sayings assigned to specific Amoraic authorities and that the two types of material—the anonymous and the attributed— are fundamentally different from each other. Halivni claims that the *Stammaim* produced most of the "give and take" that is characteristic of the Babylonian Talmud as well as much of the "legal reasoning," which explicates and comments on the Amoraic passages, that generations of the Talmud's readers have pointed to as the essential feature of Talmudic thought and logic. The *Stammaim* were interested in the argumentative process and not in producing practical legal decisions. At times, the *Stammaim* even reconstructed or (re)invented the reasoning behind the Amoraic comments in order to further their agenda of focusing on the legal reasoning of the sages whom they quoted. The Talmud's final editors, the *Stammaim*, created their passages by setting the Amoraic materials in a logical framework and supplying the underlying reasons for the Amoraic opinions.

While Halivni seems to agree with Neusner in holding that the *Stammaim* have reworked the sources they collected, unlike Neusner, he argues that in many instances we can separate the work of the *Stammaim* from the sources they wove together to complete the Talmud. Separating the *Stammaim*'s words and thoughts from the Amoraim's words and thoughts is a difficult task, whose conclusions are not always certain.[52]

Neusner and Halivni do not disagree about the role of the final editors of the Babylonian Talmud. Nor do they dispute whether in fact the final editors altered the material they amassed. The difference in disagreement is much more subtle. Halivni claims that one can separate the work of the final editors from the Amoraic materials they assembled and that one can in fact argue that much of the Amoraic strata reflect the ideas of the generation(s) in which various Amoraim lived. Neusner would argue that disengaging the Amoraic ideas from the thoughts of the Talmud's final editors is almost impossible and even irrelevant insofar as, in his view, the Talmud as a whole presents a cogent system of Judaic belief, a representation of the rabbinic worldview that is the product of the final redactors alone and that is the appropriate target of scholarly interest.

Daniel Boyarin has devised yet a different approach to moving from the text of the Talmud to the culture(s) that produced it.[53] Boyarin focuses on the Talmudic stories as we have them, without attempting to disentangle the various layers. He subjects the texts to a careful reading with the goal of unpacking the social tensions expressed in the texts which will lead us to the texts' social meanings. To Boyarin the rabbinic texts are "discourse," as Foucault used the term.[54] Literature is a process that connects to a variety of other social processes, which means that we can move from the literature to the social meanings of the culture that produced it. Literature on this reading is intimately connected to and cannot be divorced from the culture that produced it, so that the literature expresses the values and meaning of that culture.[55] Boyarin is not interested in rabbis, editors, Amoraim or *Stammaim*; he is interested in the culture that produced the Talmud—its values and its concerns. By reading the rabbinic documents as literature and not as history, law, stories or the like, Boyarin moves from the individuals who told the stories, wrote them, and edited them to the culture in which all of these individuals worked. Thus, with a good deal of care, Boyarin proposes that we move from the rabbinic documents to the social world in which they were created. Boyarin's claims and methods have stimulated a number of scholars' work.

Jeffrey L. Rubenstein's three major works analyse stories within the Babylonian Talmud.[56] In *Talmudic Stories*, he lays out the method he follows in all three volumes. He employs literary analysis, "which attends to the narrative art and rhetorical tendencies of didactic stories," along with source criticism and redaction-criticism, "which recognize the composite, multitiered nature of the Talmudic text." The Talmud's many layers were brought together by the Talmud's final editors, the *stamm*. These three methods allow the scholar to open "a window to the cultural world of the redactors."

Rubenstein sets out to uncover the tensions among these competing values in the stories he analyses.[57] Each volume attempts to discover those tensions that existed within rabbinic culture, especially within the rabbinic academies and between the values of the rabbinic academies and the demands of family life. The rabbinic academy as a formal institution was a late creation of the *Stammaim*, who were "redactors insofar as they created *sugyot* that included the Amoraic traditions they inherited," and they were the authors of the Babylonian Talmud "in that they placed those Amoraic traditions in a sustained superstructure of their own composition."[58] Because of the *Stammaim*'s dual role, we cannot always easily disentangle the two layers of the material. However, if one compares a story that appears in the Palestinian Talmud with its parallel in the Babylonian Talmud, "[b]ecause the Palestinian versions generally predate those of the Bavli [Babylonian Talmud] . . . the differences most likely result from the different interests of the Babylonian sages."[59] And most reflect the *Stammaim*'s interests and agenda. Thus, while he follows Boyarin's methods in analysing the text, he seems to accept Neusner's position that the Talmud primarily informs us about the worldviews of its final editors, and for Rubenstein they were the *Stammaim*.

In all three volumes Rubenstein examines Torah as the primary value of the Talmudic academy and discusses the means by which one gains stature in the academy: by engaging in argumentation, through one's lineage, or as a result of the breadth of one's knowledge. These competing criteria lead to a picture of "verbal" warfare within the academy, as well as extended discussions of shame. Finally, he demonstrates that the demands of Torah and life in the academy seem to have produced major social tensions between the rabbis and the non-rabbinic population as well as between the demands of the academy and those of family and home.

The majority of recent scholars' close readings of passages in the Babylonian Talmud have focused on nonlegal stories, a rather odd fact considering that the

Talmud is comprised primarily of legal materials. Barry Wimpfheimer demonstrates that a careful reading of the legal narratives can also move from the text into the culture of the creators of the Babylonian Talmud.[60] After carefully demonstrating that the widely accepted bifurcation of aggadah (nonlegal material) and halakhah (legal materials) is artificial and unproductive for understanding the narratives within the Talmud, Wimpfheimer shows that we can explore the cultural dynamics of the *Stammaim*'s academy just as easily from the legal narratives as from the nonlegal ones. In addition, instead of focusing only on relatively short stories, Wimpfheimer examines some rather long Talmudic passages, thus showing that one need not limit contemporary "literary analysis" to small units of Talmudic discourse. While Rubenstein and Boyarin reject the idea that we should read the Talmudic stories as "history," Wimpfheimer notes that many read the legal narratives as containing reliable historical information. However, he reads the legal narratives, as others have read the nonlegal narratives, as cultural creations and questions their value as historical sources.[61] Among his most interesting conclusions are the following: courtroom scenes focus on matters of status and hierarchy, which are paralleled in noncourtroom encounters between sages,[62] and although we often view the rabbis as superior moral beings, the Talmud within the context of its legal narratives shows that they act as human beings concerned with their own best self-interests.[63]

To summarize, Kalmin and Hayes argue that the final editors of the Babylonian Talmud did not homogenize what they received in such a way as to make it impossible to discover the various streams of earlier thinking within the Talmud. Along these same lines, Halivni along with Friedman developed methods to disentangle the final editors' (*Stammaim*) work from the previous generations' (Amoraim) creations. This approach in certain regards confirms Neusner's claims about the importance of the Talmud's final editors but also challenges his argument that we cannot move back from the final editing of the Talmud to previous layers. Boyarin, Rubenstein, and Wimpfheimer rejected Neusner's claims that the Babylonian Talmud must be read only in its own terms as an independent rabbinic text. At the same time, unlike earlier generations of scholars, they are less concerned with establishing the validity of the specific words attributed to a given sage than with discovering the "attitudes" and "values" the Talmudic stories convey to the reader. And even in their view, when we move from the text to the social world in which it was created, that world is dominated by the Talmud's final editors, not necessarily by the generations of Amoraim which appear throughout the document.

The implications of these ideas for the reconstructions of the history of Babylonian and Palestinian Judaism in late antiquity are significant. If we cannot easily disentangle the various layers of the Talmud, can we actually write a history of rabbinic thought that spans 500 years? If later sources elaborate on earlier material, how can we accept the Amoraim's descriptions of the Tannaim?

If the *Stammaim* created the rabbinic academies, the give-and-take of Talmudic argument, and made Torah the central cultural value, can we safely apply these values to earlier periods?

Judaism and Hellenism

In addition to rethinking the ways in which we should read the rabbinic documents, modern scholars are looking at the Jewish community and its leaders in new ways. The rabbis of late antiquity had to develop strategies to cope with the non-Jewish governments that controlled them and their non-Jewish environments in which they lived. As early as 1937, Elias Bickerman[64] argued that the Maccabees achieved and maintained power not because they opposed Hellenism but because they came to terms with it. Martin Hengel similarly developed an overarching theory that Hellenism had a profound influence on every aspect of Jewish life and thought within Palestine, as well as in the Diaspora.[65] Still, the debate concerning the "Hellenistic character" of Palestinian Judaism is far from over, as the articles collected in volumes two and three of the *Cambridge History of Judaism*[66] and *Jewish Writings of the Second Temple Period*[67] attest. In addition, the editions of First and Second Maccabees in the Anchor Bible[68] and Martin Goodman's collection of essays[69] demonstrate the current lively debate concerning the relationship of Judaism to its Hellenistic environment. Scholars have no doubt that non-Jews were aware of Jews and Judaism.[70] The question is how much Jews and Judaism adapted to and adopted from the non-Jewish cultures in which they lived.

Saul Lieberman was one of the first scholars to chart the influence of Hellenistic and Roman culture and ideas on rabbinic Judaism. Although Lieberman's goal was to explain difficult passages within rabbinic literature, the results of his studies were to demonstrate that one could not understand rabbinic literature, culture, ideas, or even exegetical techniques independently of Greek and Roman thought and culture. The rabbis did not develop their ideas and ways of thinking in a vacuum; they were deeply influenced by the cultures which surrounded them.[71] While Lieberman would not necessary have accepted the current view of scholars, his foundational studies had an important influence on those designing the new paradigm.[72]

Eric Gruen's *Heritage and Hellenism*[73] stretches the new model to its limits. He argues that

> "Judaism" and "Hellenism" were neither competing systems nor incompatible concepts. It would be erroneous to assume that Hellenization entailed encroachment upon Jewish traditions and erosion of Jewish beliefs. Jews did not face a choice of either assimilation or resistance to Greek culture. . . . The

prevailing culture of the Mediterranean could hardly be ignored or dismissed. But adaptation to it need not require compromise of Jewish percepts or practices.[74]

Jews and Rome

Seth Schwartz's work offers a somewhat more nuanced assessment, demonstrating the *complexity* of the relationship of Palestinian Jews, especially the rabbis, to Roman rule. He argues that there was a shift in the situation of the Palestinian Jews and Judaism, which altered how the Jews, especially the rabbis, dealt with Roman rule.[75] Schwartz argues that

> [a] loosely centralized, ideologically complex [Jewish] society came into existence by the second century B.C.E., collapsed in the wake of the Destruction [of the Temple and Jerusalem] and the imposition of direct Roman rule after 70 C.E., and reformed starting in the fourth century, centered now on the synagogue and the local religious community, in part as a response to the christianization of the Roman Empire.[76]

Schwartz further notes that "[n]o provincial population rebelled as many times and as disastrously as the Jews."[77] Although the Bar Kokhba rebellion was the last major Jewish action against Rome, "the Palestinian rabbis . . . never concealed their hostility [to Rome]. . . . [T]he rabbis produced a set of writings that . . . were unlike anything else ever written in the Roman world. The rabbis *performed* their political and cultural marginality in their teaching and writing."[78] The Roman defeat of Bar Kokhba in 135 severely reduced the Jewish population of the Land of Israel and also devastated ancient Palestine's agricultural economy. Schwartz argues that when the population and economy began to grow in the fourth century "some, or even many, rabbis began to accommodate themselves to Roman rule as they became part of the Roman political and social establishment."[79]

Martin Goodman also suggests that the correlation between Judaism and Hellenism was multifaceted. He writes that "some rabbis came to see Rome as wicked and malevolent and 'good' Romans as the exception." Rome was "an instrument of war" and linked to Edom, the hereditary enemy of Israel. In addition, the rabbinic texts show no great knowledge of Roman politics or political events. The rabbis applied the name of Antonius to all nonhostile Roman emperors; Antonius' major character trait was that he had the good sense to converse with the rabbinic masters and to learn from them.[80] At the same time, "the archeological and epigraphic remains from the Land of Israel for the two centuries after 135 contain little that is clearly related to Judaism"[81] and seem most unrelated to what we would expect to find based on the rabbinic collections. Goodman writes that for two centuries after 135 "[p]ublic buildings lacked any of the Jewish iconography which was to become standard on the mosaic floors of Palestinian synagogues in the late fourth to sixth centuries," including "the ram's horn, palm branch, and especially the candelabrum from the Temple."[82] Although in 212 Rome granted citizenship to everyone in the empire, none of the Jews who appear in the rabbinic collections identified themselves as Roman citizens.[83] Although the rabbinic texts paint an overwhelmingly negative picture of Rome, the archeological evidence paints a picture in which the Jews seem to be an integral part of their Roman environment. Even after the fourth century, Schwartz and Goodman argue, the rabbis worked out an accommodation with the Byzantine-Christian authorities.

Judaism and Christianity

Just as scholars are rethinking the relationship of Judaism to Roman culture, they are also reexamining the relationship of rabbinic Judaism to Christianity. Several factors complicate the possibility of our understanding the relationship between Jews and Christians in the ancient world. The rabbinic collections contain few, if any, clear references to Christians or Christianity. Some may have been altered by medieval censors, but, in fact, most rabbinic documents simply ignore Christianity. There are scattered references to Jesus or supposedly Jesus-like figures, but again they are rare and far from transparent treatments of Jesus. Therefore, uncovering the Jewish views of Christianity and Christians within the rabbinic collections is fraught with difficulty. In addition, the Church Fathers do not offer a clear or accurate picture of Jews or Judaism. Their descriptions of Jews are often paradigmatic and formulaic. The reality behind their comments is frequently difficult to ascertain. Nor can one simply move from the Byzantine law codes to any social reality, for many laws cannot be easily set at a particular time, nor do we know what was enforced and what merely existed "on the books."[84]

Becker and Reed outline the older scholarly model,[85] which posits that Judaism in the first century CE was diverse, so that Jewish and non-Jewish believers in Jesus frequently interacted with non-Christian Jews. The close relationship of the Christian Jews and the non-Christian Jews produced tension and competition. With the outbreak of the revolt under Bar Kokhba, the Jerusalem Church fled to Petra, causing Jewish Christianity to lose its institution of authority. From that point forward, non-Jewish Christians would dominate the Church, so that the center of Christianity moved from Jerusalem to the urban centers of the eastern Roman/Byzantine Empire. "Christianity emerged as a fully independent system of belief and practice, self-defined as non-Jewish in its theology, its ritual practice, and the ethnicity of its adherents." At the same time, with the rise of the rabbinic movement the diversity and vitality of Second

Temple Judaism ended. The "council of Yavneh," in about 90 CE, enacted the "benediction against the heretics," effectively expelling the Jewish believers in Christ from the Jewish community. The rabbis took control of all Jews and Judaism. From that point forward,

> Jews would choose to live in self-imposed isolation from the rest of the Greco-Roman world, just as indifferent to Christians and "pagans" as these Gentiles allegedly were to Jews and Judaism . . . Christians and Christianity remained far outside the bounds of Jewish concern, interest, or even curiosity. . . . [C]lassical Judaism successfully resisted any influence form Christian traditions, beliefs, or practices.[86]

Several contemporary scholars reject this "master narrative." Many scholars reject the idea that the rabbis controlled the Jewish population of Palestine and that Judaism developed in isolation from its non-Jewish environments. These scholars, further, understand that Christianity was a much more diverse religious system than appears to be the case when one views it from the perspective of post fifth-century Roman Catholicism. In addition some have argued that the "council of Yavneh" is a late invention and has little basis in history; the benediction against the heretics, "most likely had nothing to do with Jewish Christians," and the flight of the Jerusalem Church to Petra also may be more "historical invention" than "historical fact."[87]

Boyarin is a major advocate of this interpretation of the relationship between Jews and Christians.[88] In opposition to the model that holds that Judaism is the "mother" and Christianity the "daughter," Boyarin follows Yuval's depiction of Judaism and Christianity as sister religions.[89] Pointing to the complexity of rabbinic Judaism's identifying Christianity as Esau and Judaism as Jacob, Boyarin writes:

> [A]t least well into late antiquity . . . Judaism and Christianity never quite formed entirely separate identities. . . . [F]or at least the first three centuries of their common lives, Judaism in all of its forms and Christianity in all of its forms were part of one complex religious family, twins in a womb, contending with each other for identity and precedence, but sharing to a large extent the same spiritual food. . . . It was the birth of the hegemonic Catholic Church . . . that seems finally to have precipitated the consolidation of rabbinic Judaism as Jewish orthodoxy. . . . [T]hen Judaism and Christianity finally emerged from the womb as genuinely independent children of Rebecca.[90]

Following Ruether,[91] Boyarin argues that not until the fourth century were Judaism and Christianity recognizable as different religions.[92]

Boyarin proposes a model that shows the two systems to be in contact and interaction, "a model of shared and crisscrossing lines of history and religious development."[93] Adopting linguistic "wave theory," which argues that languages in a given linguistic group share common characteristics as a result of their continued convergence and contact, Boyarin states that "social contact and gradation of religious life were such that, barring the official pronouncements of the leaders of what were to become the 'orthodox' versions of both [Judaism and Christianity] . . . one could travel . . . from rabbinic Jew to Christian along a continuum where one hardly would know where one stopped and the other began."[94] While "orthodox" Judaism and "orthodox" Christianity are different religious systems, Boyarin offers many examples that demonstrate that Jews and Christians remained intertwined in their religious and symbolic practices throughout late antiquity.[95]

In *Dying for God*, Boyarin sets out to demonstrate that "the Talmud text reveals the blurred boundaries between Judaism and Christianity at the very moment that it is trying to insist on the clarity of those boundaries." The book demonstrates that within Judaism and Christianity, we find some voices which supported martyrdom in response to Rome, and other opinions which rejected giving up one's life in the face of Roman oppression. Boyarin argues the similarities of their responses to Roman power reflect their common task of attempting to define themselves in terms of each other as well as in terms of Rome: "[T]he making of martyrdom was at least in part, part and parcel of the process of making of Judaism and Christianity as distinct entities."[96]

In *Border Lines*, Boyarin argues that Judaism and Christianity were working in tandem in creating their independent self-definitions, and both were creating their own "orthodoxy" by defining specific others who stood in relationship to themselves as "heretics." The idea that Jewish borders were artificial and porous is not new, even if it is not widely accepted.[97] Similarly, that a group defines itself in contrast to "the other," in this case Judaism and Christianity defining themselves as not the "heretics" or *minim* has a long scholarly genealogy.[98] But Boyarin develops the idea, claiming that the rabbinic discussions of the *minim* parallel the Christians creation of heresies. Both systems were attempting to define themselves by excluding the outsiders. Boyarin contends that "orthodoxy" and "heresy" coexist and are created at the same time. He suggests that the rabbis' discussions of *minim* are their short-lived attempt to be an "orthodox religion" following the model of the emerging church.

Boyarin additionally argues that Christianity created the concept of "religion" as we know it today, and the emerging church attempted to define Judaism as a religion. Eventually the rabbis rejected that idea[99] and moved away from their concern with *minim*. Boyarin argues that Judaism and Christianity are different *categories* of things. In *Border Lines,* he argues that Christianity defines itself as religion, an orthodox doctrine besieged by heretics, of which Judaism, which was in the mind of Christians a religion, was the premier example. He maintains that for a time Judaism sought to define itself as a religion in this sense—an organized orthodox doctrine besieged by different, heretical, views. However, eventually Judaism rejected this definition as the *Stammaim* created the rabbinic intellectual debate, in which there is no single orthodox view but a variety of equally valid competing traditions. Thus, by the end of late antiquity, Judaism does not view itself as a religion in the sense that Christianity defines the term, although the Christians still maintain that Judaism is a heretical religion. The *Stammaim*'s creation of a rabbinic system of thought which is characterized by debate and disagreement stands in opposition to the theological uniformity of Nicaea and puts "rabbinic Judaism" at odds with Nicene Christianity, which privileges uniformity of ideas. By projecting rabbinic pluralism back to Yavneh, the *Stammaim* claim that the Jews were never like "the Church." In Judaism, disagreement is normative, while in the Church it is an aberration. Boyarin's work is among that of several scholars who have sought to reevaluate the interactions between Jews and Christians in the ancient words.[100]

Adiel Schremer has offered the most recent study of the *minim*[101] and challenged those who claim the *minim* in the Tannaitic materials were Christians. She draws her evidence almost exclusively from texts edited during the Tannaitic period, especially Sifré Deuteronomy, a Tannaitic collection. Therefore, she does not have the problem of dealing with materials from collections edited long after the period with which she is concerned. She argues that the Tannaim discussed the *minim* in response to the Romans' destruction of the Temple and defeat of Bar Kokhba. The Tannaim were not engaged in issues of doctrine when they contrasted the *minim* against themselves. Schremer argues that the Tannaim wanted to create a unified community in the wake of the two major disasters, because they needed to reestablish the community's identity, which had been severely undermined by what they saw to be God's allowing the Romans to vanquish the Jews. The Tannaim aimed to separate out from the community those who were different in terms of practice and ritual. Even comparatively minor deviations would lead the Tannaim to claim that the *minim* were not part of the unified community. Thus, for Schremer, *minim* were most often non-Christian Jewish groups from their community.[102]

Conclusions: New Visions of Judaism in Late Antiquity

A fairly new picture of Judaism in late antiquity is emerging. Scholars are less sanguine about accepting Talmudic statements as accurate depictions of the history of Judaism—what is historically correct cannot always be disentangled from what has been fabricated in order to make a cultural point. In addition, if we cannot automatically accept the words attributed to the generations of sages as their own and not later creations how are we to construct a development of Jewish thought? If Judaism is constantly in dialogue with its non-Jewish environment and if ideas travel back and forth between the different cultures, how do we determine what is "authentically" Jewish and where do we look to unpack the technical theological language of Judaism? In brief, contemporary scholarship is raising many questions concerning what we can accurately *know* about Judaism in late antiquity.

Whatever the difficulties, knowledge of the period is important because Judaism in late antiquity set the stage for medieval and modern Judaism. The first seven centuries of the Common Era witnessed the passing away of the core institutions of biblical and Hellenistic Judaism: The Temple cult and the priesthood. Non-Jews controlled the political, social, legal, and economic environment in which Jews lived, and Jews were dispersed throughout the known world. The Jews had to formulate a religious system absent the institutions central to the biblical and Hellenistic periods. They had to promulgate their value system against the background of powerful competing systems of meaning. All of this had to be done in line with the belief that the Hebrew Bible, especially the Torah, was Divine Revelation and forever true. The newly created Jewish way of life had to conform to biblical laws, paradigms, values, symbols, and expectations. Most importantly, it is this Jewish way of life that continued to undergird medieval Judaism and that still today stands behind all of the diverse movements within contemporary Judaism.

During late antiquity, the rabbis replaced the biblical priests as the teachers of Torah (Deut. 33.10), the "avodah" (work) of the sacrificial cult turned into the "avodah" of the prayer service, the table on which Jews ate their daily meals superseded the Temple's altar, and Jewish communities throughout the world worked to replicate the desert camp in which the Divine Presence had dwelt. Jews undertook this way of life to fulfill the demands of the covenant established at Sinai and explicated in the biblical book of Deuteronomy: Jews were obligated to obey God's revelation in their daily lives. If they obeyed that, revelation God would guide and protect them. If they did not follow God's commandments, God would punish, though not destroy, them, for God was just and merciful, a king and a father, a shepherd and an avenger. The God who created the whole world also controlled everything that happened in the world. If the Jews had lost their Temple and its priesthood, they had violated God's commandments. If they were scattered all over the world, they would return to their homeland only when their lives conformed to the revelation at Sinai.

The rabbis and their concept of the Oral Torah allowed the Jews living under postbiblical realities to conform to the Bible's demands.[103] The rabbinic class arose sometime after the end of the First Revolt in 73/74 CE. They accomplished their goal by reimagining the events on Mount Sinai. God had revealed to Moses the Written Torah—Genesis, Exodus, Leviticus, Numbers, and Deuteronomy— available to all, and an Oral Torah, which contained crucial explanations of ambiguous and repetitious laws and passages as well as the methods by which one could legitimately interpret the Written Torah overall. Both the Written Torah and the Oral Torah originated at Sinai, but only the rabbis knew both parts of God's revelation to Moses. They *alone* possessed the skills to interpret the Written Torah in legitimate ways. The Oral Torah allowed God's word to retain its validity and applicability for the Jews wherever they were and in every situation in which they found themselves. The rabbis placed Torah at the center of Jewish culture and the study of Torah as the most important activity in which a person could engage. Study of Torah was more important than performing the mandates of Torah because study leads to doing. The rabbis also emphasized that Jews were "a kingdom of priests, a holy people" (Exod. 19.6), so they appropriated many of the Bible's laws relevant only to priests and applied them to the whole people. Thus, the rabbis, their documents, and the way of life they imagined for the Jewish people became the paradigm for the way that subsequent generations of Jews would imagine and design their worlds, their symbols, and their value systems.

Notes

1. I wish to thank Alan J. Avery-Peck, Kraft-Hiatt Professor of Judaic Studies at The College of the Holy Cross. Alan's comments and correction have greatly improved this version of the essay.
2. My summary draws from the essays in Catherine Hezser (ed.) (2010), *The Oxford Handbook of Jewish Daily Life in Roman Palestine*. Oxford: Oxford University Press; William Horbury, W. D. Davies, and John Sturdy (eds) (1999), *The Cambridge History of Judaism: Volume Three: The Early Roman Period*. Cambridge: Cambridge University Press; Steven T. Katz (ed.) (2006), *The Cambridge History of Judaism: Volume Four: The Late Roman Rabbinic Period*. Cambridge: Cambridge University Press. For Babylonia, see below, note 10.
3. See Jonathan A. Goldstein (1976), *I Maccabees: A New Translation with Introduction and Commentary, The Anchor Bible*. Garden City: Doubleday & Company; Jonathan A. Goldstein (1983), *II Maccabees: A New Translation with Introduction and Commentary, The Anchor Bible*. Garden City: Doubleday & Company; Bezalel Bar-Kochva (1989), *Judas Maccabaeus: The Jewish Struggle against the Seleucids*. Cambridge: Cambridge University Press.
4. Horbury, Davies, and Sturdy, *The Cambridge History of Judaism: Volume Three*, pp. 174–90, 519–55. Each essay in Hezser's collection contains an analysis of the available sources of information.
5. E. Mary Smallwood (1976), *The Jews Under Roman Rule: From Pompey to Diocletian*. Leiden: E. J. Brill.
6. Steve Mason (2001), *Flavius Josephus on the Pharisees*. Boston and London: Brill Academic Press; Jacob Neusner (1973), *From Politics to Piety: The Emergence of Pharisaic Judaism*. Englewood Cliffs: Prentice-Hall; Jacob Neusner (1971), *The Rabbinic Traditions about the Pharisees before 70*. 3 Vols. Leiden: E.J. Brill; Ellis Rivkin (1978), *A Hidden Revolution*. Nashville: Abingdon; Gary G. Porton (1986), "Diversity in Postbiblical Judaism," in Robert A. Kraft and George W. E. Nickelsburg (eds), *Early Judaism and Its Modern Interpreters*. Atlanta: Scholars Press; Anthony J. Saldarini (1988), *Pharisees, Scribes and Sadducees in Palestinian Society: A Sociological Approach*.

Wilmington: Michael Glazier; Jacob Neusner and Bruce D. Chilton (eds) (2007), *In Quest of the Historical Pharisees*. Waco: Baylor University Press.

7. Frank Moore Cross Jr. (1958), *The Ancient Library of Qumran: a Comprehensive Survey of the Dead Sea Scrolls and the Community Which Owned Them* (revised edn). Garden City: Anchor Books; Geza Vermes (2004), *The Complete Dead Sea Scrolls in English* (revised edn). London: Penguin Books; Lawrence H. Schiffman (1995), *Reclaiming the Dead Sea Scrolls: Their True Meaning for Judaism and Christianity*. New York: Doubleday.

8. The literature on Josephus is expansive. I have found the following works useful: Steve Mason (ed.) (1998), *Understanding Josephus: Seven Perspectives* [Journal for the Study of the Pseudepigrapha Supplement Series 32]. Sheffield: Sheffield Academic Press; Steve Mason (2001), *Flavius Josephus on the Pharisees*. Boston and Leiden: Brill Academic Publishers; Shaye J. D. Cohen (1979), *Josephus in Galilee and Rome: His Vita and Development as a Historian*. Leiden: E. J. Brill; Louis H. Feldman and Gohei Hata (eds) (1989), *Josephus, the Bible, and History*. Detroit: Wayne State University Press; Louis H. Feldman and Gohei Hata (eds) (1987), *Josephus, Judaism, and Christianity*. Detroit: Wayne State University Press; Tessa Rajak (1983), *Josephus: The Historian and His Society*. Philadelphia: Fortress Press; Louis H. Feldman (1999), "Josephus (CE 37–c. 100)," in Horbury, Davies, and Sturdy (eds), *The Cambridge History of Judaism: Volume Three*, pp. 901–21.

9. Jacob Neusner (1962), *A Life of Rabban Yohanan ben Zakkai Ca 1–80 C.E.* Leiden: E. J. Brill.

10. Moshe Aberbach (1994), *Labor, Crafts, and Commerce in Ancient Israel*. Jerusalem: The Magnes Press; Ze'ev Safrai (1994), *The Economy of Roman Palestine*. London and New York: Routledge Press; Ben Zion Rosenfeld and Joseph Memrav (2005), *Markets and Marketing in Roman Palestine*, Chava Cassel (trans.). Leiden and Boston: E. J. Brill.

11. See, for example, Günther Stemberger (2000), *Jews and Christians in the Holy Land: Palestine in the Fourth Century*, Ruth Tuschling (trans.). Edinburgh: T & T Clark; Hagith Sivan (2008), *Palestine in Late Antiquity*. Oxford: Oxford University Press.

12. Most scholars date the Geonic period from the ninth to the eleventh centuries.

13. The Letter of Sherira Gaon and the *Midrash Tannaim veAmoraim* contain information about the sages of late antiquity.

14. Most recently Isaiah M. Gafni (2006), "The Political, Social, and Economic History of Babylonian Jewry, 224–638 C.E," in Katz, *The Cambridge History of Judaism: Volume Four*, pp. 792–820, especially pp. 792–3 and 793, n. 2.

15. Yaakov Elman (2007), "Middle Persian Culture and Babylonian Sages: Accommodation and Resistance in the Shaping of a Rabbinic Legal Tradition," in Charlotte Elisheva Fonrobert and Martin S. Jaffee (eds), *The Cambridge Companion to the Talmud and Rabbinic Literature*. Cambridge: Cambridge University Press, pp. 165–97. See also Yaakov Elman (2003), "Marriage and Marital Property in Rabbinic and Sasanian Law," in Catherine Hezser (ed.), *Rabbinic Law in Its Roman and Near Eastern Context*. Tübingen: Mohr Siebeck, pp. 227–76.

16. The following summary relies on Jacob Neusner (1965–70), *A History of the Jews in Babylonia*. 5 Vols. Leiden: E. J. Brill; and Isaiah Gafni (1990), *Yehude Bavel bi-tekufat haTalmud*. Jerusalem: Merkaz Zalman Shazar le-toldot Israel.

17. Christianity did play an important role in Syria and in other parts of the eastern empire. See, for example, Naomi Koltun-Fromm (2010), *Hermeneutics of Holiness: Ancient Jews and Christian Notions of Sexuality and Religious Community*. Oxford and New York; Adam H. Becker (2006), *Fear of God and the Beginning of Wisdom: The School of Nisibis and the Development of Scholastic Culture in Late Antique Mesopotamia*. Philadelphia: University of Pennsylvania Press.

18. David M. Goodblatt (1975), *Rabbinic Institutions in Sasanian Babylonia*. Leiden: E. J. Brill.
19. The name given to the Palestinian rabbis who were active in the first two and a half centuries of the Common Era.
20. The actual relationship of these two events and the exact date of Rav's migration are matters of scholarly debate.
21. The rabbis who were active in Palestine and Babylonia from 220–600(?) are called Amoraim.
22. The Palmyrenes destroyed Nehardea and its Jewish population in the 260s.
23. Sherira and *Seder Tannaim veAmoraim* are the sources. See Gafni, "The Political, Social, and Economic History of Babylonian Jewry, 224–638 C.E.," p. 800.
24. David Goodblatt (1994), *The Monarchic Principle: Studies in Jewish Self-Government in Antiquity*. Tübingen: Mohr Siebeck.
25. There are a number of discussions of these documents with which one should begin any study. Hernann L. Strack and Günther Stemberger (1991), *Introduction to the Talmud and Midrash*, Markus Bockmuehl (trans.). Edinburgh: T & T Clark; Baruch M. Bokser (1979), "An Annotated Bibliographical Guide to the Study of the Palestinian Talmud," in Hildegard Temporini and W. Haase (eds), *Aufstieg und Niedergang der römischen Welt*. Berlin and New York: Walter de Gruyter, pp. 139–256. David M. Goodblatt (1979), "The Babylonian Talmud," in *Aufstieg und Niedergang der romischen Welt*, Vol. II, 19.2, pp. 257–336; Jacob Neusner (1994), *Introduction to Rabbinic Literature*. New York: Doubleday; S. Safrai (ed.) (1987), *The Literature of the Sages First Part: Oral Tora, Halakha, Mishna, Tosefta, Talmud, External Tractes*. Assen/Maastricht and Philadelphia: Van Gorcum and Fortress Press; S. Safrai, Z. Safrai, J. Schwartz, and P. J. Tomson (eds) (2006), *The Literature of the Sages Second Part: Midrash and Targum, Liturgy, Poetry, Mysticism, Contracts, Inscriptions, Ancient Science and the Languages of Rabbinic Literature*. Assen: Royal Van Gorcum and Fortress Press. Articles on the major collections of rabbinic literature can be found in Katz, *The Cambridge History of Judaism: Volume Four*.
26. In addition to the works cited in the previous note, see also Harry Fox and Tirzah Meacham (eds) (1999), *Introducing Tosefta: Textual Intratextual and Intertextual Studies*. New York: KTAV Publish House; Jacob Neusner (1990), *The Literature of Formative Judaism: The Mishnah and the Tosefta*. New York and London: Garland Publishing, Inc.
27. The term "Tannaitic" refers to those documents that the Tannaim, the sages of Palestine who flourished during the first two and one half centuries of the Common Era, produced in Palestine.
28. Alexander lists the scholars who hold the two major positions: Mishnah as a law code or Mishnah as a handbook for students in the rabbinic academies. See Elizabeth Shanks Alexander (2006), *Transmitting Mishnah: The Shaping Influence of Oral Tradition*. Cambridge: Cambridge University Press, p. 1, n. 1.
29. Jacob Neusner (1981), *Judaism: The Evidence of Mishnah*. Chicago and London: The University of Chicago Press. Neusner argues that Mishnah lays out a philosophical system. See also, Jacob Neusner (1970), *The Modern Study of the Mishnah*. Leiden: E. J. Brill.
30. Gary G. Porton (2004), "Midrash and the Rabbinic Sermon," in Alan Avery-Peck, Daniel Harrington, and Jacob Neusner (eds), *When Judaism & Christianity Began: Essays in Memory of Anthony J. Saldarini*. Leiden: E. J. Brill, pp. 461–82.
31. Daniel Boyarin's work on Midrash was also crucial in this development; Daniel Boyarin (1990), *Intertextuality and the Reading of Midrash*. Bloomington: Indiana University Press.

32. Jacob Neusner (1970), *Development of a Legend: Studies on the Traditions Concerning Yohanan ben Zakkai*. Leiden: E. J. Brill.
33. Jacob Neusner (1971), *The Rabbinic Traditions about the Pharisees before 70*. Leiden: E. J. Brill, 3 Vols.
34. Neusner has worked out his ideas concerning rabbinic literature in literally hundreds of books. The most convenient publication is Neusner, *Introduction*.
35. Alexander Samely (2007), *Forms of Rabbinic Literature and Thought: An Introduction*. Oxford: Oxford University Press.
36. Ibid., p. 25.
37. Ibid.
38. Ibid., pp. 25–6.
39. Ibid., p. 32.
40. Ibid. Samely's conclusions have a good deal in common with Boyarin's intertextual analysis of Midrash, in that all the documents of Judaism are interconnected. Boyarin, *Intertextuality*.
41. Neusner, *Introduction*, p. 185.
42. Ibid.
43. Ibid., p. 186.
44. Richard Kalmin (1994), *Sages, Stories, Authors, and Editors in Rabbinic Babylonia*. Atlanta: Scholars Press.
45. Unfortunately his work has appeared mainly in Hebrew. He is cited throughout most of the books that deal with the literary analysis of the Babylonian Talmud.
46. Christine Hayes (1997), *Between the Babylonian and Palestinian Talmuds: Accounting for Halakhic Difference in Selected Sugyot from Tractate Avodah Zarah*. New York and Oxford: Oxford University Press, p. 25.
47. Ibid., p. 26.
48. I should note that Hayes's work engendered a stiff response from Neusner—Jacob Neusner (1995), *Are the Talmuds Interchangeable? Christine Hayes' Blunder. South Florida Studies in the History of Judaism*. Atlanta: Scholars Press. See Hayes's response: (1997), "Appendix: Response to Jacob Neusner," in Hayes, *Between the Babylonian and Palestinian Talmuds*, pp. 183–8.
49. David Weiss Halivni (1968–2003), *Meqorot U-Mesorot*. The six volumes have been published by a number of different presses in several different locations.
50. David Weiss Halivni (1986), *Midrash, Mishnah, and Gemara: Predilection for Justified Law*. Cambridge: Harvard University Press is a brief English summary of his work in Hebrew.
51. Friedman's work is virtually all in Hebrew and in the form of articles. However, the work is crucial to anyone wishing to understand the current ways one might analyse passages in the Talmud.
52. Shamma Friedman has worked out methods for separating the Amoraic passage from those of the *Stammaim*; (1978), "Complete Introduction to the Way to Study a Sugya" (Hebrew), in H. Z. Dimitrovski (ed.), *Studies and Sources*. New York: Jewish Theological Seminary of America, pp. 283–321.
53. Daniel Boyarin (1993), *Carnal Israel: Reading Sex in Talmudic Culture*. Berkeley, Los Angeles, London: University of California Press.
54. Ibid., p. 11.
55. Ibid., p. 12.
56. J. L. Rubenstein (1999), *Talmudic Stories: Narrative Art, Composition and Culture*. Baltimore and London: The Johns Hopkins University Press; J. L. Rubenstein (2003), *The Culture of the Babylonian Talmud*. Baltimore and London: The Johns Hopkins University Press; J. L. Rubenstein (2010), *Stories of the Babylonian Talmud*. Baltimore and London: The Johns Hopkins University Press.

57. Rubenstein, *Talmudic Stories*, p. 2.
58. Ibid., p. 4.
59. Rubenstein, *The Culture*, pp. 7–8.
60. Barry Scott Wimpfheimer (2011), *Narrating the Law: A Poetics of Talmudic Legal Stories*. Philadelphia: University of Pennsylvania Press.
61. Ibid., pp. 64–9.
62. Ibid., pp. 69–93.
63. Ibid., pp. 122–46.
64. Elias Bickerman (1937), *Der Gott der Makkabäer: Untersuchungen über Sinn und Ursprung der makkabüischen Erhebung*. Berlin: Schocken Verlag; in English (1979), *God of the Maccabees: Studies in the Origins of the Revolt*, Hoerst R. Moehring (trans.). Leiden: E. J. Brill.
65. Martine Hengel (1973), *Judentum und Hellenismus, Studien zu ihrer Begagnung unter besonderer Berücksichtgung Palästinas bis zure Mitte des 2 Jh.s .v.Chr* (2nd edn). Tübingen: Mohr-Siebeck. (1974), *Judaism and Hellenism: Studies in Their Encounter in Palestine during the Early Hellenistic Period,* John Bowden (trans.). Philadelphia: Fortress Press. 2 vols.
66. W. D. Davies and Louis Finkelstein (eds) (1989), *The Cambridge History of Judaism Volume Two: The Hellenistic Age.* Cambridge: Cambridge University Press. See also Horbury, Davies, Sturdy, *The Cambridge History of Judaism: Volume Three.*
67. Michael E. Stone (ed.) (1984), *Jewish Writings of the Second Temple Period: Apocrypha, Pseudepigrapha, Qumran Sectarian Writings, Philo, Josephus.* Assen: Van Gorcum and Fortress Press.
68. Goldstein, *I Maccabees: II Maccabees.*
69. Martin Goodman (ed.) (1998), *Jews in a Graeco-Roman World.* Oxford: Oxford University Press.
70. Menahem Stern (1974–84), *Greek and Latin Authors on Jews and Judaism. Edited with Introductions, Translations, and Commentary.* 3 Vols. Jerusalem: The Israel Academy of Sciences and Humanities; Louis H. Feldman (1993), *Jew and Gentile in the Ancient World: Attitudes and Interactions from Alexander to Justinian.* Princeton: Princeton University Press.
71. Lieberman's two collections of essays, *Greek in Jewish Palestine* and *Hellenism in Jewish Palestine* are now published in one convenient volume, S. Lieberman (1994a), *Greek in Jewish Palestine/Hellenism in Jewish Palestine*, with a new introduction by Dov Zlotnick. New York and Jerusalem: The Jewish Theological Seminary of America. Relevant articles are also found in S. Lieberman (1974b), *Texts and Studies.* New York: KTAV Publishing House.
72. The most convenient collection of essays is Catherine Hezser (ed.) (2010), *The Oxford Handbook of Jewish Daily Life in Roman Palestine.* Oxford: Oxford University Press.
73. Erich S. Gruen (1998), *Heritage and Hellenism: The Reinvention of Jewish Tradition.* Berkeley: University of California Press. Elias Bickerman's work is also a convenient introduction to the Hellenization of Palestinian Judaism—Elias Bickerman (1962), *From Ezra to the Last of the Maccabees.* New York: Schoken Books.
74. Gruen, *Heritage and Hellenism*, p. xiv.
75. Seth Schwartz (2010), *Were the Jews a Mediterranean Society? Reciprocity and Solidarity in Ancient Judaism.* Princeton: Princeton University Press.
76. Seth Schwartz (2001), *Imperialism and Jewish Society, 200 B.C.E. to 640 C.E.* Princeton: Princeton University Press, p. 1.
77. Schwartz, *Mediterranean Society*, p. 37.
78. Ibid., p. 43.
79. Ibid., p. 44.
80. Martin Goodman (2008), *Rome and Jerusalem: The Class of Ancient Civilizations.* New York: Vintage Books, p. 478. See pp. 482 ff., where Goodman discusses the rabbinic stories about Judah the Patriarch and Antonius.

81. Ibid., pp. 477–8.
82. Ibid., p. 478.
83. Ibid., p. 483.
84. Amnon Linder (1987), *The Jews in Roman Imperial Legislation*. Detroit: Wayne State University Press.
85. Adam H. Becker and Annette Yoshiko Reed (eds) (2007), *The Ways That Never Parted: Jews and Christians in Late Antiquity and the Early Middle Ages*. Minneapolis: Fortress Press. The volume was first published in 2003; see pp. 1–24.
86. Becker and Reed, *The Ways That Never Parted*, pp. 4–5.
87. Ibid., pp. 5–6, n. 13–15.
88. Daniel Boyarin (1999), *Dying for God: Martyrdom and the Making of Christianity and Judaism*. Stanford: Stanford University Press. Daniel Boyarin (2004), *Border Lines: The Partition of Judaeo-Christianity. Divinations: Reading Late Ancient Religions*. Philadelphia: University of Pennsylvania Press.
89. Boyarin, *Dying*, p. 2.
90. Ibid., pp. 5–6.
91. Since I first read her book many years ago, I have considered it one of the most important analyses of the relationship of early Judaism and Christianity: Rosemary Radford Ruether (1974), *Faith and Fratricide: The Theological Roots of Anti-Semitism*. New York: The Seabury Press.
92. Boyarin, *Dying*, p. 6.
93. Ibid., p. 8.
94. Ibid., p. 9.
95. Ibid., pp. 10–16.
96. Ibid., p. 93.
97. Compare Christine E. Hayes (2002), *Gentile Impurities and Jewish Identities: Intermarriage and Conversion from the Bible to the Talmud*. Oxford: Oxford University Press; Sacha Stern (1994), *Jewish Identity in Early Rabbinic Writings*. Leiden: E. J. Brill; Gary G. Porton (1988), *Goyim: Gentiles and Israelites in Mishnah Tosefta*. Atlanta: Scholars Press; Lawrence H. Schiffman (1985), *Who Was a Jew?: Rabbinic and Halakhic Perspectives on the Jewish-Christian Schism*. Hoboken: KTAV Publishing House.
98. For example, Porton, *Goyim*, pp. 288–98.
99. Boyarin, *Border Lines*, pp. 8–13.
100. See also, Judith M. Lieu (2002), *Neither Jew Nor Greek? Constructing Early Christianity*. London: T & T Clark; idem (1996), *Image and Reality: The Jews in the World of the Christians in the Second Century*. London: T & T Clark; Israel Jacob Yuval (2006), *Two Nations in Your Womb: Perceptions of Jews and Christians in Late Antiquity and the Middle Ages*, Barbara Harshav and Jonathan Chipman (trans.). Berkley: University of California Press; Günther Stemberger (2000), *Jews and Christians in the Holy Land: Palestine in the Fourth Century*, Ruth Tuschling (trans.). Edinburgh: T & T Clark; Graham N. Stanton and Guy G. Stroumsa (eds) (1998), *Tolerance and Intolerance in Early Judaism and Christianity*. Cambridge: Cambridge University Press.
101. Adiel Schremer (2010), *Brothers Estranged: Heresy, Christianity, and Jewish Identity in Late Antiquity*. Oxford: Oxford University Press.
102. She argues that in only one passage, tHullin 2:20–24 do we find *minim* unambiguously referring to Christians.
103. Jacob Neusner (1978), *There We Sat Down: Talmudic Judaism in the Making*. Eugene: Wipf and Stock Publishers; Lee I. Levine (1989), *The Rabbinic Class of Roman Palestine in Late Antiquity*. New York: The Jewish Theological Seminary of America; Marc Hirshman (2009), *The Stabilization of Rabbinic Culture: 100 C.E.–350 C.E.* Oxford: Oxford University Press; Stewart A. Cohen (1990), *Three Crowns: Structures of Communal Politics in Early Rabbinic Judaism*. Cambridge: Cambridge University Press.

New Contexts: Medieval Jews and Judaism

The Jewish Middle Ages, spanning a broad period from the close of the Talmud in the sixth century to the displacement of the Jews of Iberia in the late fifteenth, has always been a period of great interest. Until a few generations ago, the Jewish history of the Middle Ages was predominantly centered on the European, Christian West, and it was largely focused on intellectual history and the anti-Jewish polemic and activities that were part of the period. The expansion of the larger field of Medieval Studies, however, along with the discovery of new sources and fresh approaches to older material, has opened up the Jewish Middle Ages to include the experiences of many different groups within Jewish society. It has retrained attention onto issues of diversity and complexity within the Jewish community, while reevaluating the nature of the relations that Jews had with non-Jews. The recently expanded interest in Islam, along with the discovery and investigation of the rich treasures of the Cairo Geniza, have also helped to fuel new attention to the experiences of the Jews under Islam in the Middle Ages—the largest, most diverse, and yet generally least-studied group of Jews of that time.

The two essays that follow after Chapter 4 are really one essay, broken down here to allow for extended discussion, but collected in this section to afford the opportunity for comparison and contrast. Both chapters stress the unique developments of medieval Jews within their local contexts. Both chapters also reveal the intriguing continuities with the intellectual and social developments prior to the Middle Ages, as well as the important engagement with earlier Jewish thought and tradition—even amid the development of new customs and the influence of external worldviews.

In "Jews and the Islamic World: Transitions from Rabbinic to Medieval Contexts," Marina Rustow examines the Jewish communities of the Near East after the rise of Islam. She discusses the nature and impact of major demographic shifts as a result of the Islamic conquests, noting the legal status and realities of Jews as well as other groups. Comparing the experiences of Jews in Babylonia and Palestine at the end of the rabbinic period, Rustow also gives significant attention to the Karaites, who opposed much of the rabbinic system

and worldview. Islamic rule allowed for a significant measure of urbanization and geographic mobility, and Rustow assesses the implications of these opportunities for Jews. She also reviews some of the major cultural developments in the medieval Islamic world and discusses their impact on Jewish scholarship, particularly in the area of literature. The discovery of the Cairo Geniza in the late nineteenth century and the massive research on its collections since the middle of the twentieth century have changed the scope of the field of medieval Jewish history, so Rustow lavishes a good deal of attention on those documents and the various approaches to reconstructing and studying them. Rustow concludes her essay with a look at the experiences of the Jews in Iberia during the period of Islamic hegemony.

In her contribution, "Medieval Jews and Judaism in Christian Contexts," Elisheva Baumgarten likewise interweaves a nuanced historical narrative with an important discussion of recent scholarly trends and conclusions. Beginning with the significant but infrequently discussed conditions in the early medieval Byzantine Empire, Baumgarten examines Jewish settlement and migration patterns in the Middle Ages, simultaneously tracing the move of Jews from southern Italy into other parts of western Europe. Baumgarten provides a broad overview of the legal status of Jews and Jewish culture until the end of the eleventh century. She pays particular attention to the impact on the Jews of the First Crusade—an event that was seen as a watershed in Jewish history by previous generations of Jewish historians, but has been viewed less categorically in more recent scholarship, even if its impact is still assessed in dramatic tones. Turning more fully to the high Middle Ages, Baumgarten evaluates the various developments of the twelfth and thirteenth centuries, particularly cultural and intellectual advances in both Ashkenaz and Sepharad. In particular, she examines the rich theological context in which Jews polemicized with Christianity and in which Christian theologians actively sought, and frequently secured, Jewish conversion to Christianity. Baumgarten orients the reader to many of the recent scholarly discussions about the nature of Jewish and Christian exchanges in the high Middle Ages, which have challenged and complicated traditional narratives of Jewish and Christian relations as well as of Jewish identity. She concludes with a review of the later Middle Ages, and especially the persecutions and expulsions that changed Jewish existence across Europe, with particular focus on the end of the Jewish community in Iberia.

In Chapter 4, "Comparative Medieval Perspectives," which precedes the two essays, the authors offer some brief thoughts on the value and limitations of a comparative study of Jewish experiences under Islam and Christianity in the Middle Ages.

4 Comparative Medieval Perspectives

Elisheva Baumgarten and Marina Rustow

The Jewish Middle Ages, like the medieval period in western European history, has often been defined by what preceded and followed it rather than by its own characteristics. Belonging neither to the ancient nor to the modern era, the events that occurred during this period of more than a thousand years have been relegated to a common category, even though how to define it is far from simple or agreed upon.

In previous scholarship, the definitions of the period to some extent expressed historiographic principles. Heinrich Graetz and the *Wissenschaft des Judentums* scholars delineated it according to its intellectual production, beginning the Middle Ages with the close of the Talmuds. The Zionist-oriented historians, including B. Z. Dinur, ended antiquity with the Bar Kokhba Revolt (132–5 CE). Both these definitions had more to do with the ancient period than with the Middle Ages. The end of the period was no less controversial. Some historians defined it with the advent of moveable type and the printing press, others with the expulsions from Iberia in 1492 and 1497, and yet others with Emancipation and the French Revolution.

Over time, historians have generally agreed to begin discussion of the Jewish Middle Ages with the Christianization of the Roman Empire and the beginning of Islam, and to end it in the late fifteenth century with the Iberian expulsions. During the intervening millennium, Jews lived as a protected minority with religious autonomy, a certain measure of legal independence and their own structures of communal governance. And as general history has moved toward defining a separate early modern period, so, too, medieval Jewish historians have moved toward ending the period with the series of expulsions of Jews from European lands and the discovery of the New World.

There are other characteristics of the Middle Ages that are central features of the chapters that follow. During the Middle Ages, Jewish communities spread out over a larger geographic area than ever before. They were more heavily urbanized as well, and in many areas, more urbanized than other population groups—a defining characteristic given that in preindustrial societies generally and the Middle Ages specifically, the vast majority of the population engaged in subsistence agriculture or local, rural trade. Though medieval Jews were never confined to ghettos and were allowed to own land, they nonetheless tended to congregate in towns and cities. Their degree of urbanization had important consequences for their geographic mobility, the unification of their religious practices in the face of diasporic conditions, and their development of social services (including education) and an effective structure of communal organization.

Jews' communal life under Christian and Muslim rulers developed along different trajectories. Understanding it requires a constant assessment of the give-and-take between Jews and members of the majority religion among whom they lived. It makes sense, then, to discuss Jews under Christian and Islamic rule separately. In scholarly terms, the two realms are, for all intents and purposes, separate subfields, though with much to be gained from cross-comparison. This approach does, however, present an organizational challenge when it comes to the Iberian Peninsula, which came under Islamic rule in 711, but was conquered by Christians in large part by 1212. We have therefore divided our discussion of Iberia into segments under Islamic and Christian rule, treating in both places the very important period of transition between ca. 1085 and 1212, when Christian rule was pressing southward, but Jews continued to draw on the Islamic culture of the south.

Medieval Jews under Islamic and Christian rule shared a basic legal framework that had been imposed by the ruling powers in partial continuation of late Roman law. They also shared a canon of biblical and rabbinic literature from which each developed modes of interpretation and exegesis, some distinctive, some similar. Even when medieval Jews wrote treatises in fields that shared more with contemporary non-Jewish scholarship than with the sources of Jewish tradition—such as astronomy, medicine, and philosophy—those works were likely to share a common Greco-Roman legacy or to cross borders via translation. Thus Maimonides' *Guide of the Perplexed*, written in Judaeo-Arabic and completed in Egypt ca. 1190, drew on the Arabic tradition of Aristotelian commentary, especially Averroes; and Levi ben Gerson of Languedoc (1288–1344), a Talmudist, astronomer, and philosopher who knew no Arabic, read Averroes in Latin and Maimonides in Hebrew.

The sources that differentiate Jews in the Islamic and Christian worlds are no less significant than those they share. The Geniza documents have furnished the kind of detailed information on daily life of which historians of Jews in Christendom can only dream. Even those of Jews in Iberia and Italy, with their rich medieval archives, have not been able to match the density of information found in the Geniza. This difference in source survival has also shaped the scholarly consensus on the relative integration of Jews into the societies in which they lived. Historians have studied the Jews of Christian Europe primarily on the basis of Hebrew and Aramaic sources written for Jewish consumption, together with corroborating accounts in Latin. Where there are documents, they tend to have been produced by Christian institutions and so suggest that Jewish life was shaped by those institutions. The Latin sources also include a much higher proportion of polemics against Jews and Judaism than do the Arabic ones.

But if the Jews in medieval Christian Europe have been seen as not quite belonging to the society they inhabited, this is only partly due to source survival. Their history has also been read backward from the end of the period and their expulsion from large parts of medieval Europe. And the study of Jews of the Islamic world has its own set of teleologies. One debate concerns the extent to which the experience of Arabophone Jews in the Middle Ages has been read backwards from the twentieth century. An "anti-lachrymose" camp sees an Islamic world devoid of anti-Semitism until Europeans imported it to the Middle East in the nineteenth century; the "neo-lachrymose" camp draws a line from Muhammad's massacre of the Banū Qurayza to the mass exodus of Jews from Arab lands after the creation of Israel in 1948.[1]

If a single trend can be said to characterize the historiography of Jews in both regions, it is the turn to social history. Women, the family, the relationships between urban centers and their rural hinterlands, and the material culture Jews shared with non-Jews are all topics that are beginning to receive their due. A focus on nonelite Jewish groups has also meant the meaningful participation of those trained in other subfields, among them art history, archeology, and linguistics—a big-tent approach that can only enrich medieval Jewish historiography.

Note

1. Mark R. Cohen (1991), "The Neo-Lachrymose Conception of Jewish-Arab History," *Tikkun* 6 (May–June): 55–60 (cf. idem [1994], *Under Crescent and Cross: The Jews in the Middle Ages*. Princeton: Princeton University Press, chapter 1); Norman A. Stillman (1991), "Myth, Countermyth, and Distortion," *Tikkun* 6:3 (May–June): 60–4; and the authors' exchange of letters in the following issue, "Revisionist Jewish-Arab History: An Exchange," *Tikkun* 6:4 (July–August): 96–7.

5 Jews and the Islamic World: Transitions from Rabbinic to Medieval Contexts

Marina Rustow

Demographics in the Transition from Late Antiquity to the Middle Ages

At the close of antiquity, the two largest Jewish communities in the world were those of Mesopotamia and Palestine. There were other important communities in Asia Minor and Egypt, and peripheral ones in the Arabian Peninsula and (moving clockwise around the Mediterranean) Cyrenaica, central and western North Africa, the Iberian Peninsula, Sicily, the Italian peninsula, and

Greece. This meant that in the early seventh century, most Jews in the world lived in regions that the invading Muslim armies would conquer in their very first decade of campaigning outside Arabia: Palestine fell to the Muslims between 636 and 640, Egypt in 640, and Iraq in 642. Almost immediately, as a result of the conquests, most of the world's Jews came under Islamic rule. The Jews of Asia Minor, Italy, and southeast Europe remained under Christian rule whether under the Byzantines in the East or the Romans in the West.

From Iraq, Palestine, and Egypt, Jews spread East into central Asia and West across the entire Mediterranean basin. Major concentrations of Jewish population and cultural centers arose in Cordoba, Lucena, Toledo, and Granada in al-Andalus; in Fez, al-Qayrawan, Palermo, and other cities in the Maghreb and Sicily; in Fustat (the older section of the urban conglomeration that would come to be called Cairo) in Egypt, with smaller settlements in the Nile Delta and the older center of Alexandria; all over Syria-Palestine, but especially Jerusalem; and in Baghdad after its founding by the Abbasid caliphs in 762. There were smaller Jewish settlements east of Baghdad, in Iran and Transoxania (modern Afghanistan), and there is some evidence for Jewish populations in the more peripheral regions of northern Africa, such as upper Egypt and the fringes of the Sahara (e.g. the oasis town of Wargla).

By the tenth century, not only were there dense and well-organized Jewish communities all over the entire vast expanse of the Islamicate world, but also those communities were urban and prosperous to an astonishing degree. By 930, even the yeshivot of Sura and Pumbedita—ancient towns on the Euphrates—had moved to Baghdad on the Tigris, the capital of the empire and the second-most populous city on earth. (A conservative estimate puts ninth-century Baghdad at half a million inhabitants; after imperial Rome, no city in Europe would reach half a million inhabitants until seventeenth-century Paris and London.[1]) The Jewish communities in medieval Europe were tiny compared to those in the Islamic world, the smallest of them numbering a handful of families and the largest hundreds at most. By contrast, the Jews of the Islamic world numbered in the thousands and even tens of thousands in some cities—less than 1 percent of the total population of most provinces (Egypt, for instance), but 10 percent or more in urban centers.

Jews under Islamic rule would constitute the vast majority of Jews worldwide for much of the medieval period, as much as 90 percent until Islamic rule contracted on the Iberian Peninsula and the Jewish communities of Latin Christian Europe grew in size after 1200. By around 1600, Jews under Islam still constituted half the global Jewish population.[2] Any responsible picture of Jewish history in the Middle Ages must, then, devote proportional attention to Jews in the Islamic world; but for most of the twentieth century, the Jews of Latin Christian Europe received the lion's share of scholarly attention.[3]

Responses to Conquest

The notion that the Islamic conquests proceeded in an Islam-or-the-sword fashion has long been debunked. Conversion to Islam was a slow and gradual process, and the proportion of Muslims in the Middle East did not reach an absolute majority until the ninth or tenth century depending on the region. The first caliphs therefore ruled a population most of whom were Jews, Christians, and Zoroastrians (and in Transoxania, Buddhists). It is common to refer to these groups as non-Muslim "minorities," but for many generations Muslims were in fact a numerical minority in their own empire. Though most works on the early Islamic period, much like the medieval Arabic sources on which they are based, have tended to train their fascinated gaze on the origins of Islam and on the Muslim political elites who ruled in the name of the new religion, the early Islamic world was inhabited mainly by non-Muslims.[4]

There are exceptions to the scholarly focus on Islamic origins. First, a number of studies have attempted to reconstruct the history of the Jewish tribes who came under the confederation led by Muhammad. The attention has focused either on the treaty he drew up with the new Muslim converts and the clients of Arab tribes in Medina, a document historians call "the Constitution of Medina," or on the negotiations and battles between the Muslims and the three Jewish tribes of Medina in the 620s.[5] Second, a growing number of historians have emphasized the continuities before and after the conquests, arguing that for subject populations, serious change did not get underway until the end of the seventh century or later. This finding is partly confirmed in papyri from early Islamic Egypt and Palestine in Arabic, Greek, and Coptic.[6] Third, historians have attempted to understand how the conquered populations regarded or represented the conquests. Many saw the Muslims as tools of God's wrath, whether vindicating or punitive; one representative Jewish text is an Aramaic apocalypse called *The Secrets of Rabbi Shimon bar Yohai*.[7]

To the extent that one can generalize about non-Muslims' responses to the conquests, it might be hazarded that the conquests were less disruptive, or at least less traumatic, for Jews and non-Chalcedonian Christians than for Zoroastrians and the Byzantine Christians—probably the majority of Christians in absolute terms. Non-Chalcedonian Christians (East Syrians in Iraq and the Copts of Egypt, for example) came to regard the advent of Islam as a liberation from Byzantine and Chalcedonian hegemony; Zoroastrians and Christians in communion with Constantinople were relegated for the first time to second-class status. Jews, by contrast, had lived as a tolerated minority under Christian rule since the fourth century, and they continued to live as one under Islam, relying on their three centuries of experience in negotiating privileges with the ruling elite and on their preexisting communal structure and administration. But there was a major difference: while under Christian rule, Jews had practiced the only other monotheistic religion and thus attracted a disproportionate amount of attention, under Islamic rule, they constituted the least populous of the three subaltern religions, and so were singled out less than Christians.[8] And while Jews had found a stable modus vivendi under the Sasanian shahs (224–651), they rarely became active participants in high imperial culture. Under Islam, Jews rose to the highest echelons of power and contributed to and benefited from the creation of new culture whose main language was Arabic.

Legal Status

Some of the legal regulations the Muslim conquerors applied to non-Muslims are reflected in a text known as the Pact of 'Umar (*shurut 'Umar*, after the second caliph, 'Umar b. al-Khattab, 634–44). Even though the document survives only in later versions (the earliest from the ninth century), scholars agree that it reflects the treaties and capitulation agreements that the first Muslim conquerors negotiated with non-Muslims outside the Arabian Peninsula after 632.[9]

The pact promulgates as policy a basic quid-pro-quo arrangement according to which the rulers granted protection to the conquered groups and allowed them to practice their religions freely in exchange for their subordinate status. This quid-pro-quo structure resembles some of the statutes relating to Jews found in the Byzantine Codex Theodosianus of 438. The comparison is an interesting one: some other areas of Islamic administrative law likewise came not from principles stated in the Qur'an or the *hadith* (oral traditions about Muhammad and his followers), but from Roman provincial law. It also suggests why the Jews may have had no particular difficulty adapting to Islamic rule.[10]

Although the Pact of 'Umar defines non-Muslims as subalterns, prohibiting them from bearing arms and requiring them to rise from their seats when Muslims wish to sit, its statutes are not merely about subordination. It also bars them from building new houses of worship, teaching their children the Qur'an, spreading their religions through proselytizing, worshiping in public, and above all, from dressing and cutting their hair similarly to Muslims—all clauses designed to enforce social separation between the groups, to protect the fledgling *umma* (Muslim community), and to help them maintain their status as a closed ruling elite. Indeed, for the first century, the conquerors lived in garrison cities (*amsar*), sequestered from the agrarian masses; to convert to Islam, one had either to be descended from an Arabian tribe or ally oneself with one via a form of fictive kinship known as *wala'*.[11]

In practice, the rules of the Pact were rarely enforced, and when they were breached, it was generally to the advantage of non-Muslims, who mainly ignored the rules requiring visual differentiation (*ghiyar*) from Muslims and did, in fact, learn the Qur'an (fragments of Qur'an manuscripts have been found in the Cairo Geniza). Just as significantly, the pact does not prohibit non-Muslims from serving Muslim rulers as high officials: after all, the document was aimed at regulating the behavior of non-Muslims rather than that of those who made official appointments, the rulers. Complaints about non-Muslim officials would eventually surface, but not in earnest until the second half of the twelfth century. Meanwhile, plenty of Jewish officials found their way to the upper echelons of the administration, and some did after that point as well.[12]

All this added up to a great deal of latitude in practice. Islamic law categorized Jews, Christians, Zoroastrians, and later Hindus as *ahl al-dhimma*, "people of the covenant" (or in its shortened form, sing. *dhimmi*, pl. *dhimma*), guaranteeing their lives and property and granting them religious and organizational autonomy. *Dhimma* were also called by the Qur'anic term "people of the book" (*ahl al-kitab*) because of their possession of what Muslim jurists considered to be revealed scripture, itself a statement of basic respect. But there was one burden whose weight makes itself felt pervasively in the Jewish sources: male *dhimma* of legal majority had to pay the *jizya*, a head-tax or capitation tax (sometimes misleadingly translated to English as "poll-tax"). The earliest documentary sources we have on Jews who paid the *jizya*, from the eleventh century, depict it as onerous. But there were mitigating factors. The organized Jewish community and individual wealthy patrons helped poor Jews meet their *jizya* payments. (In Fustat in the twelfth century, from which more evidence has been preserved than for any other premodern Jewish community, the system of charity distribution was so well organized that many apparently converted to Judaism to take advantage of it.) Jews under Islamic rule were eventually a highly urbanized sector of the population, and urban dwellers in the aggregate enjoyed a higher standard of living than subsistence farmers regardless of *dhimmi* status. Membership in the Jewish community gave one access to powerful patrons connected to the government, at least when Jewish courtiers and bureaucrats chose to help their coreligionists. And if all else failed, premodern enforcement was remarkably lax by modern standards, so *dhimmi*s could hide from the tax-collector; or, taking the opposite tack, they could petition the ruler directly for mitigation of the *jizya* or exemption from it.[13]

Islamic rule thus perpetuated more or less the same legal status Jews had had under Roman and Byzantine rule, but offered them new opportunities. It also brought about a complete revolution in Jewish culture—both the high culture of the educated elite and the everyday life of the average Jewish inhabitants of cities and towns.

Babylonians, Palestinians, and Karaites

One index of the changes is the spread of the rabbinic construction of Judaism itself from Mesopotamia and Palestine over a huge swath of the globe, from Iberia to Khurasan. True, even before the rise of Islam there is evidence of contact between the rabbinic movement and Jews in Phoenicia, Syria, Arabia, and Alexandria, and evidence of considerable resistance to it after. But in late antiquity, rabbinic influence outside Palestine and Mesopotamia is spottily attested. After the Islamic conquests, towns and cities all over the Mediterranean littoral housed three types of congregations: those loyal to the leaders of the rabbinic movements of Palestine and Iraq (even if the details of that loyalty are vague before the tenth century); and those of a non-rabbinic movement called Karaism.

The main leaders of the rabbinic movement were the heads of the rabbinic academies (yeshivot) in Iraq and Palestine, the *geonim* (sing. *gaon*, a shortened form of *rosh yeshivat geon ya'aqov,* "head of the yeshiva of the pride of Jacob," after Ps. 47.5). The yeshivot were institutions of higher learning, high courts of Jewish law, and seats of communal leadership. There were two in Iraq, in the ancient towns of Sura (midway between the east branch of the Euphrates and the ruins of Babylon, about 15 km north of the later town of al-Hilla) and Pumbedita (about 5 km upstream on the Euphrates from modern al-Falluja), and one in Tiberias in Galilee. All three claimed ancient roots, but evidence of their existence as complex, brick-and-mortar institutions is hardly abundant prior to the ninth century.[14]

We owe information about the leadership functions that the geonim of Sura and Pumbedita exercised to three kinds of sources. The first are missives written by the geonim themselves. These include responsa, which are legal and exegetical opinions written on request, and other kinds of letters to colleagues and followers outside Iraq. The earliest surviving responsa have been dated (though not unequivocally) to the mid-eighth century, remarkably early given the general dearth of information about Jews in this period. But the responsa also present special challenges to the historian. Many gaonic responsa and letters survive not in their original form but in later medieval copies and anthologies. In some cases, the responsa include only legal argumentation and omit the kind of information that would be of greatest use to the historian—names and places.[15] Second, there are chronicles and other narrative accounts of the yeshivot in Iraq; most date to the tenth century or later.[16] Third, the Iraqi geonim and their disciples composed legal and exegetical works that attest to the kind of study that took place at the academies and their efforts to promulgate law based on the Babylonian Talmud. The earliest of these is the *She'iltot*, a book of legal homilies from mid-eighth-century Iraq by a figure named Rav Ahai of Shavha of whom practically nothing is known. There is also a pair of interrelated legal

95

codes from ca. 800 and 850 respectively called *Halakhot Pesquot* and *Halakhot Gedolot*, the first of uncertain authorship and the second by Shim'on Qayyāra of Basra.[17]

That is what survives of the early Iraqi geonim—enough to suggest that they enjoyed authoritative standing among their disciples, but not enough to demonstrate how many disciples they had or how far beyond Iraq their authority extended, with one exception: a polemical epistle written by someone named Pirqoy b. Baboy, the disciple of a disciple of Yehudai Gaon of Sura (757–61). Pirqoy wrote to the Jewish communities of al-Qayrawan and al-Andalus around 800 to convince them of the antiquity, authenticity, and superiority of Babylonian over Palestinian traditions. Though this source, too, has survived only in eleventh-century copies, it suggests the spiritual dependence of the Jews of al-Qayrawan and al-Andalus on Iraq in this period, a scenario attested in other sources.[18]

Our knowledge of the exilarchs is just as spotty. Although the office is attested in the Sasanian period and perhaps even earlier, hardly any writing by exilarchs survives at all beyond a handful of letters and responsa, making it difficult to reconstruct all the office's functions in any given period. It seems certain that the exilarch—a Hellenized rendering of the Aramaic title *resh galuta*, "head of the diaspora"—was the political leader of the Jewish community of Mesopotamia and represented the community before the state, much as the *katholikos* represented the Nestorian Christians. He also seems to have appointed local judges and supervised market transactions. Exilarchs claimed royal descent from the line of the biblical King David via King Jehoiachin (who had been exiled to Babylonia in the early sixth century BCE); the claim was probably made in competition with that of the Jewish *nesi'im* ("princes") of Roman Palestine, but it took on special meaning in the Islamic world, since Muslims regarded David as a prophet and were themselves interested in tracing and documenting descent from the prophet Muhammad.[19]

The exilarch also seems to have commanded a certain respect outside Iraq. According to two Christian chroniclers, the patriarch Michael the Syrian (d. 1199) and Bar Hebraeus (d. 1286), the Jews of Baghdad and those of Tiberias fought over the office during the reign of the Abbasid caliph al-Ma'mun (813–33), each group putting forward its own candidate. That the yeshiva of Tiberias cared so deeply about who served as exilarch suggests that at least in this period, it came under his jurisdiction. Likewise, a letter of 835–6 from the exilarch to Tiberias concedes the Palestinian gaon the privilege of determining the calendar for the entire Jewish world. Before the Fatimid conquests of 969–70, then, the yeshiva of Palestine seems to have acknowledged the Iraqi exilarch's leadership.[20]

The Palestinian yeshiva is hardly attested before the ninth century and remained completely unknown until the discovery of the Cairo Geniza (see below), after which the problem became not too little information but too much. Here, too, there is some question of the continuity between the Islamic era institution and its ancient predecessor. From the fifth century to the ninth, there is only one (late) attestation of a rabbinic institution in Tiberias, though Palestinian Jewish literary production during this period was abundant, including Midrashim, homilies, liturgical poetry (*piyyut*), and apocalypses, which suggests but does not demonstrate the existence of an organized educational institution.[21] Tiberias also housed one of three ateliers devoted to the *masora*, a project to stabilize the biblical text and provide it with vowel points and cantillation marks. (The others were in Iraq and elsewhere in Palestine; the Tiberian version eventually became the canonical one.)

Despite the vagueness with which they are attested, then, it is clear that both Iraq and Palestine housed institutions of Jewish leadership. But the power of those institutions should not be exaggerated. In an influential mid-century article, the Zionist historian Yitzhak Baer argued that the geonim and exilarchs held centralized and autocratic offices of leadership; in his view, the gaonate and exilarchate had eroded the ancient democratic traditions Jews had inherited from their commonwealth in Palestine. Geniza documents have demonstrated that, on the contrary, local Jewish communities appointed their own leaders and made decisions about how to practice Judaism without direct intervention by the geonim, who could be reached for comment only as quickly (or slowly) as caravans and ships could make it to Iraq or Palestine and back. Even in the eighth and ninth centuries, when the Abbasid Empire still ruled over all of northern Africa and Syria, the geonim depended on their followers for legitimation and donations just as much as their followers looked to them for responsa and religious leadership.[22]

As for non-rabbinic Judaism, the best attested variety is Karaism. The Karaites rejected the rabbis' claims to be the exclusive legitimate interpreters of Jewish law. They are first documented in ninth-century Iran; over the course of the tenth century, they spread to Palestine and attracted followers as far away as al-Andalus. The Karaites did not reject all rabbinic interpretations on principle, however. They simply did not accept the rabbinic system as an obligating whole, asserting instead that they were at liberty to start fresh from the biblical text and cast off rabbinic interpretation where needed. They were stalwartly experimental, adopting many fields of Islamic learning before the Rabbanites did. They were also linguistic pioneers, rejecting Aramaic as contaminated with rabbinism and embracing Hebrew for many new genres, including biblical commentaries and codes of law. There were Karaites involved in the Masoretic atelier at Tiberias; Karaite patrons commissioned some of the monumental Masoretic codices that helped the Tiberian version toward predominance among all Jews; Karaites were pioneers in Judaeo-Arabic; and by the end of the tenth century, they had transformed the intellectual landscape of Judaism.[23]

Having outlined these three kinds of Judaism, we must now ask: how many Jews in the Islamic world participated in or declared fealty to them? From the better-documented period after 1000, we know that Jews felt no obligation to make their loyalties exclusive. Perhaps a more useful way to view the question is to point to the tensions, productive and less so, between local forms of Jewish praxis and the writings of the literate elite. Those tensions existed before the Islamic conquests—the problem of how deeply rabbinized Jewish culture was is a central problem for those who study Judaism in late antiquity—and they continued to exist after. But Jewish elites after the Islamic conquests, whether Rabbanite or Karaite, had several distinct advantages over those of late antiquity: their constituents were urbanized, geographically mobile, and linguistically unified. It seems clear, then, that in explaining how all these forms of Judaism spread, one must take into account the infrastructural changes that the Islamic conquests precipitated. Without those changes, few Jews outside Iran, Iraq, and Palestine would have known or cared about the yeshivot or the Karaites.[24]

Urbanization and Geographic Mobility

Over the first few Islamic centuries, Jews came to town-based occupations in unprecedented numbers. The Jews of Palestine under Byzantine rule had lived mainly in the large villages of the north, and the Palestinian Talmud reflects a mixed urban–rural setting. Likewise, the Babylonian Talmud depicts Jews as working the land or active in trade and crafts in a local, small-scale way. But as early as the eighth century, urbanization had already wreaked irrevocable changes on the Jewish world, and even on Jewish law itself: in 786–7, the gaon of Sura and the exilarch promulgated a ruling permitting debts on the estates of the deceased to be collected from moveable property, even though the Babylonian Talmud had required them to be collected on real estate. Apparently so many Jews had given up ownership of land so as to render the old law unworkable.[25]

Why the Jews of Iraq abandoned the land has not yet been well explained. The thesis that the Jews of early Islamic Iraq lived in cities has held mainly on the strength of the contrast between the basically rural setting of the Babylonian Talmud and Jews' later concentration in cities. One spur may have been the Muslim rulers' imposition of the *kharaj*, a land tax with Sasanian roots. Even the Iraqi yeshivot eventually left their ancient towns on the Euphrates for Baghdad: Pumbedita moved around 890, and Sura followed suit before 928. These moves also marked a new intellectual porousness in the culture of the yeshivot: many of the Iraqi geonim of the tenth century were cosmopolitan, outward-looking, and educated well beyond the canon of rabbinic literature.[26]

Whatever Jews' motives for living in cities, new horizons of geographic mobility made doing so feasible and attractive. The Umayyads (661–750) and Abbasids (750–1258) expanded the infrastructure of roads in order to gather intelligence and transmit decrees and other information in writing. Over the course of the eighth and ninth centuries, overland travel became as practicable as seafaring; this opened up Asia and connected it with the Mediterranean basin. The Abbasids also established a postal system, a *barid*, with hundreds of relay points and scores of private carriers following suit, a fact that explains how the Jewish communities of al-Andalus and al-Qayrawan could stay in touch with the geonim of Iraq at all.[27]

As for the effects of geographic mobility on the economy, the Jews of Iraq can be seen as major players in long-distance trade as early as the ninth century. An oft-cited passage by an Abbasid official named Ibn Khurradadhbih, composed between 846 and 885, describes a group of Jewish traders from the region around Baghdad called Radhaniyya who traveled overland and by ship between western Europe, India, and China, covering the Mediterranean, Red Sea, and Caspian basins in between. They spoke an impressive number of languages (Arabic, Persian, Greek, French, other Romance dialects, and Slavonic—the omission of Aramaic may indicate that it was assumed of Jews), and bought and sold high-profit-margin luxury items such as slaves, furs, textiles, weapons, and spices. Gaonic responsa also mention a trade in slaves, textiles, and spices centered on Iraq, a logical place to sell luxury goods given the market provided by rulers and their entourages. S. D. Goitein argued that the Radhaniyya were an isolated phenomenon with no influence on subsequent developments such as the much better attested Mediterranean and Indian Ocean trade of the late eleventh and twelfth centuries. In fact, the Radhaniyya probably signal the beginnings of a pattern that eventually became pervasive in the Islamic east: a handful of long-distance traders would become successful as purveyors to sovereigns; they and their successors would then come to serve as sovereign bankers and counselors and, concomitantly, as powerful political patrons within the Jewish community. Just a generation or two after the Radhaniyya, a family called the Banu Netira, court bankers (*jahadhiba*; sing. *jahbadh*) to the Abbasid caliphs al-Mu'tadid (892–902) and al-Muqtadir (908–932), are attested as power brokers among the Jews: these courtiers supported two successive geonim, Kohen Zedeq of Pumbedita (926–935) and Sa'adya ben Yosef of Sura (928–942), in political battles against the exilarchs.[28]

If improvements in transportation and its accessibility meant that Jews could travel and send letters and other written compositions over great distances, political unity also meant that they could travel hundreds and even thousands of kilometers without encountering inconvenient obstacles such as borders, wars, and foreign tax regimes. The combination of these two factors led to remarkably efficient communications for a premodern diaspora—but in which languages?

Linguistic and Cultural Change

Jews—like other urban dwellers—probably adopted Arabic as a spoken language over the course of the eighth and ninth centuries. (Jews have always spoken the same language as others around them, with the notable exceptions of Judaeo-Arabic in late medieval Sicily and Judaeo-Spanish and Yiddish in the early modern period.) The first evidence that Jews also wrote sacred literature in Arabic—rather than Aramaic or Hebrew—dates to the ninth century. From the basic decision to write in Arabic there followed one of the most significant cultural transformations in all of Jewish history, one that altered the very horizons of Jewish thought in the Middle Ages, in Islamic lands and beyond.

Arabic is a language with many registers and dialects. The written variety is supra-regional (in linguistic terms, a *koine*), but it is also classicizing, aspiring to imitate the Qur'an. The vernaculars, by contrast, differ across geography, and even between cities and their hinterlands. Medieval city-dwellers used a register that linguists have dubbed Middle Arabic because it fell on the spectrum somewhere between the classical language and the vernacular; it is a phenomenon theorized to have originated in the early garrison towns and firmly attested after the Abbasids came to power in 750. Jews, being an urban population, wrote in Middle Arabic; but being Jews, they wrote it in the Hebrew alphabet.[29]

The modern scholarly term to describe Arabic written in Hebrew characters is Judaeo-Arabic—in theory, any range of Arabic registers and dialects written in Hebrew script, but in practice, usually Middle Arabic, with exceptions such as the great philosophical work by Moses Maimonides (1138–1204), the *Guide of the Perplexed*, which is in perfect classical Judaeo-Arabic interspersed with some Middle Arabic constructions and many Hebrew words. Middle Arabic facilitated communication across vast reaches of territory: just as classical Arabic was a *koine* that emerged out of contact among previously dispersed Arabian tribes, so, too, the users of Judaeo-Arabic tended to meet in the middle. Judaeo-Arabic came to be spoken by more Jews than any other language on earth and would enjoy a wider geographic reach than had either Greek or Aramaic—wider, in fact, than any language spoken by Jews until Yiddish and Ladino.[30]

But when Jews adopted Arabic, they did not simply substitute it for the previous imperial lingua franca, Aramaic. They continued to reserve Aramaic for certain kinds of texts: the *She'iltot*, *Halakhot Pesuqot*, *Halakhot Gedolot*, and some gaonic responsa are in Aramaic, though most are in Judaeo-Arabic; rabbinic legal deeds related to marriage and divorce are in Aramaic, while Karaite ones are in Hebrew. Arabic did everything else. When Jews embraced it, they also came to read and write in new genres and to abandon old genres, particularly texts of the traditional rabbinic type—the Midrash, legal commentaries, homilies, and narratives that had been produced since the dawn of the Common Era.

The old texts had been loosely and associatively organized, anonymously and/or collectively composed and orally transmitted. Beginning in the late ninth century, Jews began producing texts using an individual, authorial voice, structuring their works as monographs and transmitting them in writing. Geonim composed legal works designed for easy reference, in contradistinction to the forbidding organizational structure of the Talmuds and their commentaries. Others translated the Hebrew Bible to Judaeo-Arabic and produced verse-by-verse running commentaries that hewed closely to the plain sense of the text. And Jews wrote in a spate of new or forgotten fields: philosophical theology, linguistics, medicine, astronomy, and historiography. Just as importantly, Arabic inspired closer study of Hebrew, as well as its use in genres other than liturgical poetry.[31]

The figure who did the most to import the new Arabic models into the rabbinic canon was Sa'adya, gaon of Sura. That he embraced the new order so enthusiastically is paradoxical given that its pioneers had been Karaites and Sa'adya was a committed anti-Karaite polemicist. Perhaps both despite his anti-Karaism and precisely because of it, Sa'adya felt moved to write in disciplines and genres that had previously been off-limits to traditional rabbinic literature—a move typical of his strategy of taking from his opponents what was best and most effective. He adopted genres, ideas, texts, and ideologies from Muslims, Christians, and Palestinian Rabbanites as well; he claimed, for example, to have written his Arabic-Hebrew dictionary so that Jews would know Hebrew as well as Muslims knew Arabic.[32]

The effects of Judaeo-Arabic on Jewish literary production cannot be overstated. During the period of greatest efflorescence of Arabic literature, the fourth Islamic century and the tenth of the Common Era, Jews produced an unprecedented quantity of writing. Contact with a new literary system shattered the old vessels. New types of literature were now transmitted in writing over the entire Islamic world. Judaeo-Arabic works even circulated as far as Byzantium and Christian Europe, where efforts were made to translate them into Hebrew beginning in the eleventh and twelfth centuries. The mobility of the new literary products demonstrates the extraordinary degree of communication the Islamic conquests had allowed Jews to enjoy; their innovativeness demonstrates the unpredictable power of languages and cultures in contact. Judaeo-Arabic was one major reason why Jews under Islam felt themselves to be inhabitants of a great linguistic *oecumene* and users of a common *koine*—perhaps even a greater proportion of Jews than had felt this way in the Hellenistic world from which those two Greek terms derive.[33]

The Breakdown of Empire and the Shift Westward

No sooner had a sense of *oecumene* established itself than major cracks began to appear in the political infrastructure that had brought it together in the first place. After 900, large chunks of the empire began to fall away from Abbasid control. In 909, the Abbasids lost central North Africa to the Fatimids, a messianic movement of Shi'a who not only founded their own state but also delivered the ultimate theological affront to the Abbasids by usurping (or, in their view, restoring) the title of caliph, reserved for the Muslims' supreme guide in not merely political but soteriological terms. An amir of Cordoba in al-Andalus (which had never come under Baghdad's rule in the first place), 'Abd al-Rahman III (912–61), followed suit and took the title as well. The Islamic polity had held together for nearly three centuries under the belief that there could be only one caliph, but now there were three.

Then economic crisis took hold in Baghdad. The economy declined precipitously along with institutional structures. The Abbasid caliph al-Muqtadir's profligate spending provoked a military rebellion during which he was deposed and killed (932). In 943, the imperial administration was taken over by Persian mercenaries who ruled Iraq and Iran for the next century, reducing the Abbasid caliph to a mere puppet. The most serious blow came in 969, when the Fatimids marched westward and conquered the wealthy province of Egypt and then, with their sights set on Baghdad itself, marched on Syria as well. The Fatimids never reached Baghdad, but the crisis in the Abbasid heartland was deep and long lasting. A Muslim geographer named al-Maqdisi (d. ca. 990), whose grandfather had come from Iran to Palestine with a great wave of westward migrants in the early tenth century, described the situation this way: Baghdad "has been superseded until the day of Judgment; [Egypt's] metropole [Fustat-Cairo] has now become the greatest glory of the Muslims."[34]

The Jews of Iraq felt the shift acutely. The rabbinic academy of Sura closed its doors between 943 and 987, though it would then reopen for a few decades; but by 1040, both it and Pumbedita had ceased to be. Starting in the late ninth century, generation upon generation of migrants left Iraq and Iran for the West—not just Jews but everyone. Babylonian rabbinic loyalists spread all over the Mediterranean basin.

There is an echo of this great shift westward in the Hebrew chronicle *Sefer ha-Kabbalah* by Abraham Ibn Da'ud of Toledo, composed in 1161. The purpose of the chronicle was to demonstrate that the rabbinic scholars of the Iberian Peninsula had inherited the mantle of religious legitimacy from the Babylonian geonim in an unbroken chain of transmission. In Ibn Da'ud's zero-sum history of the rabbinate, for Iberia to triumph, Baghdad had to fall. Between 960 and 990, he writes, "It was brought about by God that the income of the yeshivot, which used to come from Iberia, the Maghreb, Ifriqiya [central North Africa],

Egypt, and the land of Israel, was discontinued." Just then, four rabbinic scholars, on their way from Bari to Baghdad by ship to study with the geonim, were
kidnapped by pirates (pirates who were acting, of course, at the behest of divine
providence). The rabbis were ransomed in four separate Jewish communities:
Fustat, al-Qayrawan, Cordoba, and a fourth that Ibn Da'ud claims not to be able
to identify (the wild card brings the number of captives to the midrashically
significant four). Each went on to found an independent center of learning.[35]

Documentary finds related to the three named rabbis have cast doubt on
whether these events ever took place. The story is patently a foundation legend,
and it conceals the fact that all three centers possessed some scholarly independence before the late tenth century and stayed in close contact with Baghdad
after. But the migrations westward permitted the geonim of Baghdad to solicit
donations beyond their own immediate eastern jurisdictions, turning to Jewish
communities around the Mediterranean basin with increasing insistence into
the eleventh century.

Nowhere were the effects of the migration more palpable—and nowhere
are they more densely documented—than Egypt and Syria under the Fatimids
(969–1171) and Ayyubids (1171–1250). Among the migrants there seems to have
been a disproportion of the literate (who in preindustrial societies rarely exceed
5 percent of the male population in any case). Like literate people in many preindustrial societies, they were the pool from which government administrators
were chosen. The Jews of the Fatimid Empire now had a steady supply of sympathetic courtiers on hand to intervene on their behalf; and they had a steady
supply of candidates for communal leadership offices, all in stiff competition
with one another. Indeed, the tenth and eleventh centuries have proven to be
enormously interesting periods of Jewish and Middle Eastern history not just
because of the wealth of documentation, but because the old elites began to be
replaced by new ones.

The Cairo Geniza

Until this point in the essay, I have discussed the social and cultural upheavals
in the three centuries following the first Islamic conquests—slow and gradual
changes at first, and then, with urbanization, geographic mobility, and linguistic change, more rapid and radical ones. While the evidence of change from the
seventh through the tenth centuries is enough to suggest patterns, much of it is
also circumstantial or indirect. There is also little information about the internal
functioning of the Jewish community.

The source silence lifts around 950 with the documents of the Cairo Geniza.
The cache comprises some 330,000 folio pages dating mostly to the period
between 950 and 1250 (there is also material from subsequent centuries, up to

the end of the nineteenth). It survived because it had been stored in the attic of a medieval synagogue in the belief that writing potentially containing the name of God should not be destroyed. What has been preserved is written on parchment and paper, with isolated items on papyrus (which was rarely used in Egypt and Syria after about 930); it is now held in 70 different libraries and private collections.[36]

The manuscripts are overwhelmingly (around 94%) copies of literary texts, in the conventional historians' sense of narrative and other compositions intended for posterity, as distinct from documents and ephemera. The largest group of literary manuscripts, perhaps as much as one-quarter, is liturgical texts—*piyyutim* (liturgical poems), prayer books, and sermons. This fact reflects the needs and habits of the synagogue's officials, who were intensive producers and consumers of texts. There are also biblical texts, translations, commentaries, as well as works from all genres of Judaeo-Arabic writing, in addition to finds in Hebrew, Aramaic, Judaeo-Persian, and even some Arabic, Ladino, Yiddish, and Greek.

The literary materials from the Geniza include works by previously unknown authors, unknown works by known authors, drafts of works long known, and enough copies of texts as to necessitate a reevaluation of books long familiar and who their audiences were. One such example is a chronicle called *Sefer Yosippon*, first composed in Hebrew in ninth-century Byzantine Italy. The work claims to be a translation of writings by Flavius Josephus (37–ca. 100), but is in fact a chronicle of Jewish and general history from the destruction of the first Judaean commonwealth to that of the second. It was not a fixed text, but subject to expansion up to and including the era of the printing press. Until the discovery of the Geniza, the Hebrew core of this evolving *Yosippon* was thought to have been composed in Italy in 953. But the Geniza preserved fragments of two Judaeo-Arabic translations of the work that made it clear that it had, in fact, been quoted decades earlier in other Judaeo-Arabic works. The entire history of the text now had to be rethought.[37]

The broad circulation of *Yosippon* proved to be a surprising discovery for two reasons. First, the work had long been thought of as a major vehicle for ancient Palestinian Jewish ideas about martyrdom, supposedly brought via Italy to the Jews of Ashkenaz, for whom sanctification of God's name in death was a religious ideal. Those ideals had supposedly bypassed the Jews of the Islamic world, who were thought to have been more likely to convert to Islam than to die in God's name. The discovery of the Judaeo-Arabic *Yosippon* made it clear that the failure among Jews of the Islamic world to produce stories of martyrdom, let alone to imitate the deeds of martyrs, cannot be attributed to lack of information. It has to be explained in some other way (absence of theological tension between Judaism and Islam and Jews' acceptance of Muslims as a "reference group" to be imitated have both been suggested). Second, Yosef Hayim Yerushalmi's influential book *Zakhor* had maintained that medieval Jews were fundamentally uninterested in reading or writing history. He thought of *Yosippon* as an exception—a book whose pedigree (the spurious attribution to Josephus) and focus on biblical-era history had earned it particular respect. But *Sefer Yosippon* was merely one of numerous chronicles the Geniza preserved; and its broad circulation and that of other works suggests that medieval Jews were just as interested in chronicles as their Arabic- and Latin-writing contemporaries, even if they had no royal courts to sponsor their composition.[38]

In rare cases, the Geniza has also offered letters by the authors of well-known works explaining their motives for composing them. One is *The Kuzari* (Kitab al-Khazari), by the Iberian physician and poet Abu l-Hasan Yehuda ben Shemu'el ha-Levi (better known as Judah Halevi, 1085–1141), a defense of rabbinic Judaism and one of the most widely circulated and translated Jewish books not just of the Middle Ages but of the entire period from its composition up until 1900. The Geniza preserved a letter by Halevi to his friend Halfon b. Netan'el al-Dimyati in Fustat in which Halevi dismisses the work as "a mere trifle" and confesses that he was writing it only because a Karaite from Christian Iberia had asked him questions he had felt moved to answer. And indeed, the third part of *The Kuzari* is a polemic against Karaism.[39]

The Documentary Geniza and Goitein

Halevi's letter is just one among thousands of documentary texts the Geniza preserved. The documentary Geniza is unrivaled in medieval Jewish and Near Eastern history for its scope, coherence, and density. The texts include letters, legal deeds, amulets, lists, petitions, edicts, communal registers, and every other conceivable type of ephemeral writing. Many are by or about people whose lives we can reconstruct in detail, and where individual biographies elude us, we can nonetheless fathom what kinds of houses Jews lived in, what they heard and smelled on the street, how many meals they ate per day (they skipped lunch), how often they cooked at home (rarely—they bought food from stalls in the marketplace), how young they married (this varied), how they dressed (mainly in linen, sometimes in wool, and generally with very few changes of clothing over a lifetime), where they stored their wheat (in earthenware jars in the sun, usually on an upper floor out of the reach of thieves), where they had it baked into bread (in communal ovens), how much money they needed to support themselves (two dinars per month for an average working family), and how a trader in Fustat could acquire and sell goods from the Malabar Coast of India without ever leaving Egypt (slave-agents, apprentices, and written correspondence).

Difficult as it is to overstate the importance of the documentary Geniza, it is also difficult to avoid blunting its impact by resorting to banal-sounding phrases such as "daily life." Another way of putting the matter is that the Geniza offers intimate knowledge of *how things worked* in the medieval Middle East—not just mundane, local matters but also lofty and trans-regional ones such as how the Palestinian yeshiva operated (it had barely been known to exist before the Geniza's discovery), how its geonim were elected (with much contention and a good dose of realpolitik), why some Jews sought justice not (or not only) from Jewish courts but from Islamic ones, or how they dared petition state officials and whether or what they heard back from them.[40]

The Geniza is distinctive not just in Jewish but in general history. Its only serious rivals for the pre-Ottoman period in Egypt (before 1517) are the Greek papyri from Byzantine Oxyrhynchus (500,000 items, the vast majority documentary) and Arabic papyri from the Fayyum and elsewhere (more than 100,000). The Geniza is different in one salient respect: not only is it later and written mainly in Hebrew script; it came into being in an urban center, a capital city no less, in one of the most geographically mobile communities in the medieval world, and at the hub of the Mediterranean and Indian Ocean trade routes. The Geniza thus reflects, either directly or indirectly, nearly every corner of the Islamic world, and sometimes beyond.[41]

Research on the documentary Geniza got seriously underway in the 1950s, when S. D. Goitein, already a mature scholar in his fifties, decided to devote all his time to it. His *A Mediterranean Society,* a five-volume compendium published over a 20-year period (1967–88), is often regarded as having exhausted the documentary Geniza. But Goitein himself, with astonishing humility, once referred to it as "only a sketch." It is a visionary sketch to be sure—not a napkin doodle but one of Leonardo da Vinci's flying machines—but no one understood better than Goitein how much work remained to be done. A remarkable number of Goitein's arguments on specific topics have been borne out by subsequent studies.[42]

After Goitein: Formalism and Informalism

In the two generations of scholarship on the documentary Geniza since Goitein, his students and successors have produced place-based studies;[43] investigations of trade and economics;[44] analyses of the organized Jewish communities of Egypt, Syria, and Ifriqiya;[45] and studies of family life and marriage, including legal traditions related to family law.[46] The approaches range between the absolute empiricism of geographic studies, in which everything from a particular place and time period is germane and requires the historian to approach the work with as few preconceptions as possible, and the modified empiricism of problem-based history, which requires enough preconceptions to consider a particular problem worthy of being solved.[47]

If there is one theoretical problem that has recurred in much of this work, it is the tension between individual social relations and institutions in the tenth-through-twelfth century Middle East—or, more precisely, the formality and structuredness of individual relations versus the continually shifting nature of relations among groups. Here Geniza historians have responded to a trend in Middle East history in general toward analyzing patron–client relations and explaining why many individual relationships (in trade, political life, and education) proved so consequential, binding and enduring even as the strength of institutions and the stability of groups could never be assumed. In Geniza studies, the emphasis on what the Arabic and Judaeo-Arabic sources call *suhba* (formal friendship) has had enormous utility. In part, this has to do with the abundance of letters, which by their nature highlight individual relationships and show them to be structured formally through recurring linguistic patterns; in part, it was an effect of the sheer mass of unofficial detail about organizations and institutions, which made them less stable than a strictly official archive might have. Goitein recognized this as a special strength of the Geniza, and insisted that offices of Jewish communal and religious leadership should be understood by separating hard prerogatives from impressive-sounding but soft titles of office, and by understanding the individual relationships surrounding them. He penetrated the sometimes opaque façade of communal institutions by peering into the delicate power negotiations behind them—the relationships of patronage, breaches of trust, failures, frustrations, and crises that authors of Geniza letters frequently negotiated.[48]

The question of how institutions and relationships combined has also proven revealing in studies of trade, which have focused not only on "hard" financial instruments—legal partnership, agency, credit—but also "soft" ones, especially the way traders used business letters to exchange and enforce commercial services outside the bounds of contractual obligation. Another example of the fruitfulness of this approach can be seen in the history of the Palestinian yeshiva in the eleventh century. The longest-serving gaon, Shelomo b. Yehuda al-Fasi (1025–51), fought off rivals repeatedly during the first two decades of his tenure: Iraqis in Palestine who sought to form their own administrative body; Hayya Gaon of Pumbedita (998–1038), who was "constantly sending letters" (as al-Fasi put it) seeking donations for his yeshiva on Palestinian turf; and a native Palestinian named Natan ben Avraham who proclaimed himself gaon and usurped some of al-Fasi's prerogatives between 1038 and 1042. Al-Fasi was, in short, set upon from all sides, and what saved him were alliances with wealthy traders, courtiers, and Fatimid bureaucrats—some of them Karaites— who could get him writs of investiture from the caliphs and threaten his enemies with imprisonment when needed. The Geniza revealed gaonic authority to have operated through the canny deployment of power relations outside the Jewish community—a point implicit in some of Goitein's work but not well elaborated until that of his successors.[49]

Islamic Iberia

Study of the Jews of Iberia is practically a subfield in itself due to its relative geographic containment, the abundance of source material and cultural milestones, and the special challenges—linguistic, archival, and conceptual—posed by studying a society over a long transition between Islamic and Christian rule. While the Jews of Muslim-ruled Iberia conform to many of the eastern patterns outlined above, they often exhibit more extreme versions of them.[50]

Jews made up a significant proportion of the population of al-Andalus: in some towns up to 20 percent (the only comparable eastern example is Sura); in most cities, between 6 and 10 percent. The Jews of Visigothic Hispania appear in Arabic chronicles as having actively aided the conquering Muslim armies in 711, hoping to find in Islamic rule a providential liberation from state and ecclesiastical persecution. While Jews in the East may have welcomed the Islamic conquests, then, those in the West are depicted as having helped bring them about.[51]

Al-Andalus appears to have come under the sway of the Iraqi geonim earlier and more completely than other areas of the Mediterranean. Later sources maintain that a deposed exilarch, named Natronai bar Havivai, arrived in al-Andalus around 772 with the entire Babylonian Talmud committed to memory and wrote it down for Andalusi Jews; since the earliest attestation of this is in a responsum of Sherira Gaon two centuries later, its veracity cannot be assumed, but even as a legend it suggests that the Iraqi geonim regarded al-Andalus as their preserve. Ninth-century responsa support this impression: Jewish communities in al-Andalus regularly queried the Iraqi geonim, especially Natronai bar Hilai of Sura (857–65); when his rival 'Amram bar Sheshna usurped his title and founded his own academy (857–75), one way he mustered authority was by responding to the query of a certain Yishaq b. Shim'on in al-Andalus with an entire monograph on prayer. Local rabbinic leaders in al-Andalus considered themselves disciples of the geonim and many went to study in Iraq. Like the Muslims of ninth-century al-Andalus, then, its Jews looked East for cultural models and religious leadership.

In 929, the Umayyad amir 'Abd al-Rahman III (912–61) proclaimed himself caliph and built a palatine city, Madinat al-Zahra' outside Cordoba, modeling it after the Fatimid capitals of Ifriqiya. He also developed a conscious program of serving as a patron of high culture, and his successor al-Hakam II (961–76) continued it. Andalusi Jews thus began to produce a steady stream of courtier-scholars. Hasdai ibn Shaprut (905–75), a physician at the Umayyad court, became the de facto head of the Jewish community of al-Andalus, taking the biblical title *nasi* (prince) and patronizing Jewish scholarship much as the Umayyad caliphs did for Islamic scholarship.

Here again, the comparison with the East is instructive: while in Baghdad the exilarchs had the Banu Netira to contend with, Andalusi Jews had their courtier-intercessor and their communal leader in one person. Hasdai may indeed have fancied himself a global Jewish leader on a par with the geonim: he wrote persistently to the Khazar ruling house, which had converted to Judaism, and ultimately received word back; and his son apparently roundly ignored the letters he received from Sherira, at least to believe the complaints he received in a Geniza letter from Sherira's son Hayya to Nissim ben Ya'aqov of al-Qayrawan. Ibn Da'ud sets his "story of the four captives" during Hasdai's tenure, claiming that he created the conditions that enabled Andalusi Jews to declare their independence from the Iraqi yeshivot, and that divine providence did the rest by sending one of the four captives, Moshe ben Hanokh, to establish a yeshiva in Cordoba. In sum, just as the Umayyad caliphate cemented its own independence from Baghdad, so did its Jews.[52]

In al-Andalus the encounter between Jewish and Arabic literature was particularly fruitful and intense; the sense of cultural competition was acute and the impact of an Arabophone milieu on the growth and creativity of literary Hebrew was inestimable. A regular participant in Hasdai's *majlis* was Dunash ben Labrat (ca. 920–90), the first to import Arabic quantitative meters into Hebrew poetry, a move that set the standard for centuries to come.[53]

The Umayyad caliphate dissolved into petty principalities during the period of the Ta'ifa Kings (1009–91); more rulers and courts meant more opportunities for patronage (as in Renaissance Italy). One result of this was continued cultural efflorescence. There were panegyrics to be written and official positions to be filled; Jews were also of special value to Muslim rulers because they could negotiate with the Christian north as trusted neutral parties. Many courtiers were themselves poets, such as Samuel ibn Naghrella (993–1056) and his son Yehosef (d. 1066), both of whom served as viziers of Granada, while in the Islamic east no Jew (and few Christians) became vizier without first converting to Islam. All this continued even when al-Andalus was conquered and politically unified by the Almoravids (1091–1135). Even though the Almoravid rulers enforced the statutes of 'Umar more rigorously than had been done before, including the *ghiyar* laws, Jews still served the court and bureaucracy, including a pair of viziers. Thus in contrast to the handful of Jewish courtiers in any given capital in the Islamic east in the tenth, eleventh, and twelfth centuries, in al-Andalus under the Ta'ifa Kings and the Almoravids, there was an entire class of them, with its own social code, ideals, and literary predilections. A Jew who migrated to the Christian-ruled north, the poet Moshe ibn 'Ezra (1060–1139), complained that he felt like "a gentleman among savages."[54]

This sense of exceptionalism—and of the impossibility and fundamental indignity of living anywhere else—was an important theme in Sephardi culture even before the late medieval expulsions. The most fascinating case of this is undoubtedly Moses Maimonides. As a boy, Maimonides witnessed the Almohad conquest of his native Cordoba (1148) and his family soon began wandering the Iberian Peninsula before settling in Almohad-ruled Fez around 1160. The Almohads conquered all of al-Andalus between 1147 and 1172, ruling it until 1269; theirs was an extreme interpretation of Islam, and one of its tenets was the abrogation of *dhimmi* law and the requirement that all non-Muslims convert or leave the realm. Some were converted forcibly; others converted for convenience's sake or went into exile. In the Maghreb—the birthplace of Augustine, Tertullian, Cyprian, and other fathers of the church—Christianity completely ceased to exist. Many Jews fled to the North, and some fled South and East; others converted or practiced Islam only outwardly. It was the death-knell of Iberian courtier life in the Islamic-ruled South.

Maimonides' family chose outward conversion to Islam. One of the greatest minds of Judaism therefore lived publicly as a Muslim during his intellectually formative years, before he and his brother (a long-distance trader) settled in Fustat around 1165, where Maimonides became a leader of the same Syro-Palestinian synagogue that bequeathed the Geniza to posterity. For years, it was debated whether Maimonides had in fact converted to Islam, but the consensus now is that he did; his Jewish scholarship has also shown to have been more deeply affected by this period of outward Islam than has previously been recognized. It was long known that Maimonides' Judaeo-Arabic philosophical works, such as the *Guide of the Perplexed*, universally considered a masterpiece of neo-Aristotelian thought, bear the stamp of deep erudition in Islamicate sources. But Sarah Stroumsa, in one of the most interesting arguments to emerge from Judaeo-Arabic scholarship in recent years, has argued that even his Hebrew legal code, the *Mishneh Torah*, contains formal and methodological innovations that are borrowed from Almohad writings: the insertion of theological principles into a legal code; terse presentations of the law without the reasoning that led to it; and rigid avoidance of anthropomorphism.[55]

For Almohad rule, the turning point came in 1212, when a coalition of Christian kingdoms defeated the dynasty at the Battle of Las Navas de Tolosa. The Islamic south was reduced to a small city-state around Granada; Andalusi culture was now fully transplanted to the Christian north. Andalusi Jews brought to life under Christian rule centuries of artistic tradition and political experience. They also brought an exceptional feature of their communal governance: sweeping powers of enforcement—up to and, in some communities, including capital punishment.

One of the ways the rabbinic segment of the courtier class in Iberia used this power was to extirpate Karaism, for them a heresy (Hebrew and Judaeo-Arabic *minut*) and a threat to their very existence. Between the courtiers Ibn Naghrella of Granada in the early eleventh century and Yosef Alfacar of León in the second half of the twelfth, a steady stream of courtiers boasted of having flogged Karaites, killed them, prohibited their beliefs, or extirpated their heresy altogether. One such reference comes from Maimonides, who wrote a Judaeo-Arabic commentary on the Mishnah while living publicly as a Muslim in Fez in the 1160s; there he noted that the Jewish laws calling for the execution of heretics "are being applied in all western lands with respect to many individuals." Another comes from a Castilian Jewish convert to Christianity, Alfonso de Valladolid (ca. 1270–ca. 1347), who wrote that in 1177–8, in the northern city of Carrión, Karaites were punished for having compelled Rabbanites to conform publicly to Karaite Sabbath prohibitions. This is, to be sure, a sign that the Karaites were still vital in late twelfth-century Iberia; but it is also the last we hear of them there.[56]

The contrast with the Islamic east is once again telling. Sa'adya's polemical campaign against the Karaites failed to bear long-term consequences; it was quickly followed by the shifting alliances among the three sectors of the Jewish community under the Fatimids and Ayyubids, with rabbinic leaders allying themselves with Karaite grandees and the rank and file following suit. But in Iberia, the persecution of Karaites during the era of the Christian conquests became definitive: Rabbanite courtiers used their proximity to the rulers to close ranks against the Karaites in the face of Christian and Muslim warfare and anti-Jewish polemics. The sweeping powers of enforcement Jewish communal leaders enjoyed would become a persistent theme in the Christian north, where fourteenth-century sources attest to Jews' right to inflict corporal and capital punishment against violators of Jewish law and "informers" on fellow Jews to the Christian authorities.[57]

The Late Medieval Period

After the closure of Sura and Pumbedita around 1040, a yeshiva would open again in Baghdad several decades later and survive until 1288; the exilarchate, too, seems to have undergone a revival in the second half of the twelfth century, though in Mosul rather than Baghdad. The best-known and most prolific gaon of this later period was Shemu'el b. 'Eli ibn al-Dastur (1164–ca. 1194–7), whose letters to Egypt survived in the Geniza. But Maimonides, who after his arrival in Egypt became head of the Jews (*nagid*, 1171–ca. 1177 and ca. 1195–1204), ridiculed Ibn al-Dastur as an ignoramus obsessed with the trappings of office. The gaonate appears by this point to have been a shadow of its former self. Indeed, that an Andalusi in Egypt could disparage a gaon of Baghdad demonstrates how rabbinic geographies had shifted by the late twelfth century—even Ibn Da'ud during the same period was more respectful of the classical geonim.

Three documents of investiture issued by Abbasid caliphs to geonim (1209, 1247–8, and 1250) suggest that on the eve of the Mongol invasion, Jews were a significant enough presence in Baghdad to warrant state appointments, but what the late geonim did with this kind of authority is a matter of speculation.

A relatively small number of Geniza documents survived from the Mamluk period in Egypt and Syria (1250–1517). The period has long been viewed as one of increased state control over *dhimmi* communal life, but this stereotype has more recently been questioned. When the state intervened in Jewish communal life, it was often at the behest of the Jews themselves.

Such was the case with Abraham Maimonides (1186–1237), the son of Moses Maimonides, head of the Jews (*nagid*) like his father and leader of a Jewish Sufi movement. (Its adherents called themselves hasidim, pious ones.) Abraham Maimonides had instituted some ritual innovations, and his enemies appealed to a state appointed *qadi* and then to the Ayyubid sultan seeking to make those innovations illegal. The Muslim authorities refused to intervene. The controversy continued under Abraham's son and successor, David, whose opponents petitioned another *qadi* about Abraham's liturgical innovations; nothing came of it, and the Maimonidean family continued to lead the Jewish community in Egypt for another three generations, until ca. 1414. In many cases, Jewish and Islamic sources alike had an interest in depicting the state as interventionist— Jewish groups on the losing side of state power resorted to tropes of oppression; Arabic chroniclers made the sultans appear more zealous by depicting them as having curbed *dhimmi* power.[58]

In one fascinating case from 1465, 24 Iberian Jewish converts to Christianity (*conversos*) arrived in Egypt professing Judaism, but proclaiming themselves biblical Jews and refusing to accept rabbinic authority. The Karaites of Cairo, from whose perspective the story is narrated, sought to win over the immigrants in light of their mutual rejection of rabbinic authority. But before recruiting them, the Karaite elders first took the precaution of querying each of the five chief Mamluk qadis on whether a change in Jewish "legal school" (in Judaeo-Arabic, *madhhab*) was permissible *according to Islamic law*. The story typifies *dhimmis'* adroitness in using the Mamluk system of legal pluralism to achieve their aims with the sanction of Islamic law—to "shop for justice," as one scholar has recently put it. It also typifies the relative latitude Egyptian and Syrian Jews enjoyed compared with Jews in fifteenth-century Iberia.[59]

Notes

1. For Baghdad, see most recently Hugh Kennedy (2001), "Feeding the Five Hundred Thousand: Cities and Agriculture in Early Islamic Mesopotamia," *Iraq* 73: 177–200; for a less conservative estimate, see A. A. Duri, "Baghdad," in *Encyclopaedia of Islam* (2nd edn). Leiden: Brill.

2. Salo Baron (1971), "Population," in *Encyclopedia Judaica* (1st edn); Sergio DellaPergola's estimate that at the end of the twelfth century, 83 percent of Jews lived on the Asian continent seems questionable, since even after openly practicing Jews had fled the Almohad realm, large concentrations remained in Egypt, Sicily, Christian Iberia, and the rest of Europe. Sergio DellaPergola (2010), "Demographics," in Norman A. Stillman (ed.), *Encyclopaedia of Jews in the Islamic World*. Leiden: Brill (hereafter *EJIW*; many of its essays on the Middle Ages will be cited here).

3. There are many more surveys covering the Jews of medieval Europe, and especially of northern Europe, than the Jews in the Islamic world. Bernard Lewis (1984), *The Jews of Islam* (Princeton: Princeton University Press) is still serviceable if synchronic; the narrative in Norman A. Stillman (1989), *The Jews of Arab Lands: A History and Source Book* (Philadelphia: Jewish Publication Society) is more historical, even if the theme of post-Fatimid twilight and decline deserves skepticism. Mark R. Cohen (2008), *Under Crescent and Cross: The Jews in the Middle Ages* (2nd edn) (Princeton: Princeton University Press) is one of very few studies to cover Jews under Islam and Christianity. In contrast see Kenneth Stow (1992), *Alienated Minority: The Jews of Medieval Latin Europe*. Cambridge, MA: Harvard University Press; Robert Chazan (2006), *The Jews of Medieval Western Christendom, 1000–1500*. Cambridge: Cambridge University Press.

4. On the conquests in general, the standard work is Fred McGraw Donner (1981), *The Early Islamic Conquests*. Princeton: Princeton University Press; see also the following notes. The pace of conversion to Islam: Richard W. Bulliet (1979), *Conversion to Islam in the Medieval Period: An Essay in Quantitative History*. Cambridge, MA: Harvard University Press; and idem (1993), *Islam: The View from the Edge*. New York: Columbia University Press. Bulliet's general conclusions have been accepted with modifications; the details and methods remain contested.

5. Moshe Gil (1974), "The Constitution of Medina: A Reconsideration," *Israel Oriental Studies* 4: 44–66; A. J. Wensinck (1975), *Muhammad and the Jews of Medina*. Wolfgang Behn (ed. and trans.). Freiburg im Breisgau: Klaus Schwarz Verlag; Moshe Gil (1984), "The Origin of the Jews of Yathrib," *Jerusalem Studies in Arabic and Islam* 4: 203–24; Uri Rubin (1985), "The 'Constitution of Medina': Some Notes," *Studia Islamica* 62: 5–23; M. J. Kister (1986), "The Massacre of the Banū Qurayza: A Re-Examination of a Tradition," *Jerusalem Studies in Arabic and Islam* 8: 61–96; Michael Lecker (1995), "On Arabs of the Banū Kilāb Executed Together with the Jewish Banū Qurayza," *Jerusalem Studies in Arabic and Islam* 19: 66–72; Rizwi S. Faizer (1996), "Muhammad and the Medinian Jews: A Comparison of Ibn Ishaq's *Kitāb Sīrat Rasūl Allāh* with al-Waqidi's *Kitāb al-Maghāzī*," *International Journal of Middle East Studies* 28: 463–89; Michael Lecker (1997), "Did Muhammad Conclude Treaties with the Jewish Tribes Nadīr, Qurayza and Qaynuqā'?," *Israel Oriental Studies* 17: 29–36; and idem (2004), *The "Constitution of Medina:" Muhammad's First Legal Document*. Princeton: Darwin Press. For a summary of the events, see Stillman, *Jews of Arab Lands*, pp. 8–19, and for a translation of the sources, pp. 119–51. See also the articles by Shari Lowin, "Constitution of Medina," "Banū Qaynuqā'," "Banū Nadīr," and "Banū Qurayza," all in *EJIW*.

6. There are also an unknown number of Hebrew-script papyri from the early Islamic period, most of them unpublished. See Chase F. Robinson (2004), *Empire and Elites after the Muslim Conquest: The Transformation of Northern Mesopotamia*. New York: Cambridge University Press; Robert Hoyland (2006), "New Documentary Texts and the Early Islamic State," *Bulletin of the School of Oriental and African Studies* 69: 395–416; Petra M. Sijpesteijn (2009), "Arabic Papyri and Islamic Egypt," in R. S. Bagnall (ed.), *The Oxford Handbook of Papyrology*. Oxford: Oxford University Press, pp. 452–72; idem (2010), "Multilingual Archives and Documents in Post-Conquest Egypt," in Arietta Papaconstantinou (ed.), *The Multilingual Experience in Egypt, from*

the Ptolemies to the *'Abbāsids*. Burlington: Ashgate, pp. 105–26; Antoine Borrut, M. Debié, A. Papaconstantinou, D. Pieri, and J.-P. Sodini (eds) (2012), *Le Proche-Orient de Justinien aux Abbassides: Peuplement et dynamiques spatiales*. Turnhout: Brepols; Petra M. Sijpesteijn (forthcoming, 2013), *Shaping a Muslim State: The World of a Mid-Eighth-Century Egyptian Official*. Oxford: Oxford University Press.

7. For a thorough collection of texts from Greek, Syriac, Coptic, Armenian, Latin, Hebrew, Aramaic, Persian, and Chinese sources (including the apocalypses in Aramaic and Syriac) and discussions of the difficulties they present, see Robert G. Hoyland (1997), *Seeing Islam as Others Saw It: A Survey and Evaluation of Christian, Jewish, and Zoroastrian Writings on Early Islam*. Princeton: Darwin Press; see also Bernard Lewis (1950), "An Apocalyptic Vision of Islamic History," *Bulletin of the School of Oriental and African Studies* 13: 308–38; John C. Reeves (2005), *Trajectories in Near Eastern Apocalyptic: A Postrabbinic Jewish Apocalypse Reader*. Atlanta: Society of Biblical Literature; and Sean W. Anthony (2012), "Who Was the Shepherd of Damascus? The Enigma of Jewish and Messianist Responses to the Islamic Conquests in Marwānid Syria and Mesopotamia," in Paul M. Cobb (ed.), *The Lineaments of Islam: Studies in Honor of Fred McGraw Donner*. Leiden: Brill, pp. 21–59. On what those sources might say about early Islam itself, see Patricia Crone and M. A. Cook (1977), *Hagarism: The Making of the Islamic World*. New York: Cambridge University Press.

8. Cohen, *Under Crescent and Cross*.

9. Albrecht Noth (1987), "Abgrenzungsprobleme zwischen Muslimen und Nicht-Muslimen: Die Bedingungen Umars unter einem anderen Aspekt gelesen," *Jerusalem Studies in Arabic and Islam* 9: 290–315; Mark R. Cohen (1999), "What Was the Pact of 'Umar? A Literary-Historical Study," *Jerusalem Studies in Arabic and Islam* 23: 100–57; Milka Levy-Rubin (2005), "*Shurūt 'Umar* and its Alternatives: The Legal Debate on the Status of the *Dhimmīs*," *Jerusalem Studies in Arabic and Islam* 30: 170–206.

10. Cohen, *Under Crescent and Cross*, p. 58; Patricia Crone (1987), *Roman, Provincial and Islamic Law: The Origins of the Islamic Patronate*. Cambridge: Cambridge University Press.

11. *Walā'*: Patricia Crone (1980), *Slaves on Horses: The Evolution of the Islamic Polity*. Cambridge: Cambridge University Press. The dress clauses have recently been argued to have precedents in the highly regimented Sasanian legislation toward non-Zoroastrians: Milka Levy-Rubin (2011), *Non-Muslims in the Early Islamic Empire: From Surrender to Coexistence*. Cambridge: Cambridge University Press, pp. 113–63.

12. Jewish manuscripts of the Qur'ān: Cambridge University Library, T-S Ar. 51.62; Aleida Paudice (2008), "On Three Extant Sources of the Qur'ān Transcribed in Hebrew," *European Journal of Jewish Studies* 2: 213–57; see also Jonathan Decter (2006), "The Rendering of Qur'anic Quotations in Hebrew Translations of Islamic Texts," *Jewish Quarterly Review* 96: 336–58. Non-Muslim officials: Luke Benson Yarbrough (2012), "Islamizing the Islamic State: The Formulation and Assertion of Religious Criteria for State Employment in the First Millennium AH," PhD diss., Princeton University (for the distinction between reflexive and imposed law, borrowed from David Freidenreich, see p. 14).

13. Camilla Adang (1996), *Muslim Writers on Judaism and the Hebrew Bible: From Ibn Rabban to Ibn Hazm*. Leiden: Brill; Camilla Adang and Sabine Schimidtke (2010), s.v. "Polemics (Muslim-Jewish)," in *EJIW*; eaedem (in process), "Polemics," in *The Cambridge History of Judaism, vol. 5: The Middle Ages*. Cambridge: Cambridge University Press. The legal status that derived from possessing revealed books held despite the Qur'ān's claim that Jews had tampered with the text of the Hebrew Bible (*tahrif*). On the *jizya* as onerous, see S. D. Goitein (1963), "Evidence on the Muslim Poll Tax from Non-Muslim Sources: A Geniza Study," *Journal of the Economic and Social History of the Orient* 6: 278–95. On Jewish communal assistance with the *jizya*, see

Mark R. Cohen (2005), *Poverty and Charity in the Jewish Community of Medieval Egypt*. Princeton: Princeton University Press, pp. 136–8; and for a thirteenth-century Coptic testimony to Jewish solidarity around the *jizya*, see Tamer el-Leithy (2005), "Coptic Culture and Conversion in Medieval Cairo, 1293–1524 A.D.," PhD diss., Princeton University, p. 45. Conversion to Judaism: Mark R. Cohen (2005), *The Voice of the Poor in the Middle Ages: An Anthology of Documents from the Cairo Geniza* (Princeton: Princeton University Press) has numerous examples of charity lists with entries marked as converts (*ha-ger* or *al-ger*), and it is difficult to sustain Goitein's argument that they were all recent arrivals from Latin Christian Europe who became poor as a result of their conversion; see S. D. Goitein (1967–93), *A Mediterranean Society: The Jews of the Arab World as Mirrored in the Documents of the Cairo Geniza*. 5 Vols. Berkeley: University of California Press, Vol. 2, pp. 299–311. Access to patrons in government: Jews were hardly alone in this, but the organized yet not entirely stratified character of the community may have facilitated access. Exemption: Geoffrey Khan (1993), *Arabic Legal and Administrative Documents in the Cambridge Genizah Collections*. Cambridge: Cambridge University Press, documents 86, 89, 136.

14. The best account of the gaonic period in Iraq in English is Robert Brody (1998), *The Geonim of Babylonia and the Shaping of Medieval Jewish Culture* (New Haven: Yale University Press), which also encompasses all earlier Hebrew-language scholarship; for gaonic historiography, see Gerson Cohen (1991), "The Reconstruction of Gaonic History," in idem, *Studies in the Variety of Rabbinic Cultures*. Philadelphia: Jewish Publication Society, pp. 99–123; Neil Danzig (1997), "Geonic Jurisprudence from the Cairo Genizah: An Appreciation of Early Scholarship," *Proceedings of the American Academy for Jewish Research* 63: 1–47. On the title gaon, see Brody, *The Geonim*, p. 49. On the problem of continuity and institutionalization of the Babylonian yeshivot, see David M. Goodblatt (1975), *Rabbinic Instruction in Sasanian Babylonia*. Leiden: Brill, and the later contributions to the debate reviewed in Sacha Stern (2008), "Rabbinic Academies in Late Antiquity: State of Current Research," *L'Enseignement supérieur dans les mondes antiques et médiévaux*. Paris: J. Vrin, pp. 221–38. On the location of Sura and Pumbedita, see the references in Marina Rustow (2008), *Heresy and the Politics of Community: The Jews of the Fatimid Caliphate*. Ithaca: Cornell University Press, pp. 7–8, n. 6.

15. Letters by Iraqi geonim: Moshe Gil (1997), *In the Kingdom of Ishmael*. 4 Vols. Tel Aviv: Tel Aviv University [Hebrew], Vol. 2. Responsa: see Brody, *The Geonim*, pp. 185–201, and for questions about the earliest attributions, Brody, *The Geonim*, pp. 185–6, n. 2.

16. Brody, *The Geonim*, pp. 19–34; 113–17.

17. Ibid., pp. 202 15, 216–32; Neil Danzig (1993), *Introduction to Hulakhot Pesuqot with a Supplement to Halakhot Pesuqot* (2nd edn). New York: Jewish Theological Seminary of America [Hebrew]; Aharon Shweka (2008), "Studies in Halakhot Gedolot: Text and Recension," PhD diss., Hebrew University of Jerusalem [Hebrew].

18. Robert Brody (2003), *Pirqoy ben Baboy and the History of Internal Polemics in Judaism*. Tel Aviv: Tel Aviv University [Hebrew]; Neil Danzig (2008), "Between Eretz-Yisrael and Bavel: New Leaves from Pirqoi ben Baboi," *Shalem* 8: 1–32 [Hebrew]. In English, see Robert Brody (2010), s.v. "Pirqoy ben Baboy," in *EJIW*. The fragments of Pirqoy's epistles have yet to be studied carefully from the point of view of the material evidence they provide for the polemic's circulation and transmission. See Moshe Gil (1992), *A History of Palestine, 634–1099*, Ethel Broido (trans.). Cambridge: Cambridge University Press, sec. 808 n.

19. On the exilarch, see Menahem Ben-Sasson (1995), "Varieties of Inter-Communal Relations in the Geonic Period," in Daniel Frank (ed.), *The Jews of Medieval Islam: Community, Society, and Identity*. Leiden: Brill, pp. 17–31; Brody, *The Geonim*, pp. 67–82; and Arnold Franklin (2012), *This Noble House: Jewish Descendants of King David in the Medieval Islamic East*. Philadelphia: University of Pennsylvania Press.

20. Arnold Franklin (2010), s.v. "Exilarch," in *EJIW*. The exilarch's letter: T-S 8G7.1, published most recently in Sacha Stern (2001), *Calendar and Community: A History of the Jewish Calendar, Second Century BCE-Tenth Century CE.* Oxford: Oxford University Press, pp. 277–83.

21. Rustow, *Heresy and the Politics of Community*, pp. 13–14.

22. Yitzhak Baer (1950), "The Origins of Jewish Communal Organization in the Middle Ages," *Zion* 40: 1–46 [Hebrew]; for opposing views, see Goitein, *A Mediterranean Society.* Vol. 2, chapter V; Menahem Ben-Sasson (1997), *The Emergence of the Local Jewish Community in the Muslim World: Qayrawan, 800–1057* (2nd edn). Jerusalem: Magnes Press [Hebrew]; and Mark R. Cohen (1997), "Jewish Communal Organization in Medieval Egypt: Research, Results and Prospects," *Judaeo-Arabic Studies* 1: 73–86.

23. The history of Karaism is currently being rewritten as scholars investigate the thousands of manuscripts collected by Abraham Firkovitch over the course of the nineteenth century, now housed in St. Petersburg and available to international researchers since 1991. Leon Nemoy (1952), *A Karaite Anthology: Excerpts from the Early Literature* (New Haven: Yale University Press) is nonetheless still a useful sampling of texts; some of the essays in Meira Polliack (ed.) (2003), *Karaite Judaism: a Guide to Its History and Literary Sources* (Leiden: Brill) provide useful introductions; Haggai Ben-Shammai (1993), "Between Ananites and Karaites: Observations on Early Medieval Jewish Sectarianism," in Ronald L. Nettler (ed.), *Studies in Muslim-Jewish Relations.* Vol. 1 (Chur: Harwood Academic Publishers) is fundamental; for Karaite interpretations of history, see Fred Astren (2004), *Karaite Judaism and Historical Understanding.* Columbia: University of South Carolina Press; on exegesis, Daniel Frank (2004), *Search Scripture Well: Karaite Exegetes and the Origins of the Jewish Bible Commentary in the Islamic East.* Leiden: Brill; on the problems associated with viewing Karaites as a sect, see Marina Rustow (2011), "The Qaraites as Sect: The Tyranny of a Construct," in Sacha Stern (ed.), *Sects and Sectarianism in Jewish History.* Leiden: Brill, pp. 149–86; and for a comprehensive bibliography, see Barry Walfish and Mikhail Kizilov (2011), *Bibliographia Karaitica: An Annotated Bibliography of Karaites and Karaism.* Leiden: Brill.

24. On the tension created "by the introduction of rabbinic Judaism into the larger social system of Judaism," see Seth Schwartz (2002), "Rabbinization in the Sixth Century," in Peter Schäfer (ed.), *The Talmud Yerushalmi and Graeco- Roman Culture.* Tübingen: Mohr Siebeck, pp. 55–69, p. 55.

25. Brody, *The Geonim*, p. 63; idem (1984–86), "Were the Geonim Legislators?," *Shenaton ha-Mishpat ha-Ivri* 11–12: 279–315 [Hebrew].

26. The moves to Baghdad: Brody, *The Geonim*, p. 36. Cosmopolitan geonim: David Sklare (1996), *Samuel ben Hofni: Gaon and His Cultural World: Texts and Studies.* Leiden: Brill, especially Chapter 4.

27. Adam Silverstein (2007), *Postal Systems in the Pre-Modern Islamic World.* Cambridge: Cambridge University Press, chapters 2 and 3; S. D. Goitein (1964), "Commercial Mail Service in Medieval Islam," *Journal of the American Oriental Society* 84: 118–23, with references to earlier studies; idem, *A Mediterranean Society*, Vol. 1, pp. 281–95; and Abraham L. Udovitch (1978), "Time, the Sea, and Society: Duration of Commercial Voyages on the Southern Shores of the Mediterranean during the High Middle Ages," *Settimane di studio del Centro italiano di studi sull'alto medioevo* 25: 503–46.

28. Rādhāniyya (also Radhanites; the Arabic name is a toponymic *nisba*): S. D. Goitein (1974), *Jews and Arabs: Their Contacts through the Ages.* New York: Schocken, pp. 105–7; Moshe Gil (1974), "The Rādhānite Merchants and the Land of Rādhān," *Journal of the Economic and Social History of the Orient* 17: 299–328; idem (1997), *In the Kingdom of Ishmael.* 4 Vols. Tel Aviv: University of Tel Aviv [Hebrew], Vol. 1, sections 344–6; Adam Silverstein (2007), "From Markets to Marvels: Jews on the Maritime Route to

China ca. 850–ca. 950 C.E.," *Journal of Jewish Studies* 58: 91–104. Banū Netīra: see most recently Gil, *In the Kingdom of Ishmael,* Vol. 1, sections 137, 144–5.

29. Writing in the alphabet associated with one's religion was common in the premodern world, and there are vestiges of the practice today: Russian is written in Cyrillic, but Polish in Latin characters; Hindi in Sanskrit-derived Devanagari script, but Urdu in an Arabic/Persian-derived script.

30. On Judaeo-Arabic and Middle Arabic, see Joshua Blau (1999), *The Emergence and Linguistic Background of Judaeo-Arabic: A Study of the Origins of Neo-Arabic and Middle Arabic* (3rd edn). Jerusalem: Ben-Zvi Institute for the Study of Jewish Communities in the East. On Middle Arabic as a *koine,* see ibid., pp. 52–4

31. Rina Drory (2010), *Models and Contacts: Arabic Literature and Its Impact on Medieval Jewish Culture.* Leiden: Brill; eadem (1988), *The Emergence of Jewish-Arabic Literary Contacts at the Beginning of the Tenth Century.* Tel Aviv: ha-Kibuts ha-meʾuhad [Hebrew].

32. See Robert Brody (2013), *Saʿadyah Gaon.* Oxford: Littman Library of Jewish Civilization.

33. That is not to say that Judaeo-Arabic left complete linguistic uniformity in its wake. East of Iraq, Jews continued to write in Persian, while the mountain communities of Kurdistan, both Jews and Christians, retained Aramaic as a spoken language (dwindling numbers of them still do today). On the Iberian Peninsula and in Sicily, Jews (and others) used Latin and Romance languages alongside Arabic.

34. al-Muqaddisī (al-Maqdisī), Muhammad b. Ahmad (1906), *Ahsan al-taqāsīm fi maʿrifat al-aqālīm (The Best Divisions for Knowledge of the Regions).* Leiden: Brill, p. 193; on his forebears, p. 357 (cf. p. 188). On the migration, see Goitein, *A Mediterranean Society,* Vol. 1, pp. 30–3; Eliyahu Ashtor (1972), "Un movement migratoire au haut moyen âge: Migrations de l'Irak vers les pays méditerranéens," *Annales: Economies, sociétés, civilizations* 27: 185–214; Mark R. Cohen (1984), "Administrative Relations between Palestinian and Egyptian Jewry During the Fatimid Period," in Amnon Cohen and Gabriel Baer (eds), *Egypt and Palestine: A Millennium of Association (868–1948).* Jerusalem: Ben-Zvi Institute, pp. 119–20.

35. Gerson D. Cohen (1967), *A Critical Edition with a Translation and Notes of the Book of Tradition (Sefer Ha-Qabbalah).* Philadelphia: Jewish Publication Society; and for an exhaustive form-critical analysis of the section discussed here, idem (1960), "The Story of the Four Captives," *Proceedings of the American Academy of Jewish Research* 29: 55–123.

36. The Cairo Geniza proper is the manuscript storage space in the attic of the medieval synagogue in Cairo where the Syro-Palestinian-rite congregation prayed, now known as the Ben ʾEzra synagogue. But there are related manuscript caches such as the Firkovitch collections, most (or all?) of which comes not from the Ben ʾEzra but from a Karaite synagogue; and there is doubt as to the provenance of some material classified in libraries as having come from the Ben ʾEzra Geniza (private dealers did not specify provenance, and many libraries assumed Hebrew script finds from Egypt to have come from the Ben ʾEzra Geniza). See Haggai Ben-Shammai (2010), "Is 'The Cairo Genizah' a Proper Name or a Generic Noun? On the Relationship between the *Genizot* of the Ben Ezra and the Dār Simha Synagogues," in Ben Outhwaite and Siam Bhayro (eds), *"From a Sacred Source:" Genizah Studies in Honour of Professor Stefan C. Reif.* Leiden: Brill, pp. 43–52. For the history of the Geniza's discovery, see the wonderfully readable and thoroughly researched book by Adina Hoffman and Peter Cole (2010), *Sacred Trash: The Lost and Found World of the Cairo Geniza.* New York: Nextbook.

37. Shulamit Sela (2009), *The Arabic Book of Josippon: A Critical Edition with Annotated Translation.* Jerusalem: Ben-Zvi Institute [Hebrew]. See also David Flusser (1979–81), *The Josippon (Josephus Gorionides).* 2 Vols. Jerusalem: Shazar Center [Hebrew].

38. Menahem Ben-Sasson (2009), "Zikkaron ve-shikheha shel shemadot: 'al qiddush ha-shem be-artsot ha-notsrut u-ve-artsot ha-islam bimei ha-benayim," in Yosef Hacker, B. Z. Kedar, and Yosef Kaplan (eds), *From Sages to Savant: Studies Presented to Avraham Grossman*. Jerusalem: The Zalman Shazar Center for Jewish History, pp. 47–72 [Hebrew]. *Yosippon* is discussed on p. 51, and see the literature cited there, n. 6; cf. Cohen, *Under Crescent and Cross*, 162–94.

39. The letter: Jewish Theological Seminary of America, ENA NS 1.5 (L 41); for a full English translation, see S. D. Goitein (1974), "Judaeo-Arabic Letters from Spain: Early Twelfth Century," in J. M. Barral (ed.), *Orientalia Hispanica: sive studia F.M. Pareja octogenario dicata*. 2 Vols. Leiden: Brill, Vol. 1, pp. 331–50. Moshe Gil and Ezra Fleischer (2001), *Judah Halevi and His Circle: Fifty-Five Geniza Documents*. Jerusalem: World Union of Jewish Studies [Hebrew]. On the circulation of the *Kuzari* up until the twentieth century, see Adam Shear (2008), *The Kuzari and the Shaping of Jewish Identity*. Cambridge: Cambridge University Press.

40. "How things worked": the phrase is borrowed from Jessica L. Goldberg (2011), "On Reading Goitein's *A Mediterranean Society*: a View from Economic History," *Mediterranean Historical Review* 26: 171–86. On Jews in Islamic courts, see now Uriel Simonsohn (2011), *A Common Justice: The Legal Allegiances of Christians and Jews Under Early Islam*. Philadelphia: University of Pennsylvania Press; on petitions to caliphs, see Khan, *Arabic Legal and Administrative Documents*, and the works cited in Marina Rustow (2010), "A Petition to a Woman at the Fatimid Court," *Bulletin of the School of Oriental and African Studies* 73: 1–27, p. 2 n. 1.

41. For the number of Arabic papyri, see Sijpesteijn, "Arabic Papyri and Islamic Egypt," p. 453 (the 150,000 she cites include paper documents dated as late as the modern period; the number of early Islamic period finds could nonetheless be in the high five or low six figures).

42. Goitein, *A Mediterranean Society*. "Only a sketch": Mark R. Cohen (1987), "Shelomo Dov Goitein [Necrology]," *American Philosophical Society Yearbook*: 117–19. On Goitein, see Goldberg, "On Reading Goitein's *A Mediterranean Society*," and Fred Astren (2012), "Goitein, Medieval Jews, and the 'New Mediterranean Studies,'" *Jewish Quarterly Review* 102: 513–31.

43. S. D. Goitein (1980), *Palestinian Jewry in Early Islamic and Crusader Times: In the Light of the Geniza Documents*. Jerusalem: Yad Izhak Ben-Zvi Publications [Hebrew]; Gil, *A History of Palestine*; Miriam Frenkel (1990), *Qehillat Yehude Halab 'al pi kitve ha-Geniza*, MA thesis, Hebrew University; Elinoar Bareket (1995), *Jewish Leadership in Fustat*. Tel Aviv: ha-Makhon le-heqer ha-tefutsot [Hebrew]; eadem (1999), *Fustat on the Nile: The Jewish Elite in Medieval Egypt*. Leiden: Brill; Menahem Ben-Sasson (1991), *The Jews of Sicily, 825–1068*. Jerusalem: Mekhon Ben-Tsevi le-heqer qehillot Yisra'el ba-Mizrah [Hebrew]; Gil, *In the Kingdom of Ishmael* (focusing mainly on Iraq but also including chapters on the Arabian Peninsula and Sicily); Miriam Frenkel (2006), *"The Compassionate and Benevolent:" the Leading Elite in the Jewish Community of Alexandria in the Middle Ages*. Jerusalem: Mekhon Ben-Tsevi le-heqer qehillot Yisra'el ba-Mizrah [Hebrew]; Roxani Eleni Margariti (2007), *Aden and the Indian Ocean Trade: 150 Years in the Life of a Medieval Arabian Port*. Chapel Hill: University of North Carolina Press.

44. Norman A. Stillman (1970), "East-West Relations in the Islamic Mediterranean in the Early Eleventh Century: A Study of the Geniza Correspondence of the House of Ibn 'Awkal," PhD diss., University of Pennsylvania; Moshe Gil (1976), *Documents of the Jewish Pious Foundations from the Cairo Geniza*. Leiden: Brill; Margariti, *Aden and the Indian Ocean Trade*; M. A. Friedman and S. D. Goitein (2008), *India Traders of the Middle Ages: Documents from the Cairo Geniza*. Leiden: Brill, plus three volumes of Judaeo-Arabic texts published with Hebrew translation and commentary; Jessica L. Goldberg (2012), *Trade and Institutions in the Medieval Mediterranean: The Geniza*

Merchants and Their Business World. New York: Cambridge University Press; Phillip Ackerman-Lieberman (forthcoming), *The Business of Identity: Jews, Muslims, and Economic Life in Medieval Egypt*. Stanford: Stanford University Press.

45. Mark R. Cohen (1980), *Jewish Self-Government in Medieval Egypt: The Origins of the Office of Head of the Jews, ca. 1065–1126*. Princeton: Princeton University Press; idem "Administrative Relations"; Menahem Ben-Sasson (1987), "Fragmentary Letters from the Geniza: On the History of the Renewed Links between the Babylonian Academies and the West," *Tarbiz* 56: 31–82 [Hebrew]; idem (1989), "The Links between the Maghrib and the Mashriq in the Ninth through Eleventh Centuries," *Pe'amim* 38: 35–48 [Hebrew]; idem, *Emergence of the Local Jewish Community in the Muslim World*; idem (2004), "Religious Leadership in Islamic Lands: Forms of Leadership and Sources of Authority," in J. Wertheimer (ed.), *Jewish Religious Leadership: Image and Reality*. New York: Jewish Theological Seminary, pp. 177–209; Rustow, *Heresy and the Politics of Community*; and Franklin, *This Noble House*.

46. M. A. Friedman (1980–1), *Jewish Marriage in Palestine: A Cairo Genizah Study*. 2 Vols. Tel Aviv: Tel Aviv University; idem (1986), *Jewish Polygyny: New Sources from the Cairo Geniza*. Jerusalem: Mosad Bialik [Hebrew]; Judith Olszowy-Schlanger (1998), *Karaite Marriage Documents from the Cairo Geniza: Legal Tradition and Community Life in Mediaeval Egypt and Palestine*. Leiden: Brill; Amir Ashur (2006), "Engagement and Betrothal Documents from the Cairo Geniza," PhD diss., Tel Aviv University. 2 Vols; Eve Krakowski (2012), "Female Adolescence in the Cairo Geniza Documents," PhD diss., University of Chicago.

47. Marina Rustow (2010), "The Genizah and Communal History," in Outhwaite and Bhayro (eds), *"From a Sacred Source,"* pp. 289–317, p. 293 (the categorizations there differ). Mention must also be made of the only book-length follow-up to Goitein's studies of material culture in *A Mediterranean Society,* Vol. 4: Yedida Kalfon Stillman (2003), *Arab Dress: A Short History from the Dawn of Islam to Modern Times* (2nd edn). Leiden: Brill.

48. This echoes the debate over how established the Mesopotamian yeshivot were in the pre-Islamic period. For the debate in the medieval Islamic context, see Roy Mottahedeh (2001, orig. 1980), *Loyalty and Leadership in an Early Islamic Society*. London: I. B. Tauris; George Makdisi (1981), *The Rise of the Colleges: Institutions of Learning in Islam and the West*. Edinburgh: Edinburgh University Press; Jonathan P. Berkey (1992), *The Transmission of Knowledge in Medieval Cairo: A Social History of Islamic Education*. Princeton: Princeton University Press; Carl F. Petry (2002), "Educational Institutions as Depicted in the Biographical Literature of Mamluk Cairo: The Debate over Prestige and Venue," *Medieval Prosopography* 23: 101–23.

49. On informalism in trade, see, A. L. Udovitch (1988), "Merchants and *Amirs*: Government and Trade in Eleventh-Century Egypt," *Asian and African Studies* 22: 53–72; idem (1977), "Formalism and Informalism in the Social and Economic Institutions of the Medieval Islamic World," in Amin Banani and Spiros Vryonis (eds), *Individualism and Conformity in Classical Islam*. Wiesbaden: Harrassowitz, pp. 71–81; Avner Greif (1989), "Reputation and Coalitions in Medieval Trade: Evidence on the Maghribi Traders," *The Journal of Economic History* 49:4: 857–82; idem (2006), *Institutions and the Path to the Modern Economy: Lessons from Medieval Trade*. Cambridge: Cambridge University Press. For a middle path between formalized legal institutions and informal mechanisms, see Margariti, *Aden and the Indian Ocean Trade*; Goldberg, *Trade and Institutions*; eadem (2012), "Choosing and Enforcing Business Relationships in the Eleventh Century Mediterranean: Reassessing the 'Maghribī Traders,'" *Past and Present* 216: 3–40; Ackerman-Lieberman, *The Business of Identity*. On Shelomo b. Yehuda, see most recently Rustow, *Heresy and the Politics of Community*, with reference to previous studies, especially Gil, *A History of Palestine*.

50. Al-Andalus is the Arabic name for the part of Iberia ruled by Muslims, whether it was great (after the initial conquests in 711) or small (after Las Navas de Tolosa in 1212, until 1492). Jews writing in Hebrew referred to the entire Iberian peninsula as Sepharad (after Obad. 1.20); Spain is a name that postdates the unification of the peninsula under the Catholic monarchs.

51. Eliyahu Ashtor (1963), "The Number of the Jews in Moslem Spain," *Zion* 28: 34–56 [Hebrew]; see also idem (1973–84), *The Jews of Moslem Spain*. 3 Vols. Philadelphia: Jewish Publication Society, still the only monographic survey of its kind in English. For a skeptical view of the claims of Jewish aid to the Muslim conquerors, see Fred Astren (2009), "Re-Reading the Arabic Sources: Jewish History and the Muslim Conquests," *Jerusalem Studies in Arabic and Islam* 36: 83–130.

52. The Khazar letter: Norman Golb and Omeljan Pritsak (1982), *Khazarian Hebrew Documents of the Tenth Century*. Ithaca: Cornell University Press; the letter from Hayya: T-S 10G5.8 and T-S 20.100, in Gil, *In the Kingdom of Ishmael*, Vol. 2, document 37. See also Jonathan Decter (2012), "Before Caliphs and Kings: Jewish Courtiers in Medieval Iberia," in Jonathan Ray (ed.), *The Jew in Medieval Iberia*. Boston: Academic Studies Press, pp. 1–32.

53. Ross Brann (1991), *The Compunctious Poet: Cultural Ambiguity and Hebrew Poetry in Muslim Spain*. Baltimore: Johns Hopkins University Press; idem (2002), *Power in the Portrayal: Representations of Muslims and Jews in Islamic Spain*. Princeton: Princeton University Press; Jonathan Decter (2007), *Iberian Jewish Literature: Between al-Andalus and Christian Europe* (Bloomington: Indiana University Press), which treats the long transition from Islamic to Christian rule as a distinctive period in its own right.

54. "Gentleman among savages": quoted in Norman Stillman (2010), s.v. "al-Andalus," in *EJIW*.

55. Sarah Stroumsa (2011), *Maimonides in His World: Portrait of a Mediterranean Thinker*. Princeton: Princeton University Press.

56. Rustow, "The Qaraites as Sect," pp. 152–7. On Alfonso, see Ryan Szpiech (2012), *Conversion and Narrative: Reading Authority in Medieval Polemic*. Philadelphia: University of Pennsylvania Press, Chapter 5.

57. Yitzhak Baer (1961), *A History of the Jews in Christian Spain*. 2 Vols. Philadelphia: Jewish Publication Society, Vol. 1, pp. 323 ff; Yom Tov Assis (1992), "The Jews in the Crown of Aragon and Its Dominions," in *Moreshet Sepharad: The Sephardi Legacy*, ed. Haim Beinart, 2 Vols. Jerusalem: Magnes Press, Vol. 1, pp. 74 ff.

58. Eliyahu Ashtor (1944–76), *A History of the Jews in Egypt and Syria under the Rule of the Mamluks*. 3 Vols. Jerusalem: Mosad Harav Kook [Hebrew]; Mark R. Cohen (1984), "Jews in the Mamlūk Environment: The Crisis of 1442 (a Geniza Study)," *Bulletin of the School of Oriental and African Studies* 27: 425–48; Marina Rustow (2009), "At the Limits of Communal Autonomy: Jewish Bids for Government Interference," in *Mamlūk Studies Review* 13: 133–59; el-Leithy, "Coptic Culture"; Elisha Russ-Fishbane (2009), "Between Politics and Piety: Abraham Maimonides and His Times," PhD diss., Harvard University; Nathan Hofer (2011), "Sufism, State, and Society in Ayyubid and Early Mamluk Egypt, 1173–1309," PhD diss., Emory University.

59. Marina Rustow (2007), "Karaites Real and Imagined: Three Cases of Jewish Heresy," *Past and Present* 197: 35–74.

6 Medieval Jews and Judaism in Christian Contexts

Elisheva Baumgarten

Introduction

Despite the common majority religion, Jewish communal life under Christianity differed significantly according to the ruling power: what remained of the Byzantine Empire (a reduced but still sizeable area compared to previous centuries), central and northern Italy (the southern part and Sicily being included in Byzantium), the Christian kingdoms of the Iberian Peninsula, and large parts of northern and central Europe.[1] Our knowledge of Jewish life in each area varies tremendously based on the kind and number of sources that have survived in Hebrew, Latin, and vernacular languages.

The history of the Jews under Christendom has often been told as one of persecutions and expulsions, starting from some of the earliest known documents that described persecutions in Visigothic Spain or early medieval Byzantium, and ending with the expulsions of the Jews from England (1290), northern France (1182, 1306, and 1394), and finally from Spain and Portugal (1492 and 1497). As early as 1928, Salo Baron called for a new narrative, one that was not "lachrymose" (as he called previous histories), but reflected the creativity and vibrancy of Jewish life and how Jews engaged with their surroundings while retaining their own separate identity.[2] The result of this call for a new approach has emerged over the past decades. At the same time, the pendulum has swung back and forth between lachrymose and anti-lachrymose histories, often varying according to the subject matter and sources. Whereas discussions of rabbinic literature have long seen this period as one of tremendous creativity, from the commentaries of Rashi and his students to the Tosafist oeuvre and Kabbalah, the narrative of a Jewish community that thrived spiritually despite their oppression and lived in relative isolation still holds currency. And despite the attempts to create a new narrative, all historians agree that the story of the Jews in medieval Europe must include some explanation and contextualization of the growing animosity toward them.

Settlement and Migration

Patterns of Jewish settlement varied across the areas under Christian rule: in some areas, Jews had lived for centuries before Christianization, whereas in others they arrived only when Christianization was already well under way. In the Byzantine Empire, Jews had to adjust to a new status when Christianity, once a persecuted religion, became the dominant one. According to principles first set out by Augustine (354–430), the Jewish presence in Christendom should be tolerated, since the political subjection of the Jews served as proof of the truth of Christianity and it expressed the hope that the Jews might still be converted. Fourth- and fifth-century Byzantine legal codes—one of the richest sources we have for the period—followed these principles in legislation concerning relationships among Jews, life in urban centers, and consideration of the formal obligation Jews had toward the empire.[3] Amnon Linder has collected and analysed the Roman legal documents according to these three categories of analysis. Jews' obligations toward the empire included, in some places, a formal requirement to serve on city councils; imperial regulation of their religious life included, among other issues, legislation about reading practices in the synagogue. This last example is a fascinating one: the church sought to legitimize the use of languages other than Hebrew in the synagogue ritual (primarily Greek and Aramaic). Jewish leaders objected strongly to this idea.[4]

The sources for medieval Byzantine Jewish history are not plentiful. Those that have survived indicate that Jews were granted freedom of settlement and movement, and that there was a Jewish presence throughout the empire, in cities from Constantinople and the rest of Asia Minor to southern Italy. The Byzantine Empire lost territory to Islam over the course of the seventh and eighth centuries. Jewish communities appear to have been affected by what has been defined as a general decline of cities throughout the Byzantine Empire after the rise of Islam. The sources provide evidence of the places of Jewish settlement, the names of some community leaders and scholars, edicts of persecution, and polemics, but little more can be said about aspects of daily and community life. There are also a few Jewish compositions—including some that are messianic in nature and some that are liturgical poems; scholars, with recently renewed interest, have suggested connections between them and the milieu in which they were written. Whereas earlier historiography tended to emphasize the tensions between Jews and Byzantine Christians, of which there is some evidence in polemics, other scholars, such as Steven Bowman, have underlined the harmony in which the Jews lived with their neighbors, especially in comparison to later periods. But with the exception of southern Italy, which will be discussed below, details of Jewish life in these areas are not abundant, and it is difficult even to estimate how large Byzantine Jewish communities were. There is especially scant information for the period following the Fourth Crusade in 1204.[5]

With the Crusader invasion of 1204, when Constantinople was sacked and then ruled by Western powers until 1261, a new chapter in Byzantine history began. After this point, Jews in the Byzantine Empire, called "Romaniot" after the Greek and Latin words for inhabitants of the empire in general (*romaioi, romani*), were as fragmented as the empire itself. The main center of Byzantine Jewish population was in the Balkans until the Ottomans captured Constantinople in 1453 and forcibly resettled Jews there. Before then, the Jewish communities were often on the move, whether to Poland and eastern Europe or to Ottoman lands.[6]

Much more is known of the Jewish community in southern Italy, especially in the ninth and tenth centuries. The sources are few but provide rich information on Jewish cultural life: *Sefer Yossipon, Megillat Ahima'az*, a number of halakhic texts, and the *Book of Yerahmi'el* (known from its later German rendition but referring back to the tenth century) have allowed scholars to outline the contours of southern Italian Jewish culture.[7] Southern Italy was seen in later generations as an important center of halakhic study; one source from the period proclaimed (after Mic. 4.2), "From Bari Torah will come forth and the word of God from Otranto."[8] It was also a center of medical and scientific practice, to judge by the writings by Shabbetai Donnolo, a physician and scholar born in Oria and known for his *Book of Remedies* and his commentary on *Sefer Yetzirah* (Book of Creation). The texts from this period, alongside archaeological evidence, begin to allow for a reconstruction of Jewish life. One theme that has emerged is the many ways in which the Jews adapted customs from their surroundings but remained distinct from their Christian neighbors. For example, the *Chronicle of Ahima'az* tells of Jews using magic in ways that replicated common Christian methods, but altering references to Jesus so as to underline the veracity of Judaism. In this way, the literary texts provide a rich tapestry of Jewish beliefs as well as hints of the culture within which the Jews lived and the beliefs that were prevalent among their neighbors.[9]

Southern Italy underwent major political turmoil. The area was conquered and reconquered by Muslims and Byzantines as described above, and then by Normans (1060–91), Hohenstaufens (1194), Angevins (1266), and Aragonese (1302). During the Norman period, Jews driven out of Iberia and North Africa by the Almohad persecutions came through southern Italy and settled there; during the reign of the Hohenstaufens, they were central in translating texts from Arabic to Latin and Hebrew, providing cultural commodities that would become important throughout western Europe in the later Middle Ages.[10] Jews in southern Italy were closely tied to those of Iberia, who experienced similar transitions in the face of the conquests. The Jews of Sicily were eventually expelled in 1492 together with the Jews of Christian Spain.

From southern Italy, Jews moved northward and westward in Latin Europe as well as to Islamic lands, founding new Jewish communities and joining older ones. Jews called the Jewish communities of medieval northern Europe Ashkenaz.[11] In modern scholarship, this term has come to include modern Germany, northern France, England, northern Italy, Bohemia, and most of central Europe until Poland. The tendency to lump these locations into one cultural entity stems from their shared halakhic and ritual traditions, but medieval Jews themselves distinguished among these different regions, based in part on the variety of languages they spoke and in part on their differing rulers.

Foundation legends relate Jewish settlement in these new communities back to more ancient periods and even to the destruction of the Temple, but the first medieval sources about Jewish settlement in northern France and Germany date to the ninth century.[12] The emigration of the Kalonymos family from southern Italy to Germany marked the genesis of the Jewish communities of Ashkenaz. In northern France, a small number of families received privileges to settle in cities and conduct trade. Little is known of these early immigrants except that they came with their families and settled along the central trade routes at the invitation of the local and regional powers, who wanted to attract Jewish trade and commerce to their territories. The first communities were small and headed by leaders who were reputed businessmen and scholars: the earliest charter inviting Jews to France was granted to two men who were relatives and their families. In the Rhineland, the Kalonymos family remained a central force in society in both business and Torah study throughout the medieval period.[13]

Legal Status and Jewish Cultural Life before the First Crusade

Jewish communities in western Europe shared some important features, especially their legal underpinnings. The first information we have for many of them are the legal charters that allowed Jews to settle in the expanding urban centers and to live as an autonomous minority, formalizing the Jews' relationships with the regional and local rulers. The most detailed documents from this period are those from the newest settlements in northern Europe; thus despite their relative youth, they are often highlighted in scholarly writings. The earliest charter dates to mid-ninth-century France, and it is typical of the language of the charters throughout the medieval period; rulers tended to draw on each other's charters, from the earliest in France to the later ones of newly conquered Christian Iberia and late medieval Poland. Jews were granted freedom of movement as well as the right to live their lives within their communities and to be judged in internal Jewish matters by their own courts of law. The early charters, which were granted by emperors, kings, and local authorities, also determined Jews' tax obligations, guidelines for trade, and their right to employ Christian servants in their homes. Some also attest to the special arrangements that were made once a new group of Jews arrived: in 1084, the bishop of Speyer, Rüdiger Huozmann, allotted the Jews whom he granted settlement rights land for a cemetery and a special Jewish quarter.[14]

Parallel to the charters, there are internal Jewish community ordinances (*takkanot*). The earliest of these are attributed to R. Gershom Me'or ha-Golah (Light of the Exile) in the tenth century. The ordinances concern community self-definition, the organization of ritual life, and the social order: the types of haircuts allowed, synagogue procedures, internal communal taxes, and marriage law (a ban on polygyny and a ban on divorcing one's wife without her consent are attributed to R. Gershom, but were probably widely accepted only later).[15]

Archeological finds from the Rhineland and northern France indicate that Jewish communities built synagogues in the center of the towns and cities they inhabited, often close to the central cathedrals. The Hebrew and Latin sources also suggest that Jews were actively involved in both agriculture and in local and regional trade.[16] One major concern of these communities, evidenced in halakhic responsa from the tenth and eleventh centuries, was their relative jurisdiction in relationship to each other. Jews traveled from place to place and conducted business transactions along the way; the question naturally arose whether their original locality still had authority over them. Responsa also discuss how communal decisions should be made and enforced—by the recognized elders or majority rule? The most plentiful Hebrew sources for the period, in addition to responsa, are commentaries on the Bible and Talmud and liturgical poems (*piyyutim*), many of which would remain part of the standard prayer rites in these areas for centuries. The centrality of *piyyut* is also attested by the large number of liturgical poets and commentaries on *piyyutim*.[17] These works were written in Hebrew and Aramaic, which were also used for communication with Jewish communities in other regions; but in daily life, medieval Ashkenazic Jews spoke the local vernaculars.

The Jewish communities were small and numbered dozens of families at most, in some places only a handful. The sources do not permit a detailed characterization of the relationships between Jews and their neighbors. On the one hand, recent scholarship has outlined the extent to which Jews were involved in local and regional trade, and the charters confirm these activities.[18] At the same time, anti-Jewish polemical writings, mainly by clergymen, expressed animosity toward Jews. The hostility toward Jews one finds in the sources was not motivated solely by theology; one can also find in them evidence of the power struggles between the church and the state. Thus Agobard, bishop of Lyons (774–840), was at odds with King Louis the Pious (778–840), who had granted a charter to the Jews to settle in France; he therefore composed a polemic against them (the earliest source to mention the *Toldot Yeshu* [Generations of Jesus], a Jewish parody of the Christian gospels).[19]

Scholars have suggested that during this period, a significant number of Jews converted to Christianity, either during attacks on the Jewish community or during the regular routine of urban life. In fact, medieval sources mention that R. Gershom Light of the Exile's own son converted, an indication of how common conversion was. Some forced converts returned to Judaism as soon as it was safe to do so. As Jacob Katz demonstrated, the accepted Jewish belief not only after but before the First Crusade was that a convert should be reintegrated into Jewish communal life, despite his or her lapse.[20]

Jews arrived in England from northern France together with the Norman conquerors of 1066. Latin legal texts attesting to Jews in England are more abundant than on the continent, while the Hebrew texts are fewer; these include charters, court rolls, and deeds, and allow for a detailed understanding of Jewish life: how Jews conducted business, patterns of landownership within certain cities, and the affairs of specific families can be traced in detail. Some English Jews who were successful in business became moneylenders to the king or to churches and monasteries.[21]

The contacts among the Jews of England, Germany, and northern France were frequent and close. While each community had its own identity and spoke different vernaculars (though those of northern France and England were mutually comprehensible), they shared customs and sources of authority. During the eleventh century, many scholars traveled from northern France to the Rhineland to study. One was R. Solomon b. Isaac (Rashi) of Troyes, who studied in Worms and returned to Champagne, becoming renowned as an exegete and scholar.[22]

The First Crusade

While tenth- and eleventh-century sources from northern Europe attest to anti-Jewish polemic among those associated with the church as well as limited cases of anti-Jewish persecution, they also depict small communities living among their Christian neighbors and engaging with them in business, living in the same town quarters and holding local celebrations together. The records from the late eleventh and early twelfth century present a gradual change from the perspective of the sources available to scholars—as the number of sources increases over time and, as a result,so do the kinds of questions historians can ask. Yet the quantity of sources is just one aspect of the changes that can be discerned in this period.[23] The more significant break between the previous century and the twelfth century are the events of the First Crusade which changed European and Mediterranean geography and politics.

The papal call to the Holy Land as part of the First Crusade was related to larger Christian and Muslim politics, both internal and between the religions. In northern Europe, the enthusiasm for the Crusade was the result of class struggles between knights and peasants as well as part of an ongoing struggle for dominance between the church and the state. As part of some of these internal debates, the Jews and their place as non-Christians within the Christian landscape became central in the rhetoric and events surrounding the Crusades. As crusaders gathered to embark, driven by an ideology that emphasized the unbelief of the Muslims, some groups and their leaders turned against the non-Christian communities they passed along the way. In the Rhineland, in the Mosel valley, in Prague, and in Bohemia—though not in the centers of Jewish life in Champagne—Jewish communities were attacked by bands of crusaders, at times joined by locals. They ordered Jews to undergo baptism, some giving them the choice between conversion and death. Both the Hebrew and Latin chronicles of these events make it clear that the Jews were often defended by the local rulers and burghers with whom they had negotiated privileges.[24]

Jews' responses to the demand for their conversion varied. Some communities converted en bloc and were later given imperial permission to return to Judaism. Others, especially in the three central Rhineland communities, Speyer, Worms, and Mainz (abbreviated in the Hebrew sources as Shum), chose instead to sacrifice themselves and their families (in the Hebrew sources, this is called sanctifying God's name, *kiddush ha-shem*). As martyrdom was not mandated by Jewish law, it required some soul searching after the events to justify this course of action. In the Hebrew chronicles, the martyrs became a symbol of Jewish devotion and piety.[25] Recent scholarship aside, the historiography has discussed the Jewish martyrs much more frequently than those who chose to convert.

Scholars have disagreed over the extent to which the Crusades changed the course of Jewish life in northern Europe and especially in the Rhineland during the early twelfth century. Nineteenth- and early twentieth-century historiography saw the First Crusade as a watershed event, a turning point after which attitudes toward Jews rapidly deteriorated and Jewish life in northern Europe and especially in the Rhineland was damaged beyond repair. More recent scholarship has maintained that the deaths during the First Crusade were far from the watershed event that previous historians had made them out to be.[26] Indeed, the Shum communities rebuilt fairly rapidly after the events, with help from the local and imperial powers; with the exception of isolated incidents, medieval Jews were fairly comfortable in their locales until the early thirteenth century. This is not to say that tensions and pressures to convert did not grow stronger. But communities that were harmed were quickly able to move beyond the traumatic events.

At the same time, the decisions many individuals had made to commit suicide and the deaths of a substantial percentage of Jews in some communities left an indelible mark on Jewish culture. In a cultural context in which Jews, like their fellow Christians, admired pious deeds, *kiddush ha-shem* was seen as the ultimate act of piety. The idea that God would take vengeance for the sake of the pious who had died remained a constant in northern European Jewish communities in later decades.

Twelfth and Thirteenth-Century Developments: Daily Life, Learned Culture, and Religious Entanglement

The post-Crusade period brought with it marked change and, from the historian's perspective, a shift that is marked by a relative abundance of sources. Many new Jewish communities can be traced to the twelfth and thirteenth centuries, springing up around older communities.[27] Another important shift was a concentration of Torah study in French—rather than German—speaking areas. Rashi's return to Champagne before the First Crusade and the establishment of a group of students around him marked a departure from the days when scholars had traveled to Germany to study. Rashi, his sons-in-law and students, and especially his grandsons R. Jacob b. Me'ir (Rabbenu Tam) and R. Samuel b. Me'ir (Rashbam) developed new ways of reading and interpreting the Bible and the Talmud, and students traveled from far to study with them. These scholars, called the Tosafists because of the additions (*tosafot*) they added to Rashi's commentary on the Talmud, wrote what became the standard commentaries on the Babylonian Talmud. During the late twelfth and early thirteenth century as Paris became a thriving urban center, centers of study developed there as well with evidence of contact between the Jewish scholars and some of their Christian counterparts, especially from the St. Victor school.[28]

In medieval Iberia, during the twelfth and thirteenth centuries there was a cultural resurgence as well. The Iberian Jews are well known for their poetry and biblical exegesis in this period, some of which continued with tropes and methods inherited from al-Andalus, whereas other commentaries and treatises contain elements that can be seen in northern Europe as well. Abraham Ibn Ezra (1089–1164) inherited a keen interest in grammar and language from his Arabic schooling, and he also traveled extensively in northern France during his lifetime, and both sets of influences can be detected in his commentary on the Bible. Travel between different centers of learning allowed Jewish scholars to share methods and knowledge, a trend that intensified in the late thirteenth and throughout the fourteenth centuries as Jews migrated from northern Europe or were expelled. For example, R. Ahser ben Yehiel (known by his acronym, Rosh, d. 1327) left Germany for Christian Iberia, where his inheritance from northern Europe became enmeshed with the norms of life in his new home. In his writings, he commented on the differences between Christian Iberia and Ashkenaz on matters ranging from repentance to capital punishment.[29] These migrations were also the impetus for encyclopedic compositions such as R. Menahem Ibn Zerah's (d. 1385) *Zedah LaDerekh* (Provision for the Way) and the Provencal rabbi, R. Aaron b. Jacob ha-Cohen's *Sefer Orhot Hayyim* (Book of the Paths of Life; composed before 1327), as exile and transition led to writing in order to preserve a world some emigrants felt they were leaving behind.[30]

Jewish religious writings in southern Europe have been situated in the context of prevailing Christian writings and beliefs. The rabbis in Provence, known for their philosophy and rationalism, have long been situated within the context of contemporary Christian belief as well as within an internal Jewish perspective.[31] Whereas previous generations of scholars saw this immersion within Christian culture as an explanation for subsequent conversion—for example, Baer explained the Jewish response to Dominican and Franciscan demands for the conversion of the Jews in Christian Iberia during the fourteenth century as the result of the philosophical beliefs as well as the Kabbalah that developed in Christian Iberia during the thirteenth century (an attitude that has since been firmly rejected)—, recent studies have presented the Jewish writings from this period both as part of the surrounding cultural environment and of local Jewish traditions. The development of kabbalistic thought has also been suggested as a response to Christian and especially Marian piety and mysticism. On the whole, Jews living in southern Europe have been presented as far more versatile and familiar with the traditions around them and as innovative when combining ancient Jewish traditions and contemporary ideas. This is not to say that Jewish rationalists and kabbalists alike were not immersed in the Jewish sources, but one of the arguments has been that their openness to their environments led to new sorts of creativity.[32]

In contrast, for many years, scholars who studied Jewish life in northern Europe viewed Jews as living within Christian urban space but in relative isolation. The pietistic self-image of Ashkenazic Jews reinforced by *kiddush ha-shem* at the time of the First Crusade as well as the pious practice encouraged by twelfth- and thirteenth-century rabbinic authorities were read as expressions of reticence and repulsion from Christianity.[33] To some extent this was a matter of definition more than of the sources, as scholars pointed to innovations within Ashkenazi culture and presented the differences rather than the similarities between these ideas and those of the surrounding culture.

The self-image and historical conception of the Ashkenazic Jews as pious and separate from their surroundings has been manifested in discussions of both Tosafists and pietists.[34] A group known as Hasidei Ashkenaz (Ashkenazi pietists) in the Rhineland promoted their own brand of devotion to God, requiring their followers to worship God in fear. These so-called pietists are best known for the three men who led them—R. Samuel b. Judah, his son R. Judah b. Samuel (d. 1217), and their disciple, R. Eleazar b. Judah (d. 1230)— and the books they produced such as *Sefer Hasidim* (Book of the Pious) and *Sefer Rokeah* (Book of the Perfumer). Some scholars have seen these pietists as a separate sect-like group, whereas others have presented them as more integrated within their communities. In any case, their writings indicate that they were searching to raise the level of piety in communal life. The pietists present themselves in their writing as practicing extreme penance and devotion, some of which scholars have seen as imitations of Christian practice. At the same time, their writings contain some of the fiercest anti-Christian expressions to be found in medieval Jewish sources, including the belief that truly pious Jews should distance themselves from Christianity to the greatest extent possible.[35]

The case of Hasidei Ashkenaz illustrates the difficulty of distinguishing between Jews' practices and their adoption and adaptation of local Christian practices. Recent scholarship has sought to understand the balance between the separate identity the Jewish communities cultivated and their involvement and entanglement with the medieval Christian environment. Studies over the past two decades, albeit in varying degrees, often argue that medieval Jews shared many ideas and practices with their surroundings. Yet they did so in distinctive ways that were meant to underline difference while using shared vocabulary and behavior. As members of medieval culture, Jews learned and appropriated beliefs from their neighbors, but they by no means adopted them lock, stock, and barrel as previous generations of scholars assumed when they spoke of influence. Instead, as Ivan Marcus has argued in his work on childhood rituals, what was at work was a process of "inward acculturation," by which Jews adapted ideas from their surroundings but then modified them according to their own needs, justifying them using Jewish sources.[36]

At the same time, and despite the mostly one-way movement in which ideas and practices on the whole are thought to have traveled, medieval Jews sought to incorporate these ideas using Jewish proof-texts, often differently from how they had previously been used. Biblical verses, Talmudic passages, poems, and Midrashim were all used as a way to incorporate new ideas into traditional frameworks or traditional beliefs into new formulations. Current scholarship has become invested in providing new understandings as to how these mechanisms work, in contrast to previous scholars, who often saw the use of a verse or a passage from late antiquity as evidence that some ideas were far from new to the Middle Ages and therefore turned the discussion into a question of origins (who held which idea first), rather than a study of lived and shared practice and thought.

The comparison between research concerning the Jews of southern France, Provence, and Christian Iberia and that concerning Ashkenaz in this context is an illustration of how research agendas and choice of sources have shaped scholars' understanding of Jewish life. Whereas the Jews of Ashkenaz were viewed as pious and isolated, those in Christian Spain were presented as an integral part of Spanish society, despite the shared majority religion and common sources of Jewish canonical authority.

Perhaps because of the Muslim chapter in medieval Iberia's history and the fact that the Jews were not the only religious minority there, historians have tended to focus on Iberia as an area of shared urban spaces, in this case among Christians, Jews, and Muslims.[37] Over time, though, Jews in Iberia came to live in more closely delimited areas, an advantage for centralized communal life, but a disadvantage when the community was under attack. In Iberia, as elsewhere, the Jews had close relationships with the king and his representatives and played vital fiscal roles. Although legal documents throughout Christian Iberia placed restrictions on Jewish movement and activities, local records indicate that Iberian Jews were economically enmeshed within the cities where they lived. Modern historiography has presented them as very much in sync with their neighbors, despite occasional violence between religious communities.[38]

Thus while both northern European Jewish communities and those in the south have histories of limiting legislation and anti-Jewish sentiment expressed against the Jews, the lives of the Jews in the south have been presented as much more harmonious with their surroundings, whereas the existence of Jews in northern Europe has been assumed to be much more isolated. This impression has been furthered by internal Jewish sources and responses to Christianity, for example attitudes toward *kiddush ha-shem* in Iberia, where Jews were more likely to convert than commit suicide. It is also a product of the sources from medieval Iberia that include far more archival data than any city or area in northern Europe. The archival data found mainly in non-Jewish municipal archives indicates Jewish involvement on all levels of urban life.

In contrast, when discussing northern Europe, due to the largely rabbinic nature of Jewish sources, the almost absolute lack of archival material (although there are some notable exceptions), and the highly polemical nature of the sources that address relations between Jews and Christians, the isolationist perspective remained prevalent until recently. Although the rabbis active in Iberia, especially during the fourteenth century, left many responsa and commentaries, these texts have been relatively understudied in comparison to the writings of their northern colleagues.

In light of these stereotypes and divisions, recent scholars have argued for changing the narrative in more than one direction. Scholars of northern Europe have suggested a kind of northern European *convivencia*, obviously differing from that in the south, but still far less isolating than conceptions that have been promoted in the past. Scholars of southern Europe have pointed to the firm divisions that existed within the *convivencia* and its limits, underlining the separatist nature of members of the different religions, even when sharing elements of culture and ideas. Thus both parts of European Christendom, south and north, had elements of separatism and *convivencia* and in both clear lines were set between Jews and their neighbors, even when sharing bathhouses and ovens as was common in Spain and in Ashkenaz. One of the features of recent research is the attempt to see a complexity in both areas that allows for a deeper understanding of the particulars in each location and this remains a challenge for future research.

Religious Polemic, Conversion, and Identity

The recent reinterpretations of the relationships between Jews and Christians have been further complicated by the way Jews in southern and northern Europe not only lived among their Christian neighbors but also constantly engaged in debate with them about the value of each religion—and in internal Jewish debates regarding the other's beliefs. Thus as Jewish settlements proliferated all over Christian Europe, with large Jewish concentrations in the expanding urban centers, so did the confrontations, both virtual and real. Jews and their supposed "blindness" to the truth of Christianity was the subject of Christian preaching and moral tales, philosophical tractates, and works of art; Christians and their errant beliefs as well as proofs of Jewish veracity were the subject of Jewish polemic compositions.[39]

Another change the twelfth and thirteenth centuries brought was increased pressure on the Jews to convert. Jeremy Cohen has noted that Augustinian ideology, according to which Jews were tolerated as a minority within Christian culture and as historic witnesses to the veracity of Christianity, lost currency during the thirteenth century. The efforts to convert the Jews were not related to attitudes toward Judaism alone; they were part of the reordering of a medieval society in which the church was asserting its power. As Christians reformed their legal and ecclesiastic systems, they sought to eradicate all heresy and instill proper order in the laity and clergy. Church leaders put forward a normative Christian ritual, encouraged popular piety, and presented Jews as aliens in their midst.[40]

The attack on the Jews can be seen on two related levels. From a theological perspective, arguments against the Jews focused on a new text—the Talmud— often with the help of recent Jewish converts to Christianity. Whereas the "classic" polemic between Jews and Christians had been over interpretation of the Bible, during the thirteenth century a new Christian awareness spread of the Talmud and the authority it commanded in Judaism. This, too, contributed to the abandonment of "witness theory" as reason for tolerance: if Jews were no longer living in accord with the Bible, why should they be tolerated as heirs to the biblical tradition? Amos Funkenstein pointed to the contribution of scholasticism alongside this new awareness of the Talmud, noting that these new emphases changed the nature of the theological debate.[41]

Yet, to characterize the twelfth and thirteenth centuries only in this way would be misleading. While theologians were attacking Jewish belief, papal authorities were also seeking ways to protect Jews and ensure tolerance. This was true from the time of the First Crusade and remained true throughout the thirteenth century: following the First Crusade, the emperors and the papal authorities had allowed Jews who had converted to return to Judaism; the papal bull *Sicut Judaeis*, first issued by Calixtus II (1119–24) protected Jews' freedom of worship, lives, and property, and it was reissued by popes throughout the Middle Ages.

The "Talmud trial" of 1240 in Paris provides an illustration of the extent to which Jewish-Christian relations depended not just on general factors such as church-state competition but also on local politics. At the behest of a Jewish convert to Christianity named Nicholas Donin, Pope Gregory IX (1227–41) wrote to all European rulers with accusations against the Talmud; the letter was ignored by all but King Louis IX of France, who at the time needed papal help gaining control over southern France. That the call to prosecute the Jews was left unanswered by all but one ruler demonstrates the degree to which anti-Jewish sentiment depended on the politics of church-state relations. In the aftermath of the trial, in which four prominent rabbis took part on behalf of the defense, hundreds of manuscripts of the Talmud were burnt. The event was followed by the Disputation of Barcelona in 1263. While each of these events had unique features, both exemplify the church's mounting efforts to delegitimize Jewish belief and to promote conversion among Jews.[42]

No less significantly, as medieval European cities expanded, Jews became increasingly pervasive as moneylenders. Throughout Europe, they were closely tied with local authorities and kings who were both indebted to and resentful of them. Opponents of the monarchs from within Christian society tended to identify the Jews as part of their critique of the monarchy in England and northern France. In thirteenth-century legal charters, Jews are called *servi camerae* (servants of the [royal] chamber), indicating their financial and legal attachment to the king—and their status as pawns in the battles between popes and monarchs.[43]

It is impossible, then, to single out one Christian attitude toward Jews and Judaism. While the period after the First Crusade brought more aggressive opposition to the Jewish presence in Christian Europe, daily life continued and there is evidence of Jewish business and neighborly relationships, medical assistance provided by members of both communities to those of the other community, as well as archeological evidence of shared neighborhoods.

Recent scholarship has taken up the challenge of presenting both perspectives. Historians have moved away from viewing the Jews as passive victims of the assault by the church and the intensifying efforts to convert them, viewing matters instead from a Jewish perspective and tracing Jewish efforts to resist Christianity. Two issues that have been central in these debates are how Jews defined Christianity and their attitudes toward Christian practices. While previous Jewish authors had considered Christians to be idol worshippers (the most derogatory category in ancient Jewish sources), Menahem Me'iri of Perpignan (1249–ca. 1310) limited that category to pagans, defining Christians as monotheists. Jacob Katz and more recently Moshe Halbertal have demonstrated that Jewish definitions of Christianity changed over time.[44]

Some texts written by the Ashkenazic Jews contained virulent anti-Christian rhetoric, with insults regularly hurled at Christianity and Christian figures. The discussion of these strategies has led to a new understanding of how Jews responded to mounting anti-Jewish rhetoric. Whereas nineteenth- and early twentieth-century scholars had portrayed Jews as the helpless victims of Christian persecution, contemporary scholars such as Israel Yuval have emphasized Jews' agency and how Jews used anti-Christian rhetoric and practices to strengthen communal boundaries.[45] Other recent scholarship has looked at how medieval sources portray Jews as living side by side with their Christian neighbors within shared urban spaces, focusing on tensions between the genders, and attitudes toward children and other groups that did not leave organized written records, but that often pointed to Christian parallels.[46]

While the twelfth and to some extent the first part of the thirteenth century was still a period of relative stability for the Jews of Christian Europe, attitudes toward Jews and Judaism were changing at the popular level in some places. In Blois in 1171, the Jews were accused of ritually killing a Christian child, a suspicion that resulted in the death of more than 30 members of the community. This event was a harbinger of similar accusations that would take place from England to Poland in subsequent centuries.[47] Jews and others also increasingly became victims of host desecration libels, the claim that Jews had harmed a host consecrated at mass, after transubstantiation was codified as a binding belief at the Fourth Lateran Council (1215).

The Lateran IV also promulgated legislation requiring Jews to wear a distinguishing symbol as well as further restrictions against Jews holding Christian servants. The council was an attempt to order Christian life—it put forward, for example, the requirement that Christians confess once a year; and regulations about Christian-Jewish contact were part of this broader effort. It is doubtful to what extent such regulations were enforced at first, though familiarity with the statutes can be found from England to Iberia.[48]

Persecutions, Expulsion, and Beyond

Throughout the Middle Ages, Jews under Christian rule experienced episodes of persecution, community members faced accusations, and some Jews were killed by judicial measures or popular violence. As the Middle Ages came to a close, anti-Jewish sentiment was on the rise throughout medieval Europe and royal powers like ecclesiastical ones were more vociferous in the edicts and laws against the Jews, demanding the clear demarcation of Jews as others and seeking to limit their activities especially in everything related to moneylending. These demands were complimented by active attempts to convert the Jews, attempts that became more persistent in Christian Iberia over the thirteenth and fourteenth centuries. In northern Europe during this same period, as the local religious authorities became convinced that the Jews would not convert, the monarchs decreed the first expulsions.

In medieval England, the Jews came under the direct protection of the king, who borrowed money from Jewish moneylenders and profited from Jewish tax revenue. An elaborate bureaucratic system had been in place to record Jews' financial transactions since the twelfth century. As the thirteenth century progressed, English subjects expressed hostility toward the Jews more frequently; the monarchs understood that their subjects expected harsher legislation toward the Jews. In 1272, Jews were prohibited from lending money, a devastating decree given that the profession had become a mainstay for many English Jews. The community was impoverished. In 1290, the king exiled all Jews from England.

Northern France and England shared many similarities. As William Chester Jordan has demonstrated, the centralization of state under the Capetian kings was at first advantageous to the Jews, but then increased their dependence on a centralized crown. Starting in the late twelfth century, the Capetians began issuing anti-Jewish measures. In 1182, Phillip Augustus called for the remission of debts to Jews (with the treasury taking one fifth of their value), expelled Jews from the royal domain, and confiscated their property, with the exception of synagogues. These decrees were meant to satisfy the church and public opinion—and to provide income for the royal treasury. The Jews were readmitted to the royal domain in 1198, a move from which the king profited by reviving Jewish moneylending and collecting Jewish tax revenue.[49]

Over the course of the thirteenth century, royal and papal opposition to Jewish moneylending increased in intensity. Lateran IV explicitly prohibited excessive usury. In thirteenth-century France, the rulers (who are noted for their piety) objected forcefully to Jewish moneylending. After the trial against the Talmud and its burning, France witnessed an accusation of host desecration in 1290; in 1306, Jews were expelled and their land confiscated (they were permitted to take moveable goods with them). They were permitted to return in 1315, but the communities that resettled never achieved the vitality of those from before 1306. The final expulsion of the Jews from France took place in 1394; they were not legally readmitted until 1790.[50]

The Jews who had been expelled from England and royal France moved to Catalan-ruled Provence and other Iberian kingdoms or to Germany and further east. Their community traditions dispersed along with them. In Germany, too, anti-Jewish accusations became more frequent over the course of the thirteenth century. Here, there was no centralization of power as in northern France and England, but instead of political fragmentation benefiting the Jews, it led to greater insecurity for the Jews who were so closely tied to the government and needed its support, and were therefore often at the mercy of specific rulers. For example, already in the thirteenth century, local tensions in Frankfurt led to an attack on the Jewish community and the death of many community members.[51]

During the summer of 1298, after a host desecration accusation, a knight by the name of Rindfleisch attacked a number of Jewish communities in Franconia, Hesse, Swabia, and Thuringia. The impoverishment and depopulation of many German communities was significant after this point. There were further attacks on German Jewish communities during the early fourteenth century, and severe violence as the Black Death spread throughout Germany during the mid-fourteenth century and Jews were associated with the spread of disease. The Jews were not formally expelled from German lands, but their communities were significantly diminished, and many chose to migrate eastward to Poland.[52]

Jews were not the only religious minority in Christian Iberia and this contributed to the way events progressed there. The large Jewish populations of Castile, Catalonia, Aragon, and Valencia came under the direct protection of the crown, as in northern Europe. The mission toward the Jews expanded throughout the thirteenth and fourteenth centuries, both in the cities and in frontier areas. In 1391, a series of forced conversions and massacres decimated the Jewish communities. The number of Jews who converted during this period has been estimated at more than 100,000. Similar numbers were killed or fled the Iberian Peninsula.[53] Central to these developments and calling for the conversion of the Jews were a number of Jewish converts to Christianity: Pablo Christiani (d. 1274) represented the Christian side against Nahmanides in the Disputation of Barcelona (1263); Paul, archbishop of Burgos (1351–1435), born Shlomo ha-Levi, attempted to convert many of his former coreligionists. Members of the Dominican and Franciscan orders, such as Ramon Llull (1232–1315), also contributed to the effort to rid Christendom of Jewish influence. Yet these developments cannot be explained only in theological terms. These attacks were closely related not only to the desire to convert the Jews but also to debts owed by the local and regal powers.

If Iberian Christians at first regarded the conversion of so many Jews after 1391 as miraculous, a half-century later, they had come to regard it as a catastrophe. Rather than eradicating Judaism, it had only brought Jews and Judaizing into the very heart of the Christian populace. Conversos began to be regarded with suspicion. During the 1440s, for the first time one finds suspicion on the grounds of "race" (*raza*), the idea that even baptized Christians possessed an ineradicable Jewishness. By 1449, some Spanish cities (Toledo was the first) passed ordinances requiring "purity of blood" (*limpieza de sangre*) of those holding public office, thus barring Jews and conversos. (It is interesting to note that this is the only medieval example of racial anti-Judaism.)[54]

But the most extreme expression of suspicion toward converted Jews (and Muslims) was the establishment of the Spanish Inquisition in 1478–80 by Ferdinand II of Aragon and Isabella I of Castile.[55] This tribunal was meant to ensure that the converts were true to their new faith. A little more than a decade later, as the whole of Iberia (now called Spain) came under Christian rule with the defeat of the Muslims in Granada, Ferdinand and Isabella expelled the Jews. One of their arguments for doing so was that they threatened all of Spanish society, since as long as they remained in the country, the conversos would never resist the temptation to Judaize. With the edict of expulsion of 1492, some Jews converted to Christianity; others fled. Those who escaped to Portugal were expelled from there or converted en masse only five years later; many Spanish Jews fled to Italy and the Ottoman Empire.

The expulsions from Iberia were without doubt the most traumatic and far-reaching of the European Middle Ages. Iberia had boasted the largest Jewish population of any European land in both absolute and proportional terms, and Iberian Jews themselves knew that Jews had already been expelled from elsewhere in western Europe. Portuguese Jews were able to maintain some group coherence for several centuries to come; after all, they had been converted en masse, while Spanish Jews endured a century of internecine strife before the expulsion, with some family members converting or fleeing and others choosing to remain Jewish. This would, then, mark a new chapter in their history. And thus the Iberian expulsions make for a fitting close to the medieval chapter of the history of the Jews in western Europe—a history that would continue only when individual princes and kings readmitted them or allowed them to settle for the first time. (See the next chapter.)

Notes

1. Interestingly, there exists no comprehensive history of medieval Jews under Christianity (as distinct from monographs on each specific geographic area). Indeed, there is not even a comparative study of Jews in southern and northern Europe. Robert Chazan (2006), *The Jews of Medieval Western Christendom, 1000–1500*. Cambridge: Cambridge University Press, excludes the Jews of Iberia and Byzantium. Michael Toch (2013), *The Economic History of European Jews: Late Antiquity and Early Middle Ages*. Brill: Leiden, provides the best and only inclusive survey to date of all these areas until the year 1000.
2. Salo Baron (1928), "Ghetto and Emancipation: Shall We Revise the Traditional View?" *Menorah Journal* 14: 515–26; idem (1952–83), *A Social and Religious History of the Jews* (2nd edn), 18 Vols. New York: Columbia University Press. See also Robert Liberles (1995), *Salo Wittmayer Baron: Architect of Jewish History*. New York: New York University Press, pp. 8–9, 340–2, where he traces how this term became central in Baron's writing and thought, especially in the second edition of his work.
3. Amnon Linder (1987), *The Jews in Roman Imperial Legislation*. Detroit: Wayne State University Press; for a social and religious history of this period, see Oded Irshai (2002), "Confronting a Christian Empire: Jewish Culture in the World of Byzantium," in David Biale (ed.), *Cultures of the Jews. A New History*. New York: Schocken, pp. 181–222 and an updated version in Robert Bonfil, Oded Irshai, Guy G. Stroumsa, and Rina Talgam (eds) (2012), *Jews in Byzantium: Dialectics of Minority and Majority Cultures*. Leiden: Brill, pp. 17–64.
4. Linder, *The Jews in Roman Imperial Legislation*. The question of language is an interesting one that has not received enough attention to date, except to note the role Jews played in translation; see below. See the recent work of Kirsten A. Fudeman (2010), *Vernacular Voices: Language and Identity in Medieval French Communities*. Philadelphia: University of Pennsylvania Press.
5. Robert Bonfil (2012), "Continuity and Discontinuity, 641–1204," in Bonfil et al. (ed.), *Jews in Byzantium*, pp. 65–100; Steven Bowman (1985), *The Jews of Byzantium 1204–1453*. Tuscaloosa: University of Alabama Press. Most recently see Joshua Holo (2009), *Byzantine Jewry in the Mediterranean Economy*. Cambridge: Cambridge University Press; Toch, *The Economic History of European Jews*, pp. 15–20.
6. Bowman, *The Jews of Byzantium 1204–1453*.
7. All these texts exist in critical editions. David Flusser (1978), *Sefer Yossipon*. Jerusalem: Mosad Bialik; Robert Bonfil (2009), *History and Folklore in a Medieval Jewish Chronicle: The Family Chronicle of Ahimaaz b. Paltiel*. Brill: Leiden; Eleazar ben Asher ha-Levi (2001), *Sefer ha-zikhronoth udivrei ha-yamim le-Yerahmi'el*, Eli Yassif (ed.). Tel Aviv: University of Tel Aviv. For scientific writings in the Byzantine Empire, see Y. Tzvi Langermann (2011), "Science in the Jewish Communities of the Biblical Cultural

Orbit," in Gad Freudenthal (ed.), *Sciences in Medieval Jewish Cultures*. Cambridge: Cambridge University Press, pp. 438–53.

8. Avraham Grossman (2001), *The Sages of Ashkenaz* (3rd edn). Jerusalem: Magnes Press [Hebrew], p. 116.

9. Bonfil, *History and Folklore*, pp. 151–87.

10. For a survey of this period in Sicily, see David Abulafia (1988), *Frederick II: A Medieval Emperor*. London: Penguin, pp. 202–25, 251–89.

11. Recent scholarship has problematized the tendency to lump all these areas into one. See Israel M. Ta-Shma (1992), *Early Franco-German Ritual and Custom*. Jerusalem: Magnes Press [Hebrew], pp. 14–16, 22–7. See further discussion of this point in Haym Soloveitchik (2008), *Wine in Ashkenaz in the Middle Ages*. Jerusalem: Merkaz Zalman Shazar [Hebrew], pp. 123–36; Ephraim Kanarfogel (2000), *Peering through the Lattices: Mystical, Magical and Pietistic Dimensions in the Tosafist Period*. Detroit: Wayne State University Press, pp. 189–250, 256–7. Although Grossman distinguishes between Germany and France in his histories of the lives of the sages, he treats them as a single region in his study of women: Avraham Grossman (2004), *Pious and Rebellious. Jewish Women in the Middle Ages*. Lebanon, NH: Brandeis University Press. Others have argued for greater differentiation: Eric Zimmer (1996), *Society and Its Customs*. Jerusalem: Merkaz Zalman Shazar [Hebrew], and reviews of this book, including Haym Soloveitchik (1998), "Review Essay of *Olam Keminhago Noheg*," *AJS Review* 23: 223–34.

12. Most recently, new discoveries in Cologne have indicated that perhaps there was a Jewish presence there in Roman times but there is no substantial evidence before the ninth century in both France and Germany.

13. Avraham Grossman (1981), *Early Sages of Ashkenaz*. Jerusalem: Magnes Press [Hebrew]; idem (1996), *Early Sages of France*. Jerusalem: Magnes Press [Hebrew]. See the recent survey of the formation of these communities and of the historiography related to them: David Malkiel (2009), *Reconstructing Ashkenaz, The Human Face of Franco-German Jewry, 1000–1250*. Stanford: Stanford University Press, chapter 1. See also, Chazan (2006), *The Jews of Medieval Western Christendom*, pp. 129–68.

14. For the Latin legal documents, see Julius Aronius (1970, orig. 1902), *Regesten zur Geschichte der Juden im fränkischen und deutschen Reiche bis zum Jahre 1273*. Hildesheim-New York: G. Olms. For a description of the struggle between church and state reflected in these documents, see the still-classic essay by Salo W. Baron (1972), "'Plenitude of Apostolic Powers' and Medieval 'Jewish Serfdom,'" in idem, *Ancient and Medieval Jewish History: Essays*. New Brunswick: Rutgers University Press, pp. 308–22. For a recent discussion of the privileges, see Jonathan Ray (2010), "The Jew in the Text: What Christian Charters Tell Us about Medieval Jewish Society," *Medieval Encounters* 16: 43–67.

15. Louis Finkelstein (1964), *Jewish Self-Government in the Middle Ages*. New York: P. Feldheim, where these statutes are translated into English. For the statutes on divorce, see Grossman, *Early Sages of Ashkenaz*, pp. 144–50; Ze'ev W. Falk (1996), *Jewish Matrimonial Law in the Middle Ages*. London: Oxford University Press.

16. For detailed information about specific cities from the ninth through the fifteenth centuries, two of the best sources remain *Germania Judaica*; Vol. 1, Ismar Elbogen, Avraham Freimann, and Haim Tykocinski (eds) (Breslau, 1934); Vol. 2, Zvi Avineri (ed.) (Tübingen, 1968); Vol. 3–4, Aryeh Maimon, Yacov Guggenheim, Stephan Rohrbacher, Michael Toch, and Israel Yuval (eds) (Tübingen, 1987–2003). For France, Henri Gross (2011), *Gallia Judaica, Dictionnaire géographique de la France d'après les sources rabbiniques*, Simon Schwarzfuchs (ed.). Paris: Peeters.

17. For recent surveys of these topics, see the studies in Christoph Cluse (ed.) (2004), *The Jews of Europe in the Middle Ages (Tenth to Fifteenth Centuries)*. Turnhout: Brepols,

where a large number of places and topics are discussed with relevant bibliographies. See also Ephraim Kanarfogel (2012), *The Intellectual History and Rabbinic Culture of Medieval Ashkenaz*. Detroit: Wayne State University Press, for a survey of commentaries.

18. Toch, *The Economic History of European Jews*.
19. On Agobard of Lyon, see Jeremy Cohen (1999), *Living Letters of the Law: Ideas of the Jews in Medieval Christianity*. Berkeley: University of California Press, pp. 123–50; Peter Schaefer (2011), "Agobard's and Amulo's Toldot Yeshu," in Peter Schaefer, Michael Meerson, and Yaacov Deutsch (eds), *Toldot Yeshu Revisited*. Tübingen: Mohr Siebeck, pp. 27–48.
20. On R. Gershom's son, see Avraham Grossman (2006), "Aggadah tipologit al hitznatz-rut bno shel Ragmah," in Avidov Lipsker and Rella Kushelevsky (eds), *Ma'asehSippur. Essays Presented to Yoav Elstein*. Ramat Gan: Bar-Ilan University Press, pp. 65–75; Jacob Katz (1984), *Halakhah ve Kabala*. Jerusalem: Magnes Press, pp. 255–69.
21. For the Jews in England, see the studies by Robert C. Stacey and Robin C. Mundill, summaries of which can be found in Patricia Skinner (ed.) (2003), *The Jews in Medieval Britain: Historical, Literary and Archaeological Perspectives*. Rochester: Boydell & Brewer.
22. See Grossman, *Early Sages of Ashkenaz*; idem, *Early Sages of France*.
23. This shift is attested in the number of manuscripts from each period. See Malachi Beit-Arié (1993), *The Makings of the Medieval Hebrew Book: Studies in Paleography and Codicology*. Jerusalem: Magnes Press.
24. The scholarship on the First Crusade in general and on how it affected the Jewish communities in northern Europe is too vast to be surveyed here. For a recent volume of essays on the Jews during this period, see Yom-Tov Assis, J. Cohen, A. Kedar, O. Limor, and M. Toch (eds) (2000), *Facing the Cross: Gezerot Tatnu in History and Historiography*. Jerusalem: Magnes Press. The Hebrew accounts of these events have also been examined at length. See the recent edition of them: Eva Haverkamp (2005), *Hebräische Berichte über die Judenverfolgungen während des Ersten Kreuzzugs*. Hannover: Hahnsche Buchhandlung.
25. Haym Soloveitchik (1986), "Religious Law and Change: The Medieval Ashkenazic Example," *AJS Review* 12: 205–22, one of the classic discussions; Jeremy Cohen (2004), *Sanctifying the Name of God: Jewish Martyrs and Jewish Memories of the First Crusade*. Philadelphia: University of Pennsylvania Press, a relatively recent study of the chronicles.
26. Simon Schwarzfuchs (1989), "Meqomam shel masa'ei ha-selav be-divre yemey isra'el," in Reuven Bonfil, Menahem Ben-Sasson, and Joseph Hacker (eds), *Culture and Society in Medieval Jewry*. Jerusalem: Merkaz Zalman Shazar, pp. 251–67; Robert Chazan (1987), *European Jewry and the First Crusade*. Berkeley: University of California Press.
27. An illustration of the geographical changes can be seen in the maps produced by the team in Trier under the direction of Alfred Haverkamp (ed.) (2002), *Geschichte der Juden im Mittelalter von der Nordsee bis zu den Südalpen*. Hannover: Hahnsche Buchhandlung.
28. Ephraim Elimelech Urbach (1980), *The Tosafists: Their History, Writings and Methods* (4th edn). Jerusalem: Mosad Bialik [Hebrew], remains the standard study of these scholars. See also, Grossman, *Early Sages of Ashkenaz*; Simcha Emanuel (2006), *Fragments of the Tablets: Lost Books of the Tosafists*. Jerusalem: Magnes Press [Hebrew].
29. Baer, *History of the Jews*, pp. 316–25.
30. Judah D. Galinsky (2008), "Of Exile and Halakhah: Fourteenth-Century Spanish Halakhic Literature and the Works of the French Exiles Aaron ha-Kohen and Jeruham b. Meshulam," *Jewish History* 22: 81–96.

31. Halbertal (2000), *Between Torah and Wisdom: Rabbi Menachem Ha-Meiri and the Maimonidean Halakhists in Provence*. Jerusalem: Magnes Press.
32. Arthur Green (2002), "Shekhinah, the Virgin Mary and the Song of Songs: Reflections on a Kabbalistic Symbol in Its Historical Context," *AJS Review* 26: 1–52. The history of Kabbalah is a topic worthy of an essay of its own. See Gershom Scholem (1941), *Major Trends in Jewish Mysticism*. New York: Schocken; Moshe Idel (1988), *Kabbalah: New Perspectives*. New Haven: Yale University Press, for two classic studies.
33. Kenneth Stow (1992), *Alienated Minority: The Jews of Medieval Latin Europe*. Cambridge, MA: Harvard University Press; Ivan G. Marcus (2002), "A Jewish-Christian Symbiosis: The Culture of Early Ashkenaz," in David Biale (ed.), *Cultures of the Jews: A New History*. New York: Schocken, pp. 449–516, assesses this conception and its development.
34. These two categories and the sharp distinctions drawn between them have been somewhat exaggerated as a result of the perspective of those discussing both groups who have read only the Hebrew sources and searched for specific modes of argumentation and intellectual thought. While this distinction is significant, it is no less important that pietists and Tosafists alike lived within the same small communities and served together as religious leaders.
35. For a summary of research on the Rhineland pietists and some of the debates in the field, see Haym Soloveitchik (1976), "Three Themes in the 'Sefer Hasidim,'" *AJS Review* 1: 311–58; idem (2002), "Piety, Pietism and German Pietism: 'Sefer Hasidim I' and the Influence of 'Hasidei Ashkenaz,'" *Jewish Quarterly Review* 92: 455–93; Ivan G. Marcus (1982), "Hasidei Ashkenaz Private Penitentials: An Introduction and Descriptive Catalogue of Their Manuscripts and Early Editions," in Joseph Dan and Frank Talmadge (eds), *Studies in Jewish Mysticism*. Cambridge, MA: Harvard University Press, pp. 57–83; idem (1981), *Piety and Society: The Jewish Pietists of Medieval Germany*. Leiden: Brill, as well as idem (1986), *The Religious and Social Ideas of the Jewish Pietists in Medieval Germany: Collected Essays*. Jerusalem: Merkaz Zalman Shazar [Hebrew], for many of the classic essays on the topic.
36. Ivan G. Marcus (1996), *Rituals of Childhood: Jewish Acculturation in Medieval Europe*. New Haven: Yale University Press; David Berger (2004), "A Generation of Scholarship on Jewish-Christian Interaction in the Medieval World," *Tradition* 38: 4–14.
37. For scholarship on medieval Iberia, the classic study remains that of Yitzhak Baer (1961), *A History of the Jews in Christian Spain*, Louis Schoffman (trans.). 2 Vols. Philadelphia: Jewish Publication Society. For more recent studies, see Yom-Tov Assis (1997), *The Golden Age of Aragonese Jewry. Community and Society in the Crown of Aragon (1213–1327)*. London: Vallentine Mitchell; Mark D. Meyerson (2004), *Jews in an Iberian Kingdom, Society, Economy and Politics in Morevedre 1248–1391*. Leiden: Brill; Elka Klein (2006), *Jews, Christian Society and Royal Power in Medieval Barcelona*. Ann Arbor: University of Michigan Press.
38. For discussions of these ideas and redefinition of some terms, see David Nirenberg (1996), *Communities of Violence: Persecution of Minorities in the Middle Ages*. Princeton: Princeton University Press; Alfred Haverkamp (1996), "Concivilitas von Christen und Juden in Aschkenas im Mittelalter," in Robert Jütte and Abraham P. Kustermann (eds), *Jüdische Gemeinden und Organisationsformen von der Antike bis zur Gegenwart*. Vienna: Böhlau Verlag, pp. 103–36; Jonathan Elukin (2006), *Living Together, Living Apart: Rethinking Jewish-Christian Relations in the Middle Ages*. Princeton: Princeton University Press.
39. For a survey of this topic, see David Berger (1979), *The Jewish-Christian Debate in the High Middle Ages: Sefer Nizzahon Vetus*. Philadelphia: Jewish Publication Society, Introduction; Cohen, *Living Letters*; Anna Sapir Abulafia (2011), *Christian-Jewish Relations 1000–1300: Jews in the Service of Medieval Christendom*. Harlow: Longman, for the most recent survey of this literature.

40. Robert I. Moore has presented a radical approach to this question in (2007), *The Formation of a Persecuting Society: Power and Deviance in Western Europe, 950–1250* (2nd edn). Malden, MA: Blackwell.
41. Cohen, *Living Letters*; Amos Funkenstein (1993), *Perceptions of Jewish History*. Berkeley: University of California Press, pp. 172–201.
42. Chen Merhavya (1970), *The Church versus Talmudic and Midrashic Literature 500–1248*. Jerusalem: Mosad Bialik [Hebrew]; See the recent essay by Robert Chazan that surveys scholarship on this topic: (2012), "Trial, Condemnation, and Censorship: The Talmud in Medieval Europe," in idem (ed.), *The Trial of the Talmud, Paris 1240*, John Friedman and Jean Connell Hoff (trans.). Toronto: Pontifical Institute of Medieval Studies, pp. 1–91. This book also contains translations into English of the Hebrew and the Latin texts; idem (1992), *Barcelona and Beyond: The Disputation of 1263 and Its Aftermath*. Berkeley: University of California Press.
43. Salo W. Baron (1960), "'Plenitude of Apostolic Powers' and Medieval Jewish Serfdom," in Salo W. Baron, B. Dinur, Shmuel Ettinger, and I. Halpern (eds), *Yitzhak F. Baer Jubilee Volume on the Occasion of His Seventieth Birthday*. Jerusalem: Ha-Hevrah ha-historit ha-Yiśre'elit, pp. 102–24; Jeremy Cohen (1989), "Recent Historiography on the Medieval Church and the Decline of European Jewry," in James R. Sweeney and Stanley Chodorow (eds), *Popes, Teachers and Canon Law in the Middle Ages*. Ithaca: Cornell University Press, pp. 251–62.
44. Jacob Katz (1961), *Exclusiveness and Tolerance: Studies in Jewish-Gentile Relations in Medieval and Modern Times*. London: Oxford University Press; Halbertal, *Between Torah and Wisdom*.
45. Israel J. Yuval (2006), *Two Nations in Your Womb: Perceptions of Jews and Christians in Late Antiquity and the Middle Ages*, Barbara Harshav and Jonathan Chipman (trans.). Berkeley: University of California Press.
46. For some examples, see Elisheva Baumgarten (2004), *Mothers and Children: Jewish Family Life in Medieval Europe*. Princeton: Princeton University Press; Ephraim Shoham-Steiner (2007), *Involuntary Marginals: Marginal Individuals in Medieval Northern European Jewish Society*. Jerusalem: Merkaz Zalman Shazar [Hebrew].
47. The classic study on this topic is Joshua Trachtenberg (1943), *The Devil and the Jews: The Medieval Conception of the Jew and Its Relation to Modern Antisemitism*. New Haven: Yale University Press. For an analysis of these accusations, see Miri Rubin (1999), *The Narrative Assault on Late Medieval Jews*. New Haven: Yale University Press. See also Sapir Abulafia, *Christian-Jewish Relations 1000–1300*, pp. 167–93.
48. Chazan, *The Jews of Medieval Western Christendom*, pp. 48, 56, 61.
49. William Chester Jordan (1989), *The French Monarchy and the Jews: From Phillip Augustus to the Last of the Capetians*. Philadelphia: University of Pennsylvania Press.
50. Chazan, *The Jews of Medieval Western Christendom*, pp. 160–7.
51. This is an interesting example, as information of this attack on the Jews is the first information about Jews in Frankfurt. See Rachel Furst (2008), "Conversion and Communal Identity: Sexual Angst and Religious Crisis in Frankfurt, 1241," *Jewish History* 22: 179–201.
52. For a recent summary, see Jörg R. Müller (2004), "*Erez gezerah*—'Land of Persecution': Pogroms against the Jews in the *Regnum Teutonicum* from c. 1280–1350," in Cluse (ed.), *The Jews of Europe in the Middle Ages*, pp. 245–60.
53. Baer, *History of the Jews*; Ram Ben Shalom (2007), *Facing Christian Culture: Historical Consciousness and Images of the Past among the Jews of Spain*. Jerusalem: Mekhon Ben-Tsevi le-heker kehilot Yiśra'el ba-Mizrah [Hebrew].
54. David Nirenberg (2002), "Conversion, Sex and Segregation: Jews and Christians in Medieval Spain," *American Historical Review* 107: 1065–93; idem, "Enmity and Assimilations: Jews, Christians and Converts in Medieval Spain," *Common*

Knowledge 9: 137–55; idem, "Mass Conversion and Genealogical Mentalities: Jews and Christians in Fifteenth Century Spain," *Past and Present* 174: 3–41.

55. The first papal Inquisition had been launched by Louis IX against Christian heretics in Languedoc. For conversos and the Inquisition, see Haim Beinart (1967), *The Records of the Inquisition: A Source of Jewish and Converso History*. Proceedings of the Akademyah ha-le'umit ha-Yiśre'elit le-mada'im 2:11. Jerusalem; Renée Levine Melammed (1999), *Heretics or Daughters of Israel: The Crypto-Jewish Women of Castile*. New York: Oxford University Press.

Changing Tempos and Foci: Looking to Modernity

The early modern period has always been presented as different from the Middle Ages and yet not quite akin to modernity. Many of the tremendous upheavals in politics, religion, technology, and social organization, however, point to an intensification of experience that makes the early modern period both exciting and increasingly relevant. Along with the massive, and at times, fairly quick, structural changes that impacted Judaism and Jewish society starting already in the late eighteenth century, the early modern and modern periods took the rabbinic and medieval inheritance and shaped it into new and often quite distinct forms. The two chapters that follow present the wide range of changes reflected across the past half millennium, while pointing to the remarkable consistency and coherence that could also link Jews together over time and across geographies. No understanding of Judaism or Jewish Studies today can be formed without serious reflection on the issues and challenges presented here.

Dean Phillip Bell's essay "Early Modern Jews and Judaism" describes the emergence of the early modern period (1450–1750) as a distinct period in Jewish history and reviews the range of sources available for its study. Bell then turns to an overview of issues of Jewish identity, settlement and demography, communal structure and governance, social dynamics (including a discussion of Jewish women and families), religious belief and praxis (including a review of Kabbalah and mysticism), and relations with non-Jews and non-Jewish society. In the conclusion, he articulates the key scholarly trends that define the work in early modern Jewish studies. Cautioning against accepting traditional narratives that are based on the recapitulation of well-known personalities and well-documented events, Bell notes that current research is increasingly attentive to questions of gender, marginal and poor groups, Sephardic culture, arts and material culture, and communal studies, while simultaneously engaging more "traditional" discussions of Jewish religious and intellectual developments on the one hand and Jewish relations with the non-Jewish world on the other. Drawing from the exciting developments in general history, Bell concludes that the early modern period has been for scholars a remarkable period of methodological experimentation and cross-fertilization, which comprises many of the broader and most innovative developments in Jewish Studies.

In "Modernity, Judaism, and Jews," Gil Graff contextualizes discussions of modernity before addressing some of the most prevalent themes associated with modern Jewish life and history. Graff orients readers toward the Jewish Enlightenment (Haskalah), Emancipation (theoretical debates and practical realities and challenges), religious currents (including the reform of Judaism and the development of confessional affiliations), and relations with non-Jews (especially within the context of political and racial anti-Semitism in nineteenth-century Europe). He outlines the important developments in East Europe, with particular attention on Jewish thought and practice (Hasidism and Haskalah), as well as demographic and political developments and the origins and context of Zionism. Importantly, Graff also deliberates on the major trends in the development of Sephardic and Middle Eastern Jewry, a subdiscipline in its own right that has begun to get much more significant and long-needed scholarly attention. Graff rounds out his overview with notes on developments in American Jewry and the impact of the Holocaust. In reviewing the major trends of current scholarship, he points to the availability of expanded archival materials, a broadening away from a Eurocentric focus, the impact of postmodernity, and increased interest in social and cultural history (notably, as reflected in the history of women). It should be noted that a number of issues raised in this essay and the essay on contemporary Jewry are advanced in the four essays that comprise Part II of the volume.

7 Early Modern Jews and Judaism

Dean Phillip Bell

Chapter Outline

Introduction

A generation or so ago this volume would likely not have included a separate essay on the early modern period. Not that the period delineated here as "early modern" was without merit or significant events or personalities. Rather, the entire epoch, from the fifteenth through the eighteenth century, was subsumed under a broad and sprawling Jewish Middle Ages that swept together the entire period from the close of the Talmud to the Haskalah (Enlightenment) and the struggle for Emancipation. Such a periodization belied a view that saw the early modern period as one that was largely "traditional" in terms of alleged Jewish belief and practice and "marginal" when it came to the legal and social position of the Jews.

The Jews most studied from this period were residents of the ghetto—in terms of physical separation as well as intellectual and cultural insularity—and largely under Christian domination. True, historians confessed that many and important Jews and Jewish communities could be found in the Ottoman Empire, but the "sick man of Europe" held out a great deal less interest for modern historians who lived and responded to modern Western society. What is more, the "less common languages" and mind-sets—at least in the West—of Jews under Islam served as a further impediment to serious engagement with non-European Jewry.[1]

In a sense, breaking free from the Jewish Middle Ages has allowed the centuries that now comprise the early modern period to be seen in a much richer and more nuanced fashion than before. Already in the 1960s, Jacob Katz, the father of Jewish social history, introduced us to the complexity of internal Jewish social formation and the diverse, multidirectional nature of Jewish and non-Jewish relations.[2] Through a number of groundbreaking studies, Jewish women and Jewish underclasses have received voices—at least to some extent.[3] Jewish praxis has become less "normative," and more complicated than was once fashionable, and the porosity of the ghetto has replaced its once-sturdy walls. Jews under Islam have begun to garner more attention, so much so that some now speak of a renaissance of Sephardic studies. At the same time, some of the more traditional themes outlined for the Jewish Middle Ages have continued to play prominent roles in the historiography, though in ways that ask about the larger, non-Jewish, context in which they were often conceived and in which they gestated and matured.

The different inflections expressed varied (and continue to vary) depending upon the particular historians or historical schools who articulated them. Some, for example, found the rabbinic casuistry (*pilpul*) as a bulwark against destructive outside influences; others found it to be stultifying and backward looking. Some historians found the mysticism of the early modern world creative and invigorating; others saw it couched in superstition and leading to various false messianic debacles. Some saw significant Jewish advances in literature and the sciences; others found such Jewish involvement to be largely traditional or derivative of external, and, by implication, superior knowledge. For some, the image of Ashkenazic Jews steeled in the face of the medieval Crusades, and early modern pogroms led to the conclusion that separation from the broader world and inward piety were the most important aspects of premodern Jewry that allowed for continuity and even survival.[4] For others, the world of Sephardic Jewry, alleged to have been more cosmopolitan and progressive—secular for some—, was the model for success that should be emulated in modernity to assure cultural vibrancy, intellectual development, and political engagement.

Recent historians have not simply asked new questions of old sources. They have simultaneously examined many different non-Jewish sources and placed

Jewish historical developments into broader historical contexts that challenge traditional understandings of the Jewish past. Contemporary scholars have also utilized a range of new sources that either were infrequently examined or yet to be uncovered. This has led to a more highly variegated and complex premodern Jewry that has forced reconsideration of notions of Jewish identity, Jewish and non-Jewish relations, and the very nature of Judaism.

The sources for early modern Jewish history are diverse and fairly extensive. They were written in many different languages, including Hebrew as well as a range of vernacular languages, and they include materials written by Jews and non-Jews alike.[5] In the early modern period, we also find a rich range of visual arts and material culture sources. While many of these sources have been known to scholars for a long time, and have often been read and studied—albeit generally with specific concerns in mind and often following prescriptive methodologies—important new sources have been unearthed in the form of archival documents (including court records) and gravestone inscriptions, for example. Added to the sources most frequently scoured by scholars, such as print and manuscript commentaries on various books of the Bible and tractates of the Talmud, as well as the rabbinic rulings compiled in responsa, hagiographies, ethical treatises, and formal scientific, philosophical, or medical writings, early modernists have utilized rabbinic sermons and many different kinds of communal documents such as communal record books (*pinkasim*); protocol books (which recorded communal statutes, litigation, and excommunications and fines); communal ordinances (*takkanot*), of both local and regional nature; memory books, which recorded the deaths (as well as the lifetime accomplishments) of certain communal members (often the wealthiest or most learned); and communal customs books, which recorded the specific religious and communal customs of individual communities. The survival of a relatively large number of such documents points to their increasing production in the early modern period, and it mirrors the important growth in formal record keeping and bureaucracy in many early modern societies. A small number of autobiographies and travelogues and a larger number of personal letters and business communications allow us the opportunity to see into the more private worlds and personal worldviews of early modern Jews. Official documents written by non-Jewish officials, such as tax registers, court proceedings, charters and privileges, and guild statutes add significant information about early modern Jewish life. Non-Jewish authors also penned travelogues and itineraries that reveal details about Jewish life, though often they are refracted through very specific lenses and anti-Jewish sensibilities. And non-Jewish scholars with interest in Hebrew language, Kabbalah, and Jewish customs and rites more generally authored a range of both popular and esoteric works that were received by hungry markets and simultaneously utilized and cast under the suspicion of academics and churchmen alike. Finally, and increasingly, various forms of popular and synagogal art, architecture, and material remains afford us the opportunity to see important Jewish culture as well as Jewish perceptions of and interactions with non-Jews and non-Jewish culture.

Defining Early Modern Jews and Judaism: Questions of Identity

We often assume that the question "Who is a Jew?" is a question made necessary by the intellectual syncretism, assimilation, and intermarriage of the modern word. But the question of how to define a Jew is in some ways as old as Judaism itself. In biblical and rabbinic texts the notion of Jewish identity was often wed with political, ethnic, cultural, religious, and sociological conditions. In the medieval and early modern periods, Jewish identity has been assumed to have been relatively stable and easy to define. For some time, however, historians have recognized the presence of dissenting views within medieval and early modern Judaism, and many have since focused on the flexibility of Jewish legal discussions and a degree of "tolerated dissent,"[6] in which Jewish society very consciously absorbed and blended a diverse range of people, in terms of socioeconomic standing and theological worldviews.

What is more, local customs and practices could vary tremendously and could at times conflict with more broadly accepted legal prescriptions. Differing ethnic and cultural orientations could be quite divisive as well. While we are accustomed to distinguish Ashkenazic Jews (Jews of German and then later eastern European background) and Sephardic Jews (Jews originally from Spain, but later a large number in other parts of Muslim-dominated lands), there were significant distinctions within and beyond these central groups, often based on customs or ethnic or geographical roots. Jews may have been forced to live with each other in some places, but that did not mean that they necessarily saw themselves as neighbors and friends, making our understanding of Jewish identity in the early modern period even more difficult.

While probably nowhere near as numerous as in the modern period, there were important numbers of Jews who converted from Judaism to Christianity and Islam, forcibly and voluntarily. Many of these converts continued to maintain close social contact with their families and Jewish communities. It should be noted that some converts, however, became the most strident opponents of their former religion and ardently campaigned against it.[7] Such individuals polemicized against Judaism, and often served as informants as well as experts, claiming to have knowledge of Jewish activities and sensibilities against the host culture and religion. The situation for individuals forcibly converted from Judaism and their descendants in Iberia in the fourteenth and fifteenth centuries and into the early modern period—with some difference, variously noted as conversos, *anusim*, Marranos, and crypto-Jews—often involved heterogeneous identities, which could mix elements of Judaism and Christianity. These individuals often practiced some elements of Judaism and were looked at with suspicion and jealousy by "old" Christians, concerned with their theological convictions and level of social and economic success and integration. Within the Jewish community itself, there was a good deal of discussion about whether such individuals were in fact to be considered Jewish or not, especially if they had an opportunity to revert to Judaism and did not.

In a different category were individuals who remained within the Jewish world, but could be considered heretics of one stripe or another. Increasingly in the early modern period, as individual Jews engaged the intellectual and philosophical streams of the broader society, Jews confronted, and often acculturated, a range of non-Jewish ideas and practices. At times, such ideas and practices were so seamlessly acculturated that we assume today that they were always part of Jewish society—consider some customs related to lifecycle events such as birth, bar mitzvah, and marriage.[8] At other times however, Jewish society castigated and tried to separate such external influences. Many secular and religious leaders in early modern Jewish communities attempted to marginalize behaviors and beliefs that did not fit within a hardening border of Judaism and Jewish communal behavior. For this reason, the ban of excommunication, *herem*, appears to have been levied with greater frequency—though perhaps less efficacy—starting in the late sixteenth century.[9]

Some Jews drew from long-standing traditions of anti-rabbinic attitudes. Karaites, for example, rejected the Oral Torah and focused their attention and practice on the Hebrew Bible. They maintained a small but visible presence in parts of the Ottoman Empire. We have evidence of other early modern Jews, who similarly rejected aspects of formal rabbinic religion or certain communal rulings and customs as well. These individuals, like the others noted above were increasingly marginalized as Judaism itself became more confessionalized and set in dogmatic structures in the early modern period.[10]

Jewish identity was also the subject of discussion and speculation among non-Jews. In many cases, non-Jews saw Jews as eternally Jewish, no matter what their outwardly stated theological positions and social behaviors might imply. "Purity of blood" laws in fifteenth-century Spain as well as suspicious attitudes of converts throughout the early modern world signaled a sensibility that Jews were an ethnic and perhaps even a biological group.[11] Many early modern polemicists quipped that "once a Jew always a Jew," often arguing that Jewish converts to Christianity were simply Jewish wolves in sheeps' clothing, who could never really embrace a new religion or worldview and were always secretly plotting against their new religion. In non-Jewish constructs, Jews were regularly regarded as a kind of conceptual category, often used in opposition to ideal categories that helped to define the community of the non-Jewish world.

Jews served as theological straw men to advance theological and philosophical positions, and they could be political foils when overlapping authorities, with various interests in or responsibilities for Jews, clashed. Jewishness, therefore, was crafted by internal and external discussions that could impact Jewish life and the position of Jews throughout the early modern period.

Settlement and Demography

The heart of early modern Jewish settlement[12] was in the expanding Ottoman Empire (including parts of the Balkans, Anatolia, the Middle East, and North Africa), and central and eastern Europe. Smaller pockets of Jews remained in western Europe—unofficially in much of France, especially port and border regions, as well as Spain and England, as conversos and crypto-Jews. In the early modern period, Jews could also be found in increasing numbers in the New World, especially in areas of South and Central America being explored and settled by European powers. Scattered Jews, or individuals and communities, with beliefs or practices approximating Judaism could be found in India and, to a lesser extent, in China. Added to this were the traveling merchants and agents, often of Sephardic background, who traversed the globe on a variety of business missions.

In the early modern period, several general demographic trends are clear. Jews had been expelled from England, France, Spain, parts of Italy, as well as from a range of towns and territories in Germany in the later Middle Ages. German Jewish population, which had been spread across more than a thousand mostly small settlements in the Middle Ages began to coagulate with several more sizeable communities and new settlement locations. In Italy, Jews migrated north and settled in the more open economic areas. Perhaps the largest and most significant demographic shift, however, was an eastward trajectory. Jews expelled from Spain and later Portugal in the late fifteenth century often traveled to Italy or North Africa on their way to destinations in the Ottoman Empire, where Jews were treated as second-class citizens to be sure, but nevertheless accorded a good deal of religious autonomy and economic opportunity. Jews also increasingly, since the late fifteenth century, made their way east to Poland in growing numbers.

In most lands, Jewish population centers tended to be rather small. Jews typically constituted far less than 1 percent, and only rarely accounted for more than 3 percent, of the local population. Most Jewish communities were small enough to be centered around a single congregation. Still, there were important and growing centers of Jewish life and even where such centers were lacking, territorial Jewish communities developed that linked residents of smaller communities to broader and more cohesive social, economic, and religious entities.

In Germany in the later Middle Ages, there were approximately 25,000 Jews; that number would grow to more than 35,000 by the early seventeenth century and grow again despite the ravages of the wars and epidemics to 60,000 by mid-century, though never reaching more than half a percent of the total population. The largest Jewish population concentrations in Germany were in Frankfurt am Main (approximately 3,000 Jews at its early modern height) and Worms (around 11% of the total population). Large rural populations of Jews emerged in villages and small towns in Germany. If the broader Holy Roman Empire is included, significant Jewish population and a robust Jewish community was to be found in Prague (estimated at perhaps as much as 30% of the total population), and, at varying times, in parts of Moravia, Bohemia, and Silesia.

In the Netherlands, Jewish settlement expanded in the sixteenth century, especially in Antwerp, and then in the early seventeenth century in Amsterdam,[13] which boasted a large and cosmopolitan Jewish community, with 3,000 Sephardic and Ashkenazic Jews by the middle of the seventeenth century. The early predominance of Sephardic Jews there was overturned with increasing population of Ashkenazic Jews by the early eighteenth century, signaling important changes in the composition of the Jewish community and the role of individual Jews.

In Italy, significant Jewish centers, with rich cultural features and important economic functions, developed in Venice[14] and her territories, and in Florence, Pisa, and Livorno as well.[15] Important Jewish settlements took shape in Bologna and Padua,[16] in part fueled by the intellectual climate of universities, and in Mantua and other locations because of political and cultural developments. A large number of Jews continued to reside in Rome and throughout the Papal States.[17] These Jews were generally well protected, though they did suffer from time to time from changes in papal policy, especially after the middle of the sixteenth century. Some Italian Jewish communities experienced a good deal of diversity, with Jews from different lands forming into multiethnic communities that could be as vibrant as they were tension-filled.

Formally expelled from England at the end of the thirteenth century, Jews were readmitted by the middle of the seventeenth century. A Sephardic community developed in London. There is some discussion among historians as to whether a small Jewish population continued to exist in England between the dates of expulsion and readmission. Similarly, in France, Jews were expelled on several occasions in the fourteenth century, and Jewish settlement remained somewhat limited through the early modern period.[18] Important Jewish communities could be found in Alsace-Lorraine, with Metz constituting a particularly large and robust community, with approximately 1,900 Jews by the early eighteenth century (approximately 7% of the total population).[19] Jews also lived in papal-controlled areas during the early modern period, such as Comtat Venaissin (especially in Carpentras) and Avignon.[20] Other, small groups of

Portuguese Jews settled in important trading centers, often along the Atlantic coast—in Bordeaux (which had as many as 93 Jewish families at the end of the seventeenth century), Bayonne, Nantes, as well as in Rouen, Paris, and other locations.[21]

One of the largest growth areas of Jewish settlement in the early modern period was in Poland. This growth continued a steady increasing trend since the later Middle Ages, when estimates of population range between 10,000 and 25,000, constituted largely by Jews from Germany, Bohemia, and Silesia, as well as from the medieval population of Kievan Jews. Some Sephardic, often from the Ottoman Empire, and Italian Jews did make their way to Poland in the sixteenth century. By the middle of the seventeenth century, some 150,000–220,000 Jews, out of an estimated total population of 11 million, inhabited the Polish-Lithuanian Commonwealth. By the middle of the eighteenth century, Jews constituted a population of some 750,000 and represented a third of world Jewry.[22] Dramatic growth of the Jewish population was facilitated by a heterogeneous Polish-Lithuanian state, in which religious diversity and some toleration combined with positive political and economic conditions, migration from other lands where Jews were persecuted, and natural increase. Most larger Polish Jewish communities were to be found in urban, commercial centers, where Jews numbered between 1,000 and 5,000 individuals, and constituted roughly 10–15 percent of the total population. Particularly large communities could be found in cities such as Cracow-Kazimierz, Lemberg, and Posen.

A large portion of the early modern Jewish population resided in Muslim lands. Some large Jewish communities were located in Iran under the Safvid Empire, as well as in other parts of the Middle East and North Africa. The latter two areas were slowly absorbed into the broad reach of the Ottoman Empire, which, in the early modern period—at least in to the seventeenth century—boasted one of the largest and most diverse Jewish populations. Many Jews and Jewish communities were native to the areas being added to the empire. This, combined with forcible movements of Jews and other minority groups as part of a larger Ottoman political policy, local and regional economic and political conditions, and the welcoming conditions for many Jews fleeing expulsion and persecution in the West, led to complex, multidimensional, variegated ethnic, and at times very large, Jewish communities. Especially big and important Jewish communities formed in the sixteenth century in Istanbul and Salonika, as well as in other major urban areas, such as Izmir and Edirne. Throughout much of the early modern period, and especially in the seventeenth century, Ottoman Jewry remained predominantly urban.[23] Istanbul may have been home to 30,000–40,000 Jews in the seventeenth century; Salonika may have been even more impressive proportionately, with Jews representing half of the population by the early sixteenth century, and numbering some 25,000 by the seventeenth century.[24] In Izmir and Edirne, approximately 5,000 Jews were present, roughly 5.5 percent of the total population in the former.[25]

Jews also ventured into parts of the New World—at first in the fairly tolerant settlements of the Dutch in South America, but also as crypto-Jews in Central America. Particularly large Jewish communities formed for a while in Curaçao and Recife. Political changes brought about by the capture of some areas by the Portuguese forced Jews to find other havens in the New World. Fleeing the persecution of the Inquisition and Portuguese and Spanish authorities, a small number of Jews made their way to North America by the middle of the seventeenth century; during the course of the eighteenth century, conditions allowed for the seeding of a North American Jewry that would begin to take root by the end of the eighteenth century.

Jewish settlement was dictated by external conditions as well as internal dynamics. Since the Middle Ages, Jewish settlement was organized according to stipulations laid down in charters granted by civic, regional, ecclesiastical, or royal authorities. Such charters generally stipulated privileges and rights to be accorded to Jews and/or a Jewish community. Such charters were often intended to help spark economic development and they outlined the responsibilities and expectations of Jews. Such charters could be a point of conflict between various sources of authority. Throughout central Europe in the early modern period local cities and towns frequently negotiated with territorial rulers to revoke such charters or to grant the privilege of nontoleration of Jews.

While Jews frequently lived in proximity to other Jews for religious, social, and economic reasons, for much of the Middle Ages and well into the early modern period, Jews did not necessarily live in the same quarters or even on the same streets. Jewish populations might be scattered across a town or village, often depending on the social status or occupation of the individual Jews. Increasingly in the early modern period, Jews were forced to live in prescribed locations and in many cases in specific quarters that were locked at night and at other times on the calendar. Such sequestration was both a hindrance and a protective measure for the Jews, who could more easily be removed from random or planned acts of violence. What is more, such ghettos were generally fairly porous, so that it is still possible to find a good deal of regular interaction, in almost all spheres of life, between Jews and non-Jews.

Jewish settlement could be highly regulated. By the end of the early modern period, many non-Jewish authorities dictated how many Jews could live in a specific area. But Jewish communities themselves could also regulate population and settlement, utilizing their own methods and tools, such as the ban on settlement (the *herem ha-yishuv*), or by working with local authorities to petition to keep out notorious criminals or even economic competitors. Settlement was also controlled, in a sense, through an elaborate structure of taxation that required financial contributions from all individuals recognized as heads of house and residents of a community—such residency could be established in many different ways. Not surprisingly many disagreements arose in the assessment and collection of such taxes, as well as in the debates over obligations for individuals who recently moved to or from another Jewish community.

Jewish Communal Structure and Governance

Jewish communal structures could vary depending on the location, size, and context of the community. Still, some basic governance and communal functions were maintained. Throughout the Middle Ages, the rabbi served in an unofficial capacity, as the expert in and arbiter through Jewish law (halakhah). His authority was dependent on a number of factors, including his own legal skills and social capital, the makeup of the community, and the approval of external authorities. In the early modern period, the rabbinate became a more formalized and official communal position, in which the rabbi was hired, by means of a contract that generally stipulated the number of years of service, key functions and responsibilities, and, often, limitations on his authority and power. Some have argued that the professionalization of the rabbinate was correspondingly weakened as a result. While some external authorities attempted to impose rabbis on local or broader regional communities, such appointments were understandably resisted by Jews and tended to be more ceremonial. Rabbis were trained in Talmudic academies (yeshivot) or individually, at the foot of a well-established rabbi. Traveling from place to place for study and work and engaged in a learned network of scholars, rabbis could be mobile and important conveyors not only of Jewish tradition but of broader Jewish culture as well.

The community was governed by other officials too. Increasingly in the early modern world, lay leaders had the lion's share of power in the Jewish communities. Such leaders, often referred to as *parnasim*, were responsible for the day-to-day governance of the community and, at times, even assumed some role in legal arbitration. These lay leaders were the primary representatives to the non-Jewish authorities and they were typically themselves among the wealthiest segment of the community. A special position of an intermediary, *shtadlan*, developed in many communities. There were, of course, benefits to holding such leadership roles; however, there were significant responsibilities and liabilities as well. As the Jewish community was generally responsible for the collection and payment of taxes in toto, lay leaders often had to make up the difference between what was collected and what was due. They also had to step up in times of emergency, when extraordinary taxes were levied or when external threats arose to endanger the community. The number of lay leaders who formed a board (*kahal, mahammad*) could vary from community to community, but was frequently seven or twelve.

A number of important, frequently paid positions also developed in the early modern Jewish communities. Individuals were engaged who were responsible for the upkeep of the synagogue, summoning people to the synagogue and for other communal events, recording of customs and legal documents, assessing and collecting taxes, and, in some larger communities, maintaining order, cleanliness, and even security in the Jewish quarter. Some formal communal appointments were related to religious and ritual functions. Individuals were responsible for the prayer services, and some communities appointed a specific chanter (*hazzan*), as well as a range of educators (particularly as communal schools began to emerge with greater frequency), ritual slaughterers (*shohtim*), and others. Societies of various stripes were also active in Jewish communities. These included the *hevra kaddisha*, or burial society, as well as societies related to charity and dowries, for example. A whole series of rules governed the election and activities of communal servants. Increasingly in the early modern world—in Jewish and non-Jewish societies—more formal and bureaucratic tools and mechanisms were adopted.

The Jewish community was, in a sense, a corporation, which associated a group of Jews on a voluntary basis. Communities were generally given a significant degree of internal autonomy by non-Jewish authorities in areas of religious custom and law. In cases of conflict with non-Jews, or when two Jews refused to be bound by the legal decisions within the community, non-Jewish courts might be involved in legal cases. Jewish communities frowned on such recourse beyond the Jewish world, in part because it diluted the Jewish court's authority and in part because it held the potential to open the community and its functions much more fully to external interference.

Community, especially in the early modern period, could be more regionally defined as well. Especially outside the largest communities, Jews often lived in smaller settlements in towns or villages. In such cases, settlements and small communities collectively formed a regional association. Many times, such associations were governed by their own constitutions and regional councils— most famous, perhaps was the Council of Four Lands in eastern Europe. These councils held annual meetings—in some places dominated by lay and in others by rabbinic authorities—that established ordinances and dealt with specific challenges facing the broader region or individual communities. At times, less regular synods of communities met to grapple with similar issues.

Jewish Social Structures and Dynamics

Although many have assumed, for a variety of reasons, that Jews were predominantly wealthy and that Jewish communities were socially well integrated, more recent studies have demonstrated that there was a great deal of diversity and social division within premodern Jewish communities. Jews practiced many different occupations, which is often surprising given frequent restrictions imposed upon them, especially in Christian lands.

Some Jews were renowned merchants, in some cases on an international scale, but primarily in local or regional trade in a wide range of products. Jews could be involved in traditional occupations as well as more entrepreneurial work, including new industries evolving in the New World, such as those related to the production and sale of sugar and tobacco. Many Jews continued to be involved in various crafts, even when technically prohibited from joining guilds or practicing certain professions. In the Christian West one might find Jews as tailors, smiths, cannon makers, engineers, and even prostitutes. Sometimes, Jews had local specialization—Jews in some northern Italian locations, for example, were renowned as tailors or dance instructors; Jews across Poland were often associated with the management of noble estates and with inn-keeping.

Under Islam, Jews often had even greater economic and occupational opportunities, in part because of the cosmopolitan and urban nature of much of Islamic society and the fact that Islam had not disparaged aspects of business and commerce as Christianity had for much of its early history. In the Ottoman Empire, Jews were regularly employed by the court or other governmental authorities in positions related to the collection of taxes and customs duties, or in supplying goods and financial services. Jews were involved with domestic and international commerce, particularly given some resistance of Muslim engagement with Europe, Jewish settlement in port cities, Jewish family and business networks, language skills, and Jews' familiarity with innovative banking methods, etc.[26] Indeed, Jews took part in the full range of commerce (including slave trading).[27] This was true of men as well as women, who often functioned as independent merchants, partners or guarantors, and even as peddlers. Ottoman Jews were involved in diverse crafts, especially in all aspects of the production of fabrics. Jews were also well represented in the processing of precious metals and gems, the production of foodstuffs (kosher as well as food for the general public), printing, brokerage, translating, and medicine, and other professions.[28] Work in financial and trading areas, as well as in positions such as servants, bathhouse attendants, fortune tellers, and lamenters for the dead—in which Jews, often women, might be engaged by Ottoman Muslims or Christians—brought Jews into daily contact and interaction with the non-Jewish world, forcing historians to reconsider Jewish culture and practices in relation to the broader societies in which Jews lived and worked.

While the majority of Jews would have fallen into a broad middle class, increasingly in the early modern period impoverishment of Jews could be found in both Ashkenazic and Sephardic communities, resulting in shifting social structures and non-Jewish perceptions of Jews.[29] Even though many sympathized with their plight, poor Jews, especially outsiders, garnered suspicion among the general populace and concern by local Jews who worried about economic competition, dependency, or poor impressions that such Jews might make on the local population or rulers.

Early Modern Jewish Women and Families

We lack a large body of sources written by early modern Jewish women directly—though there are important exceptions, especially as one moves forward in the early modern period (consider Sara Copia Sullam[30] in Italy and Glückel of Hameln[31] in Germany). Still, there are many sources that provide information about the role of women in diverse social, economic, and religious settings. Some of these sources deal with women directly. Others can be mined for what they imply more indirectly about women and perceptions of gender in the early modern world. While women were still generally excluded from the formal governing structures of the Jewish community—as they were in other communities—women influenced communal decisions in myriad ways.

Women often had important economic and social roles. This was true of widows who took over their deceased husbands' economic activities as well as other women. Increasingly, we find evidence of women engaged in fairly diverse professions and crafts to support themselves and their families. In Ottoman cities, for example, women played a vital role in the economy—dealing in property, loans, and sale of goods. They were involved in a range of craft productions and services—depending in part, of course, on their social status. The ownership of land by women was recognized in Jewish and Islamic law[32] and women were capable of a good deal of independence.

Though often ascribed an inferior social status, women had many legal and social means of self-defense at their disposal, for example through petitions and legal suits. As throughout the premodern world, female sexuality was seen as dangerous by male authorities. Segregation was generally explained as a method of guarding against the dangers associated with this sexuality and a means of protecting both modesty and chastity. While relations between Jewish women and non-Jewish men could be found, they seem to have been less common than similarly illicit relations between Jewish men and non-Jewish women. Indeed, in the Christian West it appears to have been less frequent for women to convert from Judaism and women were recognized by both Jewish and non-Jewish authorities as the member of the Jewish family, who most influenced religious connection.

Women appear in and authored important letters, of both a personal and professional nature, such as those extant from the Prague ghetto in the early seventeenth century. Such letters allow us insights into both the familial dynamics of that community and the kinship networks of individuals, as well as the occupations and economic concerns of women—single and married, as well as young and old.

In the area of religion, we find a blossoming of publications apparently geared toward a female audience, including numerous works written in Yiddish and various vernacular languages. The world of women's religious life was generally centered on the home and various printed books addressed issues related to kashrut and the household. Books of collected prayers for various occasions, including the Sabbath and holidays as well as different mitzvot (known as *tkhines*), provide evidence of central issues in women's spirituality in the early modern period. Through such works, and others, we also have some evidence of the ideal virtues ascribed to women—at least primarily by men—in the early modern world. Memory books, which recorded the deaths of prominent communal members frequently recorded the deaths of women and also indicated some of the specific acts and qualities of such women that were idealized by male authors and to be remembered. The very construction of synagogues—which increasingly in the early modern period included special sections for women—also indicate growing female attendance at public religious ceremonies.

Despite cultural constraints on women in both Christian and, some would argue even more pervasively, in Islamic society, Jewish women appear to have had a fair degree of personal freedom within the private sphere. Women were subject to both limitations and protection prescribed by Jewish law, and in some cases, by the laws of the societies in which the Jews lived. As in other areas of life, regulations on women and relations between men and women absorbed local and non-Jewish cultural elements. Legislation already from the Middle Ages that prohibited polygyny and that secured other rights for women in marriage and divorce are generally seen to have been protective measures that benefited women in premodern Jewish society. Numerous rabbinic responsa and communal documents deal with issues related to marital disputes and offer insights in to both the challenges faced by women as well as the leverage that they might be able to garner in their personal and familial affairs. Women in the Ottoman Empire frequently appealed to shari'a courts because they were quicker and simpler than going through the Jewish courts.[33] In the Christian West, we have examples of women who threatened conversion to Christianity if they were not granted a divorce.[34]

Relations between men and women (including husband and wife) as well as parents and children were generally dictated by the social norms and behaviors of the larger cultures in which Jews lived. Under Islam, for example, men and women tended to inhabit different spheres of activity—men in more public realms at work and in public institutions such as coffee houses and bathhouses, and women in more private and domestic settings, including the home and neighbors' homes. Jewish family structure also generally appears to have mirrored that of the broader society in which Jews lived—in terms of things such as kinship and family size.

Previous generations of scholars argued that premodern families were less caring and engaged with the lives of their children, especially in the face of significant childhood mortality rates.[35] In some cases, Jewish historians hailed an alleged greater concern for children in the Jewish community. Both sides of this argument have, over time, been revisited, and it is now clear that there was significant care for children and family members even before modernity and even amid the challenges of premodern life. In any event, in early modern Jewish life, the high child-mortality rate meant that many women spent a good deal of their childbearing years caring for or mourning the loss of children.

Each family member had important roles to play and families also sought means to provide education (religious and practical) for their children and to secure their future through advantageous marriages and communal positions. The core family was constituted by the immediate family in some cases and, in other areas, by an extended group that would include grandparents and perhaps other relatives. In some crowded ghettos with limited housing, we find multigenerational units and even multiple families sharing housing space. Various servants often formed part of the household unit, particularly, though not exclusively, among more well-to-do families. A wide range of rituals surrounded lifecycle events. In some cases, such rituals drew from long-standing Jewish traditions. In other cases, they absorbed elements from non-Jewish surroundings.

Religion: Belief, Praxis, Deviation

Much of the production of early modern Jewish scholars addressed hermeneutics, law, and ethics. Early modern Jews continued the efforts of their medieval coreligionists in penning commentaries to biblical and rabbinic works—activities, it should be noted, that resonated with non-Jewish scholars in the West in particular through the works of Christian Hebraists and in rampant biblicism of the Reformation era.[36] Such works had a diversity of audiences and at times the interpretations they advanced were woven into more popular sermons and even discussions of contemporary events (whether in the form of autobiographies, chronicles, or other texts and images). Commentaries were used for educational purposes, and the works of Rabbi Solomon ben Isaac (Rashi) as well as other leading medieval exegetes, as well as super commentaries upon their works, were printed and recirculated widely. But early modern Jews were not simply reactive. They penned their own commentaries that went beyond repetition of previous insights—often stringing together observations in new contexts and taking advantage of recent information. At other times,

Jewish commentaries reacted to or absorbed questions and methodologies that seeped in from outside Jewish culture. Consider the work of Azaria de'Rossi[37] or Maharal of Prague,[38] the former casting fresh glosses on a wide range of biblical and rabbinic materials; the latter covering remarkable ground that both created boundaries between Jewish and non-Jewish learning and yet demonstrated engagement with and understanding of many important contemporary scientific and educational themes and approaches.

Rabbinic responsa—that is answers written to various legal questions posed to a rabbinic authority—had also been written throughout the Middle Ages. But there was a significant publication of such literature throughout the early modern world. Some leading rabbis published hundreds, even thousands, of responsa.[39] In many cases, the questions posed were theoretical questions intended to help illustrate a point or clarify a religious ruling. Still, many questions reflected actual experiences, even if the questions and responses did not always provide much in the way of specific details that allow for dating or confirmation of the events being discussed. This situation has led many historians to be cautious in utilizing that material as historical sources, especially for the social history of early modern Jews. Nonetheless, they reveal important historical information and they can also tell us quite a bit about the legal reasoning employed by rabbis, the nature of particularly important or pressing issues, and the evaluation of previous scholarship and legal decisions.[40]

Major Jewish law codes had been authored in the Middle Ages—these included works by Isaac Alfasi, Moses Maimonides, and Asher ben Yehiel. But the early modern period, perhaps echoing the more general developments in the non-Jewish world, including expansion of printing and Confessionalization, witnessed further developments in this area.[41] Joseph Karo, for example, wrote the *Shulchan Arukh* (prepared table) in the 1560s—a more streamlined and accessible work than his previous legal codification, *Bet Yosef* (House of Joseph). Karo's code was similar in many ways to previous codes, yet it provided no citation of sources and drew primarily from Sephardic rulings and customs, with special weight given to rulings of Maimonides, Alfasi, and Asher ben Yehiel. The *Shulchan Arukh* was divided into four primary sections that treated the full spectrum of prayers, holidays, and Sabbath observance; issues of kashrut, conversion, family purity; marriage and divorce; finance, damages, and legal process. The response to this codification was boisterous, with many leading scholars rejecting the project or the approach. For some critics, Karo's sources were too narrow or partisan and, in any event, they were not cited for full discussion.[42] Moses Isserles, the great Polish legalist, wrote an extensive gloss on the code, entitled *Mappah* ("table cloth," intended to cover the "prepared table") that added a good deal of Ashkenazic and Polish customs. A variety of super commentaries also provided details about sources and alternate customs and approaches. For others, the very act of codification became a crutch that allowed individuals with too limited halakhic knowledge to venture in to halakhic decision making. Nevertheless, in an age of printing and codification of knowledge, the project gained a good deal of support. Despite at times heated opposition, the code eventually took hold and by the seventeenth century was the recognized authority of Jewish law for most early modern Jews—an honored place that the code continues to hold in Orthodox circles even today.

In some ways, the push for more universal codification was in opposition to the collection and practice of local customs. The tensions between local and universal could be quite fierce, and in the early modern period renewed energies were exerted in order to create books of customs in individual communities or regions.[43] Many customs books appear to have been relegated to communal archives and were never (or only much later) published or circulated, raising questions about their function and usage. Customs books dealt not only with legal issues. They also reflected a vast range of religious and communal rituals and sensibilities, many of which held no legal status. Of course, rituals themselves, no matter their legal status, were significant in the daily life, and communal identity of Jews in the early modern world and custom continued to be a venerable tradition and even legal decisor in early modern Judaism, with the famous quip that "the custom of our fathers is law." Custom, in conjunction with various codes and legal rulings from prior authorities, formed something of an early modern Jewish case law that was adapted in contemporary legal discussions and rulings. Added to this mix were laws and expectations imposed upon the Jews by non-Jewish authorities.

From treatises in the form of philosophical dialogues, formal work on science and politics, and the production of ethical works, philosophy penetrated Jewish life and thought. Early modern Jews drew from the well of antique thought that medieval Jews themselves had helped to transmit throughout the Middle Ages through their rendering of Greek philosophical work from Arabic into Latin. Some scholars have asserted that many Jews retreated inwardly in the early modern period. But it is clear that Jews continued to utilize language and negotiate worldviews that resonated with and borrowed from the discussions of their Christian and Islamic neighbors. Consider, for example, some of the medical writings of Tobias Cohen in the Ottoman Empire or the great legist Moses Isserles who was something of a rationalist and a warm defender of Aristotle.[44] Other central European intellectuals, such as Yom-Tov Lipmann Heller, were perhaps even more engaged philosophically.[45]

Already in a range of rabbinic texts and interpretations, mystical aspects of life and the cosmos were forwarded to address a range of intellectual and speculative concerns as well as more mundane situations. As explicated in various sectarian writings from the turn of the Common Era as well as in more "normative" rabbinic works, including tractates of the Talmud, Jewish mystical writings could be hermeneutical, explicating biblical passages. Early Jewish mysticism frequently focused on the imagery of the chariot (*merkavah*) and heavenly halls (*heikhalot*) as depicted in the book of Ezra, or in the creation stories and processes of the book of Genesis. Jewish mystical thought often reflected broad philosophical concerns as well. Many of the fundamental concepts of Jewish mysticism, such as the *sefirot* (divine emanations) and the notion of the Godhead (*En Sof*), derived important aspects from this widespread philosophical revival.[46] Although there were earlier manifestations of important kabbalistic ideas in the Middle Ages, such as those to be found in *Sefer Yetzirah* (Book of Creation), the *Zohar* (Book of Splendor)—which has been linked to Moses de Leon, a kabbalist from Castile in the thirteenth century—became a central text that helped center and advance Kabbalah well into the modern period. De Leon wrote the work in Aramaic and ascribed it to a second-century rabbinic scholar, Shimon bar Yohai. Presented in the form of biblical commentary, the *Zohar* advanced the notion that Divine Presence emanates through ten *sefirot*, noting also that man's actions can impact the divine as well. The *Zohar* was widely circulated and increasingly printed in the sixteenth century. Combined with other factors, such as growing Christian interest in Jewish esoterica, strong early modern messianism, new explorations and voyages of discovery, and the explosion of print, early modern mystical speculation grew dramatically.[47]

A particularly powerful form of Kabbalah emerged in the town of Safed in Israel, where many leading kabbalists amassed and transformed the intellectual and ritual superstructure there and later throughout world Jewry. A wave of Sephardic immigration after 1492 and again after the conquest of the Ottomans in 1516 led to the development of a large and multiethnic Jewish community that became home to a number of seminal scholars, such as Rabbis: Jacob Berab (1474–1546) (who sought to reestablish a Sanhedrin and rabbinic ordination); Joseph Karo (1488–1575), author of the *Shulchan Arukh*, but also the mystical *Maggid Mesharim* (Preacher of Uprightness); Moses Cordovero (1522–70), author of *Pardes Rimmonim* (Orchard of Pomegranates); Moses Trani (a great halakhist); and Isaac Luria (perhaps the most important kabbalistic thinker of the period), as well as his disciples. A rich ascetic and mystically oriented culture bloomed in Safed, with numerous brotherhoods and study groups holding nighttime vigils, developing important new mystical themes and seeking *devekut*, or mystical union, with God.

Isaac Luria (1534–72), known as Ha-Ari, the (sacred) lion, was the individual who transformed the very concept of the Kabbalah in the sixteenth century. Born in Jerusalem, Luria was raised in Egypt and settled in Safed only very late in his life. Luria left no writings and his thinking is known largely through the writings of his disciples, principally Hayyim Vital. Luria emphasized the doctrine of *tikkun*, or repair of the cosmos. He also focused a great deal of attention on the concept of *kavana* (intention) in prayer and the performance of the commandments. For Luria, the process of creation began when God contracted himself, allowing for an empty space for creation. Divine light, in the form of the *sefirot*, or emanations, was directed into this empty space in the form of vessels. When the vessels were broken, light remained in the shards and was reconfigured in countenances.[48] *Tikkun* would eventually lead to a messianic redemption. Luria wedded his Kabbalah with messianic strands, with some speculating that he may have revealed himself as the Messiah had he lived longer and that the redemption was imminent, perhaps in 1575.[49]

Early modern Jewish mysticism existed and at times flourished outside of the Holy Land as well. Judah ben Bezalel Loew, or the Maharal of Prague (ca. 1525–1609), is well known for the legend that he created an artificial being (*golem*). He was an advanced halakhic expert, a moralist, an educational reformer, and a man learned in the sciences, maintaining impressive connections with some of the leading scholars of his day. He was familiar with kabbalistic concepts, which he addressed in his various commentaries. Loew was particularly taken with the unique nature of the Jews, whose pure essence he described in many writings.[50]

Even as some continued to reject kabbalistic concepts, many important kabbalistic ideas and practices made their way into traditional Jewish liturgy and observance. New rituals were practiced, such as nighttime vigils on the festivals of Shavuot, Passover, and Hoshanah Rabbah, as well as regular nightly vigils such as the *tikkun hatzot*, lamenting the exile and praying for the redemption of the *Shekhinah*—a practice with roots in the Talmud and *Zohar*, but disseminated through Safed.[51] The central scholars in Safed also piloted or propagated a range of Sabbath-day rituals, as well as practices related to the synagogue liturgy, many of which have become so commonplace and accepted today that it is generally assumed they are of much older provenance than the sixteenth century.

Early modern Christians were also interested in the Kabbalah. In some cases, such interest was spurred by intellectual esotericism, especially among some Christian intellectuals operating on the margins of Christian society. At other times, however, more mainstream Christian intellectuals engaged Jewish learning. In the spirit of the Renaissance in which ancient texts were considered valuable because of their purity and original status, the Hebrew Bible as well as various rabbinic writings were increasingly utilized by Christian scholars for both exegetical as well as political purposes, as evidenced by the growing appearance of Hebrew in printed books (from individual words to entire biblical passages in a range of early modern print). Some Christian Hebraists, such as the famous Johannes Reuchlin in early sixteenth-century Germany defended the preservation of Hebrew books. While Reuchlin largely shared the anti-Jewish perspective of many of his contemporaries, and was, to an extent, concerned with the conversion of the Jews, he found value in the works of the rabbis and argued vociferously to protect Jewish books.[52] Early modern printers pursued an apparently lucrative market for Hebrew books that extended well beyond the Jewish community to include various Christian scholars. Along the way they employed Jews to proof books and to set type. The use of Hebrew was also valuable to censors, many of whom worked—though not always proficiently— with a broad range of Hebrew texts in their efforts to purge what they saw as blasphemous or problematic passages in which Christianity was allegedly attacked (subtly or directly) by Jews.[53] By the end of the sixteenth century, in many places Christians themselves had attained such proficiency in Hebrew that they began to publish their own Hebrew grammars and they depended a good deal less on Jews for Hebrew-language instruction.[54]

Christian Kabbalah reflected deeper philosophical interests among early modern Christians, and Kabbalah was adopted by some in their quest for the understanding of nature and their search for religious toleration. In some remarkable cases, as in scholarly circles in the Netherlands, as well as some intellectually vibrant princely courts from Italy through Germany and other parts of north-central Europe, Christian study of Kabbalah reached new heights, though often such study was based on translated, not original, texts.

Jewish mysticism had more practical implications as well, directed as it was toward the spiritual and medical needs of daily life through various magical and healing practices, often drawing from popular, non-Jewish practices. In both popular and scholarly works, there could be a fine line between religion and what we might today think of as superstition. While many have seen in the early modern world an increasing skepticism regarding such magic, the magical still resonated deeply in the worldviews of early modern people. As in the broader, non-Jewish world, folk beliefs often informed formal and offi- cially sanctioned religious practice.[55] Dreams could be called upon to testify to a range of personal events as well as broader religious and political develop- ments. Palmistry and astrology were also subscribed to by Jews, as they were by most early moderns. The idea of reincarnation and transmigration of the soul also circulated in segments of early modern Jewish society. Jews ascribed great power to words, especially the various names attributed to God. Masters of the art of utilizing these special names, known as *baalei shemot* (literally, mas- ters of the names) appear in a great deal of early modern literature. Folk beliefs were particularly able to cut across denominational divides, and Jews shared many customs and beliefs with the people in the broader societies in which they lived. At times, they assumed these beliefs and rituals directly; at other times, they filtered them through a Jewish prism, acculturating practices and mak- ing them ostensibly Jewish. The engagement in magic and sorcery also knew no gender boundaries, and we have many examples of women proficient in a range of magical arts and for many different purposes, often in the area of reproduction.

Messiansim, like Kabbalah, received new impetus in the years after the great expulsion of the Jews from Spain. The upheaval of a central and long-standing Jewish population, combined with the mass movement of Jews and a plethora of significant world events, seemed to be the spark for a period of messianic speculation. False messiahs abounded throughout Europe, both Jewish and non-Jewish. Some, like Asher Lemlin (who mounted something of a crusade of repentance) in Germany, had a short and more regional impact. Others, like David Reubeni and Solomon Molkho touched off a domino-like effect, especially among Marranos. They struck the fantasy of many European leaders, who for a short time entertained their supposed burgeoning campaign against the Turks—Reubeni was alleged to have come from a distant kingdom in the east to recruit military support to battle the Muslims.

Dramatic events and discoveries, especially those in the New World, further excited messianic speculation around the globe. The important Amsterdam rabbi Menasseh ben Israel (1604–57), who developed a host of relationships with Christian scholars and who advocated vociferously for the readmission of Jews to England, also speculated about the meaning of the natives in America for world history. In addition to well-known Jewish personalities and widespread speculation about the Ten Lost Tribes, numerous tales circulated about warrior Jews, penned up in the mountains, waiting to usher in apocalyptic times. This myth of the "Red Jews" provided a powerful image for a Christian society expecting the apocalypse and fearing the very real spread of the Turks west.[56] It simultaneously reenforced anti-Jewish stereotypes and the fear that the Jews were plotting, this time with military assistance, the overthrow of Christianity and dominion over the entire world.

Perhaps the best-known Jewish messianic figure, certainly of our period, but perhaps in all of Jewish history, was Shabbetai Sevi.[57] Sevi was born in Smyrna in 1626. After an extended period of semi seclusion between 1642 and 1648, he publicly proclaimed himself the Messiah. Later, in 1665, in an apparent trance, Nathan of Gaza (1644–80), who would become something like Sevi's number two man and his publicity agent, made several utterances, including referring to Sevi as the Messiah and himself as a prophet chosen by God. Sevi apparently accepted this proclamation, and in the summer of that year announced that the traditional fast of the seventeenth day of the month of Tammuz, the beginning of a three-week period of mourning for the destruction of the Temple, was turned into a feast day. While there was precedence in Jewish thought for a messianic reversion of days of sorrow to ones of joy, Sevi apparently had other questionable practices, including some related to the consumption of nonkosher food.

Sevi traveled to Jerusalem, but was summarily expelled by the rabbis there. Still, tales of his alleged miracles, such as resurrection of the dead, grew and circulated across the Islamic world and throughout all of Europe. While many discounted Sevi and his accomplice, large numbers of Jews seem to have been convinced that indeed the messianic era was beginning. In 1666, Sevi sailed to Istanbul from Smyrna, where he appeared prepared to remove the crown from the Sultan and assume rule over the Ottoman state. In February of that year, he was captured by Turkish authorities, who were careful to bring him to court without harm to avoid turning him into a martyr. After being imprisoned and given the choice between death and conversion to Islam, Sevi converted. He was eventually banished to Albania, where he died in 1676.

While many followers were quite naturally devastated, some held fast to their belief in the failed Messiah, especially convinced by the prophet Nathan that the Messiah had to penetrate the world of Islam in order to elevate the remaining divine sparks, save the Muslims from evil, and then usher in the messianic era. Others argued that Sevi was indeed the Messiah, but the Messiah son of Joseph, who would serve as a precursor to the final Messiah son of David. While small pockets of believers continued long after Sevi's conversion and death, forming sectarian groups, such belief was frequently condemned. Sabbatians were excommunicated by the Polish Council of Four Lands in 1669, for example. The Shabbetai Sevi debacle had long-standing consequences within and beyond the Jewish community. In the Ottoman Empire, for example, some scholars have maintained, the Shabbetai Sevi episode accelerated the decline of the position of the Jewish community and simultaneously spurred conservativism and the strengthening of rabbinic authority. Another fascinating epilogue to the Shabbetai Sevi story was the development of a radical group called the Frankists, followers of the charismatic Jacob Frank (1726–91) in eastern Europe. Frank crafted a new religion integrating aspects of Judaism and Christianity.[58]

Early modern Jewish society was simultaneously inward and outward looking. It was grounded in rabbinic law and interpretation, but given a far range of latitude in terms of local praxis. Fairly syncretistic in many areas, early modern Judaism often allowed for the Judaization of many non-Jewish customs and even intellectual systems. This entailed a diversity of intellectual pursuits and positions, some of which meshed nicely with inherited outlooks and others that provided points of conflict for contemporaries. Some historians, such as Jacob Katz, have described early modern Jewry as a society that could neutralize such diversity of opinions and practice and still maintain a broad cohesion.[59] That does not mean that there was no dissent, schism, or heresy in the early modern Jewish world. Increasingly over the course of the early modern period, individuals who transgressed communal regulations or authority, established rabbinic norms, or customs, were subjected to censure and, especially after the middle of the sixteenth century, excommunication. One individual, whose story reflects this development, is the famous philosopher Baruch (Benedict) Spinoza.[60] Spinoza was excommunicated, but unlike others, even in his own generation, he did not return to the Jewish community. He also never converted to Christianity. Spinoza, therefore, is perhaps the first visible example of a Jew to leave Judaism but not accept another formal religion, marking him, according to some scholars, as the first "modern Jew."

Spinoza came from a well-entrenched family in the Portuguese Jewish community in Amsterdam. He had a fairly traditional educational upbringing and may have even had some traditional yeshiva education. Spinoza clearly demonstrated familiarity with some key Jewish texts. He was affected by both internal and external influences as well as by some very significant independent thinking, not entirely unusual in the cosmopolitan Amsterdam Jewish community, which included a number of heterodox thinkers and individuals who returned to Judaism after living much of their lives nominally, at least, as Christians. Spinoza's education also included classical learning and philosophy.

There is no evidence that Spinoza sought consciously to break with the Jewish community. However, his views, which were disquieting to the communal authorities, for the doubts they might raise, were probably as problematic if seen by non-Jewish citizens and authorities as examples of Jewish religious instigation. Spinoza outlined a study of Scripture that followed a methodology for the study of nature. He differentiated philosophy and reason, which aims at truth, from theology, which seeks acts of piety and obedience. Spinoza sought to liberate reason from what he considered superstition. Spinoza opposed not so much religion as the priesthood, which he saw as a tool to dominate people. At the same time, Spinoza held miracles as unnatural events, arguing that nothing can really happen contrary to the laws of nature. In the same vein, Spinoza rejected the apparently miraculous nature of prophecy, a function of imagination according to Spinoza rather than knowledge. Spinoza rejected the notion of an unchanging and ever-enduring Bible. Mosaic Law, he argued, was created in a particular context and for specific purposes and a clearly delimited time. With his rational and historical approach to the Bible and religion, Spinoza's work was condemned not only by the Jewish community, but also by councils and synods of the Reformed Church as "the vilest and most sacrilegious book the world has ever seen."[61] After the excommunication, Spinoza studied at the University of Leiden, and he changed his name to Benedictus, a Latin equivalent of his Hebrew name Baruch. By the early 1660s, Spinoza was known both for his allegedly atheistic beliefs and his work with optical instruments. In 1664, Spinoza moved to a suburb of The Hague, and in 1670 to The Hague itself, where he stayed until he died.

Given the range of intellectual and social diversity, it should come as no surprise that there were a range of approaches to Jewish education. Formal community schools and community and individual yeshivot provided foundational instruction for boys. Individual tutors might be employed, especially in wealthier circles, to teach boys or girls. But Jews were educated in many fields beyond Judaica. Despite significant restrictions, Jews attended some

universities with increasing regularity, and they amassed a good deal of practical experience and expertise in a range of professions, always depending on local conditions. Many Jewish intellectuals were aware of advances in science and the arts, at times placing non-Jewish study within a Jewish context and at times approaching non-Jewish study outside a Jewish framework.

Relations beyond the Jewish Community

Jewish relations with non-Jews varied a great deal depending on local conditions. Individual Jews themselves might experience different relations with non-Jews depending upon their own professions, living situations, and intellectual engagement.

Jewish relations with non-Jews were still largely dictated by religious sensibilities. Jews were one of a number of religious minorities under Islam. Islamic law considered Jews to be *dhimmis*, or protected people. This meant that Jews had a certain political status that entitled them to protection from the state, but that they had to pay for such protection and that they were cast as second-class citizens, who were seen as inferior before the law. A range of obligations and restrictions impeded Jewish life. These included the head tax and a range of laws intended to segregate and humiliate Jews, and other groups as well, including restrictions on dress, mingling at bathhouses, and imposed silence in the proximity of mosques. While physical violence against Jews collectively was fairly rare under the Ottomans, mass pogroms were known for early modern Jews living in Muslim lands under extreme religious conditions—in the Safavid Empire in Iran or in North Africa at various times. In the early modern period, several waves of Islamic fundamentalism, especially in the late sixteenth and early seventeenth centuries, compromised what was generally a fairly tolerant situation for Jews, as evidenced by significant migration of Jews to the Ottoman Empire.[62] Cases of attack against individual Jews, even under Ottoman rule, are more frequently documented. Jews were at times associated with foreign Christians, an association that could be problematic in the ongoing early modern wars with the European West.[63] While Jews fared comparably well in Ottoman courts and economic spheres, Jews could suffer discrimination and were not always protected by local rulers. Jews continued to be seen as morally corrupt and problematic and Judaism was often criticized and attacked. On occasion, Jews were accused of tampering with the biblical text and of anti-Islamic statements. Constant pressure for conversion and assimilation also had an impact on Jewish individuals and communities.

In practice and in many locations, such theoretical limitations did not often come in to play as Jews enjoyed a great deal of autonomy within their own communities and a good deal of opportunity in economic and legal affairs beyond it. Jews continued to frequent Muslim courts and they were occupied in professions at all levels of society. What is more, Jewish religious development at times mirrored and drew from broader developments in Muslim society, including areas of mystical speculation. The economic decline that began to affect many in the Ottoman Empire by the end of the seventeenth century and the fomenting of Christians against Jews, as well as other episodes such as the Shabbetai Sevi debacle after the middle of the seventeenth century, often created for Jews an uneasy situation, in which ritual murder accusations—brewed in the Christian West—combined forces with accusations of Jewish conspiracy.

In the Christian world, Judaism was simultaneously seen as the religion that berthed and nourished, but was also superseded by, Christianity. With the emphasis on a return to original sources and to antiquity, Judaism and the Hebrew Bible gained a new significance in the early modern world. Expulsions in the early stages of the early modern period, especially into the sixteenth century, gave way in many places in Europe to an expansion of Jewish settlement and increased toleration of Jews by the end of the sixteenth century. Still, anti-Jewish imagery and accusations continued to mix with more normalized images of Jews and Jewish practices that could be found in a growing body of ethnographic literature that sought to present Jews and their practices, much as it did the culture and beliefs of peoples in other parts of the world, such as the Americas and the Far East. Many political authorities, from kings to local princes, found potential economic benefit by having Jews settle and work within their borders and many offered concessions that allowed Jews professional as well as religious autonomy. As a result, Jews were allowed in to many lands that had previously been closed to them—in parts of Italy, northern Germany, and even England, which finally officially readmitted Jews in the middle of the seventeenth century. Such mercantilist orientations did not necessarily do away with restrictions or negative perceptions, and the early modern period is often known as the period of the ghetto as well.

A number of rulers consigned their Jews to segregated living quarters, and for a variety of purposes—some rooted in fear of contamination and anti-Jewish sensibilities; others allegedly for the protection of the Jews themselves.[64] Indeed, interactions between Jews and Christians were closely monitored in many places. In areas where there were significant populations of Marranos, or new Christians, there was particular concern about Jewish proselytizing. In these environments, notably in Iberia, Italy, and New World colonies ruled by the Spanish and Portuguese, the Inquisition was frequently involved with New Christians accused of Judaizing and even, on occasion with actual Jews who, although not technically subject to the Inquisition could fall within its scope of operations if they were accused of impeding conversion to Christianity or winning converts back to Judaism.[65]

Changes within leadership also could affect the Jews. Individual popes and secular rulers might have very different attitudes about Jews and Judaism and advocate diverse policies of toleration or persecution as a result. Local conditions might mediate or exacerbate such policy changes. Increasingly negative laws that allowed for expulsions of Jews, stricter policies toward Judaizing, and burning of Jewish books, for example, emerged after the middle of the sixteenth century in some domains of the Catholic Church. At the same time, the diversity of religious views and growing globalization led to greater contact with people of different religious, social, and cultural backgrounds and, in some important ways, facilitated greater toleration.

As the primary non-Christian population in the Christian West, Jews were frequently cast as representing the inversion of Christian ideals. Ironically, anti-Jewish representation presented Jews as blasphemous and anti-Christian, even as alleged Jewish actions were marshaled to demonstrate that even the Jews believed in the central tenets of Christianity. Jews, for example, were accused of host desecration, which made Jews out to be enemies of Christians and Christianity at the same time that such accusations implied that Jews understood the miracle of the host as its was transformed into the body of Jesus and attempted to denigrate it, through piercing, burning, and other tortures. Jews were frequently aligned by Christian writers and artists with the devil or the anti-Christ and were seen as a people who tried to tempt good Christians in to bad behavior or away from proper Christian belief and practice. In the early modern age of Confessionalization, the full range of anti-Jewish depictions were applied by Christians of different denominations against each other in confessional battles. Lutherans, for example, were accused by Catholics of Judaizing, and Catholics were accused by Protestants of harboring Jewish rituals and labeled as new Pharisees.[66] As noted above, Jewish marginalization was at once a form of anti-Judaism and an ongoing catalyst to anti-Jewish speculation. Jews were made to live apart, to some extent, from Christian society, yet such separation spawned accusations of conspiracy and magical and diabolical machinations. Jews were often seen as in league with communal or state enemies, a motif particularly compelling with the Ottomans pressing into parts of central Europe. Frequently, Jews were dehumanized with language that cast them as animals and filth or pestilence.

Jews living in eastern Europe, especially Poland, faced the same theoretical handicaps that Jews living in the West did. In Poland in the sixteenth century and well into the eighteenth century, the Counter Reformation Church reinforced anti-Jewish provisions as it battled against Protestantism. Ritual murder charges also made their way to eastern Europe, albeit later than in the West. The first Polish accusations were from the middle of the sixteenth century;[67] 16 accusations would be heard in the sixteenth century, 33 in the seventeenth, and 32 in the eighteenth century.[68] There were also episodes of anti-Jewish violence on small scales as well as larger ones—consider, in the latter category, the massacres associated with the Chmielnicki revolt in the middle of the seventeenth century. Early modern legislation vacillated at times between positive opportunities and normal relations on the one hand and negative restrictions, anti-Jewish sensibilities, and persecution of Jews on the other.

If anything has become clear in the scholarship of the past generation, it is that Jews were not of necessity a passive group. While not always successful, Jews at times had the capacity and certainly took the initiative to defend themselves and advance their individual and communal interests. In addition, Jews might from time to time develop and circulate polemic that attacked Christians and other groups, even as such efforts were utilized to strengthen internal Jewish identity. Infamous anti-Christian writings such as *Sefer Toldot Yeshu* (Book of the Generations of Jesus), a mocking life of Jesus, and *Sefer ha-Nizzahon* (Book of the Debater), something of a handbook for debate with Christians, circulated widely in early modern Jewish communities.[69] Jews at times, as they did in the Middle Ages, advanced depictions of Muhammad that were negative, though with a great deal of care and most frequently from within the borders of Christianity.

Conclusions and Scholarly Directions

For the early modern period, as for most historical periods, we generally know the most about wealthy Jews and Jewish intellectuals. At the same time, Jews who transgressed communal or religious norms often find their way in to the records of the past—in Jewish sources as well as non-Jewish sources, such as Inquisition records. Of course, the focus on such individuals of high profile can distort our understanding of Jewish life and community. The vast majority of Jews, including the middle and lower classes, men as well as women, do not appear in many, if any, documents and we can only speculate on their day-to-day life and histories, broached at times with the occasional chronicle or memoir and through indirect gleanings.

Similarly, our perceptions of the early modern Jewish past can be overly colored by major and well-documented events. That we have more information about prescriptive laws intended to be applied to the Jews tells us a great deal about how Jews were conceptualized and were to be regulated. They may tell us less about the realities of Jewish life on the ground. More dramatic, if irregular, pogroms or trials lend the impression that Jews were constantly under existential threat. More recent findings of Jewish daily life and normalized relations with non-Jewish neighbors tend to balance that reality with a more nuanced, though no less complicated, picture of early modern Jewish experiences.

Given all of that, where is current and future research on early modern Jews and Judaism taking us? Based on recent book publications in early modern Jewish history, it is clear that the entire field is vibrant and changing. Of the books published in the past several years,[70] almost 10 percent have dealt with issues of historiography or periodization, suggesting that serious attention is being lavished on the methodologies utilized in the field and that the shape of the field is still emerging. Books, which typically reflect research conducted over the past decade, still reflect what might be seen as a rather traditional approach to early modern Jewish themes. A good deal has appeared that addresses Jewish literature and languages, as well as a diverse range of Jewish and Christian relations (especially issues of persecution and intellectual developments around themes such as messianism, economics, and conversion). Scholars appear to be interested in Shabbetai Sevi and the implications of his history, as well as some other marginalized groups, such as Karaites. Reflecting what has clearly been a renaissance of Sephardic studies, almost 10 percent of books have dealt with various related themes. Diaspora history, and especially the history of the Jews in the Americas and the Atlantic, has been well represented as has the history of the Jews in certain regions, such as Italy (particularly Venice) and Amsterdam. A look at book publications suggests a healthy balance of what we might term intellectual and social or cultural studies. Less attention has been given to communal history and identity and to women and gender, two trends that more recent scholarship, as reflected in articles and conference presentations, suggest are becoming more central.

Reviewing articles written in all languages over the past two decades in early modern fields,[71] a few general observations can be made. First, issues of Jewish and Christian relations represent the largest number of studies (around a third). This may be due to the long history of interest in the subject, the availability of documents and materials, and the backgrounds of the researchers themselves, who have frequently been trained in a broader early modern European context. The nature of the themes addressed in such studies is quite vast, however. Some staples, such as anti-Jewish representation and activities are still frequently published. Increasing attention has been paid to ethnography in the early modern period. A significant amount of attention has been given to history and themes associated with conversos and crypto-Jews, reflecting an ongoing fascination with this subject and contemporary questions of Jewish identity. Equally robust production of scholarship has addressed Christian Kabbalah and Christian Hebraism, especially as reflected in the vast array of political writings of the early modern period. The Inquisition still receives attention, but it should be noted that the Jewish side of Jewish and Christian relations is now receiving more, if still limited, play as well. There are numerous studies that look at Jewish views of and polemic against Christianity and some studies that examine Jewish crime.

As with book publications, in articles the broad field of arts and literature still receives a good deal of focus in early modern Jewish studies—some of this focus is rather traditional in terms of themes, while some studies utilize more cutting-edge methods and address new topics. A small number of studies focus on material culture; especially noteworthy is the increase in studies on architecture of synagogues and sacred spaces, such as cemeteries. Research on aspects of literature—in terms both of Jewish writing and literary representation of Jews—is vast, as is the ongoing discussion of the book and print culture in the early modern Jewish world. Approximately 2 percent of all articles deal with Yiddish and about double that with a broad category of "culture," which has been quite elastic and difficult to define with precision. Added to this group of scholarship can be more "traditional" themes. Constituting something like 6 percent of article publications are pieces on Jewish law, customs, biblical commentaries, and sermons. A third of this material now deals with a growing theme of ritual and liturgy. Here the work in early modern studies more broadly and the treasure of materials within Jewish history has helped to spark a good deal of interest. Finally, intellectual history more generally is well represented in recent studies. Philosophy, Kabbalah, and science, particularly medicine (formal and popular), continue to receive important attention and, in the case of the latter, reflect particularly significant advances. But the nature of some of the scholarship has also changed a bit from earlier scholarship. For example, one is more likely to find discussions of dissent and heretical thought than in the past. This trend is perhaps well reflected in ongoing interest in Sabbatians as well as Karaites and more recently Frankists, and something of a renaissance of interest in Spinoza and frequent, if not fully justified, associations with secularization.

Sephardic studies continue to be important in early modern Jewish scholarship, and this work increasingly transgresses previous borders between topics and even geographic regions. Here and elsewhere there have been significant strides in the study of Jews under Islam, though the bulk of scholarship still addresses Jews in western Europe. A good deal of attention continues to be paid to the move to the West and the Atlantic seaboards in Europe and the Americas. Large and well-documented communities continue to garner attention, but many studies now utilize these resources to ask questions beyond the history and development of individual communities. Still, one important trend over the past two decades has been the explosion of studies about the nature and development of early modern Jewish communities. More than 8 percent of article publications have dealt with various aspects of community structure and identity and many more have addressed such themes more indirectly or as subtopics. Issues of communal governance, memory, demography, and the implications of ghettoization have been of great interest to Jewish historians as they have to historians outside of Jewish Studies. Equally significant has been the social history of the Jews and their communities. Again, approximately

8 percent of articles have addressed issues related to women, a very promising trend that reflects a good deal of innovation in historical method, serious reconsideration of how to read historical sources and material culture, a willingness to consider a broader range of social and gender questions, and attempts to address long-imbalanced views of the past.

In recent articles, we can observe important methodological innovation. Still, the number of articles that tackle historiography is down from book publications (to about 2 percent), suggesting perhaps a maturing of the field and a clearer sense of scholarly direction and agendas. A good deal of work on the later Middle Ages continues to find its way into the early modern field, but many studies on Enlightenment and Hasidism are also now cast with a broader net and appear in the context of early modern developments.

A look at recent early modern presentations at the Association for Jewish Studies confirms some of these general impressions, but such results need to be read carefully as many sessions focus on specific themes and are organized according to the interest of a specific scholar or group of scholars. What is more, early modern Jewish papers now find homes at many diverse conferences, including the Medieval Congress, the Sixteenth Century Studies Conference, the Renaissance Society of America conference, among others, as well as discipline-specific international conferences that address many different themes and geographical regions.

Studies of early modern Jews and early modern Jewry are rich, diverse, and quite compelling. They have introduced a variety of themes in many different settings and utilized a remarkable array of sources and scholarly methodologies. It is perhaps not too much to contend that early modern Jewish studies have helped to set significant scholarly agendas and have advanced the academic field of Jewish Studies as much, if not more, than any other discipline or period of focus. Based on the field and scope of current research, as well as growing interest in the field and its many subthemes in Jewish Studies and general curricula across higher education and in the public marketplace of ideas, that trend will surely continue to be of great benefit.

Notes

1. There were and continue to be exceptions, to be sure, but the largest amount of research and publishing on the Jews and Judaism in the early modern period favors Western and European topics. The work of Bernard Lewis and Shlomo Goitein (especially for the Middle Ages), among others, has been important in keeping Jews under Islam on the academic agenda. Recent political and religious interest in Islam has stoked further interest, though the small number of Jews living in many of the once-thriving Jewish communities under Islam continues to temper such interest.
2. A number of Katz's works remain important in the study of medieval and early modern Jewish history. Consider, Jacob Katz (1961), *Exclusiveness and Tolerance: Studies in*

Jewish-Gentile Relations in Medieval and Modern Times. New Jersey: Behrman House; idem (1978, orig. 1973), *Out of the Ghetto: The Social Background of Jewish Emancipation, 1770–1870*. New York: Schocken Books; idem (1993, orig. 1958), *Tradition and Crisis: Jewish Society at the End of the Middle Ages*, Bernard Dov Cooperman (trans.). New York: New York University Press; and idem (1989, orig. 1983), *The "Shabbes Goy:" A Study in Halakhic Flexibility*, Yoel Lerner (trans.). Philadelphia: Jewish Publication Society.

3. See, for example, the recent studies that focus on the Middle Ages, but extend in some cases to the early modern period: Avraham Grossman (2004), *Pious and Rebellious: Jewish Women in Medieval Europe*, Jonathan Chipman (trans.). Waltham: Brandeis University Press; Elisheva Baumgarten (2004), *Mothers and Children: Jewish Family Life in Medieval Europe*. Princeton: Princeton University Press; and most recently, Simha Goldin (2011), *Jewish Women in Europe in the Middle Ages: A Quiet Revolution*. Manchester: Manchester University Press. Consider, as well, Natalie Zemon Davis (1995), *Women on the Margins: Three Seventeenth-Century Lives*. Cambridge, MA: Harvard University Press; and Judith R. Baskin (ed.) (1998), *Jewish Women in Historical Perspective* (2nd edn). Detroit: Wayne State University Press.

4. For a counter to this assumption, see David Joshua Malkiel (2009), *Reconstructing Ashkenaz: The Human Face of Franco-German Jewry, 1000–1250*. Stanford: Stanford University Press.

5. Among the many examples, see Dana E. Katz (2008), *The Jew in the Art of the Italian Renaissance*. Philadelphia: University of Pennsylvania Press; Marc Michael Epstein (1997), *Dreams of Subversion in Medieval Jewish Art and Literature*. University Park, PA: Pennsylvania State University Press; Petra Schöner (2002), *Judenbilder im deutschen Einblattdruck der Renaissance: ein Beitrag zur Imagologie*. Baden-Baden: V. Koerner; Vivian B. Mann (ed.) (1989), *Gardens and Ghettos: The Art of Jewish Life in Italy*. Berkeley: University of California Press; Heinz Schreckenberg (1996), *The Jews in Christian Art: An Illustrated History*. New York: Continuum; Ruth Mellinkoff (1993), *Outcasts: Signs of Otherness in Northern European Art of the Late Middle Ages*. 2 Vols. Berkeley: University of California Press. In the area of Jewish music, see Don Harrán (1999), *Salamone Rossi: Jewish Musician in Late Renaissance Mantua*. Oxford: Oxford University Press.

6. See Talya Fishman (1997), *Shaking the Pillars of Exile: "Voice of a Fool," an Early Modern Jewish Critique of Rabbinic Culture*. Stanford, Stanford University Press.

7. See Sander L. Gilman (1986), *Jewish Self-Hatred: Anti-Semtisim and the Hidden Language of the Jews*. Baltimore: Johns Hopkins University Press; Yaacov Deutsch (2012), *Judaism in Christian Eyes: Ethnographic Descriptions of Jews and Judaism in Early Modern Europe*, Avi Aronsky (trans.). Oxford: Oxford University Press; and, most recently Michael T. Walton (2012), *Anthonius Margaritha and the Jewish Faith: Jewish Life and Conversion in Sixteenth-Century Germany*. Detroit: Wayne State University Press.

8. See Elisheva Baumgarten (2004), *Mothers and Children: Jewish Family Life in Medieval Ashkenaz*. Princeton: Princeton University Press; Ivan G. Marcus (2004), *The Jewish Life Cycle: Rites of Passage from Biblical to Modern Times*. Seattle: University of Washington Press.

9. See, for example, Yosef Kaplan (1994), "The Place of the Herem in the Sefardic Community of Hamburg during the Seventeenth Century," in Michael Studemund-Halevy (ed.), *Die Sefarden in Hamburg: Zur Geschichte einer Minderheit*, Vol. 1. Hamburg: Buske, pp. 63–88.

10. See Dean Phillip Bell (2007), "Confessionalization and Social Discipline in Early Modern Germany: A Jewish Perspective," in Peter Wallace, Peter Starenko, Michael Printy, and Christopher Ocker (eds), *Politics and Reformations: Studies in Honor of Thomas A. Brady, Jr*. Leiden: Brill Academic Publishers, pp. 345–72.

11. See Haim Beinart (2002, orig. 1994), *The Expulsion of the Jews from Spain*, Jeffrey M. Green (trans.). Oxford: Littman Library of Jewish Civilization; Elisheva Carlebach (2001), *Divided Souls: Converts from Judaism in Germany, 1500–1750*. New Haven: Yale University Press.
12. In general, see Dean Phillip Bell (2008), *Jews in the Early Modern World*. Lanham: Rowman and Littlefield.
13. Amsterdam has received a good deal of attention. Particularly useful studies include: Miriam Bodian (1997), *Hebrews of the Portuguese Nation: Conversos and Community in Early Modern Amsterdam*. Bloomington: Indiana University Press; and Daniel Swetschinski (2000), *Reluctant Cosmopolitans: The Portuguese Jews of Seventeenth-Century Amsterdam*. London: Littman Library of Jewish Civilization.
14. Venice has similarly garnered important attention. See, for example, Robert C. Davis and Benjamin Ravid (eds) (2001), *The Jews of Early Modern Venice*. Baltimore: Johns Hopkins University Press.
15. See Francesca Trivellato (2009), *The Familiarity of Strangers: The Sephardic Diaspora, Livorno, and Cross-Cultural Trade in the Early Modern Period*. New Haven: Yale University Press; and Aron di Leone Leoni (2011), *La Nazione Ebraica Spagnola e Portoghese di Ferrara (1492–1559): I suoi rapporti col governo ducale e la popolazione locale ed i suoi legami con le Nazioni Portoghesi di Ancona, Pesaro e Venezia*. 2 Vols. Florence: Leo S. Olschki Editore.
16. David B. Ruderman (1995), *Jewish Thought and Scientific Discovery in Early Modern Europe*. New Haven: Yale University Press.
17. Kenneth R. Stow (ed.) (1995), *The Jews in Rome*. 2 Vols. Leiden: Brill.
18. See Esther Benbassa (1999), *The Jews of France: A History from Antiquity to the Present*, M. B. DeBevoise (trans.). Princeton: Princeton University Press.
19. See Jay R. Berkovitz (2004), *Rites and Passages: The Beginnings of Modern Jewish Culture in France, 1650–1860*. Philadelphia: University of Pennsylvania Press.
20. See, for example, Marianne Calmann (1984), *The Carrière of Carprentras*. Oxford: Littman Library of Jewish Civilization.
21. See Gérard Nahon (2003), *Juifs et judaïsme à Bordeaux*. Bordeaux: Mollat.
22. Antony Polonsky (2008), *The Jews in Poland and Russia*. 2 Vols. Oxford: Littman Library of Jewish Civilization, p. 68.
23. Yaron Ben-Naeh (2008), *Jews in the Realm of the Sultans: Ottoman Jewish Society in the Seventeenth Century*. Tübingen: Mohr Siebeck, p. 65.
24. Ibid., pp. 74–6.
25. Ibid., p. 79.
26. Ibid., p. 326.
27. Ibid., p. 331.
28. Ibid., pp. 318–42.
29. See Swetschinski, *Reluctant Cosmopolitans*, for example.
30. Umberto Fortis (2003), *La bella ebrea: Sara Copio Sullam, poetessa nel ghetto di Venezia del '600*. Torino: S. Zamorani.
31. See Glückel of Hameln (1977 reprint), *The Memoirs of Glückel of Hameln*, Marvin Lowenthal (trans.). New York: Schocken Books; Monika Richarz (ed.) (2001), *Die Hamburger Kauffrau Glikl: Jüdische Existenz in der Frühen Neuzeit*. Hamburg: Christians; Glückel of Hameln (2006), *Glikel: Zikhronot 1691–1719*, Hava Turniansky (trans.). Jerusalem: Merkaz Zalman Shazar [Hebrew]; Davis, *Women on the Margins*.
32. Ben-Naeh, *Jews in the Realm of the Sultans*, p. 368.
33. Ibid., p. 353.
34. Dean Phillip Bell (2011), "Marginalization and the Jews in Late Medieval Germany," *Das Mittelalter* 16: 72–93.

35. See the debates over the work of Philippe Ariès (1974), *Western Attitudes toward Death from the Middle Ages to the Present*. Baltimore: Johns Hopkins University Press, for example in Baumgarten, *Mothers and Children*.

36. See Stephen G. Burnett (2012), *Christian Hebraism in the Reformation Era (1500–1660): Authors, Books, and the Transmission of Jewish Learning*. Leiden: Brill.

37. See, for example, Lester A. Segal (1989), *Historical Consciousness and Religious Tradition in Azariah de' Rossi's Me'or 'Einayim*. Philadelphia: Jewish Publication Society.

38. For example, Byron L. Sherwin (1982), *Mystical Theology and Social Dissent: The Life and Works of Judah Loew of Prague*. Rutherford: Fairleigh Dickinson University Press.

39. See Matt Goldish (2008), *Jewish Questions: Responsa on Sephardic Life in the Early Modern Period*. Princeton: Princeton University Press.

40. See Hayim Soloveitchick (1978), "Can Halakhic Texts Talk History?" *Association for Jewish Studies Review* 3: 152–96.

41. See Bell, "Confessionalization and Social Discipline in Early Modern Germany."

42. In general, on Karo, see the dated but still useful, R. J. Zwi Werblowsky (1962), *Joseph Karo: Lawyer and Mystic*. London: Oxford University Press.

43. See Dean Phillip Bell (2007), *Jewish Identity in Early Modern Germany: Memory, Power and Community*. Aldershot: Ashgate Publishers.

44. Polonsky, *The Jews in Poland and Russia*, Vol. 1, p. 126.

45. See Jospeh M. Davis (2004), *Yom-Tov Lipmann Heller: Portrait of a Seventeenth-Century Rabbi*. Oxford: Littman Library of Jewish Civilization.

46. See the still-valuable work of Gershom G. Scholem (1941), *Major Trends in Jewish Mysticism*. Jerusalem: Schocken. See also the important revisions reflected in the work of Moshe Idel, including: (1988) *Kabbalah: New Perspectives*. New Haven: Yale University Press; and Jospeh Dan (1986), *Jewish Mysticism and Jewish Ethics*. Seattle: University of Washington Press.

47. For example, see Allison Coudert (1999), *The Impact of the Kabbalah in the Seventeenth Century: The Life and Thought of Francis Mercury van Helmont (1614–1698)*. Leiden: Brill.

48. For a valuable summary, see Morris M. Faierstein (1995), "Safed Kabbalah and the Sephardic Heritage," in Z. Zohar (ed.), *Sephardic and Mizrahi Jewry: From the Golden Age of Spain to Modern Times*. New York: New York University Press, pp. 196–215, pp. 201 ff.

49. See Scholem, *Major Trends in Jewish Mysticism*, regarding the significance of Lurianic thought.

50. See Sherwin, *Mystical Theology and Social Dissent*.

51. Faierstein, "Safed Kabbalah and the Sephardic Heritage," pp. 204–5.

52. Most recently, see David Price (2011), *Johannes Reuhlin and the Campaign to Destroy Jewish Books*. Oxford: Oxford University Press.

53. See Stephen G. Burnett (1994), "Distorted Mirrors: Antonius Margaritha, Johann Buxtorf and Christian Ethnographies of the Jews," *Sixteenth Century Journal* 25: 275–87; Stephen G. Burnett (1988), "The Regulation of Hebrew Printing in Germany, 1555–1630: Confessional Politics and the Limits of Jewish Toleration," in Max Reinhart and Thomas Robisheaux (eds), *Infinite Boundaries: Order, Disorder, and Reorder in Early Modern German Culture*. Kirksville: Sixteenth Century Journal Publishers, pp. 329–48; Amnon Raz-Krakotzkin (2007), *The Censor, the Editor, and the Text: The Catholic Church and the Shaping of the Jewish Canon in the Sixteenth Century*, Jackie Feldman (trans.). Philadelphia: University of Pennsylvania Press.

54. See recently, Debra Kaplan (2011), *Beyond Expulsion: Jews, Christians, and Reformation Strasbourg*. Stanford: Stanford University Press.

55. Joshua Trachtenberg (1939), *Jewish Magic and Superstition: A Study in Folk Religion*. New York: Behrman's Jewish Book House.

56. Andrew Colin Gow (1995), *The Red Jews: Antisemitism in an Apocalyptic Age, 1200–1600*. Leiden: Brill.

57. Classic is Gershom Scholem (1973), *Sabbatai Sevi: The Mystical Messiah, 1626–1676*, R. J. Zwi Werblowsky (trans.). Princeton: Princeton University Press. See also Matt D. Goldish (2004), *The Sabbatean Prophets*. Cambridge, MA: Harvard University Press; Richard H. Popkin (1994), "Three English Tellings of the Sabbatai Zevi Story," *Jewish History* 8:1–2: 43–54; Giacomo Saban (1993), "Sabbatai Sevi as Seen by a Contemporary Traveller," *Jewish History* 7:2: 105–18; and Jetteke van Wijk (1999), "The Rise and Fall of Shabbatai Zevi as Reflected in Contemporary Press Reports," *Studia Rosenthalia* 33:1: 7–27.

58. Pawel Maciejko (2011), *The Mixed Multitude: Jacob Frank and the Frankist Movement, 1755–1816*. Philadelphia: University of Pennsylvania Press.

59. See, by way of example, his (1973) *Out of the Ghetto: The Social Background of Jewish Emancipation, 1770–1870*. Cambridge, MA: Harvard University Press.

60. There is a good deal of recent interest and scholarship on Spinoza. See, for example: Steven M. Nadler (1999), *Spinoza: A Life*. Cambridge: Cambridge University Press; Don Garrett (ed.) (1996), *The Cambridge Companion to Spinoza*. Cambridge: Cambridge University Press; Harry A. Wolfson (1983), *The Philosophy of Spinoza: Unfolding the Latent Process of His Reasoning*. Cambridge, MA: Harvard University Press.

61. According to Wolfson, a leading scholar of Spinoza, Spinoza was new and daring in a number of ways. See Wolfson, *The Philosophy of Spinoza*. See also Steven M. Nadler (2011), *A Book Forged in Hell: Spinoza's Scandalous Treatise and the Birth of the Secular Age*. Princeton: Princeton University Press.

62. Ben-Naeh, *Jews in the Realm of the Sultans*, pp. 109–11.

63. See Aryeh Shmuelevitz (1984), *The Jews of the Ottoman Empire in the Late Fifteenth and the Sixteenth Centuries: Administrative, Economic, Legal, and Social Relations as Reflected in the Responsa*. Leiden: Brill.

64. On the ghetto, see Davis and Benjamin (2001), *The Jews of Early Modern Venice*; Stefanie B. Siegmund *(2006), The Medici State and the Ghetto of Florence: The Construction of an Early Modern Jewish Community*. Stanford: Stanford University Press.

65. Miriam Bodian (2007), *Dying in the Law of Moses: Crypto-Jewish Martyrdom in the Iberian World*. Bloomington: Indiana University Press.

66. See Dean Phillip Bell (forthcoming), "Polemics of Confessionalization: Depictions of Jews and Jesuits in Early Modern Germany," in James Bernauer and Robert A. Maryks (eds), *"The Tragic Couple": Encounters between Jews and Jesuits*. Leiden: Brill.

67. Polonsky, *The Jews in Poland and Russia*, Vol. 1, p. 27.

68. Ibid.

69. See Israel Yuval and Ora Limor (2004), "Skepticism and Conversion: Jews, Christians, and Doubters in 'Sefer ha-Nizzahon,'" in Allison P. Coudert and Jeffery S. Shoulson (eds), *Hebraica Veritas? Jews and the Study of Judaism in Early Modern Europe*. Philadelphia: University of Pennsylvania Press, pp. 159–80.

70. For this quick overview I chose the books listed in Harvard University's online catalogue.

71. For a representative, though by no means comprehensive, sampling I have utilized articles listed in Rambi Index (http://aleph.nli.org.il/F?local_base=rmb01; last accessed January 21, 2013).

8 Modernity, Judaism, and Jews

Gil Graff

Introduction

Modernity, characterized by scientific thought, secularization, and religious toleration and a trend toward recognizing individual status rather than corporate standing in the political sphere, wrought significant changes in Jewish life starting in the eighteenth century. Early in the nineteenth century, 80 percent of world Jewry—which numbered, in total, fewer than 3 million people—lived in

Europe. Most Jews outside western, central, eastern, and southeastern Europe lived in the Ottoman Empire, North Africa, and the Middle East.

Modernization and the Enlightenment and Emancipation that it engendered did not come to all places at once. As of 1871, only one-quarter of the world's 7.5 million Jews was emancipated; the Jews of Czarist Russia and the Ottoman Empire were not. By the 1920s, however, Jews had for the most part become citizens of modern national states.

Whether consciously recognized and articulated by those living during the era or not, a central motif of the period 1750–1945 is the tension in Jewish life between integration into the larger society and distinctiveness as Jews. While, in western Europe and the United States, Judaism was often framed in religious terms, cultural and national expressions of identity characterized Jewish responses to modernity in eastern Europe. Modernizing trends resulting from European colonialism in the Middle East and North Africa likewise evoked a variety of responses among local Jews. The theme of integration and distinctiveness was, in each setting, a significant part of the Jewish narrative, as Jews and Judaism encountered modernity.

Toward Modernity

The origins of the Jewish encounter with modernity can be seen in a gradual transition from medieval, corporate society to individual citizenship. In pre-modern European society, group membership rather than individual standing before the law defined political and social status. Throughout the Middle Ages, European Jews were, as a matter of law, bound by the regulatory authority of Jewish communal structures recognized by various rulers—often through the issuance of charters—as governing "their" Jews. The *kehillah*, the organized Jewish community, paid taxes raised in accordance with rules established and enforced by its autonomous governance for the privilege of Jewish residence and security.

Though there were, typically, restrictions as to where Jews could live and the economic pursuits in which they could engage, this "chartered" arrangement made for considerable self-government in Jewish communal life. Discipline was maintained through *herem*, the power of Jewish authorities to ban or excommunicate a noncompliant community member. In a tumultuous world in which group membership was essential, the threat of *herem* succeeded, by and large, in enforcing prevailing norms.

By the seventeenth century, in western and central Europe, rising absolutism was eroding traditional corporate structures. The leveling of the political order—with all elements subordinate to the monarch— served, paradoxically, to pave the way for later democratic currents grounded in the notion of the equality of all before the law. "Court Jews" played a significant role in the process of centralization of state authority, especially in the German states.[1]

Though small in number, Court Jews—sometimes linked to one another through arranged marriages—were crucial suppliers of munitions and food for the military. Often such Jews adopted the outer trappings of the aristocratic circles within which they operated. Yet, despite acculturation in manners and dress, social relationships between Jews and their Court colleagues were uncommon; nor were Court Jews participants in Christian intellectual life.

At the same time, the impact of the Protestant Reformation gave rise, in some circles, to challenges of traditional religious assumptions. Critiques of long-held norms were also heard within Jewish society. These ranged from calls for educational reform posed by the renowned Rabbi Judah Loew (known as Maharal) of Prague to questioning the divinity and authority of Scriptures on the part of the freethinking philosopher Baruch Spinoza.

Spinoza, though placed in *herem* by Amsterdam's Jewish communal authorities, was, in his setting—already in the seventeenth century—able to lead his life in a "semi-neutral society" (a term coined by historian Jacob Katz) that tolerated religious differences. Another example of early modernizing trends is that of the port Jews of Habsburg Trieste.[2] Yet another case study of the Jews' encounter with modernity is that of English Jewry[3] at a time when John Locke was advancing the notion of religious toleration and advocating separation of church and state.

Haskalah in Western Europe

The eighteenth century, in the western European context, is commonly termed the "Age of Enlightenment." Among the educated classes, there was a sense of progress and faith in the advance of civilization. This perception included confidence in the power of human reason; it was an age skeptical of tradition. Enlightenment ideals posited a shared human faculty for recognizing common, "self evident" truths.

Many of the intellectuals of the era conceived of God as a First Cause of the universe who, as a Watchmaker, had set the world in motion. Traditional religious beliefs gave way, in some circles, to secularism. At the same time, there was greater tolerance of diverse religious opinions.

Against this backdrop, in western Europe, the question of including Jews in civic affairs became a matter of vigorous debate in intellectual circles, particularly in Berlin. Among the widely discussed essays on the subject was a piece by a Prussian government official, Christian Wilhelm von Dohm, titled: "Concerning the Amelioration of the Civil Status of the Jews" (1781). As the title

of Dohm's essay suggests, there was an underlying assumption that amelioration of the Jews' civil status would also improve the Jews' conduct.

Dohm imagined that the Jews would, organically, reform their religious system if prejudice and exclusion were to give way to inclusion in the broader
society. They would, contrary to the view of those who argued that the Jews'
integration into the social and civic order was impossible, surely, do away
with clannishness: "They will then reform their religious laws and regulations
according to the demands of society. They will go back to the freer and nobler
ancient Mosaic law, will explain and adapt it according to the changed times
and conditions, and will find authorizations to do so alone in the Talmud."[4]

In the climate of Enlightenment ideas and debate surrounding the possibility of the Jews' civic improvement and social and political integration, Joseph
II, monarch of the Austrian Empire, promulgated an Edict of Tolerance, in 1782,
aimed at making the Jews more useful to the state. Among the key strategies of
this enactment was education in the sciences, arts, and crafts for Jewish youth.
The edict was viewed as threatening by most traditional, local Jewish authorities. There were, however, some Jews who enthusiastically greeted the new
regulations.

Responding to the Edict of Tolerance, Naphtali Herz Wessely, a Jew of traditional learning who advocated greater engagement with general education and
the broader society, wrote a pamphlet, in Hebrew, aimed at generating support for the emperor's program among fellow Jews. The treatise, *Words of Peace
and Truth*—addressed to the "Congregation of Israel that Dwells in the Domain
of the Great Kaiser Joseph II, Who Loves and Gladdens All Mankind"—
distinguished between human knowledge, the teaching of man, and divine
knowledge, the teaching of God. Regrettably, wrote Wessely, European Jewry
had long neglected the pursuit of human knowledge. The interest of Joseph II in
improving education among his Jewish subjects should be embraced; indeed,
its aims facilitated return to a Jewish ideal.[5]

Wessely, who wrote his tract while living in Berlin, was part of a circle of
Jewish intellectuals known as *maskilim*, or "the enlightened." The most prominent figure of the Berlin Haskalah (Enlightenment) was Moses Mendelssohn
(1729–86), a celebrated thinker deeply rooted in Jewish learning as well as modern philosophy, respected by such prominent public figures as Christian Wilhelm
von Dohm and the philosopher and dramatist Gotthold Ephraim Lessing. Close
friendship between Mendelssohn and Lessing reflected an expanding sphere of
social interaction. Among Christians of liberal bent, Mendelssohn—as Wessely,
an observant Jew—represented a model of the possible, in terms of Jews participating in and contributing to European society.

As interpreted by Mendelssohn in his philosophical work *Jerusalem*, Judaism
is entirely a religion of deed, not of creed. In *Jerusalem*, Mendelssohn distinguished between "eternal truths," which are self-evident principles of reason,

and "divine law," which is God's revealed will. Mendelssohn identified the doctrinal part of Judaism with natural religion; knowledge of the "eternal truths" was not a matter of supernatural revelation but, rather, a universal heritage, intelligible to all humankind. While natural religion might lapse into superstition and idolatry, the descendants of Abraham, Isaac, and Jacob were "a nation which, through its constitution and institutions, through its laws and conduct, . . . was to call wholesome and unadulterated ideas of God and His attributes continuously to the attention of the rest of mankind."[6]

Mendelssohn's rationalistic approach to the nature of Judaism was characteristic of the Haskalah. *Maskilim* saw themselves as restoring Judaism to its pure form, overcoming distortions that had materialized over the course of the medieval period. Consistent with this perspective, they emphasized the study of biblical texts rather than later rabbinic literature.

The issue of education for Jewish youth in the new age was a major topic of discussion in the circle of *maskilim* surrounding Mendelssohn. Primary themes in the educational writings of the *maskilim* were the kinship of humankind, devotion to the state and government, and the necessity of economic rehabilitation (i.e. extending beyond the narrow commercial pursuits in which—often as a matter of legal restrictions—Jews had engaged for centuries). Haskalah writings reflected a positive view of the surrounding culture, accompanied by the sense that Jews were part of a universal heritage.

New schools were launched in the curriculum of which Haskalah ideals were given expression. Companion trends included the use of Hebrew as a vehicle for engaging the interest of those involved in traditional Jewish learning in matters of broader intellectual pursuit and efforts to educate Jews in the German language. The latter goal was promoted through translation of the Bible into German, by Mendelssohn and his circle, using Hebrew characters.

David Sorkin, a noted historian of the Haskalah era, observes that the Haskalah was "the culmination of a prolonged internal development, a radicalization of ideas and impulses present in Jewish society for over a century. The (European) Enlightenment allowed those ideas to be systematized by providing the rubric of a new ideal of man."[7] While the Haskalah began in Berlin, it developed as well in Galicia, Lithuania, and Russia—with branches extending to North Africa and Jerusalem[8]—in subsequent decades under circumstances to be explored *infra*.

Embracing Citizenship

It was in France that a segment of European Jewry first experienced the status of state citizen. The Revolution of 1789 proclaimed "liberty, equality and fraternity," and the National Assembly in Paris aimed to establish a constitutional democracy translating that slogan into law. In debating the eligibility of Jews for citizenship, Count Stanislas de Clermont-Tonnerre summed up the prevailing view: "Everything must be refused the Jews as a nation; everything must be granted to them as individuals."[9] In September 1791, the French National Assembly extended the opportunity of citizenship to all Jews taking the civic oath; the communal autonomy that had characterized medieval Jewry was at an end in France.

By 1799, a revolution-weary France had conceded virtually unlimited power to General Napoleon Bonaparte. Napoleon's interest in subordinating religion to the state, combined with his assessment of the apparent failure of the Jews' "regeneration" led to the emperor's call for an assembly of Jewish notables to be gathered in Paris in July, 1806, to address the matter of the place of religion in the life of the Jews. Pursuant to Napoleon's instructions, government prefects designated prescribed numbers of distinguished Jews, including rabbis and lay leaders, to participate in the "Assembly of Notables."

Napoleon's senior commissioner to the assembly observed that though "the wish of his majesty is, that you should be Frenchmen, it remains with you to accept of the proffered title, without forgetting that, to prove unworthy of it, would be renouncing it altogether."[10] In other words, continued citizenship depended on suitable responses to the questions presented. The 12 questions put before the assembly probed whether the Jews recognized the primacy of state law, France as their nation, and all Frenchmen as their brethren.[11]

Early in August, the assembly adopted a declaration to precede its answers to the specific questions, affirming "in the name of all Frenchmen, professing the religion of Moses" that "they must, above all, acknowledge and obey the laws of the prince."[12] Self-identification as "Frenchmen professing the religion of Moses" set the context for the replies that followed. While distinctive in professing a particular religion, the Jews of the realm were, first and foremost, Frenchmen, proclaimed the assembly's deputies. The proceedings of the assembly were followed by the convocation of a Grand Sanhedrin, formalizing its pronouncements.

Napoleon's impact was felt well beyond France and the lands over which his armies held sway. In Prussia, Frederick William III responded to the loss of more than half his territory to Napoleon in 1806–7 by instituting a series of reforms designed to strengthen the power of the state. One dimension of such reform was extending citizenship to Prussia's Jews, a status welcomed by the new citizens with great enthusiasm.

The eventual defeat of Napoleon brought to an end the sweeping acts of Emancipation that had characterized the generation 1790–1815. In the reactionary period that followed, Jews struggled to preserve the political rights they had so recently acquired. Not only civic opportunities but professional and social integration proceeded quite slowly. Amid a new and changing reality, the ensuing generation in the encounter with modernity gave rise to a range of Jewish religious responses that have endured to the present day.

New Religious Currents

On the backdrop of expanded engagement with broader, western European society, a movement for the Reform of Judaism emerged, early in the nineteenth century, starting in Germany. At Seesen, in Westphalia (then under Napoleonic rule), Israel Jacobson had financed construction of a new temple attached to a school he had founded. The dedication ceremony—at which Jacobson wore Protestant garb—attracted Christians as well as Jews. Addressing the assembled audience, Jacobson observed that Jewish ritual was weighted down with customs offensive to reason and to Christian neighbors. The times seemed ripe "to make possible that which a little while ago would have appeared impossible."[13]

Owing to political upheavals in Westphalia, Israel Jacobson soon relocated to Berlin. On *Shavuoth* (Pentecost), in 1815, Jacobson initiated a reform worship service at his home in Berlin. Thereafter, services were held each Saturday morning in his home, at which both Jews and Christians were present. These services featured a choir—including Christian singers—accompanied by organ music. Prayers were recited in German and Hebrew, and the service was abbreviated by omitting the traditional repetition of the silent devotion. The *musaf* prayer relating to the sacrificial rites at the Temple in Jerusalem and expressing hope for the restoration of such rituals was also eliminated. An edifying sermon was an important component of Jacobson's service; the Berlin reform services attracted more than four hundred participants.

Inspired by the model of the Berlin services, a group of Jews in Hamburg organized the "New Israelite Temple Association" in December 1817, with the aim of arranging "a dignified and well-ordered ritual."[14] A temple was to be built for this purpose and services were to include a choir accompanied by an organ, as well as a sermon and passages of prayer in German. A ceremony, patterned on prevailing Christian practice, was to be introduced at the temple "in which the children of both sexes, after having received adequate schooling in the teachings of the faith, shall be accepted as confirmants of the Mosaic religion."[15]

Several aspects of this initiative—soon accomplished and widely replicated—are worthy of note. The focus on aesthetics and the dignity of the ritual were partly an internalization of societal norms and partly aimed at winning the respect of Christian neighbors. As with confirmation, a weekly sermon in German and choir music to organ accompaniment were practices borrowed from surrounding church usage.

The choice of the word "temple" to describe the house of worship reflected another aspect of reform: the definition of Judaism as exclusively a religious affirmation. While, at one time, Judaism had embraced nationality and people-hood, this was—for nineteenth-century reformers—no longer the case. For traditionalists, "the Temple" referred to the (one) Temple in Jerusalem—for the restoration of and return to which they continued to pray. For reformers, the Jews' Jerusalem was now the land of their citizenship.

The very word "Jew" itself had, over centuries, come to hold negative connotations. Such terms as "Israelite" and "Mosaic religion" avoided use of a negatively charged word. As for the religious instruction of children and youth, catechisms modeled on Christian works replaced the study of classical Jewish texts. Through the questions and answers of such catechisms, students learned duties to God, fellow human beings, and the state.

A response of Jewish traditionalists to the innovations of the Hamburg temple was published by the *Bet Din* (Jewish law court) of that city, in a work titled *Eleh Divrei ha-Brit* (These Are the Words of the Covenant). This book was a collection of letters from prominent rabbis of Europe, concurring with the pronouncements of the Hamburg *Beth Din* forbidding alteration of the traditional liturgy, worship in a language other than Hebrew, and use of musical instruments in the synagogue on Sabbaths or festivals, even if such instruments were played by a non-Jew. The issue that aroused the greatest concern among traditionalist respondents was denial of the Jews' national, messianic expectation of returning to the land of Israel.[16]

The generation following the Hamburg temple controversy saw a proliferation of reform associations. As German states continued (until 1876) to require that people affiliate with their religious community (although religion held no civil authority), reformers contributed funds to create and maintain institutions supplementary to the traditional structures they were obliged to help support. Gradually, the "official" communal organization came, in some cases, to be dominated by reformers, with traditionalists privately supporting alternative frameworks to meet their needs.

Michael Meyer, the preeminent historian of the Reform movement, identifies Abraham Geiger as the "founding father" of the Reform movement.[17] Although Reform ideas and innovations did not begin with him, it was Geiger who developed an ideology for the movement. For Geiger, no sacred text of Judaism, biblical or rabbinic, stood outside its historical milieu: "The Talmud, and the Bible, too, that collection of books most of them so splendid and uplifting, perhaps the most exalting of all literature of human authorship, can no longer be viewed as of Divine origin."[18]

Though not representing timeless norms, for religious reformers Jewish texts reflected Judaism's inner, creative spirit and moral ideals. Those elements that comported with modern sensibilities were worthy of reaffirmation. In the words of Geiger's contemporary and fellow reformer Samuel Holdheim, "The Talmud speaks with the standpoint of its time, and for that time it was right. I speak from the higher level of consciousness of my time, and for this age I am right."[19]

The enduring message that Abraham Geiger drew from Judaism's classical texts he termed "Prophetic Judaism." The ideals of the prophets—social justice, concern for the needy, contempt for externals, and a vision of universal peace—were the essence of Judaism. Israel was a "people of revelation" tasked with propagating the divine message throughout the ages.

Samson Raphael Hirsch, who, while a fellow student with Geiger at the University in Bonn, had studied Talmud and homiletics with the man who was to articulate the ideology of Reform, championed a different understanding of Judaism. Hirsch maintained that the lawgiving at Sinai was an irrefutable fact "which must serve as the starting point of all our other knowledge with the same certainty as our own existence and the existence of the material world we see about us."[20] Throughout his works, Hirsch affirmed that the Jew has no right to select those tenets of the Torah that he/she believes to be suitable for a particular time. Rather, the Jew must strive to raise the level of the time to that of the Torah.

Hirsch, as Geiger, affirmed that Judaism has an enduring mission: the improvement of the moral state of humankind. The idea of mission bespoke universalism while articulating a rationale for continued Jewish distinctiveness. The Jew, as a Jew, had a mission vital to the society of which he/she was an integral part.

Hirsch invoked the rabbinic teaching in the Mishnah (Avot 2.2) "The study of Torah is excellent together with *derekh eretz* (literally, 'the way of the land'; for Hirsch, Western culture)" as representing an ideal that he termed the "Man-Israel." He advocated general education alongside Jewish learning, urging a synthesis of strict religious practice and engagement with modern society. While open to aesthetic, "external" enhancements—Hirsch, for example, wore a clerical robe in his congregation and delivered a weekly sermon in German—he fiercely opposed reforms in matters he considered to be fixed halakhic (Jewish legal) norms. Hirsch's approach came to be termed "neo (new)-Orthodoxy."

In an effort to bring some cohesiveness to the emerging movement of reform, three rabbinical assemblies were held in successive years—1844, 1845, 1846—in Brunswick, Frankfurt am Main, and Breslau, respectively. Among the issues taken up at the Frankfurt Conference was whether Hebrew is an objectively necessary aspect of Jewish worship. In Geiger's view—reflecting the position of the majority of conference attendees—Hebrew represented an expression of nationalism: a distinct language is among the characteristics of a separate nation. Moreover, for Geiger, prayer in the mother tongue (German) was to be preferred as evoking greater feelings than prayers in Hebrew, a language that was no longer alive.

Zachariah Frankel, rabbi of Dresden and a conference attendee, argued that such precepts as *tefillin* (phylacteries), the mezuzah on the doorposts of Jews' homes, and the use of Hebrew in prayer services are external bonds between the Jewish people and God. For Frankel, "[T]he positive forms of Judaism are organically integrated into its character and form a part of its life and, therefore, may not be coldly and heartlessly disposed of."[21] When, on its third day of deliberations, the conference adopted the position that Hebrew was not objectively necessary, Frankel withdrew, submitting a letter of resignation.

Frankel articulated a position he described as "positive-historical" Judaism, borrowing a term then current in conservative Protestant theology. Frankel accepted the divinity of the Torah but recognized that Judaism developed within history: "The word which issued from the mouth of God is rooted in eternity. But time has a force and might which must be taken account of. . . . This (position) affirms both the divine value and historical basis of Judaism."[22] Frankel, as Geiger, shared an interest in *Wissenschaft des Judentums*, the "scientific" (critical historical) study of Judaism. Hirsch strenuously dismissed such historicism.

Most Jews in the lands of Germany continued to live in villages and small towns until the latter half of the nineteenth century. Rural Jews, by and large, maintained traditional Jewish beliefs and practices. Throughout the German states, Jews remained excluded from various political offices, associations, and clubs during the first half of the nineteenth century. Full political emancipation was not achieved until the unification of Germany in 1871.

In the second half of the nineteenth century, under the impact of the Industrial Revolution, migration from smaller communities and significant emigration to the United States altered long-standing demographic patterns. In the two decades from 1850 to 1870, the percentage of German Jews who resided in cities of over 10,000 increased from 10 to 30 percent.[23] Urbanization also gave rise to a growing Jewish middle class.

While continuing adherence to traditional religious practices often did not survive these relocations, social contact between Jews and Christians in daily life remained limited. Jews continued to interact primarily with other Jews. Despite differences in patterns of Jewish observance, German Jews, for the most part, maintained the cohesion of a distinctive subculture.

As earlier noted, traditionalist rabbis had responded to the reforms of the Hamburg temple with a collection of objections, published in the book *Eleh Divrei ha-Brit*. A key contributor to that work was Moses Sofer, rabbi of Pressburg, by that time a recognized leader of traditional Jewry in central Europe. The Hatam Sofer (as he was known) made it clear that inherited law and custom are to be preserved, and that what is new is forbidden by the Torah. Although the Hatam Sofer died in 1839, his disciples assumed leadership in combating religious innovations.

One of his students, Hillel Lichtenstein, initiated a convention of like-minded rabbis at Michalowce, in 1865, at which nine resolutions were issued to guide the conduct of Jews faithful to tradition. Interestingly, by the 1860s, the focus was no longer on the reforms of the generation of Moses Sofer. Rather, the Michalowce resolutions denounced the type of innovations introduced by neo-Orthodox rabbis such as Samson Raphael Hirsch and Esriel Hildesheimer. Those committed to tradition, urged the "ultra-Orthodox" rabbinic leaders, should know that it is, among other things, prohibited to:

(1) listen to a sermon in the vernacular;
(2) enter a synagogue for purposes of prayer in which the bimah is not in the middle of the sanctuary (one expression of modernizing trends was a stage in the front of the sanctuary from which the rabbi preached and prayers were led);
(3) use clerical vestments resembling those of other religions;
(4) listen to the prayers of a choir (even if all its members are male and there is no instrumental accompaniment);
(5) worship where there is a *mehitzah* (barrier separating men and women in the synagogue) that does not completely preclude the men from seeing women.

For the ultra-Orthodox, the challenge of the generation was the perceived threat of a modernized Orthodoxy that was a step onto the slippery slope leading to reform.[24]

Political and Racial Anti-Semitism in the Closing Quarter of the Nineteenth Century

The unification of Germany, in 1871, reflected, in part, growing German nationalism: a sense of shared history, culture, and destiny. It came not long after the appearance of Charles Darwin's *Origin of the Species* (1859), positing the theory of evolution. Though Darwin never applied his theory to distinctions among and between people, "racial science" emerged on the platform of his work. The Jews' economic success in western European society was, for some, a source of envy and cause for personal and national concern. These factors coalesced to give rise to anti-Jewish political expression.

The first effort at creating a popular political movement based on anti-Semitism dates to Wilhelm Marr's League of anti-Semites, in 1879. His pamphlet

"The Victory of Judaism over Germandom" had, by that year, reached its twelfth edition. As Marr explained:

> Jewry's control of society and politics . . . is still in the prime of its development. . . . Your generation will not pass before there will be absolutely no public office, even the highest one, which Jews will not have usurped. Yes, through the Jewish nation, Germany will become a world power, a western New Palestine. And this will happen, not through violent revolutions but through the compliance of the people.[25]

Karl Eugen Duehring, a German philosopher and economist, played an important role in framing the "Jewish question" as one of race. Arguing that Judaism should be defined as a race, not a religion, Duehring observed: "It is precisely the baptized Jews who infiltrate furthest unhindered in all sectors of society and political life. It is as though they have provided themselves with an unrestricted passport, advancing their stock to those places where members of the Jewish religion are unable to follow."[26] This infiltration, emphasized Duehring, is incompatible with German interests.

Those who were discontent with modernity saw Jews as beneficiaries of social and economic dislocations from which they felt victimized. Jews, it seemed to some, were wielding ever greater power in the new order of things. Through influence in banking, journalism, business, and politics, they were amassing instruments of control and subverting the nation. This current of thought was to gain broader support over the ensuing half century.

Eastern European Jewry

Over the course of centuries, the Polish-Lithuanian Kingdom came to be home to a majority of the Jews of Europe. Through successive partitions of Poland by Russia, Prussia, and Austria in 1772, 1793, and 1795, Russia acquired Belorussia, Lithuania, and the Ukraine. While, previously, virtually no Jews lived in Russia, the Czarist state acquired 1 million Jews through these annexations, the largest Jewish community in the world. Though Poland was dismembered, as historian Israel Bartal has aptly observed, "most Jews in the areas annexed from Poland to the neighboring states continued to maintain their old way of life. . . . They regarded themselves as 'Polish Jews,' and that is how they were seen by German, Austrian and Russian writers and bureaucrats."[27]

Hasidism, built on the teachings of Rabbi Israel ben Eliezer (better known as the Ba'al Shem Tov, or Besht)—whose charismatic leadership was accepted by existing pietistic circles—and his successors, linked adherents across national borders. In the first half of the nineteenth century, it became a mass movement, gaining hundreds of thousands of devotees. Centered around charismatic leaders (*zaddikim*) and drawing upon kabbalistic teachings, including adoption of the Lurianic liturgy, hasidism promoted both a social mission—alleviating the sufferings of poorer brethren—and the pursuit of *devekut*, communion with/ attachment to God.

The decentralization of hasidic leadership after the Ba'al Shem Tov (d. 1760) and his most prominent (though, by no means exclusive) second-generation disciple Dov Baer of Mezhrech (d. 1772) resulted in diversification of hasidic thought and emphases, with various dynasties of *zaddikim* attracting the allegiance of followers across geographic borders. Hasidic circles developed their own social and religious structures, operating outside the scope of established Jewish communal authority. Both its teachings and rejection of traditional authority systems evoked opposition; those who denounced hasidim (literally, "pietists") were termed *mitnaggedim* ("opponents").

Having inherited a substantial Jewish population, the Russian monarch, Catherine the Great, established the "Pale of Settlement," a geographic zone within which Jews under Russian rule could live; by the end of the nineteenth century, 94 percent of Russian Jewry continued to live within its borders, though there were significant demographic shifts from the north to the developing southern region, starting in the 1860s.[28]

By the close of the eighteenth century, there were a number of *maskilim* in Czarist Russia, among them disciples of the Gaon of Vilna, who maintained contact with Mendelssohn's circle in Berlin. In Galicia, that part of Poland annexed by Austria, Haskalah circles also emerged, encouraged by the reforms of Joseph II. While, in the first half of the nineteenth century, the Galician Haskalah— with centers in Brody, Tarnapol, and Lemberg—tended to focus on a critique of Hasidism, the Russian (particularly Lithuanian) Haskalah looked more broadly at the need to transform traditional Jewish society.[29]

As in Berlin, the *maskilim* of Russia called for educational reform. Isaac Dov Baer Levinsohn (Rival), considered the father of the Russian Haskalah, called for the establishment of elementary schools in which children would learn both Jewish and general studies as well as professional skills. Although opposed to Yiddish, many Russian *maskilim* wrote in the popular "jargon" to promote their ideas. As to the language of the Jewish future, there were those who favored pure German; others, Russian; and still others, Hebrew. The first Hebrew novel, *Ahavat Zion*, authored by Abraham Mapu, was published in Vilna in 1853.

During the reign of Czar Nicholas II, a number of experiments relating to the growing Jewish population were initiated. These ranged from military conscription of Jewish boys (often at age 12) for extended periods of service to "Crown Schools" at which government-sponsored education was provided. In 1844, the *kahal*—the corporate authority structure of Russian Jewry—was formally abolished by Czarist decree.

Czar Alexander II, whose rule immediately followed (1855–81), implemented a number of major reforms, extending well beyond policies associated with Jews (e.g. abolishing serfdom, in 1861). Expanded rights—which included moving beyond the Pale of Settlement—were extended to Jewish large-scale merchants, academics, craftsmen, and medical professionals. As censorship was reduced, a Jewish press in Hebrew, Yiddish, and Russian developed.

Reflecting trends that encouraged *maskilim* to imagine the possibility of acceptance in Russian society, an article (1858) in *Russky Invalid* (Russian Veteran), a publication of the Ministry of War, exhorted: "Let us be worthy of our age; let us give up the habit of presenting the Jews in our literary works as ludicrous and ignominious creatures . . . let us utilize their energy, readiness of wit, and skill as a new means for satisfying the ever-growing needs of our people."[30] In traditional Jewish circles, new yeshivot were established in the nineteenth century (at Volozhin, Mir, Vilna, Slobodka, and Telz, for example) to counter Hasidism by combining intensive scholarship with increased spirituality. In the expanding universe of emphases on various aspects of Jewish teaching, Rabbi Israel Lipkin (known as Salanter, after his place of residence, Salant, in the province of Kovno) originated a movement known as *musar*—an approach to training oneself to avoid evil and do good—in the 1840s.

Russia was comprised of diverse cultural and national groups and, while diverging as to the desirability of integration into the larger society, *maskilim* shared with traditionalists a sense of Jewish distinctiveness. As Michael Stanislawski observes, Judah Leib Gordon's famous call to "be a man in the streets and a Jew at home," expressed in a Hebrew poem, was a summons to be both an "enlightened, Russian-speaking *mensch* and a Jew at home in the creative spirit of the Hebrew heritage."[31]

Paradoxically, two reforms which represented opportunities for Jews—the expansion of free speech and the movement of (some) Jews out of the Pale, combined with their involvement in the burgeoning capitalist economy—also fueled anti-Semitism. In the 1870s, a virulent anti-Semitic press emerged in Russia, home by that time to more than half of the world's nearly 8 million Jews. The optimism of *maskilim* gave way, increasingly, to disillusionment.

Amid this changing climate, Czar Alexander II was assassinated by revolutionaries (a group that included one Jewish woman) in 1881. In April 1881, a wave of pogroms broke out in the southern provinces of the Ukraine; a year of such assaults ensued. One outgrowth of this outbreak and ensuing anti-Jewish legislation was mass emigration: from 1881 to 1914, close to 1.5 million Jews emigrated from Russia to the United States. At the same time, Jewish nationalist societies committed to purchasing land in Palestine and promoting settlement there were established; out of the pogroms of 1881–2, the *hibbat zion* (love of Zion) movement was born.

Early in the twentieth century, *Protocols of the Elders of Zion* was published in Russia. The "protocols" were purportedly the proceedings of an international Jewish conspiracy that aimed to achieve world domination. Though, initially, appearing in late imperial Russia, *Protocols* was, after World War I, translated into numerous languages, drawing broad readership throughout Europe and the United States.

Between 1917 and 1921—a period of strife between Poles and Ukrainians, Poles and Lithuania, and Poles and the Bolsheviks—many hundreds of pogroms devastated local Jewish populations. "It has been estimated that five hundred thirty communities had been subjected to more than a thousand separate pogroms in which more than 60,000 Jews were killed and several times that number were wounded."[32] A treaty between the United States, Britain, France, Italy, and Japan with the newly established Republic of Poland (1919) protected the national rights of minorities; Jews were recognized as a nationality, with attendant rights and (formally) freedom from discrimination. Similarly, national rights were extended to minorities in other new states of East Central Europe.

The Russian Revolution of 1917 granted Jews full civic rights. Yet, the Bolsheviks—and, later, the Stalinist state—viewed expressions of Jewish cultural and national identity as reactionary, unless utilized to promote communism. Zionism was banned in the Soviet Union in 1928. Comparing the relative circumstances of Jews in the USSR and those in East Central Europe during the interwar period, historian Ezra Mendelsohn aptly comments that "in the latter the environment was bad for the Jews while not necessarily being bad for Judaism . . . whereas in the former Jews as individuals were able to prosper while Judaism . . . withered away."[33]

Zionism

While several mid-nineteenth-century thinkers adumbrated the notion of Jewish renewal in Palestine in the "here and now," the establishment of *hovevei zion*, a loose-knit association of Jewish groups promoting settlement in Palestine, marked a turning point. Already in 1879, Eliezer Perlman (known as Ben Yehuda), who was to play a significant role in promoting Hebrew as the language of the *yishuv* from the time of his settlement in Palestine in 1882, wrote in an open letter in the Hebrew press: "The Jewish faith can live on in the Diaspora. It will assume new form according to time and environment, and will share the lot of all other religions. But as for the Jewish nation, it can exist only on its own soil. Only upon the soil can it find rejuvenation and bloom forth in splendor as in days of yore."[34]

The pogroms of 1881–2 served as a catalyst for the first aliyah, bringing 10,000 Jewish settlers to Ottoman-held Palestine over the course of a decade.

In addition to support from *hovevei zion* (lovers of Zion) societies, several of the newly established settlements enjoyed financial investment from Baron Edmond de Rothschild. *Hibbat zion* appealed, variously, to religionists and to secular nationalists—Jews who no longer identified with traditional religious beliefs and ritual observances, but who identified strongly with the Jewish people and sought new forms of Jewish cultural expression.

Peretz Smolenskin, a Russian-born *maskil* and the publisher of and a literary contributor to the Vienna-based Hebrew monthly *Hashahar* (The Dawn), criticized those who "have striven to remove all the bonds of love and solidarity which unite our people so that it should become assimilated among the gentiles." He observed that "Only a dog neither has nor wants a home. A man who chooses to live his whole life as a transient, without a thought for the establishment of a permanent home for his children, will forever be regarded as a dog."[35]

Leon Pinsker wrote a pamphlet, *Auto-Emancipation* (1882), pointing to the need to reclaim Jewish nationality and to establish a Jewish national home. Though, eventually, Pinsker was drawn to—and was elected to head—*hovevei zion*, he was not initially committed to Palestine as the geographic locus of Jewish national renaissance. In the 1880s and beyond, there were Jewish nationalists who envisioned the possibility of Jewish national and cultural development within Russia. As Simon Dubnow expressed it: "Jewish nationality cannot strive for territorial or political isolation, but only for social and cultural autonomy."[36] The Bund—the General Jewish Workers Union—advocated secular, socialist Jewish culture based on Yiddish within the Russian Empire.

As, in Russia, an upsurge in anti-Semitism contributed to organized Palestine resettlement efforts, rising anti-Semitism in western Europe served to galvanize the energies of Theodor Herzl—a lawyer and dramatist turned journalist—toward thinking of a solution to the problem of the Jews through creation of a nation-state. As had been the case with Pinsker, Herzl was by no means certain that Palestine was the exclusive answer; in his work *The Jewish State* (1896), he proposed Argentina or Palestine as possibilities worthy of exploration.

A capable organizer, Herzl convened a "Zionist Congress," in 1897, to initiate action toward a state of the Jews. Approximately 200 delegates from 17 countries participated. Though having planned to hold the conference in Munich, Herzl presided over the gathering in Basel, upon encountering organized opposition to the very idea of such an assembly from German Jewish leaders (both Reform and Orthodox). The Congress committed itself to promoting settlement in Palestine, fostering national consciousness and seeking the consent of governments in pursuit of its aims.

Herzl's vision of a Jewish state was of a Western-style democracy; the driving need for a state of the Jews was ineradicable anti-Semitism. Ahad Ha'am (pseudonym of Asher Ginsberg, a Russian Jew who variously served as editor of a Hebrew monthly and as representative of a tea company) championed a different aspect of the Zionist agenda than Herzl's focus on securing territorial and international political recognition. For Ahad Ha'am—who attended the First Zionist Congress and eventually settled in Palestine—the primary challenge of the era was to forge a cultural bond uniting the Jewish people: "only through the national culture and for its sake" should a Jewish state be established; a state not rooted in Jewish cultural foundations, "estranged from the living inner spiritual force of Judaism," would not add "a glorious chapter to our national history."[37]

Labor Zionists, socialist Zionists, and religious Zionists were among the ideological groups that joined with political Zionists and cultural Zionists in advancing various visions of what a Jewish state might look like. There was, to be sure, considerable opposition to the Zionist idea. This included religious groups that deemed it inappropriate to contravene God's will by seeking to end the exile (short of His miraculous intervention in history) and Jews committed to integration into various host societies who viewed Judaism and the Jewish people as no longer a nation.

As Zionist Jewish Congresses continued to meet in Europe, and efforts to secure land and recognition proceeded, a second aliyah, 1904–14, brought 40,000 additional Jewish immigrants to Palestine by World War I. Hebrew came to be the language of the new *yishuv*; a new city, Tel Aviv, was founded on the outskirts of Jaffa and Israel's first *kibbutzim* were established. In 1917, in the course of militarily ending Ottoman rule of the area, the British government announced (Balfour Declaration: November 2, 1917) that it looked with favor on the Zionist aspiration for a Jewish national home in Palestine.

With the end of World War I, the League of Nations recognized a British Mandate over Palestine. Jewish nationalism, however, confronted rising Arab nationalism; throughout the 1920s and the 1930s, tensions among the region's inhabitants mounted. Riots against Jewish settlements erupted in 1921, 1929, and 1936. Meanwhile, Zionist activism combined with escalating anti-Semitism in Europe—and immigration restrictions in the United States and much of the Western world, post–World War I—generated increased waves of Jewish immigration to Palestine; the *yishuv* was approaching 500,000 Jews by 1939.

Sephardic and Middle Eastern Jewry

The Sephardic Diaspora (post-1492) has been the subject of increased focus, in recent decades.[38] Collectively comprising twenty percent of world Jewry early in the nineteenth century, there were multiple and distinctive zones of Sephardic population and culture. Sephardic communities in the west never numbered more than a few thousand; "In the eighteenth and nineteenth centuries, these communities declined, assimilated into the non-Jewish world, or fused with larger *Ashkenazi* groups which swamped them in size."[39]

Late in the eighteenth century, Sephardic communities extended from North Africa through Syria, Iraq, Palestine and Egypt. Sephardic communities flourished under Ottoman rule in the Balkans and Asia Minor. Historical and cultural differences (separately) distinguished the Jews of Persia and Yemen. The incursion of Western powers into these areas, beginning at the end of the eighteenth century, led to reforms within the Ottoman Empire and to the emergence of new nation-states. Both trends eroded longstanding legal autonomy within Jewish communities.

Colonialism and attendant modernizing influences effected economic changes as well as religious, cultural, and educational developments. The Alliance Israélite Universelle, founded in Paris by French Jews in 1860, sought to remake "backward" Jewries; its primary areas of focus were North Africa and the Middle East. By 1913, it had established 183 educational institutions — attended by 43,700 students — in an area extending from Morocco to Iran.[40] In addition to French cultural penetration through the initiative of the Alliance, the Haskalah entered the Levant through contacts between intellectual elites; "The Hebrew newspapers of the Haskalah were to be found in towns and cities of the Islamic world from Morocco to Persia."[41]

In the absence of a Jewish religious reform movement such as emerged in the West, Sephardic rabbis, by and large, did not respond to modernizing influences with the ideological approach of those Ashkenazic traditionalists who rigidified halakhic norms in reaction to the perceived threat of Reform innovations. As Zvi Zohar has observed: "*Sephardi* rabbis felt free to continue to apply traditional canons of halakhic decision-making processes. . . . In other words, their innovativeness was not a sign of modernism but rather of traditionalism. . . ."[42]

Zionism resonated among some elements of Jewry in the Islamic world. Several hundred Jewish families emigrated from Morocco to Palestine, 1919–1923, with others coming from Iraq, Syria and Libya. Modern Hebrew schools and (Zionist) nationalist associations were established in the decades before World War II. Zionist objectives clashed with those of the Alliance which aimed to regenerate Jews within their home countries and with the vision of those Jews who identified with Arab national aspirations.

American Judaism

American Jewry numbered no more than 2,500 at the time that the 13 US colonies declared independence. Though, by the early eighteenth century, a majority of colonial Jews were Ashkenazim, each of the five congregational communities established before the Revolution followed the Sephardic ritual—reflecting the origins of the earliest Jews to immigrate to the new land. Throughout the colonial and early national periods, congregational life was led by volunteer trustees and nonordained religious functionaries; no rabbi settled in the United States before 1840.

From 1840 to 1880, the American Jewish community grew from 15,000 to 250,000, resulting primarily from the immigration of Jews from German-speaking lands. Immigrant Jews spread throughout the country; in 1850, 70 percent of the Jews in the United States were peddlers.[43] German Jewish immigrants created a broad range of social, cultural, educational and charitable organizations. One of the earliest of these organizations was B'nai Brith, composed of local lodges coordinated by district and national bodies. Established in 1843, B'nai Brith offered its members typical lodge benefits, giving loans to the needy, assisting the sick, burying the dead, and aiding widows and orphans.

The first generation of Jewish immigrants from German-speaking lands was, in the main, from small towns and villages. Traditional in their public ritual, they came in search of economic opportunity. By mid-century, more affluent, better-educated Jews made their way to the United States, some of them having embraced the movement for religious reform. Michael Meyer notes that earlier settlers saw in reform a means of religious Americanization; the German Jewish Reform leaders who came at mid-century tapped into a wellspring of readiness for an articulated vision of Reform Judaism.[44]

The master institution builder of Reform Judaism in the United States was Isaac Mayer Wise, who arrived from Bohemia in 1846. In 1873, he successfully organized the Union of American Hebrew Congregations (UAHC), with 34 participating synagogues; the union, in 1875, sponsored the establishment of the Hebrew Union College (HUC) for the preparation of rabbis. When it became clear that HUC represented what American traditionalist elites viewed as radical Reform, a group organized by Sabato Morais—a native of Leghorn, Italy, who served at Philadelphia's Mikveh Israel congregation—convened and worked to establish the Jewish Theological Seminary of America to preserve in America "the knowledge and practice of historical Judaism." Soon after the death of Morais, Solomon Schechter, reader in rabbinics at Cambridge University, assumed the presidency of the fledgling Seminary.

From 1880 to 1924, three million Russian and other—mostly, though by no means exclusively—eastern European Jews left for the United States. It is estimated that 50 to 60 thousand Sephardim were among the substantial wave of newcomers.[45] The immigrants included those for whom the Americanized traditionalism of the Jewish Theological Seminary (JTS) did not comport with eastern European yeshiva sensibilities. In 1897, RIETS—the Rabbi Isaac Elchanan Theological Seminary—was founded by a group of immigrants "to promote the study of Talmud and to assist in educating and preparing students of the Hebrew Faith for the Hebrew Orthodox Ministry."[46]

While the elites associated with JTS and RIETS, as well as many of the immigrant East European Jews identified with Zionist aspirations, the Reform movement of the late nineteenth and early twentieth centuries opposed Zionism as contrary to the Jewish mission in the modern world. Louis Brandeis, an agnostic secularist who was to become America's first Jewish Supreme Court justice, embraced Zionism and was active in the movement. Jonathan Sarna observes that, for Jews like Brandeis, Zionism provided "a way of synthesizing their Progressive ideals with their hitherto somewhat latent Jewish attachments. Zionism became, in effect, a religion for these secular Jews . . ."[47]

In the 1920s and the 1930s, Mordecai Kaplan, an early graduate of JTS, wrote extensively about the "reconstruction" of Judaism. Influenced by the writings of Ahad Ha'Am, Kaplan emphasized Judaism's ethnic orientation: its peoplehood. As to Judaism's future vitality, Kaplan averred that: "Unless its mythological ideas about God give way to the conception of divinity immanent in the workings of the human spirit, unless its static view of authority gives way to the dynamic without succumbing to individualistic lawlessness, and unless it is capable of developing a sense of history without, at the same time, being a slave to the past, the Jewish people has nothing further to contribute to civilization."[48] Even in the best case, opined Kaplan, "the Jew in America will be first and foremost an American, and only, secondarily a Jew."[49]

Alongside religious streams and their educational institutions, Yiddish secular schools (many operated by the *Arbeter Ring*: Workmen's Circle) abounded in the United States in the 1920s and the 1930s. With the relocation during the war years of leading personalities of traditionalist Jewish life in eastern Europe— for example, the Lubavitcher *rebbe* and Rabbi Aaron Kotler, a noted Talmudic scholar who, on arrival, established a *yeshiva* and *kolel* in Lakewood, New Jersey—an expanded slice of Jewish religious life took root in America. The establishment of the Joint Distribution Committee to provide Jewish war relief during and after World War I had clearly reflected the rising economic standing of the American Jewish community relative to other Jewish populations; migration and the devastation wrought during the Shoah combined to make the United States home to a substantial plurality of the world's Jews by 1945.

The Shoah: End of an Era

In the aftermath of World War I, Germany experienced acute economic distress and political instability. Between 1919 and 1933, Germany's Weimar Republic had no fewer than 20 governments.[50] In synthesizing decades of research on the causes of the Shoah (Hebrew for catastrophe; often referred to by the Greek term *Holocaust*, a translation of the Hebrew word *olah* meaning a burnt sacrificial offering dedicated entirely to God), Jehuda Reinharz and Paul Mendes-Flohr point to "a confluence of economic, psychological, political and social factors, among them a history in Germany of political and racial anti-Semitism, a dictatorship, an obedient and disciplined bureaucracy, and the technological means for industrial mass murder."[51]

Assuming power, legally, in 1933, Adolph Hitler and the National Socialist German Workers' Party that he headed rapidly undertook a legislative process of excluding Jews from Germany's social, economic, and cultural life. By 1935, the Nuremberg Laws effectively deprived Jews of citizenship and attendant civil and political rights. The assassination of a German civil servant by a disgruntled Jew, in Paris, served as a pretext for Nazi-supported pogroms in Germany and Austria the night of November 9, 1938 (*Kristallnacht*: Night of Broken Glass). Over half of Germany's more than 500,000 Jews left during the period 1933–9, many relocating to Palestine.

Immigration restrictions were in place throughout Europe and the Americas. An international conference on the Jewish refugee crisis in Evian, France, in July 1938 failed to alter this situation. In the ensuing few years—from the invasion of Poland, September 1, 1939, to the launch of the campaign against the USSR, in 1941—Germany gained control of millions of Jews.

Einsatzgruppen—special killing units—entered the Soviet Union with the German army; it is estimated that more than 1 million Jews were shot by these mobile squads. Hermann Göring expressed the nature of the battle: "This war is not the Second World War. This is the great racial war. In the final analysis it is about whether the German and Aryan prevails here, or whether the Jew rules the world, and that is what we are fighting for out there."[52] By January 1942, plans for the "final solution" of the Jewish problem were in place. While *Einsatzgruppen* had been sent to exterminate their victims, the victims were now to be dispatched to death camps for efficient destruction. Such centers at Auschwitz, Treblinka, Belzec, Sobibor, and Majdanek consumed the lives of well over 3 million Jews. Disease and privation in ghettos, bullets and mobile gassing units, and death marches took a further, massive toll in human life.

The racial state, the acts of the Nazi regime relating to the "Jewish problem," the "final solution," and the Jewish confrontation with persecution and mass murder (including the actions of *Judenräte*—Jewish councils established to manage Jews in occupied areas—and various forms of resistance, individual and collective) have been extensively studied. The stark reality is that by the close of World War II, a world Jewish population of nearly 17 million had been reduced to 11 million. Continental Europe—a center of Jewish vitality and creativity for a millennium—was, if not *Judenrein*, no longer a hub of Jewish life. By mid-twentieth century, Jewish modernity was, arguably, at a close; a postmodern era had begun.[53]

Key Research Trends

Recent decades have seen a broadening of perspectives relating to the topics explored in this essay. There are at least four significant dimensions to this expanded consideration, each of which has parallels in related disciplines. These dimensions are:

(1) newly (in the most recent decades) available archival resources in the USSR and the Soviet bloc;

(2) extending beyond a Eurocentric (particularly, West European) focus;

(3) discussion of the close of modernity and the onset of a postmodern era;

(4) greater interest in social and cultural history—beyond intellectual, political, and economic trends—including the role of women.

In the introduction to his outstanding work *Beyond the Pale: The Jewish Encounter with Late Imperial Russia*, Benjamin Nathans observes that, until the 1990s, "historians could only surmise what riches lay beyond their reach in Soviet archives, based on tantalizing citations from the works of a handful of scholars from the Czarist era. Now we face the opposite (though far preferable) problem: access to archival treasures so vast as to appear overwhelming."[54] The availability of such materials informs research on virtually every topic and subtopic explored in this essay, from the study of imperial policies relating to Jews, to Jewish communal organizations, to World War II and the Shoah. Many of the works that have appeared since the late 1990s have drawn upon these newly accessible resources, a trend that is certain to continue to enrich the field for years to come.

Only in recent decades has the study of Sephardic and Middle Eastern Jewries assumed a prominent place in the field of Jewish studies. Much remains to be learned about Sephardic and Middle Eastern communities, their relationships with local cultures and interactions, parallels and differences with Ashkenazim. In the same vein, historians who—over the course of generations—viewed the German Jewish Haskalah experience as paradigmatic of all of European Jewry and beyond, have in recent years undertaken regional studies (by city, locality, or country) yielding a far more nuanced understanding and highlighting the high degree of autonomy that characterized the Haskalah in different geographic settings.

Many authors have explored the question "Where Does the Modern Period of Jewish History Begin?" That question served as the title of a seminal article authored by Michael Meyer in 1975. Meyer reviewed the metahistories put forward by such historians as Heinrich Graetz, Simon Dubnow, Ben Zion Dinur, Gershom Scholem, and Salo Baron, and pointed to a constellation of processes that defined modern Jewry. Though elements of modernity began to appear earlier, he noted that "there remains a vast difference between the degree of modernity in evidence before the mid-eighteenth century and that apparent thereafter." Meyer suggested that "[r]ather than being concerned with the impossible task of determining the precise bounds of a single 'modern' period for all Jewries, it would be best to focus on the process of *modernization* in its various aspects."[55] Subsequently, Jonathan Israel published an important work in which he identified 1550–1750 as an early modern period—paralleling general European historiography—in European Jewish history.[56]

More recently, the question has become: "when did the modern period of Jewish history end?" Exploring the onset of postmodernity, Professor Moshe Rosman—in an important volume on postmodernism—suggested that by the late 1940s, a new, postmodern constellation of processes was in evidence. These include: a demographic leveling off (independent of the Shoah) of Jewish population; the redistribution of Jewish population among a very few large centers and scattered small nuclei; an overwhelming incidence of political equality in the societies in which Jews live; and transformation of the "nationalism" question from acquiring political sovereignty to determining how nationalist a Jewish sovereign state can be in a multicultural world.[57]

Rosman notes that conceptions of what it means to be a Jew are, today, far more variegated than at mid-twentieth century. "This," he concludes, "combined with the changing political and economic configuration of the general world context, and the expiration or transformation of most of the primary issues that preoccupied the Jews during modernity, suggests that in the postmodern period Jewish history will be as different from the modern as the modern was from the Middle Ages and antiquity."[58] Though Jewishness has always been pluralistic and multivocal, Rosman suggests that there is a constellation of elements identifying a phenomenon as "Jewish," with varying combinations of these identifying factors in evidence.

Similarly, in his introduction to *Cultures of the Jews*, David Biale observes that there were—based on literary and material cultures—multiple Jewish cultures from place to place and period to period. Yet, "the Jews throughout the ages *believed* themselves to have a common national biography and a common culture." He concludes that "on both the popular and elite level . . . the Jewish people were, at once, one and diverse."[59]

Part of the postmodernist approach has been greater emphasis on cultural history; the study of people's behavior. It is no accident that this *Bloomsbury* volume includes chapters on "Gender and Judaism" and "Jewish Arts and Material Culture." The first decade of the twenty-first century was rich in fresh research on Jewish cultural history, and there is good reason to anticipate that this trend will continue.

Rosman points to an ambitious research agenda, ahead. His comments serve as a fitting close to the historical chapter explored in these pages: "We are in a different historical period, with a new perspective on what happened before 1950. When we talk about 'the Jewish modern period' we are no longer talking about 'us'. There is a new critical distance priming reconsideration of the phenomena of modernity. . . . Jewish history will once again be rewritten."[60]

Notes

1. Selma Stern (1950), *The Court Jew: A Contribution to the History of the Period of Absolutism in Central Europe*, Ralph Weiman (trans.). Philadelphia: Jewish Publication Society of America.
2. Lois Dubin (1999), *The Port Jews of Habsburg Trieste: Absolutist Politics and Enlightenment Culture*. Stanford: Stanford University Press.
3. David B. Ruderman (2000), *Jewish Enlightenment in an English Key: Anglo Jewry's Construction of Modern Jewish Thought*. Princeton: Princeton University Press; idem (2004), "Was There a 'Haskalah' in England? Reconsidering an Old Question," in Shmuel Feiner and David Sorkin (eds), *New Perspectives on the Haskalah*. Portland: Littman Library of Jewish Civilization, pp. 64–85.
4. Christian Wilhelm von Dohm (1957), *Concerning the Amelioration of the Civil Status of the Jews*, Helen Lederer (trans.). Cincinnati: Hebrew Union College-Jewish Institute of Religion, p. 80.
5. Naphtali Herz Wessely (1826), *Words of Peace and Truth*. Vienna: n.p. [Hebrew].
6. Moses Mendelssohn (1969). *Jerusalem and Other Writings*, Alfred Jospe (trans.). New York: Schocken Books, p. 89.
7. David Sorkin (1992), "The Impact of Emancipation on German Jewry: A Reconsideration," in Jonathan Frankel and Steve J. Zipperstein (eds), *Assimilation and Community: The Jews in Nineteenth-Century Europe*. New York: Cambridge University Press, pp. 177–98, p. 186.
8. Shmuel Feiner (2001), "Towards a Historical Definition of the Haskalah," in Feiner and Sorkin (eds), *New Perspectives on the Haskalah*, pp. 184–219.
9. Jonathan Frankel (1992), "Assimilation and the Jews in Nineteenth-Century Europe: Towards a New Historiography," in Frankel and Zipperstein (eds), *Assimilation and Community*, pp. 1–37, p. 11.
10. Diogene Tama (1971), *Transactions of the Parisian Sanhedrin*, F. D. Kirwan (trans.). Farnborough: Gregg Publishing, p. 132.
11. Simon Schwarzfuchs (1979), *Napoleon, the Jews, and the Sanhedrin*. London and Boston: Routledge and Kegan Paul; Gil Graff (1985), *Separation of Church and State: Dina de-Malkhuta Dina in Jewish Law, 1750–1848*. Tuscaloosa: University of Alabama Press.
12. Tama, *Transactions of the Parisian Sanhedrin*, pp. 149–50.
13. W. Gunther Plaut (1969), *The Rise of Reform Judaism: A Sourcebook of Its European Origins*. New York: World Union for Progressive Judaism, p. 29.
14. Ibid., p. 31.
15. Ibid., p. 32.
16. *Eleh Divrei ha-Brit* (Altona: Hamburg Beth Din, 1819 reprint Jerusalem, 1970), p. 17.
17. Michael A. Meyer (1988), *Response to Modernity: A History of the Reform Movement in Germany*. New York: Oxford University Press.
18. Paul Mendes-Flohr and Jehuda Reinharz (2011), *The Jew in the Modern World* (3rd edn). New York: Oxford University Press, p. 259.

19. Plaut, *The Rise of Reform Judaism*, p. 123.
20. Samson Raphael Hirsch (1976), *The Pentateuch: Commentary on the Torah (Exodus)*. Gateshead: Judaica Press, p. 249.
21. Plaut, *The Rise of Reform Judaism*, p. 86.
22. Mendes-Flohr and Reinharz, *The Jew in the Modern World*, p. 218.
23. Steven M. Lowenstein (2005), "The Beginning of Integration, 1780–1870," in Marion A. Kaplan (ed.), *Jewish Daily Life in Germany*. New York: Oxford University Press, pp. 93–172, p. 100.
24. Michael K. Silber (1992), "The Emergence of Ultra-Orthodoxy," in Jack Wertheimer (ed.), *Uses of Tradition: Jewish Continuity in the Modern Era*. Cambridge, MA and New York: Harvard University and Jewish Theological Seminary of America, pp. 23–84.
25. Mendes-Flohr and Reinharz, *The Jew in the Modern World*, p. 306.
26. Ibid., p. 308.
27. Israel Bartal (2005), *The Jews of Eastern Europe, 1782–1881*, Chaya Naor (trans.). Philadelphia: University of Pennsylvania Press, p. 1.
28. David H. Weinberg (1996), *Between Tradition and Modernity: Haim Zhitlowski, Simon Dubnow, Ahad Ha-Am, and the Shaping of Modern Jewish Identity*. New York: Holmes and Meier, p. 34.
29. Bartal, *The Jews of Eastern Europe, 1782–1881*, p. 98.
30. Louis Greenberg (1944), *The Jews in Russia*. Vol. 1. New Haven: Yale University Press, p. 78.
31. Michael Stanislawski (1988), *For Whom Do I Toil: Judah Leib Gordon and the Crisis of Russian Jewry*. New York: Oxford University Press, p. 52.
32. Mendes-Flohr and Reinharz, *The Jew in the Modern World*, p. 415.
33. Ezra Mendelsohn (1983), *The Jews of East Central Europe between the World Wars*. Bloomington: Indiana University Press, p. 6.
34. Greenberg, *The Jews in Russia*, pp. 144–5.
35. Arthur Hertzberg (1997), *The Zionist Idea: A Historical Analysis and Reader*. Philadelphia: Atheneum, p. 157.
36. Mendes-Flohr and Reinharz, *The Jew in the Modern World*, p. 397.
37. Hertzberg, *The Zionist Idea*, pp. 268–9.
38. See, for example, Harvey E. Goldberg (ed.) (1996), *Sephardi and Middle Eastern Jewries*. Bloomington: Indiana University Press; Esther Benbassa and Aron Rodrigue (2000), *A History of the Judeo-Spanish Community, 14th–20th Centuries*. Berkeley: University of California Press; Sarah Abrevaya Stein (2002), "Sephardi and Middle Eastern Jewries since 1492," in Goodman (ed.), *The Oxford Handbook of Jewish Studies*, pp. 327–62.
39. Benbassa and Rodrigue, *A History of the Judeo-Spanish Community, 14th–20th Centuries*, p. li.
40. Ibid., p. 83.
41. Norman A. Stillman (1996), "Middle Eastern and North African Jewries Confront Modernity: Orientation, Disorientation, Reorientation," in Goldberg (ed.), *Sephardi and Middle Eastern Jewries*, pp. 59–72, p. 66.
42. Zvi Zohar (1996), "Traditional Flexibility and Modern Strictness: Two Halakhic Positions on Women's Suffrage," in Goldberg (ed.), *Sephardi and Middle Eastern Jewries*, pp. 119–33, p. 130.
43. Hasia R. Diner and Beryl Lieff Benderly (2002), *Her Works Praise Her: A History of Jewish Women in America from Colonial Times to the Present*. New York: Basic Books, p. 86.
44. Michael A. Meyer (1997), "America: The Reform Movement's Land of Promise," in Jonathan D. Sarna (ed.), *The American Jewish Experience* (2nd edn). New York: Holmes and Meier, pp. 60–83, p. 61.
45. Aviva Ben-Ur (2009), *Sephardic Jews in America: A Diasporic History*. New York: New York University Press, p. 35.

46. Gilbert Klapperman (1969), *The Story of Yeshiva University: The First Jewish University in America*. New York: Macmillan, p. 52.
47. Jonathan D. Sarna (2004), *American Judaism: A History*. New Haven: Yale University Press, pp. 204–5.
48. Mendes-Flohr and Reinharz, *The Jew in the Modern World*, p. 559.
49. Mordecai M. Kaplan (1994), *Judaism as Civilization: Toward a Reconstruction of American Jewish Life*. Philadelphia: The Macmillan Company, pp. 489–90.
50. Michael Burleigh (2000), *The Third Reich: A New History*. New York: Hill and Wang, p. 62.
51. Mendes-Flohr and Reinharz, *The Jew in the Modern World*, p. 715.
52. Burleigh, *The Third Reich: A New History*, p. 571.
53. Moshe Rosman (2007), *How Jewish Is Jewish History?* Portland: Littman Library of Jewish Civilization, pp. 64–74.
54. Benjamin Nathans (2002), *Beyond the Pale: The Jewish Encounter with Late Imperial Russia*. Berkeley: University of California Press, p. 19.
55. Michael A. Meyer (1975), "Where Does the Modern Period of Jewish History Begin?" *Judaism* 24: 329–38, p. 337.
56. Jonathan I. Israel (1985), *European Jewry in the Age of Mercantilism*. Oxford: Clarendon Press.
57. Rosman, *How Jewish Is Jewish History?* pp. 64–70.
58. Ibid., p. 81.
59. David Biale (ed.) (2002), *Cultures of the Jews*. New York: Schocken, pp. xxiv–xxv.
60. Rosman, *How Jewish Is Jewish History?* pp. 183–4.

Part II

Reorienting Contemporary Jewry and Jewish Studies

In Part II, we shift lenses to what are ostensibly more contemporary perspectives and concerns. Of course, as has been clear throughout this volume, the scholarship in all areas of Jewish Studies is indebted to and informed by current realities, interests, and trajectories. We begin with a look at some of the central developments and concerns that direct Judaism and Jewish society today. Building on all the discussions in Part I, the contemporary approach represents both continuation and disruption. New intellectual orientations and social concerns have merged with changed political landscapes as well as the unfolding implications of the dramatic events of the twentieth century. After a look at some of the key trends in play today, we turn attention to several issues and academic foci that have reached new levels in contemporary scholarship, even when their roots stretch further back into the past. We consider the role of gender, the production and impact of arts and material culture, the nature and key findings of demographic study, and the important role of Israel (especially the contemporary State of Israel) as a subject and as a catalyst for Jewish Studies and Jewish communal development.

Yehuda Kurtzer notes that Jews in the contemporary world have faced remarkable and, in many ways, unprecedented challenges internally and externally. In his essay "Mainstreams and Margins: Rethinking Contemporary Jewry," Kurtzer argues that in fact the traditional narratives of marginality—of Jews in broader society and of some Jews within Judaism—have often been overturned and have themselves become essential parts of mainstream narratives. Addressing questions of contemporary Jewish identity and the clarification of Jewish denominational borderlines, Kurtzer also explores key communal and cultural developments that have helped to shape and define Judaism today. The dynamic between an expanding Jewry in Israel and a politically significant Jewry in North America, he asserts, raises important questions about notions of peoplehood and has broader political implications. The effects on smaller Jewish population centers are also reviewed in light of this somewhat potentially polarizing development. Similarly, the Holocaust—and in particular discussions of memory anxiety and continuity—has continued to cast a shadow on and still impact contemporary Jews and Judaism. Kurtzer concludes his essay with reflections on the implications of these central issues for Jews today and for the practice and study of Judaism.

In "Women, Gender, and Judaism," Judith R. Baskin notes that only in the past several decades have Jewish women received sustained scholarly attention and that gender has only recently become a central methodological and thematic concern. Contextualizing these developments in broader social and academic contexts within and outside the Jewish community, she provides a brief outline of key themes related to women and gender in the Hebrew Bible, the Late Ancient Mediterranean Diaspora, Rabbinic Judaism, the Middle Ages (Christian and Islamic contexts), the early modern period, modernity (starting with Hasidism and Haskalah, and running through the nineteenth and twentieth centuries, with special attention to Europe, America, and Israel), as well as the contemporary world. In each case, Baskin identifies central issues that highlight both the position and perception of women and gender and that suggest how a study of gender contributes to a much richer and nuanced vision of Jewish society and history.

Aesthetics impact Jewish identity and practice. With renewed interest in material culture, there have been many opportunities to reassess Jewish participation in the arts and to incorporate arts and culture into Jewish life in various contexts and historical situations. In "Jewish Arts and Material Culture," Judah Cohen reviews the interconnection of Jewish arts with internal Jewish life and with relations with the non-Jewish world. After a quick survey of arts and material culture (and the scholarship on them) in Jewish history, Cohen identifies various methodologies (historical-contextual, text-based analysis, and ethnographic) that have been useful in work on Jewish aesthetics. For the balance of his essay, he provides an overview of key developments, themes, and figures in modern and contemporary Jewry in the fields of literature, arts and visual culture, music, folklore, dance, theater, film, and media studies. Cohen concludes with reflections on the impact of these areas for Jewish Studies as a field.

Demography, or the statistical study of human population, bridges academic disciplines and provides the opportunity for important observations about Jewish social and communal development and interaction with non-Jews. In "Jewish Demography," Sergio DellaPergola surveys the discipline of Jewish demography, covering central themes and methods. Jewish demography surfaces and helps to answer essential questions, such as who is a Jew and how is Judaism defined. DellaPergola also examines the collection and interpretation of demographic data and explores the reasons that various groups and individuals study demographic information. He considers the lessons that demographic data and demographic change can offer scholars interested in Jewish life and history. More than a methodology, demography helps to shape Jewish identity and informs key Jewish concerns. In that regard, Jewish demography reflects well the discussions of Jewish Studies at large about the connection of study and practical realities. DellaPergola concludes with brief thoughts about the future direction and orientation of Jewish demographic studies.

As noted in other places throughout this volume, Israel Studies, broadly defined, have impacted Jewish Studies in numerous ways. In "The State of Israel Studies," Michael Kotzin and Elie Rekhess contribute an overview of the state of the field of Israel Studies, mapping the field by identifying the centers, institutes, programs, and chairs in Israel Studies across the globe as well as the activities of such program centers—in terms of research, scholarly discussion, collections, and publications. They identify the central associations and publications that address Israel Studies. They also examine the key topics addressed in Israel-related courses. Turning to the growing interest in Israel Studies, Kotzin and Rekhess review the dramatic growth in Israel Studies within the context of academic developments, communal and philanthropic concerns, and political conditions (considering examples of Middle East politics and media bias as well as the role of advocacy). Their balanced approach reveals a range of issues in the content of and interest in Israel Studies, which feed on general Jewish Studies and academic themes and which add a rich dimension to a range of academic disciplines. The essay includes appendices that help provide a clear picture of current and future directions in the field.

9 Mainstreams and Margins: Rethinking Contemporary Jewry

Yehuda Kurtzer

Introduction

Virtually none of the truths—whether institutional, ideological, or philosophical—that defined Jewry in previous centuries hold true for Jewry in the present. Challenged by unprecedented internal reimagination, and confronted with unexpected external forces, contemporary Jewry is in the phase of rapid evolution at a pace of change so quick that any attempt to pause and understand its dynamics and mechanics becomes stale and outdated almost the moment it is written.

The pace of change in contemporary Jewish life might be expected given the historical circumstances that gave way to the present—the catastrophic destruction of European Jewry, the collapse of Middle Eastern Jewish communities in the wake of the rise of the State of Israel, the unprecedented success and integration of Jews in America—all of which challenge the normal evolution-ary patterns of communal life and predictable history. The story of Jewish life in the twentieth century might be described as one of profound rupture; this rupture seems to have bred or even catalyzed the innovation and creativity that has emerged as the defining story of the twenty-first century. Of course, this creativity and growth is also surprising for the same reason: these conditions of crisis, catastrophe, and change might also have bred decline and stagnancy. And though the language of crisis still permeates much of the Jewish commu-nal discourse, Jewish life has become too complex and multivalent—and there is too much unexpected growth—for it to be cast purely in the terminology of decline.

Rather than describing the extraordinarily complex world of contemporary Jewry, this essay will present a series of paradigms through which contempo-rary Jewry can be understood. This approach will emphasize both the systemic challenges that Jewish life faces today, as well as offering conceptual categories in which trends in Jewish life can be studied and understood. And while we will try to allow for the new and innovative in Jewish life to stand on its own, we will also try to demonstrate the ways in which the realities of present-day Judaism draw on its historical and conceptual antecedents.[1]

Mainstreams and Margins

The narrative of "marginality" often used to describe Jewry tends to be his-torical; Jews in America *used* to live on the margins, and can now effectively describe themselves as part of the mainstream. The Jewish people in general *used* to live outside political processes, but with the rise of Jewish sovereignty in Israel now participate among the nations of the world. This story may indeed be true, if simplistic; more important and interesting are the ways in which these categories define Jewish life in less linear ways. Within the Jewish com-munity, the category of what counts as "mainstream" is shifting constantly, and both "normal" and "normative" are evolving terms.

Perhaps the most surprising and most central manifestation of this shifting of categories is in the way in which Jews identify as Jews. In population studies,[2] the self-definition showing the greatest increase for contemporary Jewry is now "Just Jewish," a confusing designation that combines highly engaged Jews who dislike denominational labels with Jews well outside the mainstream who see the adjective "just" as something of a diminutive ("since I don't fit into or want to be identified as X, call me just Jewish"). In either case, this designation—rising to now a plurality of American Jews and outflanking in popularity all of the previously popular denominational labels—suggests a growing disin-terest in at least the structural ways in which Jewish identity is broken down, and at most a pronounced shift in what we think of as "mainstream" Judaism. Twentieth-century Jewry saw a rise in institutions, affiliations, and membership structures; Jews in the twenty-first century seem to be rejecting these organizing principles wholeheartedly.

The one denomination that is growing, meanwhile, is Orthodoxy—and in particular in its most rigid forms. The hasidic birthrate is one of the most surprising outcomes of the catastrophes of the twentieth century, the result of deliberate efforts by the leaders of the hasidic dynasties to rebuild their destroyed European communities in relocated centers. Whether in Brooklyn, Jerusalem, New York's Rockland County, the Outremont suburb of Montreal, or a number of European cities, the hasidic leaders aggressively reaffirmed the commitment to their dynasties and cultivated a culture of birth as a response to death. This has produced, for contemporary Jewry, a rapidly ascending place for ultra-Orthodoxy not just in Jewish numbers but increasingly as well in the Jewish public squares and cultural imaginations. The most publicly visible hasidic sect has long been Chabad-Lubavitch, due to its unprecedented and adaptive outreach strategy; its size and visibility may now allow it to even be described as its own denomination of American Judaism.

Centrist or modern Orthodox Jews share some of the successes marked by the growth of ultra-Orthodox Jewry, and yet also experience some of the same struggles as their "liberal" coreligionists. They, too, are caught in the classic confrontation between tradition and modernity as the rest of Jewish civilization, ever since the twin pillars of the modern turn—Enlightenment and Emancipation—called into question all of the known truths that had defined and sustained Judaism in the premodern era. If the primary and core ideological force sustaining the rise of Orthodoxy was in the formative antimodern theology of early nineteenth-century Rabbi Moses Sofer—known for his polemical invectives against anything new—modern Orthodox Jews are caught between the mainstreaming of this form of rising Orthodoxy and the other mainstreams of Judaism that are highly skeptical of this reactionary turn.[3] Alarmists will wonder whether the dwindling numbers among the denominationally affiliated, and the rising numbers of both unaffiliated and Orthodox, suggest the impending arrival of a kind of Jewish Manicheanism, a Jewish people split between the ultra-committed and the uncommitted.[4] The less alarmed dispute the meaning of the numbers, arguing that the labels with which people identify never fully tell the story of the success (or failure) of the complex ideological systems beneath the surface.

Whichever interpretation we follow, it is clear to see that the denominational ideologies that carried Judaism to the present, together with their flagship institutions, are struggling to carry it into the future. This is true as well for the organized institutional frameworks that have defined Jewish life outside the synagogue: it is increasingly difficult to imagine that the same frameworks will define Jewish life for the successive generations. Several common observations in the world of Jewish leadership bear this out: that the leadership of the classic/defensive mainstream Jewish organizations is aging dramatically, with mostly failed "young leadership" efforts not filling the succession ranks; that Conservative Judaism, once the strongest American Jewish denomination, now has a disproportionate amount of physical infrastructure in its buildings and institutions relative to its membership rolls; and that the public image of which Jewish organizations represent or can be said to speak for contemporary Jews has shifted dramatically. One need look no further than official Jewish events at the White House and the shifting guest list to see the changing image of what amounts to Jewish leadership.[5]

The world of Jewish philanthropy suggests similar seismic shifts, with a decline in the federated system that dominated Jewish philanthropy in the twentieth century to the now-predominant system of private foundations, idiosyncratic giving circles, and the rise of boutique philanthropy. In several cases, the philanthropists themselves are now running the programs that they fund (or at least serving as dominant copartners with their grantees), shifting the balance of leadership from professionals supported by funders to funders dictating the agenda of community institutions in much more explicit ways.[6]

Meantime, Jewish life is characterized by an enormous cultural productivity and creativity—even as some of its most celebrated initiatives, and critical successes, fail to achieve sustainable growth. Perhaps the most famous example of creative energy to grow out of the heavily documented "innovation sector"—a network that has received disproportionate philanthropic attention relative to its actual philanthropic dollars—is the cautionary tale of JDub records. Founded by two young entrepreneurs, JDub—a Jewish record label—made national attention in their signing and promoting of the hasidic-reggae mainstream music-icon Matisyahu, and in subsequently producing events and cultural content that uniquely captured the elusive twenties and thirties demographic so often the target of mainstream Jewish institutional attention. Within ten years, however, as the beneficiary of many small start-up grants and professional development opportunities but not 'second-stage' funding, and in spite of multiple attempts to partner with and even merge with similar cultural initiatives, JDub was forced to shutter its business due to lack of funds. The JDub story suggests that the Jewish institutional framework has not yet caught up with the speed of trends within the broader world of Jewish behaviors and cultural identity; that perhaps the issue with JDub was not its content—which reflected all sorts of new Jewish realities—but its sustained belief that it belonged as part of the mainstream Jewish establishment, which could not sustain it.[7]

Of course, there are also lasting initiatives in the world of cultural creativity as well, and they too are reshaping the locus of where the "center" of the community is—even as they and all of these trends are also fundamentally challenging the premise that "the Jewish community" can be spatially mapped in this way with obvious centers and clear margins.[8]

There is perhaps no more profound and provocative challenge to the normative than in the world of ideas. Jewish scholarship and Jewish Studies have been living a strange double life for the past two generations—on the one hand, benefiting from Jewish philanthropic largesse especially from secular Jews hoping to establish an authentically Jewish philanthropic legacy and seeing in the university a way of reaching younger Jews, and on the other hand, supporting a field that sees itself entirely unconstrained by—and in many respects a direct challenge to—classic modes of Jewish thinking and belonging.[9] Put differently, Jewish Studies has risen extraordinarily in the last few decades, one of the few remaining growth areas within the humanities at the university level, and often fueled by Jewish philanthropic objectives that do not match the much more eclectic academic interests of the scholars engaged in the work. This tension has surfaced in recent years as two major Jewish foundations—the Posen Foundation and the Tikvah Fund—have invested significant resources in the field of Jewish intellectual life with sometimes thinly veiled and sometimes explicit ideological objectives for the intended impact of the ideas they hope are generated for the public. Since scholarship is a generative and creative process, however, at play is both the historical legacy of Jewish ideas as well as the future of how Judaism is meant to be understood (and taught).[10]

So creativity can be found across the spectrum of Jewish behaviors, with all of Jewish life's main institutions—the synagogue, the community center, the federation, and the family—being redefined with and sometimes against broader cultural trends. The growth rate of so-called emergent communities is extraordinary, especially in economic conditions that should ostensibly stifle the growth rate of start-up initiatives; but the culture of belonging, and the sites of belonging, have shifted so radically in the past several decades that Jews still want to belong and participate—even if in different venues, formats and institutional frameworks than the ones they inherited.

From Ben-Gurion/Blaustein to Bibi/Barack

In the early 1950s, in a well-documented exchange, Jacob Blaustein—then the head of the American Jewish Committee—stood down David Ben-Gurion's declaration that in the wake of the creation of the State of Israel, it was incumbent on American Jewry to fulfill its destiny in mass immigration to the Jewish state.[11] Ben-Gurion and Blaustein essentially agreed to a deal, the trade-off of Jewish support and philanthropy for the nascent state in exchange for the state's tolerance of a Diaspora instead of promoting the anti-Diasporic ideology that it fundamentally held.

But viewed differently, the showdown was no less than a classic power struggle between the titular and substantive leadership of two rising Jewish communities—in retrospect, at the critical moment during which they were articulating the values that would become essential to their emerging as the two poles of today's largely bipolar Jewish world. At the time, the Jewish communities of Israel and the United States spoke to each other via their leadership: the prime minister of Israel and the leaders of the American Jewish establishment. Today, though major Jewish institutions persist in the Jewish imagination as the representative voices of American Jewry, the prime minister calls the president of the United States directly and without Jewish mediators. The Jewish community, of course, still convenes major leadership gatherings, and the White House engages this leadership—even as it changes its makeup depending on the political party in power—to gauge (and ostensibly, massage) Jewish public opinion on the issues of the day. But the nature of the intra-Jewish public leadership conversation has shifted enormously.

To be sure, this has implications for the North American Jewish community and its leadership internally; at the same time as the Israeli leadership has risen in importance, so too Jews in North America have become politically important as *American* political leaders outside of formal roles in the Jewish community. Jewish political leadership as exercised by the community itself now pales in importance to what it represented in the middle of the last century, a consequence of both of these developments as well as of the decentralization of Jewish life in general (which breeds a skepticism of organizations that purport to speak for the whole). It would be difficult to claim, in an age when an observant Jew can be a mainstream and plausible presidential candidate, and when three of the nine justices of the Supreme Court are Jewish, that Jewish political power has declined. But it must be noted that while Jews have become more powerful, the Jewish community's power may be in decline.

But at the heart of this issue of American and Israeli political divergence is the changing nature of an idea long thought to be part of the fabric of the biblical message and now emerging as a buzzword of Jewish institutions and a flashpoint in intergenerational Jewish tensions—the idea of Jewish peoplehood, that Judaism is not merely a religion in the Protestant sense but the composite, complex identity of the historically landless and disputably ethnic Jewish "nation."[12] Peoplehood, of course, is a critical component of Zionist ideology as its finds its fullest articulation in a sovereign Jewish nation-state; without a collective national identity distinctly separate from the Jewish religion, Israel would necessarily become an antidemocratic theocracy. Israel constitutes an aspirational attempt to imagine Jewishness as Irishness, and its Jewish-democratic state is the consequence of translating this ideology into the mechanisms of self-determination that enable Israel to become the Jewish member of the family of nations.[13]

For Israeli Jews, then, peoplehood is not an abstract idea but a core feature of self-definition: the sense of belonging to a people, Israel makes political sense of the State of Israel. For American Jews, however, this is increasingly called into question. After all, American Jews now belong—more than any other Diaspora Jewish community in history—to a different people, the American people, even if "American-ness" lacks some of the shared ethnic-cultural qualities that other nation-states possess, and even if its unique democracy that elides cultural difference makes the idea of "the American people" fundamentally different from other iterations of peoplehood.

Put simply, Israeli and American Jews are on different trajectories when it comes to belonging to the cultural fabric of the societies where they live. A little-noticed event in 2011 portends the profound significance of this shift: the leadership of the Anti-Defamation League and the American Jewish Committee, now no longer self-evidently the leadership of Jews in America, now capable of exercising influence only through suggestion rather than by fiat, united to plea to the American Jewish community to not allow Israel to become a partisan issue in the 2012 elections. The Republican Jewish Coalition—seeing in the Obama-Netanyahu rift an opportunity to break the back of historical Jewish support for the Democratic Party—scoffed off the suggestion. Abraham Foxman ominously noted that this refusal of the Jewish community to coalesce publicly on this issue signaled the potential decline of Jewish "soft power" in America, wherein the Jewish community was capable of wielding profound political influence outsize of its numbers precisely by thinking of itself as a sub-people in the mainstream population, rather than becoming—as Foxman indicated—merely Jewish Republicans and Jewish Democrats.[14]

In fact, much of the anxiety in the last several years about Israel's policies and the right—or lack thereof—of Diaspora Jews to publicly voice opposition to those policies—hinges heavily on this issue. As part of the launch of his book "The Crisis of Zionism"—itself a flash point of attention and criticism in the Jewish establishment—Beinart published an editorial in the *New York Times*, a bold move that invited criticism of Beinart both for the substance of his call of a boycott of Israeli settlements in the West Bank, as well as for the placement of the piece in the public arena.[15] In spite of pronounced Jewish success in the American political system, there continue to be profound anxieties about the so-called airing of Jewish dirty laundry in public, as though the Jewish community is still a subordinate, separate, and unintegrated Diasporic minority. It is probably the case that this merely reflects a gap between two (or three) generations of Jews, ranging from those for whom the American success story for Jews in the late twentieth century is still surprising, and those who have grown up taking their own cultural primacy for granted. As such, the old operating systems may just now be losing their value for significant sections of the population—those who no longer want to operate as members of a beleaguered and self-conscious minority trying to assert its place in the public square, but rather see themselves intrinsically in that square already and are tenuously holding onto the particular mechanics of their Jewish cultural identity.

But the growing gap between North American Jews and Israeli Jews does not merely reflect political realities. The demographics of both Israeli and American Jewry are changing dramatically, Israel now overwhelmingly Middle Eastern, Russian, and an ethnic hybrid. American Jewry is also increasingly being ethnically and culturally redefined by the trends toward increased conversion to Judaism as well as by the much more vexing phenomenon of intermarriage—especially between people hoping to maintain allegiance to Jewish life and community.[16] Non-Jews participate extensively in Jewish life today from Jewish Community Centers (JCCs) (where certainly no proof of Jewish heritage is required for a gym membership) to synagogues (which have been struggling for decades to calibrate precisely the line between belonging and participating for individuals who want to join in the life of the community without crossing the boundary to become a Jew).[17] Both North American and Israeli Jewry are highly creative in their cultural and intellectual output, but the cultural influences are so enormously different, that the outputs—while sharing (perhaps) a conceptual ancestry—at times appear to represent completely separate national identities.

Making this more complex is the indefinite and unstable role being played by the Jews and Jewish communities outside of these two poles, in Europe, South America, and other places. In the 1980s, the Jewish community's attention was focused on relocating Jews from the former Soviet Union and the remaining communities in the Arab world to Israel and North America, and an emphasis on aliyah to Israel remains in force. It is without a doubt a result of the success of these efforts that Israel and the United States emerged as the primary poles in this bipolar Jewish community, with an overwhelming preponderance of Jews divided almost equally between these two major centers. In the past decades, however, a meaningful shift has materialized that has made for the rapid rise of several European Jewish communities, and the shift in emphasis from resources intended to relocate these communities to resources to support their independent growth. Germany is sometimes described as the fastest growing Jewish community in the world, combining an influx of Russian immigrants heading west with internal communal efforts to rehabilitate a strong Jewish identity not predicated entirely on the history of its earlier destruction and the aftermath. Centropa is a European Jewish organization making significant strides in fostering Jewish culture throughout Europe with an emphasis on Jewish culture separate from the legacy of the Holocaust. Whether the re-rise of European Jewry and the first articulation of its independent voice—which comes with an implicit questioning of the power relationships that have existed between it and the two main poles—involves a rejection of a sense of Jewish peoplehood or an *expansion* of it remains to be seen.

The historian and then-chancellor of the Jewish Theological Seminary Gerson Cohen wrote in an extraordinary 1966 essay (actually a commencement address at Boston's Hebrew Teachers College) about "The Blessing of Assimilation in Jewish History" that it was a bad misrepresentation to view Jewish history as the efforts to preserve cultural difference in Diaspora. Rather, he described the history of Diaspora as one of successful cultural integration by Jews of the particular elements of whichever cultures they found themselves; they survived not by distancing themselves from their surrounding realities, but by adapting them. Contemporary Jewry is torn between cultural antagonists such as both ultra-Orthodox Jews and ultranationalist Jews in Israel, and cultural assimilationists living very much at home in their Diasporic environments. North American Jews in particular are breaking down the components of particularistic and separatist Jewish identity in unprecedented ways, reaping the benefits of the willingness for the first time by non-Jews to actually marry Jews—in fact, it would seem to be the case that marrying Jews has become a social commodity. The result, however, is that a success story for individuals creates a challenge for a community long held together by implicit cultural bonds reinforced by external stimuli that reiterated cultural difference to the outside.

All this is to say that the idea of a shared Jewish peoplehood across geographic, ethnic, cultural, and political divides—between American Jews internally, and all the more so across the ocean from Israel or Germany—is no longer self-evident, and there is no obvious or intuitive educational or programmatic approach singularly capable of changing this reality. This is not for lack of trying. Several major philanthropic foundations have made "Peoplehood" their singular focus (even as the programmatic experimentation under the umbrella of this goal is so profoundly varied as to call the coherence of the enterprise into question), and the organized Jewish community has been convening a public debate on the theme for quite some time.[18]

Memory Anxiety

One of the surprising and recurrent psychological trends of contemporary Jewry is a palpable "memory anxiety," a fear of the loss of the past that maps into a concerns about the future. It is worth noting, here at the outset, that it is by no means obvious why the one should implicate the other, save for the underlying assumption that Judaism is fundamentally built on a veneration of the past—or even more dramatically, to follow the traditional line of reasoning, that the past is fundamentally superior to the present. These beliefs, however, run deep even for nonbelieving Jews, and the confrontation between premodern Jewish ideas and the evolutionary, progressive sensibility of modernity continues to create anxious tremors.[19]

For contemporary Jews, the issues are increasingly less manifest in a sense of the loss of the "truths" of the past, though these concerns—borne of the scientific revolution and the encounter of traditional ideas with Enlightenment—have not gone away. This was evident in an infamous episode from 2001, when a prominent congregational rabbi critiqued the archaeological record of the Bible's stories from the pulpit on Passover to the horror and consternation of his surprisingly dogmatic audience. Contemporary Jews still do struggle to reconcile what is learned traditionally—even in nontraditional environments—with the "real" knowledge that is learned in academic and other empirical settings.

The larger concerns breeding contemporary memory anxiety have to do with the more recent past, and the beleaguering sense that we are not sure how to integrate the monumental events of recent history into the Jewish sensibility. This is most palpable in the discourse surrounding the memory of the Holocaust, as marked in a few discrete ways—in the heavy amount of archiving and museum-building, what seems like the storing of the Holocaust for the rainy days; the vehemence of the response to the periodic episodes of memoir fabrication, which spills into the tensions around all forms of literary and nonmemorial representation of the Holocaust; the tensions between descendants of survivors who refer to themselves as members of the second- or third-generation, and in doing so claim a particular right—or responsibility—to or over the memory of the Holocaust, and those other descendants who bristle at this alleged pride of place; the rhetorical use of the Holocaust as part of the discourse on Israeli foreign policy and/or world intervention in would-be genocides; and of course the recurring sensibility that appears frequently in op-ed pieces and synagogue Yom HaShoah gatherings that the day indeed looms when the witnesses will no longer be present to bear witness . . . and then what will be of us, etc.?

In all of these cases, anxiety plays a central and even defining role. And while the anxiety to preserve the integrity of the survivor experience is a live current throughout all of these preservation efforts and thus may be credited with the amount of attention and money lavished on these projects by the organized Jewish community for some time, it remains to be seen whether in the deepest sense the actual memory of the Holocaust or its prescriptive importance remains defining or alive for subsequent generations of Jews. One might argue that the defense of the Holocaust in open court by the historian Deborah Lipstadt portends tougher days ahead for the memory of the Holocaust, more than the relief that victory in that particular trial suggested. It might even be argued—as is done sharply by Ruth Wisse—that even a culture of museums and memorialization lives on precisely on the wrong side of the threshold between memory and meaning, in focusing merely on preserving just the memory of the past Holocaust, and not doing enough for preventing the next.[20] This bespeaks a profound tension in contemporary Jewry between those who claim that the Jewish history of victimhood creates a burden of responsibility for the wider world, or rather should make us focus our attention on ensuring Jewish physical security. Needless to say, there is no reason to believe these two objectives need be in opposition to one another, and the State of Israel's official efforts in recent years to be a force for humanitarianism in the world may constitute an attempt to accomplish both. But in the world of polemics, these objectives are often represented as being opposing trends.

Or we might consider the curious case of the *Yizker Bikher*, the hundreds of volumes produced by gatherings of survivors to unload their stories, memories, and name lists into print and thus posterity, and the irony of their now-frequent appearance on dusty, used bookshelves in Jerusalem and elsewhere, sold off by subsequent generations who couldn't read or understand their importance, and simultaneously largely written off by scholarship (although this is being remedied)[21] as having insufficient historical value for an authentic rendering of the historical Holocaust. Much of how the Holocaust is chronicled in scholarship tends to use German records as the more authoritative source—to its critics, this is "perpetrator history" as opposed to the more slippery evidence of the victims (who were not exactly in the equivalent position for the preservation of their records).[22] This, however, makes for the memorialization of the Holocaust in radically different ways than Jewish catastrophes were historically remembered—in liturgy, narrative, poetry, and song. The result of this confusion is that in modern Jewish consciousness, the Holocaust is both "too much" and "not enough"—a paradox that continues to vex educators and community leaders, and that stems fundamentally from a failure to integrate the recent past into the psychological state of the present.

The dysfunction connoted by this memory anxiety, however, extends beyond the Holocaust and into other realms as well. It is evident in what is anecdotally described as a growing chasm between Jews who were born before or after Israel's transformative 1967 war, and in the implicit difference between support for Israel produced by lived memory and the ambivalence produced by the lack thereof. It is evident in intergenerational (and even temperamental) tensions between traditionalists who decry the contemporary Jewish failure to embrace, support, and uphold the Jewish institutions that defined Jewish life in the past, and those others who see no particular merit in sustaining institutions beyond their present-day market value. In all of these cases, the use of the past is a defining heuristic and both a substantive and rhetorical tool.

The Jewish communal buzzword for this set of questions is "continuity"—and like all other buzzwords, it has both a strong resonance in the philanthropic sector and deep ambiguity everywhere else. Read generously, the concern over continuity is very simply an anxiety about what it is to come next—a pronounced concern for Jews who know that their behaviors depart and defy the precedents they have inherited, as well as increasingly for Jewish institutions not the future succession of their leadership. Read cynically, "continuity" is a less inflammatory way of talking about intermarriage—on the assumption that exogamy breeds discontinuity—and/or a passive-aggressive way of complaining that the coming generations are less loyal than they should be to what they have inherited. After all, the term "continuity" is in passive voice; it places no burden on the speaker to create succession, but only on the next generation to continue what they have received.[23]

"Continuity" breeds a wide range of programmatic agendas in Jewish life, and the anxiety about whether Judaism will continue informs a wide variety of Jewish subindustries—whether in the realm of Jewish education and the choice to send children to insular day schools; in the rise of Jewish camping as the now-popular Jewish educational panacea in promoting a positive, sustainable, and transmissible Jewish identity; outreach efforts on college campuses either via Hillel or Chabad; and many more. It is sometimes unclear whether these educational efforts seek to suppress meaningful Jewish content in the hope that Jews will remain attached to their future *in spite of* its complexity, or whether continuity is merely a cause that enables the spread and growth of meaningful Jewish content. There is an oft-repeated critique by many Jewish intellectuals of the continuity conversation, that "there can be no continuity without content"—mostly as a plea that serious Judaism and its ideas not be held prisoner by political concerns, as well as a demand that serious Jewish engagement be defined by the richness of Jewish tradition rather than by thin attempts at spreading ethnocentrism.

As to the issue of endogamy/exogamy itself, without a doubt it has become one of the most polarizing issues in contemporary Jewish life. It has produced public policy debates between the few prominent Jewish sociologists, and pronounced policy differences between those organizations like The Jewish Outreach Institute and Boston's Combined Jewish Philanthropies that work toward Jewish outreach to families regardless of whether the families include non-Jewish spouses or partners, and other organizations that promote endogamy more explicitly as a means of combating the continuity problem. The most prominent of such organizations is Birthright Israel, the extraordinary philanthropic success story of the beginning of the Jewish twenty-first century. In both the focus of the research data evaluating the "success" of the program—which sends young Jewish adults to Israel for intensive, short trips—as well as in the philanthropic marketing, it is clear that the goals of the program have much less to do with Israel than they do with breeding Jewish continuity (i.e. connecting young Jews with each other toward the long-term goal of stemming the intermarriage tide).

Whatever policy prescriptions abound, however, history is on the side of exogamy: it is the first time in Jewish history when marrying a Jew is even morally neutral, much less the social commodity it now appears to be in North America. Though the demographers tend to count Jews based on objective categories, the Jewish community is increasingly less a closed circle and more a Venn diagram interacting with other communities and identities in unprecedented ways. What this means for the continuation of a shared past that is simply less a part of the historical memory of more and more of its members remains to be seen.

Religion Rising

In the words of one observer, young Jewish adults engaged in Jewish life are "more self-consciously religious" today than the generation of their parents and grandparents.[24] This does not necessarily mean that Jewry, on the whole, is more religious; it is not a statistical or demographic observation. Rather, it is a suggestion that religious practice and behavior is now a more central feature of the currency of substantive Jewish engagement for the engaged and affiliated. There is sociological data to support this assertion, in the surveys of young Jewish leadership that indicate this to be the case in emerging Jewish leaders, not to mention the aforementioned 2011 New York population survey, which demonstrated an overwhelming rise in Orthodox affiliation. There is also anecdotal data, such as the rise and success of non-Orthodox religious organizations such as Mechon Hadar and dozens of other start-up congregations as part of the so-called innovation sector. After all, Orthodox and "religious" are not synonymous, and the success of a new national organization in securing funds and recruiting students for rigorous programs focused on prayer and study indicate that "the traditional forms" are alive and well, and possibly making a return.

In his famous 1923 essay "Jewish Religiosity," the philosopher Martin Buber attempted to chart a meaningful distinction between what he deemed Jewish religion and Jewish religiosity. In "religiosity" Buber saw the animating, creative spirit of Judaism, expressed in spiritual longing, awe, and wonder; "religion," meantime, described the composite dogmas over time that emerged out of the sum total of these experiences of religiosity. Religion was just the organizing principle, the stable version of living out the consequences of the living and breathing religiosity.

Predictably, the universalist and spiritually minded Buber had substantially less interest in the world of religion than in the spirit of religiosity which he sought not just to describe in the works of the hasidic masters, but indeed to bring alive as an animating force for contemporary Jewry. Indeed, it was probably in this "activism" that Buber ran awry of the scholar of mysticism Gershom Scholem and prompted their famous debate; Buber's version of the hasidic masters was too instrumental to the religiosity he sought to bring to life, and too inconsistent with the *actual* hasidic masters and their specific historical context that Scholem knew too well.[25] Still, historically accurate or not, Buber laid the foundations for a retrieval (or perhaps an invention) of a contemporary Jewish spiritually rooted at least conceptually or textually in the theology of the hasidic forbears.

In the present, both religion and religiosity are experiencing an extraordinary heyday—though those I will call the religionists might disavow the entire Buberian frame I am using to describe them, much less the category in which I have placed them. Hasidism, ultra-Orthodoxy, and even centrist/modern Orthodoxy are experiencing a substantial spike in the market share of Jewish populations and life, evident both in Israel and in North American Jewish population studies. The phenomenon of the "baal teshuva movement," so extensively documented in the previous decades, has reached fruition, and dovetails with high Orthodox Jewish birthrates to produce a palatably rising percentage of the Jewish population. Accordingly, not only are Jewish institutions catering to these populations increasing, but it is not surprising to also see an emergence in Israel of the ultra-Orthodox as a much more self-consciously powerful player in Israel's public square and political arenas.

Meantime, well outside the rise of these forms of Jewish religion, Jewish religiosity is on the rise as well. Both in North America and in Israel, myriads of initiatives promoting a Jewish spiritual sensibility—often hybridized with either forms of cultural expression, or even with the wisdom traditions of other faiths—are flowering and cluttering a landscape once much more cleanly defined between religion, culture, and ethnicity. Hundreds of Israelis gather on Friday evenings for a highly untraditional traditional Shabbat service on the Tel Aviv port, not in a veiled outreach initiative and not organized in the hope that the participants will someday, somehow drift from the port into good old-fashioned pews. Jewish spirituality and religious expression is re-rising in an innovative, eclectic relationship to Jewish belonging, and often times independent of institutional affiliation and the other usual attendant behaviors. The concern of the 1980s and the 1990s of a secular-religious divide in Israel is largely past, replaced by a Jewish society experimenting differently with religious behaviors in ways that defy classical taxonomies. The same can be said too in a North American Jewish community much more comfortable with spiritual expression, mainstream mysticism, and religious experience than previous generations (but without the accompanying denominational organizing principles that once went hand in hand with American religiosity).

Part of this evolution might date, ironically, from the attempts in the 1950s and the 1960s to soften religion by integrating it with culture and social life, what has been described as the "shul with a pool" phenomenon. When denominational affiliation could be taken for granted, the community needed to broaden the types of activities associated with communal belonging to make space for Jewish expression outside the framework of what was taking place in the sanctuary. Ironically, the opposite result has taken root: religious life has become much more central in the life of cultural and social Jewish institutions. JCCs are sites of Jewish learning, and retreat centers like Isabella Freedman offer dozens of "religious" and spiritual opportunities together with cultural, literary, and intellectual offerings. There are now humanist and multidenominational rabbinical schools to compete with the classic denominationally driven seminaries, as well as countless study opportunities and experiences available to the spiritual seekers. This phenomenon calls to mind less the legacy of Buber and more that of his longtime study partner Franz Rosenzweig, whose call for the reinvigoration of Jewish learning is finally achieving fruition decades after his death.[26]

There is no consensus, to be sure, about the religiosity itself that is rising, in content, substance, or form; even within relatively proscribed networks, substantive and polemical debates ensue about the nature of religious Jewry today and the political overlays suggested by the various ideologies. This includes a vibrant debate about the nature of religious authority in Jewish political and communal life, a particularly vexing question for a population that is experimenting with religion and religiosity without necessarily embracing the traditional authority structures usually associated with these behaviors.

Nevertheless, this rise of religion—in the wake of the massive ruptures of the twentieth century, which shattered the normal processes of religious communities just as they ruptured Jewish theology trying to make sense of it all—is nothing short of astonishing. Jews traveled through brief but dramatic epochs in the 1950s through 1970s of wrestling with the theological impact both of the divine darkness signaled in the Holocaust and the messianic glimmer of the rise of Jewish sovereignty in Israel. It might have seemed at one point that Jewry would perpetually need to embrace the theologian Eliezer Berkovits's cautioning of all those who did not live through Auschwitz to respect both the belief of the devout who walked into gas chambers singing *Ani Ma'amin*, and the disbelief of those who walked out alive—a forced pluralism of circumstance that would leave Jewry in a perpetual lurch around faith and spirituality.[27] Indeed it might be said that the secular faith of postwar Jewry that built countless communal institutions for Jews—while in some case less interested in Judaism—was propelled by this skittishness about faith combined with a conviction to survival. When we look at the reengagement with God that seems to partially define the world of contemporary Jewry, it seems that modern Jews are finally starting to reapproach God—differently, if still ambivalently—after Auschwitz.

Fate and Destiny

We have looked at a number of key trends and identifiers of contemporary Jewry, a series of conceptual lenses that helps us both name and interpret the complexity of a Jewish community spread all over the world but primarily bifurcated into two strong centers; a community in which institutions are struggling but new forms of ideological affiliation are rising; in which collective identity is both taken for granted and challenged by empirical realities; and in which the centers of gravity seem to be in constant flux.

This forces a crucial question that the dispassionate observer is loath to ask, but which highly implicates any such analysis: what does the future hold for contemporary Jewry? Or, if we want to reserve prophesy for fools, we might ask differently: what about contemporary Jewry appears to be defined and sustainable for its future, and what seems to be so dramatically in flux that we can expect it to disappear?

Contemporary Jews tend to tell two stories about their realities, stories that encompass both a sense of the past and a sense of the future: One such story, to paraphrase Rabbi Donniel Hartman, is a "crisis narrative."[28] Since Jewish self-definition has for so long been predicated on the hatred of us by others—which reinforced the need for internal cohesion and made internal strife less monumental—this narrative unconsciously seeks the language of threat, crisis, and fear to motivate and animate Jewish life. Whether the crisis is internal (intermarriage, the loss of internal civil discourse) or external (the threat of nuclear Iran, circumcision bans, swastikas on synagogues), the key lesson of the traumatic Jewish past is a constant vigilance on the borders and boundaries (real or imagined) and a Jewish public policy aimed at quelling, suppressing, and defeating these threats. This is psychologically complex, as the ultimate fear of a fearmonger is the loss of fear; does a Jew driven by a crisis narrative as the central motivating force in his/her Jewish life really want the crisis to go away? Fear, crisis, and anxiety are a cottage industry in Jewish life, and it is neither cynical nor an exaggeration to suggest that several of the major Jewish organizations that continue to dominate the landscape of Jewish leadership are predicated consciously and explicitly on the need for Jewish defense, protection, and vigilance. This is reasonable to expect in the wake of the twentieth century and in the face of meaningful ongoing external threats to Jewish survival; it is more than reasonable for Jews to take seriously Jewish protection as a dignified and ethical value and as a major feature of public policy, even—or perhaps precisely because of—a meaningful accumulation of unprecedented levels of Jewish military and political power.

A second Jewish story is the exact opposite: The Jewish moment is one of profound arrival. This same unprecedented power enables realities never thought possible, such as the idea that marrying a Jew would be not only legitimate but perhaps even a social commodity—the stuff of presidential daughters! Jews as presidential and ministerial material the world over; Natan Sharansky went from refusenik to politician in what seemed like a matter of minutes, the singular embodiment of the displacement of a narrative of despair to a narrative of hope. This is the Jewish story of the popular book *Start-Up Nation* about "Israel's economic miracle," the Jewish story of success, optimism, and unbridled pride that—unlike in previous generations—does not fear speaking of itself aloud out of fear of retribution or jealousy. Organizations such as "Reboot" explicitly envision themselves as reimagining the present and future of Jewish life in dialogue with change-agents and "catalysts" of the broader society that they lead and inhabit. In so doing, they see themselves both charting new possibilities and insinuating that what they imagine and create will, by dint of their influence, be necessarily influential. This is a signal of a Jewish optimism combined with a pragmatism of possibility that represents an entirely different narrative about the Jewish present, one that may draw on the past but sees itself largely unconstrained by it. But if the fatal flaw of the fear narrative is its unrestrained longevity and the negativity it projects as a feature of belonging to Jewishness, the flaw in the optimism narrative is its ironic complacency: is every new trend necessarily okay and worthy of integration to Jewishness? What constitutes the rigor by which a tradition with meaningful longevity preserves its unique quality? For a tradition in which journey was always more meaningful than arrival—a tradition that ends its canonical story with its people perched on the precipice of the Promised Land and not in it—what are the ethical consequences of actually arriving?

These worldviews may be otherwise articulated as "Fate and Destiny" as they are mediated through the theology of Rabbi Joseph Soloveitchik, the principal ideological architect of modern Orthodox Judaism and one of the preeminent Jewish philosophers of the twentieth century. The response to suffering in Jewish tradition, wrote Soloveitchik, can be found either in the practice of acceptance or in the ethic of behavior: I can respond through a fate framework, in which I come to terms with what I have been handed; or through a destiny framework, in which instead of wrestling with what I have been dealt I carve out a plan of action that dictates what I will *do* about it.[29] As David Hartman explains, this leaves us the productive difference between the "metaphysics or logic of description," and the "metaphysics or logic of response."[30] In other words, how we interpret the events that happen to us—the description—does not necessarily need, or perhaps should not, dictate how we react to the conditions we are given. This rabbinic approach would be to say—these are my realities; now what do I make of them? But while for Soloveitchik and Hartman there is a clear ethical difference in destiny over fate, it may be said of contemporary Jewry—the inheritors of a recent past heavy with instructive meaning—that its narratives still stand at precisely this crossroads, and that neither pathway seems obviously superior.

This may indeed be the defining question for the future of Jewry—how it holds in the balance between, on the one hand, a needed sober and prosaic memory of a very recent and horrific past, a memory that travels together with a consciousness of ongoing real threats internal and external and with an awareness of the profound fragility of the ongoing existence of Jewish life, and on the other hand, the roots for a positive optimism stemming from conditions never anticipated or experienced by Jews since the dawn of modernity revealed its first promise. One might hope that contemporary Jewry, with all its complexity, would find ways to integrate these realities—to bridge past and present as it charts its future—and not merely continue to divide in ideology and practice along precisely these lines. But if the past half-century has been in any way instructive, it is that describing present realities fails miserably at predicting future outcomes. The same may hold true about contemporary Jewry now, and ultimately, later.

Notes

1. Conversations with many colleagues working with me on projects for The Shalom Hartman Institute helped refine my thinking for this essay: these include Donniel Hartman, Suzanne Stone, Jack Wertheimer, Steven M. Cohen, Sharon Cohen Anisfeld, Shai Held, Rick Jacobs, Paul Golin, Yossi Klein Halevi, Angela Warnick Buchdahl, J. J. Schacter, and the rabbis in the fourth cohort of the Institute's Rabbinic Leadership Initiative. I have attempted to document as many as possible of the phenomena that I mention in this article, but take full responsibility for the interpretations and speculations about the meaning of this evidence.
2. See the essay by Sergio DellaPergola in this volume. My thinking on demographic issues was significantly informed by Steven M. Cohen, Jacob B. Ukeles, and Ron Miller (2011), "The Jewish Community Study of New York." UJA-Federation and by the authors' "N.Y. Jewry's Stunning Diversity, And Why That's Good," *The Jewish Week*, September 19, 2012.
3. For an example of the tension in which centrist Orthodoxy finds itself, especially on social issues, see Gail Bendheim, "When Fealty to Jewish Law Becomes Misogyny," *The Jewish Week*, January 3, 2012.
4. See for example, Jonathan Tobin, "The Beginning of the End for Liberal Jewry," *Commentary*, June 12, 2012.
5. See the allusion to this change in James Traub, "The New Israel Lobby," *The New York Times*, September 9, 2009.
6. On the rise of the foundations in the philanthropic sector, see Gary A. Tobin and Aryeh Weinberg (2007), *A Study of Jewish Foundations*. Institute for Jewish and Community Research.
7. Daniel Arkin, "Klezmer Punks, Gangsta Rabbis: An Oral History of JDub Records," *The Brooklyn Ink*, November 12, 2012. On the issue of second-stage funding, see Helen Chernikoff, "'Second Stage' for Startups," *The Jewish Week*, April, 24, 2012.
8. Jumpstart, The Natan Fund, and The Samuel Bronfman Foundation, *The Innovation Ecosystem: Emergence of a New Jewish Landscape* (2009).
9. See the Introduction to this volume.
10. See Zachary Braiterman's (problematic) critique and the ensuing comments online at http://zeek.forward.com/articles/117374/ (September 6, 2011).
11. Noam Pianko (2010), *Zionism and the Roads Not Taken: Rawidowicz, Kaplan, Kohn.* Bloomington: Indiana University Press, p. 200.

12. The recent literature in the Jewish community and in the world of Jewish think tanks is extensive: it has been usefully collected online at www.nadavfund.org.il/resources (last accessed December 16, 2012).
13. See the excellent treatment of this issue in Alexander Yakobson and Amnon Rubinstein (2009), *Israel and the Family of Nations: The Jewish Nation-State and Human Rights*. London: Routledge.
14. Nathan Guttman, "Proposed Unity Pledge Spurs More Debate," *The Forward*, October 27, 2011.
15. See Ami Eden's prescient comments at http://blogs.jta.org/telegraph/article/2012/03/19/3092214/beinarts-boycott-and-boycotting-beinart (last accessed March 19, 2012).
16. The fiercest defender of this approach to intermarriage—as a signal of American Jewish success rather than failure—is Paul Golin, for whom this translates into a public policy objective to normalize (rather than stigmatize) intermarriage. See most recently www.njjewishnews.com/article/9005/when-it-comes-to-intermarriage-experts-confuse-cause-and-effect (last accessed April 10, 2012).
17. See Michael Walzer, Menachem Lorberbaum, and Noam J. Zohar (2006), *The Jewish Political Tradition: Membership*. New Haven: Yale University Press, pp. 511 ff.
18. For a polemical/critical take on this set of issues, see Jack Wertheimer, "The Ten Commandments of America's Jews," *Commentary*, June 2012.
19. On this issue of memory anxiety, and with respect to much of the discussion that follows, see Yehuda Kurtzer (2012), *Shuva: The Future of the Jewish Past*. Waltham, MA: Brandeis University Press.
20. "How Not to Remember and How Not To Forget," *Commentary*, September 2008.
21. See, for example, Rosemary Horowitz (ed.) (2011), *Memorial Books of Eastern European Jewry: Essays on the History and Meanings of Yizker Volumes*. Jefferson, NC: MacFarland.
22. See the discussion of this term in Saul Friedlander (1992), *Probing the Limits of Representation: Nazism and the "Final Solution"*. Cambridge, MA: Harvard University Press.
23. See, for instance, the critique offered by Daniel Elazar and his "guidelines" for Jewish continuity projects in Daniel Elazar (1996), "A Statement on Jewish Continuity," *Jewish Community Studies*, available online at http://jcpa.org/dje/articles2/statement-contin.htm.
24. Personal communication with Suzanne L. Stone (November 21, 2012).
25. The literature on this debate is extensive, but see, for example, Gershom Scholem, "Martin Buber's Hasidism," *Commentary*, October, 1961.
26. This is best expressed in Franz Rosenzweig's essay "Towards a Renaissance of Jewish Learning," written originally in 1920 and reprinted (and translated) in N. N. Glatzer (ed.) (1955), *On Jewish Learning*. Madison: University of Wisconsin Press.
27. Eliezer Berkovits (1973), *Faith after the Holocaust*. New York: Ktav.
28. Donniel Hartman (2011), "Beyond the Crisis Narrative," *Havruta* 7.
29. Soloveitchik's 1956 sermon entitled "Kol Dodi Dofek" on this subject is now reprinted and translated authoritatively as Joseph Dov Soloveitchik (2000), *Fate and Destiny: From Holocaust to the State of Israel*. New York: Ktav. See a discussion similar to mine in using Soloveitchik's framework to explore the future of contemporary Jewry in Steven M. Cohen, "The Demise of the 'Good Jew': Marshall Sklare Award Lecture," *Contemporary Jewry*, February, 2012. My thanks to Professor Cohen for this reference and for his guidance with this article.
30. David Hartman (2011), *The God Who Hates Lies: Confronting and Rethinking Jewish Tradition*. Woodstock, VT: Jewish Lights, pp. 176–80.

10 Women, Gender, and Judaism

Judith R. Baskin

Introduction

Women constitute half of the Jewish people and they have always played essential roles in ensuring Jewish continuity and the preservation of Jewish beliefs and values. It is only since the 1970s, however, that Jewish women's daily lives and spiritual and cultural endeavors have received sustained scholarly attention. This burgeoning research about women and women's experiences may be attributed in great part to the emergence of women's and gender studies as theoretical academic disciplines and to the significant increase in female scholars who have earned doctoral degrees in various fields of Jewish Studies.

Women's and gender studies research methodologies have reminded scholars of what should have been self-evident: a person's gender is central to her or his cultural socialization. Along with other characteristics such as class, race, religion, and ethnicity, gender has determined and often limited a person's options and opportunities. Including gender as a category of historical analysis has transformed how many scholars approach and interpret their research data. Before the last quarter of the twentieth century, with some exceptions, historical and literary studies and reference works had little to say about the significant differences in the lives, private and public roles, and religious and creative achievements of Jewish women and men. Certainly women who were extraordinary by virtue of their portrayals in biblical and postbiblical narratives, their appearances in rabbinic texts, or the influence they exercised due to wealth and position, cultural accomplishments, or political activism were usually mentioned, at least in passing. However, references to women in general tended to be limited to their relationships with men, particularly in discussions of the legal, economic, and social implications of marriage and related personal status issues. In the 1970s and 1980s, scholars of Judaism and the Jewish experience began to investigate women's domestic, economic, creative, and spiritual contributions to Jewish life from biblical times to the present. By the early twenty-first century, attention to the constructions and consequences of gender in Jewish societies of many times and places had become an essential component of Jewish Studies scholarship.[1]

Parallel developments in the contemporary Jewish community have also played a role in new academic understandings of the significance of gender in Judaism and Jewish life. The feminist movement of the early 1970s created an atmosphere that encouraged the ordination of women as rabbis and cantors in Judaisms outside the Orthodox community and led to expanded intellectual, spiritual, and leadership roles for women in many synagogues and communal organizations. Similarly, all forms of contemporary Jewish religious life have paid increased attention to the education of girls and women.[2] In this essay I provide an overview of what recent scholarship has revealed about the impact of gender on Judaism and Jewish lives from biblical times to the present. Although space does not permit discussion of every aspect of this topic, I refer wherever possible to primary sources available in English translation and to valuable and accessible monographs and anthologies.

Hebrew Bible

The Hebrew Bible is a composite document; it preserves many types of literature that reflect the attitudes and concerns of authors writing in different times and places. An example of such significant diversity as it applies to women and gender is evident in the two biblical creation stories placed at the beginning of Genesis. The first account of the origin of human beings (Gen. 1.1–2.3) recounts that both males and females (their number is not specified) were created simultaneously in the divine image and equally charged to multiply and to steward the earth and their fellow creatures. The second narrative (Gen. 2.4 ff.) preserves a tradition of male priority where woman is a subsequent and second-ary creation, formed from man's body to fulfill male needs for companionship and progeny. Such divergent understandings of female status and capacities, and the contradictions they engender, appear throughout biblical literature.

Contemporary scholars utilize a number of strategies to contextualize and understand the diverse representations of women in biblical writings.[3] Investigations of female status in biblical law, for example, reveal that bibli-cal legislation, as Ancient Near Eastern social policies in general, assumed a woman's subordination to the dominant male in her life, whether father or husband. This man exerted control over her sexuality, including the right to challenge both her virginity and her marital faithfulness (Deut. 11.28–9; Num. 5.11–31). Indeed, legislative concerns about women's sexual activity really had to do with relations between men. A man was to be executed for having inter-course with another man's wife (Lev. 20.10) because he had committed a crime of theft against a man; similarly, a man who seduced or raped a virgin paid a bride-price to her father and married her (Deut. 22.28). In a patriarchal culture in which women functioned essentially as daughters, wives, and mothers of particular men, it is not surprising that women had virtually no property rights. Unmarried women inherited from their fathers only if they had no brothers; in such cases, women had to marry within their father's extended family to pre-vent the dispersal of tribal property among outsiders (Num. 36.2–12). Widows did not inherit from their husbands at all, but were dependent on their sons or the generosity of other heirs. According to the practice of levirate marriage, a childless widow was the legal responsibility of her husband's oldest brother; he had to marry her or release her from connection to his family to survive on her own (Deut. 25.5–10).

Priestly laws pertaining to purity also played an important role in defin-ing women in the Hebrew Bible and postbiblical Judaisms. These regulations assumed that menstruating women were ritually impure and had the potential to transmit ritual impurity to people and objects around them. During these times they were sexually unavailable to their husbands (Lev. 12, 15). A woman was also ritually impure for a period of 7 days after giving birth to a male child, and 14 days after bearing a girl. For 33 additional days after the birth of a son and 66 days after the birth of a daughter, she was forbidden to enter the Temple or touch hallowed things (Lev. 12.1–8). Although such priestly ordi-nances reflect a system of purity in which all human discharges were regarded as imparting impurity, they apply particularly to women, who are regularly subject to the biological consequences of fertility, pregnancy, and childbirth. Biblical texts provide scant information as to when, how, and whether such prohibitions were actually observed.

Little is known about women's participation in the organized worship that took place in Israelite shrines and the Jerusalem Temple. Certainly, women took part in communal festivals and brought sacrifices; references to women singing and dancing at festivals and as part of victory celebrations occur in Exod. 15, Judg. 5.1–31 and 21:19–23, and 1 Sam. 18.6–7. Hannah, the mother of Samuel, Israel's last judge, prayed alone at the Tabernacle at Shiloh (1 Sam. 1.19) and her entreaty (2.1–10) became the model for supplicatory prayer in rabbinic tradition (Babylonian Talmud *Berakhot* 31a). There is far less information on women's participation in the Temple rituals that were instituted during the monarchy period. Although it seems likely that women tended to gather with other women, there is no mention of enforced segregation of the sexes either at Shiloh or at the First Temple. During the Herodian period (first century BCE–first century CE), a women's court (*ezrat nashim*) provided a large gathering space for both men and women to the east of the Second Temple's inner court. Rabbinic sources indicate that during the water-drawing ritual on the second night of Sukkot, the autumn pilgrimage festival, women were confined to the balconies in the women's court, apparently to prevent licentious behavior during the festivities (Tosefta *Sukkot* 4:1; Babylonian Talmud *Sukkot* 51b–52a; Jerusalem Talmud *Sukkot* 55b). Although postbiblical sources indicate that women brought sacrifices and other offerings to the Second Temple, they appear to have been excluded from the Temple's central areas of sanctity that were accessible to ordinary Israelite males.[4]

There are biblical references to girls' puberty rites (Judg. 11.39–40), harvest dances (Judg. 21.20–1), and childbirth rituals (Lev. 12.6–8), but these female ceremonies and domestic rituals were not of central interest to male biblical writers and editors and are therefore not recorded in any detail. A number of scholars have discussed the persistence of goddess worship in ancient Israel and the particular place of the Near Eastern fertility goddess, Asherah. Frequent archaeological discoveries of ancient Israelite female clay figurines, particularly prominent in the period of the monarchies, indicate that aspects of such worship may have lingered in popular religious life.[5] Some authors have suggested that the female personification of Wisdom in Proverbs also preserves residual elements of female divinity. Although she serves as a divine emissary (Prov. 1.29) and not a fully independent deity, Wisdom is said to have been created before the world and its inhabitants (8.22 ff.) and functions as a cherished intermediary between the divine and the mundane (8.35–7).

Women figure in many biblical narratives, performing both positive and negative parts in the unfolding of Israel's destiny. Often these women are portrayed as using subterfuge or enticement to gain their ends; in other instances, they are the passive victims of male aggression, self-preservation, or foolishness. In both cases, their secondary place in biblical societies is evident. While a number of these episodes demonstrate the strength of sexual attraction and its potentially destructive consequences, the Song of Songs is unique in its egalitarian and erotic presentation of female–male sexuality. More typically, Proverbs warns young men to shun the snares of seductive women (5; 7; 31.2–3).

Late Ancient Mediterranean Diaspora

From at least the third century BCE on, large numbers of Jews lived throughout the Greek-speaking Hellenistic and Roman Mediterranean worlds. Evidence suggests that many aspects of Jewish life in these communities, including possibilities available for women, diverged significantly from the norms and proscriptions found in rabbinic literature, which was recorded several centuries later. Most Jewish women of these milieus lived their lives in the relative seclusion of the domestic realm, but funerary and other inscriptions in Greek and Latin indicate that some women acted independently in the social, economic, and religious spheres. Inscriptions dating from the first century BCE to the sixth century CE, found in Italy, Asia Minor, Egypt, and Phoenicia, refer to women as "head of the synagogue," "leader," "elder," "mother of the synagogue," and "priestess," indications that some Jewish women, presumably of significant economic resources, assumed positions of leadership in the public sphere of the ancient synagogue. Although it is not clear if these synagogue titles imply meaningful leadership and/or ritual obligations, or whether they are honorific recognitions of significant philanthropy, they do indicate that women could be prominent in Jewish communal life. Some scholars suggest that the female "leadership was particularly likely in Jewish synagogues with relatively high numbers of proselytes (both male and female) for whom the participation of women in public life, including religious *collegia*, was familiar and acceptable."[6] It is also significant that female characters such as Judith, Asenath (*Joseph and Asenath*), and the mother of seven sons (2 and 4 Maccabees), have frequent and diverse roles in the Hellenistic Jewish literature of late antiquity.[7] Their prominence may signal efforts to appeal to a valued audience of Jewish women and prospective female proselytes.

Some Jewish women of this milieu may have possessed significant Jewish learning. The first century CE writer Philo of Alexandria relates that a small number of upper-class, well-educated Jewish women joined the contemplative monastic Therapeutic community (located outside of Alexandria, Egypt), where they studied Jewish scriptures and allegorical commentaries and lived a life of rigorous asceticism, broken only by Sabbath and festival observances. When men and women prayed together on the Sabbath, they were separated by a partial wall which prevented visual contact but allowed women to participate equally with men in prayer and song.[8]

Women in the System of Rabbinic Judaism

The legal and literary traditions of rabbinic Judaism were primarily formed and recorded in the first six centuries of the Common Era. Rabbinic writings preserve a variety of competing interpretations and opinions; while majority views are generally privileged, minority opinions are recorded as well.[9] Given this multivocal literary structure it is not surprising that rabbinic literature expresses diverse attitudes toward women and their activities. What unites these views, however, is the conviction that women are essentially different both in innate capacities and in legal, social, and spiritual status from men (Babylonian Talmud *Shabbat* 62a). Since the interpreters and expositors of rabbinic literature were men, the ideal human society they imagined was decidedly oriented toward the centrality of their own sex. Women did not play an active part in its development, nor were they granted a significant role in any aspect of rabbinic Judaism's communal life of judicial leadership, study, and worship. It is impossible to know which of the numerous laws and ordinances were actually in effect at the time they were recorded. Moreover, the discernible anxiety in rabbinic literature regarding control of women's activities may reflect a contrast between what many women actually did and what the rabbinic sages believed that they should do. Although rabbinic ordinances may not always have been descriptive of the everyday life of most Jews in the centuries of their formulation, in the course of the Middle Ages the mandates of the Babylonian Talmud (henceforth BT) became normative, with local variations, for virtually all Jewish communities. Despite the egalitarian vision of human creation expressed in the first chapter of Genesis, rabbinic tradition is far more comfortable with the view of Gen. 2.4 ff., that women are a secondary conception, unalterably other from men, and at a further remove from the divine. This certainty of woman's ancillary and subordinate place in the scheme of things permeates rabbinic thinking; the male sages who produced rabbinic literature apportioned separate spheres and separate responsibilities to women and men, making every effort to confine women and their activities to the private realms of the family and its particular concerns.[10] These included economic endeavors which would benefit the household; indeed, undertaking business transactions with other private individuals was always an expected part of a woman's domestic role, one that is already implicit in biblical passages such as Prov. 31.10–31. However, as in that text, where the "capable wife" is praised for her accomplishments by the male elders who are "prominent in the gates" (31.23, 31), women did not participate in public worship, study of religious texts, or community leadership.

As long as women satisfied male expectations in their assigned roles, they were revered and honored for enhancing the lives of their families and particularly for enabling their male relatives to fulfill their religious obligations. As the BT *Berakhot* 17a relates, women earn merit "by sending their sons to learn

[Torah] in the synagogue, and their husbands to study in the schools of the rabbis, and by waiting for their husbands until they return from the schools of the rabbis." Rabbinic legislation goes beyond biblical precedents in its efforts to ameliorate some of the difficulties women faced as a consequence of biblical law. This includes the formulation of marriage contracts that provided financial support in the event of divorce or widowhood and mechanisms to permit women to petition rabbinic tribunals to compel divorces in specific circumstances.[11] Nevertheless, rabbinic Judaism disadvantages women in several areas of personal status, such as levirate marriage and divorce, where she is dependent on male volition to achieve her independence. The situation of the *agunah* ("anchored woman"), a wife whose husband has disappeared but cannot be proven dead, is particularly fraught because she may never remarry. Rabbinic society tolerated polygyny, although it is difficult to know its frequency, and both unmarried and married men were permitted significant sexual freedom, as long as their nonmarital liaisons were with unmarried women. Adultery applied only when a man had relations with a woman married to someone else; children of such a union, including the children of an *agunah*, were *mamzerim* (bastards), and suffered significant legal disabilities.

Women, like men, are understood to be moral and ethical beings. They are responsible for obeying all of Judaism's negative commandments and for observing the Sabbath and all of the festivals and holidays of the Jewish calendar, although male and female obligations on these days often differed. According to BT *Berakhot* 20a–20b, women are exempt from participation in time-bound communal prayers but they are not free from the obligation to pray that is incumbent on each individual (BT *Berakhot* 20b). Later Jewish tradition taught that women should make a personal address to God as they started their day and that the content of women's prayers might be spontaneous and could be voiced in a vernacular language, rather than according to an established liturgy.[12] We do not find extant versions of specific formulations of prayers for women, however, until the end of the medieval period.

Women participated in their own religious observances, including abstention from work on *Rosh Hodesh*, the New Moon (Jerusalem Talmud *Ta'anit* 1:6, 64c), however few details of these practices are known. Women also observed a number of ritual regulations within the domestic sphere. These included preparation and serving of food according the rabbinic dietary laws (*kashrut*); women were also expected to separate and burn a piece of the dough they used in making Sabbah bread (*hallah*), a reminder of Temple sacrifice (an obligation that applied to male bakers, as well), and to kindle Sabbath lights (*hadlaqah*).

The limitations on physical contact between spouses during the wife's menstrual period and for seven days afterwards (*hilkhot niddah*) were also a central component of rabbinic understandings of women's obligations and women were assumed to be trustworthy in their compliance with this legislation.

Rabbinic expansions of biblical ritual purity strictures (particularly Lev. 12, 15, and 18) forbidding contact with the *niddah* play a role, as well, in limitations on women's communal activities.[13] However, women in public were also seen as problematic because their sexual appeal to men could lead to social disruption. A significant legal argument for excluding women from synagogue participation rests on the Talmudic statement, "The voice of woman is indecent" (BT *Berakhot* 24a). This is linked to the ruling that a man may not recite the *Shema*, a central part of the worship service, if he hears a woman singing, since her voice might divert his concentration. Extrapolating from hearing to seeing, rabbinic prohibitions on male/female contact in worship eventually led to a physical barrier (*mehitzah*) between men and women in the synagogue to preserve men from sexual distraction during prayer. Indeed, rabbinic Judaism advises extremely limited contact between men and women in all circumstances to prevent the possibility of sexual contact between inappropriate partners, both in order to avert adulterous or incestuous relationships, and to prevent the conception and birth of illegitimate children (*mamzerim*).[14] These practices of separation continue to be followed today in most traditional Jewish communities.

Middle Ages

In medieval times (from approximately 600 CE to 1500 CE) most Jews lived outside the land of Israel. Large Jewish populations resided in the Muslim worlds of the Middle East, Western Asia, North Africa, and Spain (Sepharad), while smaller numbers of Jews lived in Christian Europe (Ashkenaz). While a number of sources offer useful information, including marriage contracts and other family records, historical chronicles by Jewish and non-Jewish authors, and legal and economic documents, virtually nothing written by medieval Jewish women, beyond some personal correspondence, survives.[15] Medieval Jewish communities continued rabbinic patterns in ordaining separate gender roles and religious obligations for men and women and in relegating females to secondary, enabling positions. However, the norms and customs of the environments in which Jewish communities lived were also factors in how Jewish social life developed.[16]

Jews in the Muslim world were strongly influenced by Islamic social customs and polygyny was not uncommon. While Jewish women of prosperous families were not literally isolated in women's quarters, community norms dictated that women remained out of the public eye. However, contemporaneous documents reveal that Jewish women had significant freedom of movement for visits to the synagogue, bathhouse, socializing with family and friends, and business activities, such as the buying and selling of flax and needlework. Women, who were married quite young, frequently to considerably older men, were often protected by social safeguards written into the marriage contract (*ketubah*) altering Jewish laws and practices unfavorable to women; these were particularly intended to deter polygyny, desertion, and unwanted divorce. The *ketubah* obligated the husband to provide his wife with food and clothing and to maintain her in general. Following biblical custom, Jewish grooms in the Muslim milieu also contributed a marriage gift (*mohar*), part of which was payable to the bride's father at the time of the wedding, with a portion reserved for the bride in the event of a divorce or her husband's death. Similarly the bride brought property into the marriage in the form of her dowry and trousseau.

Although boys were usually educated in both religious and secular subjects, Jewish women were rarely literate. There is no evidence in the Muslim milieu of the development of liturgical language or a spiritual literature for Jewish women, or of women prayer leaders, as in medieval and early modern Ashkenazic communities. Women who chose to attend synagogue prayed in a gallery separated from male worshipers; prosperous women often donated Torah scrolls or left legacies for the upkeep of the synagogue. Such donations were expressions of piety but also female strategies for inserting themselves into a culturally valued realm from which they were otherwise excluded. The social roles of most Jewish women in Muslim societies remained unchanged into the late nineteenth and twentieth centuries.

The small Jewish communities of medieval Christian Europe lived in an atmosphere of religious suspicion and legal disability. Following the early Crusades (1096 into the thirteenth century), Jews were barred from virtually any source of livelihood but moneylending and were often compelled to wear distinctive clothing and badges. By the end of the Middle Ages, Jews were expelled from areas where they had long lived (including England in 1290, parts of France throughout the fourteenth century, and Spain in 1492) or were forced to live in crowded urban ghettoes (Italy and German-speaking Europe). Jewish women participated in the family economy, sometimes as independent financiers, and their status was higher than that of Jewish women in the Muslim milieu. This is indicated by larger dowries, significant freedom of movement, and the eleventh-century rabbinic ruling (*takkanah*) forbidding polygyny for Jews in Christian countries, attributed to Rabbi Gershom ben Judah of Mainz. Rabbi Gershom is also given credit for the highly important ruling that no woman could be divorced against her will.

Jews in Christian Spain retained significant Muslim cultural influences, including the attitude that women should remain at home; this remained a feature of Sephardic life well into the early modern period, even when Jews lived in very different locations following the expulsion from Spain in 1492.[17] The Muslim practice of polygyny also had a significant impact on Spanish Jewry, who never wholly accepted Rabbi Gershom's ban on the practice. Widows, especially those who benefited from their husbands' recourse to the generous inheritance laws of Christian Spain for surviving wives, were often in control of significant resources. Some powerful Sephardic widows, such as Benvenida Abravanel and Doña Gracia Nasi, both of whom lived in the sixteenth century, continued their deceased husbands' businesses successfully, intervened with rulers on behalf of threatened Jewish communities, and were renowned for their philanthropy and their support of Jewish culture and learning.

Religious education for girls usually centered on domestic knowledge essential for running a Jewish household, including not only the rudiments of cooking, needlework, and household management, but also the rules of rabbinic Judaism applicable to home and marriage. Basic religious training was considered essential so that a woman would know how to observe dietary laws, domestic regulations pertaining to the Sabbath and festivals, and the commandments relevant to her intimate life with her husband. Although women's involvement in business required literacy in the vernacular language and book-keeping skills, training in Hebrew and the study of Jewish texts was rare for girls, and was limited to a few women from rabbinic families. Learned women, such as the twelfth-century Dolce (wife of the medieval rabbinic leader and mystic, Eleazar of Worms)[18] and Richenza of Nuremberg, and the thirteenth-century Urania, a cantor's daughter (also of Worms), taught and led prayers for women in their communities, sometimes in a separate room in the synagogue. From the male point of view, however, learned Jewish women were irrelevant to Jewish scholarship or communal life. Women's testimony on legal or religious matters was considered only if they were regarded as reliable witnesses to the practices of distinguished fathers or husbands.[19]

Some economically successful women in Ashkenaz expressed their high social status by assuming religious practices from which females were exempt in rabbinic law. These displays of piety were probably influenced by contemporaneous Christian religious revivals in which women took part in reshaping worship. One example is the insistence of certain prominent women in serving as godmother (*sandeka'it*) at the circumcision of a son or grandson. The fourteenth-century leader Rabbi Meir of Rothenburg attempted to abolish this innovation, arguing that the presence of perfumed and well-dressed women in the synagogue among men was immodest. However, the custom continued until the beginning of the fifteenth century, an indication of the social power that can accompany wealth. These privileges were only curtailed when the political and economic situation of European Jewish communities worsened beginning in the mid-fourteenth century and traditional male authority was gradually reasserted.[20]

In the medieval era, negative attitudes about women intensified. Secular and religious Jewish literatures, especially mystical writings, often represented women as untrustworthy, as sources of sexual temptation, and even as manifestations of the demonic.[21] Jewish practices concerning the menstruating woman became more exclusionary, particularly in the Christian sphere, and menstruants were discouraged from entering a synagogue, coming into contact with sacred books, praying, or reciting God's name. These customs have no basis in Jewish law but they were endorsed by rabbinic authorities who praised compliant women for their piety.[22]

Early Modern Period

The invention of printing in the fifteenth century made the dissemination of popular vernacular literature practicable and inexpensive and played an important role in expanding human horizons. While Jewish women were generally ignorant of Hebrew, most women in Ashkenaz were literate in the Jewish vernacular since maintaining written records was essential to their economic activities. (These dialects of German, Judaeo-German in central Europe and Yiddish in eastern Europe, were written in Hebrew characters. Both women and men, many of whom also lacked sufficient learning to read Hebrew with ease, were eager readers of these newly available books, which were printed in a special typeface called *vayber taytsh* ["women's vernacular"]). This font was based on the cursive Hebrew hand women were taught for business contracts, marriage agreements, and correspondence. The first vernacular texts to be printed were translations of the Hebrew Bible; *musar* books, ethical treatises which discussed proper conduct, female religious obligations, and a woman's relations with her husband, were also popular. One example is *Meneket Rivkah* (Rebecca's Nurse) by Rebecca bas Meir. This sixteenth-century Yiddish compendium of religious instruction for women, including biblical commentary and sermons, was published posthumously in Prague in 1609.[23] Among other works directed at women were pamphlets of *tkhines*, supplicatory prayers intended for use in Jewish rituals and worship, both in the synagogue and at home.[24] Much of this literature was written by men but there were female authors, as well. In sixteenth-century Italy Deborah Ascarelli translated Hebrew liturgical poetry into rhymed Italian, presumably for use by women. Her *Abitacolo degli oranti* (Abode of the Supplicants) completed in 1537 and published in 1601, may be the earliest published Jewish literary work written by a woman.[25] Collections of prayers and religious texts for female use in Yiddish, Ladino, and European languages were produced well into the twentieth century.[26]

The reminiscences of Glikl bas Judah Leib of Hameln (1646–1724; frequently referred to as Glückel of Hameln) interweave pious tales and moralizing with accounts of events in the author's life and those of her loved ones. Born into prosperous circumstances in German-speaking Europe, Glikl was well read in Yiddish literature, and had some knowledge of Hebrew and German. Betrothed at 12, married at 14, and the mother of 14 children, Glikl was active in business and pious in religious observance, including regular synagogue attendance.

Glikl's business activities reflect the growing economic participation of Jews in the non-Jewish world, while her religious and secular education speaks to the broader horizons and new educational opportunities becoming available to some early modern Jewish women.[27]

Hasidism

The development of Hasidism in eighteenth-century Poland did not bring improvements in women's status; the new pietistic movement perpetuated and intensified negative portrayals of women already present in rabbinic and mystical texts. Although hasidic traditions describe instances of leadership roles assumed by pious daughters, mothers, and sisters of famous rabbis, there is little external documentation for these assertions. The one apparent example of a woman who crossed gender boundaries to achieve religious leadership in a hasidic sect on her own is actually a story of female failure.[28] Hannah Rachel Verbermacher (b. 1815), who was known as "the Holy Maid of Ludmir," acquired a reputation for saintliness and miracle-working. Well educated, pious, and wealthy, she attracted both men and women to her "court" where she lectured from behind a closed door. Reaction from the male hasidic leaders of her region was uniformly negative and pressure was successfully applied on Hannah to fulfill her rightful female role in marriage. Although her two marriages were unsuccessful, they had the intended result of ending her career as a religious leader in Poland. Hannah emigrated to Jerusalem, however, where she successfully resumed her spiritual activities.[29]

Hasidism emphasized the primacy of mystical transcendence and encouraged men to spend holy days and festivals with the rabbinic leader, the *zaddik* or *rebbe*, rather than with their families; this emphasis on an exclusively male religious community played a significant role in the breakdown of Jewish social life in nineteenth-century eastern Europe. Similar tensions between family responsibility and devotion to Torah were also present among the non-hasidic learned elite of this milieu, where wives tended to assume the responsibility of supporting their families while their husbands devoted themselves to study and teaching.

Jewish Enlightenment and Modernity

Haskalah, the Jewish enlightenment movement which began in late eighteenth century German-speaking Europe, brought enormous changes to Jewish religious, political, and social life in western and central Europe. Open to modernity and European culture, Haskalah insisted that Jewish acculturation to the customs of the public sphere was not incompatible with adherence to Jewish tradition and rituals in the private domains of home and synagogue. While the goals of Jewish political emancipation and achievement of full civil rights, with their accompanying economic benefits, were central parts of this movement, some of its supporters also championed religious change within the Jewish community. Most modern forms of Jewish religious practice, including Reform Judaism, Conservative Judaism, and Modern Orthodoxy, were shaped in this milieu. Moses Mendelssohn, the founder of Haskalah in central Europe, and others of his circle, also advocated social change in gender relations. They opposed arranged marriages and supported matches based on mutual affection.[30]

Historians of nineteenth-century Jewish life have shown that the processes of acculturation to the majority culture, followed in some cases by dissolution of Jewish ties through conversion and/or intermarriage, tended to be different for women and men.[31] Men, who participated in the public realms of economic and civic life, had far more contacts with the non-Jewish world and acculturated relatively quickly. The integration of most Jewish women into their larger cultural settings was far slower; they had few external educational and vocational opportunities and their lives generally took place in domestic settings where they were encouraged to cultivate a home-based Judaism. As their husbands and sons became increasingly secularized, women were often the last family members to preserve elements of Jewish tradition.[32]

Middle-class Jewish social life not only reflected traditional Judaism's preferred positioning of women in the private realm of husband and family, but was also a form of conformity to contemporaneous Christian bourgeois models of female domesticity that assigned religion to the female sphere. This was a significant indication of acculturation in an ethnic group in which men had historically fulfilled most religious obligations, including the Jewish education of their sons.[33] The situation was somewhat different in England, where a significant number of Jewish women worked in the public domain to advance Jewish enlightenment and emancipation and to further religious reform. These activists included advocates of liberal Judaism like Lily Montagu (1873–1963) and writers such as Grace Aguilar (d. 1847) and Marion and Celia Moss (1840s); their books on Jewish themes were written in English and appealed to Jewish and gentile audiences. Scholars have pointed out that despite their uplifting messages, Anglo-Jewish women's literary success threatened many Jewish men with similar goals. While these reformers were compelled to support a degree of female emancipation in principle, they did their best to limit and undermine women's writing and influence in the public sphere.[34]

Reform Judaism sought to offer nineteenth-century central European Jews and American Jews a modernized form of Jewish belief and practice that emphasized personal faith and ethical behavior over ritual observance. Reform leaders proclaimed that women were entitled to the same religious rights and subject to the same religious duties as men in both home and synagogue. Their emphasis on religious education for girls and boys, including a confirmation ceremony for young people of both sexes, and an accessible worship service in the vernacular made the new movement attractive to many women. Pressure from young women may also have prompted the Reform rabbinate to adopt the innovation of double ring wedding ceremonies in which not only men but women also made a statement of marital commitment. European Reform Judaism, however, made few substantive changes in women's actual synagogue status, offering no extension to women of ritual participation in worship and maintaining separate synagogue seating for men and women into the twentieth century.[35] This was not so much the case in the United States where mixed seating was the norm and where women were afforded increasing opportunities to assume some synagogue leadership roles as the nineteenth century progressed. However, the Reform movement was only prepared to go so far; despite a few women who undertook and even completed rabbinic training during the first half of the twentieth century, American Reform Judaism did not ordain its first female rabbi, Sally Priesand (b. 1946), until 1972.[36] The first woman to receive rabbinic ordination was Regina Jonas (1902–44) who was privately ordained in Germany in 1935. Jonas taught and served Jewish communities in Nazi Germany until her deportation and subsequent murder at Auschwitz.[37]

Emulation of Christian models of female philanthropy and religious activism played a significant part in middle-class Jewish women's establishment of service and social welfare organizations in the nineteenth and early twentieth centuries in Germany, England, and North America. Such organizations as the Jüdischer Frauenbund in Germany (founded in 1904), the Union of Jewish Women in Great Britain (founded in 1902), and the National Council of Jewish Women in the United States (founded in 1893), cooperated in the international campaign against coercion of poor women into prostitution and argued for greater recognition of women within their respective Jewish communities. In the process, their members blurred the boundaries between traditional male and female spheres as women acquired administrative expertise and assumed authoritative and responsible public roles.[38] In the United States the proliferation of Jewish women's organizations also included synagogue sisterhoods, which devoted themselves to the "domestic management" of the synagogue, decorating the sanctuary for festivals, catering synagogue events, and performing many other housekeeping functions. National organizations of sisterhoods, separated by denomination, encouraged local groups in their activities and provided a forum for public female leadership. Jewish women also played a central role in establishing, supervising, and teaching in Jewish religious schools.[39] Through these activities, as well as through involvement with other Jewish women's groups, such as the Zionist organization Hadassah (founded in 1912), middle-class American Jewish women found opportunities to articulate their Jewish identity and values through service and philanthropy.[40]

The Jewish enlightenment movement in eastern Europe, which began in the last few decades of the nineteenth century, differed from Haskalah in the West. It did not emphasize Jewish achievement of political rights and civic equality or religious reform, since neither was likely to be achieved in the absolutist, conservative, and impoverished eastern European environment. Rather, Haskalah in eastern Europe was a secularizing process which led some Jews to abandon religious observance in favor of a Jewish national/ethnic identity, often linked to socialist political goals. Eastern European women were frequently in the forefront of these movements of cultural transformation. This was partly educational: as a result of the customary exclusion of girls from substantive Jewish educations, prosperous parents often provided secular instruction for their daughters. The Orthodox community did not begin schools for girls until after the First World War, thanks, in significant part, to the activism of Sarah Schenirer (1883–1935). Moreover, girls and women in eastern European Jewish society, where the strong capable woman shrewdly interacting with the outside world was the dominant cultural ideal, were also secularized by their active participation in public economic life.[41]

The autobiography of Pauline Epstein Wengeroff (1833–1916), written in German, is an important source for Jewish life in nineteenth-century Russia. Wengeroff was born in Bobruisk into the upper economic echelon of Russian Jewry; her entrepreneurial grandfather and father served as contractors to the Russian government, and her husband, Chonon Wengeroff, became a successful banker.[42] A very different story is told by Puah Rakovsky (1865–1955) in her Yiddish-language autobiography, which recounts her difficult life, including her break with her traditional background to become an educator and founder of a girls' school in Warsaw and her Jewish feminist leadership and Zionist political activities in Poland and Palestine.[43] The charming memoir of Bella Rosenfeld Chagall (1895–1940), also written in Yiddish, includes drawings by the author's husband, artist Marc Chagall. Writing in the voice of her childhood self, Basha, Chagall describes life in a prosperous home in prerevolutionary Vitebsk in a narrative that follows the holiday cycle of the Jewish calendar.[44]

Of the almost 2 million eastern European Jewish immigrants to arrive in the United States between 1880 and 1914, 43 percent were women, a far higher proportion than among other immigrant groups. The values these immigrants brought with them, even as they were gradually transformed by America, permitted women to play several roles in helping their families adjust to their new environment. Most women contributed to the family income and significant numbers sought the benefits of higher education. Among the agents of change were earlier-arrived Jews of western and central European origin who sought to socialize the immigrants in their own image. Young Jewish immigrant women were strongly influenced by the world of work, where they were exposed to socialist ideas and where many were ardent participants and leaders in labor activism. As these immigrants and their children became increasingly successful economically and began to enter the middle class, particularly in the period after World War II, many women who now had leisure for volunteer activities joined national Jewish women's organizations or became involved in synagogue sisterhood activities. Their daughters and granddaughters, like their Jewish counterparts in other Western countries, are generally highly educated and involved in a wide range of professional, creative, and activist endeavors that both serve the Jewish community and transcend gendered, ethnic, and religious boundaries.[45]

Not all eastern European Jews immigrated to America. Some, motivated by the goals of political Zionism, chose Palestine. The early immigrations included both men and women, some of whom had learned to work the land in Zionist training schools in Russia that stressed gender equality. On arriving in Palestine, however, most young single women, found their options limited and their choices narrowed, simply as a result of their gender. Unmarried women were virtually unemployable as agricultural workers and were forced to survive by providing men with kitchen and laundry services. A few women founded successful female agricultural and urban collectives but the majority of single women ended up working in cities as cooks or laundresses, seamstresses or clerks, or maids in private homes.[46] These traditional gendered divisions of labor and patterns of authority tended to be preserved and they continued after 1948, as well.

The kibbutz (collective agricultural settlement) movement provided an alternative for the few single women who gained entry. Many kibbutzim were dedicated to bold restructurings of the family so that men and women would be equal and independent partners sharing common goals and women would be emancipated from domestic demands to work with men in building the land. Yet even on the kibbutz, women mainly worked in kitchens and laundries and women's role in childcare was problematic. Many kibbutzim raised children collectively in children's houses under the care of nurses and teachers; parents visited with their children for an hour or two each day. These innovations were meant to free mothers to function as full members of the collective while children would benefit from feeling that their welfare was of general concern.[47] Today there is a general acknowledgment that collective child rearing asked too much of children and of parents. In the twenty-first century, the kibbutz remains but the children's house is a thing of the past.

Modern Israel continues to be far from progressive where the status of women is concerned. At the beginning of the twenty-first century, it is more conservative than most other Western democracies on women's issues. Despite significant achievements and a high level of education, Israeli women continue to earn less than their male counterparts, are less visible and influential in the political arena, do not share equal responsibilities or privileges in the military, have unequal rights and freedoms in family life, and are secondary in shaping the nation's cultural orientation. This inequality results, in significant part, from entrenched attitudes about women's appropriate roles in Jewish tradition in general, the influence of ultra-Orthodox Judaism on the larger society, and the impact of conservative Middle Eastern cultures on many Israelis from Muslim countries. One consequence of Israel's emphasis on national security is that "women's issues," particularly in areas of health, education, and welfare, have received low priority.

Efforts to advance women's status through legislative initiatives addressing equality at work, prevention of spousal violence, and welfare, health, and fertility concerns are increasing in early twenty-first-century Israel. Israel's feminist movement has begun to bring cases to Israel's Supreme Court on issues such as access to abortion, women's right to hold seats on municipal religious councils, and the ability of women's prayer groups to worship at Jerusalem's Western Wall. These initiatives, which reflect the larger gender and religious tensions that characterize modern Israeli society, offer one remedy to women's unequal roles. However, fundamental change for women will only come when the adjudication of family law and personal status issues is removed from the sole control of the Orthodox rabbinate, which has been inflexible in easing the discriminations against women inherent in the *halakhah*.[48]

Conclusions: Contemporary Challenges

One of the central contemporary changes in liberal and progressive forms of Judaism is egalitarian worship, in which women have the same responsibilities and possibilities of participation and leadership as men. In these denominations, women who successfully complete the requisite study and preparation are ordained as rabbis and cantors. Similarly, female lay leaders have emerged in most forms of contemporary Judaism. These new realities have prompted changes in the prayer liturgy (although not in Orthodox Judaisms) that include women as equal members of the congregation, recognize the matriarchs as well as the patriarchs of ancient Israel, and incorporate gender-neutral language about God into Jewish public worship. A parallel development is the formation of new lifecycle rituals that address central moments of transformation in women's lives.[49]

Many women who did not receive substantial Jewish educations in childhood have taken advantage of adult education opportunities, including participation in adult Bat Mitzvah ceremonies. While rabbinic ordination for women is still far from imminent in Orthodox communities, educational opportunities for women have expanded impressively in many traditional Jewish communities. Orthodox girls and women now have many options for serious study of traditional Jewish texts.[50] In the early twenty-first century, a small group of women knowledgeable in *halakhah* serve as rabbinic assistants in a number of Modern Orthodox synagogues in North America and others in Israel are trained to act as advocates for women on halakhic issues.

These multiple changes in the status of Jewish women have also affected Jewish men. In more liberal forms of Judaism, some observers have expressed concern that the "feminization" of Jewish leadership roles, as more women become rabbis, cantors, educators, and lay leaders, may drive men away from synagogue participation. Conversely, the dramatic shifts in gender roles may have encouraged increased rigidity and resistance to expanding opportunities for women within some forms of Orthodox Judaism.[51]

The greater visibility of lesbian, gay, bisexual, and transgendered Jews, like the impact of Jewish feminism, is linked with social change movements in the larger societies in which Jews live. While Jewish families have generally consisted of a male and a female parent and their children, an increasing openness regarding diverse sexual orientations in Western countries has altered the makeup of many Jewish families and communities.[52]

Notes

1. Works on women and gender in Jewish history and Judaism include Judith R. Baskin (ed.) (1998), *Jewish Women in Historical Perspective* (2nd edn). Detroit: Wayne State University Press; Frederick E. Greenspahn (ed.) (2009), *Women and Judaism: New Insights and Scholarship*. New York: New York University Press; Susan Grossman and Rivka Haut (eds) (1992), *Daughters of the King: Women and the Synagogue: A Survey of History, Halakah, and Contemporary Realities*. Philadelphia: Jewish Publication Society; Susannah Heschel (ed.) (1983), *On Being a Jewish Feminist: A Reader*. New York: Schocken; Paula E. Hyman and Dalia Ofer (eds) (2006), *Jewish Women: A Comprehensive Historical Encyclopedia*. [http://bibpurl.oclc.org/web/31637] Jerusalem: Shalvi Publishing; Emily Taitz, Sondra Henry, and Cheryl Tallan (2003), *The JPS Guide to Jewish Women: 600 B.C.E. to 1900 C.E.* Philadelphia: Jewish Publication Society. For a comprehensive bibliography, including monographs on specific times, places, and topics, see Judith R. Baskin (2012), "Women and Gender Relations," in David Biale (ed.), *Oxford Bibliographies in Jewish Studies*. Oxford: Oxford Bibliographies Online.
2. Recent scholarship on this phenomenon includes Sylvia Barack Fishman (1993). *A Breath of Life: Feminism in the American Jewish Community*. New York: Free Press; Elyse Goldstein (ed.) (2009), *New Jewish Feminism: Probing the Past, Forging the Future*. Woodstock: Jewish Lights Publishing; Tova Hartman (2007), *Feminism Encounters Traditional Judaism: Resistance and Accommodation*. Waltham: Brandeis University Press; Hanover: University Press of New England; Riv-Ellen Prell and David Weinberg (eds) (2007), *Women Remaking American Judaism*. Detroit: Wayne State University Press; and Tamar Ross (2004), *Expanding the Palace of Torah: Orthodoxy and Feminism*. Waltham: Brandeis University Press; Hanover: University Press of New England.

3. Valuable scholarship includes Alice Bach (ed.) (1998), *Women in the Hebrew Bible: A Reader*. New York: Routledge; Tikva Frymer-Kensky (1992), *In the Wake of the Goddesses: Women, Culture, and the Biblical Transformation of Pagan Myth*. New York: Free Press; idem (2002), *Reading the Women of the Bible*. New York: Schocken Books; Carol L. Meyers (1988), *Discovering Eve: Ancient Israelite Women in Context*. New York: Oxford University Press; idem (2005), *Households and Holiness: The Religious Culture of Israelite Women*. Minneapolis: Fortress Press.

4. Susan Grossman (1992), "Women and the Jerusalem Temple," in Grossman and Haut (eds), *Daughters of the King*, pp. 15–38.

5. Frymer-Kensky, *In the Wake*, pp. 158–61; Meyers, *Discovering Eve*, pp. 162–3.

6. Ross S. Kraemer (1992), *Her Share of the Blessings: Women's Religions among Pagans, Jews, and Christians*. New York: Oxford University Press, p. 123; and see Bernadette J. Brooten (1982), *Women Leaders in the Ancient Synagogue: Inscriptional Evidence and Background Issues*. Chico: Scholars Press.

7. Amy-Jill Levine (ed.) (1991), *"Women Like This": New Perspectives on Jewish Women in the Greco-Roman World*. Atlanta: Scholars Press.

8. Philo, *On the Contemplative Life*, §§27–9, 30, 34–9; Kraemer, *Her Share of the Blessings*, pp. 113–15.

9. On rabbinic Judaism and its literature, see the essay by Gary Porton in this volume; and Charlotte E. Fonrobert and Martin Jaffe (eds) (2007), *The Cambridge Companion to the Talmud and Rabbinic Literature*. New York: Cambridge University Press.

10. On constructions of women and gender in rabbinic writings, see Judith R. Baskin (2002), *Midrashic Women: Formations of the Feminine in Rabbinic Literature*. Hanover: Brandeis University Press/University Press of New England; Daniel Boyarin (1993), *Carnal Israel: Reading Sex in Talmudic Culture*. Berkeley: University of California Press; Judith Hauptman (1998), *Rereading the Rabbis: A Woman's Voice*. Boulder: Westview Press; Tal Ilan (1997), *Mine and Yours Are Hers: Retrieving Women's History from Rabbinic Literature*. Kinderhook: Brill; Judith Romney Wegner (1988), *Chattel or Person: The Status of Women in the Mishnah*. New York: Oxford University Press; and Dvora E. Weisberg (2009), *Levirate Marriage and the Family in Ancient Judaism*. Waltham: Brandeis University Press; Hanover: University Press of New England.

11. Hauptman, *Rereading the Rabbis*, pp. 54–5; Rachel Biale (1984), *Women and Jewish Law: The Essential Texts, Their History, and Their Relevance for Today*. New York: Schocken Books.

12. Biale, *Women and Jewish Law*, p. 20.

13. See the essays in Rahel Wasserfall (ed.) (1999), *Women and Water: Menstruation in Jewish Life and Law*. Waltham: Brandeis University Press/ University Press of New England; and Charlotte E. Fonrobert (2000), *Menstrual Purity: Rabbinic and Christian Reconstructions of Biblical Gender*. Stanford: Stanford University Press.

14. Baskin, *Midrashic Women*, pp. 29–36.

15. On the kinds of primary documents and secondary sources available, see Kenneth R. Stow (1987), "The Jewish Family in the Rhineland in the High Middle Ages: Form and Function," *American Historical Review* 92: pp. 1085–110. The Cairo Geniza documents are of overwhelming importance for the study of Jewish social life in the Muslim world, including the lives of women; see the magisterial work of Shlomo Dov Goitein (1967–88), *A Mediterranean Society: The Jewish Communities of the Arab World as Portrayed in the Documents of the Cairo Geniza*. 6 Vols. Berkeley: University of California Press.

16. On medieval Jewish women in Christian Europe, see Judith R. Baskin, "Jewish Women in the Middle Ages," in idem (ed.), *Jewish Women in Historical Perspective*, pp. 94–113; Elisheva Baumgarten (2004), *Mothers and Children: Jewish Family Life in Medieval Ashkenaz*. Princeton: Princeton University Press; Simha Goldin (2012), *Jewish*

Women in Europe in the Middle Ages: A Quiet Revolution. Manchester and London: Manchester University Press; Avraham Grossman (2004), *Pious and Rebellious: Jewish Women in Medieval Europe*. Waltham: Brandeis University Press; Hanover: University Press of New England.

17. Renée Levine Melammed, "Sephardic Jewish Women," in Baskin (ed.), *Jewish Women in Historical Perspective*, pp. 123–5.

18. On Dolce, see Judith R. Baskin (2001), "Dolce of Worms: The Lives and Deaths of an Exemplary Medieval Jewish Woman and her Daughters," in Lawrence Fine (ed.), *Judaism in Practice: From the Middle Ages through the Early Modern Period*. Princeton: Princeton University Press, pp. 429–37.

19. Judith R. Baskin (1991), "Some Parallels in the Education of Medieval Jewish and Christian Women," *Jewish History* 5: pp. 41–51; and idem (2012), "Educating Jewish Girls in Medieval Muslim and Christian Settings," in David Clines, Kent Richards, and Jacob L. Wright (eds), *Making a Difference: Essays in Honor of Tamara Cohn Eskenazi*. Sheffield, UK: Sheffield Phoenix Press, pp. 19–37.

20. Grossman, *Pious and Rebellious*, pp. 185–7.

21. See Judith Dishon (1994), "Images of Women in Medieval Hebrew Literature," in Judith R. Baskin (ed.), *Women of the Word: Jewish Women and Jewish Writing*. Detroit: Wayne State University Press, pp. 35–49; Sharon Faye Koren (2011), *Forsaken: The Menstruant in Medieval Jewish Mysticism*. Waltham: Brandeis University Press; Hanover: University Press of New England; and Tova Rosen (2003), *Unveiling Eve: Reading Gender in Medieval Hebrew Literature*. Philadelphia: University of Pennsylvania Press.

22. Shaye J. D. Cohen (2005), *Why Aren't Jewish Women Circumcised? Gender and Covenant in Judaism*. Berkeley: University of California Press.

23. Frauke von Roden (ed., with commentary) (2008), *Meneket Rivkah: A Manual of Wisdom and Piety by Rivkah bat Meir*. Philadelphia: Jewish Publication Society.

24. Chava Weissler (1998), *Voices of the Matriarchs: Listening to the Prayers of Early Modern Jewish Women*. Boston: Beacon Press.

25. Howard Adelman, "Italian Jewish Women," in Baskin (ed.), *Jewish Women in Historical Perspective*, p. 154.

26. For examples of such prayers, see Aliza Lavie (2008), *A Jewish Woman's Prayer Book*. New York: Spiegel and Grau.

27. The most complete English translation is (2010) *The Life of Glückel of Hameln, 1646–1724. Written by Herself*, Beth-Zion Abrahams (trans. and ed.). Philadelphia: Jewish Publication Society; see also, Natalie Zemon Davis (1995), *Women on the Margins: Three Seventeenth-Century Lives*. Cambridge, MA: Harvard University Press.

28. Ada Rapoport-Albert (1988) "On Women in Hasidism, S. A. Horodecky and the Maid of Ludmir Tradition," in A. Rapoport-Albert and Steven J. Zipperstein (eds), *Jewish History: Essays in Honour of Chimen Abramsky*. London: Halban, pp. 495–525.

29. Nathaniel Deutsch (2003), *The Maiden of Ludmir: A Jewish Holy Woman and Her World*. Berkeley and London: University of California Press.

30. David Biale (1992), *Eros and the Jews: From Biblical Israel to Contemporary America*. New York: Basic Books, pp. 153–8.

31. Marion Kaplan and Deborah Dash Moore (eds) (2011), *Gender and Jewish History*. Bloomington: Indiana University Press; the essays in this volume, compiled in honor of Professor Paula E. Hyman (z"l), focus on the ramifications of gender for modern Jewish history and culture in Europe, the United States, and Israel.

32. Benjamin Maria Baader (2006), *Gender, Judaism, and Bourgeois Culture in Germany, 1800–1870*. Bloomington: Indiana University Press; Marion A. Kaplan (1991), *The Making of the Jewish Middle Class: Women, Family, and Identity in Imperial Germany*. New York: Oxford University Press.

33. Paula E. Hyman (1995), *Gender and Assimilation in Modern Jewish History: The Roles and Representation of Women*. Seattle: University of Washington Press, pp. 25–30.

34. Michael Galchinsky (1996), *The Origin of the Modern Jewish Writer: Romance and Reform in Victorian England*. Detroit: Wayne State University Press; Ellen M. Umansky (1983), *Lily Montagu and the Advancement of Liberal Judaism: From Vision to Vocation*. New York: Edwin Mellen Press.

35. Kaplan, *Making of the Jewish Middle Class*, pp. 67–8; Riv-Ellen Prell (1982), "The Vision of Women in Classical Reform Judaism," *Journal of the American Academy of Religion* 50:4: 576–89.

36. Pamela S. Nadell (1998), *Women Who Would Be Rabbis: A History of Women's Ordination 1889–1985*. Boston: Beacon Press.

37. Elisa Klapheck (2004), *Fräulein Rabbiner Jonas: The Story of the First Woman Rabbi*. Hoboken: Jossey-Bass.

38. On Jewish women's organizations, see Kaplan, *Making of the Jewish Middle Class*, pp. 211–19; Ellen M. Umansky (2008), "Piety, Persuasion, and Friendship: A History of Jewish Women's Spirituality," in Ellen M. Umansky and Dianne Ashton (eds), *Four Centuries of Jewish Women's Spirituality: A Sourcebook* (revised edn), Lebanon, NH: Brandeis University Press/ University Press of New England, pp. 16–20; Mary McCune (2005), *"The Whole Wide World, Without Limits:" International Relief, Gender Politics, and American-Jewish Women, 1893–1930*. Detroit: Wayne State University Press.

39. Hyman, *Gender and Assimilation*, pp. 31–2; Umansky, "Piety and Persuasion," pp. 7–8.

40. For general histories of Jewish women in the United States, see Charlotte Baum, Paula Hyman, and Sonya Michel (1976), *The Jewish Woman in America*. New York: Dial Press; and Hasia Diner and Beryl Lieff Benderly (2002), *Her Works Praise Her: A History of Jewish Women in America from Colonial Times to the Present*. New York: BasicBooks. Collections of essays include Hasia R. Diner, Shira Kohn, and Rachel Kranson (eds) (2010), *A Jewish Feminine Mystique? Jewish Women in Postwar America*. New Brunswick: Rutgers University Press; Pamela S. Nadell (ed.) (2003), *American Jewish Women's History: A Reader*. New York: New York University Press; and Pamela S. Nadell and Jonathan Sarna (eds) (2001), *Women and American Judaism: Historical Perspectives*. Waltham: Brandeis University Press. On Hadassah, see Mira Katzburg-Yungman (2012), *Hadassah: American Women Zionists and the Rebirth of Israel*. Oxford: Littman Library of Jewish Civilization.

41. On women and gender in eastern Europe, see Eliyana Adler (2001), *In Her Hands: The Education of Jewish Girls in Tsarist Russia*. Detroit: Wayne State University Press; ChaeRan Freeze, Paula E. Hyman, and Antony Polonsky (eds) (2005), *Jewish Women in Eastern Europe. Polin: Studies in Polish Jewry*, Vol. 18; Hyman, *Gender and Assimilation*; Iris Parush (2004), *Reading Jewish Women: Marginality and Modernization in Nineteenth-Century Eastern European Jewish Society*. Lebanon, NH: Brandeis University Press / University Press of New England; and Shaul Stampfer (2010), *Families, Rabbis and Education: Traditional Jewish Society in Nineteenth-Century Eastern Europe*. Oxford: Littman Library of Jewish Civilization.

42. The most recent English translation of the first volume of this work is Pauline Wengeroff (2010), *Memoirs of a Grandmother: Scenes from the Cultural History of the Jews of Russia in the Nineteenth Century*. Trans., with an introduction, notes, and commentary by Shulamit S. Magnus. Stanford: Stanford University Press. For the complete memoir, see Pauline Wengeroff (2000), *Rememberings: The World of a Russian-Jewish Woman in the Nineteenth Century*, Henny Wenkart (trans.). Bernard D. Cooperman (ed.). Potomac: University Press of Maryland.

43. Puah Rakovska (2002), *My Life as a Radical Jewish Woman: Memoirs of a Zionist Feminist in Poland*. Paula E. Hyman (ed.). Barbara Harshav with Paula E. Hyman (trans.). Bloomington: Indiana University Press.
44. Bella Chagall (1946), *Burning Lights*, Norbert Guterman (trans.). New York: Schocken Books.
45. Joyce Antler (1997), *The Journey Home: Jewish Women and the American Century*. New York: Free Press; Hyman, *Gender and Assimilation*; Riv-Ellen Prell (1999), *Fighting to Become Americans: Assimilation and the Trouble between Jewish Women and Jewish Men*. Boston: Beacon Press; see also, Beth S. Wenger, "Constructing Manhood in American Jewish Culture," in Kaplan and Moore (eds), *Gender and Jewish History*, pp. 350–66.
46. For primary sources, see Rachel Katznelson-Shazar (ed.) (2002), *The Plough Woman: Records of the Pioneer Women of Palestine: A Critical Edition*, Mark A. Raider and Miriam B. Raider-Roth (eds). Hanover: University Press of New England for Brandeis University Press; and see Deborah Bernstein (1986), *The Struggle for Equality: Urban Women Workers in Pre-State Israeli Society*. New York: Praeger; idem (ed.), *Pioneers and Homemakers: Jewish Women in Pre-State Israel*. Albany: State University of New York Press; and Ruth Kark, Margalit Shilo, and Galit Hasan-Rokem (eds) (2008), *Jewish Women in Pre-State Israel: Life History, Politics, and Culture*. Waltham: Brandeis University Press; Hanover, NH: University Press of New England.
47. Michal Palgi (ed.) (1983), *Sexual Equality: The Israeli Kibbutz Tests the Theories*. Norwood, PA: Norwood Editions.
48. On these topics, see Esther Fuchs (ed.) (2005), *Israeli Women's Studies: A Reader*. Piscataway, NJ: Rutgers University Press; and Kalpana Misra and Melanie S. Rich (eds) (2003), *Jewish Feminism in Israel: Some Contemporary Perspectives*. Hanover, NH; London: University Press of New England [for] Brandeis University Press.
49. Rochelle L. Millen (2004), *Women, Birth, and Death in Jewish Law and Practice*. Hanover and London: University Press of New England for Brandeis University Press; Vanessa Ochs (2007), *Inventing Jewish Ritual*. Philadelphia: Jewish Publication Society; Debra Orenstein (ed.) (1994), *Lifecycles, Volume One: Jewish Women on Life Passages and Personal Milestones*. Woodstock, VT: Jewish Lights Publishing; Sylvia Rothschild and Sybil Sheridan (eds) (2000), *Taking up the Timbrel: The Challenge of Creating Ritual for Jewish Women Today*. London: SCM Press.
50. See Hartman, *Feminism Encounters Traditional Judaism*; and Tamar El-Or (2002), *Next Year I Will Know More: Literacy and Identity among Young Orthodox Women in Israel*. Detroit: Wayne State University Press.
51. Sylvia Barack Fishman and Daniel Parmer (2008), *Matrilineal Ascent/Patrilineal Descent: The Gender Imbalance in American Jewish Life*. Waltham: Cohen Center for Modern Jewish Studies and Hadassah Brandeis Institute; Nurit Stadler (2009), *Yeshiva Fundamentalism: Piety, Gender, and Resistance in the Ultra-Orthodox World*. New York: New York University Press; Elana Maryles Sztokman (2011), *The Men's Section: Orthodox Jewish Men in an Egalitarian World*. Waltham: Brandeis University Press; Hanover: University Press of New England.
52. Recent books include Noach Dzmura (ed.) (2010), *Balancing on the Mechitza: Transgender in Jewish Community*. Berkeley: North Atlantic Books; Steven Greenberg (2004), *Wrestling with God and Men: Homosexuality in the Jewish Tradition*. Madison: University of Wisconsin Press; and David Shneer and Caryn Aviv (eds) (2002), *Queer Jews*. New York and London: Routledge.

11 Jewish Arts and Material Culture

Judah M. Cohen

Introduction

Aesthetics play an important role in defining Jewish identity and practice. At all stages in history, with every ritual action, and in each philosophical construct, people's understandings of Judaism have been paired with specific images, sounds, movements, and tastes. Merely viewing or using Hebrew characters, for example, ties Jews to long-standing practices of visual culture, and the value placed on writing these characters "correctly"—particularly when creating sacred texts—speaks to deeper values about the acceptable boundaries of Jewish expression. Likewise, the intricate textual descriptions of the Ark of the Covenant and the Bet HaMikdash that pervade the Hebrew Bible and rabbinical writings provide insight into the ways that Jews conceived of sacred spaces over time. Although we do not have sound recordings from before the late nineteenth century, and musical notations are scarce before the seventeenth century, plenty of rabbis have weighed in over history on the kinds of chants they preferred (and, more often, did not prefer) to accompany sacred texts in communal prayer. Food regulations link aesthetic qualities with fitness for Jewish consumption, whether through appearance (such as requiring a cloven hoof or disallowing bruises among land animals), preparation (soaking and salting of meat, for example, to drain it of blood), and claims of ethnic authenticity (such as the numerous recipes for the Passover *charoset*, or the composition of an "Israeli" salad). Appearances, clothing, and adornment have been indicators of Jewish identity in all walks of life, whether propagated within Jewish communities, such as the practice of male facial hair among some religious Jewish populations, or imposed by host populations, such as required hats or cloth patches in medieval/early modern Europe, or yellow stars in Nazi-occupied areas during the 1930s and the 1940s. The depth and complexity of the aesthetic choices people make to determine what is "Jewish" can easily be taken for granted, or dismissed as subservient to other, better documented, forms of expression. Yet upon closer inspection, we can see how pervasive creative expression has been in forging Jewish civilization, helping to align individuals with larger ideas of community, and elevating everyday practices into broader concepts of tradition.

Community, after all, requires dynamic and constant action to bring together people's internal feelings and beliefs. We cannot know what others are thinking unless they give us an indication, showing us who they are in ways that we can understand. Consider how a religious service allows people to display their particular forms of Jewish practice through the movements they make, the music they use, the prayer books they employ, the layout of their sanctuary, their dress and religious accouterments (such as head coverings and prayer shawls, not to mention who wears them), their Torah and ark adornments, and even the shape of the synagogue building itself. Consider also the many ways people have attempted to define and evaluate the "Jewish" home over the ages: through objects such as a mezuzah/door amulet, seder plate, menorah, *tzedakah/* charity box, candlesticks, Jewish toys, etc.; rituals such as food preparation or bedtime prayers; and through differentiation from a "non-Jewish" home, excluding a December "Christmas tree," for example, in many Euro-American communities. These seemingly mundane activities highlight but a few of the innumerable ways that creativity becomes a basis for participating in Jewish life, as shared and negotiated by all who associate with the community.

While nearly everyone has ideas about how Judaism should be represented, however, and most participate in its creation in some way or another, populations often recognize a subset of specialists as propagators of "the arts." Bezalel, the biblical designer of the Tabernacle from Exodus 31, became the inspiration for Palestine's first major art academy in the early twentieth century. In the Jerusalem Temple, the Levites had a reputation as music makers as well as ritual specialists, and their symbolic roles held on in communal memory well after the Temple's destruction. In the eighteenth and nineteenth centuries, Jews saw art as a point of entry into modern society; thus dancers, composers, visual artists, sculptors, and architects became the focus of commissions to create "Jewish" works. While communities as a whole engaged in broad debates over identity, in other words, artists often assumed the responsibility of crystalliz-ing those debates in individual art works. These formal art creations and their creators became emblems of place, era, and practice. Scholars of the arts have subsequently deemed them worthy of investigation on their own terms.

In looking at Jewish creative works, then, we may begin with the assumption that Jews *always* expressed themselves to each other through their creations, even when the temporary nature of some artistic forms leads to lacunae in the historical record. We may assume that non-Jews used art to portray Jews also, often in counterpoint to Jews' own ideas. By developing and deploying a series of analytical techniques for studying these forms of expression, scholars can access a complex and nuanced portrayal of Jewish life that dovetails with other approaches in history, philosophy, and critical studies.

Creativity and Jewish Populations

Creative expressions in Judaism sit at the crossroads of philosophy and prac-tice. In many ways, areas such as music, dance, visual art, film, museum stud-ies, theater, new media, material culture, and folklore integrate deeply with the canonical written texts so central to the core of Jewish Studies. Yet seen from within the field of Jewish Studies, these art forms' frequent lack of linguistic fix-ity offers logistical challenges. How can scholars incorporate the (often nonver-bal) arts into a field that privileges the written word? One strategy has involved emphasizing each art form's intellectual history, its particular mode of sensing the world, its recommended (or required) technical training, and its spectrum of analytical methods in bringing a new angle to the Jewish experience. Such perspectives, scholars of the arts argue, reconfigure questions of meaning, ide-ology, and tradition within Judaism in ways that can complicate Jewish Studies' philological foundation.

While different art forms have developed their own disciplinary conversa-tions (such as art history, musicology, film studies, and so forth) in the broader world of scholarship, they have often found themselves grouped together under the rubric of "the arts" in Jewish Studies circles. Academic convention, which tends to separate the arts from the humanities, plays some part in this designation. Governmental conventions support this approach as well: in the United States, as elsewhere, funding structures provide for (or threaten) the arts and humanities differently. Within Jewish Studies, the repercussions of such configurations, combined with the arts' comparatively specialized models of discourse, has led these fields to the margins of conversation. At times scholars in the core of the discipline questioned them as modes of legitimate scholarly inquiry, or dismissed them as incompatible with prevailing forms of analysis. At other times, these same scholars promoted the arts for practical purposes, as forms of recreation or student engagement. Aware of such challenges, scholars who study the arts thus must mediate between using a scholarly voice to contribute to the academic literature, and a creative voice to promote and curate new artistic activity.

Just as text study straddles the practice of Jewish faith and Jewish scientific inquiry, then, so do these fields exist in dual, often inseparable worlds. Scholarship on creativity and Judaism inevitably serves both to study Jewish artistic activity and to promote it; to question Jewish "traditions" and to propagate them (in cantorial schools, for example); to interrogate the structure of Jewish identity, and to reinforce it (through Jewish theater groups, Jewish film festivals, and studies of Jews in new media). While academics in these fields continue to argue for the inclusion of their disciplines into core Jewish Studies contexts, organizations that support Jews and the arts (such as the Foundation for Jewish Culture) have commissioned some of the same scholars to study various aspects of "culture" as investments in Jewish communal life. Thus "the arts" in some ways represents the conundrum of Jewish Studies itself: seeking new, sometimes difficult insights into Judaism, while facing conservative expectations.

Scholars of Jewish creative production have used a number of strategies to assert the importance and longevity of these expressive forms. They have presented the arts as significant case studies in the emerging field of Jewish Cultural Studies. They have sought to extend each area's specialized analytical languages across art forms into a more layered and rich conversation. They have used examples based in Jewish Studies to reexamine the intellectual basis of their own individual disciplines. They have attempted to use artistic expression as a means for exploring Jews' relationships with host societies. And they have asked the separate question of how societies picture Jews, whether actual or imaginary. Throughout, these related fields have also faced larger, Jewish studies-specific questions: should these disciplines band together to create common paradigms, should they individually seek a greater presence in the field, should they seek deeper integration with the core fields, should they work from existing institutional alliances that link scholarship with outreach and creativity, or should they search for primary alliances outside of Jewish Studies? The broad variety of responses to these questions speaks to the difficulty involved in framing this set of disciplines as a cohesive unit.

A comprehensive discussion of each field of "the arts" would thus be unrealistic in the space provided here. Instead, this chapter aims to offer an introduction to the broad questions these areas of study pose, both as a group, and individually, while proffering some points of convergence in relation to the broader goals of Jewish Studies.

Historical Perspectives

The nature of aesthetics within Jewish life has long occupied Jewish thinkers, though explicit discussions of the arts often refer less to art itself then to the writers' larger philosophical contexts. Rabbinical writings, for example, have included periodic commentary on music, art, and architecture. Among many examples: in the eleventh–twelfth centuries, Judah Halevi produced poetry that conformed to classical Arabic poetic styles, while Maimonides wrote a responsum on music, and incorporated thoughts on sculpture and other forms of art into his writings; in the sixteenth–seventeenth centuries, Venice-based Rabbi Leon de Modena used the arts (especially music) as an exemplar for his progressive views of Jewish identity, and Moses Mendelssohn, in the eighteenth century, wrote several passages about the arts in his oeuvre. Scholars addressing these texts as core materials in Jewish Studies have subsequently engaged with aesthetics as a key part of the discipline through to the present day.[1] Yet even in recent writings, this philosophical tradition has led to an idiosyncratic treatment of creative production that engages with art and artists even as it relegates them to a separate (often secondary) plane of discourse.[2] The arts have consequently remained visible within the core conversations of Jewish Studies, but scholars coming from individual arts fields, due in part to the specificity of their skills, have faced challenges in making their own perspectives and scholarly trajectories heard.

Arts-focused scholarly traditions have developed along parallel timelines and topographies to the core philosophical tradition, and can generally be traced to the mid late nineteenth-century "aesthetic turn" in European Judaism. At that time, Jews attempted to link scholarship with identity politics in order to gain greater acceptance in the "modern" world around them. As part of a drive to create a *Wissenschaft des Judentums* (science of Judaism), the attempt to understand the arts through a Jewish lens helped establish Jews as a distinct people among peoples, while opening up a search for expressive culture to supplement and deepen reforming movements. Performance and display helped to illustrate contemporary Jews' search for "essential" elements—qualities that could differentiate Jews from others and publicly represent their specific points of view.

Ancient Judaism, with its foundational status for both Jews and Christians, consequently became an anchor for creating and performing new artistic approaches to Jewish modern life. Cantors, for example, used the search for a "pure" (read Temple-period) Jewish liturgical sound as the basis for distilling a series of musical modes in the 1880s, paralleling similar developments among monk-scholars of Gregorian chant. Museum curators and artists, both Jewish and non-Jewish, used ancient lineage as a lens for collecting, displaying, evaluating, and creating Judaica collections. Yiddish theater, meanwhile, leaped from the realm of the private Purimspil to the musical theater stage in eastern Europe by the 1880s, with early productions such as Avram Goldfadn's *Shulamith* trading on biblical themes; by the early twentieth century, the proper theater was addressing the role of the Jew on stages across the Western world. Complementing a renewed interest in Jewish folklore that appeared in Jewish periodicals as both a mode of preservation and a prescriptive storehouse for future creativity, these initiatives capitalized on popular understandings of Jews as an "ancient" people to reassert their significance in contemporary public culture and its conjoined intellectual life.

Jewish artistic movements arose alongside efforts to institutionalize Jewish life. By the 1930s, genres of "Jewish music," "Jewish art," "Jewish folklore," and so forth had gained traction through such initiatives as St. Petersburg Folk Music Society and Jewish Historical-Ethnographic Society (1908–ca. 1928), New York's Jewish Museum (est. 1904), Jerusalem's Bezalel School of Arts and Crafts (1906–29), and theatrical works such as Israel Zangwill's *The Melting Pot* (1908) and S. Ansky's folklore-inspired play *The Dybbuk* (written 1914). Particularly influential during this time were attempts to include artists in the Zionist nation-building project: in addition to the founding of musical groups (such as the Palestine Philharmonic and the Erez Israeli Opera company), dance groups (Rina Nikova's Biblical Ballet, 1933), theater troupes (Habimah, 1928), and radio stations (Radio Tel Aviv [1930], Palestine Broadcasting Service [1932]), institutions such as the revived New Bezalel School (1935) and the World Centre for Jewish Music in Palestine (1936–40) sought to reshape to Jewish creativity in a Zionist mold.

American Jewish artists, in contrast, looked to include Judaism within a "great" aesthetic society that drew from European traditions. When Ernest Bloch premiered his *Sacred Service* in 1935, for example, he continued the prestigious European practice of creating high-concept, concert-worthy liturgical music, only using the American Reform movement's *Union Prayer Book* rather than Christian liturgy. In most cases, these efforts proved continuous with contemporary movements in the arts in general, as Jewish artists valued their inclusion in circles of respected colleagues. Just as important, these artistic movements existed concurrently with attempts to create a thriving Jewish intellectual culture and scholarly community (embodied by the establishment of Hebrew University in Jerusalem [1925] as well as Baltimore's Hebrew College [1919], Boston's Hebrew College [1921], the Chicago College of Jewish Studies [1924; today the Spertus Institute for Jewish Learning and Leadership], and the opening of an enlarged 92nd St. Y building [1930]). Several artist/scholars ascended to significant institutional positions during this period, and actively contributed through both words and actions to contemporary discussions of Jewish identity, tradition, and culture.

The establishment of the State of Israel in 1948 expanded the need to create a national "Israeli" culture. Institutions created in the 1920s and the 1930s, including the Hebrew University, the new Bezalel School of Art, the Habimah theater troupe, and a contemporarily written folk-song repertoire, contributed to a broad expansion of cultural activity that engaged both formal and leisure time. Song competitions, dance festivals, literary salons, museums, a film industry, and schools for music and drama often overlapped with communities of scholarship that valorized artistic efforts. Scholars of Hebrew literature, for example, interacted with the authors themselves while establishing canonical works for further study. Likewise, Israeli musicology promoted scholarly and institutional attention to new composers and compositions. Historical projects looking at the development of particular Israeli styles of expression gave the state a stronger ideological foundation, while also allowing research to interrogate more thoroughly creativity's political roots. As a result, "Israeli" arts became a prominent category of inquiry among studies of Jewish creative expression by the late twentieth century.

More recently, arts-based scholarship has tracked closely to periods of communal anxiety about the Jewish future, often coinciding with philanthropic and social science-based decisions to fund "culture" initiatives: particularly during the 1940s and the 1950s, with the rise of liberal Jewish youth movements, Israel, and the new role of the United States in world Jewry; during the 1970s, as young Jews sought to revamp Jewish education and ethnic identity (including new efforts in the field of Jewish Studies); and during the late 1990s–2000s as groups called for initiatives to ameliorate worrying statistics about Jewish "engagement" and endogamy in North America, Europe, and Israel. The opportunities such efforts have presented to scholars of the arts characterize the complex relationships that Jewish Studies in general has with Jewish communities and the organizations that represent them. But in its particular vulnerability to communal premises and expectations, arts-based research (as with social science) has often had to balance claims of scholarly rigor with funders' calls to research (and celebrate?) the latest ideas.

Methods

Scholars who specialize in the intersection of Judaism and the arts must find ways to translate the sensory world onto the written page. In addition to asking foundational questions about how images, sounds, or gestures generate meaning within the context of Jewish life, therefore, studies also tend to comment on the "print culture" of scholarship—that is, the convention of disseminating ideas through published words. What may appear self-evident based on the arts' integration into communal activities through homes, museums, or other "Jewish" activity, in other words, requires a great deal of mediation. Paul Ricoeur, Judith Butler, and others have written convincingly on the essential impossibility of scholars to make objective cultural observations (i.e. describing things "as they are"), and ethnographers from Paul Rabinow to James Fischer have commented extensively on the scholar's dilemma in translating personal ethnographic experience into the written word. The arts present these layers of complication in full force. Arts practitioners often choose their forms of expression specifically because of the ways they differ from a strictly verbal expression; thus print becomes a less-than-ideal means for explaining or describing their ideas. In addition, artistic concepts of tradition and dialogue, while accepted as intellectual pursuits, often differ markedly from those of exegetical or literary traditions. The experience of internal reference in music, an artistic motif in visual art, or the hallmarks of a theatrical directing school, for example, are long-standing practices that exist almost entirely outside of verbal representation. Bringing these experiences into the verbal "art" of scholarship thus serves as a central preoccupation for the field.

The wide variety of topics addressed in scholarship on the arts therefore utilizes a broad series of methods and approaches. First and foremost, scholars engage with discipline-specific topics and materials. A musicologist might attempt to use a musical score or a notated transcription to address a point of ideology or history, triangulating those materials with archival or secondary scholarly accounts. An art historian might similarly work within the framework of a specific established period or area, bringing together art works, artist statements, and contemporary intellectual treatises to comment on key ideas. For dance historians and ethnographers, particular motions and gesture combinations gain historical relevance within a broader historical framework. These kinds of explorations typically incorporate images, video, audio, and nonstandard notational materials, sometimes created from live performances by the scholars themselves. Although such methods require special knowledge for analysis, they serve the overall purpose of allowing nonverbal materials to enter the realm of scholarly conversation.

Amid these different ways to assemble materials, studies in the arts tend to take three major approaches:

(1)   Historical-Contextual: Scholars of Historical-Contextual approaches seek to place existing groups, works of art, or artists within a social, cultural, and historical context. Most compatible with mainstream Jewish Studies scholarship, scholarship of this sort tends to draw heavily on documentary evidence, including contemporary theoretical works. Depending upon the time frame of the topic being investigated,

scholars might supplement their documentary research as necessary with interviews and/or observation.

(2)   "Text"-based analysis: Drawing from scholarship that frames all objects as repositories of cultural knowledge, these studies tend to approach specific artistic, theatrical, musical, or choreographic pieces as "texts" to be "read," usually through a combination of critical theory and specialized, discipline-specific techniques (such as an analysis of musical scores, gestures, images, and/or theatrical conventions).

(3)   Ethnographic: Ethnographic works involve learning about a culture, population, or phenomenon through extended contact with individuals and/or communities. A bundle of methods developed in conjunction with the social sciences, and adopted differently in individual subfields, the method is itself a subject of scholarly innovation and discussion. Ethnography as practiced by sociologists for commissioned studies, for example, can include focused observation of events, structured interviews, and surveys; in anthropology-based fields, the process may involve extended immersion for periods of a year or more, open interviews, and long-term relationships. Ultimately all these techniques aim to document human behavior as it happens, and seeing how both special and everyday activities can offer insight into the human condition. Topics addressed with ethnography can include learning the practices and patterns of Jewish identity in a Judaica store, exploring a specific Israeli folk dance session, documenting the training of cantors, learning about the values underlying attendees of Jewish "hipster" events, or conducting a survey of non-Jewish synagogue attendees.

Based on the nature of a particular project, researchers may use these methods alongside each other in various constellations. More often than not, scholarship will distill a combination of methods that satisfy the conventions of their major field(s) and fit their topic's needs. Ideally, these approaches will allow researchers to link specific, unique, and deeply researched case studies with broader historical contexts, find ways to address the nonverbal nature of the artistic endeavors often represent, and create a common and acceptable scholarly language for considering the larger implications of such studies.

Scholarship in the arts also tends to incorporate the use of media as both a research tool and a mode of presentation. Technological developments have assisted researchers in facing the dilemma of having to translate forms of expression into durable and reproducible entities for scholarly conversations by "fixing" images and performances for later use and analysis. These forms have also led to different presentational formats: from full-color plates and CD/DVDs bundled into books, to media materials coupled with extensive scholarly liner notes, to digital presentation approaches, to predominantly creative forms such as films, workshop performances, websites, and art exhibitions. Rapidly changing technology and storage formats, moreover, have created complications in preserving and maintaining these materials, particularly when compared with the more durable conventions of the printed/written word; this situation has led to extensive "best practices" conversations among archivists and a significant need to migrate formats for both personal and commercial materials among researchers.

These considerations have led each of the disciplines that address creative activity to face its own spread of questions in canonicity, inclusion and exclusion. As with other aspects of Jewish Studies, the arts have been shaped by conversations about the generative aspects of Jewish identity. When applied to creative forms, these considerations have come to include the parameters for clarifying the identity of the work itself: whether as a function of the person or people making it, its context of usage, and its relevance for dialogues about identity more generally.

The sections that follow present brief accounts of the subsequent development of different fields. As earlier, the boundaries between scholarship and active advocacy, as well as the boundaries between the fields themselves, tend to blur and shift based both on contemporary trends and on the configuration of support and resources. Nonetheless, amid these dynamics scholars have sought to develop discipline-specific conversations that more effectively establish their chosen art form's position within Jewish Studies. In dialogue with their larger theoretical bases in musicology, art history, and so forth, these conversations ask a number of parallel questions: How does the art form break into regional or historical subcategories (and how do those subcategories compare with accepted categories within Jewish Studies)? How should the idea of the "Jewish" integrate with the creation, display of, and discussion around "art" (should "Jewish" art be defined according to the subject, the artist's identity, the conversation in which art is created, or other criteria)? How can researchers create a scholarship that coexists with both the needs of supporting institutions and the artists themselves? While each conversation has a unique character, and involves intimate knowledge of the artistic communities in question, they collectively seek more rigorous theoretical foundations as a means for asserting legitimacy within the broader Jewish Studies field.

Individual Fields

Literature

The comparatively vast academic field of Jewish literature dwarfs the other disciplines outlined here in its size and influence, and could easily occupy its own chapter in this handbook. In numbers of scholars and academic programs alone, literature scholarship holds the critical mass to generate ideas that can subsequently be adopted by other smaller disciplines. As an intellectual pursuit that focuses on creative texts, moreover, literature studies do not, on the surface, require extraordinary artistic training in order to engage with the primary materials. Literature consequently integrates more smoothly into the major intellectual goals of Jewish Studies, retaining the discipline's tendencies toward textual authority and analysis while offering meaningful meditations on the different forms of writing that comprise the Jewish literary tradition. Literature-focused essays routinely appear across the spectrum of Jewish Studies journals. In addition to specific literature journals such as *Studies in American Jewish Literature* and *Magid: A Journal of Jewish Literature*, moreover, the field has its own high-level journal in *Prooftexts: A Journal of Jewish Literary History*, and popular periodicals such as the *Jewish Literary Review,* the *Jewish Review of Books,* and *Tablet* (formerly *NextBook*) offer space for lay-conversation that present literature as a generative force of intellectual culture.

As chroniclers of literary culture, scholars engaging with this field have largely followed a paradigm of artist/author as intellectual, wherein a single work often corresponds to a single expansive or enlightened mind, even when that author is not explicitly known. The elevated position of literature in intellectual circles, reinforced by the frequency with which noted thinkers illustrated their ideas through fiction and vice versa, thereby established literature as a standard bearer for intellectual achievement and aspiration. Written texts themselves, moreover, could be interpreted as existing at the meeting point of Western scholarship and Jewish exegetical tradition. The resulting field that emerged facilely attributed to these works Jewish philosophical concepts, literary technical analysis, and the evaluation of historical/contextual paradigms.

Strategies in defining the field of Jewish literature, which helped to frame the emerging field, thus yielded models that paralleled the religious tradition of sacred textual interpretation. Late nineteenth-century scholars of Jewish literature, including Israel Abrahams, saw the topic as comprising a trajectory of creative writings from the Bible to the present day.[3] Others attempted to group literature according to national tradition, addressing recurring motifs or concepts as related to the particular experiences of Jews within a given nation's history—an approach that held great power when addressing "emerging" nations such as the United States and Israel. Still others organized their canons along linguistic lines in order the document and follow predominant intellectual movements in Jewish history. Yiddish literature serves as a good example here: whereas scholars and supporters of Yiddish argued that the language was a legitimate form of Jewish expression in 1908 at a now-legendary conference in Czernowitz, and individuals writers such as Sholem Aleichem and Mendele Mocher Sforim attempted to show how the language could be elevated to literary status, the formal modern study of Yiddish literature largely emerged through the efforts of Ruth Wisse in the 1970s and the 1980s. Literature studies of other "Jewish" languages, such as Hebrew and Ladino, emerged in the 1950s and the 1990s respectively. As the field of Jewish literature diversified, scholars began to organize themselves along the ancient/medieval/modern schema that had emerged as a dominant outline for Jewish history. Later, a fourth category of twentieth / twenty-first-century Jewish literature, including works in English and Russian, emerged as a way to expand the borders of the field and establish scholarship as gatekeeper for canonicity.

Literature thereby became a vessel through which scholars could experiment with new academic trends, and one of the leading means for introducing new directions in contemporary Jewish life to Jewish Studies. In addition to a steady stream of curated anthologies,[4] literature became a key part of Holocaust memory studies, several area studies (including Latin American Jewish Studies and cultural studies among others), and modern/postmodern/critical studies discourses, including the introduction of Mikhael Bakhtin and Frantz Fanon into the field.

Recent literature scholarship has taken an expansive approach to the idea of the canon, seeking new themes and genres that challenge existing conceptions of Jewish creativity, and often, therefore, of Judaism itself. Scholars have explored literature in relation to contemporary concepts of "culture." They have framed literature as a means for experiencing Jewish encounters with the "other," both real and imaginary, including African Americans, Native Americans, and Orthodox Jews.[5] They have evaluated new literature and connected it with established legacies and literary discourses, and they have helped maintain literature as a bellwether of Jewish cultural creativity, assisting in the establishment and administration of numerous Jewish book awards.

Art and Visual Culture

Evidence suggests that Jews have had a thriving visual culture since the start of Jewish identity. Just as others, Jews fashioned objects for everyday, ritual, and ornamental usage.

The nineteenth-century development of the field of archeology, and the expansion of a museum culture intended to bring works of art to a broader public, opened a new interest in material objects as clues for understanding human cultures. American and European ethnological societies gathered artifacts from expeditions to current and ancient sites, placing them on display to illustrate the cultures of premodern civilizations, and art museums displayed the heights of cultural achievement for all to see. For Jews who strived to join that culture, objects consequently became an important mode of entry, connecting Jews to the story of Western civilization while positively distinguishing them from other national cultures. A culture of Judaica collection consequently emerged in the mid-nineteenth century that would help fuel the rise of museum collections, and the subsequent desire to view Jewish art as a genre. Scholarship followed, largely attempting to reconstruct older Jewish artistic styles to assist in creating prescriptive models for contemporary activity. One of the first published studies on a Jewish art topic focused on the fourteenth-century Sarajevo Haggadah.[6] For the most part, however, Jewish art studies retained a fascination with the ancient and the religious: the 1901–6 *Jewish Encyclopedia*, for instance, included articles entitled "Art Among the Ancient Hebrews" and "Art, Attitude of Judaism Toward," but relegated all Jewish artists of the modern period to a brief, list-like "Pictorial Art" entry. Part of this perspective included an over-zealous interpretation of the second commandment, leading scholars to explain Jews' historic exclusion from major artistic movements as religiously dictated until the reforming movements of the nineteenth century. As a result, contemporary artists initially appeared as outliers to the discussion, treated as relative newcomers who lacked a "racial" tradition.[7]

In developing a Jewish identity in art, scholars began to draw heavily on Middle Eastern and Mediterranean area archeological expeditions through the 1930s, building off of discoveries of ancient places of worship and other important sites. The detailed mosaic floors found in the Tiberias (third–fourth century, discovered 1920) and Dura-Europos (second- to third-century Syria, discovered 1932) synagogues achieved particular prominence in the conversation as sources of Jewish iconography that connected religious practices in antiquity to contemporary worship. Such glimpses into ancient Israelite society, while speaking to the use of art in early religious settings, offered icons of Jewish longevity and national pride. Publications on this and other topics largely served to catalogue motifs and images, while attempting to reconstruct the values of the ancient societies that created them. Several images from this period, including the seven-branched candelabrum (menorah), were adopted as symbols of the Zionist movement, and eventually became signifiers of Israeli nationalism, appearing on currency, monuments, and state buildings.

While some ancient materials had been central to the religious practice of Judaism, the category of ritual art in Judaism skewed more toward recent objects, gathered by collectors and eventually serving to endow the core collections of emerging Jewish museums. Often deemed as crafts pieces more often than the work of individual artists, these objects served to define Judaism largely along lines of religious practice. They subsequently generated scholarship that largely aligned with the field that came to be known as museum studies. Presenting Judaism in a somewhat more recognizable form than the ancient artifacts, these objects emblematized the Jewish move into modernity as they shifted from active ritual accessories to museum pieces valued for their aesthetic qualities.

Modern art studies corresponded more directly to the field of art history, where specific, trained individuals are credited with creating bodies of work corresponding with certain locations, historical periods, and schools of thought. Although there have been many self-identified Jewish artists since the mid-nineteenth century, interest in these figures within Jewish Studies usually corresponded with a desire to define a "Jewish art" genre and style, in some cases born of innate artistic urges as well as external decisions.

Within this schema, the art of modern Israel developed as its own category. Boris Schatz's 1906 founding of the Bezalel art center in Jerusalem opened a space for émigré artists to guide their European training toward subjects and techniques appropriate to the Zionist nation-building project. Early iterations of the Bezalel School (1906–17, 1919–29, and 1935–55) encouraged students to engage with images of the ancient world, while linking those images to a sense of Middle Eastern exoticism. Other groups of artists, including modernists who came to Palestine in the 1920s, continued to explore the idea of an artistic style emerging from the Jewish/Hebrew experience into a nationalist form.[8] Over time, these efforts migrated selectively into the national consciousness. The third incarnation of the Bezalel School started receiving Israel state funding in 1952, and by the following decade came under the supervision of the Ministry of Education and Culture. State-sponsored museums fashioned Israel-centered timelines of Jewish people; in the case of the Israel Museum, this process of remediation involved importing Bezalel's art collection, as well as its concept of a national style, into a specific "Israeli Art" wing in 1965.[9]

Art came into its own as a sweeping topic in Jewish Studies at this time as well. Cecil Roth's 1957 (Tel Aviv; Hebrew, with Zussia Efron)/1961 (New York/London; English) edited collection *Jewish Art* became a defining publication for the field, presenting sections on art in ancient, medieval, and modern times, and formulating a broadly inclusive view of the topic that intended "to describe . . . the artistic achievements in every medium of Jews and persons of Jewish birth, from the earliest times down to the present day, together with objects and buildings of specific Jewish ritual use, whether their authorship was provably Jewish or not."[10] While this framing included all types of architecture, ritual objects, sculpture, and visual art, it notably excluded depictions of Jews by non-Jewish artists. Roth and Efron's book crystallized debates about the nature of defining "Jewish art" within a broad narrative structure, while consolidating the field for both Israeli and American audiences. Art critics Clement Greenberg and Harold Rosenberg, meanwhile, engaged concurrently with similar questions specifically about modern artistic creation during the same era, asking direct questions about the place of Jewish identity within the contemporary art world. Greenberg argued that the experience of Jews in the modern world lent itself to a sense of abstraction, almost to the point of being considered a Jewish "style." Rosenberg, in contrast, famously saw Judaism as one among many motivations for artistic creation, held in reserve by artists and brought to the fore as determined by the work, the venue, or the discussion. These three highly influential perspectives on "Jewish art" consequently served as touchstones for exploring Jewish motivation and the creative process in both classroom and museum settings.

Subsequent generations of scholars, including a number of important curators, have developed these different strands in challenging ways, slowly shifting to a broader concept of "visual culture" that placed art within a complex cultural context. In Israel, efforts spearheaded by Bezalel Narkiss (1926–2008) helped institutionalize Jewish art studies at Hebrew University's Center for Jewish Art (founded 1979), and Narkiss's Index of Jewish Art project, created to be compatible with Princeton's Index of Christian Art, began an inventorying project that as of this writing has extended to more than 200,000 items from 41 countries. Bar-Ilan University's museum and department of Jewish art, established in 1989/1990, extended the conversation with degree programs and conferences. These two centers have played leading roles in directing scholarly conversations about Jewish art and art curation; the Index, now online, remains a major resource, and in 2007, a third program at Tel Aviv University established by the Goldstein-Goren Diaspora Research Center, attempted to add European institutions to the discussion as well. Motivated by Israel's self-perception as a center for Jewish gathering and cultural preservation, these efforts have continued to map Jewish visual culture in its broadest dimensions, ancient, medieval, modern, and "contemporary."

Other scholars came to the material as modern historians interested in addressing art's place within Jewish life. Richard I. Cohen and Ezra Mendelssohn's historical investigations of Jews and European art in the nineteenth and twentieth centuries, for example, view the artistic urge as a rich area for exploring Jews' engagement with modern society, claiming that "visual arts talk history and constitute history."[11] American voices have emphasized the encounter of Jews and art with art history, exploring the work and writings of contemporary artists through a Jewish lens (such as R. B. Kitaj and his 1989 *Diasporist Manifesto*), including art as a subgenre of Holocaust study, and attempting to address Jewish artistic expression through alternative (i.e. nonreligious or non-Zionist) Jewish frameworks. Curators developed their own voices as well, offering their perspectives by conceiving and mounting meaningful exhibits for an interested public. Jewish Museum of New York curator Norman Kleeblatt's provocative projects "Too Jewish?: Challenging Traditional Identities" (1996) and "Mirroring Evil: Nazi Imagery/Recent Art" (2001), for example, brought artists, scholars, and the public into direct, sometimes contentious, interactions and fostered new models for conceiving of the museum's role in Jewish culture in the process.

A number of journals have been created to support scholarly discussion about Jews and art, including the Israeli journals *Rimonim* (Hebrew, 1983–89), *The Journal of Jewish Art* (English, 1974–99, 24 vols [later just *Jewish Art*]), published by the Center for Jewish Art, and *Ars Judaica* (English, 2005–, 8 vols), a publication of the Bar-Ilan program.[12] *Images* (2007–, 6 vols), published in conjunction with the Jewish Art and Visual Culture program at New York's Jewish Theological Seminary, continues to provide an American perspective on the field as well. The seemingly reenergized publication field has benefited from both improved technology for presenting the graphic-intensive discipline, an increased presence of scholars trained in Jewish art, and the improved (if perhaps temporary) availability of resources.

This range of voices, combined with art's permanence compared to other forms of expression such as dance, has brought the field into a relatively successful if still somewhat uneasy exchange with central ideas of Jewish Studies.[13] A new round of Jewish art survey publications starting in the mid-2000s has attempted to consolidate and reorient the field. Moving beyond an all-inclusive approach, scholars have added nuance to issues of identity and motivation developing since the 1990s, shifting critical emphasis to the modern period in the process.[14] Matthew Baigell's account of American Jewish art ostensibly establishes a new historical structure for further research, introducing a succession of artists and their works within a decade-by-decade narrative of American Jewish life.[15] Samantha Baskind and Larry Silver seek new paradigms for understanding art and Judaism by exploring "how aspects of the diverse and complex Jewish experience find expression(s) in modern art."[16] The early period has seen significant reshaping as well, with scholars such as Steven Fine placing archeological evidence of artistic expression in dialogue with existing written (often rabbinic) sources to reveal a more complex and culturally diverse picture of ancient Jewish/Israelite society.[17] These publications speak to a desire to understand the nature of "Jewish art" through a shift to "visual culture,"[18] placing images and objects within an increasingly layered context of discourse, reception, and experience. While outside perceptions of second commandment, restrictions persist both among scholars unfamiliar with the field and in popular culture, the voluminous and creative discussions now being produced by specialists in the area speak to the field's increasing sense of establishment and sophistication.

Music

As much as art, arguably, music has served as an important means for Jews to refashion themselves in the modern world. Propagated in communal settings that often emphasized Jewish identity, such as home gatherings, religious rituals, and youth activities, music served as a mode of flexible communication with varied amounts of required skill. The meaning of a musical performance, moreover, could completely redefine itself with each repetition depending upon the setting, and types of instruments used, and the surrounding conversations. Such widespread use of music in Jewish history and culture has caused research on the topic to take various forms, occasionally serving to forward the political and philosophical agendas of each scholar.

From the nineteenth century and well into the twentieth, research on music and Judaism has largely been based on defining and clarifying two related realms of practice: the synagogue and "folk" music. In both cases, musician/ scholars typically became the most prominent and enthusiastic proponents of research, emboldened by their training and their public roles in communal leadership. These researchers brought a varied combination of theory, history, composition, and performance practice to argue for the existence of centuries-old musical traditions, or for the legitimacy of new ones. Support for these forms of research had clear practical purposes: in addition to giving Jews a place at the table alongside other national musical "styles" promoted at the end of the nineteenth century, such scholarly work contributed to the modernization of liturgy, the sounds of the Zionist movement, and the development of "Jewish" art music repertoires. In 1886, for example, in the midst of internal debates among cantors about the codification of a Jewish synagogue musical style, Vienna cantor Josef Singer distilled three main synagogue "modes" (musical scales, loosely defined) that he claimed to embody the breadth of synagogue chant. Both descriptive and prescriptive, these modes helped practitioners of synagogue music to identity what "was" Jewish music, and to create new idiomatic compositions. By 1893, Baltimore cantor Alois Kaiser and New York cantor William Sparger had refined this system further, incorporating a series of "ancient" melodies that retroactively strengthened Singer's theory. Australian cantor Francis L. Cohen wrote a series of entries in the *Jewish Encyclopedia* that placed these musical practices into a broad historical trajectory that traced the development of Jewish music in the form of melody, as it took root in the gaonic period, interacted with non-Jewish melody during the Middle Ages, and gained instrumental accompaniment in the mid-nineteenth century.

Others, inspired by increasing late nineteenth-century interest in folk materials as the basis of popular ideology, sought to collect and elevate the musical styles of rural Jews in Russia (see the section on Folklore, below). In St. Petersburg, composer Yuli/Joel Engel established with several other composers and musicians a New Jewish School in music between 1908 and the late 1920s. In conjunction with a series of expeditions organized by the writer and activist S. Ansky, these composers continued a trend started by Peysekh Marek and Shaul Ginsburg to develop a Jewish folk music repertoire. Members of the society, which also established a branch in Moscow, arranged and adapted the

collected folk songs into art music compositions, thereby attempting to legitimize Jewish musical identity through public concerts and scholarly lectures.

Abraham Zvi Idelsohn (1880–1938), however, consolidated the field. As a
trained cantor inspired by both Zionism and emerging sound-recording technologies, Idelsohn conducted about 14 years of fieldwork in Palestine in an effort
to distill a Middle-Eastern-based music that could serve as the basis for a future
Jewish state. These efforts led to extensive recording and transcription projects,
as well as a detailed schema that attempted to establish a comparative scale of
Jewish musical conservatism organized by national community. In the early
1920s, Idelsohn moved to the United States and reorganized his history around
Reform Judaism, teaching at Cincinnati's Hebrew Union College and attempting to create a Reform musical idiom that would attract liberal Jews back to
their synagogues. His *Thesaurus of Hebrew Oriental Melodies* (1914–33) and *Jewish
Music in Its Historical Development* (1929) became cornerstones in the field as a
result, remaining to many the most comprehensive books on the topic to date.

By the 1930s, a thriving exchange on musical scholarship existed between
Europe, Palestine, and the United States, perhaps best exemplified by the World
Centre for Jewish Music in Palestine and the short-lived journal *Musica Hebraica*.
The decimation of European Jewish communities in the Holocaust, however,
shifted scholarship on music and Judaism to the United States, which had the
most stable system of higher education and a larger population of (heavily émigré) musicologists. Brief attempts to ameliorate the state of research took place in
New York's Jewish Music Forum; ultimately, however, the era's greatest accomplishment was the establishment of cantorial schools at the New York branch
of the Hebrew Union College (1948), the Jewish Theological Seminary (1952),
and Yeshiva University (1954). Modeled after European Jewish teacher-training
schools, these institutions centralized the academic field of Jewish music around
religious practitioners, and promoted religious music, particularly in an eastern
European tradition, as the primary topic of Jewish music research.

Through the 1970s, "Jewish music" studies focused on projects that chronicled musical tradition and survival with an emphasis on Ashkenazic musical
styles that contributed to cantorial practices. Eric Werner, who founded the first
of these schools, dominated the field through this time, pursuing a program
that included imbuing composer Felix Mendelssohn-Bartholdy with a (now
disputed) bold Jewish identity, exemplifying Ashkenazic synagogue chant as a
paragon of Jewish musical innovation, and claiming a musical "Sacred Bridge"
between Jews and Catholics during the Middle Ages (a theory that has largely
been disproven). Lacking opportunities for scholarly dialogue during this time,
Werner's claims appeared to emerge from the losses in eastern Europe: he based
a significant part of his arguments on Jewish moral imperatives that touched
Jewish populations emotionally even when the scholarship itself seemed to
drift into speculation.

Starting in the 1960s, a new generation of scholars in both Israel and America began to explore and eventually question ideas of tradition in much greater detail. The field shifted to focus on two major methodologies: in Israel, in line with the nation-building project and European models of "comparative musicology" (*vergleichende Musikwissenschaft*), a paradigm of an East/West musical duality took hold. Building upon the work of Idelsohn and his Palestine-based successor Robert Lachmann (1892–1939), scholars such as Hanoch Avenary (1908–94) and Edith Gerson-Kiwi (1908–92) combined ethnographic observation with a large folk-song archive gathered at the Hebrew University (later brought into the Jewish Music Research Centre) to explore the musical traditions of various Jewish communities. Taking to some extent after Idelsohn's Palestine work, these studies contributed to a vast cultural mapping project that sought to highlight the range of Jewish musical "traditions" in the young state, preserve them for posterity, and use them to highlight both the richness and interrelatedness of Jewish musical identity.

In America, in contrast, the field shifted toward ethnomusicology—a field that concerned itself more with the ways self-identified Jews employed music as a way to invoke past and current identities through extended field research. Studies by Kay Shelemay, Mark Slobin, and Philip Bohlman characterized this work in their focus on specific communities and a methodology that avoided national, cultural, or religious agendas. Shelemay studied the liturgical chants of the Beta Israel community in Ethiopia in the early 1970s, and discovered that this repertoire more closely resembled Ethiopian Christian chant than documented Jewish chant; Bohlman's work on German Jewish communities in Israel explored how the European middle-class tradition of classical music making sustained itself within a national setting that sometimes viewed such music with skepticism after the Holocaust; and Mark Slobin's work on Yiddish music in America became a cornerstone of the 1970s movement that led to a national revival of eastern European Jewish identity. Each of these works helped to clarify or contradict broadly held assumptions about Jewish heritage and/or senses of tradition.

Several publications emerged as part of this era, including *The Journal of Synagogue Music, Musica Judaica*, and *The Journal of Jewish Music and Liturgy* (United States), and the *Yuval* publication series (Israel). Though sponsored by organizations aiming to preserve Jewish heritage for moral purposes, they became sites of active dialogue that allowed scholars, cantors, composers, and educated laypeople to exchange their ideas about the purpose, repercussions, and practical needs of scholarship on Jews and music well into the twenty-first century.

The university-based model of Jewish music research expanded in the 1990s, led by such scholars as Edwin Seroussi and Don Harrán in Israel, Shelemay, Slobin, and Alexander Ringer in the United States, and Bohlman in Europe's reemerging Jewish Studies programs. Their students, in turn, have joined with other scholars of music and Judaism—including those in the seminaries—to push for more active dialogue and critical engagement. Studies that interrogate how senses of Judaism are consciously constructed, whether in historical situations such as the St. Petersburg Folk Music Society or the compositions of Ernest Bloch, or in contemporary populations such as Syrian Jewish community of Brooklyn, New York, American Reform Jewish cantorial students, or the Lower Manhattan "Radical Jewish Culture" scene, move toward what Seroussi has called a "musicology of the Jewish": an approach that recognizes the myriad ways that people use music to think about Judaism, rather than aiming to affirm a largely ideology-driven Jewish music "tradition." As evidenced by a revived Jewish Music Forum, an invigorated Jewish Music Research Centre at Hebrew University, and the establishment of Jewish music interest groups in a number of professional academic music societies (including the Society for Ethnomusicology, the Society for American Music, and the American Musicological Society), these activities portend a more robust conversation.

Folklore

Folklore (or folklife) encompasses a broad array of activities associated with communal activity. From stories (folktales and narratology), to the creation of objects (folk art), to patterns of food preparation (foodways), to the conventions of community life (more generally, folkways), folklore seeks to understand how populations forge their values through everyday interaction. While its roots go back to at least the eighteenth century, with such central thinkers as Johann Gottfried von Herder, the field gained popularity during the mid-nineteenth century, as it brought the expressions of so-called common people into a form that could contribute to scholarly conversations. As with the other artistic pursuits addressed here, Jews became increasingly involved in this pursuit by the turn of the twentieth century, seeing it as an important means for Jewish populations to preserve and present their heritage in the modern world. In Vienna, Rabbi Max Grunwald (1871–1953) led what has been described as the first Jewish Folklore Society between 1898 and 1929. Joseph Jacobs (1854–1916) helped establish the field through his articles in the 1906 *Jewish Encyclopedia*. Louis Ginzburg's 1909–10 *Legends of the Jews* collected and arranged stories from rabbinic literature according to a biblical timeline. S. Ansky in Russia and the YIVO Institute in Vilnius put out calls to collect folklore at this time as well, seeking to document vastly changing times among the largely Yiddish-speaking populations of eastern Europe. In the United States, meanwhile, folklorists attempted to preserve a body of Jewish folk tales and beliefs from first-generation eastern

European Jewish immigrants in the hope of documenting their lives before they assimilated into the American scene.

While the field's aims of collecting and publishing or displaying materials from the common people changed little over the following decades, upheavals of central and eastern Europe brought by the Nazi period necessitated radical revision. In 1944, with European folklore institutions largely obliterated, Raphael Patai (1910–96) founded the Palestine Institute of Folklore and Ethnology, and in 1946 he laid out a program for establishing the field of folklore in Palestine/Israel.[19] Mark Zborowski and Elizabeth Herzog's 1952 publication *Life Is with People*, developed through interviews with eastern European Jewish immigrants to the United States, crystallized the idealized eastern European *shtetl* culture as an emblem of heritage loss for American Jews after the Holocaust. These and other projects emphasized the need to preserve memories, stories, and objects as cultural artifacts.

In 1955, Dov Noy established the Israel Folklore Archives in Haifa, a center for collecting stories and legends among immigrants to Israel—and a part of the country's desire to document the lives of the immigrants in preparation for assimilation into Israeli society. Arranged according to ethnic group, it eventually grew to contain well over 20,000 stories and served as a source for many subsequent publications, including the eight volumes of the *Folklore Research Center Studies* (1970–83).

The development of folklore graduate programs in the United States, especially at Indiana University and the University of Pennsylvania, served to shape the next direction of Jewish folkloristics. The combination of collection fieldwork, theme classification, and literary presentation that had largely shaped the field until then began to diversify in the 1960s and the 1970s into a more ethnographic mode that began to take a broader range of performance practices into account. An influx of Jewish students to these programs in the 1970s, combined with the growing acceptability in the academy of researching one's own ethnic groups, led to a broad reinvention of Jewish folklore studies, as exemplified by the creation of the *Jewish Folklore and Ethnography Newsletter* at Indiana University in 1978 (later renamed the *Jewish Folklore and Ethnology Review* [1987–2000]).[20] Outside of the academy, this period included a revival in Jewish storytelling as a literary and performance art, as spearheaded by Howard Schwartz, Peninnah Schram, Gerald Fierst, and Shlomo Carlebach. Beyond collecting, these developments showed researchers' interests in the ways people's spoken and creative interactions indicated cultural changes and norms, whether through the use of humor or the employment of narrative in creating a communal mind-set in Israel.

These two centers of Jewish-folklore study in the United States and Israel have remained active into the twenty-first century, with leading folklorists such as Haya Bar-Itzhak and Galit Hasan-Rokem in Israel and Simon Bronner and

Dan Ben-Amos in the United States continuing to welcome scholars who explore a wide variety of creative expressions and research methods. Recent published collections by Eli Yassif and Dan Ben-Amos have garnered international recognition.[21] In other cases the field looked to the discipline of performance studies to examine the ways that people create and present folktales and folk arts: Barbara Kirshenblatt-Gimblett's *They Called Me Mayer July*, which recounts the ways the author's father described his prewar European life through his paintings, offers one perspective on this process.[22] The Jewish Folklore and Ethnology section of the American Folklore Society, in recognition of this broadening disciplinary base, initiated the occasional publication *Jewish Cultural Studies* in 2008.

Dance

"Who are Jews dancing, and how does dance enhance Judaism and Jewish identity?"[23] So Judith Brin Ingber states as one of the organizing questions of the field of Jewish dance. As the practice of embodying Jewish history and identity, dance has held a significant role in public culture, while being more difficult to document than music. Moreover, as seen most visibly at weddings and celebrations of ethnicity or nationhood, dance has been used as an active mode for determining identity.

In Palestine/Israel, national forms of dance developed as an extension of European modern dance and folk dance movements: two interrelated forms from the start of the twentieth century that sought freedom from the restrictive norms of classical dance, and attempted to engage groups of people in identity-defining physical activity. Zionist groups incorporated these interests when developing their rituals and cultural institutions, and brought dance into their own events while publishing collections of "Palestinian Dances" in the 1920s and the 1930s for export around the world.

The need to give these practices an intellectual history and philosophy opened the door for the form's most active participants to become its first scholarly voices: most notably Benjamin Zemach, Dvorah Lapson, Sara Levi-Tanai, and Fred Berk. Through a combination of teaching and promotion, these key figures imbued Jewish dance with historical (largely biblical) roots, and helped to develop the field both as a form of performance (including Levi-Tanai's *Inbal* dance troupe, founded 1949) and as a communal activity (such as Berk's founding of the first Israeli folk-dance session in America at New York's 92nd St. Y in 1952). While producing a number of instructional handbooks and recording inserts on the art form, their publications were limited, with Fred Berk's edited pamphlet *The Jewish Dance* perhaps the most prominent.[24]

Dancer-scholars have remained highly visible in the field ever since, serving the professional dance community, the scholarly community, and the lay public through their work. Accomplished dancer and choreographer Ruth Eshel, for example, was active in Israel's art dance community in the 1970s and the 1980s, published a history of Israeli art dance in the early 1990s, edited a pair of professional journals during the 1990s, lectured at the University of Haifa from 1991–2005, served as a dance critic for *HaAretz*, ran her own dance troupe, and completed her PhD in dance history in 2002.[25] Judith Brin Ingber has also been highly influential in shaping the international scholarly field: cofounding *Machol Be-Yisrael* (the *Israeli Dance Annual*) with Giora Manor in 1976, writing the first history of Israeli Folk Dance, producing a scholarly biography of Israeli dance proponent Fred Berk (1911–80), and editing two related collections on Jewish dance (*Jewish Folklore and Ethnology Review* 20, #1–2 [2000], and the 2011 volume *Seeing Israeli and Jewish Dance*). Ingber's work focuses on identifying and documenting important dance movements in modern Jewish history, and she frequently illustrates her scholarship with live dance demonstrations. Their work has paved the way for younger scholars such as Naomi Jackson, Dina Roginsky, Rebecca Rossen, Nina Spiegel, and Joshua Perelman, who have contributed to a deeper understanding of dance history through a written idiom that, like the rest of the dance studies field, addresses motion and gesture in a mode compatible with document-based scholarship. Their works have explored the relationship of Jewish/Israeli identity with corporeality, interrogating how different dancers, choreographers, and institutions chose to frame the nature of Jewish experience through their communal initiatives and rehearsed movements.

Theater

Scholarship on Jews and theater presents a relatively heterogeneous field that has only recently attempted to consolidate to some extent. In many cases, documentation and preservation served as a major motivation for conducting research, reflecting both amateur ("folk") theatrical practices and specialized/professional productions. At the same time, the scholarship has held an important symbiotic relationship with theater performance itself, helping to generate both institutional and popular interest in the field, while incubating new works and innovative stagings of existing works.

Yiddish culture has played an important role in shaping the discipline. Some of the earliest scholarly work on Jewish theater emerged as part of Yiddish intellectualist movements, with histories, lexicons, and accounts of key personalities in the Yiddish theater scene emerging in the 1920s.[26] Theater also factored into Yiddish ethnographic expeditions, perhaps best exemplified by Moisei Beregovskii's considerable yet largely unpublished work on the amateur Purimspil (Purim play) in Soviet Russia. After World War II, scholarship on Yiddish theater shifted from a largely internal literature in the immediate postwar period into an important aspect of the Yiddish revival starting in the 1970s. Nahma Sandrow's 1977 book *Vagabond Stars: A World History of Yiddish Theater* reflected this historical moment, and launched another round of scholarship on the topic.

In the 1980s, the formative questions of the discipline began to take on broader questions of identity within history, literature, performance studies, and film. Scholarship in the field, consequently, cleaves along a number of areas that reflect the broader disciplinary topography of Jewish Studies as well as theater's performative nature. Studies classified according to spoken language, for example, overlap with Israel Studies as a self-sustaining culture region (Hebrew), the expansion of Yiddish secular studies, emerging scholarship on Sephardic history and culture (Ladino), the growth of "Jewish theater" in the United States and England (English), and additional sociolinguistic considerations. Work on the cultures of "Israeli theater," "Russian theater," "American theater," "Argentine theater," and so forth frame performance practices as phenomena that emerge from a population's history, experiences and particular constellation of theatrical development, institutions, and support. Important individual figures and institutions (playwrights, actors, directors, and troupes) receive their own literature as producers, shapers, and philosophers of theatrical performance: from actor Jacob Adler, to playwright Hanokh Levin, to the Israeli Russian-speaking Gesher troupe.[27]

A second realm of scholarship on theater links with literature studies, involving textual analyses of Jewish-themed play scripts. Taking the work itself as the primary source, studies of this type attempted to explore the minds and philosophies of the plays' authors in order to gain insight into major literary figures. Holocaust representation constitutes one particularly notable topic within this area, with studies often evaluating works by significance, historical accuracy, and honor to the dead.[28] Researchers have built literature around canonical theater works as well, such as *The Merchant of Venice* and *The Dybbuk*, in effort to chronicle Jewish responses and reinterpretations. From another perspective, scholars have presented editions of theatrical works themselves, whether classic or (mostly) new, in an effort to establish a repertoire for both performance and analysis.[29]

By the start of the twenty-first century, attempts to consolidate the field had resulted in the "All About Jewish Theater" website (www.jewish-theatre.com) that chronicled Jewish theater-based activity around the world. Gatherings of scholars, meanwhile, such as the 2009 "Jews/Theater/Performance in an Intercultural World" conference convened by Edna Nahshon at the Jewish Theological Seminary, have attempted to organize the discipline around a set of parameters and common themes, leading to a series of edited volumes as well as a recent Jewish-themed issue of *The Drama Review*.[30]

Film

While parallel in some ways to theater scholarship, the field of film studies has developed along its own trajectory since the 1960s, partly emerging from critical theory projects developed by such scholars as Gilles Deleuze and Christian Metz. In addition to exploring the narratives and subjects themselves, researchers have engaged broad philosophical questions about the relationship of technology to human experience, including the processes of creating, developing, and distributing films, the modes of film viewing and consumption, and the implications of a film industry.[31]

Jewish communal interest in film as a mode for promoting social adherence and "Jewish values" in the late 1970s and the 1980s developed alongside the emergence of the first large-scale scholarly works on Jews and film, which identified and categorized Jewish film characters and plot arcs by historical time period.[32] By the mid-1990s, the field had developed some historical depth. Yet Joel Rosenberg, writing in the 1996 *American Jewish Year Book*, found the existing field relatively insular, and called on future scholarship to integrate more fully with the broader field's critical engagement, while seeking to situate Jews within a broader international and intercultural context.[33]

Although quite a few subsequent studies addressed the rubric of "Jewish film," the field itself has not enjoyed as much academic organization as other areas discussed here. Some scholars have responded (directly or otherwise) to Rosenberg's call, defining the boundaries of discourse by establishing criteria for "Jewish film" studies, proposing large-scale questions for further investigation, or organizing films into meaningful categories.[34] Award-winning or landmark films with Jewish themes, such as *The Jazz Singer* (1927), have received considerable analysis as mass-mediated products, as have Holocaust-centered films such as *Schindler's List* (1993) and *Life Is Beautiful* (1997).[35] Isolated works have explored Jews' association with particular filmic techniques and styles (such as the film noir).[36] A distinct subfield of Israeli film studies has addressed political, ethnic, sexual, and creative power struggles in the state.[37] And an emerging interest in documentary film studies has led to important questions about Jews' mediated portrayals of themselves in the (post)modern world.[38]

The increasing availability of technology for making, storing, and distributing films, whether through commercial or institutional channels, has helped to expand the field rapidly. Hebrew University's Steven Spielberg Jewish Film Archive, for example, was established in 1971 (and named for Spielberg in 1988) as a repository for hundreds of professional and amateur films about Israel since the start of the twentieth century; these films became available through the internet starting in 2002, making obscure resources widely accessible for viewing, teaching, and research. These and other collections, augmented by internet-based on-demand services for more commercial fare, continue to create rich scholarly opportunities.

The proliferation of Jewish film festivals around the world since the 1980s has also increased awareness of the genre and promoted community participation. A meeting ground for artists and scholars in front of an interested public, they have become notable forums for intellectual debate, growing a support structure in conjunction with the National Center for Jewish Film at Brandeis University (founded 1976), and even becoming themselves subject for study as ritualized, nonreligious forms of Jewish observance and identification.[39]

The continued growth and organization of this field appears assured, as indicated through well-attended conference sessions, increasing scholarly and curricular interest in popular media (see below), the 2013 debut of the self-described "international journal" *Jewish Film and New Media*, the annual appearance of over a dozen monographs on the topic as a global phenomenon,[40] and ever-advancing consumer-grade technologies easing film composition, distribution, and analysis.

Media Studies

The most recent of the fields, Media Studies (and its growing associated study of "New Media") explores forms of expression made possible by the mass dissemination of new communications technologies. Emerging alongside scholarship on postmodernity, performance studies, and critical studies, the field recognizes the potential of these technologies to affect the ways that individuals perceive knowledge, identity, and their place in the world. At the same time, it has become an important interdisciplinary meeting place for scholars interested in the broader impact of the modernist project.

The "Jews and Media" field emerged with particular energy at the turn of the twenty-first century, as scholars increasingly found these technologies affecting their own lives. Collectives of scholars such as the Working Group for Jews and Media at the New York University Center for Religion and Media (est. 2003) have developed this field rapidly, bringing these questions enthusiastically into the Jewish Studies field. Scholars have reassessed the impact of older media forms, such as print media, radio, film, and television, upon the Jewish populations that used them.[41] They have also have made deep inquiries into the ways that the internet, forms of mass media, and the consumer electronics industries (among others) have combined with new perceptions of Jewish identity to redefine the concepts and precepts of Jewish communities. Artists have engaged openly in these discussions as well, and helped inform such works as Melissa Shiff and Louis Kaplan's "Post Modern Jewish Wedding" (2003) as well as Shiff's 2011 "Mapping Ararat: An Imaginary Jewish Homelands Project."

By the mid-2000s, a wide variety of scholars from many disciplines had made a presence for themselves at annual meetings of the Association for Jewish Studies. Under the leadership of Barbara Kirshenblatt-Gimblett and Jeffrey Shandler, among others, scholars produced collective efforts at redefining parts of the field, nurtured each others' long-term research projects, and sought to energize the field of Jewish Studies more generally. From this synergy have come studies of immersive online environments, graphic novels, home movies, youth culture, and avant-garde performance among other topics.[42]

The Media Studies field, by including such a broad variety of disciplines, has seen particular success at engaging Jewish Studies at a variety of levels, largely by eschewing a specific methodology in favor of a more inclusive approach that highlights meaningful recent phenomena inadequately covered by existing Jewish Studies methodologies. Jeffrey Shandler's call, as president of the Association for Jewish Studies, to engage "Judaism in the Public Sphere" in all its robustness at the association's annual conference in 2012, exemplifies the inroads this approach has made since 2000.

Conclusions: The Arts in Jewish Studies

Since the turn of the twenty-first century, the arts have factored differently into two coexisting models of Jewish Studies. A more classically oriented model acknowledges the significance of the arts and creative expression to Jewish life, but tends to situate them around a core trajectory of scholarship in classical, medieval, and modern Jewish history and philosophy. *The Oxford Handbook of Jewish Studies*, published in 2002, reflects this arrangement: although including five chapters on the arts (on "Art, Architecture, and Archeology," Music, Theater, Film, and Folklore), the volume relegates them to the back of the book (chapters 33, 34, 35, 36, and 38 out of 39; the current volume follows this model as well).[43] A contrasting model, characterized by David Biale's edited history *The Cultures of the Jews* (also 2002), integrates creative production into history itself. While remaining with a roughly chronological perspective of Jewish civilization, Biale's model opens extensive space for creative expression as a form of Jewish mediation with host societies.[44] Arts and culture consequently receive significant attention, with several specialists in these fields contributing chapters. These two approaches in some ways serve as poles for exploring the ways Jewish Studies programs organize themselves in the United States: older, more established programs tend to value (and hire faculty based on) the more classical model, while newer programs tend toward the latter schema for a variety of reasons.

The arts have also shown up in a number of significant Jewish Studies initiatives since 2000. In Fall 2000 / Spring 2001, the Katz Center for Advanced Judaic

Studies at the University of Pennsylvania held its annual fellowship program on "Jews and the Arts," leading to a volume that aimed for a collective rethinking of the topic.[45] The Conney Project on Jewish Arts, a five-year initiative started at the University of Wisconsin, Madison, in 2007, brought scholars and artists together in large events and conferences to encourage "new narratives of Jewish identity in all the arts, both traditional and contemporary."[46] Indiana University established the Lou and Sybil Mervis chair in Jewish Culture and the Arts in 2005, and the University of California, Los Angeles, announced a search for its Mickey Katz chair in Jewish Music in 2010. In 2011, meanwhile, The George Washington University initiated its Master of Arts program in Jewish Cultural Arts. These significant moments complemented numerous other field-specific conferences, panels, and initiatives exploring Jewish identity and the arts in all its detail.

While these initiatives may seem to illustrate cultural expression's rising status in Jewish Studies, other factors suggest a strong connection with patterns of funding based on communal concern for the future. This same time period (ca. 2000–12) coincided with a ramping up of philanthropically supported cultural initiatives intended to reenergize a Jewish youth population deemed at risk for religious attenuation—a position established in collaboration with commissioned (but often not peer reviewed) sociological studies. Projects such as the Joshua Venture (The Nathan Cummings, Righteous Persons, and Walter and Elise Hass Foundations), Reboot (The Andrea and Charles Bronfman Philanthropies), and the Six Points Fellowships (Jewish Federation of New York), among many others, targeted young adults with performance spaces, journals, media, and other inducements to create and present their own "culture" as a form of Jewish engagement. The recipients of these grants, in turn, directed their attention to college students and young adults, and the grant programs themselves retained artists, critics, and PhDs as consultants, researchers, and employees.[47] A perfect storm consequently arose whereby philanthropies, interested in Jewish "continuity" among young adults, inspired legitimacy through direct academic involvement. Subsidizing both the programs and (to some extent) scholarly attention to these programs, philanthropic organizations ultimately treated Jewish Studies as both a respected institution and an instrument for outreach to a desired demographic. Such a complicated relationship between community and academy has long been endemic to Jewish Studies as a field, and in this instance, that relationship seems to have generated its own legacy and literature, along with new intellectual directions for understanding the intense connections between Jews, scholarship, and the arts.

The long-term impact of this era is yet to be fully determined in studies of creative expression and Judaism, though it has opened up new possibilities for configuring and expanding its study. Increasingly sophisticated research on the arts will hone our understanding of these important modes of discourse in

Jewish life and history. Still, studies of "creative Judaism" face ambivalence in some areas of Jewish Studies: their overlap with the practical nature of artistic endeavor and the difficulty associated with their translation into a standardized academic language remains a barrier. Nonetheless, efforts continue to bridge the areas' different methodological palettes, often in collaboration with other artists, in the hopes of exploring Judaism's creative and multisensory richness.

Notes

1. See, inter alia, Kalman P. Bland (2000), *The Artless Jew: Medieval and Modern Affirmations and Denials of the Visual*. Princeton: Princeton University Press and Michael Steinberg (2007), *Jews Musical and Unmusical*. Chicago: University of Chicago Press.
2. Recent examples of this kind of scholarship include Michael Brenner (1998), *The Renaissance of Jewish Culture in Weimar Germany*. New Haven: Yale University Press; Zachary Braiterman (2007), *The Shape of Revelation: Aesthetics and Modern Jewish Thought*. Palo Alto: Stanford University Press; Jonathan Freedman (2008), *Klezmer America*. New York: Columbia University Press; and Ken Koulton-Fromm (2010), *Material Culture and Jewish Thought*. Bloomington: Indiana University Press.
3. Israel Abrahams (1999), *Chapters on Jewish Literature*. Philadelphia: Jewish Publication Society of America.
4. David Stern (ed.) (2004), *The Anthology in Jewish Literature*. New York: Oxford University Press.
5. Stephen Katz (2009), *Red, Black and Jew: New Frontiers in Hebrew Literature*. Austin: The University of Texas Press; Rachel Rubenstein (2010), *Members of the Tribe: Native America in the Jewish Imagination*. Detroit: Wayne State University Press; Ethan Goffman (2000), *Imagining Each Other: Blacks and Jews in Contemporary American Literature*. Binghamton: SUNY Press; Nora Rubel (2010), *Doubting the Devout: The Ultra-Orthodox in the Jewish American Imagination*. New York: Columbia University Press, among many others.
6. David Heinrich von Müller, Julius von Schlosser, and David Kaufmann (1898), *Die Haggadah von Sarajevo: Eine spanisch-jüdische Bilderhandschrift des Mittelalters*. Vienna: Hölder.
7. See for example S. J. Solomon (1901), "Jews and Art," *Jewish Quarterly Review* 13:4: 553–66.
8. Dalia Manor (2005), *Art in Zion: The Genesis of Modern National Art in Jewish Palestine*. New York: Routledge.
9. See also Gideon Ofrat (1998), *One Hundred Years of Art in Israel*. New York: Basic Books.
10. Cecil Roth (ed.) (1961), *Jewish Art: An Illustrated History*. London: W. H. Allen, col. 30.
11. Richard I. Cohen (1998), *Jewish Icons: Art and Society in Modern Europe*. Berkeley: University of California Press, p. 8; see also Ezra Mendelsohn (2002), *Painting a People: Maurycy Gottlieb and Jewish Art*. Waltham: Brandeis University Press.
12. The Bar-Ilan program also published one special of *Timorah*, a Hebrew analog to *Ars Judaica*, in 2006.
13. Larry Silver and Samantha Baskind (2011), "Looking Jewish: The State of Research on Modern Jewish Art," *Jewish Quarterly Review* 101:4 (Fall): 631–52.
14. The ancient period has not been abandoned, however, as illustrated by Lee I. Levine (2002), "Art, Architecture, and Archaeology," in Martin Goodman and Jeremy Cohen

(eds), *The Oxford Handbook of Jewish Studies*. New York: Oxford University Press, pp. 824–51.

15. Matthew Baigell (2007), *Jewish Art in America: An Introduction*. Lanham: Rowman and Littlefield.

16. Samantha Baskind and Larry Silver (2011), *Jewish Art: A Modern History*. London: Reaktion Books, p. 13.

17. Steven Fine (2005), *Art and Judaism in the Greco-Roman World: Toward a New Jewish Archeology*. New York: Cambridge University Press. This work has continued Fine's exploration of Jewish/Greek/Roman interaction dating back to the late 1980s.

18. See also Maya Balakirsky Katz (2010), *The Visual Culture of Chabad*. New York: Cambridge University Press.

19. Raphael Patai (1946), "Problems and Tasks of Jewish Folklore and Ethnology," *Journal of American Folklore* 59:231: 25–39.

20. See also Dan Ben-Amos (1991), "Jewish Folklore Studies," *Modern Judaism* 11:1: 17–66.

21. Eli Yassif (2009), *The Hebrew Folktale: History, Genre, Meaning*. Bloomington: Indiana University Press; Dan Ben-Amos (ed.) (2006–11), *Folktales of the Jews*. New York: Jewish Publication Society. 3 Vols.

22. Barbara Kirshenblatt-Gimblett (2007), *They Called Me Mayer July: Painted Memories of a Jewish Childhood before the Holocaust*. Berkeley: University of California Press.

23. Judith Brin Ingber (2011), "Coming into Focus," in Judith Brin Ingber (ed.), *Seeing Israeli and Jewish Dance*. Detroit: Wayne State University Press, p. 1.

24. Fred Berk (1960), *The Jewish Dance: An Anthology of Articles*. New York: Exposition Press.

25. Ruth Eshel (1991), *Dancing with the Dream: Art Dance in Israel, 1920–1964*. Tel Aviv: ha-Sifriya le-Mahol be-Yisrael.

26. B. Goren (1923), *Di geshikhte fun yidishn teater*. New York: Max N. Mayzel, for example.

27. Edna Nahshon (1998), *Yiddish Proletarian Theater: The Art and Politics of the Artef, 1925–1940*. Westport: Greenwood Press; Jeffrey Veidlinger (2000), *The Moscow State Yiddish Theater: Jewish Culture on the Soviet Stage*. Bloomington: Indiana University Press; Olga Gershenson (2005), *Gesher: Russian Theater in Israel*. New York: Peter Lang.

28. Robert Skloot (1988), *The Darkness We Carry: The Drama of the Holocaust*. Madison: University of Wisconsin Press; Gene Plunka (2011), *Holocaust Drama: The Theater of Atrocity*. Cambridge: Cambridge University Press.

29. Edna Nahshon (2005), *From the Ghetto to the Melting Pot: Israel Zangwill's Jewish Plays*. Detroit: Wayne State University Press; Ellen Shiff (1995), *Awake and Singing: Seven Classic Plays from the American Jewish Repertoire*. New York: Signet.

30. Edna Nahshon (ed.) (2011), *Jewish Theater: a Global View*. Leiden: Brill; (2011), *The Drama Review* 55:3 (Fall): Special issue on Jewish American performance, coedited by Jill Dolan and Stacy Wolf.

31. See Moshe Zimmerman (2002), "Jewish and Israeli Film Studies," in Martin Goodman (ed.), *The Oxford Handbook of Jewish Studies*. New York: Oxford University Press, pp. 911–42.

32. Patricia Erens (1984), *The Jew in American Cinema*. Bloomington: Indiana University Press; Lester Friedman (1987), *The Jewish Image in American Film*. Secaucus, NJ: Citadel Press.

33. Joel Rosenberg (1996), "The Jewish Experience on Film: An American Overview," *American Jewish Year Book* 96: 3–50.

34. Omer Bartov (2005), *The "Jew" in Cinema: From the Golem to Don't Touch My Holocaust*. Bloomington: Indiana University Press; Judith E. Donseon (1987), *The Holocaust in American Film*. Philadelphia: Jewish Publication Society.

35. Yosefa Loshitzky (ed.) (1997), *Schindler's Holocaust: Critical Perspectives on Schindler's List*. Bloomington: Indiana University Press.
36. Vincent Brook (2009), *Driven to Darkness: Jewish Emigré Directors and the Rise of Film Noir*. New Brunswick: Rutgers University Press.
37. Ella Shohat (1989), *Israeli Cinema: East/West and the Politics of Representation*. Austin: University of Texas Press; Amy Kronish and Costel Safirman (2003), *Israeli Film: A Reference Guide*. Westport: Praeger; Nir Cohen (2004), *Beyond Flesh: Queer Masculinities and Nationalism in Israeli Cinema*. New Brunswick: Rutgers University Press; Miri Talmon and Yossi Peleg (eds) (2011), *Israeli Cinema: Identities in Motion*. Austin: University of Texas Press.
38. Alisa Lebow (2008), *First Person Jewish*. Minneapolis: University of Minnesota Press.
39. See, for example, Mikel Koven (1999), "'You Don't Have to be Filmish': The Toronto Jewish Film Festival," *Ethnologies* 21:1: 115–32.
40. Lawrence Baron (ed.) (2011), *The Modern Jewish Experience in World Cinema*. Hanover: Brandeis University Press; Nathan Abrams (2011), *The New Jew in Film*. New Brunswick: Rutgers University Press.
41. Jonathan Boyarin (1993), "Voices around the Text: The Ethnography of Reading at Mesivta Tifereth Jerusalem," in Jonathan Boyarin (ed.), *The Ethnography of Reading*. Berkeley: University of California Press, pp. 212–37; Jeremy Stolow (2010), *Orthodox by Design: Judaism, Print Politics, and the ArtScroll Revolution*. Berkeley: University of California Press; Ari Kelman (2009), *Station Identification: A Cultural History of Yiddish Radio in the United States*. Berkeley: University of California Press; Jeffrey Shandler (2000), *While America Watches: Televising the Holocaust*. New York: Oxford University Press.
42. Vincent Brook (ed.) (2006), *You Should See Yourself!: Jewish Identity in Postmodern American Culture*. New Brunswick: Rutgers University Press; (2007) *Material Religion* 3:3: Special Issue: Material Cultures of American Jewry; Samantha Baskind and Ranen Omer-Sherman (eds) (2010), *The Jewish Graphic Novel: Critical Approaches*. New Brunswick: Rutgers University Press; Jeffrey Shandler and Barbara Kirshenblatt-Gimblett (eds) (2012), *Anne Frank Unbound: Media, Imagination, Memory*. Bloomington: Indiana University Press; Judah M. Cohen (2009), "Hip Hop Judaica: Representin' Heebster Heritage," *Popular Music* 28:1: 1–18; The Modiya Project (http://modiya. nyu.edu).
43. Martin Goodman (ed.) (2002), *The Oxford Handbook of Jewish Studies*. New York: Oxford University.
44. David Biale (ed.) (2002), *The Cultures of the Jews: A New History*. New York: Schocken.
45. Barbara Kirshenblatt-Gimblett and Jonathan Karp (2007), *The Art of Being Jewish in Modern Times*. Philadelphia: University of Pennsylvania Press.
46. http://conneyproject.wisc.edu/about/.
47. Among the numerous studies commissioned by these groups is Steven M. Cohen and Ari Y. Kelman (2007), *The Continuity of Discontinuity: How Young Jews Are Connecting, Creating, and Organizing Their Own Jewish Lives*. New York: 21/64 [commissioned by the Andrea and Charles Bronfman Foundation].

12 Jewish Demography: Discipline, Definitions, Data, Investigators, Interpretations

Sergio DellaPergola

Chapter Outline

Introduction: Demography and Jews

Demography[1] is the statistical study of human population.[2] With its inductive-deductive, theory-informed, and fact-dependent approach, demography as a discipline is centrally positioned in the sphere of the social sciences and constitutes a natural bridge between disciplines in the humanities and the natural sciences. Jewish demography[3]—the specialized study of Jewish population characteristics and trends—operates within the distinctive parameters of the general discipline applying, if anything, a somewhat expanded investigative scope to a more narrowly focused research subject. Over time, the study of

Jewish demography has attracted significant amounts of scholarship as well as public debate. Such extended interest often touched upon specific and limited aspects of Jewish population trends globally and locally, but it also sometimes addressed the whole gamut of past, present, and future connections between an unfolding Jewish *population* and the underlying existence of a Jewish *peoplehood*. The concept of a *population* refers to an aggregate of individuals falling under one definition, but not necessarily linked by meaningful mutual relations. The concept of *peoplehood* implies a deeper layer of voluntary interconnectedness among the relevant individuals. Some of these linkages between an amorphous aggregate of individual Jews, and a socially meaningful representation of the collective, were solidly grounded on scientific research; some tended to express merely ideational propensities and states of mind; and some offered intriguing blends of both.

Major predicaments emerged in relation to defining the subject matter of Jewish population studies, the boundaries of the Jewish collective at the global and local level, the quality of the data, the nature of the principal investigators, their backgrounds and commitments, and the main interpretative directions and implications of investigative work. These issues are dealt with in this essay in some detail, followed by short mention of the two substantive areas that have attracted most of the recent discussions and disagreements: evaluating the demographic trends of Jews in the United States in their broader identificational context, and appraising the demographic trends of Jews in Israel within the broader Middle Eastern sociopolitical context.

The Discipline of Demography

The preoccupation with, and art of counting, the Jews, describing their characteristics, analyzing their developments, and even projecting their future—commonly known as the core issues of Jewish demography—is as old as the Bible.[4] Since the outset, Jewish population studies always had to cope with the possible interference between pure and neutral research, and ulterior motive. In the modern era, since Leopold Zunz in the 1820s,[5] through Abraham Moses Luncz in the last quarter of the nineteenth century,[6] Jewish population studies not only dealt with methodological and substantive research, but also reflected the widely differing intellectual backgrounds of the scholars themselves. Under the broad umbrella of demography, many different topics came under the scrutiny of specialists and practitioners. The same topics more often attracted the attention of publicists, community activists, and sometimes motivated the work of planners and policy makers. These topics included estimating the number of Jews; assessing their rate of growth versus other populations; anthropological similarity or dissimilarity within what was the long held credo of race; health and behavioral patterns involving the respective merits of mutable environment versus inherited character; and the role of the Jews in the national society and economy. What was often clear was the existence of persisting differences between Jewish and non-Jewish marriage, fertility and mortality levels, composition by age and marital status, geographical and socioeconomic mobility, and social structure and occupational skills. Quite different and unique patterns were detected of Jewish population growth or decline, concentration and dispersion among the broader population, and socio-demographic structure.[7] These studies often served as baseline tools to shape idealistic analyses and concrete programs for the improvement and promotion of the Jewish condition and fate.[8]

As against the determinist explanations of earlier researchers in the biological and social sciences,[9] and facing widespread forms of anti-Jewish prejudice in society, one important thread developed by later scholars was the effort to provide the apparently unique characteristics of the Jews with rational and systematic explanation.[10] Another main theme intertwined with scholarly research was the preoccupation of sustaining Jewish continuity as against perceived threats from the outside, such as physical violence, or from the inside, such as a loss of cultural identity and community cohesion.[11] The early study of Jewish demography was often strictly related to the study of physical anthropology. Later, the relationship between population characteristics and cultural identity tended to occupy a more central place in Jewish demographic studies. In the more recent period, the growing volatility and emotionality of some of the issues dealt in the realm of Jewish demography tended to generate more eclectic materials, focused on particular contents and policy implications rather than on broader conceptualization and method. In this context, it would seem useful for those engaged in the substantive discussion to agree on some common procedural grounds. But a perusal of relevant research and publicist literature clearly shows that this was not the case.

One of the reasons for such analytical diffusion is the somewhat unbounded contour of demography itself as a discipline. As with any discipline, population studies constitute an ever-expanding body of accumulated knowledge, theories and hypotheses, analytic tools and techniques, empirical observations usually synthesized in the form of quantitative data, and emerging policy options and directions. In terms of subject matter, as noted, demography is an empirical discipline at the crossroads of the social sciences and the humanities. But in order to produce its verifiable results demography also draws from methods and hypotheses originally developed for the natural sciences, with an important input from mathematical statistics.

The multidisciplinary nature of demography/population studies is one of its major strengths, but may also turn into one of its perceived weaknesses. As a discipline and profession, the subject is not usually taught in the framework of a separate university department but as part of a broader program—mostly in sociology or statistics.[12] Even more debatable is a specialization in Jewish demography which—with the possible exception of receiving some attention at the Hebrew University—did not rise, nor pretend to rise, to the status of an independent field within a certain discipline (in the footsteps of the widely practiced separate status of Jewish history vs. history, or Jewish thought vs. philosophy). Jewish demography mostly evolved at the borderline between the social sciences and Jewish studies.

Demography substantively deals with the fundamentals of human behavior, some quantifiable, others better appreciated in qualitative terms. At the core of demography stand the basic facts of the lifecycle: birth, death, household composition, living in a certain place at a certain time, and moving from place to place. Demography of a specific group also essentially involves sharing one's group identification with others, or shifting from one particular group identification to another. Demographic trends thus concern human development all along the basic lifecycle processes and stages, as well as a significant amount of widespread interactions with other aspects of social life—from the basically biologic through the environmentally acquired, the cultural and the socioeconomic. As such, in general as in the Jewish case, demographic variables powerfully reflect and affect the internal fabric of relations within a given society or community, as well as mutual relations between societies or communities.

Naturally, any serious discussion of Jewish demographic trends should proceed from understanding the broader processes that generally determine the development of a population. Population is a collective, macro-social concept, but its changes reflect events that mostly occur at the individual, micro-social level. All changes in world population size result from the simple balance between births (reflecting fertility levels and a population's age composition) and deaths (reflecting life expectancy and age composition). When a population is considered within a definite geographical area where in- and out-migration is possible, such geographical mobility must be accounted. And when a population is also defined by culturally determined characteristics (such as religion, ethnicity, language, or other divisions), a somewhat more complex *balancing equation* becomes necessary to express population change over time. The important underlying principle is the continuity of a human population that is not created from a vacuum (besides quite rare cases of *ethnogenesis*—the initial act of a new group coming into existence) but constantly evolves in the longer term following a circumscribed set of drivers.

The principal factors at work are specified in Figure 12.1, which outlines the main drivers of change, the intervening operational variables of population change, and the final product in terms of Jewish population size and composition. It should be noted that demography of the Jews may serve, and has served, as a paradigm for the more general case of subpopulations whose existence and development over time is determined not only by demographic-biological factors, but also by cultural-ideational factors.

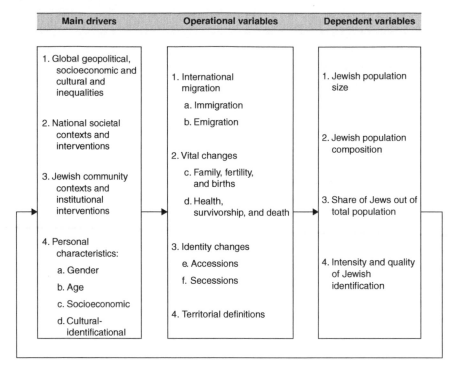

Figure 12.1 Main Determinants of Jewish Demographic and Identificational Change

Four main measures, or dependent variables, each alone or better in combination, allow for an evaluation of Jewish population trends: (1) Jewish population *size*; (2) Jewish population *composition*; (3) Jewish *share* out of total population; and (4) the *intensity and quality* of Jewish identification and interactions.

Each of these dependent variables at a given point in time reflects the status of the same variable at an earlier point in time, plus the impact of six intervening operational variables over the span of time considered: (1) *vital changes*, which comprise marriage and fertility levels, affecting the *birth rate*,[13] and health and survivorship, affecting the *death rate*;[14] (2) *migration*, which comprises *immigration*[15] and *emigration*[16] between different areas—whether international or internal; (3) *identificational changes*, which comprise the balance of *accessions* to Judaism[17] and *secessions* from Judaism[18]—often, but not exclusively, dealt with under the heading of "conversions."

The impact of each of these factors can be of varying magnitude at different stages of a population's history. In the case of world Jewry, the frequencies of birth rates, death rates, migrations into and out of an area, and conversions to and from Judaism have undergone drastic variations in the course of history. Demographic events occurred and occur at times because of the individual actors' determined decisions, and at times because of circumstances beyond the free will of the individuals concerned. Often, changes reflected the scope and balance of external factors that were forced upon Jews, as well as internal factors that operated from within the Jewish community itself.

A seventh factor should be added to the six main operational variables of population change, not related to personal transformation but rather to the corporate environment. Changes in the *territorial boundaries* within which a given Jewish population lives may play an important role in determining its size, characteristics, relative weight versus the surrounding population, and identificational quality. Several examples in history concern boundary changes and the passage of territories inhabited by Jews from one power to another—such as the partition of Poland, the creation of the Pale of Settlement in the late eighteenth century, or the definition and redefinition of the State of Israel's boundaries relative to the total territory of Palestine that was under British Mandate jurisdiction until 1948.

Each component of demographic change influences the various age cohorts in a population in different and specific ways. Age, in turn, functions as a powerful intermediary referent, synthesizing past demographic change and significantly affecting the likelihood of future demographic events and overall population change. It is therefore necessary to disaggregate the whole demographic process into its various component parts—vital events, geographical mobility, identity shifts—as much as possible in order to reach a deeper understanding of the mode of operating and effects of each component separately. It is also necessary to obtain information on population trends and composition according to sex, age, and other relevant characteristics that can influence the likelihood of a certain event occurring to a given person. At the same time, other important transformative mechanisms within a given population, such as lifecycle transitions of personal status, educational attainment, social stratification and mobility, welfare policies, and cultural persuasions, may generate further significant changes in the socio-demographic profile of a population. Population characteristics and the components of population change stand in tight mutual relationship. Analyses that ignore these basic relationships spread over time, thus basically "inventing" a population disconnected from its continuously evolving context, do not help much to advance our understanding of the issues—hence the advancement of the research field.

Definitions

Studying the Jew's socio-demographic characteristics and trends requires in the first place some conceptual grounding concerning the nature of the main variable of reference. Therefore, before addressing the more famous "Who is a Jew?" issue, we need to briefly address the question "What are the Jews?" Jews are posited here as one modality within the broader class of groups defined by *religious, ethnic, geographic, cultural,* or more broadly *civilizational identities,* often abridged in the research literature under the rubric of *ethnicity.* But it should be clarified that the answer to the question may be different according to the disciplinary approach adopted. In the dialectics between boundary and contents,[19] demography, as we shall argue, would primarily insist on boundary, that is population size, while acknowledging the mutual relationship between the two dimensions of population size and characteristics. Sociology, anthropology, and social psychology would mostly focus on contents, that is norms, values, and behaviors, while not neglecting the mutual relationship between these personal interactions and collective social space.[20] Population genetics — especially after the breakthrough of human genome's sequencing — would try to uncover boundary-contents correlations at the basic DNA, that is chemical-biological level without addressing issues of culture, collective values, and personal identification.[21]

From a demographic perspective, then, scholarly debates suggest four main approaches regarding the referent variable's basic nature and societal role. In the particular case of the Jewish group, these approaches may be defined as: (1) *maximizing*: viewing Jewish populations as the largest possible conglomerate of all populations that can be defined through one or more criteria possessing any pertinence or affinity with a Jewish category of any sort;[22] (2) *consolidationist*: viewing Jewish populations as discrete objects for conceptual definition and empirical measurement based on coherent and comparable criteria;[23] (3) *situational*: viewing Jewish populations as groups that can be recognized and studied at a given point in time but not really quantified in the longer term — the elusive product of ever-changing exogenous and endogenous circumstances and attitudes;[24] (4) *manipulative*: viewing Jewish collectives as lacking historical continuity and essentially generated by the calculated interventions of elites or special interest groups, hence lacking serious claim to empirical reality or even legitimacy.[25]

Mainly out of a *consolidationist* point of view, and paying due attention to the *situational* claim, we maintain that Jewish communities in the Diaspora and in Israel in the past or present do constitute a target for empirical investigation. Jewish populations are composed of people, accordingly, who are identifiable to specified, multiple criteria for inclusion and exclusion, featuring definite individual perceptions of group boundaries and collective identities, and unique and recognizable patterns of social and demographic composition and mobility. This paradigm suggests a powerful, relevant, and necessary approach to establishing the theoretical and empirical foundations to scientific investigation and public discourse on Jewish population.

A major challenge that unavoidably ensues when considering Jewish population studies is the definition of the boundaries of the collective — in itself one and not the least of the topics for empirical investigation, as well as a factor of empirical uncertainty and internal conflict. The paradigmatic "Who is a Jew?" question constitutes an ever-elusive issue in Jewish population studies. A major problem bedeviling Jewish population estimates available in the literature, whether by individual scholars or by Jewish organizations, is a lack of coherence and uniformity in the definitional criteria they follow.[26]

Jewish population estimates may rely on *normative* or on *operational* definitions. Traditional halakhah (Jewish rabbinical law) provides a clear and authoritative normative definition of who is a Jew, long—though not in an earlier past[27]—based on matrilineal descent and codified rules for cooptation better known as *conversion*. Alternatives stemming from the adoption of a patrilineal definition in the attribution of a Jewish identity, while admittedly competing with traditional halakhah, remain essentially normative in that they still offer positive and determinate criteria for determining one's Jewishness—even as they part with traditional formulations. However, in empirical research, it is not possible to undertake the stringent controls involved in ascertaining each individual's Jewish identity according to such criteria because they would be overwhelmingly costly and time consuming. Therefore, Jewish populations are usually identified in censuses or surveys through operational criteria, such as the more or less accurate proxies offered by generally elective individual responses to simply precoded variables like *religion* or *ethnic origin*, or based on indirect and rougher information such as countries of origin, languages, and the like.[28]

One important complicating factor in contemporary population definitions is the increasing frequency of out-marriage. Intermarriage generates a growing number of individuals whose Jewish identification is one among their several possible or shared ancestries. Moreover, such personal Jewish identities may become the object of controversy between different religious or legal authorities. Consequently, many eligible individuals may not know whether, when, or how to identify as Jewish, and may prefer not to. Others do not deem their Jewishness mutually exclusive with other religious or ethnic identities, in contrast with the normative assumption that Jewish identity is incompatible with other religious identities. Many more do not deem it important to the point of feeling compelled to declare it.

Appropriate appraisals of Jewish population trends thus require addressing the broadest possible definition of the collective so as to capture the full dynamics of ongoing change. Yet, to meaningfully address a population, we need working definitions. Definitions imply certain standards, the alternative being an amorphous approach unable to generate analytic conclusions of any sort. Data collectors should allow for wide and flexible analytic opportunities for data users who within the broadest possible initial definition may later decide on more restrictive definitional typologies according to their own assumptions and research goals.

A major problem with Jewish population estimates produced by individual scholars or Jewish organizations concerns the lack of uniformity in definitional criteria—when the issue of defining the Jewish population is addressed at all. The study of a Jewish population (or of any other population subgroup) requires undergoing three main steps and solving the respective problems: (1) *defining* the target group on the basis of conceptual or normative criteria aimed at providing the best possible description of that group—which in the case of Jewry is no minor task in itself; (2) *identifying* the group thus defined based on tools that operationally allow for distinguishing and selecting the target group from the rest of the population—through membership lists, surnames, areas of residence, or other random or nonrandom procedures; and (3) *covering* the target group through appropriate field work—in person face-to-face, by telephone, by internet, or otherwise.

Most often in the actual experience of social research, the definitional task is performed at the stage of identification, and the identificational task is performed at the stage of actual fieldwork. It thus clearly appears that the quantitative study of Jewish populations only relies on *operational*, not *normative*, definitional criteria. Its conceptual aspects, far from pure theory, heavily depend on practical and logistical feasibility.

The ultimate empirical step—obtaining relevant data from relevant persons—crucially reflects the readiness of people to cooperate in the data collection effort. In recent years, as survey-cooperation rates have decreased, the amount, content, and validity of information gathered has been affected detrimentally. These declining cooperation rates, besides more general causes, also reflect the identification outlook of the persons who are part of the target population—that outlook which is itself an integral part of the investigation. No method exists to break this vicious cycle. Therefore, research findings reflect, with varying degrees of sophistication, only that which is possible to uncover. Anything that cannot be uncovered directly can sometimes be indirectly estimated through various imperfect techniques. Beyond that, we enter the virtual world of myths, hopes, fears, and corporate interests. To the extent that some of these claims lack empirical backing, no way exists to demonstrate their actual nature—at least not within the limits of a nonfictional investigation such as inherent in demographic work.

Keeping this in mind, three major definitional concepts have been suggested to help provide solid comparative foundations to the study of Jewish demography, in historical perspective, and more cogently in the present (Figure 12.2).

Today, in most Diaspora countries, the concept of a *core Jewish population*[29] includes all persons who, when asked in a socio-demographic survey, identify themselves as Jews; who are identified as Jews by a respondent in the same household; or who have Jewish parentage and are identificationally indifferent

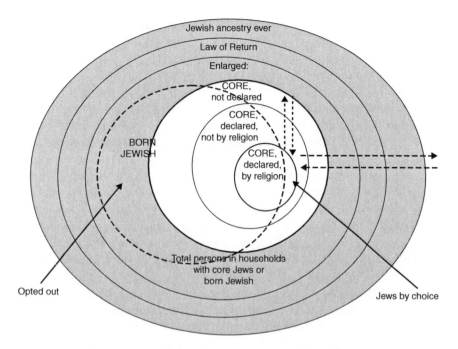

Figure 12.2 Defining Contemporary Jewish Populations

or agnostic, but do not formally identify with another monotheistic religion. Such a definition of a person as a Jew, reflecting *subjective* perceptions, broadly overlaps but does not necessarily coincide with halakhah or other normatively binding definitions. Inclusion does *not* depend on any measure of that person's Jewish commitment or behavior in terms of religiosity, beliefs, knowledge, communal affiliation, or otherwise. The *core Jewish population* includes primarily those who define themselves as Jews by religion. But as Judaism cannot be reduced to a solely religious concept, a second component of the core is Jews who define themselves as such by ethnicity or nationality or culture, outside a religious concept. All of these together form the more visible *declared* part of the core. But there are further individuals who, when asked, would not immediately unveil their Jewish identity, although they are the descendants of Jewish parents and do not possess an alternative identity. These *undeclared core* individuals can be detected with the help of inquiring in greater detail about the interviewee's parentage and childhood. It is important to note that, reflecting the increasingly fluid character of contemporary identities, there can be continuous and frequent passages of individuals moving in both directions between the more consolidated and declared part, and the undeclared part of the core Jewish population.

As just noted, it is customary to include in the *core* Jewish population persons of Jewish parentage who claim no current religious or ethnic identity. The *core* also includes all converts to Judaism, regardless of the conversion procedure they may have followed, as well as other people who declare they are Jewish even without conversion. On the other hand, persons of Jewish parentage who have formally adopted another monotheistic religion are usually excluded, as are persons who in censuses or socio-demographic surveys explicitly identify with a non-Jewish religious group without having formally converted out.

The *core* concept therefore offers an intentionally comprehensive and pragmatic approach, basically relying on self-assessment and reflecting the nature of most available Jewish population data sources. In the Diaspora, such data often derive from population censuses or socio-demographic surveys where interviewees have the option to decide how to answer relevant questions on religious or ethnic identities. In Israel, personal status is subject to the rulings of the Ministry of the Interior, which relies on criteria established by rabbinic authorities and by the Israeli Supreme Court.[30] In Israel, therefore, the *core* Jewish population does not simply express subjective identification but reflects definite legal rules. This entails matrilineal Jewish origin, or conversion to Judaism, and not holding another religion. Documentation to prove a person's Jewish status may include non-Jewish sources.

The question of whether *core* Jewish identification can or should be mutually exclusive with other religious and/or ethnic identities is a major bone of contention. The issue emerged on a major scale for American Jews in the course of developing and analysing the 2000–1 National Jewish Population Survey (NJPS 2000–1). The solution preferred by the National Advisory Technical Committee (NTAC)—after much debate—was to allow for Jews with multiple religious identities to be included under certain circumstances in the *core* Jewish population definition. This resulted in a rather multilayered definition of the United States Jewish population.[31] A category of *Persons of Jewish Background* (PJBs) also was introduced by NJPS 2000–1. Some PJBs were included in the *core* Jewish population count and others were not, based on a thorough evaluation of each individual ancestry and childhood.

Following the same logic, persons with multiple ethnic identities, including a Jewish one, have been included in Jewish population counts for Canada. The adoption of such extended criteria by the research community tends to stretch Jewish population definitions with an expansive effect on Jewish population size beyond usual practices in the past and beyond the limits of the typical *core* definition. These procedures may respond to local needs and sensitivities but tend to limit the actual comparability of the same Jewish population over time and of different Jewish populations at one given time.

The *enlarged Jewish population*[32] includes the sum of (a) the *core* Jewish population; (b) all other persons of Jewish parentage who—by *core* Jewish population criteria—are *not* Jewish at the time of investigation (non-Jews with Jewish background); and (c) all respective non-Jewish members (spouses, children, etc.) in mixed religious households.

Non-Jews with *Jewish background*, as far as they can be ascertained, include: (a) persons who have adopted another religion, or otherwise opted out, although they may claim to be *also* Jewish by ethnicity or in some other way—with the caveat just mentioned for recent United States and Canadian data; and (b) other persons with Jewish parentage who disclaim being Jewish. As noted, most PJBs who are not part of the *core* Jewish population naturally belong under the *enlarged* definition.[33]

It is customary in socio-demographic surveys to consider the religio-ethnic identification of parents. Some censuses, however, *do* ask about more distant ancestry. For both conceptual and practical reasons, the *enlarged* definition usually does not include other non-Jewish relatives who lack a Jewish background and live in exclusively non-Jewish households. Historians might wish to engage in the study of the number of Jews who *ever* lived and how many persons today are the descendants of those Jews—for example conversos who lived in the Iberian Peninsula during the Middle Ages and whose descendants may be numerous today in Mediterranean, Central, and South American countries. The ancient Jewish backgrounds of some currently non-Jewish population groups have been uncovered in recent studies of population genetics.[34] These long-term Jewish roots attract growing interest as a topic for analysis and also for the purposes and mandate of some Jewish organizations which actively operate to bring back to Judaism what they call the Lost Tribes.[35]

The *Law of Return*, Israel's distinctive legal framework for the acceptance and absorption of new immigrants, awards Jewish new immigrants immediate citizenship and other civil rights. According to the current, amended version of the *Law of Return*,[36] a Jew is any person born to a Jewish mother or converted to Judaism (regardless of denomination—Orthodox, Conservative, or Reform), who does not have another religious identity. By ruling of Israel's Supreme Court, conversion from Judaism, as in the case of some ethnic Jews who currently identify with another religion, entails loss of eligibility for *Law of Return* purposes. The Falash Mura—a group of Ethiopian non-Jews of Jewish ancestry—must undergo conversion to be eligible for the *Law of Return*, even if such conversion sometimes occurs after they have actually immigrated to Israel. The law as such does not affect a person's Jewish status—which, as noted, is adjudicated by Israel's Ministry of Interior and rabbinic authorities—but only the specific benefits available under the *Law of Return*. This law extends its provisions to all current Jews, their children, and grandchildren, as well as to their respective Jewish or non-Jewish spouses. As a result of its three-generation and lateral extension, the *Law of Return* applies to a large *aliyah eligible* population whose scope is significantly wider than the *core* and *enlarged* Jewish populations defined above.[37] It is actually quite difficult to estimate the possible total size of the *Law of Return* extant population.

Similarly to the fluidity that may characterize the positioning of Jewish individuals within the different circles that form the core population, there may be increasing two-way identificational migrations all across the *core, enlarged, Law of Return* domains, and between inside and outside them. What once upon a time was not conceivable—that a person may feel Jewish one day and non-Jewish another day—can today occur and has in fact been documented by those who have been involved in survey fieldwork.[38] This logically determines an ever-changing personal composition of the different analytic categories just outlined, although it affects to a lesser extent the very existence and mutual relationship of those Jewish population categories as such.

Several major Jewish organizations in Israel and the United States—such as the quasi-governmental Jewish Agency for Israel, the global social-service oriented American Jewish Joint Distribution Committee (JDC), or the Jewish Federations of North America (formerly UJC and CJF)—have sponsored data collection and tend to influence the rules of research rendering them more complex and policy sensitive. Organizations are motivated by their mission toward their respectively perceived constituencies rather than by pure scientific research criteria. In turn, the understandable interest of Jewish organizations to function and secure budgetary resources typically influences them toward defining Jewish target populations increasingly similar to the *enlarged* and *Law of Return* definitions rather than to the *core* definition. Some socio-demographic surveys, by investigating people who *were born* or were *raised* or are *currently* Jewish, may have envisaged a population that *ever* was Jewish, regardless of its present identification.

In spite of these growing complexities, the *core* definition is the necessary starting point for any elaboration about the *enlarged* definition or broader definitions such as the *Law of Return*. But it is also true that the distinction between the cluster of Jews and others who share their daily lives in the same households corresponds to trying to trace virtual boundaries where in reality such distinctions have become increasingly flexible, porous, and interchangeable. A great amount of latitude hence characterizes the definitional solutions adopted in socio-demographic research, with obvious consequences for the ensuing population counts and their policy implications. Unfortunately, these various definitional concepts are often confused, which makes the comparison and discussion of trends increasingly confused. It should be noted that a given *enlarged* Jewish population may be growing at the same time that the respective *core* Jewish population is declining.

The question remains of how to define the present Jewish population in coherent and meaningful ways. We remain with a significant, growing amount of ambivalence in the definition of the collective whose profile and transformations research is supposed to unveil. It is legitimate to posit that these difficulties pinpoint the challenges inherent in the effort to conceptually synthesize the observation of Jewish peoplehood. The empirical Jewish population equivalent of *Klal Israel*—the normative Jewish collective—implies not only a given aggregate of people, no matter how well technically defined, but also the bonds of mutual responsibility that provide it contemporary meaning and long-term resilience. The better and sounder research strategy, however, seems to create a set of alternative definitions and to provide the empirical evidence that will allow the investigations appropriate to each of those definitions. If individual investigators will carry the responsibility of explaining their own choices, the possibility of meaningful comparisons across the gamut of possible plausible definitions will be preserved.

Data

Data on population size, characteristics, and trends are a primary tool in the evaluation of Jewish demography, and consequently of community needs and prospects at the local, national, and international level. In modern historical experience, the database for the study of Jewish demography has been a mixed and complementary pool of state-sponsored data collections—mainly through national and local censuses and vital statistics records—and independent data collection initiatives sponsored a large variety of public and private organizations, namely by Jewish organizations often in collaboration with scholarly bodies.

From the Jewish side, there were successful efforts to create stable institutional bases for research and a systematic output of studies. One important example in the late 1920s were the *Bureau fuer Juedische Statistik* in Berlin and its publication *Zeitschrift fuer Demografie und Statistik der Juden*, or YIVO and its *Bleter far Yidishe Demografye, Statistik un Ekonomik*, where mostly European Jewish social scientists started confronting the whole range of issues related to the broad subject matter and its implications for Jewish society. The Shoah and the destruction of European Jewry caused a tremendous impediment to the available demographic documentation about Jews, because most of the communities destroyed lived in countries with an established tradition to document religious and ethnic origins of the population. Moreover, the flow of Jewish migrations led to the strengthening of communities in countries like the United States or France, where, because of the separation between church and state, no such documentation was legally allowed.

After World War II, Israel's Central Bureau of Statistics and the Hebrew University of Jerusalem played a central role in promoting the study of Jewish population. The former—long headed by Roberto Bachi who built it upon the foundations of the British Mandate's Palestine Department of Statistics—since inception has represented the state's central authority for data collection and processing. While an integral part of Israel's government, CBS was able to establish a solid and respected reputation of independence from political pressure. The Israeli component of world Jewry was growing from quite a small to a very large size and share of the global total, hence in a global perspective increasing numbers of Jews were covered by sound demographic documentation. Moreover, Israeli data provided important insights on the characteristics of Jews who previously had lived in other countries. The Hebrew University—through the *Division of Jewish Demography and Statistics* at the Institute of Contemporary Jewry (ICJ; established by Bachi with the help of Oscar Schmelz in 1959) and its publications series *Jewish Population Studies* (reaching 29 published volumes and numerous occasional reports)—was instrumental in creating a central database and library stressing more rigorous criteria about the definitional paradigm, the investigative tools, and a global-comparative analytic framework.[39]

Some of the more important institution-building efforts in Jewish population research occurred in the United States. The *Bureau of Jewish Statistics* long headed by Harry Linfield published its findings in the *American Jewish Year Book*. The AJYB (1899–2008)—sponsored by the *American Jewish Committee*—offered a central podium for its own research, largely consisting of systematic documentation of Jewish life in the United States, as well as for American and other researchers to disseminate independent and innovative analyses of current Jewish affairs globally. The stopping of AJYB publication in 2008 represented one of the saddest landmarks in a rapidly changing Jewish institutional landscape in the United States and internationally. The research division of the Council of Jewish Federations (CJF)—later United Jewish Communities (UJC), currently the Jewish Federations of North America—provided systematic updates on Jewish population spread and change all across the United States locales. The *North American Jewish Data Bank* (NAJDB), born at the initiative of Mandell Berman in the fold of the Federations with the scientific sponsorship of Brandeis University and the Hebrew University's ICJ, later moved from New York to Brandeis, and finally found a permanent seat at the University of Connecticut at Storrs.[40] Brandeis established the *Steinhardt Social Research Institute* (SSRI) at the *Maurice and Marilyn Cohen Center for Jewish Studies*[41]—currently, in terms of budget and manpower probably the largest academic institution specialized in Jewish social scientific research. The *Association for the Social Scientific Study of Jewry* (ASSJ) reunites many of the mostly American experts and practitioners in the field, publishes the journal *Contemporary Jewry*, and awards the coveted Marshall Sklare prize.

Over the past decades, the efforts to clarify the worldwide Jewish demographic picture have expanded significantly. Some coordinated work aimed at studying scientifically the demography of contemporary world Jewry benefited from the collaboration of scholars and institutions in many countries.[42] Worth mentioning are the efforts initiated by the Jewish Agency through its Demographic Initiative at the beginning of the 2000s,[43] and the subsequent foundation and activity of the Jewish People Policy Institute (JPPI, formerly JPPPI).[44]

It should be emphasized, however, that the elaboration of truly comparable estimates for the Jewish populations of the various countries is beset with difficulties and uncertainties.[45] The problem of data consistency is particularly acute given the very different legal systems and organizational provisions under which Jewish communities operate in different countries. The basic typology must refer to: (a) whether or not a country conducts a national population census including a category *Jewish* or similar in one of the census variables;[46] (b) whether or not a country holds a central national population register with such a category; (c) whether or not a country has a central Jewish community organization, or a set of smaller communities somewhat coordinated by a central Jewish body, whose membership covers the vast majority of existing Jews. Today, the situation is highly variable country by country, but it should be stressed that two of the largest Jewish populations in the world, in the United States and France, live in countries where none of the above conditions exist. In spite of keen efforts to create a unified analytic framework for Jewish population studies, users of Jewish population estimates should be aware of these difficulties, of the inherent limitations, and of the paradox of the *permanently provisional* character of Jewish population estimates.[47]

While the quantity and quality of documentation on Jewish population size and characteristics are far from satisfactory, over the past 20 years important new data and estimates were released for several countries through official population censuses and Jewish-sponsored socio-demographic surveys. Updated information on Jewish population became available following the major round of national censuses and Jewish socio-demographic surveys in countries with large Jewish populations. During the first decade of the twenty-first century, national censuses yielded results in countries with large Jewish populations such as Israel, Canada, the United Kingdom, the Russian Republic, Australia, Brazil, Ukraine, South Africa, Hungary, and Mexico. Population censuses in the United States do not provide information on religion, but have furnished relevant data on countries of birth, spoken languages, and ancestry. Permanent national population registers, including information on Jews as one of several documented religious, ethnic, or national groups, exist in Israel and in several European countries with admittedly small Jewish populations.[48]

In addition, independent socio-demographic studies have provided valuable information on Jewish demography and socioeconomic stratification, as well as on Jewish identification. In the United States, important new insights were provided by several large national surveys: the *National Jewish Population Survey*

(NJPS 2000–1), the *American Jewish Identity Survey* (AJIS 2001), the *Heritage, Ancestry, and Religious Identity* Survey (HARI 2001–2), the *American Religious Identification Survey* (ARIS 2008), and the *Pew Forum on Religion and Public Life* (2008). Smaller Jewish samples are routinely obtained from the *General Social Survey* and similar national studies (see below throughout this section on Data). Moreover, numerous Jewish population studies were separately conducted in major cities in the United States[49] and in several other countries, like France, the United Kingdom, Argentina, Australia, Hungary, Mexico, and the Netherlands.[50] Since 2000, either a national census with data on Jews, or a specially focused population survey, or a Jewish community population register has been available in each of the countries with a Jewish population of 30,000 and over, with the exception of Belgium. Synoptic studies of several Jewish communities in different countries were undertaken as well.[51]

Additional evidence on Jewish population trends may come from the systematic monitoring of membership registers, vital statistics, and migration records available from Jewish communities and other Jewish organizations in many countries or cities.[52] In some cases, such as in Buenos Aires and in London, research centers devoted to Jewish data collection, analysis, and publication were established, but some of these operations were intermittent, or ceased altogether. Detailed data on Jewish immigration routinely collected in Israel help to assess Jewish population changes in other countries. The cross-matching of more than one type of source about the same Jewish population, although not frequently feasible, can provide either mutual reinforcement of, or important critical insights on, the available data.

National boundaries have constituted a powerful defining constraint for Jewish population studies—perhaps underlying the more powerful issue of the characterization of Jewish identity as a derivative of national identities or as a transnational construct.[53] A very large segment of the available information—historically and currently—reflects the data collection initiatives undertaken by public or private bodies whose mandate corresponded with given national boundaries. Geopolitical changes—such as the disaggregation of countries into small independent state (as in the case of the USSR, Yugoslavia, or Czechoslovakia), or the reverse process of the merging of individual countries into broader sociopolitical conglomerates (as in the case of West and East Germany and—at a looser level of aggregation—of the European Union) have influenced only to a limited extent the nature of demographic research of the respective Jewish populations. Availability of data has mostly continued along the preexisting patterns, introducing—if anything—greater variation in definitions.[54] The need and advantages to coordinate data collection and analysis at the broader, supranational level has been perceived and discussed, but not systematically implemented in the lack of adequate community institutions and resources.

Investigators

In the rather eclectic conceptual and definitional context of Jewish demography, a significant part of the final product—insofar as the numbers reflect clear definitions—derives from assumptions and choices determined by the investigators, and by their employers. Who the investigators and their employers are, therefore, becomes an integral part of the analytic process at stake.[55]

Early researchers principally grounded in Europe included Zionists of the Herzlian (political), Ahad Ha'amian (cultural), or socialist varieties, like Alfred Nossig,[56] Arthur Ruppin,[57] or Jacob Lestschinsky,[58] alongside diasporists, Bundists, like Liebmann Hersch,[59] or more traditional encyclopaedists, like Joseph Jacobs,[60] as well as non-Jewish scholars, like Corrado Gini[61] or Livio Livi.[62] Later production reflected the dominance of Jewish investigators in the United States, like Nathan Goldberg,[63] Salo Baron,[64] or Simon Kuznets,[65] and in Israel, like Arieh Tartakower,[66] Roberto Bachi,[67] or Oscar (Uziel) Schmelz.[68] Among the living we shall only mention Sidney Goldstein at Brown University.[69]

While ideological biases need to be taken into account in reading the literature, taken as a whole, the study of Jewish population resulted in a remarkable output of scholarly work. European and later Israeli scholars, as well as the Americans who worked through Jewish organizations were primarily concerned with data collection and applying sophisticated—or at least feasible—techniques of population analysis to the available database. Those American scholars who were located in a variety of academic centers, played a leading role in developing social theory especially oriented toward a better understanding of the large Jewish community in the United States. All in all, having to confront the peculiar challenges of investigating a relatively small and somewhat elusive subpopulation stimulated the development of innovative research methods and analytic approaches.

Jewish population studies have been carried out by a variety of investigators—often referred to as *demographers*. In contemporary practice, the *demographers* should be those experts who study (Jewish) demography, but the appellative has often been attributed to a wide range of specialists and nonspecialists, trained or untrained, who have had a saying about (Jewish) population data. The inflation, devaluation, or absence of professional requirements needed to carry the title would not be tolerated with *engineer, physician,* or *psychologist*, the reason being perhaps that few untrained would dare—or be legally allowed—to excavate the foundations of a new building or provide clinical care to a patient. However, quite a few people think they are sufficiently knowledgeable when it comes to discussing population numbers. Indeed, several researchers, commonly called by others "demographers," would consider themselves experts in other disciplines, like sociology, geography, or psychology, rather than in population studies.

The progressive privatization of research initiatives entails a growing direct involvement of investigators in the creation and processing of the database, whereas when the data stemmed from governments or other public bodies, investigators were principally the users of those data. Hence, data quality increasingly reflects the characteristics of the investigators and their analytic assumptions and hypotheses. No less important is the question of who the commissioning bodies of demographic research are. This raises the issue of the relationship and sometimes conflict of interests between research-sponsoring organizations and the community of professional investigators—a topic worth of special attention but seldom discussed in the framework of Jewish social studies.

Researchers depend in their work on resources provided by sponsoring organizations. The mode of operating of the sponsor-researcher relationship and the amount of independence available to investigators may critically affect the results of research. Indeed, at least three types of situations can be singled out: (1) *tenured academics* who work as *employees of public universities or research institutes*, similar to civil servants and part of an epistemic community regulated by academic rules. This is the situation that grants highest independence and professional controls on research; (2) *investigators who work in the framework of projects or institutions supported by renewable budgetary resources*—known as "soft money." Here, rules for quality control and personal advancement may be similar to those under the previous type. However, especially when funding comes from private sources, the need to provide results that are not significantly incompatible with the expectations of the commissioning person or body may create some constraints to academic freedom; (3) *entrepreneurs in the private sector* whose income depends on contracts in a competitive market. Here a researcher's dependency on the employing body and its needs and expectations is highest.

International experience shows that studies commissioned by organizations with an agenda focused on specific research needs even unintentionally risk producing biased findings, not because the findings are not true or seriously researched, but because not all of the relevant questions may come under scrutiny. Ideally, research should be undertaken by independent high-quality professional bodies isolated from organizational agendas and, as far as possible, budgetary pressures. But this ideal is clearly not easily attainable.

Interpretations

The problem of explanation in Jewish demography was often elusive and elicited responses that drew from the—in today's eyes often dated—major scientific paradigms of each period. Jewish social research was no mere exercise of human curiosity or analytical skill, but often was a means of advancing specific theses regarding the nature of the Jews vis-à-vis world society, their unique character, their just claim to respect, equality, individual and corporate rights, and the quest for cultural resilience or assimilation into surrounding societies—up to the ultimate goal of political sovereignty.

Descriptive and interpretative efforts were strongly imbued of the emancipatory ethos of the *Wissenschaft des Judentums* in the nineteenth century. Remarkably, some ideas originally developed in the particularistic framework of Jewish demography, like Ruppin's ideas about models of assimilation,[70] actually anticipated by 20 years or more similar approaches developed by Robert Park and his fellows of the Chicago school of sociology.[71] Likewise, Shmuel Eisenstadt's models of immigrants' absorption in the specific context of early Israeli statehood[72] largely anticipated more general models, such as Milton Gordon's assessments of assimilation in American society.[73] Jewish social scientists produced a critical mass of studies far heavier and probably more articulated than that available for most other religious, ethnic, or cultural groups, although in a sense the main scope of the debate remained within a Jewish context, and the struggle to find a definitive place in the mainstream of general scholarship cannot be said to have been convincingly won.

In the twentieth century, these efforts often drew from the ferments of the national reconstruction ethos and the engagement of nation building in Israel, but also reflected the non-Zionist aspirations of Jewish autonomism in different times and places. At the turn of the twenty-first century, analytic efforts more often have become cognate to postmodern relativism. The struggle between affirmation and denial of Jewish demographic uniqueness was there all along the way. Sometimes the boundary was unclear between the struggle between neutral scientific research and apologetic public advocacy.

Over time, the initial concern with race and physical anthropology gave way to more qualitative insights on the mutual relationships between demographic patterns and Jewish identification. Social scientific studies of the effects of assimilation were ultimately an inquiry into collective Jewish identity, historical and contemporary, the changing boundaries of the collective, and the question of Jewish corporate survival in the longer term. The central issue of survival of the Jewish Diaspora in the post-emancipation era[74] was to be joined by a growing emphasis on assessing the demographic, socioeconomic, and cultural role for global Jewish continuity of a growing community in Palestine, and later in the State of Israel. Important research strands were assessing the determinants and consequences of an early Jewish demographic transition in most European and Middle Eastern countries vis-à-vis the majority populations of the same countries, and the direct and indirect consequences of Shoah for Jewish demography.[75] Eventually, assessing the socio-demographic and identificational trends of American Jewry became the central fixture in the field.[76] One important analytic thread was, and is, the competition between a mainly locale-oriented versus a global-comparative approach in Jewish population studies. While the distinction mainly and naturally reflected immediate research needs and data resources available, it also stemmed from contrasting ideational views of Jewish peoplehood as one overarching global entity as against the emphasis on a constellation of local and national, largely unrelated experiences.[77]

Keeping in mind the peculiar subject area of Jewish demography, there is a great variety of interpretative approaches from which to choose in order to make sense of the empirical data collected. Quite a few observers have been tempted to provide mono-causal and narrow geographically defined explanations. At the one end of the continuum there stands the inside-oriented view of a Jewish world that is generated and evolving uniquely in function of its own culture—if not destiny—regardless of the intervention of what happens in the outer, non-Jewish world. By this view, grounded in Jewish mysticism, Jewish communities are inherently self-generating, and—regardless of possible temporary ups and downs—their existence merely reflects the *eternal Israel*.[78] A less ambitious version would focus on the more active component of the identifiable collective, reaching the conclusion that there always exists a lively Jewish community, regardless of the changing size and characteristics of those uninvolved in the visible part of the community.[79] At the opposite end, there stands the purely outside-oriented view that all is determined by social class and political power conflicts, and no apparent role is left to the specific culture of the group. On the contrary, culture is viewed as a subordinate by-product of the more powerful external determinants.[80] By this interpretation, grounded in historical materialism, Jewish communities are merely the contingent product of processes unavoidably bound to make them disappear on the way of human society toward a new order.

As against these deterministic points of view, a more balanced interpretative strategy would argue that three major types of explanatory factors should be considered in assessing the social and demographic trends of any subpopulation, namely Jews: (1) the complex of *distinctive* religious imperatives, ethic values, social norms, ancestral traditions, popular beliefs, local customs, and community institutions peculiar to the given group; (2) the legal and other *interactive* modes between that group and the rest or the majority of society; and (3) the circumstances *shared* by the specific group and the majority concerning the general character of society, its patterns of modernization, economic resources, modes of production, social structures and stratification, political institutions, level of technology, and climatic and other environmental conditions.[81]

From this pragmatic perspective, inclusive of both internal and external factors,[82] Figure 12.3 schematically outlines the expected causality chain for socio-demographic events among a minority or subpopulation—moving from the most general, diffuse and global, to the most particular and individual, through the national and the communitarian. The chart not only assumes gradual passages from the broader to the more particular, but also considers direct influences from the broader and more diffused societal frame to the individual process, as well as the admittedly weaker reverse influences from the individual-micro level to the broader-macro level.

Such a flowchart may be understood as the underlying scheme for quantitative analyses bound to use multivariate analyses of data, that is data-processing tools aiming at uncovering the causation of events based on inference about a limited set of variables that operationally represent the selected hypotheses. Precisely in this perspective, it is imperative to clarify at the outset that the goal of statistical "explanation" of human behaviors is very imperfect and cannot be

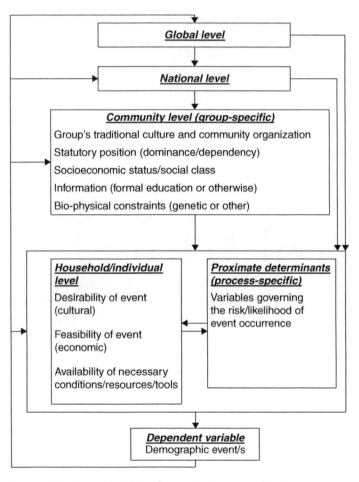

Figure 12.3 Causality Chain for Socio-Demographic Events Among
a Minority/Sub-Population

undertaken without stressing that there always is a substantial, often dominant, unexplained residual that encompasses individual psychological affinities, personal traits and considerations, and other specific contextual factors.

The main drivers of each possible component of demographic change operate at different levels of societal aggregation, flowing from the broader global and national levels, through an intermediate community level, to the individual level where demographic events actually occur. Consequently, Jewish population changes prominently reflect: (1) transformations in the *world societal system,* namely geopolitical, socioeconomic, and cultural changes across the world's different regions, and extant inequalities among countries; (2) the respective contexts of the *national societies* in which Jewish communities are located, including the nature of the relationships between the majority of society and the Jewish minority, and policy interventions by national governments and other authorities; (3) the specific internal context of *Jewish communities,* each including various types of interventions enacted by the Jewish institutional system internationally and locally; (4) the *personal* characteristics of individual Jews, and in particular their gender, age, socioeconomic status, and cultural-identificational patterns.[83]

Globalization results in powerful influences on individual demographic processes, although this is less true in reverse. Global patterns mostly escape influences by specific individuals, community groups, or even countries, but they do reflect the influences of events and changes within large and powerful nations during certain periods of time, and of widespread communities—such as global religions—in the longer run. In turn, national experiences may be powerfully influenced by patterns and transformations that operate at the global level. The analyst should keep this in mind, especially when working on such large and apparently self-sufficient aggregates like the Jewish population in the United States.

Religio-ethnic communities are affected by the overall context of the national societies of which they are part and parcel, but they also reflect transnational processes and influences somewhat indifferent to space, and in some cases to time as well. To some extent, and according to the variable circumstances in each country, such communities may operate to influence national patterns—for example by advocating particular policy interventions—in order to advance their own corporate interests. While demographic events always concern one specific individual, as a rule individuals are subject to significant influences that originate in the community or communities of which they are part.

The intensity and quality of group identification—in this case, Jewish identification—is not only a matter of interest regarding the cultural style and tastes of a community, but also a fundamental mechanism of population growth or decline. A major constant throughout history is the Jews' exposure to contextual circumstances simultaneously perceived in different and parallel national-territorial divisions. Population studies predominantly aim at the national society of a given country, and this is true to a large extent of the investigation of local Jewish communities as well. But with periodically different incidence over time, the latter were and are affected by sweeping trends of a broad international or global nature. Wide geographical dispersion through large-scale migration and the progressive deepening of globalization and transnational networks and identification patterns across Jewish communities make it essential to address world-system structure and change as a necessary background for understanding the position of Jewish communities internationally and locally.[84]

Five variables that operate at the community level in particular determine a parsimonious analytic framework for the preferred strategies that may lead or not toward the given demographic event: (1) the group's unique *traditional culture and organization* with special reference to religious and social norms relevant to the given demographic event, as well as community frameworks and institutions established to implement those norms; (2) the group's legal status or—more relevant to the contemporary situation—subjective perceptions of its own *dominance/dependence* versus the majority of society or other minorities within it; (3) the group's *social-class stratification*, implying significant inter- and intra-group differences in perceived interests and access to resources relevant to the demographic event; (4) the group's available *knowledge* with respect to the given socio-demographic process, whether acquired through formal education or other channels, and the consequent behavior relative to the given demographic event; (5) group-specific *biological constraints* of genetic or other nature, namely in relation to inherited properties that may enhance or hinder exposure to the given demographic event.

Population composition by a variety of personal characteristics is a crucial factor in the chain of demographic events. Individual characteristics, hence, directly or indirectly reflect the influence of broader determinants, such as religious and social norms and institutions; legal frameworks; economic development; levels of modernization; political regimes; available technologies; environmental constraints; and other variables that simultaneously shape the lives of many contemporaries.[85]

As noted, the ultimate dependent variable is the occurrence or nonoccurrence of a given single event of demographic relevance. Most socio-demographic processes functionally depend and probably can be statistically explained by an appropriate set of proximate determinants or intermediate variables. One typical example is viewing birth rates as the joint product of couple formation frequencies, natural fertility levels, and fertility control.[86] Each of these proximate determinants evidently is by itself the dependent variable of a more complex explanatory chain. In this sense, demographic events reflect the integrated strength of three main factors that operate at the individual or household level: (1) the event's cultural *desirability*, that is its compatibility with the prevailing social norms within a given population; (2) its economic *feasibility*, that is the presence of the material resources needed for the event to happen; and (3) the *availability* of instrumental tools and conditions necessary for the event to occur.[87]

Different likelihoods of desirability, feasibility, and availability tend to determine the occurrence of socio-demographic events in a given religio-ethnic community—namely among Jews versus others, and regarding patterns of variation within and across Jewish communities. Explanation and interpretation will particularly focus on the frequency of events, their distribution over the lifecycle, particularly with regard to age at event, and their distribution over calendar time measured in months and years. In community comparisons, no less important than intensity and frequency is the role played by a community as a forerunner or a late-joiner in the occurrence and diffusion of a given phenomenon,[88] and sometimes in being the unique actor and carrier of the given circumstance and process of demographic interest.

Relationships between these various factors and processes usually run from the main drivers through the operational variables, down to the dependent variables. However, to some extent, the final product becomes in turn a determinant of further change. Jewish—and any other—demographic trends are therefore embedded in an eminently dynamic, interactive, and in fact iterative process. The process itself is in no way deterministic because no relations are expected to occur necessarily, hence affecting a final result known in advance. However, the logic of the relationships in Figure 12.3 is expectedly verifiable, hence somewhat predictable. Such an approach mainly aims at circumscribing the range of possible occurrences, rather than indicating what the actual occurrences will be.

The rational and pragmatic analytic outlook described here obviously needs validation through empirical data. Interestingly, the very role of data in such explanatory efforts has become a target of growing skepticism in recent interpretative debates. Critiques aimed at diminishing the role played by data in leading to valid conclusions have included the following: (1) data are not important for revealing or assessing the given process; (2) data are important, but those needed to assess the given process are not available; (3) the needed data are available, but they are not reliable enough, or are reliable but have been misused, to adjudicate on the given process; (4) the available data are reliable, and have been used appropriately, but they are not conclusive enough to adjudicate in a given process; (5) the data do adjudicate in the given process, but the process is unimportant in light of a broader set of conceptual considerations and normative goals.

Such differences about the data often are not easily adjudicated on the basis of research and tend to become a bone of contention of broader significance for Jewish communal discourse. In the past, the conventional wisdom was that ascertained facts affect interpretations whose implications in turn affect the processes of policy decision making and implementation. More recently, a more complex and reciprocal interplay of facts, interpretations, and policies has emerged. The reading of basic findings about Jewish populations is increasingly influenced by preexisting interpretative assumptions. Positive or negative interpretations of the trends often precede in-depth analyses. If one sweeping critique can be put forward of the more recent research efforts, it is not that the data stand sometimes quite far from ideal quality, but that the available data are underutilized, thus lending a shallow factual basis to the substantive debates. In turn policies—in particular the different choices made by various large Jewish organizations in determining their target constituencies—tend to directly affect not only the interpretations but judgments about the data. One of the more intriguing propositions in recent population debates is that the data may indeed indicate the nature and implications of a given process, but if reality is nevertheless perceived—or needs to be perceived—differently, then reality *is* different.[89]

One final, quite extreme, position is that the very existence of the data is inherently responsible for creating social and political issues that would not otherwise exist. In this perspective, data are seen as instrumental in the misrepresentation, manipulation, and domination of society.[90] These critics often find a connection between data biases and the personal background of the analysts allegedly responsible for those manipulations. According to this opinion, it is denial of the legitimacy of the Diaspora on the side of biased Zionist intellectuals that would explain the emphasis on the downward population trends in the Diaspora—namely among American Jewry.[91] By the same token, it is an exploitative concept of group relations expressed through the establishment of imaginary analytic categories like "Europe/America/Asia/Africa" or "Jewish/Arab" that would explain the emphasis on, and alleged failure of, ethnic and sub-ethnic integration in Israel.[92] And, from a diametrically opposed perspective, it is dearth of roots in Israeli authenticity that would explain the emphasis on the vanishing Jewish dominance in the Israeli-Palestinian population contest.[93] The common thread of all these different critical instances is that authors' preconceptions and hidden agendas percolate into the data, and thus affect interpretations and, quite possibly, the ensuing debates about possible policy interventions. The fact that the critics themselves may have their own agendas is not a matter they would care to discuss.

In the global perspective offered by these more specific predicaments, today the collective Jewish peoplehood essentially comprises two separate situations, each of which requires somewhat different, if not contrasting, sets of analytic tools. Jews in Israel operate in the context of a Jewish *majority* within a sovereign state. The rest of world Jewry operates as a set of *minorities* of different absolute sizes, which also constitute small to minuscule shares of the total populations of their respective countries. While demographic expectations for the two typological components of world Jewry cannot be the same, it is important to verify whether commonalities of patterns and outcomes do exist among the Jewish global collective. What is probably true as a whole in historical perspective, needs validation in contemporary research through the development of comparable, coherent, and complementary description and theory. Keeping this in mind, it is easier to understand why the greatest research emphasis has been placed upon the research predicaments concerning Jewish population trends in the two numerically dominant and quite different contexts of the United States[94] and Israel.[95]

Conclusions: Toward the Future

A final reflection touches on the future of Jewish demographic studies. A first remark concerns how one perceives the topic facing the two watersheds of *the Jews* as a definitionally *identifiable* or *nonidentifiable* subpopulation, and of *Jewish demography* as an academically *respectable* or *less respectable* specialization. This in turn revolves around different and competing conceptions of Jewish peoplehood, the diverse relationships these entail between cultural, social, and biological processes, and the more appropriate methodologies for the study of such a complex cluster of issues. Demographic research, as such, is not responsible for these different predicaments, but it can and should meaningfully reflect them at the empirical and interpretative level, if it has to preserve a sustained level of scientific and public relevance.

In the demographic domain, there cannot be waterproof separation between substantive analytic answers, on the one hand, and acknowledging several sensitive aspects of the relationship between research-oriented and public-applied domains, on the other hand. Frank discussion, sincere introspection, and significant investments are needed concerning the future of serious research on "State of Israel" and "world Jewish community" populations. In turn, any effort to develop policy planning and management programs cannot proceed without the foundations of sound Jewish population research. This requires constant monitoring of ongoing trends, of their expected projection and development, and of their longer-term implications.[96] This also implies the awareness that the resources necessary to such research effort should be secured with high priority.

The analytic goals and contents of systematic Jewish population studies, namely the respective merits and complementarities of qualitative versus quantitative research and of scientific-oriented versus policy-oriented research go hand in hand with the professional competence and decisional autonomy of the investigators involved in research design, data collection, and analysis. One important challenge relates to the ability of the organized Jewish polity in Israel and of the central Jewish community institutions elsewhere to withstand objective scrutiny of their own trends and characteristics, and to learn from scientific research facing possible gaps between the results of systematic research and existing conceptions, hopes, and fears. Public leaders and opinion makers should hopefully base their policy conclusions and programs upon sound and systematic research.

All of this conspicuously reasserts the need to understand the nature of demographic facts and their determinants and consequences, and responsibly face institution building to promote future Jewish population research and its manifold knowledge-bound and applied—including policy oriented—uses.[97]

Notes

1. Some of the materials in this essay draw from: Sergio DellaPergola (2002), "Demography," in Martin Goodman (ed.), *The Oxford Handbook of Jewish Studies*. Oxford: Oxford University Press, pp. 797–823; idem (2010), "World Jewish Population 2010," Current Jewish Population Reports 2. Storrs: North American Jewish Data Bank; idem (2011), Jewish Demographic Policies: Population Trends and Options in Israel and in the Diaspora. Jerusalem: Jewish People Policy Institute; and idem, in a forthcoming article in Vol. 27 of *Studies in Contemporary Jewry*, Uzi Rebhun (ed.). New York: Oxford University Press.
2. See for example, Paul Demeny and Geoffrey McNicoll (eds) (2003), *The Encyclopedia of Population*. New York: Macmillan Reference USA.
3. I use here the terms *demography* and *population studies* as synonyms, although sometimes the distinction is suggested between demography as more formal and population studies as more descriptive. See Geoffrey McNicoll (1992), "The Agenda of Population Studies: A Commentary and Complaint," *Population and Development Review* 18:3: 399–420.
4. "Take ye sum of all the congregation of the children of Israel, by their families, by their fathers' houses, according to the number of names" (Num. 1.2).
5. Leopold Zunz (1823), "Grundlinien zu einer künftigen Statistik der Juden," *Zeitschrift für die Wissenschaft des Judentums* 1: 523–32.
6. Abraham Moses Luncz (1991–03), *Jerusalem; Jahrbuch zur Beförderung einer wissenschaftlich genauer Kenntniss des jetzigen und des alten Palästinas*. Jerusalem. 6 Vols [Hebrew and German]. Vienna: Georg Brög.
7. See one early example in G. Lagneau (1882), *Remarques à propos du dénombrement de la population sur quelques différences démographiques présentées par le catholiques, ler protestants, les israélites*. Paris: Académie des Sciences Morales et Politiques.
8. Mitchell B. Hart (2000), *Social Science and the Politics of Modern Jewish Identity*. Stanford: Stanford University Press.
9. See, for example, Jean Christian Boudin (1856), *Traité de géographie et de statistique médicales*. Paris: J.B. Bailliere et Fils. Vol. 2; Fishberg (1911), *The Jews: A Study in Race and Environment*. New York: Walter Scott. For a broader overview, see Léon Poliakov (1973), *Le mythe aryen*. Paris: Calmann-Lévy.

10. See, for example, Roberto Bachi (1976), *Population Trends of World Jewry*. Jerusalem: The Hebrew University; DellaPergola, *Jewish Demographic Policies*.

11. See, for example, Felix A. Theilhaber (1911), *Der Untergans der deutschen Juden*. Munich: Reinhardt.

12. At the Hebrew University of Jerusalem, demography is taught at the Faculty of Social Sciences in the Department of Sociology, but was initially taught in the Department of Statistics, and for several years constituted a separate department. Demography of the Jews was taught primarily in the Department of Contemporary Jewry, until its recent merger with the Department of Jewish History.

13. Paul Ritterband (ed.) (1981), *Modern Jewish Fertility*. Leiden: Brill; Eric Peritz and Mario Baras (eds) (1992), *Studies in the Fertility of Israel*. Jerusalem: The Hebrew University of Jerusalem; Sergio DellaPergola (2011), *Fertility Prospects in Israel: Ever below Replacement Level?* New York: United Nations Secretariat, Department of Economic and Social Affairs, Population Division, *Expert Paper* No. 2011/9: 1–36.

14. U. O. Schmelz (1971), *Infant and Early Childhood Mortality among the Jews in the Diaspora*. Jerusalem: The Hebrew University.

15. Moshe Sicron (1957), *Immigration to Israel 1948–1953*. Jerusalem: Central Bureau of Statistics, Special publication n. 60; Sergio DellaPergola (1998), "The Global Context of Migration to Israel," in E. Leshem and J. Shuval (eds), *Immigration to Israel: Sociological Perspectives*. New Brunswick and London: Transaction, pp. 51–92; idem (2009), "International Migration of Jews," in Eliezer Ben-Rafael and Yitzhak Sternberg (eds), *Transnationalism: Diasporas and the Advent of a New (Dis)order*. Leiden and Boston: Brill, pp. 213–36.

16. Uzi Rebhun and Lilach Lev Ari (2010), *American Israelis: Migration, Transnationalism, and Diasporic Identity*. Leiden and Boston: Brill.

17. See DellaPergola, *Jewish Demographic Policies*, Chapter 7.

18. Sylvia Barack Fishman (2004), *Double or Nothing? Jewish Families and Mixed Marriage*. Hanover and London: Brandeis University Press; Shulamit Reinharz and Sergio DellaPergola (eds) (2009), *Jewish Intermarriage around the World*. New Brunswick and London: Transaction.

19. See Zvi Gitelman, Barry Kosmin, and Andras Kovacs (eds) (2003), *New Jewish Identities: Contemporary Europe and beyond*. Budapest: Central European University; Steven M. Cohen (1994), "Jewish Content versus Jewish Continuity," in Robert Seltzer and Norman Cohen (eds), *The Americanization of the Jews*. New York: New York University Press, pp. 395–416; Shlomit Levy, Hanna Levinson, and Elihu Katz (2002), *Believes, Observances and Values of Jews in Israel 2000*. Jerusalem: Guttman Center, The Israel Institute for Democracy, Avi Chai.

20. See the different levels and directions of conceptualization in: Shmuel Noah Eisenstadt (1992), *Jewish Civilization: The Jewish Historical Experience in Comparative Perspective*. Albany: State University of New York Press; Marshall Sklare (ed.) (1958), *The Jews: Social Patterns of an American Group*. New York, London: The Free Press-Collier-Macmillan; Simon N. Herman (1977), *Jewish Identity: A Social Psychological Perspective*. Beverly Hills-London: Sage Publications.

21. See Michael F. Hammer, Alan J. Redd, Elizabeth T. Wood, M. R. Bonner, Hamdi Jarjanazi, Tanya Karafet, Silvana Santachiara-Benerecetti, Ariella Oppenheim, Mark A. Jobling, Trefor Jenkins, Harry Ostrer, and Batsheva Bonné-Tamir, "Jewish and Middle Eastern Non-Jewish Populations Share a Common Pool of y-Chromosome Biallelic Haplotypes," *Proceedings of the National Academy of Sciences*, June 6, 2000, 97:12: 6769–74; Doron M. Behar, Bayazit Yunusbayev, Mait Metspalu, Ene Metspalu, Saharon Rosset, Juri Parik, Siiri Rootsi, Gyaneshwer Chaubey, Ildus Kutuev, Guennady Yudkovsky, Elza K. Khusnutdinova, Oleg Balanovsky, Ornella Semino, Luisa Pereira, David Comas, David Gurwitz, Batsheva Bonné-Tamir, Tudor Parfitt,

Michael F. Hammer, Karl Skorecki, and Richard Villems (2010), "The Genome-Wide Structure of the Jewish People," *Nature*, www.nature.com/dofinder/10.1038/nature09103, pp. 1–6; see also Batsheva Bonné-Tamir and Avinoam Adam (1992), *Genetic Diversity Among Jews: Diseases and Markers at the DNA Level*. New York: Oxford University Press.

22. Abraham Moles (1965), "Sur l'aspect théorique du decompte de populations mal definies," in Centre national des hautes études juives—Bruxelles, Institute of Contemporary Jewry of the Hebrew University of Jerusalem, *La vie juive dans l'Europe contemporaine*, Bruxelles: Editions de l'Institut de Sociologie de l'Université Libre de Bruxelles, pp. 81–7.

23. Sergio DellaPergola (2000), *World Jewry beyond 2000: The Demographic Prospects*. Oxford: Oxford Centre for Hebrew and Jewish Studies.

24. Dominique Schnapper (1994), "Israélites and Juifs: New Jewish Identities in France," in Jonathan Webber (ed.), *Jewish Identities in the New Europe*. London: Littman Library of Jewish Civilization.

25. Baruch Kimmerling (1999), "Conceptual Problems," in D. Jacoby (ed.), *One Land, Two Peoples*. Jerusalem: The Magnes Press [Hebrew], pp. 11–22; Shlomo Sand (2009), *The Invention of the Jewish People*. New York: Verso.

26. Interesting surveys of alternative definitions of the Jewish population target are reported in: (1945) Yiddish Scientific Institute—YIVO, *The Classification of Jewish Immigrants and Its Implications—A Survey of Opinions*, New York: YIVO; Sidney B. Hoenig (ed.) (1965), Baruch Litvin (comp), *Jewish Identity: Modern Responsa and Opinions on the Registration of Children of Mixed Marriages—David Ben-Gurion's Query to Leaders of World Jewry—A Documentary Compilation*. Jerusalem-New York: Feldheim.

27. Shaye Cohen (1999), *The Beginnings of Jewishness: Boundaries, Varieties, Uncertainties*. Berkeley: University of California Press.

28. Eric Rosenthal (1975), "The Equivalence of United States Census Data for Persons of Russian Stock or Descent with American Jews: An Evaluation," *Demography* 12: 275–90; DellaPergola, *World Jewish Population*.

29. The term *core Jewish population* was initially suggested in Barry A. Kosmin, Sidney Goldstein, Joseph Waksberg, Nava Lerer, Ariela Keysar, and Jeffrey Scheckner (1991), *Highlights of the CJF 1990 National Jewish Population Survey*. New York: Council of Jewish Federations.

30. Michael Corinaldi (2001), *The Enigma of Jewish Identity: The Law of Return, Theory and Practice*. Srigim-Lion: Nevo [Hebrew].

31. In the NJPS 2000–1 version, initially processed and circulated by United Jewish Communities, a Jew is defined as *a person whose religion is Judaism, OR whose religion is Jewish and something else, OR who has no religion and has at least one Jewish parent or a Jewish upbringing, OR who has a non-monotheistic religion and has at least one Jewish parent or a Jewish upbringing*. See Laurence Kotler-Berkowitz, Steven M. Cohen, Jonathon Ament, Vivian Klaff, Frank Mott, and Danyelle Peckerman-Neuman (with Lorraine Blass, Debbie Bursztyn, and David Marker) (2003), *The National Jewish Population Survey 2000–01: Strength, Challenge, and Diversity in the American Jewish Population*. New York: Mandell J. Berman Institute. The issue of *Contemporary Jewry* (the scholarly journal of the Association for the Scientific Study of Jewry, edited by Samuel Heilman), 25, 2005, is devoted to critical essays and analyses of NJPS method and findings.

32. The term *enlarged Jewish population* was initially suggested by Sergio DellaPergola (1975), "The Italian Jewish Population Study: Demographic Characteristics and Trends," in U. O. Schmelz, P. Glikson, and S. J. Gould (eds), *Studies in Jewish Demography: Survey for 1969–1971*. Jerusalem, London: Hebrew University, Institute of Contemporary Jewry, pp. 60–97.

33. Kotler-Berkowitz et al., *National Jewish Population Survey 2000–01.*
34. See Hammer et al., "Jewish and Middle Eastern Non-Jewish Populations Share a Common Pool of y-Chromosome Biallelic Haplotypes"; Doron M. Behar, Michael F. Hammer, Daniel Garrigan, Richard Villems, Batsheva Bonné-Tamir, Martin Richards, David Gurwitz, Dror Rosengarten, Matthew Kaplan, Sergio DellaPergola, Lluis Quintana-Murci, and Karl Skorecki (2004), "MtDNA Evidence for a Genetic Bottleneck in the Early History of the Ashkenazi Jewish Population," *European Journal of Human Genetics*, pp. 1–10; Behar et al., "The Genome-Wide Structure of the Jewish People."
35. Tudor Parfitt (2002), *The Lost Tribes the History of a Myth.* London: Weidenfeld and Nicholson.
36. Ruth Gavison (2009), *60 Years to the Law of Return: History, Ideology, Justification.* Jerusalem: Metzilah Center for Zionist, Jewish, Liberal and Humanistic Thought.
37. For a concise review of the rules of attribution of Jewish personal status in rabbinic and Israeli law, including reference to Jewish sects, isolated communities, and apostates, see Michael Corinaldi (1998), "Jewish Identity," in idem, *Jewish Identity: The Case of Ethiopian Jewry.* Jerusalem: The Magnes Press, Chapter 2.
38. Barry A. Kosmin, personal communication. Professor Kosmin was the scientific director of NJPS 199.
39. U. O. Schmelz (ed.) (1976), *Demography and Statistics of Diaspora Jewry 1920–1970; Bibliography.* Vol. 1. Jerusalem: The Hebrew University of Jerusalem; Roberto Bachi (1997), "Personal Recollections in the History of Research in Jewish Demography," in Sergio DellaPergola and Judit Even (eds), *Papers in Jewish Demography 1993 in Memory of U.O. Schmelz.* Jerusalem: The Hebrew University, pp. 33–7.
40. Currently directed by Arnold Dashefsky.
41. Currently directed by Leonard Saxe.
42. Many of these global activities have been promoted, executed, or coordinated by the Division of Jewish Demography and Statistics at The A. Harman Institute of Contemporary Jewry (ICJ), The Hebrew University of Jerusalem.
43. Two major projects sponsored in this framework were a survey of the Jewish population in Buenos Aires, see: Yaacov Rubel (2005), *La Población Judía de la Ciudad de Buenos Aires, Perfil Socio-Demográfico.* Buenos Aires: Agencia Judía para Israel, Iniciativa de Demografía Judía; and *Fertility Levels in Israel: Jewish Population Performances and Attitudes*, conducted in Israel in 2004–5 by Sergio DellaPergola, Mina Tzemach, Rimona Viesel, and Moran Neuman.
44. See the institute's annual reports, and DellaPergola, *Jewish Demographic Policies.*
45. For overviews of subject matter and technical issues see Paul Ritterband, Barry A. Kosmin, and Jeffrey Scheckner (1988), "Counting Jewish Populations: Methods and Problems," *American Jewish Year Book* 88: 204–21; DellaPergola, "Demography"; idem, "World Jewish Population 2010."
46. From this point of view, Jews in the former Soviet Union—whose quantitative assessment has often been deemed to rely on weak ground—have constituted one of the best-documented sections of world Jewry. See Mordechai Altshuler (1987), *Soviet Jewry since the Second World War: Population and Social Structure.* Westport: Greenwood Press; Mark Tolts (2001), "Jewish Demography of the Former Soviet Union," in Sergio DellaPergola and J. Even (eds), *Papers in Jewish Demography 1997.* Jerusalem: The Hebrew University, pp. 109–39.
47. DellaPergola, "World Jewish Population 2010."
48. Ibid., for a more detailed review.
49. See a synopsis of the main findings in Ira M. Sheshkin (2001), *How Jewish Communities Differ: Variations in the Findings of Local Jewish Demographic Studies.* New York: City University of New York, North American Jewish Data Bank.

50. DellaPergola, "World Jewish Population 2010."

51. Andras Kovacs and Ildiko Barna (2010), *Identity à la carte: Research on Jewish Identities, Participation and Affiliation in Five European Countries. Analysis of Survey Data.* Budapest: The American Joint Distribution Committee.

52. Notably in Buenos Aires at the Centro de Investigaciones Sociales, in the United Kingdom at the Community Research Unit of the Board of Deputies of British Jews, in Germany at the Zentralwohlfhartstelle, in Italy at the Unione delle Comunità Ebraiche Italiane, and in São Paulo at the FISESP.

53. See the reviews in Eliezer Ben-Rafael and Yitzhak Sternberg (with Judit Bokser Liwerant and Yosef Gorny) (eds) (2009), *Transnationalism: Diasporas and the Advent of a New (Dis)order.* Leiden-Boston: Brill.

54. Mark Tolts (2011), "Demography of the Contemporary Russian-Speaking Jewish Diaspora," a paper presented at the conference on the contemporary Russian-speaking Jewish Diaspora. Cambridge, MA: Harvard University.

55. See recent work on this matter by Bethamie Horowitz (2006), *Enhancing "Knowledge Production" to Inform Decision-Making in the American Jewish Communal World.* New York, 2006.

56. Alfred Nossig (1887), *Materialien zur Statistik des jüdischen Stammes.* Vienna: C. Konegan.

57. Arthur Ruppin (1904), *Die Juden der Gegenwart.* Berlin: Calvary; idem (1930), *Soziologie der Juden.* Berlin: Jüdischer Verlag; idem (1940), *The Jewish Fate and Future.* London: Macmillan. See also Sergio DellaPergola and Ruppin (1999), "Revisited: The Jews of Today, 1904–1994," in S. M. Cohen and G. Horenczyk (eds), *National Variations in Modern Jewish Identity: Implications for Jewish Education.* Albany: SUNY Press, pp. 53–84.

58. Jacob Lestschinsky (1926), "Probleme der Bevölkerungs-Bewegung bei den Juden," *Metron,* 6:2: 1–157; idem (1930), "Die Umsiedlung und Umschichtung des jüdischen Volkes im Laufe des letzten Jahrhunderts," *Weltwirtschaftliches Archiv* 30: 123–56; 32: 563–99; idem (1948), *Crisis, Catastrophe and Survival.* New York: Institute of Jewish Affairs. See also Paul Glikson (1967), "Jacob Lestschinsky: A Bibliographical Survey," *The Jewish Journal of Sociology* 9:1: 48–57.

59. Liebmann Hersch (1931), "International Migration of the Jews," in W. Wilcox (ed.), *International Migration.* Vol. 2. New York: National Bureau of Economic Research, pp. 471–520; idem (1938), *Le juif delinquant: Ètude comparative sur la criminalité de la population juive et non-juive de la République Polonaise.* Paris: Librairie Félix Alcan.

60. Joseph Jacobs (1891), *Studies in Jewish Statistics.* London: Nutt.

61. Corrado Gini, the developer of the index of income inequality, was interested in the Karaite communities in eastern Europe and wrote: "Alcune ricerche demografiche sugli Israeliti in Padova," in *Atti della R. Accademia di Scienze, Lettere e Arti* 32: 4 (1916): 467–85.

62. Livio Livi (orig. 1918–20; reprinted 1978, Forni Sala Bolognese), *Gli ebrei alla luce della statistica.* Firenze: Libreria della Voce.

63. Nathan Goldberg (1946), "Occupational Patterns of American Jews," *Jewish Review* III: 4.

64. Salo W. Baron (1971), "Population," *Encyclopaedia Judaica,* Vol. 13: col. 866–903. Large amounts of demographic materials are interspersed in Salo Baron's monumental work (1952–83) *A Social and Religious History of the Jews.* New York: Columbia University Press, 18 Vols.

65. Simon Kuznets (1960), "Economic Structure and Life of the Jews," in L. Finkelstein (ed.), *The Jews: Their History, Culture and Religion* (2nd edn). New York: Harper, pp. 1597–666; idem (1972), *Economic Structure of U.S. Jewry: Recent Trends.* Jerusalem: The Institute of Contemporary Jewry, The Hebrew University of Jerusalem; idem

(1975), "Immigration of Russian Jews to the United States: Background and Structure," *Perspectives in American History* 9: 35–124.

66. Arieh Tartakower (1958), *In Search of Home and Freedom*. London: Lincoln-Prager.

67. Bachi (1976), *Population Trends of World Jewry*; Roberto Bachi and Sergio DellaPergola (1984), "Did Characteristics of Pre-Emancipation Italian Jewry Deviate from a General Demographic Paradigm for Jewish Traditional Communities?" in G. Wigoder (ed.), *Contemporary Jewry, Studies in Honor of Moshe Davis*. Jerusalem: The Institute of Contemporary Jewry, The Hebrew University of Jerusalem, pp. 159–89.

68. U. O. Schmelz (1970), "A Guide to Jewish Population Studies," in U. O. Schmelz and P. Glikson (eds), *Jewish Population Studies 1961–1968*. Jerusalem: The Hebrew University of Jerusalem, pp. 11–94; idem (1981), "Jewish Survival: The Demographic Factors," *American Jewish Year Book* 81: 61–117; idem (1981), *World Jewish Population: Regional Estimates and Projections*. Jerusalem: The Hebrew University of Jerusalem.

69. Sidney Goldstein and Calvin Goldscheider (1968), *Jewish Americans: Three Generations in a Jewish Community*. Englewood Cliffs: Prentice Hall; Sidney Goldstein (1992), "Profile of American Jewry: Insights from the 1990 National Jewish Population Survey," *American Jewish Year Book* 92: 77–173; Sidney and Alice Goldstein (1996), *Jews on the Move: Implications for Jewish Identity*. Albany: State University of New York Press.

70. Arthur, *Die Juden der Gegenwart*.

71. Robert Park, R. D. McKenzie, and Ernest Burgess (1925), *The City: Suggestions for the Study of Human Nature in the Urban Environment*. Chicago: University of Chicago Press; Louis Wirth (1928), *The Ghetto*. Chicago: University of Chicago Press.

72. Shmuel Noah Eisenstadt (1954), *The Absorption of Immigrants*. London: Routledge and Kegan Paul.

73. Milton M. Gordon (1964), *Assimilation in American Life: The Role of Race, Religion and National Origins*. New York: Oxford University Press.

74. Ruppin, *The Jewish Fate and Future*; Schmelz, "Jewish Survival."

75. Sergio DellaPergola (1983), *La trasformazione demografica della diaspora ebraica*. Torino: Loescher; idem (1992), "Major Demographic Trends of World Jewry: The Last Hundred Years," in Batsheva Bonné-Tamir and Avinoam Adam (eds), *Genetic Diversity among the Jews*. New York: Oxford University Press, pp. 3–30; idem (2001), "Some Fundamentals of Jewish Demographic History," in Sergio DellaPergola and J. Even (eds), *Papers in Jewish Demography 1997*. Jerusalem: The Hebrew University, pp. 11–33; idem (1996), "Between Science and Fiction: Notes on the Demography of the Holocaust," *Holocaust and Genocide Studies* 10:1: 34–51. See also H. S. Halevi (1963), *The Influence of World War II on the Demographic Characteristics of the Jewish People*. Jerusalem: The Hebrew University.

76. See the several volumes devoted to the topic by the journal *Contemporary Jewry* issued by the Association for the Social Scientific Study of Jewry.

77. Compare the local-national oriented approaches in Jeffrey Lesser and Raanan Rein (2008), *Rethinking Jewish Latin-Americans*. Albuquerque: University of New Mexico Press versus the comparative-transnational approaches in Judit Bokser Liwerant, Sergio DellaPergola, Haim Avni, Margalit Bejarano, and Leonardo Senkman (2011), "Cuarenta años de cambios: transiciones y paradigmas," in Haim Avni, Judit Bokser Liwerant, Sergio DellaPergola, Margalit Bejarano, and Leonardo Senkman (eds), *Pertenencia y alteridad: Judíos en/de America Latina: cuarenta años de cambio*. Madrid, Frankfurt am Main, Orlando, and Mexico: Iberoamericana-Vervuert-Bonilla Artigas Editores, pp. 13–83.

78. "The eternal glory of Israel shall not fail" (1 Sam. 15.29).

79. See, for example, Calvin Goldscheider (1986), *The American Jewish Community: Social Science Research and Policy Implications*. Atlanta: Scholars Press; Steven M. Cohen

(1988), *American Assimilation or Jewish Revival?* Bloomington-Indianapolis: Indiana University Press.

80. This view is classically reflected in Karl Marx (1844), "Zur Judenfrage," *Deutsch Franzosische Jahrbücher*; but it also appears—in the totally different context of the revival of an autonomous Jewish society in Palestine—in the writings of Arthur Ruppin. See his 1971 *Memoirs, Diaries, Letters*, A. Bein (ed.). London: Weidenfeld and Nicholson.

81. DellaPergola, *Jewish Demographic Policies*.

82. On which might be the most appropriate interpretative framework, see the review of Marshall Sklare (1982), "On the Preparation of a Sociology of American Jewry," in Marshall Sklare (ed.), *Understanding American Jewry*. New Brunswick-London: Transaction, pp. 261–71.

83. Sergio DellaPergola (2000), "Jewish Women in Transition: A Comparative Sociodemographic Perspective," in Jonathan Frankel (ed.), *Jews and Gender: The Challenge to Hierarchy. Studies in Contemporary Jewry, An Annual* 16: 209–42; Harriet Hartman and Moshe Hartman (2009), *Gender and American Jews: Patterns in Work, Education, and Family in Contemporary Life*. Hanover-London: Brandeis University Press.

84. Sergio DellaPergola, Uzi Rebhun, and Mark Tolts (2005), "Contemporary Jewish Diaspora in Global Context: Human Development Correlates of Population Trends," *Israel Studies* 11:1: 61–95.

85. For an interpretation of Jewish demographic patterns focusing on minority-majority interaction, see Calvin Goldscheider (1971), *Population, Modernization and Social Structure*. Boston: Little Brown, Chapter 10. For a similar approach focused on explaining the peculiar economic profile of Jewish populations, see Kuznets, "Economic Structure and Life of the Jews" and *Economic Structure of U.S. Jewry: Recent Trends*. See also Barry Chiswick (1999), "The Occupational Attainment and Earnings of American Jewry, 1890–1990," *Contemporary Jewry* 20: 68–98; idem (2006), *The Earnings of American Jewish Men: Human Capital, Denomination and Religiosity*. Bonn: IZA Discussion Paper No. 2301.

86. See, for example, Kingsley Davis and Judith Blake (1956), "Social Structure and Fertility, an Analytic Framework," *Economic Development and Cultural Change* 4: 211–23.

87. See, for example, Ruth Dixon (1971), "Explaining Cross-Cultural Variations in Age at Marriage and Proportions Never Marrying," *Population Studies* 25:2: 215–33.

88. Massimo Livi Bacci (1986), "Social-Group Forerunners of Fertility Control in Europe," in Ansley Coale and Susan Cotts Watkins (eds), *The Decline of Fertility in Europe*. Princeton: Princeton University Press, pp. 182–200.

89. In the words of an Israeli-elected politician to this author around the year 2000, "Do not bother us with your data, we know the situation."

90. Anat Leibler (2004), "Statistician's Ambition: Governmentality, Modernity and National Legibility," *Israel Studies* 9:2: 121–49.

91. Charles E. Silberman (1985), *A Certain People: American Jews and Their Lives Today*. New York: Summit.

92. Yehouda Shenhav (2006), *The Arab Jews, A Postcolonial Reading of Nationalism, Religion, and Ethnicity*. Stanford: Stanford University Press.

93. Yoram Ettinger, *The Ettinger Report*, www.theettingerreport.com.

94. See Sophie M. Robison and J. Starr (1943), *Jewish Population Studies*. New York: Conference on Jewish Relations; Sidney Goldstein and Calvin Goldscheider (1968), *Jewish Americans: Three Generations in a Jewish Community*. Englewood Cliffs: Prentice Hall; Sidney Goldstein (1992), "Profile of American Jewry: Insights from the 1990 National Jewish Population Survey," *American Jewish Year Book* 92: 77–173; Roberta

Rosenberg Farber and Chaim I. Waxman (1999), *Jews in America: A Contemporary Reader*. Hanover and London: Brandeis University Press; Uzi Rebhun (2001), *Migration, Community and Identification: Jews in Late 20th Century America*. Jerusalem: Magnes Press [Hebrew]; Sergio DellaPergola (2005), "Was It the Demography? A Reassessment of U.S. Jewish Population Estimates, 1945–2001," *Contemporary Jewry* 25: 85–131; Len Saxe and Sergio DellaPergola (eds) (2013), *Contemporary Jewry* 33, Special issue on Jewish Demography in the United States.

95. Roberto Bachi (1977), *The Population of Israel*. Jerusalem: The Hebrew University of Jerusalem and Prime Minister's Office; Dov Friedlander and Calvin Goldscheider (1979), *The Population of Israel*. New York: Columbia University Press; U. O. Schmelz, Sergio DellaPergola, and Uri Avner (1991), *Ethnic Differences among Israeli Jews: A New Look*. Jerusalem: The Hebrew University of Jerusalem and The American Jewish Committee; Calvin Goldscheider (ed.) (1992), *Population and Social Change in Israel*. Boulder: Westview Press; Sergio DellaPergola (1993), "Demographic Changes in Israel in the Early 1990s," in J. Kop (ed.), *Israel Social Services 1992–93*. Jerusalem: The Center for Social Policy Studies in Israel, pp. 57–115; Calvin Goldscheider (1996), *Israel's Changing Society: Population, Ethnicity, and Development*. Boulder: Westview Press; Uzi Rebhun and Chaim I. Waxman (eds) (2004), *Jews in Israel: Contemporary Social and Cultural Patterns*. Hanover and London: Brandeis University Press.

96. Israel Central Bureau of Statistics, *Statistical Abstract of Israel*. Jerusalem (yearly); U. O. Schmelz (1981), *World Jewish Population: Regional Estimates and Projections*. Jerusalem: The Hebrew University of Jerusalem; Vivian Klaff (1998), "Broken Down by Sex and Age: Projecting the American Jewish Population," *Contemporary Jewry* 19: 1–37; Sergio DellaPergola, Uzi Rebhun, and Mark Tolts (2000), "Prospecting the Jewish Future: Population Projections, 2000–2080," *American Jewish Year Book* 100: 103–46; Sergio DellaPergola (2001), "Jerusalem's Population, 1995–2020: Demography, Multiculturalism and Urban Policies," *European Journal of Population* 17: 165–99; idem, "Demographic Trends in Israel and Palestine," *American Jewish Year Book* 103: 3–68.

97. For comprehensive statements of the case for policy-oriented research, see Sergio DellaPergola and Leah Cohen (eds) (1992), *World Jewish Population: Trends and Policies*. Jerusalem: The Hebrew University of Jerusalem; DellaPergola, *Jewish Demographic Policies*.

13 The State of Israel Studies: An Emerging Academic Field

Michael Kotzin and Elie Rekhess

Part I: Introduction

Over the past decade-and-a-half, Israel Studies has grown rapidly in North America as a distinctive academic field. The purpose of this chapter is to provide updated data on this development, advance understanding of the field, discuss certain challenges faced by the field, and identify directions for future growth.

Following this introduction, in Part II the chapter maps the current state of Israel Studies at universities around the world exclusive of Israel, with an emphasis on universities in the United States. This data includes information about various centers and institutes for Israel Studies; programs of Israel Studies; chairs, professorships, and lectureships; and other pertinent aspects of the field. The information is as accurate and complete as we could make it, though it should be noted that not all the desired details are readily available or easily identifiable. Furthermore, as up-to-date as we have tried to make this report, some of the data in it no doubt will be at least somewhat obsolete by the time this book appears in print.

Part III charts the development of the field while elaborating on the various conditions that have coalesced to trigger its rapid and considerable growth over the past decade. This section addresses the influences that have impacted the way in which the field has taken shape and the broadening of the subject matter being studied and taught within it. It also considers the challenges that have been encountered regarding the legitimacy of Israel Studies as an academic field, tied significantly to the role played by donors in the Jewish community in the growth of the field. This section of the chapter closes by considering issues involved in determining where Israel Studies programs are "housed" on various campuses. Then, in Part IV, the chapter concludes with an anticipation of future directions for this still-evolving field.[1]

Part II: Mapping the Field

In 2012, Israel Studies was being taught in 12 centers and institutes, 11 in the United States and 1 in Canada; in 9 programs, 7 of which are in the United States; and in 2 MA programs in the United Kingdom[2] (see Appendices). In 2012, there were 19 permanent chairs and professorships in Israel Studies, 13 of which are in the United States, and 34 visiting professorships in Israel Studies, all in the United States (Table 13.1).

Altogether, there are 21 chairs, professorships, and lectureships in Israel Studies: 13 in the United States and 8 outside the United States (excluding Israel). Of the 13 in the United States, 8 are within an existing center or program of Israel Studies and 5 are independent or affiliated with centers for Jewish Studies.[3] Of the eight outside the United States, six are independent from a center or program of Israel Studies, and two are part of these centers/programs.[4]

There are currently 34 universities in the United States that host visiting professors and scholars in Israel Studies. Seventeen of those universities established the positions,[5] 18 have one-year Schusterman Visiting Israeli Professors,[6] and one has a program with two positions supported in part by the Jewish Federation of Metropolitan Chicago.[7] Two of these universities (Boston University and the University of Maryland) have both established their own positions and also host Schusterman Visiting Professors.

Of the universities with centers, institutes, or programs of Israel Studies, two (University of California, Los Angeles [UCLA] and New York University) grant doctoral degrees in Israel Studies. Three of them (University of Calgary, University College London, and University of London) offer an MA, three (American University; California State University, Chico; and University of Maryland) offer

Table 13.1 Centers, Institutes, Programs, and Chairs in Israel Studies (2012)

	United States	Elsewhere	Total
Centers and institutes	11	1	12
Programs	7	2	9
MA programs	–	2	2
Chairs and professorships	13[a]	6	19
Visiting professorships	34[b]	–	34

[a] Eight of these positions are within a center or program of Israel Studies, and five stand independently of such institutions. For details, see Appendices 4 and 5.

[b] Twelve of these positions are within a center or program of Israel Studies, and 22 stand independently of such institutions; 34 institutions host visiting professors, so that number is the minimum number of visiting professorships, as several institutions have more than one position. Additionally, 17 of these positions have been established by the universities themselves, 18 are Schusterman Visiting Professors, and 2 are visiting postdoctoral fellows funded by the Jewish Federation of Metropolitan Chicago (there is some overlap because 2 institutions have both established positions themselves and host Schusterman Visiting Professors). For details, see Appendices 7, 8, and 9.

minors, and two (University of Florida, Wesleyan University) offer a concentration/certificate in Israel Studies. Four universities (Columbia University, New York University, University of Texas, and University of Washington) do not grant degrees in Israel Studies specifically, but offer related degrees in Jewish or Hebrew Studies or a similar field. Four (Brandeis University, Emory University, University of Nebraska, and Concordia University) of the institutions do not currently grant degrees in Israel Studies at all. Finally, one school (Moscow State University) offers a major in the Politics and Economics of Israel.

The topics of Israel-related courses vary, and they address a number of fields and themes. History courses in Israel Studies range from general surveys of the nation's history, to narrowly focused topics, such as "Historical Evidence and Interpretation: Israel and the 1967 June War." Common topics include the history of Zionism (ideology, organization, institutions), immigration, the British Mandate, the first decade of statehood (1948–58), and the 1960s, 1970s, and 1980s.[8] Popular subtopics within the category of Israeli society include Israel's identity; social, ethnic, communal, religious, and national cleavages; urbanization; the kibbutz; economic development; socioeconomic gaps; and the Arab minority in Israel.[9] In courses about state institutions, topics that may be examined include the study of the executive branch, the legislative branch (the Knesset), and the judicial system, with special emphasis on the constitutional aspect, and the nature of Israel as a Jewish and democratic state.[10] Both historical and contemporary aspects of the Israeli political system are usually analyzed in these courses. Major subtopics within this category include the prestate political system; political parties, movements, institutions, practices, and culture; election campaigns and results; leading political figures; and the place of the judiciary and religion in politics. The Israeli case is sometimes used in teaching comparative politics.[11] Courses on Israeli culture and art examine historical and contemporary examples of the literature, poetry, film, music, theater, and other art forms of Israel. They may study how literature, poetry, and various art forms reflect the development of Israeli identity, including its different subcultures and distinct ethnic/cultural groups; divisions within past and present-day Israel (Jews/Arabs, religious/secular Jews, Sephardic/Mizrahi communities, Holocaust survivors, the Sabra ideal, gender issues).[12] Courses on the Arab-Israeli conflict and peace process may examine the topic from different disciplinary viewpoints, such as history, political science, international relations, or security studies. Subtopics include the origin of the conflict; the 1948, 1967, 1973, and 1982 wars; the refugee problems, Israel and the PLO, the Israeli rule of the West Bank and Gaza Strip; history of the peace process; the two Intifadas; Israeli and Palestinian identity; and regional security.[13] Subtopics often addressed in classes on Israel's foreign policy include relations with the United States; European nations, USSR-Russia, Asian countries, and the Arab world; national security; nuclear weapons, arms control, and terrorism.[14] Subtopics that may be taught in courses about Israel's Arab minority may include Israeli Arabs' legal status; national identity; relations with the PLO; political activity; voting patterns; local government; socioeconomic development and gaps; the Druze, Christian, and Bedouin communities; and government policies.[15] Courses focusing on the topic of Israel and the Diaspora often address the connections and conflicts between Jews in Israel and in the Diaspora, as well as other subtopics, such as American Jews and the pro-Israel lobby in the United States.[16]

Hebrew is the most common language affiliated with Israel Studies; it is offered by 20 of the universities.[17] Yiddish is less common, offered by six of the universities,[18] and only one offers Ladino (Judeo-Spanish).[19]

Research and Programs

Although the majority of the institutions of Israel Studies focus on teaching, several conduct research projects related to the field. For example, the Gildenhorn Institute for Israel Studies at the University of Maryland has initiated a research project on "Israel 2023," exploring alternative scenarios for the Israeli polity and society when Israel reaches its seventy-fifth anniversary.[20]

The organization of academic events is an integral part of all centers, institutes, and programs of Israel Studies. Typical academic events include conferences,[21] symposia, colloquia, workshops, lectures, talks, forums, seminars, and panel discussions. Typical Israel Studies cultural events include film screenings and film festivals; concerts; exhibitions, showcases, and demonstrations; poetry readings; Israeli dance instruction; and theatrical performances.[22]

There are a number of central publications in the field of Israel Studies. Brandeis University's Schusterman Center for Israel Studies publishes the Schusterman Series in Israel Studies and books on Jewish Studies, Zionism, and Israel Studies. It also cosponsors the academic journal *Israel Studies* with Ben-Gurion University of the Negev. The University of Maryland's Gildenhorn Institute for Israel Studies publishes *Israel Studies Review* (ISR, the official periodical of the Association for Israel Studies [AIS]), as well as research papers and position papers.

Other related programming includes a range of summer institutes. The Schusterman Center at Brandeis University organizes an annual Summer Institute for Israel Studies (SIIS). Faculty from universities in North America and around the world participates in seminars at Brandeis and in Israel that will help them design courses in Israel Studies for their home universities. The SIIS has had 185 faculty members from 175 universities worldwide who have completed the program and taught thousands of students with syllabi designed at SIIS. SIIS fellows spend the first two weeks in residence at Brandeis and participate in seminars taught by distinguished Israel Studies scholars focusing on the society, history, politics, economics, culture, foreign affairs, and diplomacy of Israel. In Israel, participants connect with scholars, government officials, writers, artists, public intellectuals, and Jewish and Arab community leaders.[23] Additionally, the SIIS was used as a model for a series of workshops/seminars at Peking and Shandong Universities in China in the summer of 2009.[24] UCLA and the University of Maryland hold contests for student academic essays about Israeli politics, society, or culture. The University of Maryland hosts the Washington Israel Seminar, in which about 20 scholars who study Israel from universities around Washington, DC, meet to talk about, develop, and cooperate on projects.[25]

Many of the institutions surveyed offer study abroad programs in Israel. Most schools are affiliated with the leading Israeli universities. Some have more than one program, and several universities have as many as seven.[26] Denver University organizes student diplomacy trips to Israel and the West Bank through the Student Interfaith Peace Project. The University of Nebraska sponsors the Bethsaida Excavation Project. Emory University offers undergraduate internships in the United States and Israel. At University College in London, all undergraduate students in the Department of Hebrew and Jewish Studies spend their third year at the Hebrew University of Jerusalem, whose faculty members regularly come to teach in the department.[27]

Some centers offer important collections and sources. Emory University, for example, has a long list of primary source materials on its website.[28] UCLA has the Israeli Film and Media Collection. Yeshiva University has the Yeshiva

University Museum,[29] the Mendel Gottesman Library of Hebraica/Judaica,[30] and the Arch of Titus Digital Restoration Project.[31]

As a maturing field, Israel Studies is now represented by academic associations. The AIS is "an international, interdisciplinary scholarly society devoted to the academic and professional study of modern Israel"[32] founded in 1985. It organizes an annual conference, which, in 2012, was held in Haifa and dealt with "Multicultural Israel in a Global Perspective: Between One Society and Many Societies." The AIS publishes the *Israel Studies Review*,[33] which examines contemporary Israel from multiple disciplines, including the social sciences, history, the humanities, and cultural studies and also focuses on Israel's connections with the region and world. AIS promotes workshops and panels, including some at the International Studies Association's and the American Political Science Association's meetings, and hosts a reception and board meeting at the yearly MESA conference. In Israel, AIS collaborates with various scholarly associations, institutes, and universities. AIS members consist of academics from all disciplines in the social sciences and the humanities.[34] The European Association of Israel Studies (EAIS) is "an independent, international and scholarly association devoted to the academic study of Israel." For its first four years, it will be housed in the University of London's School of Oriental and African Studies (SOAS). Its inaugural conference was held in September 2011. Another conference, entitled "Israel and Europe: Mapping the Past, Shaping the Future," was held in September 2012. According to its charter, the EAIS "will promote, encourage, and sponsor scholarly activities" such as meetings, conferences, panels, workshops, research projects, scholarly investigations, a website and publications, and networking opportunities to spread "scholarly academic conference."[35]

A variety of foundations and institutions support Israel Studies on multiple campuses. The Charles and Lynn Schusterman Family Foundation, created in 1987, has played a major role in promoting Israel Studies in the United States by providing the chance for the study of contemporary Israel throughout the country and broadening and improving the quality of formal and informal Israel education.[36] One of its programs, the American-Israeli Cooperative Enterprise (AICE), offers information and training about Jewish history, culture, and politics for students and institutions. AICE, founded in 1993, implements the Schusterman Visiting Scholars Program, which places about 20 scholars at colleges in the United States each year, and the Schusterman Israel Scholar Awards, which give scholarships to graduate students studying fields related to Israel Studies. The Pears Foundation, which is funded by "a British family rooted in Jewish values," supports, among other things, positions in Israel Studies at the University of Manchester, the University of Leeds and SOAS, as well as support for the EAIS.[37] The Jewish Federation of Metropolitan Chicago operates an Israel Studies Project that supports Israel Studies programs on four campuses:

Northwestern University, the University of Chicago, the University of Illinois at Chicago, and the University of Illinois at Urbana-Champaign.[38]

Part III: Development of the Field

Israel Studies consists of multidisciplinary academic scholarship, research, and teaching on Israeli history, politics, society, and culture. It is focused on the modern State of Israel in the context of the historical developments that preceded its founding, its current characteristics, and its place in the Middle East. Israel Studies may be institutionalized in large university centers and institutes or smaller programs, or it may simply be taught by a chair or other faculty members. Research in this field aims to inform, raise awareness, and increase the knowledge and understanding of students, academics, decision makers, and other individuals with particular interest in the subject. The missions and priorities of Israel Studies programs may vary among scholarship and teaching, research, programming and events, the advancement of public understanding, and the preparation of policy studies.

Israel Studies as an academic discipline has developed significantly in the United States since the mid-1990s. Israel was previously taught about at times, but mostly in the context of the Israel-Arab conflict or in the framework of international relations. Israel was also often taught about in sociological and anthropological curricula, with a focus on modernization and immigration. However, as Ilan Troen, the Stoll Family Chair in Israel Studies and Director of the Schusterman Center for Israel Studies at Brandeis University, has observed, "Israeli history and society has only recently become a discrete topic or field of study within the humanities and social sciences, and included in university curricula."[39]

Troen believes that a foundational date in the establishment of Israel Studies was the appointment of Professor Ben Halpern to Brandeis University in 1960. A master historian of Zionism and the Yishuv, Halpern trained the first scholars who made Israel a major part of their oeuvre, among them Jehuda Reinharz and Ian Lustick.[40]

The founding of the AIS in 1985 was another key development.[41] However AIS was not involved in institutionally promoting the teaching of Israel Studies, and the major initial growth of the field took place in the 1990s. First came the establishment of the Jacob and Libby Goodman Institute for the Study of Zionism and Israel at Brandeis in 1992.[42] Then came the establishment of the Institute for the Study of Israel in the Middle East at the University of Denver in 1996,[43] to be followed by the Institute for the Study of Modern Israel at Emory University[44] and the Center for Israel Studies at American University[45] in 1998. Six additional centers for Israel Studies were then established between 2003 and

2010.[46] In addition, during these early twenty-first century years, seven programs for Israel Studies were established and more than 25 chairs, professorships, and visiting professorships were formed.

Since early in this century, there has been a particularly notable surge of academic interest in Israel Studies. As Gal Beckerman has observed, "a study conducted by the Cohen Center for Modern Jewish Studies at Brandeis University found that among 246 American campuses surveyed, there was a 69 percent increase in the number of courses that mainly focused on Israel from the 2005–2006 academic year to the 2008–2009 year. Only 28 percent of these courses dealt with the Israeli/Arab conflict. Most of them examine Israel as a culture, society, political system, and historical entity instead of simply a point of international conflict."[47] Similarly, Ilan Troen has pointed out that in 2010 "there [were] some 1,300 courses on the State of Israel [taught] . . . in U.S. universities. That is three times as many as there were three years ago."[48] Likewise, Yoram Peri, the Abraham S. and Jack Kay Chair in Israel Studies and the Director of the University of Maryland Gildenhorn Institute for Israel Studies, indicated that the number of students enrolled in Israel Studies course there rose from 200 in 2009–10 to 500 in 2011–12.[49]

The growing interest in Israel Studies has also been visible outside the classroom. Over the last two decades, three new journals have appeared in English: *Israel Studies*, published by Indiana University Press; *Israel Affairs*, published in London by Frank Cass Publishers; and *Israel Studies Review*, the official periodical of the Association for Israel Studies, published by the University of Maryland's Gildenhorn Institute for Israel Studies.[50] These periodicals operate with multidisciplinary editorial boards composed of scholars from the United States, Israel, and Britain. Moreover, academic publishers offer a greater number of monographs whether originally written in English or translated from Hebrew. The largest list is the State University of New York's Series on Israel Studies, initiated in 1988 and edited by Russell Stone, with dozens of books in print.[51]

Before moving forward in analyzing the factors that have contributed to the recent growth of this academic discipline, it is worth noting that the expansion has taken place in the context of controversy, a factor that outside commentators often dwell on. On one side are those who challenge the academic bona fides of Israel Studies altogether, charging that it is just a form of advocacy. On the other side are those who, arguing that practitioners in the field are as committed to observing academic standards as any other scholars, assert that the field fills an important pedagogical and scholarly niche and is no less legitimate than other fields that deal with complex subjects.

Media reporting on the matter has often focused on this debate, which at times mirrors aspects of the conflict that has engaged Israel since its establishment. For example, in June of 2005, at a time when the current growth in the field was first gaining traction and attracting significant attention, *The Chronicle of Higher Education* produced an extensive piece with the headline "The Politics of Israel Studies." In that article, Ali Banuazizi, a Professor of Psychology at Boston College and then the president of the Middle East Studies Association (which itself has at times been accused of anti-Israel partisanship), charged that people being hired to hold chairs in Israel Studies "would like . . . the academic study of Israel to be commensurate with the attention, special attention, that Israel receives in the United States, particularly in U.S. foreign policy." In contrast, Ronald Zweig, an Israeli who a short time before had been engaged to fill just such a chair at New York University, was cited as saying "that his own politics have nothing to do with his courses, and that he does not function as a classroom spokesman for the Israeli government. 'I don't consider presenting the Israeli perspective as part of my job,' he says."[52] Zweig had elsewhere declared that in accepting the chair he had "insisted that this job is not advocacy. . . . It's about scholarship."[53]

Taking its cue from what it called "a heated discussion" at the then just-completed annual meeting of the AIS held in Tucson, Arizona, the *Chronicle* article focused extensively on a somewhat related difference of opinion. Taking one side, Ian Lustick, a Professor of Political Science at the University of Pennsylvania, proclaimed that "Israel is now seen more as a function of the conflict than as the result of the Zionist blueprint," and he asserted that teaching should reflect that dynamic. The alternative position was presented by Kenneth Stein, Director of the Institute for the Study of Modern Israel at Emory University, who claimed that "the teaching of Israel's history has been hijacked" and went on to say: "We need to . . . put Israel . . . into the context of Jewish history."[54] Ilan Troen was also quoted in the article, saying: "Imagine if in America there were only people who studied Russia in terms of the Cold War or France and Germany only in terms of their conflict with each other. [That] would be a gross distortion of what those societies are really about." Echoing Stein's approach, Michael Stanislawski, Professor of History at Columbia University and head of a search committee filling the first chair in Israel Studies there, said: "In place of the sense of crisis, there should be recognition of a growing interest in Israel from the academic point of view."[55]

As philanthropic support for Israel Studies programs has expanded and gained attention, such debates have continued to preoccupy many of those reporting on the subject.[56] All the same, though, with a host of scholars on the scene and with more and more universities embracing the field, Israel Studies has taken its place as a solid academic discipline whose impressive growth can be attributed to a number of factors.

The first cause of the emergence of Israel Studies at this time has involved the post–Cold War world's growing sense of globalization, driven in part by a technological communications revolution that has brought about greater mutual dependency between countries. The need for understanding these developments and for enabling educated students to flourish within today's global environment has increasingly permeated academic life throughout North America and has been a major factor driving university administrators to introduce courses on international affairs into their curriculums, including courses on Israel.

Thus, Daniel Linzer, at the time Dean of Northwestern University's Weinberg College of Arts and Sciences, declared that "a priority for Northwestern and Weinberg College is expanding opportunities for students to learn about, and to participate in, international studies," as he described the university's establishment of an Israel Studies postdoctoral fellowship program in 2005, at the same time that a new offering in Turkish Studies was introduced there. Linzer went on to say: "Based on the vibrancy of our other international offerings, I expect that these new activities will find a ready audience."[57] In the same publication, Henry Bienen, then-president of Northwestern, was quoted as saying that "Northwestern students live in an increasingly interdependent world," and that "it is thus ever more important for Northwestern students to engage the world around them and to do this with a knowledge of cultures, languages, and the political economy of nations and peoples."[58]

Along with the advancement of a broad interest in international affairs, recent years have seen a particular rise in academic interest in the Middle East, long a region of cultural fascination and economic involvement for Americans. The region became especially central in the American consciousness following the terror attacks of September 11, 2001, and the subsequent invasion of Iraq. The interest has increased further with the evolution of American geopolitical and strategic involvements in the region and the drastic changes that have taken place there. The centrality of Israel as a key factor in much of that has been evident. This argument has also been stressed by university administrators.

Thus, when Eran Kaplan was recently named a Professor in Israel Studies at San Francisco State University, he expressed the hope to "show students how to move past the black and white of the issues involving Israel and invite them to apply what they learn to other global issues."[59] Similarly, in England, where new programs and chairs have also recently been established, *The Guardian* described the approach of Colin Shindler, Professor of Israeli Studies at the School of Oriental and African Studies at the University of London and soon-to-be chair of the newly created European Association of Israel Studies, by saying that "the decision to expand Israel Studies is a response to growing demand from students to know more about the political, cultural, social, and economic background to events in the Middle East and is an attempt to offer an academic alternative to what he [Shindler] terms 'the megaphone war.'"[60]

A second factor that has contributed to the dramatic growth in Israel Studies programs and chairs relates to funding. The above-noted developments have played out at a time of financial stress, and at most universities the urge to enlarge the curriculum with Israel-related material has not easily translated into a readiness or ability to provide their own funds to support the introduction of these courses. Much of that load has instead fallen upon outside donors. And here too, external trends at hand during the opening decade of the twenty-first century have played a significant part in the process, stimulating a readiness by Jewish donors to help make these programs feasible.

Jewish support for higher education is hardly a new phenomenon. Members of the Jewish community have long been generous in giving to their alma maters and to universities in their communities. Indeed, most of the fields supported by this largesse are unrelated to issues of particular Jewish communal interest, and many gifts reflect personal preferences, a sense of "paying back" by donors who have "made it" in fields of their own professional accomplishment, or in the case of the teaching hospital, a desire to make a contribution helpful in effecting cures in areas where loved ones have suffered.

One major area in which communal interests have helped to drive the readiness to support programs has been the field of Jewish Studies—a subject that developed significantly several decades earlier than did the growth of Israel Studies. While the broader subject of Jewish Studies is the focus of this entire volume, it is useful to reflect here on the intended purposes of that support, which reflect a somewhat different orientation from what has been manifested regarding Israel Studies.

Briefly put, it can be suggested that support for Jewish Studies in general has, for one thing, reflected pride in the academic endorsement of the entrance of Jewish history, learning, and thought into the mainstream of American intellectual life and a desire to advance academic treatment of those subjects. Additionally, at a time when research carried out by community organizations was showing that Jewish continuity was in jeopardy and that the level of young people's Jewish literacy was low, many in the community saw university courses as a way to fill a major communal gap. Meanwhile, a great deal of early donor backing for Jewish Studies was aimed at supporting Holocaust education, reflecting an urge to advance understanding and sustain knowledge of the Holocaust, particularly at a time when it was increasingly seen as "ancient history," with fewer and fewer survivors, eyewitnesses, and others for whom it was a personal experience still alive.

The motivation for advancing Israel Studies, it can be suggested, has come from similar but also different sources. In part, this urge was also driven by a desire to reach Jewish students—in this case, by connecting them with Israel as a means of enhancing their sense of Jewish identity. As Ilan Troen observed in commenting on the interests of members of the Jewish community in the mid-1990s: "The problem for them was less the status of the state of Israel and more the recognition of Israel as a vital component in building the Jewish identity of

Jewish youth in the U.S."[61] In the past decade, similar impulses and goals have led to the creation of the project known as Birthright Israel, through which the community provides free organized trips to Israel, which have been seen as offering highly positive experiences to Jewish youth.[62]

In part, the impetus for developing the field was also closely tied to developments in the region—and in this case the goal was not only to reach Jewish students. Russell A. Stone, a Professor Emeritus at American University and one of the founders of the Association for Israel Studies, has noted that the fiftieth anniversary of Israel's independence, commemorated in 1998, generated much interest in the field, along with the outbreak of the Second Intifada in 2000.[63] In fact, the collapse of the Oslo Peace Process in the fall of 2000 was accompanied by two unfolding sets of events which had a significant impact: the escalating terror war against Israeli civilians, which was embodied in the Second (or al-Aksa) Intifada, and also a concomitant campaign aimed at challenging Israel's moral legitimacy and its right to exist as the nation-state of the Jewish people.

The terror war, though eventually contained, caused thousands of casualties and replaced the hope—held by many in the nineties—that peace was about to be achieved with a sense that Israel's physical security was at risk in ways it had not been thought to be for some time. Meanwhile, the anti-Israel war of words and images continued to grow in scope, creating a strong feeling of how much was at stake for Jewish communities and the sense that America itself—especially its college campuses—had to a certain extent become a battleground.

Many of Israel's supporters saw the intensifying anti-Israel political campaign as distorting historic and contemporary truths in advancing a polemical case driven by ideology and, in numerous instances, by bias. While activity of that sort has been more widespread in Europe than in the United States, its most congenial home in North America has been on university campuses, which in general have been more sympathetic to the Palestinian narrative and cause and more critical of Israel than the broader American population commonly is.

The campus-based agitation which has advanced this hostility—including pro-Palestinian demonstrations and street theater; vigorous promotion of boycotts, divestment, and sanctions; and disruptions of pro-Israel demonstrations and programs—has mostly been carried out by students, with some faculty involvement or support. But faculty-driven classroom activity has also raised concerns. This has pertained not only to courses with a specific Middle Eastern focus, but also to classes taught in a wide range of areas—including archeology, history, geography, sociology, and literature—where faculty members have exploited the classroom setting to convey messages that have been seen as factually questionable and hostile to Israel.

A groundbreaking study of the earlier development of these trends was Martin Kramer's 2001 book *Ivory Towers on Sand: The Failure of Middle Eastern Studies in America*.[64] The June 1967 War, Kramer asserts, was a turning point in the nature of Middle East Studies in the United States:[65] "From 1967," he writes, "the Arab-Israeli conflict made for a deepening politicization of the field, clouding the reputation for disinterested objectivity so important to the founders [of Middle East Studies]."[66]

A decade later, according to Kramer, "Middle Eastern Studies came under a take-no-prisoners assault, which rejected the idea of objective standards, disguised the vice of politicization as the virtue of commitment, and replaced proficiency with ideology. The text that inspired the movement was entitled *Orientalism*, and the revolution it unleashed has crippled Middle Eastern Studies to this day."[67]

The author of *Orientalism* was Edward Said, a well-known Palestinian American Professor of English at Columbia University in New York. Elaborating on the impact of his book 20 years after its publication in 1978, Kramer said: "*Orientalism* made it acceptable, even expected, for scholars to spell out their own political commitments as a preface to anything they wrote or did. More than that, it also enshrined an acceptable hierarchy of political commitments, with Palestine at the top, followed by the Arab nation and the Islamic world. They were the long-suffering victims of Western racism, American imperialism, and Israeli Zionism—the three legs of the Orientalist stool."[68] In this context, then, when Israel was taught, it was most often in the framework of the Israeli-Palestinian conflict—with the likelihood of the approach being sympathetic to the Palestinian side. For friends of Israel, not only was there a considerable and serious gap in the curriculum, but also when the subject of Israel was treated, it was not necessarily done according to strict academic standards.

This perceived slant of the Middle East Studies centers was seen as resulting from—or at least being made possible by—funding from Iran and oil-rich Arab Gulf countries that wanted to improve their images beginning in the mid-seventies, at a time when federal and foundation funding for Middle East Studies was drying up. A notable example, discussed by Kramer, was a major endowment that Georgetown University secured from Libya in 1977—and returned in 1981.[69] Such giving continued in the 1980s and the 1990s, including a 1986 donation of $5 million made by Saudi arms dealer Adnan Khashoggi to American University for a sports center and a 1998 gift from the Sultan bin Abdulaziz al Saud Foundation to the University of California at Berkeley's Arab and Islamic Studies Center.[70] Especially controversial was a gift from the president of the United Arab Emirates to Harvard Divinity School in 2000. It was returned in 2004 after it was disclosed that the donor had also supported a policy for engaging in discourse that "contradicted the principles of interfaith tolerance."[71]

Another burst of giving could be seen following the September 11, 2001, World Trade Center and Pentagon terror attacks, when Muslim countries were especially eager to advance a positive image of Islam. For example, in 2005,

Harvard University and Georgetown University each announced $20 million gifts from the Saudi businessman and member of the Saudi royal family, Prince Alwaleed bin Talal bin Abdulaziz Alsaud. As the *New York Times* reported at the time, both gifts were made to support Islamic Studies, with the goal of advancing greater understanding of Islam.[72]

It was in this context, seeing a considerable gap in the curriculum, and believing that Israel, when included, was taught often in a fashion more appropriate to the realm of partisan debate, that members of several Jewish communities concluded that the playing field was not level. Resigned to the fact that most universities on their own were not going to remedy that condition, they considered it appropriate and desirable to play an ameliorative role. Some universities then came on board with matching funds.[73]

As the authors of a study produced in 2006 by the Israel on Campus Coalition wrote: "Conceptually, Middle East study centers are supposed to provide students and professors with the opportunity to examine the complexities of that region from a variety of perspectives and dimensions. Yet today, the approximately 125 Middle East study centers that exist across America tend to view Israel solely through the lens of the Arab-Israeli conflict or not at all. This situation, and the frequent complaints of hostility toward Israel within those departments, has stimulated the creation of Israel Studies programs and departments."[74]

Notwithstanding these factors, while the motivation for supporting the establishment of Israel Studies programs may have been driven in great part by a concern about Israel's image, administrators, faculty members teaching Israel Studies courses, and funders as well, by and large acted with recognition and respect for academic norms and principles.

Thus, for example, the *New York Times* column that focused on the NYU appointment reported that "Professor Zweig assigns readings from Arab and Arab-American scholars like Rashid Khalidi, as well as dissident Israelis including Avi Shlaim."[75] Similarly, Ilan Troen is described by Liel Leibovitz as denying "the allegation that he, or any other endowed Israel Studies professor, was appointed as a foot-soldier in a war against pro-Palestinian scholarship. 'I don't agree with the notion of combat,' he said. 'It suggests propaganda. It suggests advocacy. I don't think that's what any of us are about. We're real academics . . . we're there to combat ignorance, not advocate a particular line."[76]

On that theme, Alex Joffe, a research scholar with the Institute for Jewish and Community Research, wrote: "American Jews are unquestionably dedicated to the ideals of the American university. . . . Donors to Israel Studies programs also know that their critics have knives sharpened and are ready to strike at the first sign of excessive enthusiasm. Therefore, intellectual leaders of Israel Studies have repeatedly emphasized that their goal is academic inquiry, not advocacy." Joffe concluded, "Israel Studies programs promise to represent Israel seriously rather than as a cartoon villain in a post-colonial morality play and to use the best intellectual tools to hearken back to nearly-vanished ideals of academic integrity."[77] Substantiating that kind of a claim, Yitzak Benhorin observed in 2010 that "whoever visits the University of Maryland campus could not possibly make the mistake of thinking that Israel Studies department is a mouthpiece for Israeli PR efforts."[78]

While the Lustick-Stein debate described in the *Chronicle of Higher Education* may have represented the prevailing situation in 2005, as Israel Studies has grown in the past half-dozen years, it is the Stein perspective that seems to have held greater sway. This is documented in the extensive January 2010 "Report on the Teaching of Israel on U.S. College Campuses 2008–09" carried out at Brandeis University. The authors, Annette Koren and Emily Einhorn, making a comparison to an earlier study of courses offered in 2005–6, noted that their current study "finds a 'normalization' of Israel study within the university curriculum. From course titles and descriptions, we see a move toward viewing Israel as a culture, society, political system, and historical entity rather than solely as a locus for international conflict."[79] Colin Shindler identified a similar trend in England on the occasion of the expansion of Israel Studies there. As *The Guardian* reported: "For Shindler, the increasing interest being shown by students in different aspects of Israel, from its politics to its art and films, is part of a drive to understand the country and people outside the context of the Israel/Palestine conflict."[80]

A third factor contributing to the current growth in Israel Studies, in this case by adding to the interest, has been a development in Israel itself that can be seen both in the cultural realm and in academia. The trend has expressed itself in a "turn inward" that has included a shifting of the focus of academic research from the traditional study of the history of Zionism, the establishment of the State of Israel, and Israel's conflict with its Arab neighbors, to a wider examination of the sociology, anthropology, politics, ethnicity, culture, literature, art, theater, and cinema of Israeli society. With the emergence of the "New Historians" in the late 1980s significantly contributing to this trend,[81] these developments within Israeli academia have added insights and data for those teaching these subjects in North America in a way that has made such coursework both deeper and more rounded. Meanwhile, as Israeli literary figures and visual artists have also turned inward for subject matter in their way, leading to greater personal introspection and to sharper focusing on personal relationships in their writings, art, and films, the resulting cultural products have become both more particular and at the same time more universal and thereby more accessible to audiences and students in the United States. At the same time, Israeli life, while retaining its particularity, has in certain ways also come to more greatly resemble the American condition—making the art that reflects this life more accessible in that way too. And so, for example, Israeli television shows have become virtual templates for such powerful, popular American television dramas as "In Treatment" and "Homeland."

Returning to the practical realm, a fourth factor that has helped enable Israel Studies to grow in North America over the past decade has been the greater availability of Israeli academics. Given the belt-tightening policies adopted by Israeli universities and the decreasing number of employment opportunities in Israeli institutions of higher learning, a growing number of faculty members have taken leave from their positions in Israel and have responded to the demand in North America.

This availability has made it possible for a gap to be filled, since American universities have been far from able to produce a sufficient number of scholars and teachers in the field able to teach the many courses that have been added to the curriculum. There has thus been a fortunate confluence of circumstances where a newly created demand has been filled by visitors coming for limited timeframes or by professors taking long-term appointments, with many of the visitors brought to campuses around the country by the AICE with funding from the Charles and Lynn Schusterman Family Foundation, which in many ways has been a major force in advancing Israel Studies nationally. Meanwhile, some communities and schools have taken similar steps on their own, as exemplified by the programs carried out on four Illinois campuses thanks to the support of the Jewish Federation of Metropolitan Chicago, or the Younes and Soraya Nazarian Center for Israel Studies at UCLA, which represents another major community-supported effort.

Universities that have embraced the programs and courses that have brought about the growth in this field have struck a chord. The Israel Studies courses that have entered the curriculum at many institutions of higher learning have not only provided an academically sound alternative to treatments of the subject matter to those that previously prevailed in a number of places, but they have also filled a widespread vacuum elsewhere. This growth in Israel Studies has brought into many institutions' course listings an approach that is aimed at seeing Israel whole and as a member of the family of nations worthy of study and understanding in reference to its history, economy, sociology, political structure, culture, and other fields of inquiry that are regularly applied to other nations and regions. As Jan Jaben-Eilon notes, referencing an observation made by Russell Stone, "academic programs that revolve around Israel parallel other programs like Russian Studies or Latin American Studies, which are usually interdisciplinary programs."[82]

This overall development can be seen as paralleling a broader situation of the past decade as well, for it is occurring at a time when a range of activities in Israel have blossomed in ways that are fascinating in themselves, of global significance, and of interest to the North American university student population. We refer, in particular, to the burst of technological advances that has characterized the past several years in Israel; to the economic stability and growth that have been achieved in a time of economic difficulty throughout the world; and to a veritable renaissance in literature, film, theater, dance, and other creative arts, all of which are drawing increasing attention to the Israeli scene. The result has been an enriched curriculum responding to and generating student interest of a sort that has made these courses very popular on university campuses where they have been offered, with student enrollment and responsiveness demonstrating that the appeal of these courses is not at all limited to Jewish students.

Testimony to this fact is provided by the heads of three of the key programs in the field cited in Jan Jaben-Eilon's *Jerusalem Post* article "Studying Israel: Israel Has Finally Arrived."[83] Attributing the growth of the field in part to "academic interest by students," Arieh Saposnik, Director of the Younes and Soraya Nazarian Center for Israel Studies at the UCLA, is quoted as saying that "the Israel-Palestinian conflict is very hot," and Jaben-Eilon then paraphrases what he went on to say, adding that "ideally, students will develop an interest beyond the conflict and, in fact, all the Israel Studies programs offer a variety of courses." Jaben-Eilon goes on to say that, "according to [Ilan] Troen [at Brandeis], [Ron] Zweig [at NYU], and [Arieh] Saposnik [at UCLA], courses around the country are so oversubscribed that they must turn away students."[84]

In sum, the growth of Israel Studies at this time, and the way the field is being defined, is very much a result of conditions that have emerged during the past decade. A desire to address a burgeoning interest in international affairs has been joined by the identification of a gap in academically sound and wide-ranging instruction in a particular area of international studies. Donors have stepped forward with an interest in filling that gap, and suitable faculty members have been supplied to meet the demand for teaching experts in the field. The result has been that larger numbers of courses in Israel Studies are being offered, and they have been greeted by a strong response from the student population—which has, in turn, stimulated further growth in the field. Given the controversies and differences surrounding the Israeli-Palestinian conflict, not to mention the potential structural tension between community interests and academic values, this has not all happened without suspicion and criticism from some quarters. But university officials have been comfortable in validating the academic bona fides of these programs, and Israel Studies has emerged as a vigorous, still-growing, multifaceted field.

One question, however, remains to be answered. Where, in each university's structure, should these programs and courses be placed? While venues like the Middle East Studies centers established at many American universities in the 1980s and the 1990s might have seemed a logical choice, many of them were inhospitable to an unbiased and broadly based treatment of Israel. Those centers dealt with Israel mostly in connection with its conflict with Palestinians and often included faculty members with political leanings sympathetic to Palestinian positions on the conflict. Similar circumstances could be seen regarding many other Middle East programs. In light of that situation, as Israel Studies has grown as a discipline in the past decade, it has generally either been housed in Jewish Studies frameworks or established in stand-alone programs. As Liel Leibovitz observed, "discouraged by the risk of donating money to Middle East departments, some Jewish donors are opting to establish Israel chairs within a Jewish Studies department where they perceive faculty committees are more likely to be sympathetic to Israel."[85] However, while the decisions about where to place Israel Studies may have made sense, certain complexities have emerged.

As far as placement in Jewish Studies goes, there clearly is a natural alignment based on a number of factors, and the newer field of Israel Studies has been making its way into this broader field in recent years.[86] The affinity starts with modern Israel's geographical location on the land where the Jewish people lived and ruled in ancient times and where they had a continuous presence, albeit drastically reduced during most of the centuries of exile, and with which they felt a strong connection. Similarly, the history of Zionist thought and activity is tied to the history of Jews in Europe and elsewhere, while prestate Zionist immigration and settlement, and then the establishment of the State of Israel, can be connected with the Holocaust and other aspects of Jewish experience in both early and mid-twentieth century Europe, as well as with the experience of the Jews in Arab lands. The identification of Israel as a "Jewish state" provides further justification for placing Israel Studies in Jewish Studies. Meanwhile, a growing attention to the concept of Jewish peoplehood and to Israel-Diaspora relations bears appropriately on these matters. As Ilan Troen, Director of the Schusterman Center for Israel Studies at Brandeis University, has noted, "within 60 years, Israel's relative share of the Jewish world grew from 6 percent to 40 percent, and the specialists in Jewish Studies are beginning to realize that this is where the future is."[87]

All the same, many of these ways of looking at the subject need not necessarily be associated with Jewish Studies, and they certainly do not cover the totality of the Israel Studies curriculum. Furthermore, not only does Israel Studies not need to be subsumed under the broader heading of Jewish Studies, but there are even those who say that putting Israel Studies there leads to handling it in a limited fashion which might cut Israel Studies off from other profitable areas of study.

In a nutshell, placement in Jewish Studies can lead to a form of "ghettoization"—to the treatment of Israel not as a country in the world but merely as a manifestation of Jewish life, a tendency which could drive away examination by scholars in other fields and be off-putting for students. Rather than facilitating the study of Israel as a nation with a history and identity that, although greatly defined by Jewish-related themes, is not limited to them, placement in Jewish Studies can be counterproductive to the achievement of that goal.

Furthermore, as attendance at Jewish Studies conferences and conversations with Jewish Studies and Israel Studies faculty reveal, there is an element of tension involved here. In particular, a degree of protectiveness and even resentment has surfaced among some longstanding Jewish Studies faculty members as Israel Studies has emerged as a "growth area." In their eyes, Israel Studies is an upstart promoted by community members with nonacademic interests, and, when added to the curriculum, threatens to overwhelm less fashionable subjects while draining budgets needed to sustain more traditional Jewish Studies curriculum.

As Leonard Binder, a distinguished veteran in the field of Middle East Studies, said: "When framed by these well-established academic tracks [i.e. Middle East and Islamic Studies on the one hand and Jewish Studies on the other], Israel Studies are limited by the paradigms that channeled these alternative academic schemas."[88]

Different universities have found their own solutions to these issues. Where lone courses have been offered, either as permanent components of the curriculum or taught by visitors, they most often have been handled either through Jewish Studies programs or simply through the disciplines in which those specific courses fit (e.g. history, sociology, literature, etc.). When there has been enough magnitude to create a program in Israel Studies, those programs have tended to be established either as units within Jewish Studies or in a standalone fashion, with the scholars frequently appointed within the framework of their individual academic disciplines. This pattern has enabled the programs to avoid the strain of being part of Middle East Studies and the potential ghettoization of simply being part of Jewish Studies, while at the same enabling Israel Studies to achieve its own identity.

Exactly what it is that defines the field of Israel Studies is a matter still in flux. But what emerges from examination of the way the field is establishing itself is that Israel is today being studied internally as well as in a wider range of contexts. External approaches include looking at Israel in relationship to the history of the region and of the world; considering it within the framework of political, sociological, cultural, and economic developments in the region and of the world; and so on. When looked at internally, Israel becomes a more closed-in unit, to be studied intensely with in-depth reference to a single discipline or in a holistic, interdisciplinary fashion. This, for example, could mean considering the interlocking connections between Israel's literature, sociology, history, and political affairs, as well as other dimensions of the Israeli reality.

All in all, then, while continuing to evolve, Israel Studies has firmly taken its place in higher education as a serious academic field.

Part IV: Conclusion: Future Directions

Given the factors that have led to the growth of Israel Studies over the past decade, it appears safe to predict that the field of Israel Studies will continue to grow and develop, rewarding scholarly investigation and stimulating increased student interest, along with cementing university and community support.

As this happens, one further development will probably grow increasingly essential: the expansion, growth, and advancement of degree-granting programs in Israel Studies throughout North America—programs producing PhD graduates in the field and creating academic positions to which those scholars may aspire on an increasing number of campuses.

The current abundance of Israel-trained scholars, as visitors to North American universities or with permanent appointments there, is something that will probably continue to be seen in the short as well as the long term. But with the field growing and its increasing professorial needs being met by other means as well, those scholars will inevitably cease to be the predominant holders of chairs in the field as they currently are.

In conclusion, like practically anything having to do with Israel in today's world, there are plenty of issues in play surrounding Israel Studies at North American universities. In addition—and also like so much having to do with Israel—the field is characterized by vibrancy, accomplishment, meaning, and value. As Israel takes its place among the nations of the world, Israel Studies is taking its place in the realm of academia.

Part V: Appendices

Appendix 1: Israel Studies Programs

United States

1. The Center for Israel Studies, American University.[89]
2. The Center for Israel Studies, American Jewish University.[90]
3. The Schusterman Center for Israel Studies, Brandeis University.[91]
4. The Institute for Israel and Jewish Studies, Columbia University.[92]
5. The Institute for the Study of Modern Israel [within the Institute for Jewish Studies], Emory University.[93]
6. The Taub Center for Israel Studies [within the Skirball Department of Hebrew and Judaic Studies], New York University.[94]
7. The Younes and Soraya Nazarian Center for Israel Studies, University of California, Los Angeles.[95]

8. The Institute for the Study of Israel in the Middle East, University of Denver.[96]
9. The Joseph and Alma Gildenhorn Institute for Israel Studies, University of Maryland.[97]
10. The Natan and Hannah Schwalb Center for Israel and Jewish Studies, University of Nebraska, Omaha.[98]
11. The Center for Israel Studies, Yeshiva University.[99]

Canada

1. The Azrieli Institute of Israel Studies, Concordia University.[100]

Appendix 2: Programs of Israel Studies

United States

1. Modern Jewish and Israel Studies, California State University, Chico.[101]
2. The Program on Israeli Law, Economy and Society, University of California, Berkeley.[102]
3. The Israel Studies Track in the Center for Jewish Studies, University of Florida.[103]
4. The Schusterman/Josey Program in Judaic and Israel Studies, University of Oklahoma.[104]
5. Israel Studies in the Department of Middle Eastern Studies and the new Israel Studies Collaborative in the Schusterman Center for Jewish Studies, University of Texas at Austin.[105]
6. The Modern Hebrew and Israel Studies Program in the Department of Near Eastern Languages and Civilization, University of Washington, Seattle.[106]
7. The Jewish and Israel Studies Program, Wesleyan University.[107]

Canada

1. The Israel Studies Program, University of Calgary.[108]

Russia

1. The major in Politics and Economics of Israel in the Department for Jewish Studies, Moscow State University.[109]

Appendix 3: MA Programs in Israel Studies

There are two Israel Studies programs that grant only MA degrees, both of which are in the United Kingdom:[110]

1. The MA in Modern Israeli Studies in the Department of Hebrew and Jewish Studies, University College London.[111]
2. The MA in Israeli Studies in the Centre for Jewish Studies in the School of Oriental and African Studies, University of London.[112]

Appendix 4: Chairs, Professorships, and Lectureships in the United States within Existing Centers or Programs of Israel Studies

1. The Stoll Family Chair in Israel Studies in the Schusterman Center for Israel Studies, Brandeis University.[113]
2. The Yosef H. Yerushalmi Professor of Israel and Jewish Studies, in the Institute for Israel and Jewish Studies, Columbia University.[114]
3. The William E. Schatten Professor of Contemporary Middle Eastern and Israeli Studies in the Institute for the Study of Modern Israel, Emory University.[115]
4. The Marilyn and Henry Taub Professor of Israel Studies in the Taub Center for Israel Studies, New York University.[116]
5. The Rosalinde and Arthur Gilbert Foundation Lecturer in Israeli Law, Economy and Society in the Berkeley Institute for Jewish Law and Israeli Law, Economy and Society, University of California, Berkeley.[117]
6. The Rosalinde and Arthur Gilbert Foundation Chair in Israel Studies in the Younes and Soraya Nazarian Center for Israel Studies, University of California, Los Angeles.[118]
7. The Abraham S. and Jack Kay Chair in Israel Studies in the Joseph and Alma Gildenhorn Institute for Israel Studies, University of Maryland.[119]
8. The Schusterman/Josey Chair in Judaic History in the Schusterman/Josey Program in Judaic and Israel Studies, University of Oklahoma.[120]

Appendix 5: Chairs, Professorships, and Lectureships in the United States Independent of a Center or Program of Israel Studies

1. The Michael and Elaine Serling Chair in Israel Studies in the Jewish Studies Program, Michigan State University.[121]
2. The Saul and Sonia Schottenstein Chair in Israel Studies in the Melton Center for Jewish Studies, Ohio State University.[122]

3. The Stampfer Professor of Israel Studies in the Harold Schnitzer Family Program in Judaic Studies, Portland State University.[123]
4. The Richard and Rhoda Goldman Chair in Israel Studies in the Department of Jewish Studies, San Francisco State University.[124]
5. The Harvey M. Meyerhoff Assistant Professor of Israel Studies, University of Wisconsin.[125]

Appendix 6: Chairs, Professorships, and Lectureships Outside the United States

1. The Leon Liberman Research Chair in Modern Israel Studies in the Australian Centre for the Study of Jewish Civilisation, Monash University.[126]
2. The Stanley Lewis Professor of Israel Studies, Oxford University.[127]
3. The Yossi Harel Chair in Modern Israel Studies in the School of History, Art History and Philosophy, Sussex University.[128]
4. A lecturer/senior lecturer in Israel and Middle East Studies based in the School of Politics and International Studies, University of Leeds.[129]
5. An Israel Studies lectureship, University of Manchester.[130]
6. The Andrea and Charles Bronfman Chair of Israeli Studies, University of Toronto.[131]
7. The Chair of the Department of Modern Israel Studies, Canada Christian College and the School of Graduate Theological Studies.[132]
8. The Kahanoff Chair in Israel Studies in the Israel Studies Program, University of Calgary.[133]

Appendix 7: Visiting Professorships in Israel Studies at US Universities[134]

1. Visiting faculty in Israel Studies hosted by the Elie Wiesel Center and the Department of Religion, Boston University.[135]
2. The Aaron and Cecile Goldman Visiting Israel Professorship in the Department of Government, Georgetown University.[136]
3. The Nachschon Visiting Professorship, Harvard University.[137]
4. The Ginor Visiting Professor of Israel Studies in the Program in Modern Jewish Studies, Jewish Theological Seminary.[138]
5. The Mirowski Israel Studies Visiting Scholars Program, Temple University.[139]
6. The Charles and Lynn Schusterman Visiting Professor in Israel Studies, the David and Andrea Stein Visiting Professor of Modern Israel Studies,

and the Arizona Center for Judaic Studies' Visiting Professor in Modern Israel Studies (in past years), University of Arizona.[140]

7. The David Bornblum/Lemsky Visiting Scholar in Israel Studies, University of Memphis.[141]

8. The Efroymson Visiting Israeli Scholar in the Department of Jewish, Islamic, and Near Eastern Languages and Cultures, Washington University, St. Louis.[142]

9. Visiting faculty members (from the University of Tel Aviv, Sapir College, and the Hebrew University of Jerusalem) in the Institute for Israel and Jewish Studies, Columbia University.[143]

10. Israeli Visiting Professor Program in the Institute for the Study of Modern Israel, Emory University.[144]

11. The Michael and Elaine Serling Visiting Israeli Scholars Fund in the Jewish Studies Program, Michigan State University.[145]

12. Visiting scholars and postdoctoral fellows in Israel Studies in the Taub Center for Israel Studies, New York University.[146]

13. The Richard and Rhoda Goldman Visiting Israeli Professor, Visiting Professor in Israeli Law, Economy and Society, and two visiting scholars in the Berkeley Institute for Jewish Law and Israeli Law, Economy and Society, University of California, Berkeley.[147]

14. A visiting research fellow and postdoctoral fellow in the Younes and Soraya Nazarian Center for Israel Studies, University of California, Los Angeles.[148]

15. Visiting professors and assistant professors in the Gildenhorn Institute for Israel Studies, University of Maryland.[149]

16. Visiting lecturers in the Natan and Hannah Schwalb Center for Israel and Jewish Studies, University of Nebraska.[150]

17. A visiting scholar in Jewish and Israel Studies, Wesleyan University.[151]

Appendix 8: US Universities that Hosted a Schusterman Visiting Israeli Professor in 2011–12

According to "AICE Visiting Israeli Professors 2011–12 Academic Year," the following schools hosted a Schusterman Visiting Israeli Professor in that year:

1. American University
2. Boston University
3. California State University, Chico
4. Indiana University
5. Northeastern University
6. Rutgers University

7. San Diego State University
8. Stanford University
9. State University of New York Binghamton
10. Tulane University
11. University of California, Davis
12. University of Denver
13. University of Illinois at Urbana-Champaign
14. University of Maryland
15. University of Michigan
16. University of Minnesota
17. University of Texas, Austin
18. University of Virginia

Appendix 9: Positions Supported by the Jewish Federation of Metropolitan Chicago Israel Studies Project

Since the fall of 2005, Northwestern University has maintained a program for Israeli postdoctoral fellows who come for two years at a time. The program was established through a direct agreement between Henry Bienen, then the president of Northwestern, and Itamar Rabinovich, then the president of Tel Aviv University, with Asher Susser, then the director of the Moshe Dayan Center for Middle Eastern and African Studies at Tel Aviv University, playing an instrumental role in putting it together.

At the University of Illinois at Urbana-Champaign, a project which was inaugurated in the fall of 2005 annually brings writers in residence or scholars in residence for visits that have gone anywhere from one week to the entire school year. In the fall of 2009, the university hired a full-time, tenure track assistant professor in Comparative and World Literature who teaches courses on Israeli Literature and Culture.

Since the school-year 2007–8, semester-long visiting professors have been brought to the University of Illinois at Chicago. And since the school year of 2008–9, with a one-year hiatus, quarter-long visitors have been brought to the Divinity School of the University of Chicago through a program called "Religion and Culture in the 21st Century: New Perspectives from Israel."

Notes

1. The authors wish to thank Ilan Troen, Alan Dowty, and Itamar Rabinovich for reading the manuscript and for their most helpful and insightful comments. The authors are also grateful to Elisabeth Boeck for her assistance in meticulously collecting data on Israel Studies.

2. Arranged alphabetically according to university.
3. See Appendices 4 and 5.
4. See Appendix 6.
5. See Appendix 7.
6. See Appendix 8.
7. See Appendix 9.
8. Authors whose works are often assigned for history courses include Shlomo Avineri, Dan Bar-On, Michael J. Cohen, Motti Golani, Yosef Gorny, Ben Halpern, Arthur Hertzberg, Dan Horowitz, Moshe Lissak, Israel Kolatt, Walter Laqueur, Adel Manna, Benny Morris, Sari Nusseibeh, Robert I. Rotberg, Howard Sachar, Anita Shapira, Avi Shlaim, Michael Stanislawski, Kenneth Stein, and Ilan Troen. For a list of books related to Israel Studies recently published by members of the Association for Israel Studies, see www.aisisraelstudies.org/new_books.ehtml.
9. Some of the major authors whose works are assigned for this topic include Michael N. Barnett, Eliezer Ben-Rafael, Sami Shalom Chetrit, Yossi Dahan, Alan Dowty, Dan Horowitz, Aziza Khazzoom, Baruch Kimmerling, Moshe Lissak, Yiftachel Oren, Yoav Peled, Uzi Rebhun, Nissim Rejwan, Amnon Rubinstein, Gershon Shafir, Anita Shapira, Yehouda A. Shenhav, Ella Shohat, Sammy Smooha, Melford E. Spiro, Chaim I. Waxman, and Alexander Yakobson.
10. Assigned readings may include those by Gad Barzilai, Ariel Bin-Nun, Asher Landau, Chaim Gans, Ruth Gavison, Gary Jeffrey Jacobsohn, Amnon Rubinstein, Anat Scolnicov, Carmel Shalev, and Yedidia Z. Stern.
11. Assigned readings often include works by Asher Arian, Myron Aronoff, Shlomo Avineri, Gad Barzilai, Ahron Bregman, Asher Cohen, Avraham Diskin, Eliezer Don Yehiya, Gideon Doron, Alan Dowty, Yaron Ezrahi, Adam Garfinkle, Arthur Hertzberg, Dan Horowitz, Baruch Kimmerling, Charles Liebman, Moshe Lissak, Noach Lucas, Gregory Mahler, Peter Medding, Jonathan Mendilow, Benyamin Neuberger, Yoav Peled, Yoram Peri, Don Peretz, Aviezer Ravitzky, Howard Sachar, Gershon Shafir, Michal Shamir, Yedidia Z. Stern, Bernard Susser, Ilan Troen, and Yael Zerubavel.
12. Major authors on these topics include Robert Alter, Nathan Alterman, Yehuda Amichai, T. Carmi, Nurith Gertz, Hayim Gouri, Peter Gradenwitz, Benjamin Harshav, Arthur Hertzberg, Tamar Katriel, Baruch Kimmerling, Charles Liebman, Yosefa Loshitzky, Tamar Manor, Alan Mintz, Gideon Ofrat, Amos Oz, Derek Jonathan Penslar, Dalia Ravikovitch, Motti Regev, Alexander L. Ringer, Edwin Seroussi, Natan Shahar, Anton Shammas, Anita Shapira, Assaf Shelleg, Ella Shohat, Scott Streiner, Ram Uri, A. B. Yehoshua, Yigal Zalmona, and Yael Zerubavel.
13. Those authors that appear to be assigned most often for this topic include Rashid Khalidi, Aharon Klieman, Walter Laqueur, Ian Lustick, Joel S. Migdal, Aaron David Miller, Benny Morris, William Quandt, Itamar Rabinovich, Eugene L. Rogan, Barry Rubin, Yezid Sayigh, Gilead Sher, Avi Shlaim, Kenneth Stein, and Mark Tessler.
14. Authors whose works are commonly assigned for this subject include Uri Bar-Joseph, Yaacov Bar Siman Tov, Yehuda Ben Meir, Uri Bialer, Michael Brecher, Naomi Chazan, Gabriel Gorodetsky, George Gruen, Efraim Inbar, Yosef Lamdan, Zeev Maoz, Sergio Minerbi, Arie Oded, Joel Peters, Raanan Rein, Shmuel Sandler, Shai Shabtai, Gabi Sheffer, Yaacov Shimoni, Zev Sufot, David Tal, Angelika Timm, Dominique Trimbur, and Moshe Yegar.
15. Authors whose works are commonly assigned for this topic include As'ad Ghanem, Oded Haklai, Amal Jamal, David Kretzmer, Jacob Landau, Binyamin Neuberger, Ilan Peleg, Yochanan Peres, Yitzhak Reiter, Elie Rekhess, Nadim Rouhana, Emile Sahliyah, and Sammy Smooha.

16. Prominent authors in this category include Yossi Beilin, Peter Beinart, Zvi Ganin, Hillel Halkin, Elihu Katz, Shaul Kelner, Charles Liebman, Gabriel Sheffer, and Yael Zerubavel.

17. American University; American Jewish University; Brandeis University; California State University, Chico; Columbia University; Concordia University; Emory University; New York University; University of Calgary; University of California at Berkeley; University of California at Los Angeles; University College London; University of Florida; University of London; University of Maryland; University of Nebraska; University of Oklahoma; University of Texas; University of Washington; Wesleyan University.

18. American Jewish University; Columbia University; Emory University; University of California at Berkeley; University College London; University of Oklahoma.

19. University of Oklahoma.

20. Information provided by the director, May 30, 2012.

21. Recent conferences include Berkeley Law's "Israel through the High-Tech Lens"; American University's "Greener, Cleaner, Better: Israeli Innovation in Greentech" and "Strengthening Israel's Democracy: Arab Citizens of Israel"; and UCLA's "In the Mirror's Reflection: The Encounter between Jewish and Slavic Cultures in Modernity."

22. Recent film events include Wesleyan's Ring Family Israeli Film Festival: Restoration; a screening of award-winning Israeli films *My Australia* and *Mabul*, followed by a discussion at American University; and a screening of *West Bank Story*, with a question and answer time with the composer and live performance after the film at UCLA. Concerts include one by Hadag Nahash, "Israel's best-selling hip-hop act" at UCLA and one by Sheshbesh, the Arab-Jewish Ensemble of the Israel Philharmonic Orchestra at American University. Additionally, UCLA recently hosted "My Heart Is in the East: A Lecture-Demonstration on Sacred Israeli Music."

23. www.brandeis.edu/israelcenter/SIIS/aboutSIIS.html.

24. www.brandeis.edu/israelcenter/SIIS/siis_related.html; see also comments by Ilan Troen in Benhorin, "Israel Studies Increasingly Popular in U.S."

25. www.israelstudies.umd.edu/WashingtonIsraelSeminar.html.

26. University of Maryland: Culture in Tel Aviv (winter term), semester study in Israel: Maryland-in Haifa (spring semester); UCLA: UC Study Abroad Program at Hebrew University of Jerusalem; Columbia University: programs at Ben-Gurion University, Hebrew University, Tel Aviv University, and University of Haifa; California State University, Chico: programs at the University of Haifa, Hebrew University/Rothberg International School, and Tel Aviv University; American University: seven study abroad programs in Israel; New York University: New York University academic center in Tel Aviv; University of California at Berkeley: six study abroad options in Israel; University of Florida: programs at the Hebrew University of Jerusalem, Tel Aviv University, University of Haifa, and Ben-Gurion University of the Negev; University of Texas: the University of Haifa, the Hebrew University, Tel Aviv University, Ben-Gurion University of the Negev (Beer Sheva); University of Washington: the Hebrew University of Jerusalem, Tel Aviv University, University of Haifa; University of Nebraska: a program in the Bethsaida Excavations, affiliated with a program of the Institute for Study Abroad in Jerusalem; Wesleyan University: programs in Israel at the Hebrew University of Jerusalem, Ben-Gurion University, Tel Aviv University, and University of Haifa; Yeshiva University: YU Summer Israel Experience (archaeological excavations organized by Bar-Ilan University); University of Oklahoma: Huqoq Excavation Project in Israel, Hebrew University of Jerusalem; "Journey to the Middle East."

27. www.ucl.ac.uk/hebrew-jewish/department. Additional educational trips which are not directly organized by Centers for Israel Studies include the University of Chicago Spring quarter Study Abroad program entitled: "Jerusalem in Middle Eastern Civilizations" (http://study-abroad.uchicago.edu/programs/jerusalem-middle-eastern-civilizations).
28. www.ismi.emory.edu/primarysource.html.
29. www.yumuseum.org/.
30. www.yu.edu/libraries/about/mendel-gottesman-library/.
31. www.yu.edu/cis/activities/arch-of-titus/.
32. www.aisisraelstudies.org/.
33. Originally, the AIS published the *Israel Studies Forum*. In 2011, it was relaunched as ISR, housed at the Gildenhorn Institute for Israel Studies at the University of Maryland.
34. www.aisisraelstudies.org/.
35. www.soas.ac.uk/eais/.
36. www.schusterman.org/.
37. www.pearsfoundation.org.uk/#4/who-we-are.
38. For further details, see Appendix 9.
39. Ilan Troen (2002), "Settlement and State in Eretz Israel," in Martin Goodman, Jeremy Cohen, and David Sorkin (eds), *The Oxford Handbook of Jewish Studies*. Oxford: Oxford University Press, p. 445.
40. Ilan Troen, interview with the authors, June 20, 2012.
41. www.aisisraelstudies.org/about.ehtml, last accessed June 15, 2012. All websites pertaining to Israel Studies that are cited in this article were last accessed on June 15, 2012.
42. When the Goodman Institute was founded, it was organized and managed under the Tauber Institute for the Study of European Jewry, which had been founded in 1980. When the Schusterman Center for Israel Studies was later created in 2007, the Goodman Institute was subsumed under its auspices. Sylvia Fuks Fried, email correspondence with the authors, June 25, 2012.
43. www.isime.org/about/mission-vision-goals/.
44. www.ismi.emory.edu/About.html.
45. Mitchell G. Bard, "Introducing Israel Studies in American Universities," *Jerusalem Center for Public Affairs*, December 23, 2008, last accessed June 15, 2012, http://jcpa.org/article/introducing-israel-studies-in-u-s-universities/. Information also provided by acting director of American University's Center for Israel Studies.
46. New York University, 2003; Columbia University, 2006; Brandeis and Yeshiva Universities, 2007; University of Nebraska Omaha, 2009; University of California, Los Angeles, 2010.
47. Gal Beckerman, "Israel Studies: Scholarly Pursuit or Public Diplomacy?" *Forward*, May 26, 2010, http://forward.com/articles/128346/israel-studies-scholarly-pursuit-or-public-diplom/; also see Michael D. Colson, "Searching for the Study of Modern Israel," *Jerusalem Post*, January 13, 2010.
48. Yitzhak Benhorin, "Israel Studies Increasingly Popular in U.S.," *Ynetnews.com*, May 10, 2010.
49. Information provided by the Institute to the authors, May 30, 2012. The reports cited above deal with courses that may or may not be offered in the framework of formal Israel Studies programs.
50. Troen, "Settlement and State in Eretz Israel," p. 445.
51. Ibid.
52. Jennifer Jacobson, "The Politics of Israel Studies," *Chronicle of Higher Education*, June 20, 2005.

53. Samuel G. Freedman, "Separating Political Myths from Facts in Israel Studies," *The New York Times*, February 16, 2005.
54. Jacobson, "The Politics of Israel Studies."
55. Nathaniel Popper, "Israel Studies gain on Campus as Disputes Grow," *The Forward*, March 25, 2005.
56. For example, Beckerman, "Israel Studies: Scholarly Pursuit or Public Diplomacy?"
57. Northwestern University, "Widening the Global Path to and from Northwestern," *Crosscurrents* (Spring/Summer 2005): 10–12.
58. Ibid. The quotation from Linzer was also cited in the fall 2005 issue of *Northwestern*, the university alumni magazine. Demonstrating one aspect of the climate in which such Israel Studies programs have been established, the Northwestern University announcement evoked a hostile letter to the editor in the next issue of that publication from an alumnus who referred to Israel as "more of a pariah state in that part of the world than a true representative of the Middle East" and who charged that the Israeli postdoctoral fellows would "lecture Northwestern undergraduates insidiously" (Letter to the Editor, *Northwestern Magazine*, Winter 2005, www.northwestern.edu/magazine/winter2005/mailbox/mailbox_print.html). Similarly, an initiative to promote Israel Studies at the University of Illinois at Urbana-Champaign has been attacked several times by an individual who has described the program on that campus as having "nothing to do with the serious study of Israel, and everything to do with promoting support for its criminal political behavior" (David Green, "Propaganda Disguised as Academic Inquiry at the University of Illinois," *The Electronic Intifada*, December 4, 2009, http://electronicintifada.net/content/propaganda-disguised-academic-inquiry-university-illinois/8564).
59. Denize Springer, "Eran Kaplan Was Named the Goldman Endowed Chair in Israel Studies," San Francisco State University, March 1, 2011, www.sfsu.edu/~news/2011/spring/18.html.
60. Harriet Swain, "SOAS Creates Two New Posts in Israel Studies," *The Guardian*, April 11, 2011.
61. Benhorin, "Israel Studies Increasingly Popular in U.S."
62. Leonard Saxe and Barry Chazan (2008), *Ten Days of Birthright Israel: A Journey in Young Adult Identity*. Waltham: Brandeis University.
63. Jan Jaben-Eilon, "Studying Israel: Israel Has Finally Arrived," *The Jerusalem Post*, September 7, 2011.
64. Martin Kramer (2001), *Ivory Towers on Sand: The Failure of Middle Eastern Studies in America*. Washington, DC: Washington Institute for Near East Policy.
65. See similar comments by Howard Sachar, who considered the 1967 Six Day War between Israel and its Arab neighbors to be "the dramatic impetus" for the establishment of "more and more chairs devoted to the Arab-Israel problem in Middle East Studies centers and departments." Liel Leibovitz, "Battle of the Chairs: Arab Princes and Wealthy Jews Vie for Influence on American Campuses," *Moment Magazine*, February 2006, 16.
66. Kramer, *Ivory Towers on Sand*, p. 16.
67. Ibid., p. 22.
68. Ibid., p. 37.
69. See ibid., pp. 20–1, and the chapter notes on p. 26, especially note 64, which lists a number of articles that appeared on the subject between 1976 and 1984.
70. On that and for other examples see Julia Duin, "Saudis Give Big to U.S. Colleges," *Washington Times*, December 10, 2007.
71. Stephanie Strom, "Arab's Gift to Be Returned by Harvard," *The New York Times*, July 28, 2004.

72. Karen W. Arenson, "Saudi Prince Gives Millions to Harvard and Georgetown," *The New York Times*, December 13, 2005.
73. For more examples of Arab giving and a perspective on this overall matter see Leibovitz, "Battle of the Chairs."
74. *In Search of Israel Studies: A Survey of Israel Studies on American College Campuses*, Israel on Campus Coalition (Boston, 2006).
75. Freedman, "Separating Political Myths from Facts in Israel Studies."
76. Leibovitz, "Battle of the Chairs," p. 18.
77. Alex Joffe, "Israel Studies 101," *Jewish Ideas Daily*, October 3, 2011.
78. Benhorin, "Israel Studies Increasingly Popular in U.S."
79. "Executive Summary," *Searching for the Study of Israel: A Report on the Teaching of Israel on U.S. College Campuses 2008–09*. Cohen Center for Modern Jewish Studies, Brandeis University, 2010, p. 1. The Brandeis University Summer Institute for Israel Studies, established in 2004, which enables faculty members in various fields to enhance their abilities to develop courses with Israel-related content, has itself contributed to this development.
80. Swain, "Soas Creates Two New Posts in Israel Studies."
81. Laurence Silberstein (2008), *Postzionism: A Reader*. New Brunswick: Rutgers University Press.
82. Jaben-Eilon, "Studying Israel: Israel Has Finally Arrived."
83. Ibid.
84. Ibid.
85. Leibovitz, "Battle of the Chairs."
86. See presentation by Alan Dowty, "Israel Studies—The International Dimension," Colloquium on Trends and Challenges in Studies of the State of Israel, Ben-Gurion University of the Negev, Beer-Sheva, Israel, June 4, 2008.
87. Amiram Barkat, "A Major in Israel," *Ha'aretz*, October 4, 2005.
88. Leonard Binder, "Perspectives on Israel Studies: A Personal View," originally in *Intersections*, the newsletter of the UCLA Center for Near Eastern Studies, 2006. Posted on the UCLA website.
89. www.american.edu/cas/israelstudies/.
90. http://cpo.ajula.edu/Default.aspx?id=684.
91. www.brandeis.edu/israelcenter/index.html.
92. http://iijs.columbia.edu/.
93. www.ismi.emory.edu/.
94. http://hebrewjudaic.as.nyu.edu/page/taub.
95. www.international.ucla.edu/israel/.
96. www.isime.org/.
97. www.israelstudies.umd.edu/.
98. www.unomaha.edu/israelcenter/index.php.
99. www.yu.edu/cis/.
100. http://azrieli-institute.concordia.ca/about-us/.
101. www.csuchico.edu/mjis/.
102. www.law.berkeley.edu/10095.htm.
103. http://web.jst.ufl.edu/israel_studies.shtml.
104. http://judaicstudies.ou.edu/.
105. www.utexas.edu/cola/depts/mes/israel_studies/israel_studies.php; information about the new "Israel Studies Collaborative" is from Ami Pedahzur, email correspondence with the authors, February 10–14, 2012.
106. http://depts.washington.edu/neareast/modheb/.
107. www.wesleyan.edu/jis/.
108. http://arts.ucalgary.ca/isst/.

109. http://cjs.iaas.msu.ru/index.php?page=31.
110. Arranged alphabetically.
111. www.ucl.ac.uk/hebrew-jewish/postgraduate/ma-mis.
112. www.soas.ac.uk/jewishstudies/.
113. www.brandeis.edu/israelcenter/about/staff.html.
114. http://iijs.columbia.edu/Faculty.php.
115. www.ismi.emory.edu/stein.html.
116. http://hebrewjudaic.as.nyu.edu/object/ronaldzweig.html.
117. www.law.berkeley.edu/10097.htm.
118. www.international.ucla.edu/israel/about/index.asp.
119. www.israelstudies.umd.edu/director.html.
120. http://judaicstudies.ou.edu/faculty.htm.
121. Data from the director of the Jewish Studies program (February 14, 2012).
122. http://israbib.wordpress.com/2011/09/24/ssscisosu12/.
123. http://mideast.unc.edu/2011/08/31/portland-state/.
124. http://jewish.sfsu.edu/sf-state-names-eran-kaplan-endowed-goldman-chair-israel-studies.
125. http://polisci.wisc.edu/people/person.aspx?id=1069.
126. www.monash.edu.au/news/releases/show/245.
127. Jeevan Vasagar, "Oxford University Appoints Israel Studies Professor with £3m Donation," *The Guardian*, May 25, 2011, last accessed June 15, 2012, www.guardian.co.uk/education/2011/may/26/oxford-university-israel-studies-professor.
128. "New Professor Will Develop Modern Israel Studies," University of Sussex, last updated April 26, 2012, last accessed June 15, 2012, www.sussex.ac.uk/students/newsandevents/?id=11967.
129. "University of Leeds and Pears Foundation Partner to Create New Lecturer / Senior Lecturer Post in Israel & Middle East Studies," University of Leeds, July 12, 2011, last accessed June 15, 2012, www.leeds.ac.uk/news/article/2233/university_of_leeds_and_pears_foundation_partner_to_create_new_lecturer__senior_lecturer_post_in_israel_and_middle_East_studies.
130. This position is on the list of the Association for Israel Studies, but it is not listed on the university's website (www.manchesterjewishstudies.org/).
131. www.acbp.net/canada/unitoronto.php.
132. www.canadachristiancollege.com/programs_israel_studies.htm.
133. http://arts.ucalgary.ca/isst/node/39.
134. Excluding the Schusterman Visiting Israeli Professor Program and the Jewish Federation of Metropolitan Chicago's Program.
135. www.bu.edu/judaicstudies/courses/israel-studies-at-bu/.
136. http://spme.net/cgi-bin/articles.cgi?ID=7230.
137. Fred Berkovitch (assistant dean for Faculty Affairs in Harvard's Faculty of Arts and Sciences), email correspondence with the authors, February 23, 2012.
138. www.jtsa.edu/Academics/Registrar/Academic_Bulletin/AB_Modern_Jewish_Studies.xml.
139. www.cla.temple.edu/about/submit-events/mirowski/.
140. http://judaic.arizona.edu/peo-faculty?value_1=Visiting+Faculty.
141. "Visiting Lecturer and Middle East Analyst Chodoff Will Teach Course at U of M," University of Memphis, January 8, 2007, last accessed June 15, 2012, www.memphis.edu/newsarchive/jan07/middleeast.php.
142. JoAnn Achelpohl (the department's administrative assistant), email correspondence with the authors, February 10, 2012.
143. http://iijs.columbia.edu/Visiting%20Faculty.php.
144. www.ismi.emory.edu/VisitingProfessorProgram.html.

145. "Michael Serling: A Legacy of Support to Enhance Jewish Life at MSU," Michigan State University, December 27, 2011, last accessed June 15, 2012, www.givingto. msu.edu/article.cfm?articleNum=361.
146. http://hebrewjudaic.as.nyu.edu/object/taub.visitingscholars.
147. www.law.berkeley.edu/10097.htm.
148. www.international.ucla.edu/israel/people/index.asp.
149. www.israelstudies.umd.edu/faculty.html.
150. www.unomaha.edu/israelcenter/core.php.
151. www.wesleyan.edu/jis/.

Part III

Resources

Glossary

Note: The glossary includes items that appear across the essays in the volume with some regularity or that benefit from a separate and brief explanation. Many broader concepts are described in individual essays, and readers are advised to use the Index to locate specific topics.

Aggadah: narrative, often categorized as nonlegal, writings of the rabbis. Aggadah could take diverse forms—though it was frequently presented as a form of biblical exegesis or the narration of legends—and address a wide range of issues, such as morals. The origins of aggadah seem to be the Second Temple period in Palestine; aggadic works continued to be produced throughout the Talmudic period.

Agunah: "tied"; refers to a woman who cannot remarry because she is separated from her husband, and she cannot secure a bill of divorce (*get*) or it cannot be determined if her husband is still alive. This issue has garnered a good deal of discussion in Jewish law and remains a significant issue in some parts of contemporary Jewish society, with some authorities advocating for prenuptial agreements or investigating into the possibility of the annulment of the original marriage in cases when the husband refuses to grant his wife a divorce.

Aliyah: "ascent"; refers to Jews moving permanently to the Land of Israel (leaving Israel is "descent"). In the modern period, aliyah referred to immigration to Israel, especially from eastern Europe and by individuals fleeing persecution or actualizing Zionist ideals.

Allliance Israélite Universelle: founded in 1860, the AIU was an international organization of Jews involved in political defense of Judaism and the expansion of Jewish education. Its central committee was headquartered in Paris, though its reach was global, with special emphasis on bringing modernization (and Westernization) to Jews in the Middle East and North Africa.

Amidah: "standing"; a central prayer in Jewish liturgy, to be recited standing. Recited individually at each of the three daily-prayer services (as well as repeated communally in the morning and afternoon services), the *amidah* is typically composed of 18 benedictions, though the number and focus vary on the Sabbath, festivals, and fast days. The weekday *amidah* is directed at praise for and thanks to God, petitions to God for wisdom, forgiveness of sins, redemption and ingathering of the exiles, healing of the sick, agricultural productivity, restoration of righteous judges, rebuilding of Jerusalem, and the establishment of the kingdom of David and God's return to Zion. The prayer also requests the destruction of enemies, generally taken to refer to slanderers or heretics. There is some debate about whether the prayer was instituted in the Second Temple period or after the destruction of the Second Temple.

Amoraim: "speaker" or "interpreter"; refers to the rabbinic sages referenced in the Talmud from Palestine and Babylonia from the middle of the third to the early sixth century, who commented on the various discussions of their predecessors, the Tannaim. Amoraim are referenced in the Talmud as well as Midrash collections. The great sage Rav (Abba b. Aivu), who founded the academy of Sura and was a student of Rabbi Judah ha-Nasi (Judah the Prince), is generally credited with transporting the Mishnah to Babylonia and inaugurating the Amoraic period. Primary centers of Amoraic study in Palestine included Caesarea, Lydda, Sepphoris, and Tiberias; in Babylonia, Sura and Pumbedita.

Anti-Judaism: hostility toward Judaism. Prior to the modern period, the term expresses anti-Jewish actions and laws more generally.

Anti-Semitism: since the last quarter of the nineteenth century, the term refers to hatred of Jews that is rooted in arguments that Jews are of different, inferior, racial and biological constitution. The term is often associated with the German-writer Wilhelm Marr, who cast the Jews as a distinct race that had overthrown the German nation. Anti-Semitism developed in the context of social Darwinism and expanding colonialism and the associated deprecating representation of colonized people.

Apocalyptic writing: "revelation"; writing that claimed to tell about the unfolding of events often associated with messianisim. The genre is related to the experiences of postexilic Judaism and the early church, though it has been present in many cultures at various times. Apocalyptic literature was quite common in the Middle Ages and early modern period in Europe, for example. Many apocalyptic elements could be found or derived from a range of passages in both canonical and noncanonical Scripture.

Apocrypha: collection of books not included in the canon of the Hebrew Bible, but included in the scriptural canon of the Roman Catholic and Greek Orthodox churches. Among these books are Esdras, Tobit, Judith, additions to Esther, the Wisdom of Solomon, Ecclesiasticus (Wisdom of Ben Sira), Baruch, the Song of the Three Holy Children, Susannna, Bel and the Dragon, The Prayer of Menasseh, and I and II Maccabees. A central focus of these works is the battle against idolatry.

Apostasy: conversion from Judaism is discussed in writings and rulings since the rabbinic period. Conversion could be forced (e.g. at times of anti-Jewish repression or pogroms) or voluntary (often for a wide range of reasons, from genuine belief, to perceived opportunities for social or economic advancement). Well into the modern period, apostates often remained closely connected with their families and former coreligionists. Indeed, one of the main reasons articulated by royal authorities for the expulsion of the Jews from Spain was the alleged negative influence that Jews continued to have on converts to Christianity, supplying them with information about and facilitating Jewish observance. On the other hand, many of the most violent anti-Jewish polemicists were converts from Judaism, who used their status as former Jews to provide "insider" information on Jewish practices and to stir sentiments against the Jews.

Arab-Israeli Conflict: conflict between Arabs and Jews already since the late nineteenth century, pitting Arab nationalism and Zionism against one another, resulting in a number of anti-Jewish riots. After the creation of the State of Israel in 1948, the conflict escalated militarily, with Israel winning important victories to solidify the nascent state. In 1967, the Six-Day War and in 1973 the Yom Kippur War helped to establish the position of Israel, while further sowing seeds of territorial conflict that continue until today in the form of the First (1987) and Second (2000) Intifadas, or Palestinian uprisings, and ongoing military and diplomatic tensions.

Aramaic: an ancient northwest Semitic language, closely related to biblical Hebrew. A small portion of the Bible is written in Aramaic, including several chapters each of Ezra and Daniel. In the rabbinic period, Aramaic was the primary spoken language of Jews, and was the central language of the Talmud and important in the liturgies of some eastern Christian churches.

Ashkenaz (Ashkenazic/Ashkenazim): term used generally to designate Jews of northwest, central, and eastern European descent. The term "Ashkenaz" appears in the book of Genesis; though referencing a Near Eastern location, the term was taken to refer to Germany already in the Middle Ages.

By the early modern period, the term began to be used to represent Jews in eastern Europe, especially Poland, as well.

Bar Kokhba Revolt: or Second Jewish War (132–5) was the last, and an unsuccessful, Jewish revolt against Roman rule in Israel. The leader, Simon bar Koseva, was seen by some as a messianic figure. Repressive legislation was imposed on Jews in Israel, especially in Judea, as a result.

Bet Din: "house of law"; refers to Jewish legal court. The Sanhedrin of the Second Temple period was comprised of 71 judges; lesser courts had 23 or 3 judges. Throughout the medieval, early modern, and modern periods, a court of 3 rabbis was typical. After the Temple period, such courts dealt with civil and family matters, and not cases of criminal or capital offenses, which typically had to be released to non-Jewish courts of the dominating society. The use of non-Jewish courts was consistently legislated against in the Middle Ages and early modern period, suggesting that some Jews frequented such courts instead of Jewish courts.

British Mandate: the establishment of Palestine as a national home for the Jews proclaimed by the British government in the Balfour Declaration of November 1917. With the defeat of the Ottomans in World War I, the British were accorded permission to govern Palestine by the League of Nations in 1922, leading to economic, administrative, and cultural development, an increase in the migration of Jews, and opposition of Arabs.

Confessionalization: the process of forming denominations according to theology in the aftermath of the Protestant Reformation. The process is often associated with modernization and with the creation of normative theologies and practices and a system of social disciplining to enforce such norms.

Converso(s): Christian(s) of Jewish descent; frequently accused of secretly maintaining Jewish rites; also known as *anusim* (coerced) or Marranos (a derogatory term). The issue of conversos became particularly complicated in Spain in 1391 with the anti-Jewish pogroms and forced conversions of Jews. A good deal of debate ensued among late medieval rabbis about the Jewish status of these converts. On the Christian side as well, a good deal of ambivalence colored attitudes toward conversos, who were frequently portrayed as secret Judaizers and who were seen to be serious economic and social competitors to "Old Christians."

Dead Sea Scrolls: hundreds of documentary fragments, including texts of the Bible and biblical commentaries, as well as otherwise unknown writings dating from the later part of the Second Temple period that were discovered in caves in the Judean Desert, most near Qumran in the mid-twentieth century. The documents include copies of biblical books, apocrypha and pseudepigrapha, as well as a range of sectarian documents, associated by many scholars with the Essenes, an isolated group focused on spiritual development and active in the area around Ein Gedi by the Dead Sea.

Denominations: in the nineteenth and twentieth centuries, various denominations developed within Judaism. Today they are referred to as Orthodox (with various strands, including ultra-Orthodox (*haredim*), as well as more modern-oriented groups (represented by the flagship institution Yeshiva University and several important Israeli yeshivot); Conservative (with its center at the Jewish Theological Seminary of America and focused on accommodation to modern life and the notion of adaptation to changing historical conditions); Reform (centered at the Hebrew Union College-Jewish Institute of Religion, with its reform of Jewish liturgy and expansive notion of Jewish identity with the acceptance of patrilineal as well as matrilineal determinations of Jewishness). Reconstructionist Judaism (founded by Mordechai Kaplan) and various renewal movements have gained adherents and developed over the course of the later twentieth and into the twenty-first century.

Dhimma: protected people; refers to Jews, Christians, and other tolerated people under Islamic hegemony. Such people are considered second-class citizens, responsible for tributes (such as poll taxes and land taxes) and restrictions on behavior (such as dress, arms-bearing, and construction of new houses of worship), as stipulated in the medieval "Pact of 'Umar."

Dina de Malkuta Dina: the "law of the land is law"; the principle that Jews are subject to the laws regnant in the country of their residence. In different contexts and situations, limitations were placed by rabbinic authorities on the scope of this law, particularly as it might conflict with halakhah.

Documentary Hypothesis: this thesis proposes that the Torah (Five Books of Moses) is comprised of various independent narratives that were shaped by redactors. The thesis is often associated with the German biblicist and Orientalist Julius Wellhausen (1844–1918) in the last quarter of the nineteenth century, though there were earlier scholars back into the early modern period who anticipated some of these ideas. Source critics evolved over time to consider four main sources, seen as incomplete and at times inconsistent, though other smaller bodies of sources have also been identified. The primary four sources were designated as J (Yahwist/Jahwist), E (Elohist), D (Deuteronomist), and P (Priestly), reflecting the focus of the sources' alleged authors. The first is often ascribed to the tenth century BCE (Kingdom of Judah), the second to the ninth (Kingdom of Israel), the third to the seventh (Jerusalem), and the last to the sixth (Babylonian exile). For many, though not all, source criticism challenges the sacrality of the Bible (its authorship as well as its inherent holiness). It should be noted that not everyone accepts this approach and many scholars prefer other explanations for apparent inconsistencies in the biblical text, which they assert are intended to prod investigation.

Edom: refers to a region south of Judea and the Dead Sea. It came to be associated with the biblical Isaac's son Esau. The term was used to discuss military enemies of Israel and was later used to refer to Rome and to Christianity.

Essenes: a sectarian group from the Second Temple period, known for focus on religious observance and purity. Some connect them with a Dead Sea sect at Qumran. The group was described by Josephus and Pliny the Elder. (See Dead Sea Scrolls.)

Exegesis: Jewish interpretation of Scripture, as it developed in the rabbinic period and the Middle Ages, was focused around four approaches, mirroring but distinct from Christian exegetical approaches. The four senses of Jewish exegesis are referred to as "PaRDeS" (orchard) and include: peshat (simple or plain); remez (allegorical); derash (comparative, based on similar occurrences); and sod (esoteric or mystical).

Exilarch: head of the Jews in Babylonian exile, as referenced by Parthian and Sasanian authorities.

Gaon (pl. Geonim): "excellency"; title of heads of the two leading Babylonian academies between the end of the sixth and end of the twelfth centuries. A gaon was also regnant over Palestinian Jewry, centered in Tiberias, where he appears to have been less focused on Talmudic study and more on communal matters.

Genizah: perhaps originally a Persian word, it denotes a storage area for ritual objects or texts that are no longer usable but that contained or might contain sacred material, such as God's name. As a result, we find copies of sacred literature, as well as heretical or sectarian works, in additional to troves of secular letters, contracts, and documents. The largest preserved *genizah* is in Cairo, with more than 200,000 preserved fragmentary documents spanning the broad medieval period. The collection—well preserved because of the unique climate conditions of the location—is especially rich for the Near Eastern Jewish communities, but contains materials related to Jewish communities across Europe as well. The collection was uncovered by Solomon Schechter, who secured permission to move some 140,000 fragments to the Cambridge University library in 1897.

Ghetto: "to cast"; the word is derived from the Italian for activity related to the area of the foundry where the Jews were relocated in Venice in 1516. Jews had often lived in separate quarters or along the same street in medieval towns, and probably the first enclosed separation occurred in Frankfurt am Main in 1462. Still, the Venetian ghetto is often seen as the first important step in what some would later label the "age of the ghetto," when Jews were increasingly separated from non-Jewish society. Ghettoization could serve multiple functions: removing Jews from the general public at certain set times, but also as a means of protection and, some have argued, as a way of organizing them communally. In some cases, segregation was seen as a positive development even in some Jewish eyes. There were, at times, even in cities with a Jewish ghetto, some rich Jews who managed to maintain living quarters outside the ghetto. Although locked at night, the ghetto walls could often be quite porous, with Jews traveling out and Christians entering in for a variety of social and business functions. Forced ghettoization during the Holocaust served as a means to corral and dehumanize Jews, many of whom were murdered on the spot or prepared for shipment to death camps.

Haggadah: "telling"; refers to the key text that explicates the Passover seder, which is read aloud at the evening meal and which fulfills the obligation to retell the experience of the Jews' slavery in and exodus from Egypt. The textual components of the Haggadah draw from biblical and rabbinic texts, and were probably assembled during the rabbinic period, though some scholars argue that pieces of the Haggadah are of a later provenance and may have been a polemical response to Christianity. Many Haggadot were beautifully illustrated, a practice that continues through today. The images, as well as occasional marginal notations, have been utilized by historians to understand the conditions under which certain editions were created and used.

Halakhah: from the Hebrew root "to walk"; Jewish law that prescribes behavior and obligations based on divine commandments as articulated in the Bible (numbering 613) and as explicated by the rabbis (including at times the addition of ordinances and customs). Codes of Jewish law were assembled in the rabbinic period (including the Mishnah) and throughout the Middle Ages (including the codes of Isaac Alfasi, Moses ben Maimon [Maimonides or Rambam], Asher ben Yehiel, Jacob ben Asher, and Moses ben Jacob of Coucy, among others) and early modern period (most famously by Joseph Karo, in the *Shulhan Arukh* [Prepared Table]). Codification continued into the modern period and individual denominations have dealt with halakhah in their own particular ways.

Herem: ban of excommunication, which separated an individual or group from the Jewish community, prohibiting any kind of social or business interaction, including synagogue attendance and participation in religious services. There were varying levels of excommunication, depending on the nature and severity of transgressions. Excommunicated individuals were not allowed to rejoin communal life until they expressed contrition and fulfilled any financial penalties or bore stipulated punishments. Excommunication proved to be fairly successful, particularly in the Middle Ages when individuals had no option other than reconciling with the Jewish community or converting from Judaism. The incidence of excommunication appears to have increased in the seventeenth century, perhaps as a result of growing Confessionalization and hardening of orthodoxies. Baruch Spinoza represents perhaps the best-known case of excommunication; in the case of Spinoza, however, we find the beginning of a new era. Spinoza did not reconcile with the Jewish community and also did not convert to Christianity; rather he lived the remainder of his days after his severe excommunication outside the Jewish community.

Inquisition: a papal legal procedure instituted throughout the Middle Ages to identify and extirpate heresy, and at times utilized for other political purposes as well. The Inquisition was established in Spain in 1480 to uncover cases of converso Judaizing. Technically the Inquisition could not try cases of Jews, who were not subject to its authority, though some Inquisitions in Italy have been shown to have dealt with cases of Jews. The Inquisition utilized torture to elicit confessions from its victims. Feared well into the modern period, the Inquisition tried many more people than it killed. The Inquisition was instituted in the New World in the sixteenth century, especially in areas under Portuguese or Spanish control to ferret out alleged crypto-Jews.

Israel: the Land of Israel refers to the biblical region promised to the descendants of the biblical patriarchs and matriarchs, and conquered over a period of time after the exodus from Egypt. The Kingdom of Israel was established in the tenth century BCE, when 10 of the 12 tribes seceded from the United Monarchy to form the large and wealthy northern kingdom (as distinct from the smaller southern kingdom of Judah). The Assyrians conquered the northern kingdom in the early eighth century BCE. In modern times, the State of Israel was founded in 1948. (See also Arab-Israeli conflict above.)

Kabbalah: "tradition"; refers to secret traditions of Jewish mysticism. Drawing from earlier rabbinic and biblical texts and concepts, Kabbalah incorporated various magical and philosophical streams. Medieval developments occurred in the late twelfth and early thirteenth century in northern Germany and France and in Spain, where the *Zohar* emerged (see *Zohar* below). A particular form of Jewish mysticism developed in Safed in the middle of the sixteenth century by Isaac Luria (1534–72) and his adherents. That Kabbalah was infused with a number of practices and theological teachings that would be engaged in the messianic speculation of the seventeenth century (notably around the figure of Shabbetai Sevi) and later in various forms of Hasidism.

Karaism: in opposition to rabbinic Jews, Karaites reject the Oral Torah of the rabbis and instead take the Written Law (the Hebrew Bible) as the supreme source of authority in law and theology, hence their name, which is derived from the Hebrew "mikra," for Scripture. For some, Karaism is related to sectarian Judaism from the Second Temple period, perhaps as a remnant of the Sadducees, though the unclear origins of the movement first come in to focus in the eighth century in Babylonia, with Anan ben David, taken to be the founder of the movement in opposition to the Exilarch. A large number of Karaite works were produced in the Middle Ages under Islam (especially in the tenth and eleventh centuries) and substantial numbers of Karaites were active in Russia in the nineteenth century and Israel today.

Kashrut: Jewish dietary laws, based on biblical injunctions (especially in the books of Leviticus and Deuteronomy) and rabbinic law that stipulated what foods and what food combinations are permissible or forbidden, pure or impure. The discussion of kashrut has grappled with many issues, particularly as new foods have been discovered or been imported to areas with large Jewish populations (consider the introduction of coffee in the early modern period) or with increased processing of food in contemporary times.

Kehillah: community; kehillot were autonomous Jewish communities in the medieval and early modern periods that controlled various religious institutions (such as synagogue, *mikveh*, cemetery), and that oversaw a range of other functions, including appropriation and collection of taxes, record keeping, adjudication of cases involving Jewish law, and, increasingly, Jewish education. The kehillah was governed by a council of lay leaders and various officials and functionaries appointed for prescribed tasks. In the early modern period, rabbis were engaged by the community and given contracts for their services. In some cases, a number of smaller kehillot might form a broader regional association; larger kehillot often had authority over the Jews in their town or city as well as in outlying areas and smaller, proximate settlements or communities.

359

Ketubah: Aramaic document of a bridegroom's obligations toward the bride as a prerequisite to marriage. The document was intended to protect a woman financially. At times ketubot have been highly decorated, reflecting prevailing cultural tastes in the Jewish communities and the broader world in which Jews lived.

Lachrymose conception of Jewish history: a traditional notion that Jewish history has been one long trail of tears. For some historians, Jewish history has been narrated along two main lines—the history of suffering and the history of scholars. Over the past half-century, the notion that Jewish history is one of constant suffering has been revisited and frequently rejected. Historians note extended periods of rather normative relations between Jews and non-Jews throughout historical periods and they argue that the language of persecution and suffering has at times been more rhetorical than reflective of constant persecution.

Ladino: Judaeo-Spanish language that was utilized by Sephardic Jews exiled from Spain at the end of the fifteenth century into modernity in their new lands of settlement, especially in the far reaches of the Ottoman Empire. The language is based on Spanish grammar but utilizes Hebrew letters.

Law of Return: Israeli legislation enacted in 1950 that allows any Jew the right to return to Israel and secure Israeli citizenship. A Jew is defined in this and subsequent legislation as "a person who was born of a Jewish mother or has become converted to Judaism and who is not a member of another religion." This distinction has caused some debate, for example related to individuals whose father (but not mother) was Jewish, who converted but did not have an Orthodox-recognized conversion, and individuals or groups whose genealogy cannot be adequately determined.

Levirate marriage: from Latin for brother-in-law; refers to the biblical command that if a man dies with no sons, his widow must marry the deceased husband's oldest brother as a way of maintaining the family line. Many halakhic discussions address this issue. A ritual known as *halitzah* is required to free the widow from this obligation.

Masoretes: Masorah refers to scribal transmission of the Bible to correctly reproduce the biblical text. Masoretes, scholars active from the seventh through eleventh century CE in Israel, added vowel signs to the biblical text as well as signs for accentuation and cantillation. There were different schools of Masoretes with different traditions.

Messiah: in Hebrew "mashiach" refers to someone anointed—anointing being associated with royal or divine roles. Biblical texts mention an anointed king who will rule with righteousness and justice; a human who will restore Israel. In various noncanonical and rabbinic-period writing, messianism is associated with strong militarism expected to subdue those who have attacked Jerusalem or the Jews. In the medieval and early modern periods, episodes of messianism erupted at times of great turmoil or speculation within the Jewish community or the larger communities in which Jews lived, for example, in Yemen in the twelfth century as described by Maimonides and in western Europe in the sixteenth and seventeenth centuries during periods of geographical expansion, religious upheaval, and social tension.

Midrash: from the Hebrew root derash to investigate, Midrash refers to rabbinic interpretation of texts, generally the Hebrew Bible, which preserves oral traditions and provides background information and fills in apparent gaps in either legal or narrative texts. Most Midrashic compilations date from the fifth century into the Middle Ages, in a wide range of forms that are frequently difficult to date with precision.

Mikveh: ritual bath for various forms of purification likely with Second Temple period origins, and often related to the immersion of women after a period of time following their menstrual cycle, but also to the ritual purity of various vessels. The waters of the *mikveh* are collected from rainwater in a reservoir. There is a good deal of discussion in Jewish law about the parameters of *mikva'ot* and in Jewish communal documents about the financing, construction, and use of *mikva'ot*.

Mishnah: "repetition" or "teaching"; refers generally to the Oral Law—legal traditions codified and written down around the end of the second century CE. The first major work of the rabbinic movement, the redaction of the Mishnah is generally ascribed to Rabbi Judah ha-Nasi, drawing from earlier collections and covering a broad range of Jewish case law. The six divisions of the Mishnah deal with: prayers and blessings, as well as tithing and laws related to agriculture; laws related to the Sabbath and festivals; laws pertaining to women, such as marriage and divorce, as well as various oaths; a range of civil and criminal concerns, including discussions of idolatry; sacrificial rites and dietary laws; and issues of purity and impurity.

Mitzvah: "commandment"; laws imposed by or derived from biblical texts or through rabbinic interpretation and ordinances. The total number of mitzvot prescribed in the Hebrew Bible is 613, dealing with all aspects of life and ritual observance.

Mizrahi: refers to "eastern" Jews and Jewish communities, specifically those from North Africa and the Middle East. At times associated with Sephardic Jewry, the two have many varying customs and orientations.

Musar: moral and religious ethical instruction. A good deal of *musar* literature was produced in the medieval and early modern periods, for example in the works of Bahya ibn Pakuda. As a movement, *musar* is often associated with the teachings of the Vilna Gaon (Rabbi Elijah ben Solomon Zalman [1720–97], Moses Hayim Luzzatto [1707–47], and Rabbi Israel Salanter [1810–83].

Mysticism: esoteric speculation about the divine, drawn from some biblical and rabbinic works, such as the divine chariot (*merkavah*) referenced in Ezra and heavenly palaces (*hekhalot*) discussed in some apocryphal and pseudepigraphic literature and in other rabbinic writings. Mystical speculation developed during the rabbinic (third through seventh centuries) in works such as *Sefer ha-Rezim* (Book of Secrets), and later in the medieval periods, in such works as *Sefer Yetzirah* (Book of Creation), and works of the Hasidei Ashkenaz (German Pietists). (See also Kabbalah.)

Nasi: patriarch; hereditary leaders of Palestinian Jewish communities in the first five centuries of the Common Era. With some precedent of individuals who presided over the Sanhedrin at certain times, the position of nasi is generally associated with the descendants of the figure of Gamliel. The nasi developed significant communal authority and served as a key representative of the Jewish community with Roman authorities.

Near East, Ancient: Refers to areas of the "East" closer to Europe (as opposed to the Far East of Asia). The geographical span of the Near East crosses from Iran to Egypt and Turkey through Arabia. The Ancient Near East was dominated by Egypt and the major Mesopotamian empires of Assyria and Babylonia. The area included the Land of Israel, under various Canaanite tribes and in the form of the United Monarchy of the Israelites (and later the Kingdoms of Israel and Judah). A good deal of literary, legal, and material remains allow for remarkably rich understanding and comparison of Israelite and other Ancient Near Eastern development in the biblical and rabbinic periods.

Pale of Settlement: boundary or enclosure; an area of permitted Jewish settlement in part of western Russia, gained with the partition of Poland in the late eighteenth century. Jewish settlement outside this area was often prohibited. Various restrictions on the large population of Jews in the area, as well as several large pogroms (particularly in the late nineteenth and early twentieth centuries) often led to very negative associations of the Pale with anti-Semitism and mass migration.

Parnas: "presider"; religious or administrative functionary noted in Talmudic literature. In the Middle Ages, the position tended to be that of a lay communal leader, responsible for a range of communal activities and forming, together with other parnasim, a community governing council. In the early modern period in some communities, different parnasim were assigned various administrative functions for varying lengths of time.

Pharisees: a group of Jews active in the period of the Second Temple. Many scholars speculate that these Jews were forerunners of the rabbis, though this view has increasingly been challenged. In any event, Pharisees, as described by Josephus and others, were known for their concern with purity and their strict observance of the Law. As represented in the New Testament and well into the modern period, the term Pharisee was often used in a derogatory sense by Christians, arguing that the Pharisees were indeed the Jews, with their overemphasis on the Law and ceremonials and their rejection of Jesus.

Piyyut: liturgical poem, often according to an acrostic spelling of the author's name or the letters of the Hebrew alphabet, starting in the fourth century and focused on the fast day of Tisha b'Av as well as the high holy days to add to and adorn those occasions. *Piyyutim* became popular in the Middle Ages and have been analysed for their literary production as well as what they reveal about the cultures in which they were created and recited. Many *piyyutim* of the Hebrew poet Eleazar ben Killir from the sixth and early seventh century survive and continue to be recited today.

Pseudepigrapha: books not included in the Hebrew canon and included only partially in the eastern Christian churches. Among the many books of pseudepigrapha are The Book of Enoch, Jubilees, The Ascension of Isaiah, the Assumption of Moses, The Book of Adam and Eve, and the Testaments of the Twelve Patriarchs. These works were often attributed to sectarian groups.

Rabbi: derives from the Hebrew root rav, "great"; refers to Jewish religious authority and/or teacher. The process of rabbinic ordination was ended in late antiquity, though several attempts to restart rabbinic ordination, for example in Safed in the sixteenth century, were made. In the medieval period and forward, rabbis were so designated with a license or appointment based upon the mastery of a specific body of halakhah and jurisprudential expertise. In the early modern period, the position of rabbi became an increasingly formalized and professionalized position, which regulated its scope but may simultaneously have weakened its authority, subordinating it to communal oversight.

Responsum: response to questions of Jewish law and observance provided by rabbis in reply to inquiries addressed to them. Responsa originated in the period of the Geonim and are still produced. A particularly vibrant traffic in responsa existed in the Middle Ages and early modern periods. Responsa cover a remarkable range of topics. At times they reflect actual events or concerns; at other times they deal with theoretical halakhic issues. As such, responsa provide useful insights into rabbinic decision making, and they may at times offer useful information about historical events and personalities. However, the highly formalized structure and the infrequent mention of specific names, dates, and contexts limits the extent to which many responsa can be used as historical sources.

Sadducees: A group of Second Temple Jews, generally from higher social and economic levels, known for their emphasis on the Written Torah and their rejection of the Oral Torah, that is, many rulings of the Pharisees and rabbis.

Samaritans: defined as Jews or non-Jews in various rabbinic discussions (as well as in the New Testament), the Samaritans deviated in many customs from rabbinic norms and were frequently disparaged in rabbinic writings as a result. Their origins appear to go back to the eleventh century BCE in a schism in which they abandoned the shrine at Shechem for one at Shiloh; the Samaritans cast themselves as the true keepers of the law.

Sanhedrin: assembly of ordained scholars who served as a supreme court and legislating body in Jerusalem during the Second Temple period. (See Bet Din.)

Savoraim: a group of rabbinic scholars who served as intermediaries between Amoraim and *Stammaim* and performed some editorial functions of rabbinic units prior to the seventh century CE.

Sepharad (Sephardic/Sephardim): the place name Sepharad is first mentioned in the biblical book of Obadiah, though probably referring to a Middle Eastern location. In the Middle Ages, Jews took Sepharad to refer to Spain and so the Jews in Spain under Islam and Christianity were labeled Sephardic. This term was also extended to include the many Jews who resided in the Ottoman Empire later, after the expulsions from the Iberian Peninsula.

Septuagint: "seventy"; translation of the Hebrew Bible into Greek, said to have been conducted simultaneously by 72 translators and yielding identical versions. This Greek rendering has a somewhat different organization from and includes some books not included in the canon of the Hebrew Bible.

Servi camerae: servants of the chamber, that is, the position of medieval Jews as the dependents of the royal powers.

Shehitah: method of Jewish ritual slaughter of animals and birds permitted under Jewish law. Shehitah has been banned at times in parts of Europe and it has been utilized by anti-Semitic polemicists to allege Jewish cruelty—as in some Nazi-propaganda films—when in reality Jewish law requires a good deal of sensitivity to the animals being slaughtered and prescribes careful processes for valid slaughtering.

Shtetl: market town in eastern Europe, generally with a significant Jewish population. Developed in the early modern period, the *shtetl* has been represented in diverse ways in modernity, though generally to depict an idealized and traditionally observant Jewish population, segregated from non-Jews. In reality, *shtetl* life could be quite complex, with internal Jewish divisions and a good deal of interaction between Jews and non-Jews.

Sifre: rabbinic Midrashic and exegetical works on the biblical books of Numbers and Deuteronomy.

Stammaim: anonymous rabbinic sages who in the sixth or early seventh centuries CE edited and reworked various earlier traditions into the Babylonian Talmud.

Supercessionism: fulfillment and replacement of the Old Testament (Mosaic Law) with the New Testament and the Jews as the Chosen People of God by Christians.

Synagogue: "assembly"; place of Jewish worship and Torah study. Origins of the synagogue may extend to the period of Babylonian exile, but the synagogue was well established by the start of the Common Era. Synagogues functioned as central communal spaces in medieval and early modern Jewish communities. Architectural designs of synagogues frequently mirrored the regnant architecture in the places where they were constructed.

Takkanah: ordinances established by rabbis or communities. *Takkanot* are identified already in biblical sources and throughout the rabbinic period by the Sanhedrin and various leading sages. *Takkanot* could deal with religious observance as well as a range of communal matters and business practices. Such legislation was often included in medieval and early modern communal ledgers and constitutions.

Talmud: from the root to "teach" or "study"; commentary on and discussion of the Oral Law (Mishnah), redacted in the late fourth or early fifth century in Tiberias (Jerusalem, Yerushalmi) or from the late fifth into the eighth century in Persia (Babylonian, Bavli). The Babylonian Talmud is larger and more developed in ways than the Jerusalem Talmud. In 63 tractates, the Talmud provides the text of Mishnah as well as additional writings of the Tannaim, called baraitot (or outside material), as well as the Gemara, or discussion of these texts, and it addresses both halakhah and aggadah. The first complete edition was printed in the early sixteenth century.

Tannaim: repeaters, from the time of the dissolution of the Great Assembly until the period of Judah ha-Nasi (the redactor of the Mishnah), who circulated the oral traditions that would form the key pieces of the early rabbinic corpus, such as the Mishnah and Tosefta.

Temple: the First Temple, or Solomon's Temple, was constructed in the tenth century BCE. It was destroyed by the Babylonians (Nebuchadnezzar II) in 587 BCE when Jerusalem was besieged. The Second Temple was constructed in 516 BCE, with the encouragement of the Persian King Cyrus the Great who had allowed Jews in exile to return to Jerusalem. The Second Temple was expanded by Herod the Great in the first century BCE. It was destroyed in 70 CE, as a culminating act of the First Jewish War against Rome (66–70 CE). The construction of a Third Temple is generally relegated to the messianic era.

Tisha b'Av: the ninth day of the Hebrew month of Av (summer), on which particular suffering of the Jewish people occurred, including the destruction of both Temples and other pogroms throughout history. Various lamentations are read and Jews are to abstain from eating, drinking, bathing, application of oils, sexual relations, and wearing leather shoes.

Tosefta: legal supplements to the Mishnah, compiled by Tannaim and most likely datable to early third century. Longer than the Mishnah, it covers similar ground as the Mishnah.

Va'ad: committee or council; assemblies of representatives of Jewish communities were called at various times throughout the Middle Ages and early modern period to address a range of internal communal and external political issues. The early modern Council of Four Lands of the Polish-Lithuanian Commonwealth was perhaps the largest and most developed council, which exercised great influence, even though it, like other councils, was not recognized by some rabbis as an autonomous institution.

Yavneh: an ancient city on the southern coastal plain of Israel. Referred to in the Bible, it is often taken to be the place where the Sanhedrin was transferred when the Second Temple was destroyed.

Yeshiva: from the root "to sit"; refers to a Talmudic academy for advanced study. Dating to the Geonic period, with academies in Jerusalem, Sura, and Pumbedita, a yeshiva served as an educational institution for rabbis.

Throughout the medieval and early modern period, yeshivot were generally small and often housed at the residence of the rosh yeshiva, head of the yeshiva. Yeshivot served a range of students, often from outside the town or city in which they were located. Curricula might vary, but focused upon discussion of Talmud and halakhah.

Yiddish: a Jewish vernacular language that is a Germanic language written in Hebrew characters, traceable back to the high Middle Ages. Some have contended that Yiddish is a Slavic language, but that is very much a minority opinion, although Yiddish does borrow a range of words from the host societies in which the specific version of Yiddish developed. Yiddish was a primary spoken language of German Jews in the medieval and early modern periods and of Jews in eastern European in the early modern and modern periods.

Yishuv: "settlement"; the Jewish community in Palestine prior to the founding of the State of Israel. (See Israel.)

Zohar: "The Book of Splendor," a primary kabbalistic text authored in large part by Moses ben Shem Tov Leon (ca. 1240–1305) in Spain. Written in Aramaic and comprised of a range of biblical commentary, with various legends and secrets, and ascribed to the Talmudic figure Rabbi Shimon bar Yohai. Reprinted frequently in the early modern period, the *Zohar* became a central text in mystical and kabbalistic speculation.

Maps

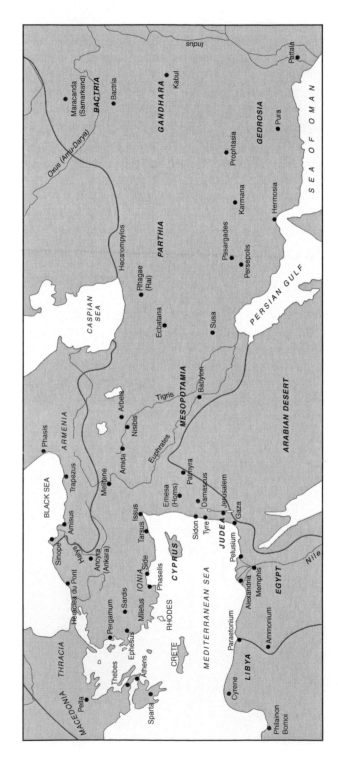

Map 1 The Ancient Near East.

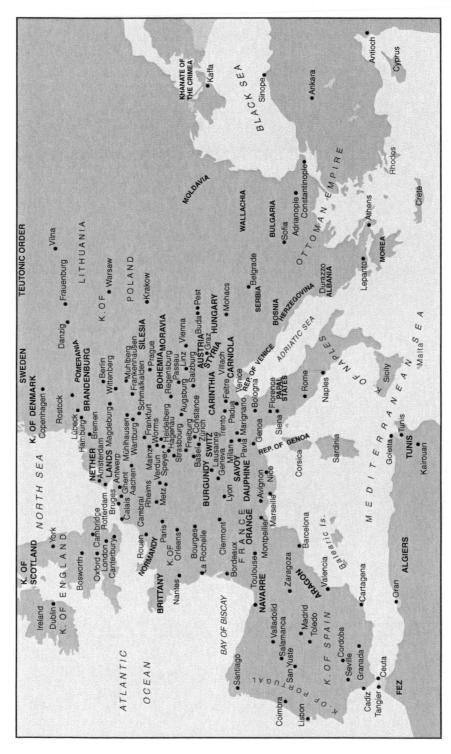

Map 2 Europe and the Ottoman Empire

Map 3 Greatest Extent of the Polish-Lithuanian Commonwealth in the 17th Century.

Map 4 Select Locations in Central and South America

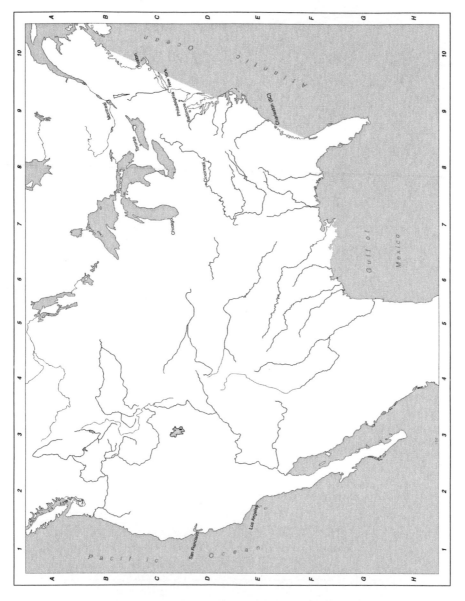

Map 5 North American Jewish Communities Referenced

Timeline

Before the Common Era (BCE) [Note: some of these dates are speculative]

Nineteenth–seventeenth centuries: Biblical Patriarchs and Matriarchs

1792–50: Hammurabi [Babylonian king]

1312: Exodus from Egypt

Thirteenth century: Israelite conquest of Canaan

1150–1025: Period of the Judges

1025–07: King Saul

1010–970: King David

1001–931: King Solomon

1000 (or before): Pre-monarchic period

960: Solomon's Temple in Jerusalem completed

931: Split between northern kingdom of Israel and southern kingdom of Judah

930: Aleppo Codex

740–22: Kingdom of Israel falls to Assyrians

701: Assyrian ruler Sennacherib besieges Jerusalem

649–09: King Josiah of Judah

586: Jerusalem falls to Nebuchadnezzar and destruction of Temple

539: Cyrus, King of Persia, allows Jews to return to Jerusalem and rebuild Temple

516: Second Temple consecrated

460: Reforms of Ezra

333: Alexander the Great arrives in Palestine

320–168: Judaism under Greek Ptolemies and Seleucids

250: Septuagint translation of Torah into Greek

200–135: Qumran community

167/66: Maccabean War

164: Dedication of the Temple

157–129: Hasmonean dynasty
129/28: John Hyrcanus establishes independent Jewish State
120–220: Parthians
Second century: Final redaction of book of Daniel
63: Pompey conquers Palestine
37–4: Herod the Great
4–33 CE (?): Jesus of Nazareth

Common Era (CE)

2–35: Anileus and Asineus establish Jewish enclave in Parthia
66/67–73/74: Great Revolt against Rome
70: Second Temple destroyed
70s: Yohanan ben Zakkai at Yavneh
70–200: Tannaim
73/74: Fall of Masada
132/33–135/36: Bar Kokhba Revolt
Third–seventh century: Sasanian rule in Babylonia
200–20: Editing of Mishnah
220: Babylonian Academy founded at Sura by Rav
220–500: Amoraim
Ca. 250: Tannaitic period ends
250: Compilation of Tosefta
250–300: Early Midrashic collections
312: Conversion of Constantine to Christianity
333: Council of Nicaea
400s: Palestinian Talmud
500s–800s: Babylonian Talmud
Ca. sixth century: Amoraic period ends
632: Death of Muhammad
638: Islamic conquest of Jerusalem
694–711: Judaism outlawed in Visigothic Spain
700–1250: Geonim
711: Muslim invasion of Spain
Ca. ninth century: Saboraic period ends
1040–1105: Rabbi Solomon ben Isaac (Rashi)
1084: Charter for Jews in Speyer, Germany
1096: First Crusade
1138–1204: Rabbi Moses Maimonides
1144: Blood Libel in Norwich, England
1165: Forced Conversions in Yemen

1179: Third Lateran Council of the Christian Church

1215: Fourth Lateran Council of the Christian Church

1240: Disputation and burning of Talmud in Paris

1263: Disputation in Barcelona

1286: Completion of *Zohar*

1290: Expulsion of Jews from England

1306: Expulsion of Jews from France

1348–50: Black Death

1391: Persecution and forced conversion of Jews in Spain

1453: Ottoman Conquest of Constantinople (now Istanbul)

1457: First book printed by Gutenberg

1462: Jewish Ghetto formed in Frankfurt am Main

1469: Union of Castile and Aragon

1475: First Hebrew book printed

1475: Trent ritual murder accusation and trial

1480: Inquisition in Spain

1488–1575: Rabbi Joseph Karo

1492: Expulsion of Jews from Spain and Moors from Granada

1496: Expulsion of Jews from Portugal

1506: Attack on New Christians in Lisbon

1516: Creation of Venetian Ghetto

1516: Ottoman conquest of Israel

1531: Portuguese Inquisition established

1534–72: Rabbi Isaac Luria

1538: Attempt of Jacob Berab to reinstitute *semikhah* (Rabbinic Ordination)

1553: Burning of Talmud in Italy

1555: Pope Paul IV Edict "Cum Nimis Absurdum," enforcing Segregation of Jews

1565: First Printing of *Shulhan Arukh*

1580: Council of Four Lands formed in Poland

1603: Synod of German Jews

1618–48: Thirty Years' War in Europe

1648: Chmielnicki massacres

1654: Jews forced to leave Recife with Portuguese incursions; settlement of First Jews in New Amsterdam (Later New York)

1656: Reentry of Jews to England; excommunication of Baruch Spinoza

1665: Shabbetai Sevi declares himself the messiah

Ca. 1700–60: Israel ben Eliezer (Ba'al Shem Tov), father of Hasidism

1720–97: Elijah ben Solomon Zalman (Vilna Gaon)

1729–86: Moses Mendelssohn

1772, 1793, 1795: Partitions of Poland (by Prussia, Russia, and Austria)

1781: "On the Civil Improvement of the Jews" is published by Christian Wilhelm von Dohm

1782: Edict of Tolerance, Joseph II; *Divrei Shalom ve-Emet* (Words of Peace and Truth) published by Naphtali Herz Wessely

1783: Mendelssohn's *Jerusalem* is published

1789: French Revolution

1791: Civil rights to Jews in France

1791: Creation of Pale of Settlement

1806: Assembly of Jewish Notables convenes in Paris (at the direction of Napoleon)

1807: Paris Sanhedrin

1810: Dedication of Reform synagogue in Seesen

1818: Hamburg Temple

1819: *Eleh Divrei ha-Brit*: traditionalists respond to Reform innovations; Hep-Hep riots in Germany

1844–6: Reform rabbinical conferences

1810–83: Rabbi Israel Lipkin (known as Salanter, after the place of his residence), founder of Musar movement

1853: First Hebrew novel (*Ahavat Zion*, by Abraham Mapu)

1855–81: Reign of Czar Alexander II, in Russia

1860: Alliance Israélite Universelle founded in Paris

1870: Roman ghetto abolished

1871: Unification of Germany

1875: Establishment of Hebrew Union College, in Cincinnati

1881: Assassination of Alexander II; pogroms erupt the next month

1882: Leon Pinsker publishes "Auto-Emancipation"

1882: First aliyah begins

1856–1927: Asher Ginsberg (Ahad Ha'Am)

1860–1904: Theodor Herzl

1887: Jewish Theological Seminary opens, in New York

1894: Dreyfus case begins

1896: Herzl publishes *The Jewish State*

1897: First Zionist Congress is held in Basel

1897: RIETS (Rabbi Isaac Elchanan Theological Seminary) is established in New York

1903: Kishinev pogrom

1904: Second aliyah begins

1904: New York's Jewish Museum founded

1905: First Russian public edition of *Protocols of the Elders of Zion*

1906: First iteration of the Bezalel art center founded by Boris Schatz in Jerusalem

1908: Czernowitz Yiddish Conference held

1908–ca. 1928: St. Petersburg Society for Jewish Folk Music Active

1909: Founding of Tel Aviv; founding of Deganyah (first kibbutz in Palestine)

1914–18: World War I

1917: Balfour Declaration

1917: Russian Revolution

1920 (December): First production of *The Dybbuk* by the Habinah Theater Troupe in Warsaw.

1921, 1929, 1936: Arab riots in Palestine

1924: Founding of College of Jewish Studies in Chicago [today the Spertus Institute for Jewish Learning and Leadership]

1925: Opening of Hebrew University

1933: Hitler is appointed Chancellor of Germany

1935: Nuremberg Laws

1936–40: World Centre for Jewish Music in Palestine active

1938: Evian Conference; *Kristallnacht*

1939–45: World War II

1942: Wannsee Conference: Plans for "Final Solution"

1944: First folk dance festival in Palestine held at Kibbutz Dalia

1946–56: Discovery of Dead Sea Scrolls

1947: UN adopts Palestine Partition plan

1948: Establishment of the State of Israel

1948: Hebrew Union College-School of Sacred Music founded [today the Debbie Friedman School of Sacred Music]

1949: Inbal Dance Troupe founded in Jerusalem by Sara Levi-Tanai

1952: Cantors Institute founded at the Jewish Theological Seminary [today the H. L. Miller Cantorial School]

1952: First Israeli Folk Dance session in America started by Fred Berk at New York's 92nd St. Y

1955: Israel Folklore Archives founded in Haifa by Dov Noy

1964: Jewish Music Research Centre founded in Jerusalem by Israel Adler

1967: Six-Day War

1969: Founding of Association for Jewish Studies

1971: Steven Spielberg Jewish Film Archive founded at Hebrew University

1973: Yom Kippur War

1976: National Center for Jewish Film founded at Brandeis University

1979: Hebrew University Center for Jewish Art founded

1981: The first Jewish Film Festival held in San Francisco

1987: Beginning of First Intifada

2000: Beginning of Second Intifada

Select Bibliography by Period

Note: This bibliography is very selective. It is not intended to be comprehensive and there are many central scholars and seminal works that are not included. Its goal is to provide some key works in English, which may serve as useful introduction to broad periods and themes.

General

Baskin, Judith R. (ed.) (2011), *The Cambridge Dictionary of Judaism & Jewish Culture*. Cambridge: Cambridge University Press.
—. (ed.) (1998), *Jewish Women in Historical Perspective* (2nd edn). Detroit: Wayne State University Press.
Baskin, Judith R. and Seeskin, Kenneth (2010), *The Cambridge Guide to Jewish History, Religion, and Culture*. Cambridge: Cambridge University Press.
Ben-Amos, Dan (ed.) (2006–11), *Folktales of the Jews*, 3 vols. Philadelphia: Jewish Publication Society.
Biale, David (ed.) (2002), *Cultures of the Jews: A New History*. New York: Schocken.
Cohen, Shaye J. D. and Greenstein, Edward L. (eds) (1990), *The State of Jewish Studies*. Detroit: Wayne State University Press.
Goodman, Martin (ed.) (2002), *The Oxford Handbook of Jewish Studies*. New York: Oxford University Press.
Greenspahn, Frederick E. (ed.) (2009), *Women and Judaism: New Insights and Scholarship*. New York: New York University Press.
Meyer, Michael A. (1987), *Ideas of Jewish History*. Detroit: Wayne State University Press
Roth, Cecil (ed.) (1971), *Jewish Art: An Illustrated History* (rev. edn). London: Valentine Mitchell.
Skolnik, Fred (ed.) (2007), *Encylopaedia Judaica*. Detroit: Macmillan.

Biblical

Alter, Robert (1981), *The Art of Biblical Narrative*. New York: Basic Books.
—. (2011), *The Art of Biblical Poetry* (2nd edn). New York: Basic Books.
Berlin, Adele and Brettler, Marc Zvi (eds) (2004), *The Jewish Study Bible: Featuring the Jewish Publication Society TANAKH Translation*. New York: Oxford University Press
Brettler, Marc Zvi (2005), *How to Read the Bible*. Philadelphia: Jewish Publication Society.

Cherry, Shai (2007), *Torah through Time: Understanding Bible Commentary from the Rabbinic Period to Modern Times*. Philadelphia: Jewish Publication Society.

Cohn Eskenazi, Tamara and Weiss, Andrea L. (eds) (2007), *The Torah: A Women's Commentary*. Cincinnati: URJ Press.

Coogan, Michael D. (2008), *A Brief Introduction to the Old Testament: The Hebrew Bible in Its Context*. New York: Oxford University Press.

Dever, William G. (2012), *The Lives of Ordinary People in Ancient Israel: When Archaeology and the Bible Intersect*. Grand Rapids: Eerdmans.

—. (2006), *Who Were the Early Israelites and where Did they Come from?* Grand Rapids: Eerdmans.

Finkelstein, Israel and Silberman, Neil Asher (2007), *David and Solomon: In Search of the Bible's Sacred Kings and the Roots of the Western Tradition*. New York: Free Press.

Fishbane, Michael (1998), *Biblical Text and Texture: A Literary Reading of Selected Texts*. Oxford: Oneworld.

Friedman, Richard E. (1987), *Who Wrote the Bible?* (2nd edn). New York: Summit Books.

Greenspoon, Leonard J. (2008), "By the Letter?/Word for Word? Scripture in the Jewish Tradition," in Frederick E. Greenspahn (ed.), *The Hebrew Bible: New Insights and Scholarship*. New York: New York University Press, pp. 141–63.

—. (2003), "Jewish Translations of the Bible," in Adele Berlin and Marc Zvi Brettler (eds), *The Jewish Study Bible*. New York: Oxford University Press, pp. 2005–20.

—. (2006), "The Septuagint," in Fred Skolnik (ed.), *Encyclopaedia Judaica* (new edn). Jerusalem: Jerusalem Publishing House, vol. 3, pp. 595–8.

Heschel, Abraham J. (2010; orig. 1962), *The Prophets*. New York: Harper Perennial Modern Classics.

The Jewish Bible: A JPS Guide (2008). Philadelphia: Jewish Publication Society.

The JPS Torah Commentary. Philadelphia: Jewish Publication Society: *Genesis*, commentary by Nahum M. Sarna (1989); *Exodus*, commentary by Nahum M. Sarna (1991); *Leviticus*, commentary by Baruch A. Levine (1989); *Numbers*, commentary by Jacob Milgrom (1990); *Deuteronomy*, commentary by Jeffrey H. Tigay (1996).

Kugel, James L. (1999), *The Bible as It Was*. Cambridge, MA: Harvard University Press.

Levenson, Jon D. (1987), *Sinai and Zion: An Entry into the Jewish Bible*. San Francisco: HarperOne.

Orlinsky, Harry M. and Bratcher, Robert G. (1991), *A History of Bible Translation and the North American Contribution*. Atlanta: Scholars Press.

Sandmel, Samuel (1978), *The Hebrew Scriptures: An Introduction to their Literature and Religious Ideas*. New York: Oxford University Press.

Schiffman, Lawrence H. (1994), *Reclaiming the Dead Sea Scrolls: The History of Judaism, the Background of Christianity, and the Lost Library of Qumran*. Philadelphia: Jewish Publication Society.

Sternberg, Meir (1987), *The Poetics of Biblical Narrative: Ideological Literature and the Drama of Reading*. Bloomington: Indiana University Press.

Sweeney, Marvin A. (2012), *TANAK: A Theological and Critical Introduction to the Jewish Bible*. Minneapolis: Fortress Press.

Rabbinic

Baskin, Judith R. (2002), *Midrashic Women: Formations of the Feminine in Rabbinic Literature*. Hanover, NH: University Press of New England.

Becker, Adam H. and Reed, Annette Yoshiko (eds) (2007), *The Ways that Never Parted: Jews and Christians in Late Antiquity and the Early Middle Ages*. Minneapolis: Fortress Press.

Boyarin, Daniel (2004), *Border Lines: The Partition of Judaeo-Christianity*. Philadelphia: University of Pennsylvania Press.

—. (1993), *Carnal Israel: Reading Sex in Talmudic Culture*. Berkeley: University of California Press.

—. (1999), *Dying for God: Martyrdom and the Making of Christianity and Judaism*. Stanford: Stanford University Press.

Fine, Steven (2005), *Art and Judaism in the Greco-Roman World: Toward a New Jewish Archeology*. New York: Cambridge University Press.

Fonrobert, Charlotte Elisheva and Jaffee, Martin S. (eds) (2007), *The Cambridge Companion to the Talmud and Rabbinic Literature*. Cambridge: Cambridge University Press.

Goodman, Martin (2008), *Rome and Jerusalem: The Clash of Ancient Civilizations*. New York: Vintage Books.

Halivni, David Weiss (1986), *Midrash, Mishnah, and Gemara: Predilection for Justified Law*. Cambridge, MA: Harvard University Press.

Hauptman, Judith (1998), *Rereading the Rabbis: A Woman's Voice*. Boulder, CO: Westview Press.

Hezser, Catherine (ed.) (2010), *The Oxford Handbook of Jewish Daily Life in Roman Palestine*. Oxford: Oxford University Press.

Horbury, William, Davies, W. D., and Sturdy, John (eds) (1999), *The Cambridge History of Judaism: Volume Three: The Early Roman Period*. Cambridge: Cambridge University Press.

Kalmin, Richard (1994), *Sages, Stories, Authors, and Editors in Rabbinic Babylonia*. Atlanta: Scholars Press.

Katz, Steven T. (2006), *The Cambridge History of Judaism: Volume 4: The Late Roman-Rabbinic Period*. Cambridge: Cambridge University Press.

Levine, Lee I. (1989), *The Rabbinic Class of Roman Palestine in Late Antiquity*. New York: The Jewish Theological Seminary of America.

Lieberman, Saul (1974a), *Greek in Jewish Palestine/Hellenism in Jewish Palestine*. New York: The Jewish Theological Seminary of America.

—. (1974b), *Texts and Studies*. New York: Ktav Publishing House, Inc.

Neusner, Jacob (1970), *Development of a Legend: Studies on the Traditions Concerning Yohanan ben Zakkai*. Leiden: E.J. Brill.

—. (1965–70), *A History of the Jews in Babylonia*, 5 vols. Leiden: E.J. Brill.

—. (1994), *Introduction to Rabbinic Literature*. New York: Doubleday.

—. (1973), *From Politics to Piety: The Emergence of Pharisaic Judaism*. New York: Prentice-Hall.

—. (1978), *There We Sat Down: Talmudic Judaism in the Making*. New York: Ktav.

Safrai, Shmuel (ed.) (1987), *The Literature of the Sages First Part: Oral Tora, Halakha, Mishna, Tosefta, Talmud, External Tractes*. Minneapolis: Fortress Press.

Safrai, Shmuel, Safrai, Z., Schwartz, J., and Tomson, P. J. (eds) (2006), *The Literature of the Sages Second Part: Midrash and Targum, Liturgy, Poetry, Mysticism, Contracts, Inscriptions, Ancient Science and the Languages of Rabbinic Literature*. Assen: Royal Van Gorcum and Fortress Press.

Samely, Alexander (2007), *Forms of Rabbinic Literature and Thought: An Introduction*. Oxford: Oxford University Press.

Schiffman, Lawrence H. (1995), *Reclaiming the Dead Sea Scrolls: Their True Meaning for Judaism and Christianity*. New York: Doubleday.

Schürer, Emil (1972–87), *A History of the Jewish People in the Age of Jesus Christ (175 B.C.– A.D. 135)*. Revised and ed. Geza Vermes and Fergus Millar, 4 vols. Edinburg: T&T Clark.

Schwartz, Seth (2010), *Were the Jews a Mediterranean Society? Reciprocity and Solidarity in Ancient Judaism*. Princeton: Princeton University Press.

Strack, Hernann L. and Stemberger, Günther (1991), *Introduction to the Talmud and Midrash*, trans. Markus Bockmuehl. Edinburg: T&T Clark.

Vermes, Geza (2004), *The Complete Dead Sea Scrolls in English* (rev. edn). London: Penguin Books.

Medieval

Ashtor, Eliyahu (1973–84), *The Jews of Moslem Spain*, 3 vols. Philadelphia: Jewish Publication Society.

Baer, Yitzhak (1961), *A History of the Jews in Christian Spain*, 2 vols. Philadelphia: Jewish Publication Society.

Baumgarten, Elisheva (2004), *Mothers and Children: Jewish Family Life in Medieval Ashkenaz*. Princeton: Princeton University Press.

Berger, David (1979), *The Jewish-Christian Debate in the High Middle Ages: Sefer Nizzahon Vetus*. Philadelphia: Jewish Publication Society of America.

Chazan, Robert (1987), *European Jewry and the First Crusade*. Berkeley: University of California Press.

—. (2006), *The Jews of Medieval Western Christendom, 1000–1500*. Cambridge: Cambridge University Press.

Cohen, Jeremy (1999), *Living Letters of the Law: Ideas of the Jews in Medieval Christianity*. Berkeley: University of California Press.

Cohen, Mark R. (2005), *Poverty and Charity in the Jewish Community of Medieval Egypt*. Princeton: Princeton University Press.

—. (1994), *Under Crescent and Cross: The Jews in the Middle Ages*. Princeton: Princeton University Press.

Finkelstein, Louis (1964 repr.), *Jewish Self-Government in the Middle Ages*. New York: Feldheim.

Funkenstein, Amos (1993), *Perceptions of Jewish History*. Berkeley: University of California Press.

Gil, Moshe (1992), *A History of Palestine, 634–1099*. Cambridge: Cambridge University Press.

Goitein, S. D. (1967–93), *A Mediterranean Society: The Jews of the Arab World as Mirrored in the Documents of the Cairo Geniza*, 5 vols. Berkeley: University of California Press.

Grossman, Avraham (2004), *Pious and Rebellious: Jewish Women in Medieval Europe*, trans. Jonathan Chipman. Waltham: Brandeis University Press.

Holo, Joshua (2009), *Byzantine Jewry in the Mediterranean Economy*. Cambridge: Cambridge University Press.

Kanarfogel, Ephraim (2000), *Peering through the Lattices: Mystical, Magical and Pietistic Dimensions in the Tosafist Period*. Detroit: Wayne State University Press.

Lewis, Bernard (1984), *The Jews of Islam*. Princeton: Princeton University Press.

Linder, Amnon (1987), *The Jews in Roman Imperial Legislation*. Detroit: Wayne State University Press.

Marcus, Ivan G. (1981), *Piety and Society: The Jewish Pietists of Medieval Germany*. Leiden: Brill.

—. (1996), *Rituals of Childhood: Jewish Acculturation in Medieval Europe*. New Haven: Yale University Press.

Marcus, Jacob (1938), *The Jew in the Medieval World: A Source Book, 315–1791*. Cincinnati: HUC Press.

Nemoy, Leon A. (ed. and trans.) (1952), *Karaite Anthology: Excerpts from the Early Literature*. New Haven: Yale University Press.

Nirenberg, David (1996), *Communities of Violence: Persecution of Minorities in the Middle Ages*. Princeton: Princeton University Press.

Rubin, Miri (1999), *Gentile Tales: The Narrative Assault on Late Medieval Jews*. New Haven: Yale University Press.

Rustow, Marina (2008), *Heresy and the Politics of Community: The Jews of the Fatimid Caliphate*. Ithaca: Cornell University Press.

Sapir Abulafia, Anna (2011), *Christian-Jewish Relations 1000–1300: Jews in the Service of Medieval Christendom*. Harlow: Logman.

Stow, Kenneth (2006), *Alienated Minority: The Jews of Medieval Latin Europe*. Cambridge, MA: Harvard University Press.

Toch, Michael (2013), *The Economic History of European Jews: Late Antiquity and Early Middle Ages*. Leiden: Brill.

Yuval, Israel J. (2006), *Two Nations in Your Womb: Perceptions of Jews and Christians in Late Antiquity and the Middle Ages*, trans. Barbara Harshav and Jonathan Chipman. Berkeley: University of California Press.

Early Modern

Beinart, Haim (2002, orig. 1994), *The Expulsion of the Jews from Spain*, trans. Jeffrey M. Green. Oxford: Oxford University Press.

Bell, Dean Phillip (2008), *Jews in the Early Modern World*. Lanham: Rowman and Littlefield.

Bell, Dean Phillip and Burnett, Stephen G. (2006), *Jews, Judaism, and the Reformation in Sixteenth-Century Germany*. Leiden: Brill.

Bodian, Miriam (1997), *Hebrews of the Portuguese Nation: Conversos and Community in Early Modern Amsterdam*. Bloomington: Indiana University Press.

Bonfil, Robert (1994), *Jewish Life in Renaissance Italy*, trans. Anthony Oldcorn. Berkeley: University of California Press.

Burnett, Stephen G. (1996), *From Christian Hebraism to Jewish Studies: Johannes Buxtorf (1564–1629) and Hebrew Learning in the Seventeenth Century*. Leiden: Brill.

Carlebach, Elisheva (2001), *Divided Souls: Converts from Judaism in Germany, 1500–1750*. New Haven: Yale University Press.

Coudert, Allison P. and Shoulson, Jeffery S. (eds) (2004), *Hebraica Veritas? Jews and the Study of Judaism in Early Modern Europe*. Philadelphia: University of Pennsylvania Press.

David, Abraham (1999), *To Come to the Land: Immigration and Settlement in Sixteenth-Century Eretz-Israel*, trans. Dena Ordan. Tuscaloosa, AL: University of Alabama Press.

Foa, Anna (2000), *The Jews of Europe after the Black Death*. Berkeley: University of California Press.

Fram, Edward (1997), *Ideals Face Reality: Jewish Law and Life in Poland, 1550–1655*. Cincinnati: Hebrew Union College Press.

Gampel, Benjamin R. (1989), *The Last Jews on Iberian Soil: Navarrese Jewry 1479–1498*. Berkeley: University of California Press.

Gerber, Jane (1992), *The Jews of Spain: A History of the Sephardic Experience*. New York: Free Press.

Goldish, Matt (2004), *The Sabbatean Prophets*. Cambridge, MA: Harvard University Press.

Harrán, Don (1999), *Salamone Rossi: Jewish Musician in Late Renaissance Mantua*. Oxford: Oxford University Press.

Heller, Marvin (2004), *The Sixteenth Century Hebrew Book*, 2 vols. Leiden: Brill.

Horowitz, Elliot S. (1989), "Coffee, Coffeehouses, and the Nocturnal Rituals of Early Modern Jewry," *AJS Review* 14(1): 17–46.

Hsia, R. Po-chia (1988), *The Myth of Ritual Murder: Jews and Magic in Reformation Germany*. New Haven: Yale University Press.

Israel, Jonathan (1998), *European Jewry in the Age of Mercantilism, 1550–1750* (3rd edn). London: Littman Library of Jewish Civilization.

Kaplan, Yosef (1989), *From Christianity to Judaism: The Story of Isaac Orobio de Castro*, trans. Raphael Loewe. Oxford: Littman Library of Jewish Civilization.

Katz, Jacob (1980, orig. 1961), *Exclusiveness and Tolerance: Studies in Jewish-Gentile Relations in Medieval and Modern Times*. Westport, CT: Greenwood Press.

—. (1993, orig. 1958), *Tradition and Crisis: Jewish Society at the End of the Middle Ages*, trans. Bernard Dov Cooperman. Syracuse: Syracuse University Press.

Levy, Avigdor (ed.) (1992), *The Jews of the Ottoman Empire*. Princeton: Princeton University Press.

Nadler, Steven M. (1999), *Spinoza: A Life*. Cambridge: Cambridge University Press.

Polonsky, Antony (2008), *The Jews in Poland and Russia*, 2 vols. Oxford: Littman Library of Jewish Civilization.

Ruderman, David B. (ed.) (1992), *Essential Papers on Jewish Culture in Renaissance and Baroque Italy*. New York: New York University Press.

Saperstein, Marc (1989), *Jewish Preaching, 1200–1800: An Anthology*. New Haven: Yale University Press.

Scholem, Gershom (1973), *Sabbatai Sevi: The Mystical Messiah, 1626–1676*, trans. R. J. Zwi Werblowsky. Princeton: Princeton University Press.

Stillman, Norman A. (1979), *The Jews of Arab Lands: A History and Source Book*. Philadelphia: Jewish Publication Society of America.

Swetschinski, Daniel (2000), *Reluctant Cosmopolitans: The Portuguese Jews of Seventeenth-Century Amsterdam*. London: Littman Library of Jewish Civilization.

Weinryb, Bernard D. (1973), *The Jews of Poland: A Social and Economic History of the Jewish Community in Poland from 1100 to 1800*. Philadelphia: Jewish Publication Society of America.

Weissler, Chava (1998), *Voices of the Matriarchs: Listening to the Prayers of Early Modern Jewish Women*. Boston: Beacon Press.

Modern

Bartal, Israel (2005), *The Jews of Eastern Europe, 1782–1881*, trans. Chaya Naor. Philadelphia: University of Pennsylvania Press.

Baskind, Samantha and Silver, Larry (2011), *Jewish Art: A Modern History*. London: Reaktion Books.

Benbassa, Esther (1999), *The Jews of France: A History from Antiquity to the Present*, trans. M. B. DeBevoise. Princeton: Princeton University Press.

Benbassa, Esther and Rodrigue, Aron (2000), *A History of the Judeo-Spanish Community, 14th–20th Centuries*. Berkeley: University of California Press.

Berenbaum, Michael (ed.) (2007), "Holocaust," in *Encyclopedia Judaica* (2nd edn). Detroit: Macmillan, pp. 324–493.

Bohlman, Philip (2010), *Jewish Music and Modernity*. New York: AMS Press/Oxford University Press.

Breuer, Mordechai (1992), *Modernity within Tradition: The Social History of Orthodox Jewry in Imperial Germany*. New York: Columbia University Press.

Cohen, Richard I. (1988), *Jewish Icons: Art and Society in Modern Europe*. Berkeley: University of California Press.

Diner, Hasia R. (2004), *The Jews of the United States, 1654–2000*. Berkeley: University of California Press.

Diner, Hasia R. and Benderly, Beryl Lieff (2002), *Her Works Praise Her: A History of Jewish Women in America from Colonial Times to the Present*. New York: BasicBooks.

Dubin, Lois (1999), *The Port Jews of Habsburg Trieste: Absolutist Politics and Enlightenment Culture*. Stanford: Stanford University Press.

Feiner, Shmuel (2002a), *Haskalah and History*. Portland: Littman Library of Jewish Civilization.

—. (2002b), *The Jewish Enlightenment*. Philadelphia: University of Pennsylvania Press.

Ferziger, Adam S. (2005), *Exclusion and Hierarchy: Orthodoxy, Nonobservance, and the Emergence of Modern Jewish Identity*. Philadelphia: University of Pennsylvania Press.

Freeze, ChaeRan, Hyman, Paula E., and Polonsky, Antony (eds) (2005), *Jewish Women in Eastern Europe*. Polin: Studies in Polish Jewry 18.

Fuchs, Esther (ed.) (2005), *Israeli Women's Studies: A Reader*. Piscataway, NJ: Rutgers University Press.

Goldberg, Harvey E. (ed.) (1996), *Sephardi and Middle Eastern Jewries*. Bloomington: Indiana University Press.

Hertzberg, Arthur (1997), *The Zionist Idea: A Historical Analysis and Reader*. Philadelphia: Jewish Publication Society.

Hess, Jonathan M. (2002), *Germans, Jews and the Claims of Modernity*. New Haven: Yale University Press.

Hyman, Paula E. (1995), *Gender and Assimilation in Modern Jewish History: The Roles and Representation of Women*. Seattle: University of Washington Press.

Hyman, Paula E. and Ofer, Dalia (eds) (2006), *Jewish Women: A Comprehensive Historical Encyclopedia* [http://bibpurl.oclc.org/web/31637]. Jerusalem: Shalvi Publishing.

Kaplan, Marion (1994), *The Making of the Jewish Middle Class: Women, Family, and Identity in Imperial Germany*. New York: Oxford University Press.

Kaplan, Yosef (2000), *An Alternative Path to Modernity: The Sephardic Diaspora in Modern Europe*. Leiden: Brill.

Kark, Ruth, Shilo, Margalit, and Hasan-Rokem, Galit (eds) (2008), *Jewish Women in Pre-state Israel: Life History, Politics, and Culture*. Waltham: Brandeis University Press.

Katz, Jacob (1973), *Out of the Ghetto: The Social Background of Jewish Emancipation, 1780–1870*. Cambridge, MA: Harvard University Press.

Kirshenblatt-Gimblett Barbara and Karp, Jonathan (eds) (2007), *The Art of Being Jewish in Modern Times*. Philadelphia: University of Pennsylvania Press.

Lowenstein, Steven M. (2005), "The Beginning of Integration, 1780–1870," in Marion A. Kaplan (ed.), *Jewish Daily Life in Germany*. New York: Oxford University Press, pp. 93–172.

Malino, Frances and Sorkin, David (eds) (1990), *From East and West: Jews in a Changing Europe, 1750–1870*. Cambridge, MA: Blackwell.

Mendelssohn, Ezra (1983), *The Jews of East Central Europe between the World Wars*. Bloomington: Indiana University Press.

Mendes-Flohr, Paul and Reinharz, Jehuda (eds) (2011), *The Jew in the Modern World* (3rd edn). New York: Oxford University Press.

Meyer, Michael A. (1988), *Response to Modernity: A History of the Reform Movement in Germany*. New York: Oxford University Press.

—. (1975), "Where Does the Modern Period of Jewish History Begin?" *Judaism* 24: 329–38.

Nadell, Pamela S. (1998), *Women who Would be Rabbis: A History of Women's Ordination 1889–1985*. Boston: Beacon Press.

Nadell, Pamela S. and Sarna, Jonathan (eds) (2011), *Women and American Judaism: Historical Perspectives*. Waltham: Brandeis University Press.

Nathans, Benjamin (2002), *Beyond the Pale: The Jewish Encounter with Late Imperial Russia*. Berkeley: University of California Press.

Petrovsky-Shtern, Yohanan (2010), *Lenin's Jewish Question*. New Haven: Yale University Press.

Sarna, Jonathan D. (2004), *American Judaism: A History*. New Haven: Yale University Press.

Shapiro, Anita (2012), *Israel: A History*, trans. Anthony Berris. Waltham: Brandeis University Press.

Silber, Michael K. (1992), "The Emergence of ultra-Orthodoxy," in Jack Wertheimer (ed.), *Uses of Tradition; Jewish Continuity in the Modern Era*. Cambridge, MA: Jewish Theological Seminary of America, pp. 23–84.

Umansky, Ellen M. and Ashton, Dianne (eds) (2008), *Four Centuries of Jewish Women's Spirituality: A Sourcebook* (rev. edn). Lebanon, NH: Brandeis University Press.

Wengeroff, Pauline (2010), *Memoirs of a Grandmother: Scenes from the Cultural History of the Jews of Russia in the Nineteenth Century*, trans. Shulamit S. Magnus. Stanford: Stanford University Press.

Wisse, Ruth R. (2000), *The Modern Jewish Canon: A Journey through Language and Culture*. New York: The Free Press.

Contemporary

Baron, Lawrence (ed.) (2011), *The Modern Jewish Experience in World Cinema*. Waltham: Brandeis University Press.

Ben-Amos, Dan (1991), "Jewish Folklore Studies," *Modern Judaism* 11(1): 17–66.

Berk, Fred (1960), *The Jewish Dance: An Anthology of Articles*. New York: Exposition Press.

Bial, Henry (2005), *Acting Jewish: Negotiating Ethnicity on the American Stage and Screen*. Ann Arbor: University of Michigan Press.

Biale, Rachel (1984), *Women and Jewish Law: The Essential Texts, their History, and their Relevance for Today*. New York: Schocken Books.

Boyarin, Jonathan (ed.) (2003), *The Ethnography of Reading*. Berkeley: University of California Press

Brin Ingber, Judith (ed.) (2011), *Seeing Israeli and Jewish Dance*. Detroit: Wayne State University Press.

Cohen, Shaye J. D. (2005), *Why Aren't Jewish Women Circumcised? Gender and Covenant in Judaism*. Berkeley: University of California Press.

DellaPergola, Sergio (2011), *Jewish Demographic Policies: Population Trends and Options in Israel and in the Diaspora*. Jerusalem: Jewish People Policy Institute

—. (1999), *World Jewry beyond 2000: The Demographic Prospects*. Oxford: Oxford Centre for Hebrew and Jewish Studies.

Hartman, Tova (2007), *Feminism Encounters Traditional Judaism: Resistance and Accommodation*. Waltham: Brandeis University Press.

Heschel, Susannah (ed.) (1983), *On Being a Jewish Feminist: A Reader*. New York: Schocken.

Idelsohn, A. Z. (1929), *Jewish Music in its Historical Development*. New York: Henry Holt & Company.

Jackson, Naomi (2000), *Converging Movements: Modern Dance and Jewish Culture at the 92nd St Y*. Hanover: University Press of New England.

Lassner, Jacob and Troen, Ilan S. (2007), *Jews and Muslims in the Arab World: Haunted by Pasts Real and Imagined*. Lanham: Rowman and Littlefield.

Misra, Kalpana and Rich, Melanie S. (eds) (2003), *Jewish Feminism in Israel: Some Contemporary Perspectives*. Hanover, NH: University Press of New England.

Nahshon, Edna (ed.) (2009), *Jewish Theater: A Global View*. Leiden: Brill.

Rosenberg, Joel (1996), "The Jewish Experience on Film: An American Overview," *American Jewish Year Book* 96: 3–50.

Shandler, Jeffrey (2009), *Jews, God, and Videotape: Religion and Media in America*. New York: New York University Press.

Shelemay, Kay K. (1995), "Mythologies and Realities in the Study of Jewish Music," *The World of Music* 37(1): 24–38.

Shneer, David and Aviv, Caryn (eds) (2002), *Queer Jews*. New York: Routledge.

Shohat, Ella (1989), *Israeli Cinema: East/West and the Politics of Representation*. Austin: University of Texas Press.

Skloot, Robert (1988), *The Darkness We Carry: The Drama of the Holocaust*. Madison: University of Wisconsin Press.

Troen, Ilan S. (2003), *Imagining Zion: Dreams, Designs, and Realities in a Century of Jewish Settlement*. New Haven: Yale University Press.

Webber, Jonathan (ed.) (1994), *Jewish Identities in the New Europe*. London: Littman Library of Jewish Civilization.

Wirth-Nesher, Hana and Kramer, Michael P. (eds) (2003), *The Cambridge Companion to Jewish-American Literature*. New York: Cambridge University Press.

Yassif, Eli. (2009), *The Hebrew Folktale: History, Genre, Meaning*. Bloomington: Indiana University Press.

Index